Lieder began with words, with the composer's discovery of a poet but the study of lieder has tended to bypass those origins. Schub has traditionally come under fire for the preponderance of mediocre talent, and yet many of these writers were highly esteemed in their day. The author has chosen four such poets – Gabriele von Baumberg, Theodor Körner, Johann Mayrhofer, and Ernst Schulze – in order to re-examine their lives, works, and Schubert's music to their verse. Schubert gravitated to different poetic repertoires at different times and for different musical purposes, such as the anticipations of *Winterreise* one hears in the Schulze songs or the radical tonal experimentation of the Mayrhofer songs. All four poets were vivid inhabitants of a vivid area, and their tribulations afford us added insight into the upheavals, the manners and the mores, of their day.

Schubert's poets and
the making of lieder

Schubert's poets and the making of lieder

SUSAN YOUENS

Professor of Musicology
Department of Music,
University of Notre Dame,
Indiana

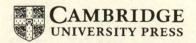

CAMBRIDGE
UNIVERSITY PRESS

Published by the Press Syndicate of the University of Cambridge
The Pitt Building, Trumpington Street, Cambridge CB2 1RP
40 West 20th Street, New York, NY 10011–4211, USA
10 Stamford Road, Oakleigh, Melbourne 3166, Australia

First published 1996
Reprinted 1998
First paperback edition 1999

Printed in the United Kingdom at the University Press, Cambridge

A catalogue record for this book is available from the British Library

Library of Congress cataloguing in publication data

Youens, Susan.
Schubert's poets and the making of lieder / Susan Youens.
p. cm.
Includes bibliographical references and index.
Contents: "The Sappho of Vienna": Gabriele von Baumberg and the disasters of war – The lyre and the
sword: Theodor Körner and the lied – Chromatic melancholy: Johann Mayrhofer and Schubert – En route
to *Winterreise*: Ernst Schulze and the sisterly muses, or a study in romantic psychopathy.
ISBN 0 521 55257 5 (hardback)
1. Schubert, Franz, 1797–1828. Songs.   2. Songs, German – 19th century – History and criticism.
3. Poets, German – 18th century – History and criticism. Choirs (Music) – England.   4. Poets, German –
19th century. I. Title.
ML410.S3Y73   1996
782.42168'092 – dc20   95–19069   CIP   MN

ISBN 0 521 55257 5 hardback
ISBN 0 521 77862 X paperback

MX/CP

Contents

Illustrations

Preface

IN THIS BOOK, I have borrowed the resonant nineteenth-century notion of *Charakterbilder* (character portraits) in music in order to turn it upside down and transmogrify it as scholarship. Rather than words engendering music to depict such symbolic archetypes as Faust and the commedia dell'arte figures, or real-life artists en route to mythification in their own medium (Chopin and Paganini in Schumann's *Carnaval*), I wish to paint "character portraits" of a different sort – biographical and poetic – in order to create richer associations around a body of music: four groups of songs by Franz Schubert on texts by four different poets. Organizing a book on lieder around a song composer's poets is perhaps a novel approach, but song, after all, begins with poetry. The assumption that music is at the center of lied creation requires, I believe, a more nuanced account in which words share the stage at all times and thereby permeate the music. It is my hope that a portrait gallery in language which begins with matters seemingly extraneous to lieder will conclude by conducting the reader back to the song, there to discover aspects previously veiled from sight and sound.

I do so against prevailing notions of song scholarship. Poets and even their poetry are too often regarded as somehow ancillary to the study of lieder, as if poets are merely the provisioners of fodder for music. Once the names and dates, perhaps a capsule biography, of the poets are given, one can rush forward to the heart of the matter: the songs themselves, or rather, the *music* of the songs. Even when the poet is of the empyrean likes of Goethe or Schiller, musicians seem curiously uninspired to delve into literary waters, to discover the when, where, how, what, and why of the verbal text. When the poet is not a household word, not one of Germany's literary gods, it is all too customary to decry his or her works as unworthy of scrutiny and thereby excuse oneself from the task of discovering anything further about the poet's life, literary and historical context, themes and preoccupations, strengths and weaknesses, or the precise nature of the attraction these poems had for song composers. Thousands of people know and love Schubert's "Im Frühling" (In the spring), D. 882, composed in 1826, but Ernst Schulze, the poet who made it possible, is a faceless name for all but a few. Who was he? What were his experiences in life, and what did those experiences have to do with the verse he created? What did he write? How was his poetry received in his own day and later? What was the attraction for Schubert of *this* verse at *that* time? What did Schubert choose for musical setting, and what did he reject? Can we speculate why? Did other composers set this poetry and if not, why? In sum, what was the pre-history of the song? What of that pre-history might Schubert have known? Even in those frequent instances where we cannot ascertain with any certainty who or what he knew of the personal history surrounding the poetry he set to music, we should remember that these poets were his contemporaries. The possibility that he heard "through the grapevine" both gossip and fact which neither he nor his friends bothered to record for posterity should not be discounted.

There are over a hundred poets whose poems were set to music by Schubert. Even if one discounts the truly obscure writers of whom we know little or nothing, there are still too many for a comprehensive study. Not wishing to pick at random from among such a horde, I relied on the following criteria as the basis for inclusion, starting with chronology: I wanted to discuss poets important to Schubert at different times, extending from the very beginning of his compositional life to the final years. In doing so, I am not attempting to demonstrate some sort of "development" but rather to show that there is a correlation between his attraction to a particular poet and the vicissitudes of his own situation at different turning points in his life. Thus, the first poet to appear in these pages is possibly the first poet who inspired Schubert not only to set her verse to music but to pursue an artistic calling, and I have ended with the poet of a group of songs in 1825–26 which paves the way for the late masterpiece *Winterreise*, D. 911. Because creative artists, no matter how avowedly apolitical, do not create in a vacuum, I also chose poets whose lives were particularly vivid and whose activities provide what I judged to be the greatest insight into the larger cultural-social-historical milieu in which poetry and lieder are born. As Roger Parker has observed, *petites histoires* and minor figures in many ways recreate their age more faithfully than the great can now do for us. Reading these poets' works, their diaries and letters, the chronicles of those who knew them, one discovers a rich social world in which poets and composers hobnobbed with one another, fell in love, created poetry and music side-by-side, and responded in a variety of ways to the upheavals and aftermath of the Napoleonic wars – the Chinese curse "May you live in interesting times" comes to mind often when one reads these accounts. One need not deny the self-sufficiency of the artistic work or fall into the trap of confusing the poet/composer with the persona of a lied in simplistic ways if one acknowledges that the extra-musical factors impinge on creativity and even appear, whether blatantly or covertly, in the works themselves.

Furthermore, I have chosen poets little-known to modern readers, underrated and misunderstood where they are known at all, writers exiled from what Jane Brown amusingly dubs the "Goetheandschiller" ambitus of those whose reputations have endured to the present day. Three of the four members of my portrait gallery were not, however, obscure in their own times; one in particular (Ernst Schulze) was highly esteemed throughout much of the nineteenth century, before later critics besmirched his name or dropped him from the canon altogether. When read in fuller knowledge of their varying purposes and contexts, however, these poets emerge as more interesting, even more skilled, than their detractors past and present would have us believe. We, after all, read with great approbation, even enthusiasm, many late twentieth-century writers who will certainly vanish from sight when the cultural winds shift; post-post-post-modern historians might have as much difficulty reclaiming reasons for our interest in these "marginal figures" as present-day scholars have with Schubert's attraction to mediocre poets and poems. Those "mediocrities," I would argue, had much to offer Schubert, who knew them better than we do.

The portrait gallery begins with two poets who belong to the history of Schubert's youth: Gabriele von Baumberg (1766–1839), known to musicians only (if at all) for Mozart's passionate setting of her poem "Als Luise die Briefe ihres ungetreuen Liebhabers verbrannte," K. 520 (As Luise burned her faithless lover's letters), and Theodor Körner (1791–1813). This book began many years ago when I first asked, "Who is Gabriele von Baumberg?" – there are, after all, only a few women among the Schubert poets (Caroline Pichler, Karoline von Klenke, Wilhelmine von Chézy, and Marianne von Willemer are the others) – and then discovered a riveting tale of intrigue, with no less than Napoleon and Metternich as players in the drama. Gabriele's life will seem particularly grim to present-day feminists: this woman, who believed fervently in her poetic destiny and claimed Olympian status as a poet, was silenced long before her death as a consequence of her marriage to a fellow-writer, an ardent Jacobin whose political activities ruined both of their lives. Schubert subsequently found in her poem "Lebenstraum" the inspiration for one of his earliest compositions and, speculatively, a source of artistic self-assertion. He also received direct encouragement for his creative aspirations from the subject of chapter 2, Theodor Körner, whom the young composer met in 1812. Körner, a battlefield martyr before his twenty-second birthday, was one of the most idolized figures of the War of Liberation, his every word and deed recorded in great detail and hymned throughout the nineteenth century and beyond; as late as the 1980s, there was yet another novel telling the tale of the Lützower Volunteers and Körner's death at Gadebusch. The story of his battlefield extinction is a reminder to musicians of the wartime turbulence that is the insistent backdrop to much of what is recounted in this book. Of all the connecting links between these four tales, the war is the most tragic.

The latter half of the portrait gallery belongs to Schubert's maturity. If the Baumberg and Körner songs are admittedly small repertoires within this composer's gigantic song oeuvre, the same is not true of Johann Mayrhofer (1787–1836), perhaps the single most important influence on Schubert's thought between the years 1817 and 1820. Mayrhofer's poetry was the inspiration for many of Schubert's greatest lieder, such as "Auf der Donau" (On the Danube), D. 553; "Freiwilliges Versinken" (Voluntary descent), D. 700; and "Auflösung" (Dissolution), D. 807, to cite only three of the forty-seven Mayrhofer songs, more than any other poet except Goethe and virtually all of them representative of Schubert at his best. And yet, the tormented poet, whose lifelong depression culminated in suicide in 1836, is still little known, his best poetry not appreciated as it should be for its proto-Expressionistic power, radical experimentation with form and meter, and Romantic appropriation and warping of Greek mythology. From the tangled strands of his own complex, difficult being, he devised either overtly autobiographical verse in futuristic forms or poems in which gods, goddesses, and Homeric figures tell of *his* distress, his rare joys, and his wish for transformation into pure spirit in a "gentle land" beyond death's frontiers. For these often vatic words, Schubert devised songs which run the gamut from the smallest and gentlest of miniatures ("Schlaflied," D. 527) to immense, heaven-storming lieder, including some of this composer's most intellectually challenging works. The enigmas of Mayrhofer's life and verse, the two closely interwoven, and Schubert's music to such powerful words deserve re-examination.

Beyond a plea for recognition of poets now lost from view, I have been captivated by the complex alliance of life and art in these tales, life borrowing from art which in turn borrowed from life in a fusion both selective and transformative. One sees the phenomenon at its most pathological in Ernst Schulze (1789–1817), the last and perhaps most tragic of the four portraits. Despite a posthumous biographical cover-up designed to save the dead young poet's reputation from tarnish, Schulze had already versified his own case history of delusion in the poems Schubert set to music; if his distressing prose diary and even more distressing letters were not accessible to the reading public for a long time, the poems were. When one realizes the intertwining of art and near-madness in his poetry, that knowledge forever changes the way in which one hears these songs. The discovery is hardly a cheerful one, but it is closer to the truth than the longstanding myth of Schulze the grief-stricken, sickly-sweet, pure-hearted poet-minstrel of Romantic love. Lawrence Kramer, in *Music and Poetry: The Nineteenth Century and After* (University of California Press, 1984), pp. 143–44, points to "An mein Herz" – "a breathtakingly banal poem by Ernst Schulze" – as evidence of a "tepid, ruminative, resigned poem" crushed by music that is "distraught, manic, defensive, duplicitous." But Schulze, who would nowadays either be jailed or hospitalized as a "stalker," was indeed distraught, manic, defensive, duplicitous and more, the indices of mental illness writ large in his poetry. Schubert, unlike his later critics, read Schulze's entire *Poetisches Tagebuch* in search of composable poetry; he did not fail to observe the poet's desperate condition, minutely recorded in that quasi-autobiographical collection, and to incorporate that knowledge into his settings. In each of his nine completed Schulze songs (a tenth was abandoned in fragmentary form), he registers every twist and turn of a diseased mind. Madness or incipient madness has often fascinated composers because of its beckoning to extremity and hence to virtuosity, also because of the delicate balancing act required of the composer – how does one portray the looming loss of control in a controlled artistic form? Whether for those reasons or others, Schubert found in Schulze's poetic diary the forerunner for his second Müller cycle, *Winterreise*, D. 911, in which one can hear many instances of "harking back" to the devices of the Schulze songs.

It will already be apparent to the reader that this book is centrally concerned with the interplay between those Siamese twins, life and art. The recent swirl of publicity about Schubert's sexuality and how it might or might not pertain to his music, a discourse which has run the gamut from valuable to vitriolic, has re-opened the old question of how later generations judge the relationship between an artist's life and personality and the work he or she creates, and has revealed yet again how deeply scholars' passions can be stirred by the imputation of human foibles to particularly beloved figures. The issue of life vis-à-vis art, vexed wherever it occurs, is further complicated in the nineteenth century by the mythology of the Romantic artist, which converted real-life creators either into Promethean demi-gods (the Beethoven model) or frail, misunderstood, refined "shrinking violets" (the Chopin model) or *gemütlich* inhabitants of operetta plots (the Schubert model) and postulated direct connections between the weather and what a composer wrote that day. Infuriated by simplistic equations between the "dancer and the dance," scholars revolted, and the pendulum for a time swung to the opposite extreme, the denial of any connection whatsoever between the life and the oeuvre; such was the creed when I was in graduate school. But the transactions between art and life not only exist but assume numberless idiosyncratic guises, all the more complex when both a poet and a composer share the stage. In an attempt to sort out those transactions in the four case-histories which follow, I have arranged each chapter along similar lines, beginning with an introduction to the lives-and-works of the poets and culminating in an examination of their effect on Schubert and commentaries on selected songs to texts by those poets. The space devoted to biographical matters, then to musical matters, necessarily shifts from one chapter to the next – we know relatively little about the reticent Mayrhofer's life while Schulze poured out his misery in page after page of documentation – but the order is the same, duplicating that of real life: to bring the poet onstage first, then the composer.

Where the repertoires are small, as they are with the Baumberg, Schulze, and Körner songs, I have discussed all of them, but only the most encyclopedic dimensions would permit commentary on all forty-seven of the Mayrhofer settings. After earlier drafts of this manuscript in which I greedily attempted to find a place for vast numbers of songs, reason returned, and ruthless selectivity became the order of the day. My decisions about which Mayrhofer lieder to include and which to omit were dictated by considerations both of variety and quality; only the best – but not all of them – and/or the most representative works have found a home in these pages. Even with a shortened list, reproducing examples from each Schubert song I invoke would swell the book to unmanageable girth, and therefore, I have only included a limited number of examples pertaining to less well-known songs; elsewhere, I have assumed that readers will consult both the old and new Schubert editions as they read my discussions of the music. I am grateful to Dover Editions, Inc. for permission to print examples from the old Breitkopf & Härtel Schubert edition and to Professor Walther Dürr and Bärenreiter-Verlag for permission to reproduce passages from the *Neue Schubert-Ausgabe*.

Examples from works long out of print, however, abound. Because I believe, in company with many scholars, that the fullest possible knowledge of the context surrounding a work can only enhance understanding and appreciation of it, one of the primary purposes of this book is to place Schubert's songs in the company of other lieder and to reintroduce neglected, and often very lovely, songs to texts by these same poets. I do so for a variety of reasons: Schubert was not only of his era in gravitating to these poems, but on certain occasions, especially in his youth, took his cue from an existing work; for example, I believe that the Viennese composer Stephan Franz's *Sechs Gedichte von Theodor Körner* perhaps influenced Schubert in his choice of five of the same texts for musical setting. Because Körner and Schulze were popular with so many composers, I could not include examples from all of the extant lieder to their verse and therefore have chosen what I considered to be the most representative and interesting specimens as a set of *Albumblätter* of fragments in chapters 2 and 4; perhaps an anthology of these songs in their entirety can follow after this book someday. Many scholars are now discovering treasures within the vast repository of neglected nineteenth-century song, and it is a trend I hope will continue to flourish in future years.

I owe a great debt of gratitude to the many people and institutions who have supported me throughout the work on this book. The National Endowment for the Humanities awarded me a travel grant in the summer of 1992 for a research trip to Budapest and a research fellowship for the academic year 1994–95; without its generosity, it would have been far more difficult for me to locate either the financial resources or the time necessary to complete this book. The American Philosophical Society and the Institute for Scholarship in the Liberal Arts at the University of Notre Dame funded a research trip to Berlin and Vienna in October 1993; during my stay in those two cities, the curators of the Bartsteingasse music collection of the Wiener Stadt- und Landesbibliothek, the music collection and theater collection of the Österreichische Nationalbibliothek, and both houses of the Deutsche Staatsbibliothek graciously allowed me access to all of the manuscripts and printed material I wished to consult. I am especially grateful to Johann Ziegler of the Wiener Stadt- und Landesbibliothek for his unfailing helpfulness and courtesy.

I also owe debts of gratitude to the Library of Congress, the British Museum, the New York Public Library, the Beinecke Library at Yale University, the Eda Kuhn Loeb Music Library at Harvard University (my special thanks to Millard Irion), and the Newberry Library in Chicago for coping both with large orders for photocopies and microfilm and, on numerous occasions, with my presence. The Staats- und Universitätsbibliothek in Göttingen, the Niedersächsische Hauptstaatsarchiv in Hannover, the Stiftsarchiv at St. Florian bei Linz, the Genealogisch-Heraldische Gesellschaft in Göttingen, the Niedersächsischer Landesverein für Familienkunde, the Deutsche Zentralstelle für Genealogie Leipzig, the Lutheran Kirchenbuchamt Göttingen and the Stadtarchiv in Göttingen have aided me enormously with various genealogical investigations; this book would not have been possible without their involvement. I am also grateful to the curators of the Galerie der Romantik at the Schloß Charlottenburg in Berlin for photographing Georg Friedrich Kersting's beautiful painting *Theodor Körner, Friesen und Hartmann auf Vorposten* for me and granting permission to reproduce it in chapter 2. In 1993, I sent a preliminary version of the chapter on Schulze to the British pianist Graham Johnson in order that he might use some of the information therein for his essay on "Schubert and the Strophic Song" in vol. 18 of *The Hyperion Schubert Edition* (Hyperion CDJ33018), which appeared later that year; this unfurling edition-in-sound of Schubert's entire lieder oeuvre is one of the most valuable Schubert projects of them all, and I felt very honored indeed to play a small part in it. The discussions I so enjoy with my friend and fellow-Schubertian, the brilliant coach-accompanist John Wustman, are woven into the fabric both of this book and my life. Brae Korin has been my collaborator in the German translations, as with my previous books; both her bulldog tenacity in researching early nineteenth-century usage and her desire to reflect each poet's style as clearly as possible in English translation have proven an invaluable aid to me these past six years of our friendship. Roger Parker, who helped me in my struggles with an early draft of an earlier book, generously agreed to sign on for a second shift at the same exercise; there are no words sufficient for my gratitude. Whatever may be felicitous in my writing reflects his generous tutelage. My graduate assistants Maryalice Mohr and Aaron Gauthier have helped with everything from sorting piles of photocopied lieder to researching publication dates for nineteenth-century sheet music, dates notoriously difficult to pinpoint, to the tedium of proofreading and checking translations. I could not have asked for more willing or able assistance. Lisa Feurzeig of the University of Chicago, my student, friend, and colleague, whose work on the Schlegel songs of Schubert confirms for me that the next generation of Schubert song scholars will be a brilliant one, has generously run various errands for me in Vienna during her stay there as a Fulbright scholar, and I am deeply indebted to her for such selfless and time-consuming aid.

Finally, this book, in company with my previous endeavors, is dedicated to the memory of my friend and mentor Paul Amadeus Pisk, who died on 12 January 1990 after a long and brilliant life as a composer, musicologist, critic, and teacher *extraordinaire*. It was from his example that I learned to be skeptical of received opinions, especially where they are dismissive in nature, and to trust my own intuition that the lives and works of artists are not nearly so disjunct as I was formerly taught. From his profound insight into human nature, I too became fascinated by artists as people and came to see their works not solely as isolated artifacts but as creations woven into the very warp and woof of their lives. On better days, when optimism about this book runs higher than usual, I like to think that he would have enjoyed reading about the colorful dramatis personae who appear in these pages, had he only lived to do so.

Music examples nos 1, 7, 16, 21, 23, 24 appear by permission of Bärenreiter-Verlag, and nos 34 and 35 by permission of the Staatsbibliothek zu Berlin, Preussische Kulturbesitz-Musikabteilung.

Chapter One

"The Sappho of Vienna": Gabriele von Baumberg and the disasters of war

IN THE FIRST VOLUME of her memoirs, *Denkwürdigkeiten aus meinem Leben* (Reminiscences of My Life), and the second volume of her *Zerstreute Blätter* (Scattered Album Leaves), the Viennese writer Caroline Pichler briefly invokes a friend of her youth, "one of the most interesting women in Vienna": the poet Gabriele von Baumberg (1766–1839).[1] This gifted poet was indeed fascinating, but her renown died long before she did. Despite her often-stated desire for poetic immortality, the public turmoil of revolution and the private turmoil of her marriage to another poet silenced her voice and stopped her pen well before physical extinction. The elderly Caroline Pichler, poignantly aware of having outlived her own era, lamented her old friend's obscurity and sang her praises before her own death in 1843, but oblivion returned when the loyal advocate was no more.[2]

There are many reasons to resurrect the extraordinary life and works of Gabriele von Baumberg – if the connection with Schubert is the principal impetus to do so in this context, it is not the only cause for curiosity. She was a local literary celebrity in Schubert's youth, although her fame did not endure: eighteenth- and nineteenth-century women *were* able, despite considerable obstacles, to publish their works and garner a measure of critical acclaim in their own day, but the approbation seldom lasted. Gabriele von Baumberg, whom Carl August von Schindel praises in his 1823 compendium of female authors, *Die deutschen Schriftstellerinnen des neunzehnten Jahrhunderts* (German women writers of the nineteenth century),[3] perfectly exemplifies the phenomenon; the association with Mozart's and Schubert's names (Mozart's "Als Luise die Briefe ihres ungetreuen Liebhabers verbrannte," or "When Luise burned her faithless lover's letters," K. 520, on a text by Gabriele is among his most beautiful songs) was not sufficient to attract more than passing mention from later music historians.[4] Where her name *has* resurfaced, it is primarily as an appendage to her spouse; Schindel was not alone in speaking more of Gabriele's husband, the Hungarian poet Batsányi János, than of Gabriele herself. The couple was still alive at the time Schindel's encyclopedia was published, but he was right to speak of them in the elegiac terms of a tragedy long past and beyond reparation. Batsányi's political troubles and his jealousy of her writing constituted a juggernaut that crushed her creativity

I

altogether for the last thirty years of her life. At the nexus where history at its most violent collides with personal and artistic destiny, theirs is a tale of love, art, and revolution with a special poignance.

Before disaster struck, Gabriele's works were regularly published in the *Wiener Musenalmanach* (Viennese Almanac of the Muses), an artistic periodical founded by two of the leading figures of the Austrian Enlightenment, Lorenz Leopold Haschka and Johann Baptist von Alxinger;[5] Gottlieb Leon, another member of the circle, called her "our poetess."[6] She was evidently a music-lover: in a poem entitled "An den grossen unsterblichen Hayden [*sic*], bey Gelegenheit als die Schöpfung diess Meisterstück der Tonkunst im k. k. Nationaltheater aufgeführt wurde" (To the great, immortal Haydn on the occasion of his *Creation*, this masterpiece of music, performed at the Royal-Imperial National Theater), she hails the composer as "the God of harmony."[7]

Erquickend – sanft – wie alles Schöne	Refreshing – gentle – like everything beautiful,
Entzückend, feurig und doch rein,	Enrapturing, fiery and yet pure,
Strömt oft der Zauber deiner Töne	the magic of your tones often flows
Durch's Ohr in unser Herz hinein.	through the ear deep into our hearts.
Jüngst schuf dein schöpferisches Werde!	Recently you created your creative "Become!"
Den Donner durch den Paukenschall;	the thunder resounding through the drum-rolls;
Und Himmel, Sonne, Mond, und Erde,	And heaven, sun, moon, and earth,
Die Schöpfung ganz – zum Zweytenmal.	the entire creation, for the second time.
Gefühlvoll – staunend – Wonnetrunken!	Full of emotion – astonished – drunk with joy!
Wie Adam einst im Paradies	Like Adam once in Paradise
Am Arm der Eva hingesunken,	leaning on Eve's arm,
Zwar sprachlos den Erschaffer pries,	almost speechless, praised the Creator,
So huld'gen wir, im Aug' die Thräne,	so we laud, with tears in our eyes,
Dem Kunstwerk deiner Phantasie –	the artistic work of your fantasy,
Der Allmacht deiner Zaubertöne –	the power of your magical tones,
Und Dir, dem Gott der Harmonie!![8]	and you, the god of harmony!

Her passionate evocations of feminine experience and her preoccupation with what it meant to be both a poet and a woman played a little-recognized part in Schubert's development at a critical juncture. One of his first extant attempts at lieder composition is an incomplete sketch of her lengthy poem "Lebenstraum" (Dream of life), D. 39 (21A), composed in 1810 (?) at a time when he too had perhaps begun "dreaming of life" and wondering what its future course would be. Because the teenage composer gravitated for several years thereafter to ballad compositions and Baumberg was not a ballad poet, Schubert did not return to her verse until August 1815. When he did, it was from an altered perspective. In the midst of a spate of Goethe settings (the conjunction is not, I believe, coincidental), he set five of her poems to music in a single three-day span: "Lob des Tokayers" (In praise of Tokay wine), D. 248; "Cora an die Sonne" (Cora to the sun), D. 263; "Der Morgenkuss" (The morning kiss), D. 264; "Abendständchen: An Lina" (Evening serenade: To Lina), D. 265; and "An die Sonne" (To the sun), D. 270. The 1815 settings, especially "Der Morgenkuss," betray in every measure the influence of Mozart and Gluck on the young Schubert, whose enthusiasm for *Iphigénie en Tauride* is well-documented and who studied composition with Gluck's student Antonio Salieri. Schubert, I believe, associated the elevated language of love in Gabriele von Baumberg's poetry with the invocations of noble passion in eighteenth-century opera, in particular, the works in which Orestes and Pylades value love for one another before their own lives and Pamina and Tamino prove worthy of the most exalted conception of love. Indeed, as Ewan West has pointed out, operatic models were crucial to the formation and continued life of Viennese song before 1815;[9] that Schubert should engage in yet another experiment with opera-in-the-lied, and should do so in his own individualistic way, is not surprising. But let us first meet the poet and come to know something of her troubled life and the poetry she was able to write before history intervened, something of the context from which "Der Morgenkuss" and other such delicately radical poems emerged.

A TEMPEST-TOSSED LIFE

In "Liebel an mich" (To me from Liebel), Ignaz Liebel,[10] a professor of aesthetics at the University of Vienna, hails her as the Sappho of Vienna:

Du Sappho Wiens, in deren holden Blicken	Thou Sappho of Vienna, in whose gentle gaze
Der Dichtkunst und der Liebe Feuer glänzt;	poetic art and the fire of love glow,
Die selbst die Musen mit dem Lorbeer schmücken,	whom the Muses themselves adorn with laurel
Und Amor mit der Myrthe kränzt![11]	and Love crowns with myrtle!

The sobriquet, whether or not Liebel was the first to use it, evidently caught on. Among the extant depictions of Gabriele, the best-known is an undated painting, now in Kaschau, Hungary, by the Viennese *Historienmaler* (history painter) Heinrich Füger in which she is depicted as Sappho, a pseudo-Grecian veil draped about the head, shoulders, and arms, with a lyre cradled to her bosom. In another contemporary painting (fig. 1) she is quite beautiful, with an oval face and high forehead, a sensitively modeled mouth, and large, dark eyes, her intensity and melancholy disposition apparent. The designation as Sappho – Plato's "Tenth Muse" – is a commonplace for women poets through the ages, multiply emblematic of the equation between sexual passion and poetry, the taint of the perverse ("unnatural" women, both poetically and sexually), and the solitude of the woman poet. Given Gabriele's determination to attain Parnassus, comparisons to Sappho might well have been both the ultimate accolade and cause for pangs of fear: Sappho, after all, was alone.[12]

Perhaps Gabriele would have been better so, although she, I suspect, would not have agreed. She was born on 24 February 1766, the third child of Johann Florian Baumberg, a high-ranking official at the imperial court, and his wife Maria Christina Rodius.[13] (The couple had four children, but the other three all died in infancy.) Florian Baumberg was an educated man with a particular interest in literature and

Figure 1.   Portrait of Gabriele von Baumberg (1766–1839) in 1791

art who encouraged his daughter's literary pursuits; Gabriele idolized him, but had a difficult relationship with her mother.[14] Her father began his career at the court as a clerk in charge of purchases and transportation, but was transferred to the court chambers, where he became first a secretary and finally director of the court archives. He was Gabriele's principal teacher (she also had a piano instructor and a dancing master) until the age of eleven, when she was sent to a Catholic public school; it was her father who introduced her to the works of Goethe, Schiller, the Virgil translator and poet Johann Heinrich Voss, and Salomon Gessner. Whether he did so for lack of any other family members with whom he could share his interests or as an expression of liberal principles regarding women's education (perhaps both, perhaps neither), she was grateful for the early fostering of her gifts as a writer.

Educated or no, she was expected, and would herself expect, to be married. Gabriele was, from all accounts, much courted by young noblemen, but her first important love, whom she calls "Eduard" in her poems, was a poverty-stricken, albeit cultured and well-educated, young man named Anton Bernhard Eberl (1762–1805). He was the impetus for her first published poem, which appeared anonymously in the *Wienerblättchen*; he replied in the same journal, and their poetic love-letters continued until the journal announced in 1785 who the authors really were. Although Gabriele was reportedly distressed about the revelation, it drew the attention of such established writers as Alois Blumauer and Alxinger to her and resulted in entrée to the highest literary circles in Vienna. Her first poem published under her own name was an occasional piece in honor of her father's birthday, printed in the *Wiener Musenalmanach* in 1785,[15] when Gabriele was nineteen years old. Thereafter, between 1785 and 1796, sixty-nine of her poems appeared in the *Musenalmanach*,[16] also in Christoph Martin Wieland's *Der teutsche Merkur*, a leading periodical in German intellectual life for thirty-seven years; Johann Wilhelm von Archenholtz's *Literatur- und Völkerkunde*, which ran from 1782 to 1791; and the *Österreichischer Taschenkalender*. If her reputation was primarily local, she did have readers elsewhere in the German-speaking world.

The learned, lively Caroline Pichler, whose salon was one of the most important centers of Viennese cultural life in the early nineteenth century, was always interested in the conjunction of love and art – women writers, who had to construct their own unique mélange of those two concerns and then justify the inclusion of art, could hardly escape the subject. The one event from Gabriele's life that she recounts in some detail (she says nothing about the events of 1809) is the young Gabriele's unhappy love affair with Eberl; this tragedy, in part, made Gabriele into a practicing poet and provided her with her principal poetic material thereafter, openly auto-biographical in nature. The couple are believed to have met in 1783 when they both performed in one of the theatrical performances at the Greiner household on Monday evenings. In such domestic theatres, the melancholy Eberl was a favorite for the role of the gallant lover. Pichler describes him as follows:

A dark disposition, a sharp intellect, a melancholy view of the world drew the attention of his acquaintances, particularly that of women, to him. His circumstances (he held a small post in a government accounting office); his character, which was not without ambition and the desire for distinction; his limited means; and his sickliness which … hindered each of his aspirations, failed to lighten his melancholy aspect. But these same traits rendered him, with his refined manners, pleasing demeanor, and cultivated mind, a very significant personality in society. When he made his appearance in the role of the actor [Joseph] Lange in private theatricals, roles in which he was equally striking in figure, bearing, and motions, many glances and hearts flew his way.[17]

Caroline Pichler herself felt the attraction of this saturnine creature and later based the novella "Das gefährliche Spiel" ("The dangerous play," Pichler's pun on play-acting both in love and on the stage) on this incident.[18] But if she turned away from a more serious involvement with Eberl, Gabriele did not, to her mother's displeasure.[19] The relationship, however, ended when he left Vienna in December 1786 for a post in Brussels. Gabriele, according to Pichler, was devastated: she was sick with grief for a year and did not fall in love again until she met Batsányi thirteen years later. The parting with Eberl was the impetus for the poem "Fragen an mein Schicksal" (Question to my destiny):

O Schicksal! musstest du mein Herz mit Lieb' erfüllen,	O Fate! Must you fill my heart with love,
Mit Liebe für den Mann, der nie die Seufzer stillen,	love for the man who will never still the sighs,
Die Thränen trocknen wird, die er mir ausgepresst?	never dry the tears, which he has forced from me?
Und bin ich nie ein Gast bey Amors Wonnefest?	And will I never be a guest at Love's feast of rapture?
Lernt' ich den edelsten der Männer darum kennen,	Did I therefore come to know the noblest of men
Um stets von ihm verkannt, im Stillen nur zu brennen?	only to be continually misunderstood, left to burn for him in silence?
Soll dieses arme Herz der Jugend beste Kraft	Shall this poor heart expend youth's best strength
Verschwenden in dem Streit mit Pflicht und Leidenschaft?	in the strife between duty and passion?
Und soll ein Mann, wie Er, versehn mit tausend Gaben,	And should a man like him, graced with a thousand gifts,
Von tausend Fehlern frey, den Einen Fehler haben:	free from a thousand faults, have this one fault:
Dass er mich Liebe lehrt, die Schülerinn nicht liebt,	That he taught me love, but did not love his pupil,
Und durch Entfernung nur die Ruh' ihr wieder giebt?[20]	and only through distance can restore peace to her?

Gabriele's friendship with Caroline Pichler seems to have suffered as a result of Eberl's greater interest in Caroline upon his return to Vienna; the two women did not see much of each other after 1787. And yet, the friendship with Caroline was important to Gabriele, who met the leading Viennese literati at the Greiner household. Gabriele was even appointed to the court in the early 1790s, although her connections with the aristocracy were not sufficient to help her uncle Franz Rodius, a cavalry captain who was imprisoned on charges of Jacobin ties; despite a verdict of innocence, he was exiled.[21] A similar fate would later befall Gabriele and her husband, János Batsányi, born 5 September 1763 in Tapolcza, Hungary.[22]

From the portrait by Heinrich Füger, he was indeed an arresting figure, ramrod-straight, with a stern face, high forehead, Roman nose, and piercing gaze (fig. 2). As a young man in Pest, he was befriended by Baron Lörinc Orczy, who aided the young commoner in his literary ambitions. The first fruit of Batsányi's nascent patriotism was the poem "A magyarok vitzsége" (The Valor of the Magyars), published in Pest in 1785. Three years later, Batsányi founded the literary quarterly

Figure 2.   Engraving of János Batsányi (1763–1845) after a painting by Heinrich Füger

Magyar Múzeum (Hungarian Museum), with two associates, but the journal ended that same year when he was fired, in part because he challenged his employer to a duel, in part because of his support of French revolutionary principles. The poem "A franciaországi változásokra" (On the changes in France), written in 1789, exemplifies his vision of poetry as social philosophy and prophesy:

Nemzetek, országok! kik rút kelepcében	Nations still trapped within the snare of servitude!
Nyögtök a rabságnak kínos kötelében,	Peoples who groan in pain, by iron bonds subdued,
S gyászos koporsóba döntö vas-igátok	who have not shaken off the collar of the slave,
Nyakatokról eddig le nem rázhatátok;	the yoke that drags you down into a wretched grave!
Ti is, kiknek vérét a természet kéri,	You also, sacred kings, who consecrated kill
Hív jobbágyitoknak felszentelt hóhéri!	– since earth cries out for blood – the subjects of your will
Jertek, s hogy sorsotok elöre nézzétek,	to Paris turn your eyes, let France elucidate,
Vigyázó szemetek Párizsra vessétek!	for king and shackled slave, a future and a fate!
	(trans. Matthew Mead)[23]

In his German poetry (he wrote in Hungarian, German, French, and Latin), he took his cue from Friedrich Klopstock, as in the following extract from a poem written in the aftermath of hearing the blind virtuoso Marie Theresia von Paradies perform in 1798. This is the rhapsodic-grandiloquent style he would press upon Gabriele as more elevated than her own, a model she should emulate.

Nach langem Sehnen, endlich sah und hört' er Sie	After long desiring it, at last he [the Poet] saw and heard you.
Er hörte Sie mit toller Seele; und verlor	He heard you with frenzied soul, and lost
Von ihres sichern Spieles reizenden Getöne	not a single sound from your assured
Nicht einen Laut – ganz Sinn, ganz Ohr.	playing of bewitching tones – all senses, all ears.
…	…
Rief er mit Staunen aus: "Groß! groß und herrlich sind	He cried out with astonishment: "Great, great and majestic
Die Wunder Deiner Macht, o Kunst Du Himmelskind! –	are the wonders of your power, o Art, Thou child of heaven!
…	…
So rief erstaunt der Dichter aus. Er sprach	So cried the poet, astonished. He spoke
Zu sich gekehrt, kein Wort mehr. Er fühlte nur,	not a word more, turned in upon himself.
Und dachte schweigend dann noch lange nach;	He only felt, and pondered silently a long time after
Welch unbekannte Kraft in Dich verborgen liege	What unknown power lies hidden in you,
Du Menschen-Seele! Gottes-Haupt!	Thou human spirit! Godhead!
Und ob der Geist, der solche Wunder wirkt, wohl auch	And does the spirit that works such wonders vanish
(Wie mancher wähnt) mit diesem Leben einst verfliegen?[24]	(as many believe) when this life is gone?

In 1794, Batsányi was accused of participation in a Jacobin-inspired conspiracy[25] and, despite being cleared of the charges, was imprisoned in the fortress of Kufstein for a year in 1795–96, where he wrote the powerful *Kufsteini elégiák* (Elegies from Kufstein). After his release, he went to Vienna and worked in the finance ministry as a clerk, but his political interests were not in abeyance. The mixture of personal anguish and revolutionary fervor typical of this poet are evident in the massive poem, *Der Kampf* (The Struggle), completed in 1801 and published anonymously in 1810, along with a lengthy prose appendix entitled "On the feudal system and the new European state system, or the republican constitutional monarchy," written in August 1809 (the date is significant). The political ardor was fuelled in part by disgust: like many revolutionaries, he was repulsed by most individual specimens of the humanity whose lot he ostensibly wished to better, writing that "Man is false and horrible and wicked! Hostile and malicious wherever I find you! A lowly poisonous race of snakes!"[26] Rather, he envisioned humanity as he dreamed it would become in the wake of revolution, free from the "grim priests' blood-altar," and he claims for poets the truest democracy because they are not bound to time and place: their Fatherland is the world. The desperation of this self-styled "Sohn des Unglücks" (son of misfortune) is palpable from the beginning: "The path of life grows ever darker and more confused, and all my energies can hardly suffice to bear the heavy burden. Where should I go? What can I, what dare I, the weary one, hope for? Gods! Shall there never be an end to my suffering?"[27] He had apparently not met Gabriele when he wrote the lines, "Alas, and no beloved woman! Who could harken to the straying man's fearful, anxious cry! No one who, pitying him, lovingly extends a lifeline to him! From the heights showing him the divine light in his last struggle! Saving him from certain and nearby fall! No one! No one!" He was prone to this hyper-exclamatory – dare one say hysterical? – vein.[28]

For all that Batsányi wrote political poetry and Gabriele poetry of love, friendship, and poetic art in a woman's voice, the two were akin in their intensity and their sense of isolation from others. The thirty-six-year-old Batsányi and the thirty-three-year-old Gabriele met on 17 October 1799 at a soirée given by the artist Vincenz Georg Kininger (1767–1851). Shortly thereafter, Batsányi lent Gabriele his copy of Herder's *Zerstreute Blätter* (Scattered album leaves), and she wrote on 4 November to thank him and to tell him, with remarkable frankness, about the effect on her of their conversation the previous day. In a wonderfully extravagant analogy, she compares her state to that of an exotic plant left untended in a kitchen garden to wither in the cold, obdurate ground until Destiny's storm shatters the greenhouse windows and lets in the sun and rain so that the plant might revive. Only then does the astonished gardener notice what a rare botanical specimen had been in his keeping all along.[29] Batsányi was clearly "Destiny's storm," and both her sense of her own uniqueness and the impact of their meeting are measurable in the vivid letter.

That was the start of an extraordinary correspondence, or what remains of it (only fifty-eight of their over five hundred letters have been preserved) – fragments from an extraordinary relationship. Encouraged by her dazzled reaction, Batsányi evidently suggested love-making after less than a month, or so one infers from Gabriele's witty reference to "your lengthy prescription from Doctor Ovid." The phrase occurs in her "Grosse Antworth" (Great answer) of 18 November, less a conventional letter than a manifesto of her beliefs and a disquisition on her life before she met him.[30] "Frostige" (cold) men nipped the bud of her springtime, she writes; her summer skies were darkened by storm clouds, and autumn makes her fear the winter to come. (It is an eloquent reminder of life expectancy in late eighteenth-century Europe that she characterizes thirty-three as autumnal.) Concerning marriage, she confesses, "I try to attend all wedding ceremonies out of an utterly singular species of curiosity because *until now, I have never seen a wife whom I envied on account of her husband* [Gabriele's italics]." And yet, she desired love and marriage, but only according to her own proud ideals.

I know of no pageantry more festive, no ceremony more solemn than a wedding, when a gentle bride comes to the altar accompanied by a worthy matron, and with indescribable feelings of overpowering sweetness, with tears in her eyes, looks into the future which hangs over her that very night, in clear expectation of those things that will follow, extends her trembling hand to the husband who will lead her through life, and whose worth is thereby ennobled and elevated, who is sacred to him right up to the final moment when he may say: *now she is mine!*

I have gone to weddings where I have crept away from the press of people and thanked Heaven, with gentle tears, that it had *joined together two equal souls* [Gabriele's italics], but nowadays one sees few such instances.

In this letter and others, she provided him with a primer on how to win her heart, and Batsányi responded to every cue, including Gabriele's fear that she would go to her grave without ever having known love. "We have found one another late – perhaps too late," he told her. "Our remaining years vanish quickly … the autumn of life is upon us … with every day, every hour, we draw closer to the grave and what will we have found on the long, hard, thorny path?"[31] Gabriele was not easily persuaded, however. Her importunate lover in December 1799, having seen her in a dream, told her ("thou cold, hard maiden") that his nights were more fortunate than his days, that she could become Héloïse to his Abélard, if only she would consent to love him as he loved her (the analogy seems an unfortunate one).[32] That same month, after they had quarreled about her reluctance to trust him and accede entirely to his love, he wrote that God had never created so equal a pair, two instruments more exactly and harmoniously tuned to praise His might.[33] He was not only eloquent but insistent, and his efforts were successful, from the evidence of their increasingly incendiary letters. Exclamation marks and ecstasy fill the pages, as in Gabriele's "poetische Idee über das Ja – bei der Heirath" (poetic idea on "Yes" with regard to marriage):

Stop! – Not yet is the powerful word, whose monosyllabic sound makes the difference between happiness and sadness for humanity, spoken aloud, the word that rules over life and death, that often frees the slave, yet often binds free people and chains them for their entire lives. Mighty word! so gently resounding in the ear of a loving youth, like the silvery tone of a flute, when he draws you forth from his pitiless sweetheart's lips after a long trial. Mighty word! You teach the doubting one faith, call back the dying man from Orcus and elevate the submissive son of destiny above the clouds.

Magic tone, that, avowed before human witnesses, sanctions your sacred right … This "Yes"! Soon it shall resound in my ears from the mouth of the one I love, that through the echo of my stammered response will be transformed from "brother" to "husband." O that the power of these tones does not make the sweetest of husbands into a despot and never lowers me to a slave's state. I would willingly wear chains, but would not hear them rattle nor be made to feel their weight, which none save thou, O Death, can release.[34]

The cataclysm of those first months after meeting her future husband coincided with another milestone in her life: the publication of her collected *Gedichte* in 1800. Looking at the "Catalogue of Subscribers," a literally princely list which includes Franz II and Maria Theresia, Archduke Rudolph, Count Franz Xaver von Auersperg, and others, one realizes anew the courtly circles to which she belonged until her husband's political misfortunes deracinated her, cutting her off from the milieu of her youth and stopping both her patronage and her pen. She even sought her inspiration in courtly circles, in France as well as Austria; several of her poems are paraphrases of works by another aristocratic woman dubbed "The Tenth Muse": Antoinette du Ligier de La Garde Deshoulières (1638?–1694),[35] a "femme sçavante" whose "Sonnet Burlesque, sur la Phèdre de Racine" earned her that great writer's enmity. Of her poetry, the nineteenth-century critic Charles-Augustin Sainte-Beuve wrote that one finally waxes impatient "contre ses petits moutons toujours ramenés," but her powerful late poems on death hardly accord with that pompous dismissal. In her earlier works (idylls, eclogues, chansons, and rondeaux), she writes, in shifting combinations and moods, about love, poetry, women's experiences, and seventeenth-century *mœurs*. She might well have provided Gabriele both with the comforting reassurance that writers of her own sex – women closer at hand than Sappho – had wrestled with many of the same difficulties besetting Gabriele's life and with a model she could transcend; her German paraphrases are exercises in intensification surpassing the French original.[36]

Paging through Gabriele's *Gedichte*, one repeatedly discovers meditations *in* verse *on* verse by women: a Poetess, she reminds us over and over, is an exalted being, the insistence necessary because to be a woman and a poet meant being labeled shameless (poets wear their hearts on their sleeves and make public that which other people hide), pretentious (for claiming that which is supposedly not theirs to claim), and a traitor to their sex (for espousing an occupation other than motherhood). Gabriele announces her principal themes – poetry itself and love's frequent sad aftermath for women – in the engravings on the title pages, the first being a vignette of a *putto* with its back turned and its head twisted around as if to look at the reader while proclaiming, "Ich führe dich in jenen Hayn, komm mit!" (I will lead you into this grove – come with me!). The line is taken from the first poem in the anthology, "Ein Jugendtraum" (A dream in youth), and the *putto* is the "kleine Genius" who appears to her in a dream and leads her to the Muses' meadow, where Apollo has commanded that she receive his lyre. Across from the title page, one sees the engraving of a woman clad in classical drapery and standing by a marble column placed in a darkly-shaded Arcadian grove; she has broken Cupid's arrow in two, and the bow lies on the ground. With that eloquent image, Gabriele claims both the mantle of classical antiquity and the antique role of the lovelorn, abandoned woman. If the role was no longer appropriate to her at the time of publication, it was nonetheless the country and climate in which many of her best poems were created.

For Sappho's descendants, poetry was a realm apart, where a woman could express – and turn into art – erotic emotion, the physicality of passion, the terror of abandonment, the aftermath of desertion, all the experiences and fears forbidden honest revelation in prosaic speech and everyday life. Gabriele is at her most eloquent in this sphere and for this purpose; here is where her poetry finds its truest *raison d'être*. Batsányi failed either to apprehend or appreciate her "Beweggründe zur Dichtkunst" (The motives for poetic art), but Gabriele knew why she wrote poetry and told her readers so in a poem with that didactic title. There, in an example drawn, as usual, from her own life, she writes that an unmarried woman who cannot say "I love" openly can do so in poetry, can send forth the otherwise inexpressible decked out in the trappings of rhyme and meter. And yet, she was aware of the dangers of exposure; according to the ancient formula for women poets, "poetry equals abandonment and abandonment equals shamelessness."[37] In "An einen Freund bey Uebersendung meiner noch unbekannten Manuscripte" (To a friend [Batsányi?] upon consignment of my as yet unknown manuscripts), she confesses her trepidation that the smallest crevices of her heart now lie revealed to the reader's eye – and yet, what pride is evident in the words "my *as yet unknown* manuscripts"! Always, she writes about her inner emotional world; the external world only appears as a reflection of her own feelings, and her infrequent imagery drawn from Nature has little of the passionate conviction with which she writes about women's emotions. The tone she takes and the stance she adopts in her love poetry are notable for the lack of sentimentality and for the often pointed commentary on manners, as when she tweaks the fashion for wearing watches pinned to the bosom:

Verkündet's laut, ihr Grazien und Musen!	Proclaim it aloud, ye graces and Muses!
Die Damen tragen itzt die Uhren in dem Busen.	Women now wear clocks on their breasts.
Weh dem, der Liebe heischt, der hinfühlt tief bewegt,	Woe to him who asks for love, who feels deeply moved,
Und glaubt, es sey ein *Herz*, was ihm entgegen schlägt.[38]	and believes it is a *heart* that beats against him.

It was not only men whose failures of love she observed.

And yet, this is poetry insistently in a woman's voice, the poetic personae nearly always feminine. Gabriele's lineage from Sappho seems especially compelling when she catalogues, as in Sappho's Second Ode, the terrifying, almost unendurable loss of self in the presence of the beloved. The poetic persona of "Das liebende Mädchen" (The young woman in love) recites a catalogue of all the chaotic sensations of a young woman in love, each verse ending with a different question: "was? … warum? … wo? … wohin? … worauf? … wann? … wie?" (what, why, where, where to, what, when, how). No matter what question the poetic persona asks, there is no answer, no terra firma, only a whirlwind in which the beloved seems a divinity and his godliness an intimation of mortality. It is not by coincidence that Gabriele writes of "Sterbens-Wörtchen" (dying little word).

Jüngling, wenn ich Dich von fern erblicke,	Young man, when I glance at you from afar,
Wird vor Sehnsucht mir das Auge nass;	my eyes grow moist with longing;
Nahst Du dich, so hält es mich zurücke	if you draw near, I am held back as if
Wie mit Felsen, – und ich weiss nicht, was?	by stones – and I do not know what it is.
Fern von Dir, hab' ich so viel zu klagen,	Apart from you, I have so much to lament
Und Dir gegenüber sitz' ich stumm,	and next to you, I sit mutely,
Kann Dir nicht ein Sterbens-Wörtchen sagen,	cannot say a dying little word to you,
Stammle nur, – und weiss doch nicht,	but only stammer – and I don't know why.
warum?	
Unwillkührlich hangt an Deinem Blicke	Involuntarily, my eyes are drawn
Oft mein Blick; allein, begegnen so	to yours; alone, should they happen
Beyde sich, – dann fährt er scheu zurücke,	to meet, my gaze withdraws shyly,
Will sich bergen, – ach! und weiss nicht, wo?[39]	and would hide – ah, and knows not where.

(stanzas 1–3 of 7)

And yet this poem, in which language is deployed to record language's failure in the face of passion, is immediately followed in the 1805 revised second edition of the anthology by "Die weggeworfene Rose" (The discarded rose). The placement is surely not coincidental: *this*, she tells her female readers, is the danger you incur when you place your destiny in the hands of someone who may well discard you when you are no longer young and beautiful.

So lange Sie noch frisch am Strauche glühte,	As long as she still glowed afresh on the bush,
War sie der Wunsch des Jünglings, – dann	she was the desire of young men, then his
sein Raub;	booty;
Und nun, – da sie an seiner Brust	and now, when she has faded on his breast,
verblühte, –	cold and uncaring,
Wirft er sie kalt und achtlos in den Staub! …	he throws her on the ground!
Soll ich vielleicht an ihr mein Schicksal lesen,	Shall I perhaps read in her the fate
Das mich bedroht, wenn mein Jugend flieht?	that threatens me when my youth flees?
O Gott! so lass mich sterben und verwesen,	O God, let me die and pass away
Bevor noch ganz mein kurzer Lenz verblüht![40]	before my brief springtime is entirely gone!

Male poets have for centuries sung of women as roses whose beauty and brief flowering become a metaphor for seizing the sexual advantage with young women, as a seducer's ploy (Pierre de Ronsard's "Mignonne, allons voir si la rose" comes to mind), but it is the aftermath of such scenarios in abandonment that is Gabriele's subject. For present-day readers, what is most affecting about this poem is the dilemma at its core: she recognizes the injustice of it all, her anger evident in the words "Raub," "kalt und achtlos," and yet her fear that this fate might become her own compels the wish for death before her youth is entirely over. Gabriele was, one realizes with a pang, true to her perception that anything at all was better than abandonment and paid a terrible price for her resolution.

    Over and over again, Gabriele tells her readers that a woman loses control of her destiny when she deeds her heart to the man she loves (did she, one wonders, ever read these poems in the wake of the 1809 disaster and shudder at the applicability of her earlier words to her own fate?). In "Grosse Wirkungen aus kleinen Ursachen" (Great effects from little causes), revised as "Warnung der Mutter" (A mother's warning) in the 1805 edition, a mother tells her daughter that the most seemingly inconsequential motions can give rise to great and unforeseen effects. Just as a single drop of water poured from a glass makes everything in the glass shudder, move, and overflow, so too, a single kiss from a young man can lead to the loss of peace and happiness.

So, Mädchen! ist ein Kuss des Jünglings, den Du liebst,	Just so, maiden, is a kiss from the young man you love,
Ein Tropfen Deinem übervollen Herzen.	one little drop from your overflowing heart.
D'rum, willst Du, sorgenlos, nicht Glück und Ruh verscherzen,	Therefore, lest you carelessly forfeit your peace and happiness,
So fürchte jeden Kuss, eh' Du ihn nimmst und giebst!⁴¹	beware each kiss before you give or take it!
	(3rd and final stanza, 1805 edition)

In "Schwur und Glaube" (Vow and belief), she tells, in a nutshell, the age-old story of a maiden who believed "Siegmund's" vows of undying love, his proclamation that "Should this heart, which loves you so sweetly, so passionately, ever be untrue to you, then, linden leaves, fall to the ground, and you, beloved stream, turn to ice!" But "he fled; she wept; he never came again," and the poem ends with the woman's voice saying:

"Ach, Gott! er hat nicht falsch geschworen,	O God, he did not swear falsely –
Ich hab ihm nur zu leicht geglaubt!	I believed in him too easily,
Denn alle Quellen sind gefroren,	for all streams are frozen
Und alle Bäume sind entlaubt."⁴²	and all trees lose their leaves.

And yet, whatever the warnings, with whatever justification, she prized love and friendship, specifically, erotic love between men and women and friendship between women, above all else in life. Titles such as "Bey dem Kuss einer Freundinn" (Upon kissing a friend), "Freundschaftsbund an Elisen" (Bonds of friendship with Elise), "Am Geburtstag meiner geliebtesten Freundinn Constance" (On the birthday of my most beloved friend Constance), "Auf die Genesung einer Freundinn" (On a friend's recovery), and "Der Schwesternbund an Fanny" (The sisterly alliance with Fanny) attest to the importance of female friendship in her life – a poetic motif that is almost on a par with erotic love in the 1800 original edition, far less so in the 1805 edition after Batsányi had deleted those poems he considered too slight. Occasional poems about unexalted creatures such as his fiancée's women friends would not have passed muster as sufficiently "noble" subjects.

But love did, and the nexus of love, poetry, and life was Gabriele's principal concern. No coward she, Gabriele knew that, whatever the difficulties and dangers, we learn more from Dido than we do from Aeneas. In "An Ihn" (To him), she joins the throng who parodied Friedrich Matthisson's "Ich denke Dein" (Goethe's is the most famous of the lot), but seldom inverted in this fashion: the poetic persona who hymns the beloved is female, the beloved is male:

Ich denke Dein, wenn sich die Aussicht
  trübet,
Wenn Nacht und Stille jedes Herz,
  das liebet,
In süsse Träume wiegt.

Ich denke Dein, wenn mir der Tage schon
  grauet,
Der Mond noch winkt,
Und dort im Busch, vom Regen überthauet
Die Ros' entblättert sinkt.

...

Ach! komm, Du Licht und Wonne meiner
  Seele!
Komm endlich doch!
Denn sonst verschmachtet Deine Gabriele
Und stirbt vor Sehnsucht noch![43]

I think of you, when the prospects that lie
  before me are gloomy,
when night and quietness cradle every loving
  heart
in sweet dreams.

I think of you when the day already dawns
  gray for me,
the moon still shines,
and there in the bushes, dewed with raindrops,
the withered rose falls

...

Oh come, light and delight of my soul!

Come then at last!
For your Gabriele pines for you
and dies for longing!   (stanzas 2, 3, and 8 of 8)

No wonder she was dubbed "the Sappho of Vienna." To love, to be loved, in the manner she considered worthy of human beings at their best was for her the non plus ultra. But she was keenly aware of the tribulations inherent in love as well as in lovelessness; rose-colored glasses were not her wont. In "Selbstgespräch," one of her most eloquent and beautiful poems, she poses the question "What is life with and without love?" and comes to the pessimistic conclusion that sorrow is plentiful in either condition:

Was ist ein Leben ohne Liebe?
Ein ödes Daseyn, dumpf und trübe,
Das uns nicht Schmerz, nicht Lust gewährt,
Das kein Gefühl als Unmuth nährt;
Ein martervolles Nichtbehagen
An allem, was uns sonst entzückt,
Das, unberechtiget zu Klagen,
Doch jeder Freude Keim erstickt;
Ein kalter Hinblick auf die Scenen
Der allbelebenden Natur,
Ein Mittelding von Scheu und Sehnen
Beym Anblick jeder Creatur.
Ein dämmernd Licht, das auf die Wonne
Des Lebens Riesenschatten streut,
Und einer künft'gen Glückessonne
Schon zweifelhafte Flecken leiht;
Ein Unkraut, das der Hoffnung Blüthen
Im Herzen nicht gedeihen läßt ...

...

Was ist ein liebesvolles Leben?
Ein langes Fieber, das zuletzt

What is life without love?
A barren existence, dull and dark,
that vouchsafes us neither sorrow nor joy,
that nurtures us with no feeling other
than ill-temper; an excruciating malaise
with everything that once delighted us,
that, unentitled to lamentation,
yet nips every joy in the bud;
a cold prospect of the scenery
of all-revivifying Nature,
a middling thing between shyness
and desire at the sight of every creature.
A twilight that casts giant shadows
on all the joys of life,
and already casts wavering flecks
on the sun of future fortune,
a weed that the flowers of hope
in the heart should not allow to flourish.

...

What is a love-filled life?
A long fever, that finally becomes

Unheilbar wird; ein banges Schweben	incurable; a fearful swaying
In einem schwanken Schiff, das jetzt	in a weak ship, that now
Auf ruhigen Gewässern gleitet,	glides on peaceful waters
Und Hoffnung an dem Steuer hat,	and has hope at its helm,
Jetzt, wenn der Sturm der Meer bestreitet,	now, when an ocean tempest besieges it,
Herumgeweht wird, wie ein Blatt,	tosses like a leaf,
Bald auf ein wüstes Eiland treibet,	at times driven ashore to a barren
Bald nieder in die Flut sich senkt,	island, at times submerged in the flood,
Auf Felsenklippen hangen bleibet,	left hanging on the rocky crags,
Und dann die Schiffenden ertränkt.[44]	and then those aboard drown.

Whatever the risks, whatever the inevitability of sorrow, she wanted a "liebesvolles Leben" and recognized, well before meeting Batsányi, that she could not marry an ordinary man. In a punning couplet entitled "Aeusserung über die Wahl eines Gatten" (Dictum about the choice of a husband), she observed, "Mein künftiger Gemahl muss eigensinnig seyn; / Dann liebt er mich vielleicht aus Eigensinn allein" (My future husband must be headstrong; then perhaps he will love me out of self-will alone).[45] He was and he did – and the result was every bit as stormy as she had predicted.

When the *Gedichte* appeared, however, she had love in the particular rather than the poetic to decipher. The new century had brought her to a crossroads, and by Sylvester's Eve, she had all but capitulated, telling him, "I am no more my own – what more do you want? Your fate is now bound to mine ... why do you wish me to bind myself to you by means of a ring? Do you think I love you less when I am supposedly free and unbound?"[46] On 5 January 1800, Gabriele sought once again to extricate herself from a love whose power she feared, but was unsuccessful and wrote to him, saying, "Only you can see through all the crevices of my soul; in your vicinity, I am entirely light, but when you are distant from me, I am once more obscured by a thousand clouds, imprisoned within myself, a stranger to myself."[47] Fiordiligi's capitulation "Fa di me quel che ti par" (Make of me what pleases you) in act 2 of *Così fan tutte* comes unbidden to mind when one reads her words, all the more so as the operatic figment of the imagination and the real-life poetess seem related in their proud characters, their emotional extravagance, and the belittling, silencing effect of the loves to which they accede.

There are few things in life more seductive than the promise to subordinate one's own gifts to those of the beloved. Batsányi swore that he believed absolutely in her poetic genius, that he wanted nothing more in life than to be remembered as the one who fostered her verse and stood by her side, but the reality was otherwise. In a mammoth letter of 1 February 1800 to Gabriele, he criticizes an ode she had sent him. "I have already marked the prosodic faults, which must be corrected," he says, and then tells her that she can never write poetry expressive of the highest ideals until "your poetic language resembles that of Klopstock more closely than it already does, until it is even more refined in construction than it already is, and until you have had even greater practice and facility in the highest kind of versification and poetic technique."[48] The letter is particularly ghastly because he mixes rapturous praise with dictatorial advice whose effect was ultimately to undermine her confidence in her own creativity. She is already a true poet, he assures her, and, with his help, she will become even greater; he asks for nothing more from fate than that he should be the one who provides her with the means for immortality.[49] Despite the underlying admonition that she become something other than she was, Gabriele was grateful for his tutelage, calling him "my beloved, dear, good Apollo!" in March 1800.[50] His intent to become her very own self-appointed god of poetry may have been well-meant, at least on the surface, but the execution (indeed the apposite word) recalls Apollo and Marsyas more than anything else in classical mythology. In effect, Batsányi flayed the pen right out of her hand.

The concern for her poetic renown was an effective means of eliciting the physical response he desired, from the evidence of a rhapsodic letter in which Batsányi proclaims: "Hail to thee, firstborn of the Divinity! ... The noblest, the most proud, and highest! The most unique of your gender! The worthiest and most resolute of all maidens!" etc.[51] Prevented by bad weather on 26 February 1800 from venturing forth to see her, he writes a letter that is either the erotic fantasy of a longed-for future or evidence of a physical relationship already commenced.[52] In late September, Gabriele wrote a series of fragmentary "Reflexionen und Entwürfe" (Reflections and sketches) about the alliance between passion and art in her life; in these aphoristic sketches, she planned to hold the "Mirror of Truth" up to him (she capitalizes the pronoun "Er" throughout, as if he were God). He would, she writes, see therein what he refused to understand; she would then take him by the hand and lead him back to the boundaries of friendship, whose borders he had so rashly transgressed.[53] It was a resolution she did not enact.

Gabriele's mother did everything she could to separate the lovers, especially when Batsányi returned to Hungary to see his dying mother. The situation became so tense that Batsányi ceased visiting the Baumberg house, although his correspondence with Gabriele continued. Gabriele's father died on 13 April 1801, after sending his blessings to Batsányi from his death bed; his death was followed by that of Gabriele's mother on 3 August of that same year. Although the lovers could then marry, their poverty forced them to delay the marriage until 1805, when Batsányi was promoted to a position as a junior civil servant at court. Whatever one thinks of Batsányi's behavior, Gabriele loved him, and the poem she wrote on their first anniversary is a measure of that adoration. "Today it has been a year," she begins, "since, with the seventh hour of evening, struck the end of my last freedom, where friendship in gentle league with brotherly love stirred the spark of flame in our hearts, where I, illuminated in the sunlight from your eyes, saw my greatest happiness and my pride, where the rays of the most angelically pure rapture melted, Seclusion, your cold seal."

Als mich dein erster Bruderkuss entzückte,	As I was enraptured by your first
Da stand mein Blut in seinem schnellen Lauf,	brotherly kiss, my blood was arrested
Dein heisser Mund berührte mich und drückte	in its swift course; your warm mouth
Ein göttlich Siegel meinen Lippen auf.	touched mine and pressed a divine seal on
	my lips.

Ich war entrückt aus meinem Alltagskreise,	I was enraptured, carried away from my
Die Seele schwamm in einem Wonnenmeer;	everyday surroundings; my soul swam in a
Mistrauisch in mich selbst, fragt' ich Dich leise:	sea of rapture; mistrustful of myself, I asked
Ist diese Bruderliebe nur – nichts mehr?	you softly: Is this only brotherly love –
	nothing more?
Du weihtest mich zur Priesterin heil'ger	You consecrated me as the priestess of
Flammen,	sacred fires,
Und keusch wie Westa selbst bewahr' ich sie,	and, chaste as Vesta herself, I guarded them;
Eh' würde ich mich zum Opfertod verdammen,	sooner would I damn myself to a sacrificial
Als zu entweihn den Bund der Sympathie.	death than profane the ties of sympathy.
Kein Mann nach Dir darf diesen Mund	No man after you may touch this mouth,
berühren,	
Den Deine Zärtlichkeit der Welt verschloss;	which your sweetness has closed away from
Soll heisse Sehnsucht mich zum kühlen Grabe	the world; should passionate longing lead me
führen,	to the cool grave,
So sink' ich ungeküsst hinab in seinen Schooss.[54]	then I will sink, still unkissed into its bosom.

If ever there was anyone capable of sustaining so high-flown a conception of love, it was Gabriele, but even a saint would have had difficulty keeping such a "sacred flame" alive in the midst of the conflagration that overwhelmed them both in 1809, when Napoleon occupied Vienna and Batsányi had the opportunity to put his political ideals into practice.

While the couple waited for the means to marry, Batsányi directed the revision of her *Gedichte* (would she, one wonders, have felt the need to revise her poems without his prodding?), which was published in 1805, the year of their wedding. For the occasion, the writer Friedrich Ludwig Wilhelm Meyern wrote a lengthy introductory essay entitled "Ansichten eines Freundes der Kunst und der Dichterinn" (Opinions of a friend of Art and of the Poetess) in which he first defines in the abstract what a poet is and does and then justifies on that basis both the existence of female poets and Gabriele's choice of love as her principal subject matter. "To ask whether there should be female poets," he states, "seems to me the same as asking: do women think and feel?"[55] Should we not rejoice, he asks, in the art born of another way of feeling, another mode of perception, a new way of speech? Women poets should beware only that they do not echo masculine modes but speak in their own voices, an ironic observation in light of Batsányi's heavy-handed direction of this very volume. It is often debated, Meyern continues, whether women should talk openly about love "without the horrible propriety the world demands." Is a false silence better than the truth, he asks? Should not the pure, free spirit dare to unveil, even with the dangers of misunderstanding by coarser souls, what she knows of love as a matter of the most refined emotions?[56] For all the forward-looking feminism of Meyern's essay, he too dispensed mixed messages in which the insistence upon the traditionally feminine qualities of gentleness, sweetness, and purity resides side-by-side with praise for one who foreswore hypocrisy.[57]

Under Batsányi's direction, Gabriele's poetic anthology shrank from its prior 297 pages to 152 pages in 1805, from 155 poems to forty-two, many of them renamed and revised. While the collection itself diminished, individual poems grew; his crusade to make her poetic tone more elevated often involved greater verbiage. To cite only a few such instances, "Ein Jugendtraum" becomes "Lebenstraum" – she was no longer young, and the "Song of Innocence" is now a "Song of Experience" – and is vastly expanded, while "An ein Brautpaar" is also augmented and becomes "Guter Rath, an ein Brautpaar" (Good advice to a newly-married couple). "Schwärmerey in einer sterneheitern Frühlingsnacht" (Emotions on a starry spring night) is revised and renamed "Melancholie" (Melancholy), the tone more solemn than before. At her husband's urging, Gabriele experimented with classical meters in such poems as "Begleitung, bey Übersendung eines Gemäldes" (Accompaniment to the presentation of a painting [by Heinrich Füger of Lucius Junius Brutus, the first consul of Rome]), but the attempts are not successful: she was writing pseudo-Batsányi, not Baumberg, and her heart was not in it. And yet, he was the inspiration for the happiest poems she was ever to write; she had at last found the love she had longed for and wanted to broadcast the glad tidings to the entire German-speaking world. The 1805 anthology ends with the poem "Die Glückliche (Nach Pfeffel.) Zum Gedächtniss des 10. Junius 1805" (The Fortunate Woman [after Gottlieb Konrad Pfeffel]. In Celebration of 10 June 1805) – her wedding day. In this poem, she hymns Batsányi as friend, brother, teacher, and lover. "Only God and the Fatherland are dearer to me than his heart," she wrote in the fifteenth stanza, words that may well have come back to haunt her four years later. In stanzas 6–10, she praises him as her instructor in poetry:

Und einen Lehrer! ... Dieser borgt	And a teacher! ... this one never borrows
Nie fremdes Licht; und mehr	illumination from strangers,
Für mich und meinen Ruhm besorgt	and no one could care more about me
Kann keiner seyn, als Er.	and my fame than he does.
Die Weise, wie man richtig denkt,	The manner by which one thinks aright
Und, fern von Schein und Wahn,	and, far from mere appearance and delusion,
Den freyen Geist im Fluge lenkt	guides the free spirit in flight
Den Sonnenweg hinan:	out into the sunlit way:
Die Art, wie man die Leyer stimmt,	The art by which one tunes the lyre
Dass nie der Ton verhallt, –	so that the tone never dies away –
Dass er den Weg zum Herzen nimmt,	so that each finds its way to the heart
Es zwingt mit Allgewalt;	and overcomes it with almighty power;
Und jene seltne hohe Kunst,	And that rare high art,
Die mich sein Beyspiel lehrt,	which his example teaches me,
Wie man die wandelbare Gunst	by which one lightly dispenses
Fortunens leicht entbehrt:	with Fortune's changeable favor;
All' diess verdank' ich Ihm allein,	For all this, I am grateful to him alone,
Ihm alles, was ich bin!	to him I owe everything I am!
D'rum soll auch laut und ewig seyn	Therefore his pupil's thanks
Der Dank der Schülerin![58]	shall be loudly proclaimed!

No matter what one thinks, and however rightly, of his influence, "Die Glückliche" is a happy and touching way in which to end the anthology, all the more so as she was shortly to become "Die *Unglückliche.*" It is no wonder that the mournful engraving of the earlier edition had to be replaced, although one notes that the classical female figure seated in an Italianate landscape outside a small temple in the 1805 frontispiece is alone, unaccompanied by any male figure. Sappho is ever thus, and Gabriele still proudly claimed to be her descendant.

Between her marriage and the catastrophe of 1809, she wrote her largest and most ambitious poem: *Amor und Hymen, Ein Gedicht zur Vermählung einer Freundinn* (Amor and Hymen, A Poem on the Wedding of a Friend) of 1807.[59] In this work, perhaps inspired by Christoph Martin Wieland's neo-Grecian romances, she preaches the gospel of right and worthy marriage. As the title proclaims, this is an allegory of Love and Marriage, who were friends until they both saw a myrtle entwined with a thornless rosebud and fought over possession of the rose. A "heavenly maiden" told the two miscreants that flowers thus woven together by the gods for the benefit of humanity must not be destroyed, but Amor stole the rosebud and ran away with it. The maiden then commanded Hymen to take the myrtle and told him that he was the more fortunate of the pair because the rose, love, and "the free republic of young hearts" would vanish with the spring, but Hymen's myrtle grove would provide the best refuge of all, although one could enter the myrtle grove of marriage only through Love's kingdom. After various adventures,[60] Love himself leads a pair of emblematic lovers across the waters to Marriage's kingdom and a *lieto fine* at the end of the fifth canto. The lovers are easily recognizable as Gabriele and Batsányi, whatever the veil of allegorical universality: for an all-too-brief period of her life, she believed that her long travail had turned to enduring joy, and she made the voyage to happiness into a work whose expansiveness seems emblematic of larger ambitions and the peace in which to pursue them – but it was not to be.

There are still mysteries surrounding the descent into tragedy. According to Eduard Wertheimer's 1884 *feuilleton* on Gabriele in the *Neue Freie Presse*, the powerful head of the Imperial Police Department, Count Josef von Sedlnitzky, whose nephew was one of Batsányi's rivals for Gabriele's hand, may have been responsible for the couple's misery,[61] but it now seems certain that the forces of history, not romance, were the cause. The tale begins with Napoleon's proclamation of 15 May 1809 to the Hungarians to rise up in revolt against their Austrian rulers, a proclamation printed in two variants: one in French- German-Hungarian and one in French-Latin-Hungarian (Latin was the official language of Hungary until 1844).

Hungarians! The Austrian emperor, unfaithful to his treaties, ignoring the generosity with which I have treated him after three consecutive wars, and notably after the war of 1805, has attacked my armies. I have beaten back this unjust agression. The Lord who grants victory, who punishes the ingrate and the liar has looked kindly on my army: I have entered the capital of Austria and am now on your borders. It is the emperor of Austria, not the king of Hungary, who declared war on me; according to your laws, he should not have been able to do so without your consent, etc. etc.[62]

Historians have long debated about who translated the proclamation into Hungarian and who wrote the inflammatory tract "Nobilis Hungarus ad Hungaros," dated 19 May 1809, designed to popularise the proclamation among the uncultivated minor nobility. Batsányi always denied the charge that he had written the tract, calling it a "travail bâclé" (a botched piece of work), but he could not deny complicity in the proclamation. For all Batsányi's pleading that he only "completed" or "corrected" the work of another translator, Gilbert Schuy has demonstrated that the Hungarian text reflects Batsányi's orthography throughout[63] and that Batsányi even inserted additional fiery phrases to give the proclamation a more passionate character. When he did so, he placed himself – and his wife – at the center of a conflagration that would engulf their entire lives thereafter.

After Batsányi fled Vienna at the end of 1809, Gabriele was interrogated several times, but denied knowing anything about her husband's whereabouts or his reasons for departing. Because she was surrounded by spies, with both her maid and caretaker on the police payroll, she sent her letters to Batsányi via secret couriers. Correspondence by such circuitous means was very slow; Gabriele heard nothing until early 1810 and was terrified that he might be ill, in need, or even dead.[64] In despair, she went to the noted Orientalist Joseph von Hammer-Purgstall, soon to leave for Paris to study Oriental manuscripts, and asked him to bring her news and letters. Batsányi at last wrote on 1 March 1810 to say that God had helped to foil his foes and preserve his life, although she did not receive the letter for a month.[65]

It was at this time, with Gabriele's life in turmoil, that her husband's literary jealousies became especially intense. In that first letter from exile, he forbade her to write, with the only exceptions being permission to finish her "better" fragments, such as "Schillers Bild" (a poem in praise of a suitably revered model) and revise poetry from her previous anthology; it would be deleterious to her health, he told her, to do anything more.[66] The real reason was that he did not want her writing poetry he could not control for purposes he did not endorse. Two anecdotes in particular from the letters of 1810 confirm that there was an active rivalry between them, fanned by Gabriele's disclosures of literary success in his absence. In her reply on 4 April 1810 to his first Parisian letter, she gleefully recounts that in the most recent issue of the *Vaterländische Blätter*, Batsányi's fame was compared to a moon that only borrowed radiance from the sun, the sun being herself.[67] Even though she hastily exclaims "Quel Unsinn!!" (What nonsense!), she promises to send him a copy of the paper as soon as she can obtain an extra one.[68] How interesting that she would thus insist that he see the evidence of her greater literary acclaim – but then, he had assured her that his life's mission was service to her Muse. If she ever believed that this could occur without friction, the next such instance might well have cured her of the notion.

The second time, Batsányi lashed back. The Archduchess Marie Luise of Austria was married to Napoleon in 1810, and Gabriele wrote a celebratory poem entitled "Das Waisenlied" (The Orphan's Song) for the event.[69] In an undated letter, Gabriele recounted to Batsányi all the details of her coup, as she conceived it.[70] When she took the manuscript of her poem to the Archduchess's court, she was told that the work must be submitted directly to the king for him to give to the bride. Gabriele, fearing the king's displeasure because of her husband, then gave the poem as an anonymous work to Prince Trautmannsdorf, who assured her that he would personally deliver it to the king. Anxiety about the monarch's permission for publication cost her a sleepless night, but the permission was duly granted. Gabriele delightedly lists the number of copies in vellum bound in bridal-white or kingly red, the 500 copies printed for general distribution, the requests by the likes of Prince Auersperg and the Duchess Colloredo for copies, and the praise she has received. "You cannot believe, dear heart, how much attention and public notice I have won since that time. People come from everywhere and bring copies to the house ... and vie for the honor of participating in such a great event"[71] – one realizes anew how thoroughly Viennese she was. She even wanted Batsányi to translate the poem into French so that the bridegroom could understand it better.

Far from sharing her delight, Batsányi was furious. In a letter of 13 May 1810, he excoriated her for relishing the approbation of his enemies, for acting as if he were already dead and buried, for selfishly pursuing her own interests, for behavior unworthy of his wife.[72] She should remember whose name she bears, he wrote: it is his name, and he wishes to take it pure and spotless to his grave. He accused her of having decided to go her separate way out of weariness at the long wait for his return and played the martyr, telling her that he was not born to luck and Heaven alone knows what he has had to endure and must yet endure. Seven days later, he resumed the attack, telling her that he could not believe she had been seduced by mere praise into an action that could only be a triumph for his enemies.[73] Gabriele at first attempted to placate him, telling him on 14 July 1810 that her poem was printed anonymously, that he must forgive her "sin in Apollo" – a revealing choice of words. But by the end of the month, she had changed her tune and told him spiritedly that of everything she had written, this had pleased her and everyone else the most. One must seize the moment, she declared, and the poem was a means of reaching those who could help them out in their predicament and even bring them to safe harbor.[74] Furthermore, she informed him that thirty years before she ever became his wife, she had learned to be proud of her name – a flash of self-assertion one can only applaud.[75]

But, despite behavior that made a mockery of his wish to serve her Muse, Gabriele remained faithful to Batsányi in his tribulations. She could not follow him to France until April 1811, however, and only after delicate negotiations with Metternich to obtain the necessary passes for legal departure. Although Gabriele assured her husband on 31 July 1810, "I am resolved and ready to follow you unquestioningly wherever you go, to share your destiny with you,"[76] she had also made her fears apparent in another letter written that same month: "My heart bleeds at the thought, should posterity ever come to discover it, of two such singular people, parted by malign destiny, condemned to wander about the world, shunned by their own fellow-citizens and driven from their midst ..."[77] and her despair was to escalate as the prospect came closer. Her age – she was forty-four at the time – and delicate health made the thought of exile all the more difficult; in one letter, she made a painful jest that "antique heads also have their worth – you should write an ode to my silver hair," to which Batsányi replied, "Gray hair means nothing. Every season has its virtue."[78] Only her bitterness at "the thousandfold deceits that have been done to us both" made the thought of leaving Vienna possible.[79]

One could cry aloud to the heavens at the conduct of your friends and enemies!! They have persecuted you, slandered you, and robbed me of ten years of my life; they have deceived you with hopes, fed you promises, and for this entire year done *nothing* for you. This does not accord at all with the high ideals I have of friendship.[80]

She made no secret of her forthcoming voyage, she told him in a letter of 25 September 1810, and was engaged in selling her books, paintings, and drawings to various members of the nobility; the negotiations go slowly, she writes ruefully, because one dare not press these people for payment.[81]

Throughout the autumn and winter of 1810, the pair pinned their hopes on Metternich's good offices. On 23 September, Batsányi told Gabriele that he had spoken to Metternich, who was returning to Vienna from Paris in two days, and that she should seek an audience with this "just and noble man" to request his help.[82] Gabriele complied, telling her husband on 14 October, "Leave everything to your Joan of Arc."[83] After her meeting with Metternich, she recounted the proceedings in a gigantic letter begun on All Souls' Day "under the muffled sounds of the bells for the dead."[84] Fascinatingly, she writes out verbatim the dialogue between herself and the powerful minister, including Metternich's unflattering assessment of Batsányi's character. "I pity him," Metternich stated, "but he is himself guilty [for his plight]. He is one of those men who conform to no mold and who, being of lively imagination, are easily led astray into paths that bring about their misfortune, especially as they seize upon everything with great energy." He would be unfortunate anywhere, in any society, the minister continued, because he did not know how to compromise; Metternich did, however, agree that others were also to blame for Batsányi's misfortunes. When Gabriele bravely stated that she alone was fortunate enough to harmonize with "this noblest of men," Metternich replied that this was perhaps more to her credit than Batsányi's and asked whether she wished to be re-united with her husband. "It is my greatest and only wish, and the reason why I have sought an audience with you," she replied. The difficulty was gaining permission from the king, ill-disposed to granting favors for anyone connected with the "traitor" Batsányi. Batsányi's flight was not in his favor, the minister observed, to which Gabriele replied that friends had feared for his life and she herself had begged him to leave.

As the negotiations proceeded, Batsányi became alarmed by what he perceived as her wavering resolve to join him. In a letter of 9 November 1810, he told her that if she decided to remain in Austria, she would never see him again.[85] He need not have feared – that same day, she wrote him from Vienna with a detailed itinerary of her journey, coupled with complaints about travelling in the depths of winter.[86] She was clearly both embittered by what she perceived as Vienna's mistreatment of her husband and filled with anguish at the thought of leaving her homeland and native city.

The part that I play is not a joyful one, I agree, and at my age and in this season, one does not make a trip to Paris as a tour. But this is the only way I can see my husband, and no one in the world will prevent me from doing so. And for the rest, what do I have to lose here? My parents are dead, and thank God, they will not see the day I leave these walls, the sole and only witnesses to all my troubles, all my joys, all my sorrows. My friends? They are unmasked to their disadvantage andar e not worthy of remembrance – I will forget those ingrates. I will leave my childhood home without a tear and my country without a sigh in order to rejoin the only friend I have in the world.[87]

Batsányi renewed the threat of perpetual banishment from his side several times. He did not receive Gabriele's account of the meeting with Metternich until late November 1810, and he reacted angrily, vowing never to return and excoriating those "phlegmatic temperaments" who objected to his fieriness. He would not be lured back in order to be betrayed and perhaps even murdered, and he repeated his previous injunction: "If you would ever see me again in this life, if you are unalterably bound to share my destiny, then you must follow me into exile." We want no more mercy, he wrote,[88] and told her to put a final close to her life in her native city. If homesickness for the Stephansdom overwhelmed her and she wished to go back, she would do so without him.[89]

The delicate diplomatic maneuvering to obtain a passport out of the country was finally accomplished. On 17 December 1810, Gabriele wrote to her husband to say that Metternich had appeared "like an angel from Heaven" to tell her that the king was in a receptive mood.[90] The necessary permission was granted on 5 January 1811, and Gabriele both thanked her monarch and bade him farewell on 13 March, followed by a series of farewell visits to various members of the nobility.[91] On 6 April 1811, two weeks after her forty-fifth birthday, she left Vienna; Napoleon had in the meantime offered a pension of 2,000 francs a year to Batsányi as a "man of letters," thus rescuing the couple from complete penury. Misery at the now-inescapable fact of exile overwhelmed any happiness at the thought of seeing her soul-mate once again: "But when I think that I must begin setting up house in a strange land, starting from the beginning, I shudder. Good night! It must be! This is the last sacrifice that I can bring to you! Consummatum est!"[92] On 22 April, she wrote to tell him of the imminent deaths of various statesmen who had been his enemies. If she were not so far along in her journey, she tells him, she would turn back; in a bitter reversal of his repeated threats to her, she states that if he wished to see her again, he would have to come to Vienna. But it is too late now: she must, she writes in palpable anger, finish eating the sour apple into which she has already bitten. Batsányi's threats, coupled with her love for him, had sufficed to uproot her from her native country, but she was unhappy about it, and she let him know it. Nowhere, one notices, in the extant letters does he make any attempt to comfort her or to assume the burden of responsibility, to say, "I did this to you … my misfortune has cost you your home … I am so sorry."

The couple arrived together in Paris on 27 April and lived there quietly, in modest circumstances, for the next three years. By 1814, they were apprehensive about their future: the political situation in Paris was uncertain, and Batsányi's pension, their only source of income, was in danger. When Emperor Franz I received Gabriele benevolently upon his visit to Paris in 1814, the couple decided to return to Vienna. Gabriele arrived first on 11 September 1814, in order to make sure that Batsányi could return safely. She received little help from either her friends or the emperor, however, and was so poor that she was forced to support herself by selling needlework. When she fell ill and went to Baden-Baden, she encountered Marie Luise there, and the empress promised to intervene to her father on Gabriele's behalf.

After Napoleon's final defeat at Waterloo, the Austrians flooded into Paris, and on 5 August, Batsányi was arrested. To the old charge of translating Napoleon's proclamation, a new charge was added: he was said to have abused the Austrian emperor verbally and in public. When Gabriele received his letter ten days later, she was struck dumb with grief. "Since I received your letter, I have been in mute despair. I have said not a word to anyone – I have borne the entire weight of my misery locked silently in my breast." Batsányi was brought to Brünn on 15 October and imprisoned in Spielberg Castle, while Gabriele, whose circumstances soon became dire, was taken in by a Countess Kokorsova who had befriended her in earlier days. Gabriele wrote to Batsányi of weeping unnoticed into the expensive vintages served at the countess's table; she felt, she told him, like Goethe's Harper (in "An die Türen will ich schleichen," with its lines "A kind hand will offer food / And I shall go on my way"). To alleviate her financial woes, she planned to write her autobiography, but that project, along with plans for an autobiographical play, never came to fruition. If only she had done so – what, one wonders, would she have made of her fate for a public readership?

When the investigation ended, Batsányi was found innocent of treason in the matter of the proclamation, while the other charge was dismissed for lack of evidence. His release was again due to Gabriele's efforts: she had obtained an audition with the emperor in the summer of 1816 and pleaded her husband's cause. When Franz I married Charlotte von Wittelsbach (Franz's fourth marriage) in November 1816, Gabriele wrote an epithalamium entitled "Die deutsche Muse" (The German Muse), a not-so-covert plea for mercy directed to Charlotte. "Yes, more beautiful times have finally come again!", the poet sings, after celebrating the end of war:

Vorüber sind die langen, wilden Stürme,	The long, wild storms are over,
Gehemmt zu Land und See dies Krieges Lauf;	war's path arrested on land and sea;
Die Erde, sicher unterm Schutz und Schirme	the earth, secure under the shelter and protec-
Der Friedensgöttinn, athmet freyer auf.	tion of the goddess of peace, breathes freely.
Versöhnt und einig sind die Nationen, –	The nations are reconciled and united –
Die Menschenfreunde steh'n erwartungsvoll,	the friends of humanity stand expectantly
Und blicken segnend hin, wo auf den Thronen	and look reverently hence, where Justice only
Mit Huld gepaart das Recht nur herrschen	should reign, together with kindness, on
soll.[93]	the thrones.

She even published two poems "Schillers Bild" (On an Image of Schiller) and "An Füger" (To [Heinrich] Füger), in the *Taschenbuch Aglaja* for 1816 and did so under the name Gabriele Batsányi.[94] But despite her efforts on her husband's behalf,

Sedlnitzky sent the poet into internal exile in Linz and offered Gabriele a pension if she remained in Vienna. Gabriele, however, refused the offer and went to share her husband's fate in Linz, where they lived at first in miserable poverty. Sedlnitzky initially blocked all their attempts to win support from the court, but by 1817, Batsányi again received his pension from the French government and Gabriele regained the small pension from her father's estate. The couple found prestigious friends in their new environment, including the governor of Upper Austria and his family.

The last years, however, were grim. Shortly before her death, she wrote to a friend to say that she had been unable to leave her lodgings for three years; a doctor had recommended medicinal spa baths, but she could not afford the treatments, despite a charitable grant from the emperor. At 11 o'clock in the evening on 24 July 1839, she died; that night, Batsányi wrote on a scrap of paper, "Half of my life is gone. Fate, do not delay, take the other half soon." He would have six more years to wait before Fate complied. Four days after Gabriele's death, her poem "An mein Mann" (To my husband) was printed in Vienna at the instigation of Joseph von Hammer-Purgstall, despite initial reluctance on the part of the censors (interestingly, Hammer-Purgstall does not mention Gabriele or her husband once in his memoirs). One hardly knows what to think: that her elegy should be a poem in praise of her husband seems both bitterly ironic and yet appropriate, given his mammoth impress on her life and art.

"DURCH LIEDER GERN GESTÖRT": SCHUBERT AND THE BAUMBERG SONGS

What did the young Schubert find in Gabriele's poetry to beguile him to musical setting on two different occasions? They seem so utterly unlike, the melancholy, intense older woman from the fringes of the Austrian *ancien régime* and the adolescent son of a bourgeois schoolmaster, especially as Gabriele was obsessed with the contemporary debate about women-as-creative-artists and with the perils peculiar to her gender – hardly the young Schubert's concerns – and yet an extended song-fragment and five completed small songs attest to episodes of musical empathy with her verse. For all the obvious differences in their emotional worlds, there are reasons for his attraction to certain poems of hers at those two moments in his life, uses to which he could, and did, put her poems of *Empfindsamkeit* in a feminine voice.

Among the first extant vocal compositions by Schubert are a lengthy fragment (231 measures) of a setting of "Lebenstraum" (Dream of life), the opening poem of Gabriele's 1805 revised anthology, in C major, D. 39 (intended for mezzo-soprano? – there is much use of the lower register and little of the high tessitura) and an even longer fragment in C minor (394 measures), D. deest, for baritone with a large range, the autograph manuscript (Wiener Männergesang-Verein, Ms. A) wholly devoid of text. These two unfinished compositions are related in that the uncompleted Allegro moderato in G major with which D. 39 "ends" is much the same as the Allegro moderato in mm. 245–303 of the C minor fragment, which therefore surely precedes Schubert's first Baumberg setting, although not by much.[95] If the tentative date of early 1810 which Walther Dürr proposes for D. 39 is correct, Schubert's attention could well have been drawn (anew? for the first time?) to Gabriele's anthology by the political brouhaha of 1809–10. Whether rumor-mongering about Batsányi's flight and Gabriele's subsequent plight was a factor in his choice of this text at this time or whether a composer perhaps already launched on a lifetime of omnivorous reading in search of texts for music would have known "the Sappho of Vienna" anyway cannot be determined, but it is intriguing to speculate that the couple's involvement in Napoleon's imperialistic ambitions might have led to one of Schubert's first extant vocal works. Gabriele's autobiographical long poem, however, proved to be unamenable material for the apprentice-composer, an experiment he probably abandoned, I would guess, when the experiment of putting a previously composed passage to new use displeased him. But the attempt is not without interest for Schubertians – far from it; the fragment is more revelatory than one might initially suspect.

Present-day Schubertians can only admire (with an accompanying chuckle) the audacity of the thirteen(?)-year-old composer in tackling this huge poem, with its 221 lines spread over thirteen pages; anyone other than a neophyte whose lifelong large-scale ambitions are evident from the start in this choice of text would have known to pass it by. Nor is it typical of the other ballad-cantata texts Schubert chose shortly thereafter, at least one of which (Schiller's "Der Taucher," or "The Diver") is even longer than Gabriele's poetic dream: "Lebenstraum" has little or none of the action-packed heroic derring-do of Schiller's ballads and few of the overt invitations to harmonic richness and pianistic virtuosity one finds in the dramatic narratives to which Schubert gravitated in his youth. If Gabriele invokes storms of passion, even thunder and lightning, on occasion in "Lebenstraum," it is within the context of a neo-classical allegory, or rather, autobiography allegorized, the whole poetic enterprise fundamentally incompatible with the depictive nature of ballad-setting, although Schubert tries to impose some of the formulae of balladesque musical excitement – saber-rattling dotted rhythms, thirty-second note scale figures shooting upwards, and, first and foremost, harmonic radicalism – on this text. And yet, for all the seeming oddity of D. 39 (the self-justification of a woman poet set to music by a teenage boy), Schubert's attraction to this poem is perhaps explicable on autobiographical grounds – the composer's rather than the poet's – in a manner consistent with Schubert's other youthful textual choices.

Those choices, both for ballad and lied, can be directly linked to issues in Schubert's own life. At some length, Gabriele insists in "Lebenstraum" that artists should follow the vocation they know to be theirs, that the true artist should listen to her heart, not the advice either of well-meaning friends or an ill-disposed society, no matter what price the world exacts in scorn and disapproval. Schubert, disputing with his father about his future course in life, could have found in Gabriele's poetic dream additional justification for belief in himself as a composer, all the more so because the obstacles faced by women were even more extreme than those of men. We can readily assume that he was drawn to texts such as Gottlieb Konrad Pfeffel's "Der Vatermörder" (The patricide), D. 10, in which a son who kills his father is punished by madness and execution; to Schiller's "Eine Leichenphantasie" (A Funereal Fantasy),

D. 7, in which a father mourns his heroic and beautiful dead son; even to Clemens August Schücking's "Hagars Klage" (Hagar's Lament), D. 5, in which a mother weeps over an endangered child destined for future glory, because of his own situation in early adolescence, that is, his attachment to his mother and his struggles with his father. Even the archetypal adolescent who sits by the stream in Schiller's "Der Jüngling am Bache" (Schubert's first setting of three was D. 30 in 1812), longs for love, and laments the passing of time could have seemed an alter ego to the young composer. It is possible that he was drawn to Gabriele's poetry out of a feeling of kinship with a similarly high-minded artist, her aspirations not small, who also encountered obstacles and yet insisted upon her right to join the company of the immortals. Furthermore, "Lebenstraum" is the first extant instance of Schubert's marked musical sympathies with female personae in poetry ("Hagars Klage" and "Des Mädchens Klage" are other early examples), whether those personae were conceived by male or female poets. What, one wonders with amusement, would he have made of the lines "Klagt' ich? – so galt's dem oft gekränkten Rechte / Vom ganzen weiblichen Geschlechte," had he gotten that far in "Lebenstraum"?

"Lebenstraum" is a revelation of Gabriele's greatest hopes and worst fears as a poet, and, sadly, it was the latter that would come true. The poetic "I" unfurls a vision of her poetic vocation throughout her life to date: as she sat in the meadow of the Muses at sunset, she saw the throne of the gods on the mountaintop, the hallowed abode of those poets both bygone and modern whose songs still delight readers. Those idolized in their day, but no more, sleep unknown and forgotten in the "giant shadows of oblivion." Out of the depths arose a dark and massive figure, its obscure contours inspiring terror, who offered her a chalice wreathed in poppies and filled with Lethe's waters. When the apparition vanished, a guiding spirit or "Genius" appeared and said, "Come with me! Leave this fearful twilight, which saddens the sunshine of Truth … I will lead you to the myrtle grove where … an undying poet's garland blooms for you in the bright spring radiance, a garland entwined with myrtle." There, she found Apollo's golden lyre, which the "Genius" promises will outstrip Time's swift flight, assuage all misfortunes, and resound every-where. At first, not yet confident of the lyre's powers, she sang "only small songs," and Echo carried them far and wide, as they spoke of that which every young heart desires. But "this no longer pleased the young woman" after a time, and she decided to write of the "Hochgefühl" (high emotion) of love instead.

Diess Hochgefühl, das kein Geschick verleidet,	This great emotion, that no destiny can
Nach welchem jede bess're Seele strebt;	destroy, to which every better soul strives,
Das von dem Thier den Menschen scheidet	which separates humanity from the beasts
Und himmelan zu Göttern hebt;	and raises us heavenwards to the gods,
Der edelste, der reinste aller Triebe,	the noblest, the purest of all instincts,
Die unschuldvolle, wahre Liebe:	innocent, true love:
Schien mir (mit höhern Wesen schon verwandt)	it seemed to me (already bound to higher ways)
Des Liedes würdigster und schönster Gegenstand.[96]	the worthiest and most beautiful circum-stance for poetry.

If she has lamented, she insists that it is women's right, born of men's inconstancy. In proud assertion of difference and plea for understanding, she writes, "I left the merry crowd and withdrew into myself. Loneliness brought quiet happiness and a better, higher way of life. In this way, I sang out, at times happily, at times sorrowfully, my springtime of life." When storms have battered her soul, however, she begs Apollo to take back his gift. Ever a sensitive creature, she was hurt by dismissals of her poetry as mere effusions and her dedication to poetry as unwomanly.

Die schöne, feine Welt, um sich an mir zu rächen,	The world of high society, to revenge itself upon me,
Hiess mein Lieder – Schwärmereyn!	calls my poems "gushing"
Und, Deinem Dienste mich zu weihn,	and dedicating myself to your service
Ein unverzeihliches Verbrechen! –	an unpardonable offense.
Nicht achtend ihrer Klügeleyn,	Not heeding their caviling,
Liess ich mein Herz allein nur sprechen,	I only let my heart speak to me
Und folgte meinem Genius.[97]	and followed my genie.

"I have lived only for Truth and for you – give me immortality!", she demands. Apollo's winged steed Pegasus draws near, and, borne aloft, she surveys the passing eras, her genie guiding her past such dangers as false friendship, envy, jealousy, and will-o'-the-wisps. With immortality assured, she is awakened from her long dream by an unintelligible murmuring. Reading this poem, which is given pride of place in both editions of her verse, one is struck by her fear of literary oblivion after death and by the sad irony of the fact that those fears were realized. She could turn away the dark spectre with his poppy-laced Lethean waters in her poetry, but not in actuality.

The young composer only set the first twenty-nine lines of Gabriele's poem and only provided the text underlay for the first few phrases (lines 1–4).

Ich sass vor eines Tempels Halle	I sat before the great hall of a temple
Am Musenhayn, umrauscht vom nahen Wasserfalle,	in the meadow of the Muses, the nearby waterfall murmuring
Im sanften Abendschein.	in the soft evening glow.
Kein Lüftchen wehte; – und die Sonn' im Scheiden	No breath of wind stirs – and the departing sun
Vergüldete die matten Trauerweiden.	gilds the languid weeping willows.
Still sinnend sass ich lange da,	Quietly musing, I sat there a long time,
Das Haupt gestützt auf meine Rechte.	my head leaning to the right.
Ich dachte Zukunft und Vergangenheit; und sah	I reflected on the future and the past and saw
Auf einem Berg, dem Thron der Götter nah,	the throne of the gods nearby on a mountain,
Den Aufenthalt vom heiligen Geschlechte	the dwelling place of the divine beings,
Der Sänger alt' und neuer Zeit,	the singers of olden and newer times
An deren Liede sich die Nachwelt noch erfreut.	in whose songs posterity still rejoices.

Todt, unbemerkt, und längst vergessen schliefen	Dead, unnoticed, and long-forgotten,
Fern in des Thales dunkeln Tiefen	the idols of their time sleep far-off in the
Die Götzen ihrer Zeit, –	dark depths of the valley –
Im Riesenschatten der Vergänglichkeit.	in the giant shadows of transitoriness.
Und langsam schwebend kam auf jenem dunkeln Thale,	And slowly swaying, there now came to this dark valley,
Entstiegen einem morschen Heldenmahle,	arisen from a decaying heroic monument,
Jetzt eine düstere Gestalt daher,	a dark creature from thence
Und bot (indem sie wie von ohngefähr	who offered me (as it was passing by)
Vorüberzog) in einer mohnbekränzten Schale	Oblivion from Lethe's
Aus Lethe's Quelle mir – Vergessenheit!	springs in a poppy-garlanded chalice.
Betroffen, wollt' ich die Erscheinung fragen:	Dazed, I wanted to ask the apparition,
Was dieser Trank mir nützen soll?	"What will this drink avail me?",
Doch schon war sie entflohn: ich sah's mit stillen Groll;	but it had already vanished; I saw it with quiet anger.
Denn meinen Wünschen – konnt' ich nicht entsagen.	But my wishes – I could not abandon them.
Da kam in frohem Tanz, mit zefyrleichtem Schritt,	There came, merrily dancing, with zephyr-light step,
Ein kleiner Genius ge-[sprungen … the setting breaks off in mid-word]	a little genie springing up …

(lines 1–29)

After m. 20, where the text underlay breaks off in mid-word ("sanf-[ten]"), one must guess what of Gabriele's words belong with Schubert's melody, a process rendered more complex by the fact that the fragment is itself fragmented: mm. 1–140 are in the collection of the Bibliothèque Nationale in Paris (ms. 281), while mm. 141–231 are in a private collection in Louisville, Kentucky. There is also an incomplete autograph sketch, twenty measures in length, on folio 5r of the autograph of the C minor fragment for baritone, D. deest (Wiener Männergesang-Verein, ms. A), probably intended as an insertion between measures 221 and 222; Schubert evidently realized that he had omitted two lines of text ("Doch schon war sie entflohn: ich sah's mit stillem Groll, / Denn meinen Wünschen – konnt' ich nicht entsagen") and therefore composed a passage fifteen measures long to accommodate those two lines, placed just before the return of the Allegro moderato which he borrowed from D. deest (see ex. 1 for the entire fragment, with the interpolation inserted in brackets).[98]

Musically, the fragment is a mixture of youthful ineptitude, radical experimentation awkwardly handled, classical textures and gestures, and the through-composed alternation between recitative and song that one also finds in Johann Rudolf Zumsteeg's ballads, which Schubert both admired and felt he could modernise. For example, the piano introduction is remarkable for its asymmetries (Schubert's wont both in early youth and thereafter); although the broken-chordal accompanimental figuration in the left hand continues spinning nonstop throughout ten measures, the harmonic progression and the melodic line in the right hand (also without a single pause or break for the entire duration) imply a phrase structure of 3 + 4 + 3, the

Gabriele von Baumberg

Example 1. Franz Schubert, "Ich saß an einer Tempelhalle," D. 39, mm. 194–221 and insertion following m. 221 (Wiener Männergesang-Verein, Ms. A), mm. 222–36. From the *Neue Schubert-Ausgabe*, Series IV: *Lieder*, vol. 6a, ed. Walther Dürr.

Example 1. *cont.*

latter three measures a slightly varied repetition of mm. 5–7. The classical mordents, texture, and diatonicism combine oddly with this asymmetry, leaving the listener aware of palpable awkwardness. The harmonic radicalism that was to shock some critics and delight others in Schubert's later life is already evident: Schubert pays Gabriele a harmonic compliment when his "ich" thinks truly deep thoughts in the recitative beginning at m. 37 ("Still sinnend saß ich lange da …"). The three soft, unharmonized "drum-tap" C♯s preceding the recitative become the pivot tones for a sudden move to the dark side – multitudinous flats equal profundity in this context, I suspect. This tonally unsettled passage eventually moves to a brief cadence on B-flat major (m. 47), but B-flat is then jolted upwards a semitone to a pounding, *fortississimo* emphasis on B major in mm. 50–52 – was Schubert perhaps tonally symbolising "Zukunft und Vergangenheit" (future and past) by means of radically opposite harmonic emphases? Both here and in the *Tempo presto* which follows ("und sah auf einem Berg dem Thron der Götter nah"), Schubert transmogrifies Gabriele's reflective tone into dramatic power, the vocal line of the F minor *Tempo presto* broken into gasps and underlaid with heavy octaves extending to the bottom of the fortepianos of Schubert's day. The metamorphosis is almost comically indicative of the poet's and composer's different ages and conditions in life, of different creative imaginations.

The way in which Schubert's musical imagination was moved by words is already evident in D. 39, however inept or awkward the handling might be. When the menacing "dark creature" ("düstere Gestalt") appears, Schubert bursts forth into *Presto vivace* fieriness on a prolonged G minor chord, succeeded by a fermata-sustained sudden hush on a Neapolitan sixth of G minor; that A-flat harmony then becomes tonic for the "poppy-garlanded chalice" in mm. 196–206. Schubert sets the invocation of Lethean oblivion over a rocking, cradling pedal point in the bass, hypnotic in effect, with the diminished seventh harmony at the word "Lethe" an appropriately horrific detail. But the G major passage at the end, sufficiently diatonic as to rival Muzio Clementi's easiest works for unskilled musicians, seems too musically uninspired even for Apollo's most junior-grade emissary (the prosody is, diplomatically speaking, unimpressive as well). Schubert only copied ten measures of the corresponding fifty-nine-measure section in D. deest and then struck through the entire passage, his dissatisfaction evident graphically. Thereafter, I would guess, he abandoned a text he may have realized by this point was ill-suited for musical setting. If he did any further work on "Lebenstraum," the manuscript has subsequently vanished without a trace.

Gabriele's other works are, as we have seen, primarily small lyric poems, and Schubert did not become interested in their like for musical purposes until a few years later, when he set "Cora an die Sonne" (Cora to the sun) and "Der Morgenkuss" (The morning kiss) on 22 August 1815, "Abendständchen. An Lina" (Evening serenade. To Lina) on 23 August, "An die Sonne" (To the sun) on 25 August, and "Lob des Tokayers" (In praise of Tokay wine), also in August 1815. At the time, Schubert was principally occupied with the composition of small strophic songs patterned after folksong – the *Volkston*. In the days preceding the composition of the five Baumberg songs, all of them strophic, Schubert set twelve poems by Goethe, one after another:

"Der Gott und die Bajadere," "Der Rattenfänger," "Der Schatzgräber," "Heiden-röslein," "Bundeslied," the first version of "An den Mond," "Wonne der Wehmuth," "Wer kauft Liebesgötter?", "Die Spinnerin," "Liebhaber in allen Gestalten," "Schweizerlied," and "Der Goldschmiedsgesell." All are strophic, and all, despite the compositional subtleties one finds in works such as "Heidenröslein," simple. But in the midst of a spate of lieder that seem tailored to Goethe's own preferences in song composition, one finds an astonishingly different kind of strophic song: "Der Morgen-kuss," D. 264, perhaps the gem of the Baumberg songs. In this work, lied and opera fuse in a novel way, and the *Volkston* is replaced by a mere nine measures of opera at its highest and purest. The worlds of Gluck and Mozart, whom Goethe also revered, converge on the strophic lied, impelled by Gabriele's distinctive poetic voice.

Schubert's love of Mozart is well-known, but the importance of Christoph Willibald Gluck's operas for the young composer is also documented in anecdotes by his friends. In early 1813, Joseph Spaun took the young composer, nine years his junior, to hear the great soprano Anna Milder and Johann Michael Vogl sing in a performance of Gluck's *Iphigénie en Tauride*, first performed in Paris in 1779 and revived in Vienna from 1809 on. After the performance, Spaun and Schubert dined with the already famous young poet Theodor Körner. The audience was sparse, "to the disgrace of the Viennese" in the heady flush of the Rossini craze, but Schubert was profoundly moved. He even exchanged heated words with a pedant at a neighboring table, a professor who disparaged Milder's and Vogl's performances. According to Spaun in several of his later reminiscences, "that evening's effect on him he could never forget, and it was followed by the keenest study of all Gluck's scores, which quite enraptured Schubert for years."

That "keen study" left its mark on Schubert's own music, especially the lieder on mythological themes that perhaps inevitably recalled Gluck's favorite operatic realms, such as the settings in 1817 of Johann Mayrhofer's "Der zürnenden Diana" (To Diana in her wrath), D. 707; "Memnon," D. 541; and "Iphigenia," D. 573. What Schubert took from Gluck were the older composer's richly animated Classical accompanimental figuration; the Gluckian scena, including passages in arioso, reci-tative, and aria styles, compressed into lied; and, less easily definable, an atmosphere both dramatic and yet noble, classicizing in a larger sense. We know that Schubert singled out "O malheureuse Iphigénie!" (Oh, unhappy Iphigenia), a lament in G major — was it in part from Gluck that Schubert learned to use major mode on occasion as more deeply expressive of grief than minor mode? — for Iphigenia and the choir of priestesses, as incomparably beautiful, and this lament exemplifies the style to which Schubert would later adapt his own harmonic language. The duet between the solo oboe and Iphigenia, whose broad melodic arches at times span intervals of a thirteenth in a mere two or three measures, is accompanied by a layer of accompanimental patterns, with the violas trilling their repeated eighth notes throughout, with mid-measure accents in the second violins' broken-chordal figu-ration, and a syncopated pedal point in the first violins. The effect is typically rich, an eloquent backdrop and foundation for Iphigenia's melodic lament; it is also perhaps one of the sources of Schubert's musical language in "Der Morgenkuss."

1. Even before the mythological songs of Mayrhofer, Gabriele von Baumberg's poems prompted Schubert to the most miniature condensations of operatic language at its most intense, miniatures as small as nine measures – the length of the thrice-repeated strophe in Schubert's setting of Gabriele's "Der Morgenkuss nach einem Balle" (The morning kiss after a ball).

Durch eine ganze Nacht sich nahe seyn,
So Hand in Hand, so Arm im Arme weilen,
So viel empfinden ohne mitzutheilen –
Ist eine wonnevolle Pein!

To be close the whole night long,
to linger hand in hand, arm in arm,
to feel so much, without revealing
it in words, is blissful torment.

So immer Seelenblick im Seelenblick
Auch den geheimsten Wunsch des Herzens
   sehen,
So wenig sprechen, und sich doch verstehen –
Ist hohes martervolles Glück!

To gaze constantly into each other's soul,
to see into the heart's most secret desire,
to speak so little, and yet to
understand each other, is sublime,
anguished happiness.

Zum Lohn für die im Zwang ver-
   schwundne Zeit
Dann bey dem Morgenstrahl, warm, mit
   Entzücken
Sich Mund an Mund, und Herz an Herz
   sich drücken –
O diess ist – Engelseligkeit! [99]

Then, in the morning light,
as a reward for time of necessity wasted,
warmly, rapturously to press

mouth to mouth and heart to heart –

oh, that is angelic bliss!

This poem has as much to do with social constraints upon passion as with passion itself. Words tell of constraints on words, of the failure of language itself in the face of love; words say that there is communication without words. The context of a ball is particularly apt because the late eighteenth-century formal dances to which the Viennese were addicted allowed those in love to ape intimacy but in company, with the social "police" of etiquette present at all times and therefore a frustration to true intimacy. Lovers were permitted to be in close physical proximity on these nocturnal occasions, if resolutely vertical, but they could not say aloud what they felt nor proceed beyond a certain point. That the constraints were an instrument by which to increase passion, as well as frustrate it, is made explicit in Gabriele's phrase "wonnevolle Pein" (blissful torment) at the end of stanza 1. The poem manages to be both luxuriant in the emotional world it evokes and economical in its concentration, the *mise-en-scène* limned in as few words as possible; for example, we are not told how the lovers manage, after an entire night of togetherness-in-company, to snatch privacy for a single kiss, but they do – and there, the poem discreetly ends. As Graham Johnson points out, her reference in the final stanza to "time of necessity wasted" in the observation of the social niceties is disarmingly frank. [100] Many a woman in love may have thought so at the time, but few could have said it so simply and artfully, or had the audacity to publish the observation in verse and under her own name.

   The artfulness deserves attention in part because of Gabriele's past and present literary eclipse and because it has been fashionable to decry that she had any pretensions to artistry at all. The combination of luxuriance and economy to which I have already alluded is inherent in the form she used to express it, three short quatrains (a b b a rhyme scheme) in which the first three lines of each stanza are in iambic pentameters mostly with feminine endings (eleven syllables) rather than shorter line lengths. A statelier, more solemn pace, the poet lingering reverently over each line as if it were the lover's body or eyes, is induced in this way. Gabriele's concern with the alliance of sound and sense in poetry is evident in the -a vowels that recur, like sighs of wonderment, throughout the first line of stanza 1 ("Durch *ei*-ne g*a*n-ze N*a*cht sich n*a*h zu s*e*yn") and the percussive -z,-ts consonants that accentuate "time of necessity wasted" in the first line of stanza 3 ("Zum Lohn für die im Zwang verschwundne Zeit") at beginning, middle, and end. Each time, the pentameter lines culminate in a fourth shorter line in iambic tetrameters with stressed endings (eight syllables), and it is in those climactic end-lines that the situation unfurled at length in the three preceding lines is defined succinctly in emotional terms. At the ends of stanzas 1 and 2, the lovers' frustration is rendered in oxymoronic compounds of bliss and pain; notably, the elements of the compound are reversed from one stanza to the next in a progression from greater to lesser anguish en route to fulfillment (for the moment) in a kiss. "Pain" takes pride of place as the noun, modified by "blissful" in stanza 1, but in stanza 2, it is "happiness" that is emphasized when it becomes the noun, modified by the adjectives "sublime" and "anguished." Only when the lovers are alone and at last can kiss does erotic torment disappear from the summations at the close of each verse, replaced by "angelic bliss," noun and adjective merged in one word, fused as are the lovers. Throughout the poem, Gabriele reiterates paired expressions – "Hand in Hand," "Arm im Arme," "Seelen-blick im Seelenblick," "Mund an Mund," and "Herz an Herz" – to demonstrate that the lovers are both separate entities and yet a couple. Poised between the two poles that have aroused the poet's wonder, "to feel so much … to say so little," the poem attempts to do likewise, to say only a little, if lingeringly, and thereby evoke an awe-filled world of erotic feeling from a woman's point of view. The lack of references to "he" or "him" heightens the erotic charge of the poem by underscoring the feint that the beloved is present and does not require identification, thereby enveloping the poem in a bubble of intimacy, a *hortus conclusus* of passion into which the reader or listener is admitted.

Schubert omitted Gabriele's qualifying phrase "nach einem Balle" from the title of his lied, perhaps because the music has nothing dance-like about it and he may have wanted to obliterate any such expectations from the start. Rather, it is the world of late eighteenth-century opera at its most elevated that comes to mind when one hears "Der Morgenkuss" in its original version. Like Gabriele herself, Schubert disposes solemn, complex strains within the smallest of frames, honoring in music her awestruck polarity between "feeling so much" and "saying so little" by compressing the undiluted language of opera within the bounds of a small lied – the very look of it on the printed page is startling. Every aspect of the music is challenging, from its dauntingly high vocal tessitura to its seamless flow, as if in unbroken rapture, to the chromatic details that give the tonal structure its profundity and to much else, a match in music for Gabriele's vision of eros as the noblest and most challenging of emotions. The seeming paradox of operatic style and lieder dimensions – no paradox, of course, but a perfectly attuned musical reading of the poem's essence – and the sheer difficulty of the music seem to have so flummoxed Diabelli when the firm first published the song in book 45 of the *Nachlass* that the editors tampered mightily with the work, transposing it down a third, simplifying the introduction, rebarring it in doubled note values so as to appear less complex, and cutting the interludes between strophes; thus, a different, lesser, imbalanced song emerged and was subsequently printed in volume 6 of the Peters Edition. Only in the original version and key can we appreciate the true nature of Schubert's experimental hybrid of opera-in-the-lied and its rightness for these words.

The long and luxuriant piano introduction seems a reminiscence, not of the actual music itself but the atmosphere, of the even lengthier orchestral introduction preceding the countess's first aria, "Porgi amor," in the same E-flat tonality at the beginning of act 2 of *Le nozze di Figaro*. Like the countess, the wordless instrument speaks for Gabriele's love-possessed persona before a word is sung, and like that aria, this song is simultaneously a woman's hymn to love and a plea for love's surcease ("qualche ristoro"), imbued with the same profound feeling and the same elevated conception of love. Nor is that the only Mozartian reminiscence. The solemn fanfare with which "Der Morgenkuss" begins echoes those which issue from Sarastro's halls in *Die Zauberflöte*, where Pamina and Tamino learn of love in the same vein and key. Everything about the introduction bespeaks extraordinary richness: the breadth of the 4/4 meter, with the eighth note as the tactus rather than quarter notes; the thirty-second note scale figures in the right hand and the Mozartian extension and development of those figures, especially the interval of the fourth with which Schubert's lieder personae customarily hail the dawn; the secondary dominants; the slow harmonic rhythm; and the way the singer's anacrusis ascent from $\hat{5}$ to $\hat{1}$ in m. 3 echoes the previous thirty-second note figures in rhythmic augmentation. The chromaticism with which the song is so distinctively tinged begins with the flatted $\hat{6}$ – $\hat{5}$ scale degrees at the end of m. 1 and beginning of m. 2, that is, with passing motion from C to C-flat to B-flat in the inner voice, bridging the antecedent and consequent phrases – it is as if emotions first expressed formally, solemnly, symmetrically, in accord with convention and etiquette, then immediately become more intense and flower into fuller expression. Even before the formal first phrase ends, Schubert descends to the second scale degree in the right hand part, but retains the tonic pitch in the bass, dissonant with it, and then prolongs the dissonant outer voices of the seventh chord for an instant. The consequent phrase then begins with the same supertonic seventh chord, this time with the fifth lowered, the inner voices redistributed and the soprano lifted upwards an octave; the tension-filled element at the end of the first phrase thus becomes the impetus for the phrase to follow, the composer dwelling upon and exploring the mild harmonic "anguish" just as the poetess explores the "wonnevolle Pein" she celebrates (ex. 2).

In m. 3, the C-flat / B-flat pitches are respelled as B-natural in the inner voice of a passing chord in which the chromatic tone does not resolve upward as expected but down to B-flat, the progression all the more emphatic for the trill in the topmost voice that resolves to the high A-flats one subsequently hears over and over in the texted body of the song. The same pitches are enriched with still more chord tones and reheard in m. 7 at the words "[wonne]-volle Pein" – Schubert thus underscores the word "Pein" unforgettably (and the progression was surely conceived for stanza 1) when the voice-leading for "wonnevolle" does not lead to what one would expect but instead to tonal "Pein." The bass pitch, one notices, is E-natural, so near and yet so far from the E-flat tonic of "Engelseligkeit." There is a lovely additional subtlety to this climactic passage as well: at the words "mitzutheilen, ist eine wonnevolle" in mm. 6–7, Schubert sounds a cluster of relative minor harmonies, including the dominant seventh, the dark and dramatic Neapolitan sixth, and "tonic" of C minor, although he never establishes the key or remains on the submediant for long. Rather, the leap to "Pein" and the simultaneous side-slipping jolt in the accompaniment deflect the patch of intensified minor darkness and impel a repetition of the phrase leading to the re-establishment of E-flat, a key associated with pure devotion and awe ("Du bist die Ruh'," D. 776; "Am See," D. 746; "Im Freien," D. 880; and "Litanei auf das Fest aller Seelen," D. 343, are other lieder in that tonality).

The texted body of the strophe is as rich and remarkable as the introduction. The vocal line is pure opera, as distant from the *volkstümlich* lied as one can possibly be. Schubert's propensity for high tessituras is here lent in the service of literally elevated passion: four times in four measures, the enraptured woman in love soars to high G or A-flat, only briefly descending to medium register and then rising once more. Schubert does not notate a single rest in the vocal line from beginning to end: as

Example 2. Franz Schubert, "Der Morgenkuss," D. 264, mm. 1–9

Example 2. *cont.*

if she were lingering on the melodic line and reluctant to leave it, Schubert's poetess can only snatch a breath in the interstices between the sixteenth notes at the end of one phrase and the beginning of the next; even at a *langsam* pace, one must gasp as if in the throes of passion, especially if one is to imbibe enough oxygen to ascend yet again into the empyrean upper reaches of the soprano's range. To compound it all, each time the singer vaults into the stratosphere, she is bidden to linger on the high note a trifle longer until, at the end of the strophe, she climbs by degrees to a high A-flat quarter note prolonged by double-dotting – as sumptuously graphic a means of emphasizing the adjective "wonnevolle" as Schubert could devise. At the start of the texted body of the strophe, Schubert brings back the harmonic progression of mm. 1–2 and a thoroughgoing variant of the right-hand line; one notes, for example, the reversed direction of the phrase ending in mm. 1 and 4 ("sich *nah zu sein*") in order to emphasize the word designating proximity ("nah"). The operatic hallmarks cluster thick and fast, such as the affective intervallic leaps of a diminished seventh, a tritone, and a diminished fourth, which one finds in *recitativo accompagnato* or in such passionate arias as Pamina's "Ach, ich fühl's," from *Die Zauberflöte*, and the changes of accompanimental figuration, unlike the often unified accompaniments of small-scale lieder, classical figuration right out of Gluck's Iphigenia operas. After all those high A-flats and in the wake of such a literally elevated atmosphere, one expects to hear – and does – a reverential plagal cadence with lingering suspensions before resolution.

2.   That same day in August 1815, Schubert also set "Cora an die Sonne" in the same key as "Der Morgenkuss" and a similarly reverent mood, but with a difference. Whether "Cora an die Sonne" was written before "Der Morgenkuss," which was then an elaboration of the song to the sun, or whether "Cora an die Sonne" was distilled from the previous lied-cum-aria is impossible to determine, but the relationship between the two songs is apparent.

Nach so vielen trüben Tagen	After so many gloomy days
Send' uns wiederum einmal,	take pity on our lament,
Mitleidsvoll für unsre Klagen,	and send us once again
Einen sanften milden Strahl.	a soft, gentle ray of light.
Liebe Sonne! trink den Regen,	Dear sun, drink up the rain
Der herab zu stürzen dräut,	that threatens to pour down;
Deine Strahlen sind uns Segen,	your rays are a blessing to us,
Deine Blicke – Seligkeit.	your glances bliss.
Schein', ach scheine, liebe Sonne!	Shine, oh shine, beloved sun!
Jede Freude dank' ich dir;	I thank you for every delight;
Alle Geist- und Herzenswonne,	every joy of heart and spirit,
Licht und Wärme kommt von dir.	light and warmth, comes from you.

Anyone who has endured a lengthy spell of gray, rainy weather can chime in fervently with Gabriele's plea for the restoration of the sun and her assignment of every benefice to its presence. Because what she hymns is less complex than the experience and emotions of "Der Morgenkuss nach dem Balle," however, the form is likewise simpler: quatrains in trochaic tetrameters and a simple a b a b rhyme pattern. She anthropomorphizes the sun as a lover, a beloved creature who bestows joy, but because there is no eroticism, no pain, in the transaction, the poem has all the hallmarks of a heartfelt hymn.

In his setting, Schubert makes the sun come out in musical tones that wax warmer and richer and quicker from beginning to end until at last the E-flat sun comes out fully with the word "Strahl" at the end of stanza 1. Not until then, in a lovely tonal conceit, does one find root position tonic and dominant chords – *complete* chords – rather than chord fragments and chord inversions, and even then, tonic closure in the topmost voice is postponed until the end of the piano postlude. The strophe begins without an introduction, the singer pleading in unharmonized fervor. The adjective "viel-[en]" on the first downbeat of the little song is prolonged in unmistakeable emphasis, even its unaccented second syllable on the third and weakest beat intensified by means of an appoggiatura against the harmonic intervals in the right hand, not yet fully emergent chords. With his customary sensitivity to these matters, Schubert both acknowledges that "Nach" is the accented syllable of the first trochee in "Cora an die Sonne" and yet does not place it on a downbeat, making it rather part of a prolonged anacrusis to his interpretive stress on "vie - [len]." At the words "trüben Tagen," not only is E-flat tonic darkened by the addition of the flatted seventh degree, but that chromatic addition intensifies the subdominant harmony in perfect accord with the prayerful plea "send' uns … "; the accented syllable of the adjective "trüb - [en]" is placed on the downbeat in further emphasis, but Schubert bids the singer hurry through it to the noun "Tagen." "*Wie* - [derum]" too is emphasized by downbeat placement, by the high F that surpasses the E-flat apex of the first phrase, by prolongation that underscores the poet's longing. Schubert's liking for asymmetrical phrase structures is evident here in the 3 + 3-bar setting of lines 1 and 2, followed by 2 + 4 bars for lines 3 and 4, the composer lingering upon the words "*einen sanften milden* [Strahl]," "deine Blicke Seligkeit," and "Licht und Wärme," prolonging them in apt depiction of the poetic persona's longing for the sun. As tiny and unpretentious as this song is, the details are finely honed: one notes the repetition of the hymn-like fourth B-flat E-flat in the piano in m. 6 ("Mitleidsvoll") while the voice in *Terzensteigerung* vaults to high G in intensified pleading, and the lower neighbor-note inflection in m. 7 at the word "Klagen," with its weak-beat accent and augmented triad simultaneity underscoring the lamentation by means of dissonance and a slight rhythmic jolt. B-flat is then triply reinstated in m. 8 in the right-hand part when the sun is invoked, beginning the greater motion that culminates in the postlude. That postlude is yet another variation of the gestures stated earlier – the B-flat E-flat interval at the beginnings of phrases and descending scalewise melodic lines – but in rhythmic diminution. In m. 12, the accent on the second, weak beat reappears from m. 6, but this time not on a dissonant appoggiatura but on the dominant seventh harmony with A-flat in the topmost voice, overtopping the high G in the vocal line. This song, and most of the other Baumberg songs, are reminders that small size did not preclude a multiplicity of structural and text-setting refinements on Schubert's part – "Auch kleine Dinge können uns entzücken" indeed ("Even small things can delight us," the first song in Hugo Wolf's *Italienisches Liederbuch*).

3.   Three days later, on 25 August, Schubert set to music another of Gabriele's hymns to the sun: "An die Sonne," D. 270. It too is in the same E-flat tonality in which Sarastro sings "Die Strahlen der Sonne / vertreiben die Nacht" at the end of *Die Zauberflöte*, when the stage is transformed into an Enlightenment sun in full glory. (There was a spate of songs to the sun from Schubert's pen in August 1815, including "Lilla an die Morgenröthe," D. 273, poet unknown; Friedrich Leopold

Graf zu Stolberg's "Morgenlied," D. 266, with its lines "O Sonne, sei mir Gottes Bild, / Der täglich dich erneut, / Der immer hehr, und immer mild, / Die ganze Welt erfreut!;" and Christoph August Tiedge's "An die Sonne," D. 272.) In her sun-hymn, Gabriele hails the sun, not at its appearance, but at its *dis*appearance and anticipates with joy both its return and her lover's. The delicate inference that she and her beloved are not married and that night entails separation, day togetherness, is at the heart of the poem. Since evening has come and the lovers must part for the sake of the proprieties, she bids night run its course as swiftly as possible so that day might reassert its primacy — in this poem, the sun is given power over the moon and bids the moon rise in its place — and her lover might return. "*Liebe* Sonne" leads in short order to "meinen *Lieben* mir" and the end of the poem.

Sinke, liebe Sonne, sinke!	Sink, dearest sun, sink!
Ende deinen trüben Lauf,	End your dusky course,
Und an deine Stelle winke	and in your place soon bid
Bald den Mond herauf.	the moon to rise.
Herrlicher und schöner dringe	But tomorrow come forth
Aber Morgen dann herfür	more glorious and more beautiful,
Liebe Sonn'! und mit dir bringe	dearest sun! and with you,
Meinen Lieben mir.	bring my love.

"An die Sonne" is written in the same trochaic tetrameters as "Cora an die Sonne," but Schubert treats them differently (triple meter in "Cora an die Sonne," duple meter in "An die Sonne"). "An die Sonne" begins with a plea-command in the imperative tense, so Schubert reverses the former B-flat E-flat "sun interval" in order to sound E-flat first on the verb of command, "Sinke," which then sinks to B-flat; conversely, when he bids the moon rise ("[Bald den] Mond herauf") at the end of stanza 1, the same interval appears in ascending guise. Even more, Schubert, who knew the reverent intensity which Gabriele brought to matters of love, invests this song with those shadings; if one takes the poem as an isolated entity, it would be possible to treat it more lightly than Schubert does here, the *sehr langsam* tempo, double-dotted rhythms, chromatic touches, and high tessitura, all indices of a literally elevated, ethereal and yet solemn atmosphere. It is little wonder that the song is seldom performed, despite its beauty, since the vocal line never descends below B-flat but hovers, like the moon in the sky, about and above E-flat for most of its length. No more than Gabriele herself would Schubert condescend to ease the performers' path, however small and intimate the context. Even the piano accompaniment is lifted into the treble empyrean realm: the left-hand part only descends into the bass clef range three times in the stanza, the first time in mm. 8–9 at the cadence on the dominant for the "trüben Lauf," darkening it and weighting it down, at the end of the texted body of the strophe (but with the low E-flat still notated in the treble clef), and again at the very end of the postlude for the tonic cadence, as if in fulfillment of the singer's plea.

Schubert uses a similar harmonic progression, especially the tonic and submediant initial harmonies, at the beginning both of Gabriele's "An die Sonne" and Tiedge's

"An die Sonne" ("Königliche Morgensonne, / Sei gegrüsst in deiner Wonne"), marked "Mit Majestät" and more proclamatory in tone than Gabriele's poem, evoking Beethoven in his hymnic mode. In the introduction, varied as the postlude to the song, Schubert invests the dominant and approach to the dominant with multiple chromatic voice-leading, with passing tones and neighboring tones that both darken the "trüben Lauf" and give these musings a slight but perceptible erotic languor well before the cause for such languorous hints is revealed. One notices in particular the extended rising chromatic line in the inner voice of mm. 15–16, leading to the words "meinen Lieben mir" at the end of stanza 2 (and it was those words, I believe, that inspired the voice-leading in that passage rather than the final line of stanza 1), all the more as the previous G-flats here become F-sharp in ascending motion to G rather than descending motion to F. As in "Cora an die Sonne," the relationship between the piano and the right-hand part in this song is a beautifully-calibrated balance between doubling and independence, unlike straightforward hymns; in the first phrase, they begin paired and then diverge when the voice rises to F at the words "liebe Sonne," after which the piano echoes, in elision, the singer's plea "sinke" in m. 6, repeating the figure and thereby underscoring it. And for all the slow solemnity of the tempo and the hymn-like atmosphere, Schubert heeds the verbs of motion ("sinke," "dringe," "winke," "bringe"), the images of rising and falling celestial orbs, the expectation of the lover's arrival, and keeps the voice-leading in motion throughout the song, especially in the piano accompaniment bridging the vocal phrases and in m. 11, where the voice prolongs the word "Stelle" while the accompanimental voice-leading shifts and changes.

4. "Abendständchen: An Lina," D. 265, is even tinier than "An die Sonne" and, with its high B-flat, even more remarkable for its high tessitura—the vocal line never descends below B-flat above middle C.

Sei sanft, wie ihre Seele,	Be as gentle as her soul,
Und heiter, wie ihr Blick,	and as serene as her gaze,
O Abend! und vermähle	o evening, and reward
Mit seltner Treu das Glück.	such rare constancy with happiness.
Wenn alles schläft, und trübe	When all sleep,
Die stille Lampe scheint,	and the silent lamp burns dimly
Nur Hoffnungslose Liebe	only hopeless love
Noch helle Tränen weint:	still weeps shining tears.
Will ich, laß mir's gelingen!	If only I may succeed in my desire
Zu ihrem Fenster gehn	to go to her window,
Ein Lied von Liebe singen;	sing a song of love,
Und schachtend nach ihr sehn.	and gaze longingly at her!
Vielleicht, daß Klagetöne	Perhaps the sorrowful tones
Von meinem Saitenspiel	of my strings
Mehr wirken auf die Schöne,	will touch the fair maiden more deeply,
Mehr reizen ihr Gefühl;	will charm her feelings;

Vielleicht daß meine Saiten	Perhaps my strings
Und meine Phantasie'n	and my improvisations
Ein Herz zur Liebe leiten,	will awaken love in a heart
Das unempfindlich schien.	that seemed unfeeling.
Wenn sie, im sanften Schlummer	When happily aroused from gentle
Durch Lieder gern gestört,	slumber by my songs,
Halb träumend meinen Kummer	she hears, half-dreaming,
Und meine Leiden hört;	my grief and suffering,
Dann bang, und immer bänger	Then ever more anxious,
Von ihrem Lager steigt,	she will arise from her bed,
Und was er litt, ihr Sänger,	realizing how her minstrel
Sich selber überzeugt:	has suffered.
Dann leucht' aus deiner Höhe	Then, beloved moon, shine down
Herab, geliebter Mond!	from on high,
Daß ich die Tränen sehe,	that I may see her tears
Die meinen Schmerz belohnt.	reward my pain.

It is fascinating to encounter from this poet a nocturnal serenade to a woman, as if sung by a male minstrel. But Gabriele's serenade is as much and more about the workings of song on the beloved, that is, about the power of art, as it is about love. His song will, the lover hopes, touch the unfeeling beloved's heart as mere words cannot; if this is the *raison d'être* for all song-serenades, Gabriele makes it explicit. The poem also tells of the commonplace wish that the beloved should, by the power of empathy, feel what the lover feels and, even more interestingly, about the strain of vengefulness implicit in the wish. "I am suffering, therefore you should suffer too," the lover-serenader says forthrightly. The poem ends, significantly, with the lover bidding the moon rise so that he might see the beloved's tears, not with any fantasy of reciprocity. "He" has already declared the love to be hopeless – fidelity, he says bitterly, is uncommon – and asks only that she weep for him.

One Schubert scholar writes that the composer seems to have ignored the vein of passionate feeling in the Baumberg songs, but it seems more likely that Schubert honored Gabriele's eighteenth-century *Empfindsamkeit* by garbing it in reminiscences of operatic formality.[101] In this song too, he might well have paid heed to the poet's initial injunction to Evening that it be "gentle" and "merry" when he devised the dotted rhythmic figures of the piano introduction (mm. 1–5) and the beginning of the texted strophe in B-flat major, a *plein-air* key in Schubert's song oeuvre. And the passion is indeed present, albeit constrained by its formal classical evocations, and is especially evident in such gestures as the dramatic ascent to high B-flat at the word "Abend" in mid-measure, extending the phrase in an unmistakably passionate manner. The way in which Schubert restores the diatonic pitch E-flat in the next measure, leaping to it on the offbeat, sounding it in the topmost voice as a tritone dissonance against the bass, prolonging it via a fermata on the verb "vermähle" (reward) in gently pleading emphasis, is another such thumbprint of classical profundity of feeling. The chromatically ascending bass line in mm. 14–15 ("[mit] selt'ner Treu' das Glück"), the diminished seventh chord on the adjective "selt'ner," and the semitone- and dissonance-laden setting of that same word when Schubert repeats the last line of Gabriele's stanza are still other indices of passion that may be somewhat muted but cannot be denied and even increases throughout the strophe.

5. In "Lob des Tokayers,"[102] Gabriele once again undertook an almost-exclusively male genre: the drinking song, although one might note in amusement that she praises, not strong spirits but relatively innocuous and expensive *Tokay aszu*, a tipple of Hungarian vintage readily available in Gabriele's and Schubert's Vienna. Gabriele both invokes her standard pose of antiquity, here in an Anacreontic vein, when she sings of her lyre and yet "modernises" the genre by hymning this Austro-Hungarian wine made from grapes whose *pourriture noble* (Botrytis cinerea, or "noble rot") produces the sweetness that made it popular.

O köstlicher Tokayer, o königlicher Wein!	O exquisite Tokay, king among wines!
Du stimmest meine Leier zu seltnen Reimerei'n.	You inspire my lyre to rare rhyming.
Mit langentbehrter Wonne	With long-desired rapture,
Und neu erwachtem Scherz	and newly-awakened gaiety,
Erwärmst du, gleich der Sonne,	like the sun, you warm
Mein halberstorbnes Herz.	my half-frozen heart.
Du stimmest meiner Leier zu seltnen Reimerei'n.	You inspire my lyre to rare rhyming.
O köstlicher Tokayer, o königlicher Wein!	O exquisite Tokay, king among wines!
O köstlicher Tokayer, du königlicher Wein!	O exquisite Tokay, king among wines!
Du giessest Kraft und Feuer durch Mark und durch Gebein.	You pour strength and fervor through my very bones.
Ich fühle neues Leben	I feel new life
Durch meiner Adern sprühn,	sparkling in my veins.
Und deine Nektarreben	I feel your nectar grapes
In meinem Busen glühn.	glowing in my breast.
O köstlicher Tokayer, du königlicher Wein!	O exquisite Tokay, king among wines!
O köstlicher Tokayer, du königlicher Wein!	O exquisite Tokay, king among wines!
Dir soll, als Gramzerstreuer, dies Lied geweihet sein!	To you who allay grief I dedicate this song!
In schwermutsvollen Launen	In melancholy moods
Beflügelst du das Blut,	you fire the blood;
Bei Blonden und bei Braunen,	to blonde and brunette both,
Gibst du dem Blödsinn Mut.	you give the bashful courage.
Dir soll, als Gramzerstreuer, dies Lied geweihet sein!	To you who allay grief I dedicate this song!
O köstlicher Tokayer, du königlicher Wein!	O exquisite Tokay, king among wines!

There is something wonderfully, comically bibulous about the refrain-structure of this poem; like a true inebriate, the poetic persona repeats the same words of praise for her liquid relief at regular intervals. The refrains look all the funnier on the printed page because the hexameter refrain lines that frame each stanza on either side are twice the length of the internal four lines in trimeters. It is characteristic of Gabriele that the first beneficent effect of wine that she hails is its effect on her poetry, in particular, its ability to inspire "rare" rhymes, and it is equally characteristic that Schubert would respond to the invocation of the poet's "lyre" with a particularly frisky triplet flourish in the treble, all the more effective because both hands have to fly up in the space of a single beat from lower to higher registers as if suddenly inspired. The prolonged high G and the full harmonization after two measures of unison texture emphasize "Leier" even more; poet and composer are thus co-conspirators in the importance they ascribed, however merrily, to their art.

The poet may invoke "uncommon" poetic flights of fancy as a gift from Bacchus, but the inside joke (one Schubert caught quite nicely) is that alcohol-induced grandiosity makes what is actually commonplace seem, but only seem, uncommon or "rare." Certainly there is nothing "selten" about the hearty B-flat major strains (Schubert seems to have associated that key with heartiness, bluster, conviviality, and the like), almost entirely restricted to tonic, dominant, and the occasional V/IV or V/V chords. If Gabriele had a more refined crowd in mind when she wrote the poem, Schubert adapts it to more convivial and decidedly less refined contexts. D. 248 keeps the pianist active indeed: accompaniments to drinking songs are often bombastic because they must support group singing, and the *fortissimo* introduction in octaves is in accord with the conventions of the genre. Nonetheless, there are some delightful comic touches in the song. In order to enact the way in which alcoholic exuberance overflows into physical gesture when words cease, Schubert extends the postlude by means of a hilarious crescendo; over and over again, he repeats the tonic harmony, accentuated by neighbor-note dotted rhythms and rising higher and higher. (Hugo Wolf would later do likewise, in his own post-Wagnerian idiom, in his settings of Goethe's Hafiz-inspired drinking songs such as "Erschaffen und Beleben." He would also echo his predecessor's triplet arpeggiated flourishes in the piano at the ends of phrases, as in m. 24 of "Lob des Tokayers," far more extensively in his setting of Joseph von Eichendorff's "Der Glücksritter," a tavern-song with a difference.) Furthermore, hilariously, the postlude begins with a harmonic "surprise," a *forzando* diminished seventh chord not heard anywhere in the texted body of the song – a chromatic hiccup let loose when there are no more words to hold such comic crudeness in check.

With that jolly entry into the lists, the Baumberg settings come to an end, a happier end than Gabriele's own. There is no precise dating for "Lob des Tokayers," and we do not know where it falls in the brief roll-call from August 1815 of Baumberg songs, but certainly it gives the impression of a merry release of tension after the solemnity and intensity which characterize the other five lieder to her poems. The compound of those elements is distinctive to this poet and these songs: in a year of many small songs, Gabriele's poetry inspired a vein of experimentation and a style different from that of the Goethe songs earlier that month, the Klopstock settings that followed in September, or the Stoll and Körner settings in October, to mention only a few of the clusters composed that amazing year. If it is a style redolent of the late eighteenth century, transmuted through the filter of lied rather than opera, that is only appropriate to Gabriele's poetic voice.

CONCLUSION

"I wish that I had died after the publication of my first book. Then the Sappho of Vienna would still be an idol today – all the men of genius would have accompanied my coffin and strewn my grave with elegies. But now I must wander my own homeland as if I were a foreigner and as a wandering Muse can find no employment." Gabriele could not have predicted when she wrote those bitter words in 1816 that another twenty-three years of this shadowy half-life remained to her. The politics of turbulent times engulf the apolitical as well as those who engage actively in political strife; Gabriele, who wrote of love, friendship, and poetry, not of politics, was forced to share her husband's political misfortunes for almost the entire so-called Biedermeier period, the age between revolutions. And yet, there were other reasons as well for her status as an unemployed Muse during all those long years, reasons she could, in proud bitterness, recognize. She was no friend to the Romantic poets and the latest developments in music; she compared Schlegel's sonnets unfavorably to her revered Schiller, and she disparaged the piano virtuosos of the post-Napoleonic concert halls as lacking in true art, especially in comparison with Mozart. She was a phenomenon of the Josephinian Enlightenment from which she came, and her continued adherence to its ideals rendered her a fossil in her own lifetime – this may, speculatively, have had as much to do with the silencing of her Muse as her husband's political misfortunes and literary meddling. If he indubitably belonged to the nationalistic, revolutionary and individualistic movements of the late eighteenth century, she spoke in a different voice.

Ironically, the same year in which Gabriele mourned her premature passing as a poet, Batsányi wrote her a poem of praise as the perfect wife, one of only three poems dedicated to her. The poem merits quotation in full because in it he defines a wife's nature and vocation, except with regard to the children they did not have. "Duty," "fidelity without lies or deception," "love without coercion," no laziness in attending to household chores, virtue, purity, propriety, and modesty are all present and accounted for in a short poem whose Biblical echoes are no accident. There is, one notes, no mention of poetry.

Wem ein Weib von Tugendart,	Whoever has a virtuous wife,
Solch' ein Weib bescheret ward;	such a wife was bestowed on him as a gift;
Über Perlen geht sein Gut.	his good fortune is beyond pearls,
Fest an ihr ist Mannes Mut.	her husband's courage has strength in her.
An ihr hat er Beute genug;	In her, he has bounty enough:
Treue, sonder List und Trug,	fidelity, without lying or deceit;
Liebe, sonder Leid und Zwang,	his entire life, she gives him love
Gibt sie ihm sein Lebenlang.	without sorrow or constraint.

Und ihr Schmuck ist Reinigkeit,	And her adornment is purity,
Froher Blick auf späte Zeit.	a cheerful regard for future times.
Klugheit öffnet ihren Mund,	Wisdom issues from her mouth,
Huld und Sitte tut er kund.	she makes grace and propriety known.
All' ihr Haus durchschauet sie,	She oversees her entire house,
Gibt ihr Brot der Faulheit nie.	never eats the bread of idleness.
Darum pr 't sie ihr Geschlecht,	Therefore, she is praiseworthy among
Und ihr Mann frohlocket recht:	her sex, and her husband rightfully rejoices:
"Viele Frauen, frisch und reich	"I saw many women, young and rich,
Sah ich; Dir war keine gleich.	but none were your equal.
Aller Schönheit Reiz vergeht,	All of beauty's charms vanish,
Gottesfurcht im Weib' besteht.	the fear of God in a wife endures.
Solch ein Weib verdienet Ruhm,	Such a wife deserves praise,
Ihrer Tugend Eigentum,	her virtue a possession.
Gebt ihr ihrer Hände Lohn,	Give her your applause,
Dank und Preis im Heldenton."[103]	thanks and praise in heroic tone."

Perhaps (being charitable), he wished to console her for the loss of one vocation with utmost praise for her other vocation, but one rather doubts it. He surely knew that she wished to be heralded for something other than Godfearing adherence to housewifely responsibilities.

Gabriele's story is tragic in large measure because history and society did not allow her to resolve, despite her best efforts, the conflicts engendered by her longing for love and marriage on the one hand, for creativity and recognition of her poetic gifts on the other. The tale is all the more affecting because Batsányi both professed utmost support for his wife's writing and yet preached the conventional gospel of wifehood to her; she in turn both accepted its premises, took pride in them, and yet rebelled against definition only in those terms. If there were undeniably women practicing their poetic arts and sympathetic chroniclers such as Schindel, those who inveighed against female writers were far more numerous. To cite an example from Gabriele's own Vienna, another of the Schubert poets, Johann Gabriel Seidl (1804–75), published the first volume of his collected poems in 1826, including a poem that would surely have added to Gabriele's depression if she encountered it. In "Einer jungen Dichterin" (To a young poetess), Seidl "exalts" women both as phenomena of Nature and as domestic goddesses while forbidding them creative gifts other than motherhood. "Throw the pen and the half-written sheet away," he commands at the beginning of his lengthy injunction, the heavy trochaic rhythms adding emphasis. Obviously attracted to the young woman, he writes of electricity emanating from her hands, of Life itself burning in her eyes and her breast. "Will you sit at your table and write something cold and unliving, as thinkers do? Will you spoil your freshness, with its promise of so many beautiful flowers? Shall we read in books of how lovely springtime is?" he asks. No, he enjoins, Life itself will be your poetry; to love, to serve, your versification. Marry, have children, practice wifeliness, find your pleasure and pastime in household duties, he counsels. In their proper sphere, women can indeed rule, can hold sway like moonlight or springtime. They are, he implies, creatures of Nature, not art, and attempts to become poetic artificers ill become them.

Sei die Heiligkeit im Bilde,	Be the image of holiness
Und ein Bild der Harmonie,	and the picture of harmony,
Sei der Welt ein Stern der Milde,	be a star of gentleness to the world –
Wärm', erhell', entzücke sie.	warm, brighten, and delight it.
Darum laß das Reimeschmieden,	Therefore leave off concocting verses,
Denn der Jungfrau ziemt es nicht:	for that is not suitable for a young woman –
Ist sie, was sie soll, hiernieden,	she herself is, as she should be,
Ist sie selbst schon ein Gedicht![104]	down here on earth, already a poem!

Seidl was clearly an old fogey in the making (he was twenty-two years old when this anthology appeared), but he had a great deal of company, including János Batsányi. Whatever else it is, Seidl's poem is a response to a contemporary debate on the subject of literary women, a debate rekindled by the likes of Dorothea von Schlegel, Bettina von Arnim, Rahel Varnhagen von Ense, the Baroness Karoline de la Motte-Fouqué, Caroline Pichler, and others; his was, unfortunately, the view that would prevail long after these saccharine words, devoid of any knowledge of female realities, were penned. To modern readers, the poem would inspire only equal measures of irritation and laughter if we did not know of women such as Gabriele von Baumberg who were destroyed by the conflict between their quest for love – it is, after all, the desire of everyone human – and their literary ambitions. In Gabriele's case, the tragedy is all the blacker for Batsányi's assurances of support, his purported abnegation of his own interests to serve her Muse.

In the end, those who best served her cause were the composers who set her verse to music – they provided the Pegasus-like wings to set her words in flight. Both Mozart in "Als Luise die Briefe" and Schubert in "Der Morgenkuss" were her "gleichgestimmten Seelen," her kindred spirits, especially Mozart; the accord between word and tone in "Als Luise die Briefe" is of a different and closer order than the 1815 Schubert settings, for all their felicities.[105] The unanimity between the two eighteenth-century artists is hardly surprising: Mozart and Gabriele, despite the differences in destiny and much else, were of the same generation and shared a similar Enlightenment *Weltanschauung* and proximity to courtly circles, if not full entrée; one can even, somewhat fancifully, imagine how Mozart, a writer of vivid letters in an epistolary age, would be drawn to Gabriele's poetic imagery of letters. But for Schubertians, what is perhaps most striking of all in the tale of Gabriele von Baumberg is the distance between the emotional worlds of these two creators; the more one discovers about her life and art, the more one becomes aware of how little they had in common with one another. I have suggested that Schubert may have been drawn to her verse because he found in it confirmation of his own assertions of an artistic calling in the face of paternal opposition, but could not complete the musical "collaboration": not only were his compositional capacities not yet equal to the task, but it is one thing for an adult woman to defend the rights of her entire gender to a creative destiny and quite another for a teenage boy in conflict with his father over a *Brotwissenschaft* to do so. And yet, whatever initially drew him to this poetry in a female voice brought him back to Gabriele in the wake of "Gretchen am Spinnrade" and in the same month as his setting of Goethe's "Die Spinnerin," a small masterpiece both of the strophic lied and empathy with a female persona. But Schubert echoing Mozart is not the same as Mozart per se: he must, I would guess, have known it and gone on to other voices, other verses, never more to return to the poetry of Gabriele von Baumberg.

Chapter Two

The lyre and the sword
Theodor Körner and the lied

IN THE EIGHTH CANTO of his epic poem *Cäcilie*, the young Ernst Schulze hymned Theodor Körner, dead on the battlefield at age twenty-one, in these words:

So sankst auch du jüngst in der heil'gen Schlacht,	You too recently died in the holy battle,
O Theodor, du Zweig aus Deutschlands Siegeskrone!	O Theodor, thou scion of Germany's crown of victory!
An edler Kühnheit reich und reich an Liedesmacht,	Rich in noble audacity and the power of song,
Nahmst du für Lieb' und Lust den schönen Tod zum Lohne!	In recompense for love and joy, you died a beautiful death!
Was weinst du, Vaterland, dem tapfern Heldensohne?	Why, Fatherland, do you weep for your valiant hero-son?
Er schlummert sanft und kühl in grüner Eichen Nacht;	He sleeps softly, in the cool shade of the green oak;
Er schlummert nur, auch in den fernsten Jahren	He but sleeps, that in the most distant years
Wird Schwert und Leier stets sein Leben uns bewahren.	the sword and lyre will preserve his life for us to eternity.

Schulze was not alone in his veneration for the ebullient young playwright who used his facile poetic gifts and fervent patriotism to rouse the German-speaking world in its final revolt against Napoleon and then died in battle on 26 August 1813. For a century, his name was synonymous with the rebirth of German nationalism; of all the heroes of the War of Liberation, it was Körner who most captured the public's imagination. He was buried under an oak-tree, symbolic of Germany itself, and instantly became a mythical figure, the subject of plays, poems, novels, paintings, and operas well into the late twentieth century; Ulrich Völkel's *Mit Leier und Schwert: Roman um Theodor Körner* (With lyre and sword: a novel about Theodor Körner) of 1986 is the latest in a long line of such works. Körner was considered a model for youth – episodes from his life adorn a children's calendar for 1890 – and a pattern of patriotism, a Germanic David who sang songs and helped to slay the giant Napoleon.[1] His heroic status is evident in the ten-foot-high statue of him completed in 1871 by Julius Hähnel in the poet's native Dresden

Figure 3.   The monument to Theodore Körner in Dresden (1871), sculpted by Julius Hähnel

(Fig. 3), a monument which depicts him in the uniform of the Lützower Volunteers, holding a roll of poems in his right hand, his left hand clutching his sword to his breast. That he did not live to see the denouement of the real-life drama in which he participated made him all the more compelling a martyr – "the Rupert Brooke of his generation," John Reed calls him.[2] In one sense, this is the tale of all the ardent young men throughout history who have thrown themselves on the point of a sword for their patriotic ideals.

The year after his death, his grieving father, Christian Gottfried Körner, gathered together thirty-six patriotic poems his son had written between 1811 and 1813 and published them under the title *Leier und Schwert* (The lyre and the sword).[3] Collections of patriotic poetry abounded at a time when nationalistic sentiments had spilled over into war, but Körner's verses were especially appealing because he had died a hero's death and because his poems lent themselves so well to music in their "drum-beat" rhythms and passionate imagery. They were *poesia per musica* from their inception – Körner had written them as *contrafacta* and designated the desired folk-tunes and chorale melodies for most of the poems[4] – and attracted a swarm of composers, including Schubert, who set five poems from the famous collection ("Jägerlied," or "Hunting Song," D. 204 and "Lützows wilde Jagd," or "Lützow's wild hunt," D. 205 for two voices or two horns; "Trinklied vor der Schlacht," or "Drinking song before the battle," D. 169 for two unison choruses with piano accompaniment; the "Schwertlied," or "Sword-song," D. 170, for solo voice, unison chorus, and piano; and the solo song "Gebet während der Schlacht," or "Prayer during the battle," D. 171). None of them are especially memorable: the composer, while he took part in the musical celebration of a glamorous young war-hero he knew personally, was nevertheless unmoved by the white-hot militaristic fervor for which the poet was famous. If Schubert writes "At the 'Hurrah!' with swords clinking" in the manuscript of the "Schwertlied," that only proves that he knew the clichés of the genre, not that he was inspired by them.

The nineteenth-century Körner-cult has received only sporadic attention in the years after World War I, since Körner's literary sun fell into eclipse and other war-martyrs captured public attention. Despite his undeniable facility, his verse is marked more by promise than by profundity (with one or two exceptions). And yet, as the symbol and rallying cry of German liberation from Napoleonic rule, he continues to lead an echoing half-life in historical novels and in music history. This last scion of a remarkable family inspired a quantity of music, some of it deserving resurrection and all of it deserving commentary for its role in those turbulent times. Wars require propaganda, and the arts lent their services to the call-up, including songs to words by Theodor Körner; given his anti-Napoleonic ardor, it is no wonder that he found his way onto the emperor's blacklist of "traitors" and became the very pattern of the patriotic German for a century thereafter. The model was all the more powerful because he was an artist who devoted his art to nationalistic purposes at the moment of Germany's rebirth from the ashes, *Kultur* and *Vaterland* thus mingled in the most potent way. Given the glamor of this brief life-turned-into-legend, it is not surprising that Körner's fame was resurrected in the years just before World War I, when the German nation sought hundreds of thousands of new Körners to die for their country as he had done. Fritz Jöde, in his 1913 songbook *1813 im Liede* (1813 in song), ended the preface by hoping "that we might be heartened by the remembrance of this high time of German conviction and strength" a century earlier. The collection includes more songs to texts by Körner than by anyone else, except the ubiquitous "Anonymous."[5]

FROM SUNSHINE TO STORM: THEODOR KÖRNER'S LIFE AND WORKS

Theodor grew up in a remarkable household led by a remarkable man: one investigates the father's background initially to learn more about his son and becomes fascinated by an extraordinary parent. In the portrait of Christian Gottfried (1756–1831) by Anton Graff (Fig. 4), one sees a handsome man with the high forehead and strongly marked features that he would bequeath to his son in softer

Figure 4. Portrait by Anton Graff of Christian Gottfried Körner (1756–1831)

guise. In accordance with family tradition, Christian Gottfried began theological studies in 1772 at the University of Leipzig, but conflicts with his father arose over religious doubts that Christian Gottfried had already begun to experience at the Landesschule in Grimma as a result of his studies in philosophy. Abandoning theology, he studied law as the means of earning a livelihood, although his varied interests in natural science, mathematics, and economics eventually took him away from what he called "das starre, tötende Recht" (rigid, deadly law). While at the University of Göttingen, he belonged to a circle of friends "who served the Muses" and was particularly drawn to music, although he realized that "I am lacking, not in pleasure in my own work in this medium, but in hopes of success, not in … good ideas, but in the means to execute them."[6] Nonetheless, he composed music, opened his home to musicians, sang in various choral organizations, and taught his children to love music. Theodor would learn to play the violin, fortepiano, and guitar and to sing in a melodious baritone voice; in their letters, he and his father enthusiastically discussed performances of Handel's oratorios and the latest Beethoven symphony.[7]

After a European journey in 1780–81, Christian Gottfried went to Leipzig, where he became the youngest councillor in the parliament and met Anna Maria Jacobine Stock, known as Minna (born 11 March 1762 in Nuremberg), the daughter of the well-known engraver Johann Michael Stock, who counted Goethe and his own daughter Johanna Dorothea, or Dora, among his more gifted students. Christian Gottfried asked Minna to marry him in 1782, although an immediate wedding was impossible because of his father's objections; when Christian Gottfried attempted to give his father a painting of Minna by Anton Graff as a birthday present, Johann Gottfried was furious, crumpled the canvas and threw it away. His son, however, remained adamant and left for a new post in Dresden with his future wife's support, if not his father's.

Once settled in Dresden, Christian Gottfried and Minna were married on 7 August 1785. Dora and Dora's fiancé Ludwig Ferdinand Huber (the relationship would later sour and Dora would remain unmarried) became the friends and sponsors of Friedrich Schiller, then at a crossroads in his life due to financial exigencies, cabals at the Mannheim theatres where he was dramatist-in-residence, and a hopeless relationship with a married woman.[8] Nor was Schiller the only famous guest in the Dresden household. The gregarious Körner kept open house for all manner of thinkers and artists, including Wilhelm von Humboldt, the Danish poet Jens Immanuel Baggesen, the Countess Elise von der Recke, and Mozart, who came to the Saxon capital on 12 April 1789 and visited almost daily during his brief trip; it was on this occasion that Dora Stock created her famous profile portrait of the thirty-three-year-old composer. In June 1803, Johann Friedrich Zelter visited the household, prompting a characteristically astute analysis of Zelter's musical tastes from Christian Gottfried:

According to him [Zelter], only Fasch, Handel, Bach and a few others are at all worthy. I believe, however, that the kingdom of music is much greater than that and has room for many others. He passes judgement in a disparaging manner on many a first-rate talent, for which he is perhaps lacking in discernment, and much of what he prizes above all seems to me like strict textbook writing. I would like to discuss the philosophical aspects of music theory with him, but I will have to keep some of my opinions to myself since he is not deeply enough steeped in philosophy and holds too closely to authority. There is, to be sure, a certain effeminacy [Weichlichkeit] in modern music, a base striving to tickle the ear without gratifying the heart and the spirit, against which it is a duty to be hard and inflexible. But to limit ourselves only to robust northern art would be another extreme. In music as well, what is exalted does not lie only in the realm of what is complex, and there are beautiful forms that one cannot achieve through correct but arid drawings. Zelter would have to scorn the greater portion of his own works if he is to be consistent.[9]

Several Schubert poets also visited the house on the Kohlenmarkt, including Friedrich von Matthisson in early 1795 (neither Christian Gottfried nor Schiller was enthusiastic about his poetry) and August Wilhelm Schlegel and his brother Friedrich. Through the auspices of a family friend named Ernst von Pfuel, the Körners met Heinrich von Kleist in late 1807, and Kleist thereafter became a frequent guest, along with Ludwig Tieck, Madame de Staël, and Gotthilf Heinrich von Schubert, the author of *Ansichten von der Nachtseite der Naturwissenschaften* (Views from the night-side of the study of nature).

It was in this household, where the brightest people in all manner of the arts, letters, and sciences came and went, that Emma Sophie was born on 20 April 1788 and Theodor on 23 September 1791. Christian Gottfried's greatest gift may have been as a parent. Unlike the autocratic Prussian fathers of legend, he took delight in his son's burgeoning imagination and awakened his nascent dramatic sensibilities by creating domestic festivals for the two children, complete with poetic declamations, music, and dramatic scenes. Although it was a pious household, Christian Gottfried wanted his children to think of religion "not as a gloomy taskmaster and a kill-joy of innocent pleasures, but as a soul-uplifting friend." On Theodor's birthday in 1802, his father wrote him a distich: "Full of hope, I take this sheet of paper; a father is fortunate if there remains for him a worthy place among his son's friends."[10] His goal was to raise his son in such a way that father and son would become close friends and confidants in adulthood; that his goal was achieved makes the tragedy of his son's premature death all the greater.

Körner's first poems were of the "clever schoolboy" variety, including, inevitably, paraphrases of Schiller; his 1804 farewell to his tutor Wilhelm Gottfried Küttner begins "Will sich Küttner ewig von mir wenden" (Will Küttner forever turn away from me), casting his erstwhile teacher in the role of a male Andromache from Schiller's poem "Hektors Abschied" (which Schubert would set to music in 1815, D. 312). The same year, the thirteen-year-old Theodor wrote a maladroit poem in French about his hatred of Napoleon and his allegiance to the German language; those same sentiments at fierier temperatures would send him to his death nine years later.

Oui, je trouve le Français charmant	Yes, I find French charming
Pour dire aux dames des compliments,	for paying compliments to ladies,
Mais les mots addressés aux tyranns,	but the words spoken to tyrants
Cela seule exprime l'allemand.[11]	can only be expressed in German. (stanza 4)

Another of his early poems is a parody of Matthisson's "Ich denke Dein" (there was a growth industry in parodies of this popular poem), written in 1805 for his first sweetheart, followed by an entire series of poems with titles such as "An Augusten," "An Theresen," "An Henrietten," and "An Amor." He also translated segments from James MacPherson's Ossian poems, from *King Lear* and *Timon of Athens* and Anacreon's poems from the Greek, as well as writing dramas with titles such as "Francesco and Francesca's unfortunate love and terrible death, brought into the light of a godless world by a friend" and the comedy "Cupid and his disciples." If little of this youthful production is memorable, one can nevertheless trace his increasing fluency from year to year.

In June 1807, Theodor went to study at the famous mining school in Freiberg, twenty miles southwest of Dresden, where the distinguished mineralogist Abraham Gottlob Werner (immortalized by Novalis in *Die Lehrlinge zu Sais* and *Heinrich von Ofterdingen*) was his teacher. Christian Gottfried was of his age in his choice of livelihood for a budding writer like Theodor; Goethe, Novalis, Clemens Brentano, Gotthilf Heinrich Schubert, Alexander von Humboldt, Johann Friedrich Reichardt, and many others were either mine administrators or studied mining, an area which exercised a potent symbolic attraction for the late eighteenth- and early nineteenth-century German mind.[12] Theodor, however, was only interested in literature. "If I did not sacrifice every day to my household gods, Schiller and Goethe, I would die of boredom," he wrote to a friend, and then, with characteristic optimism, declared that matters would soon be better because he was meeting new people and receiving many invitations.[13] Although the rumors of war between France and Austria in 1808 aroused the peace-loving Körner family's interest, Theodor paid little attention to the troop movements near Freiberg, while in 1809, the year war actually broke out, father and son alike were principally preoccupied with Theodor's growing disinclination for mining. In that year of rekindled Napoleonic strife, he enclosed the following poem in a letter to his father:

Laßt uns nicht bangen im Kampf der Zeit	Let us not be afraid in the battles of the age,
Tobt auch auf den Feldern der blutige Streit;	even when bloody combat rages in the fields;
Wem das Herz in heiliger Ruhe schlägt,	he whose heart beats in holy peace
Der wird nicht vom Sturme des Schicksals bewegt.[14]	will not be moved by the storms of fate.

Theodor even went on a walking trip from 22 to 29 July 1809 in the Bohemian mountains and, in August, to the Riesengebirge, where on 21 August, he wrote "Auf der Riesenkoppe" – "It rains sonnets," he told his parents.[15] By that time, Christian Gottfried had sympathetically conceded that he did not want his son to sacrifice "the loveliest years of his youth" in an occupation Theodor found inimical, although he cautioned that young men do not often consider with sufficient thoughtfulness the means to make a living. If his son would finish his two-year course of study in Freiberg, Theodor could then go to university.[16]

Before Theodor left for the University of Leipzig in summer 1810, he compiled a book of forty-three poems modestly entitled *Knospen* (Buds). Those who appreciate the Schillerian school, Theodor's father wrote to the publisher Göschen, might find these poems – hardly the work of a master but full of talent and heart – pleasing. Concerned lest Theodor's feelings be hurt by bad reviews, Christian Gottfried warned him that even the Olympians among writers were regularly roughed up by critics: "Jacta est alea. Arm yourself against stringent and malicious critics … recently there was even a rude attack on Goethe."[17] The Schubert texts "Liebeständelei," "Das war ich," "Sängers Morgenlied," and "Sehnsucht der Liebe" all come from *Knospen*, which was, in general, kindly received when it appeared, despite critiques of the young author's too-faithful echoes of Schiller. Far from being discouraged, no sooner was *Knospen* published than Theodor conceived the notion to found a *Taschenbuch* for Christians – the family theological heritage emerging in literary guise – that would include historical essays, religious poems and musical settings, woodblock illustrations of Biblical scenes, and the like. His father entered into the plan with enthusiasm and formulated a slate of co-editors, including Zelter, Jean Paul Richter, Ludwig Tieck, and others, all to be directed by Friedrich Schleiermacher, but the plan came to nought.

En route to Leipzig, the Körners went to Karlsbad, where Theodor spent the month of July writing poetry in which German pride at a time of German humiliation comes to the fore. Moved by the sight of the ancient oaks in the Dallwitz Park in Karlsbad, Körner wrote one of his most famous poems, "Die Eichen" (The Oaks), a clarion call for renewal of ancient Germanic glory.

Ach, was hilft's, daß ich den Schmerz erneue?	Oh, what is the use of renewing my pain?
Sind doch alle diesem Schmerz vertraut!	All are familiar with this sorrow!
Deutsches Volk, du herrlichstes von allen,	German people, the noblest of all,
Deine Eichen stehn, Du bist gefallen![18]	your oak trees stand, but thou art fallen!

(final stanza)

Both this poem and the sonnet "Andreas Hofers Tod" (Andreas Hofer's death), written on 19 July 1810, were later included in *Leier und Schwert*. Andreas Hofer was a Swiss patriot who, with Austrian encouragement, led a successful Tyrolean uprising against the French and their Bavarian allies in April 1809; the Austrian defeat at Wagram and the Treaty of Schönbrunn, however, spelled his doom, and he was shot under martial law on 20 February 1810. Theodor, along with other patriotically inclined writers such as Karl Immermann, Max von Schenkendorf, and Julius Mosen, found Hofer's fate a compelling symbol of anti-Napoleonic sentiment. These invocations of Teutonic pride were perhaps also the vehicle for Körner's individuation from Schiller, the means to become less Schiller-like and more his own poet. Although Schiller's ghost was at the heart of nationalistic sentiment among the young literati-turned-soldiers (Immerman wrote that "Schiller was the strongest influence on us by far – our enthusiasm for him amounted to reverence"), Körner's brand of popularizing patriotism would be different in tone and temper from that of his great predecessor.

In August 1810, Theodor went to Leipzig and promptly became embroiled in *Burschenschaft* politics. At that time, the student societies were divided into two warring factions of nobility ("Adeligen") and a local Thuringian organization;

Theodor rapidly became one of the most ardent members of the anti-aristocratic Thuringian club. If at first he found time to participate in literary societies, he was soon so caught up in the student unrest that his studies were no longer the subject of discussion with his family. Christian Gottfried was alarmed, but tried both to reassure himself that the wildness he had heard bruited about was exaggerated and to counsel his son against undue influence. "You have idealized the student societies, and I have nothing against that, but stay true only to your ideals! Don't sink to the level of your surroundings," he wrote urgently. It is very natural, he stated, his pride in his son always apparent, that Theodor would be considered a prize acquisition, but he knew the arts by which someone of Theodor's temperament could be seduced into actions unworthy of him and begged his son to leave Leipzig and go to Berlin, where things were quieter.[19]

Shortly after the start of the winter semester, the conflicts smoldering between the Thüringer and the Adeligen broke out in duels and street-fighting, in which Theodor played a major role. When he came home at Christmas, he wrote three opera texts, *Der Meistersänger* (The Mastersinger), *Alfred der Große* (Alfred the Great), and *Chlotilde*,[20] while waiting to hear whether his bellicose behavior had angered city authorities. When the coast seemed clear, he returned to Leipzig, where yet another bout of fisticuffs with the rival *Burschenschaft* led to an eight-day prison sentence. His father advised him to wait for the Leipzig town council to mete out judgment, and, in the meantime, he [Christian Gottfried] would intervene. It would be dishonorable, he wrote, to sneak out of Leipzig as a lawbreaker and might thereby put an end to his university prospects.[21] But Theodor proceeded to do something so harmful to his own cause – this was clearly a test of his father's remarkable sweetness – that he did indeed have to leave the city under cover of darkness. On 17 March 1811, the young hothead fought a duel and was wounded on the forehead. Despite his attempt to hide his latest contretemps from the council, the authorities discovered the matter and Theodor fled the city, as he describes in his poem "Meine Flucht" (My flight). One can only sympathize when his father wrote, more in sorrow than in anger, to say, "You know that it is difficult for me not to give up on you entirely when I have such cause to be upset … after what has happened, I can well imagine you would rather leave Leipzig secretly than be in danger of spending half-a-year locked up in jail."[22] The danger was worse than he thought: one of Theodor's companions was given an eight-year sentence, the first year on bread and water only.

By 27 March, Theodor was in Berlin, where he participated in the Singakademie, performing in Zelter's oratorio *Die Auferstehung Christi* (The Resurrection of Christ), and works by Handel, Benda, Graun, and Bach. For his father's delectation, he wrote a lively account of Zelter's rehearsals.[23] At first, however, he again disobeyed his parents' wishes. His father had urged him to stay with the Parthey family (the Hofrat Friedrich Parthey, 1745-1821, was head of a distinguished Berlin family and longtime friend of the Körner family), but Theodor, his rebellious streak not yet concluded, seems to have stayed with his *Burschenschaft* friends in a disreputable area of the city and not to have contacted Parthey père at all. His sister Emma reproached him spiritedly in a letter of 1 April, telling him that their father had not spared any unpleasant task that might alleviate his son's predicament and bidding him in no uncertain terms to spare his family any further anxiety.[24] Christian Gottfried had already written to the rector and the University Senate in Leipzig, asking for mercy on account of his son's youth. The matter was all the more serious because Leipzig, Wittenberg, Berlin, and others belonged to a group of universities who would not admit those students expelled from one of their number. When news of the judgment against Theodor reached Berlin, he was formally excluded on 14 August 1811, or placed under "Relegat." By that time, he was already in Vienna.

Reading Theodor's letters from Berlin to his *Burschenschaft* comrades and Freiberg friends, one discovers the prelude to the Lützower Volunteers, the combination of blood-brotherhood and patriotism he found irresistible. He makes the connection explicit when he wrote to a friend as follows:

But consider, too, that after our youth is over, this fellowship loses the greatest part of its special bond, that you must enter a cold Philistine life, where nothing then will remain of it for you but the memory and the conviction that the brothers of our society will always recognize one another, will aid one another in the battle for freedom, should that day dawn – thus our closer union will be re-established and our society can attain its highest secret meaning![25]

But he did not have much time in Berlin to pursue his *Burschenschaft* allegiances. In May 1811, he fell seriously ill with a fever, and on 4 June returned home to Dresden to be cared for by his family, first at home and then in Karlsbad. While in Karlsbad, he wrote a romantic opera text entitled *Die Bergknappen* (The mountain miners), subsequently set to music by six composers, among them, Friedrich von Flotow; a sequence of poems entitled *Erinnerungen an Karlsbad* (Memories of Karlsbad), and various individual poems. Then he left for Vienna, arriving on 26 August.

His worried father's letters during those first months regarding the choice of a profession and the means to procure the necessary training for that profession in the wake of the Leipzig debacle are examples of parenthood at its best. Rather than hectoring his son about economic realities (he had seen at first-hand how even Schiller found it difficult to make a living solely by writing) or attempting to undermine Theodor's confidence in his creativity, Christian Gottfried was concerned that Theodor know how to define happiness properly, that is, to strive for peace with one's self and a worthy goal in life. He knows, he writes, young men of great ability who have a wide field of occupations from which to choose, but wrongly follow the crowd or false glory, thereby shutting themselves away from the prospect of lifelong happiness. Ironically, he includes soldiering as a possible choice of profession only to reject it, concluding that battle for a worthy cause may be necessary, but in "today's warfare," there is little opportunity for an individual soldier to distinguish himself from the crowd and therefore be honored for his feats.[26] One wonders whether he ever re-read this letter after his son's death and realized the tragic irony of his words. At the time, he urged his son to study history and Greek, subjects he felt could only enrich poetry, and preferably either in Munich, where Friedrich Schelling and Friedrich Heinrich Jacobi could be his teachers, or Weimar, as soon as Christian Gottfried could succeed in having the interdiction against his son lifted.

But Theodor had fallen in love with Vienna, in particular, with its theatrical life. He wrote to his family on his birthday (23 September) to say that he would remain there for the winter to study history, Greek, and other languages, clearly as a way of placating his father's concerns and putting a temporary halt to Christian Gottfried's plans for enrolling him in universities elsewhere. In the house where he lodged, many of Vienna's young actors took their meals, and Theodor began writing plays for them; by Christmas 1811, he had written the comedies *Die Braut* (The bride) and *Der grüne Domino* (The green mask), as well as the opera texts *Das Fischermädchen* (The fisher-maiden), and *Der Kampf mit dem Drachen* (The battle with the dragon), the latter based on the famous poem by Schiller.[27] Both of the comedies, written in the alexandrines his father had designated in his essay "Über das Lustspiel" (Concerning comedy) as the best for comedy, were accepted for performance at the Hofburgtheater. In late December, he began another one-act comedy in Knittelvers entitled *Der Nachtwächter* (The Nightwatchman)[28] – the fiery young student Ernst Wachtel, who is placed under "Relegat," is clearly the author himself, the tale exaggerated for comic effect. The fact that Theodor could thus turn his recent past into a comedy was a sign that the days of wild oats were on the wane, and his father was increasingly reassured of a new-found sense of stability. On 6 January 1812, Theodor wrote to his father to argue eloquently that he should pursue a playwright's vocation. "Now more than ever, I am convinced that God put me into the world to be a poet. Talent is not the possession only of an individual: it belongs to the nation, which desires that a poet expend his talent prodigiously."[29] If he succeeds, he tells his father, he will remain in Vienna and continue to write plays; if not, he will pursue some "Brotwissenschaft" (breadwinner's profession) and dedicate his leisure hours to sonnets. He is satiated, he assures his father, with student excesses and will never again place his future in jeopardy for such games. "This is my plan for the future – it could only be altered if Prussia goes to war … people might tell me that I am meant for better things, but there is nothing better than to fight or die for what one knows to be the highest in life." Whatever his preoccupation with the theater, Theodor paid heed to the rumblings of imminent war.

When the Burgtheater staged a rehearsal on 17 January 1812 for the forthcoming performances of *Die Braut* and *Der grüne Domino*, the young playwright met the actress Antonie Adamberger (1790–1867), soon to become his fiancée, for the first time. Antonie, or "Toni," came from a theatrical family:[30] her father Valentin was a famous tenor for whom Mozart wrote the concert arias "Per pietà non ricercate" and "A te fra tanti affanni" from the *Davidde penitente*, and her mother, Maria Anna Jacquet, was a court actress renowned for ingenue roles. When both of her parents died in 1804 of tuberculosis, Antonie became an actress in order to support her five sisters and herself. Her roles included parts in August von Kotzebue's comedies, Desdemona in *Othello*, Beatrice in Schiller's *Die Braut von Messina*, and Clärchen in Goethe's *Egmont*.[31] She was, for a time, aided by the family friend Heinrich von Collin (a famous playwright and brother of the Schubert poet Matthäus von Collin), but Collin too died suddenly on 28 July 1811, another of many losses Toni endured in her youth. There is a charming anecdote of her meeting with Beethoven as he was composing the incidental music for *Egmont*: when he asked her, "Can you sing?", she replied "No!", at which Beethoven laughed and replied, "No? But I'm supposed to set the songs from 'Egmont' for you."[32] He subsequently taught her the songs, enjoining her not to add "even a single mordent."

For her return to the stage in January 1812, after an absence due to a cold, the elderly actor Karl Friedrich Krüger suggested the plays by an unknown poet from Germany. "So much sorrow and yet such holy joy followed that evening for me! I thank God for having allowed me to experience both," she wrote in her fragmentary memoirs from 1855–56.[33] She could not, however, bring herself to speak of him in much detail.

How we saw each other often thereafter [after the first rehearsal of the "Domino" and "Die Braut"]; how all those in my family were won over by his noble, true-hearted ways; how he later told me that he had lost his heart to me in an instant; how his talent developed and how he wrote 'Toni' for me; how his passionate patriotism overcame every other feeling, so that he left the next year, never to return – it is ever and always difficult for me to tell of it, even after forty-four years,

she wrote.[34] After the rehearsal, Theodor wrote to his family to say that he would never have dreamed that he, a mere beginner, should have two works played at the Burgtheater, that "die Adamberger" had only to open her mouth to enchant everyone, that *Die Braut* pleased the audience more than *Der grüne Domino*. The plays were performed three times to full houses, and the critics were friendly, the writer for the *Wiener Beobachter* observing that seldom had the first-born of a dramatic poet been baptized more pleasingly than these.[35]

His initial success was followed by more. The first performance of *Der Nachtwächter* on 8 February was also well-received, despite a dismal first performance in which the lead actor, perched on a stage roof, became dizzy and forgot his words. Theodor, encouraged by his success, next turned to serious drama and wrote a three-act play entitled *Toni*, based upon Kleist's novella *Die Verlobung* (The betrothal) – one suspects it was the name Toni and the subject of betrothal that spurred him to adapt a novella he had earlier considered converting into an opera text. When it was first performed on 17 April, the audience again gave its approbation, although the play compares badly with its masterful source; Kleist's moment of alchemical transformation in the character Toni's soul from evil to knowledge of compassion and love is not present at all in Theodor's version, with its two-dimensional silhouette of noble feminine heroism. Nevertheless, it was a success and brought Körner into contact with Caroline Pichler for the first time. Theodor had been given a letter of introduction from a mutual friend in Dresden, but did not avail himself of it during his first months in Vienna. Pichler, mildly piqued that he did not beat a path to her door and curious to discover what he was like, sent word through another court playwright that if he did not want to visit her, he should at least return the letter from their Dresden link so that she would not miss a communiqué from a friend. This gentle machination worked: Körner came to pay a visit on 17 April 1812, and the two instantly took to one another, Körner thereafter a frequent guest at the Pichler salon.[36] At the

Pichlers, he met the beautiful and cultivated Baroness Henriette von Pereira-Arnstein, the arbiter of another Viennese salon and one of Theodor's closest friends during the year that remained to him in his adopted city. Theodor contributed to the literary activities of the two salons; Pichler marveled at the young man's facility and wrote in her memoirs that he covered entire folios with scarcely a thought or a line altered in the process (she does not say that his writings would have benefited from revision and greater thought, but present-day readers are wont to do so). It was at her salon that he read *Rosamunde* on 18 November 1812 and improvised the ghost stories "Die Tauben" (The Pigeons) and "Die Rosen" (The Roses), which Pichler wrote down in 1819 and sent as a gift to Henriette von Pereira-Arnstein.

During the winter and spring of 1812, Theodor wrote poems to Toni and his best comedy, *Die Vetter aus Bremen* ("The Cousins from Bremen") – Goethe spoke highly of this work – searched for the subject of a historical tragedy, and wooed Toni. On 16 May, he wrote an ecstatic letter to a friend, saying "At last, I am entirely, completely happy; death can now call for me whenever it wants!," and on 20 May, he wrote to his father: "Father, dear, dear friend, I have found that goal where I shall throw my anchor – Father, I'm in love."[37] He had not said anything of the matter to his parents earlier, and he identifies her only as "Toni," possibly out of fear that his father would object to his son's marrying an actress. In the next letter, he told his father, in a youthful gush of words, the entire tale, upon which his parents immediately made plans to visit Vienna in the summer. In June, Theodor went to Döbling and there wrote his tragedy *Zriny,* based on an incident from Hungarian history, in a mere three weeks. He certainly wrote rapidly and easily. Despite troubles with the censors, the play was finally performed on 30 and 31 December 1812 and 1 January 1813. It is no wonder that the censors were nervous, as Theodor's fictive sultan clearly represents Napoleon Bonaparte:

Ich hab' gekämpft, genossen und bezwungen;	I have waged war, relished, and conquered,
Den Augenblick hab' ich mit Blut erkauft	I have bought the moment with blood,
Und seine ganze Wollust ausgekostet.	and enjoyed its debauchery to the utmost.
Mein Thatenruf hat rings die Welt durchbebt,	The fame of my deed resounds through the
Der Mitwelt Furcht und Zittern aufgedrungen,	entire world, has impelled fear and trembling
Der Nachwelt ihre Stimme abgetrotzt	in our times, has bullied posterity out of its
Und sich die Bahn zur Ewigkeit gebrochen!	voice and broken the pathway to eternity!
Daß ich auf Trümmern und auf Leichen ging,	That I went my way through the wreckage
	and over dead bodies,
Daß ich Millionen in den Tod geschmettert	that I have shattered millions of people to
Wenn's mein Gelüsten galt, das mag der Wurm,	death when it so pleased me, thus may the
Der unter mit im Staube sich gewunden,	worm that has wound its way in the dust
	beneath my feet,
Der Welt erzählen; sein Gekrächz' verstummt;	Tell the world; its croaking falls silent;
Das Große nur bleibt ewig, unvergessen,	only greatness remains eternal, unforgotten,
Und hat kein Ende in dem Grab der Welt![38]	and has no ending in the world's grave!

(Act 4, sc. 4)

The lines with which the Hungarian nobleman Lorenz Juranitsch casts his lot with that of his lord Zriny, both of them doomed to die in the siege of Sigeth, were to become Theodor's own fate a few months after the premiere of his drama:

Daß ich dem Tod mich weihte, gilt nicht viel;	That I dedicated myself to death is not much;
Mein Leben schlug ich oft schon in die Schanze.	I have often thrown my life into the breach.
Doch daß ich's that mit diesem Recht an Glück,	Yet that I did it with such right to happiness,
An Seligkeit und höchste Erdenwonne,	to ecstasy, and the greatest joy on earth, that
Das war des Kampfs, das war des Preises wert;	was worth the battle, worth the price.
Mein Vaterland sei stolz auf dieser Opfer![39]	My Fatherland can be proud of such a
	sacrifice! (Act 4, sc. 9)

At the end, Zriny cries out, "Stirb, wack'res Volk! für Gott und Vaterland!" (Die, brave folk! For God and the Fatherland!), and all reply, "Dir nach! Dir nach! für Gott und Vaterland" (After you! For God and the Fatherland!), Körner already warming up his pen for the fervent recruiting speeches he would write shortly thereafter.

Theodor's parents and sister came to Vienna in August and early September 1812 to see their son and meet his fiancée, Minna giving Toni a pearl necklace for the occasion. "I have never worn it," she wrote in her memoirs, "without being aware of the proverb now engraved in my heart: pearls signify tears."[40] Upon their departure, Theodor went back to work on various theatrical projects, including the Singspiel *Der vierjährige Posten* (which Schubert set to music in May 1815, D. 190), a three-act play *Hedwig*, the comedy *Der Wachtmeister*, and the five-act tragedy *Rosamunde* about Rosamunde Clifford, one of the mistresses of Henry II. In early 1813, he was named as imperial-royal court theater poet, contractually obligated to write two large plays and two small "Nachspiele" (sequels) per year for a salary of 1,500 gulden annually. After his appointment, he wrote the last of his comedies, *Die Gouvernante* (The governess) and the one-act tragedy *Joseph Heyderich, oder Deutsche Treue* (Joseph Heyderich, or German faithfulness), written in prose and based on an anecdote from Napoleon's Italian campaign of 1800. The title character, an elderly corporal, offers his life to save that of his lieutenant in the Austrian defeat at Montebello on 9 June 1800; as in *Zriny*, one hears Theodor himself speaking in lines such as these from a soliloquy by the lieutenant in the fourth scene, when he believes he is dying:

I never thought, when I was in school and translating Horace, that I would someday apply the phrase "dulce pro patria mori" to myself. – Yes, by the Almighty, the immortal poet was right: it *is* sweet to die for the Fatherland! – Oh, if I could only stand before all the young, true hearts among my people and thunder forth, with the last remaining strength of my fast-fleeting life, "It is sweet to die for the Fatherland!" Death is not dreadful when it winds the bloody laurels about the pale sleepers' brows – if they knew that the cold egoists, who creep behind the ovens when the Fatherland calls its sons to its banners; if they knew that the cowardly, vile souls, who consider themselves to be wise and prudent, when they make a parade of their empty talk, – let it go on without them; two fists more or less do not matter in the scales of victory – if they had imagined the bliss that a brave soldier feels when he bleeds for a just cause, they would have forced themselves into the ranks … Go quickly to the banners, when the inner voice drives you to do so; leave father and mother, wife and child, friend and beloved firmly behind; thrust them from you when they would hold you back – the Fatherland has first place in your heart![41]

The play ends with the lieutenant proclaiming, "See here, Fatherland, what hearts beat in your sons' breasts, what deeds come to fruition under your sun – Fatherland, you can be proud!" With this work, Theodor's playwriting career was at an end: he had seen it coming and had incorporated his farewell into his last play for Vienna.

The nationalistic pride exhorted by Ernst Moritz Arndt in his verse and prose and by Johann Gottlieb Fichte in his 1808 *Reden an die deutsche Nation* (Addresses to the German nation) had seemed in vain for a time, but Theodor took part in the metamorphosis by which a humiliated and divided nation awoke to reclaim its heritage from the Corsican emperor. After the horrors of the Russian campaign in 1812, the German-speaking world began slowly, because of petty jealousies and disunity, to organize against Napoleon. The hesitant Friedrich Wilhelm had to be compelled into compliance with the uprising, but finally, on 28 February 1813, Prussia entered into a formal alliance (the Convention of Kalisch) with Russia for the liberation of Europe. On 3 February, Friedrich Wilhelm called for volunteer corps to be formed, and on 17 March, he issued the "Aufruf an mein Volk," the general call-up of the Prussian people. German soldiers, he announced, "will fight for our independence and the honor of the *Volk*. Both will only be secured if every son of the fatherland participates in this battle for honor and freedom ... My cause is the cause of my *Volk*, and of all well-intentioned Europeans." This was followed on 25 March 1813 by a "Proclamation to the German People and Princes," issued in the names of Tsar Alexander and Friedrich Wilhelm and containing a mélange of threats and inducements to such reluctant states as Theodor's native Saxony.

Theodor had been following the great historical drama closely, with every intention of becoming a participant. On 27 January 1813, he wrote to his family to say, "A great moment in life is drawing near. You may be sure, it will not find me unworthy when it comes to the test."[42] On 10 March, he told them of his resolution to join the Prussian volunteer corps formed by Major Adolph Freiherr von Lützow:[43]

My dear father! I am writing you concerning a matter that I have the strongest trust will neither alienate nor frighten you. Recently I already gave you a hint of my purpose, which has now reached fruition. – Germany is arising; the Prussian eagle, with the bold beating of its wings, has awakened the great hope of German, or at least North German, freedom in all true hearts. My future sighs after its Fatherland – let me be its worthy youth! – Yes, dearest father, I will become a soldier, will joyfully cast aside the happy and carefree life I have won here in order to fight for my Fatherland, even if it is with my own blood. – Do not call this bravado, frivolity, or wildness! Two years ago, I would have designated it thus; now, when I know what happiness this life affords; now, when all the stars of my happiness shine down on me in soft beauty; now, by God, it is a worthy sentiment that impels me; now it is the mighty conviction that no sacrifice is too great for the greatest earthly good, for the freedom of one's nation. Perhaps your fatherly heart is tempted to say: Theodor is intended for greater goals, he could accomplish weightier and more meaningful things in another sphere, he still owes humanity a great talent. But Father, my opinion is this: no one is too good for a sacrificial death in the cause of freedom and the honor of his nation, but many are too base for it![44]

His father replied with a brief note to say "You have not been mistaken in me. We are of one mind," followed by a longer letter, now lost, telling of his pride and love.

Figure 5.   Engraving after an oil painting of Adolph von Lützow (1782–1834)
by W. Witting

Theodor's Viennese friends attempted to dissuade him from his resolution, Prince
Lobkowitz finally releasing him from his contract with the promise that the position
would be held open for him. Louis Spohr writes in his autobiography that he and
Theodor were about to collaborate on an opera based on the Rübezahl theme when
he heard of Theodor's decision to volunteer for the Prussian war against France,
adding (incorrectly) that Antonie Adamberger's refusal to reciprocate Theodor's love
for her was an element in the young poet's decision to go to war.[45] Certainly
Theodor was much loved in Vienna, according to the Viennese dramatist, patriot
and Schubert song poet Ignaz Franz Castelli, who wrote in his memoirs that

there are few youths to whom one is drawn at first sight, at the first words they speak, and with whom one feels such empathy as Theodor Körner … he had such a fiery soul, burning brightly for justice and truth, and yet such deep sensitivity that any sufferer found in him a sympathizer and, wherever it was possible, a helper. He was serious with those who were serious and merry with those were merry – in short, he was loved by all the world, and he loved the entire world.[46]

Despite his friends' pleading, however, Theodor left Vienna forever on 15 March 1813 for the Golden Scepter tavern in Breslau, where Lützow (Fig. 5) had set up a bureau to form his volunteer corps, and was signed into the ranks of the volunteers by Lützow's wife Elise Davidia Margarethe, Gräfin von Ahlefeldt-Lauwig, as charismatic a figure as her husband.

Once enlisted, Theodor kept both a diary-letter for Henriette von Pereira and a *Taschenbuch* containing poems and brief entries of troop movements and locations. Humorous descriptions of a court theater poet doing military exercises, tales of his fellow volunteers singing "a quantity of songs that have flowed from my pen,"[47] and a fervent account of the swearing-in ceremonies at the church in Rogau on 27 March (Fig. 6), all appear in his letters. To his parents and sister, he wrote, "I cannot tell you how pleasant are the circumstances in which I live, where the most cultured and learned folk in all of Germany are arrayed next to me. One could carry out a great publishing project with the best writers, since there are so many among 'the black ones' [the uniform of the Lützowers was black with gold trim]."[48]

Figure 6. *Einsegnung des Lützowschen Freikorps in der Kirche zu Rogau*, 27. März 1813 (The swearing-in of the Lützower Volunteers in the church at Rogau, 27 March 1813), painted by F. Martersteig. Körner is the kneeling figure in the left foreground, with Fritz Friesen standing next to him

Figure 7.   Engraving of Theodor Körner in Lützower uniform from the portrait
in pastels by Emma Körner (April 1813)

He indeed had distinguished company in the corps, including Ludwig Jahn, Karl
Immermann, Joseph von Eichendorff, and Friedrich Förster. Förster, who had been
a friend of the Körner family before the fresh outbreak of Napoleonic strife, later
wrote an account of Theodor at the Lützower encampment as part of his [Förster's]
three-volume history of the War of Liberation:

[After describing the evening activities] Some are already toasting good comradeship; one of
the men tries on a recruit's tschako, one goes deer-hunting, a third slings on his rifle. But not
all misgivings are set aside – then one hears from the first watch-fire, "Welcome!" and the
joyful cry, "Körner has a new song for us." "Here it is!", cries Körner, the wildest and handsomest
of the black-clad soldiers, with his pearl-bedecked letter-case, a gift from his fiancée, held up
high in his hands. "I'll sing it to a well-known melody and you chime in with the chorus and
sing the refrain loudly with me. The song is called "Men and boys" ("Männer und Buben").[49]

Theodor also wrote a prose "Aufruf" (Call-up) printed on 12 April in the *Leipziger Zeitung* and distributed throughout Saxony. It has every ingredient of the genre, from invocations of German justice in German lands to calls for an end to shame and subjugation.

Brothers! Countrymen! Through the threefold bond of blood, of language, of the oppression that enslaves us, we come to you. Open your hearts to us, as you have opened your doors. The long night of shame has made us well acquainted; the dawn of a better time shall find us in league together. We are countrymen and brothers; in the firm faith of your return to the good, to the holy matter of God and the Fatherland, many among us boast of having been born in your company and raised according to your custom. As is now becoming to brothers, we want to wander through your valleys. To whom would their native earth, this one great paternal house of all German hearts, not be holy? Who cares more about the security, the prosperity of a land for whose freedom we have gladly sworn to sacrifice blood and life? – We want to fight for the freedom of our country and, as God wills, triumph or die. – Shall the foreign tyrants mock our sacred commandments, the honorable traditions of our ancestors?[50]

In April, the Lützower company marched to Dresden, where Theodor saw his family on the 6th. It was on that occasion that Emma drew a portrait in pastel of her brother (Fig. 7), and Theodor wrote "Dresden. 1813," attempting to explain his love of country more fully to Toni. Evidently, he felt guilty about earlier excoriations of his native land (for Saxony's alliance with Napoleon) and wished to make reparations.

Hab' ich die Heimath geschmäht, vergieb's inneren Grimme,	If I have inveighed against my home-land, may my inner wrath redeem it –
Das fatale Gesicht regte die Galle mir auf. –	the deadly face incited my rancor.
Ach! das Herz war so voll, so glühend in Lieb' und Begeist'rung,	Oh, my heart was so full, so glowing with love and enthusiasm,
Wie ein gefrorner Blitz schlug die Erbärmlichkeit drein.	the misery was driven inwards like a frozen lightning bolt.
Sieh, da trieb mich die heimliche Wuth zur beißenden Rede,	See, my secret rage drove me to biting speeches,
Und der giftige Groll warf mir die Galle hinein.	and poisonous complaints thrust the bitterness inward.
Nein, Geliebte, so mein' ich's nicht mit dem heimischen Lande,	No, beloved, I did not really mean it thus about my homeland,
Und ich ehre mein Volk …[51]	and I honor my people …

It is heart-breaking to read the letters in which Christian Gottfried presses money worriedly on his son, lest Theodor be wounded and need extra care. "Do not laugh at us for our concern!" he writes, and later readers are indeed not moved to laugh.[52] In mid-April, Theodor and his company were in Leipzig, and the irrepressibly ebullient Theodor wrote to Henriette von Pereira, "It was a wonderful sensation for me to parade in military splendor through the place I had to flee a year-and-a-half ago."[53] During his stay, he was preoccupied with arrangements to publish his war poems, which he hoped would have the same effect as the Spartan poet Tyrtaeus' war-songs to the Lacedaemonians in the last half of the seventh century BC ("For it is a fair thing for a good man to fall and die fighting in the vanguard for his native land," Tyrtaeus wrote in fragment ten of his extant verse[54]), hence Theodor's later designation as "the German Tyrtaeus." His friend Wilhelm Kunze undertook to oversee the publication, and Theodor wrote the "Zueignung an das deutsche Volk" (Dedication to the German people) and "Lützows wilde Jagd" (Lützow's wild hunt) on 24 April before leaving the city the next day.

The early victories belonged almost entirely to the French; Theodor's "Letzter Trost" (Last comfort) was written after hearing of the defeat at Groß-Görschen on 2 May. On 15 May, three days after another defeat at Dannenberg, a discouraged Körner wrote to Henriette von Pereira, saying,

> What should I write to you? – my despondence? What should I confide in you? – my fury? It gnaws at me horribly! ... Before the cannons began to thunder on the 12th, I slept a half-hour at a watch-fire. There I had a dream, the most vivid and horrendous in my entire life, in which I was eternally silenced. You and Marianne [Saaling, a longtime friend] were important in the action, particularly Marianne, whom I saw with long, black ringlets and in old-fashioned mourning garments ... God be with us, or Death.[55]

He was to have other premonitions of death. In mid-June, as Lützow was leading his troops through enemy territory to the Prussian boundary, Theodor's horse sank momentarily into a burial pit at Groß-Görschen, and Theodor shuddered, convinced it was an ill-omen. Lützow, he wrote, laughed at him for his "poet's impressionability" and told him to banish poetry from real-life ("die Poesie aus dem Leben zu verjagen").

Theodor's premonitions, however, were accurate: he would shortly be wounded and then killed in battle. On 17 June, a force consisting of the cavalry and about one hundred newly inducted Lützower volunteers reached the town of Kitzen and there encountered an enemy column of French and French-allied Württemberger troops under the command of General Friedrich Lebrecht von Normann. The Lützowers obtained a promise from a lieutenant named von Kechler to allow them free passage to Leipzig in accord with the Armistice of Pleischwitz, a seven-week armistice that began on 2 June 1813 after the battle of Bautzen. But Napoleon himself had instructed the French commander, General Fournier, to treat Lützow and Körner not as soldiers but as brigands marked for murder; according to Normann's reports, Fournier wept in fury at the thought that Lützow might escape his vengeance. When Lützow and Körner rode out to tell Fournier that he must respect the armistice, the infuriated general replied, "L'armistice pour tout le monde, excepté pour vous!" (Cease-fire for everyone but you!).[56]

The Lützowers were hacked to pieces. Friedrich Förster recounts that it was due to the heroic actions of one Beczwarzowski that Lützow, although wounded, was able to get away – was this Gustav Beczwarzowski, the nephew of the Bohemian composer Anton Felix Beczwarzowski who would set Körner's *Leier und Schwert* to music the next year? Körner too was wounded, struck across the forehead and cheek by a saber-blow; only his horse springing away saved his life. He reached the woods near the village of Groß-Zsocher and there, so goes the legend, wrote the sonnet "Abschied vom Leben" (Farewell to life), first published in the *Berlinischen Nachrichten* for Sunday, 21 August 1813. Two children found him unconscious by a stream and fetched their father, a gardener who took the wounded poet to his home until Theodor was well enough to make his escape in disguise to Karlsbad.[57] Concerned about his family's fears, he wrote to his father under the pseudonym "Lorenz Juranitsch" (one of Zriny's most ardent compatriots) on 18 June to reassure them that he was among friends, that he was "sound and as yet my own master." He stayed in Karlsbad until 15 July and then left in order to return to Prussia, although his wound broke open again in Reichenbach, where he stayed from 19 to 31 July. It was in Reichenbach on 27 July that Austria and Prussia struck an alliance against Napoleon, followed by the Emperor Franz's declaration of war on 11 August and the end of the cease-fire.

The sands were swiftly running out of the hourglass. Only three days later, on 14 August, a grief-stricken Toni wrote to Theodor to tell him that Krüger, the actor who had brought them together, was dead and that everyone was still worried about his [Theodor's] wound. This was the last letter he would receive from her. On 18 August, Theodor told Henriette that in two days "we await the death-wedding" in which the army would liberate Hamburg. During the cease-fire, Lützow had gathered his scattered forces and organized a new cavalry division, garnered into the third Prussian army corps under the direction of General Friedrich Wilhelm Freiherr von Bülow. A variegated mixture of troops – a Russian-German division, a British-German division, Mecklenburgers, Hanoverians, and more, with an avant-garde of Cossacks, volunteer Jägers, and the Lützowers – were then engaged in a diversionary "Kleinkrieg" (small war) along the Elbe designed to harass the French, cut their communication lines, capture their munitions and supply transports, and stop their couriers from reaching their destinations. It was in an outbreak of the "small war" that Körner met his end.

Theodor rejoined the troop on 9 August. The day after, the Lützowers were ordered to send a division to Gadebusch in Schwerin. On 24 August, Lützow heard that the French had been seen on the Gadebusch post-road and devised a plan to hide a group of soldiers, with Theodor commanding, in the pine forest near the village of Rosenberg (later, the history painter Richard Knötel would fashion a woodcut depicting Körner waiting for the French to arrive, from a round slice taken from the evergreen tree by which Körner fell). In the painting *Theodor Körner, Friesen und Hartmann auf Vorposten* (Körner, Friesen and Hartmann on guard duty) of 1815 by Theodor's fellow Lützower Georg Friedrich Kersting (who enlisted in the Volunteers due to Körner's influence), Kersting converts the trees where Körner (seated at the left), Karl Friedrich Friesen (standing at the right), and Hartmann (lying in front of Körner) keep watch into more symbolically resonant oak trees (Fig. 8).[58] The Lützowers were to ambush two enemy infantry companies and thirty-eight wagons with munitions and supplies on 26 August 1813, but their plan went awry. According to the testimony of a farmer named Dühring who observed the battle from the top of a nearby hill, Theodor saw the elderly cavalry master Fischer in his company wounded by a French marksman who had pretended to surrender and then reached for his gun. Theodor, angered by the spectacle, called out, "Züchtigt die Halunken!

Figure 8. Georg Friedrich Kersting, *Theodor Körner, Friesen und Hartmann auf Vorposten, 1815*

Wer ein braver Kamerad ist, folgt mir!" (Thrash the scoundrels! Whoever is a brave comrade, follow me!) and sprang from the woods, followed by his comrades Friesen and Hugo Helfritz. He was struck immediately by a bullet; depending upon whose eyewitness report one reads, he whispered "Da habe ich eins; es schadet aber nichts" or "Da hab ich auch eins weg!" or "Mich haben sie gut getroffen" (I've got one ... it's not doing any harm ... I've got one too. They've really got me) before he listed to the right and fell dead from his horse,[59] but those accounts were possibly

Figure 9. Otto Donner von Richter, *Die Lützower an der Leiche Theodor Körners in Wöbbelin, 27 August 1813* (The Lützowers by the body of Theodor Körner at Wöbbelin) in the Körner-Museum, Dresden (Fischer and Fritz Friesen are the two figures at the far left)

concocted to comfort Körner's grieving parents – still another eyewitness stated that Theodor lived for two hours after being shot. According to Adolph Bäuerle's *Allgemeine Theater-Zeitung* for 14 December 1842, Körner may well have been killed, not by a Frenchman but by a German musketeer named Franz (no last name given), a farmer still living when the article appeared. He had been in the transport caravan along with a Lutheran schoolmaster named Schönborn, who later told the story to a Lützower first lieutenant named Storck.[60] It was a commonplace tragic irony of the War of Liberation that German shot German from opposite sides of the Napoleonic divide.

Whether French or German, his aim was true, and the dead hero was subsequently buried by his comrades under a great oak tree at Wöbbelin, south-east of Gadebusch. Friedrich Förster, in a letter to Theodor's family on 28 August 1813, describes how the body was brought to its burial-place in a wagon, how his comrades chose two giant oak trees as the grave-site and wove a garland of oak-leaves to place on their dead friend's brow, and how they found the "Schwertlied" (Sword song), written only the day before, in his letter-pouch. They had already chosen the site and dug the grave when General Graf Thedel von Wallmoden sent word that he had selected a smaller, inconspicuous plot, less likely to attract the nearby enemy's notice. The dismayed Förster and two other friends of Körner's went to the General to plead in person for the symbolically-resonant burial ground, and Wallmoden sympathetically acceded to their request. In his letter to the Körners, Förster recounts his last conversation with Theodor on the night before the poet's death, when Theodor reassured Förster, overcome by premonitions of his friend's death, by saying, "Since Kitzen, when I believed it was truly all over for me, I have been bullet-proof, so no more of that [Förster was sobbing] – be of good cheer and don't pay any attention to such fearful visions. Sleep well!"[61] Wallmoden had forbidden a parting salvo at the burial because of the enemy's proximity, so his comrades sang, in hushed farewell, the "Gebet während der Schlacht" and "Lützows wilde Jagd."[62] A painting by Otto Donner von Richter of *Die Lützower an der Leiche Theodor Körners in Wöbbelin, 27 August 1813* (The Lützowers by the body of Theodor Körner at Wöbbelin, Fig. 9), with its weeping maiden, passionate farewells, and fellow soldiers overcome by grief, gives us a glimpse of the adulation Körner inspired. He was not yet twenty-two years old, and he never knew of the "Völkerschlacht," the great Battle of the Nations at Leipzig that began on 16 October 1813 and raged for three days.[63] It was effectively the death-knell of Napoleon's imperium, although the aftermath continued through the final chapter at Waterloo. But Theodor saw none of it, not the bloody victory at Leipzig, not the 100 Days' Reign, not Elba – nothing.

The first news of Theodor's death appeared in the Berlin newspapers for 3 September and was immediately contradicted by a report that he had only been wounded. Hardly had his father found cause for hope than he heard of a full account of his son's death and burial in the *Berliner Zeitung* for 13 September and wrote a pitiful letter to Kunze in Leipzig, begging for copies of the newspapers, so that he could ascertain which was the latest. Not until 8 November did the family receive an official military report of Theodor's death. "I shall revere him as my guardian angel and will spend the rest of my life working to the best of my abilities for the great cause for which he sacrificed himself, in order that I might be worthy of him," his heartbroken father wrote to Kunze.[64] The next day, 9 November 1813, he published an announcement of Theodor's death in the *Leipziger Zeitung*.[65] Shortly after, a friend of Christian Gottfried's, a Dresden architect named Gottlob Friedrich Thormeyer, designed a grave-monument at Wöbbelin, the completed sculpture unveiled on 29 September 1814. On the front was – what else? – a lyre and sword surrounded by a garland of oak leaves and the inscription: "Hier wurde / Karl Theodor Körner / von seinen Waffenbrüdern / mit Achtung and Liebe / zur Erde bestattet" (Here Theodor Körner was buried by his comrades-in-arms with reverence and love). On the back was another inscription and a condensed biography, with quotations from his poems on the sides of this four-sided altar.[66]

Christian Gottfried devoted his remaining years to his son's cause, although at a heavy cost – later images depict a haunted, bereft-looking man. Two days after he sent the notice of his son's death to the *Leipziger Zeitung*, Dresden capitulated, and the Körners returned to their home. A friend of the family wrote to another friend to say, "Körner has aged by twenty years but he doesn't grieve aloud. He only says to me, when we are alone, with a gentle face and tone of voice: 'It was a beautiful vision that now is gone' [Es war eine schöne Erscheinung, die nun dahin ist]."[67] The return of the victorious armies only worsened their sorrow, as Emma wrote to Henriette von Pereira, saying, "We live without hope and joy from one day to the next, and only the certainty that the freedom of our German Fatherland has been secured in the great war, which has cost us so much, holds us upright. The present times are little guaranteed to soften our sorrow – the return of so many fortunate ones to their homes, where their families can receive them with the greatest rejoicing, tears open our wounds anew, for no one comes home to us."[68] She never recovered. One wonders about the relationship between brother and sister: Theodor was clearly the "Lieblingskind," the heart of the family, and the unmarried Emma, twenty-six years old when her brother died, was grief-stricken to a degree that provokes both pity and the desire to know more. Before she herself died on 15 March 1814 of "nerve fever," the family made a pilgrimage to Wöbbelin which she described in letters to Henriette (not, one notices, to Toni).[69] At her wish, she was buried alongside her brother. As each of Theodor's relatives died, they too were buried at Wöbbelin: the seventy-five-year-old Christian Gottfried on 13 May 1831, the seventy-two-year-old Dora Stock on 26 May 1832; and Theodor's eighty-one-year-old mother on 20 August 1843.

One also wonders about Toni in the aftermath of Theodor's death, all the more so because there is evidence of hard feelings between the Körners and Theodor's fiancée. We know little about the relationship between Toni and Theodor: Minna burned Toni's letters to Theodor, and it seems likely that Toni did likewise with Theodor's letters to her. She was certainly reticent on the subject in later life. Her son Alfred von Arneth wrote that his mother said "nothing of their [Toni's and Theodor's] theatrical collaboration, nothing of the sorrowful parting between them, nothing of the manner in which she heard the shattering news of his death, nothing of how she lived through the period afterwards," despite discoursing often and in a lively manner on other aspects of her youth.[70] In her fragmentary memoirs, she wrote only a single eloquent sentence about her fiancé's death: "When Theodor was struck and killed, he had my picture, painted on leather, on his breast; a ring I had given him with a little heart on his finger; and my letter in his letter-pouch," before describing, at much greater length, the Viennese public's sympathy and applause for her when she returned to the theater. This, she stated somewhat mysteriously, was like a "forged copper shield" against the subsequent "moral griefs [moralischen Leiden]."[71] What she meant is uncertain, but she could have been referring either to the unsubstantiated rumor that Theodor's love for her had either grown cold or flickered out altogether in his last months in Vienna, a rumor fed by Theodor's close association with Henriette von Pereira, or to the Körners' hostility. In 1837, Minna wrote to a friend, describing Toni as "very beautiful, very sweet" but adding that Toni had married again only half-a-year after Theodor's death and that she [Minna] felt this was too soon and had hardened her heart against Toni in consequence. Her chronology was wrong, blurred by time and perhaps also by ill-will. Toni met Joseph von Arneth at Caroline Pichler's salon in early 1817 and married him on 19 June, four years after Theodor's death and well within the bounds of propriety. When Minna heard that Toni's eldest son was named Theodor, she relented somewhat, but the sense of suppressed resentment on both sides is very strong.[72]

If anonymity was the lot of most soldiers, it was not Theodor's: the German-speaking world, especially the literati, honored him upon his death. Among those who wrote poems in his honor were Friedrich von Stägemann, at whose house in Berlin *Die schöne Müllerin* was born; Friedrich Rückert (1788–1866), whose *Zeit-gedichte* (Poems of the age) of 1814–15 include the poem "Körners Geist" (Körner's spirit); Caroline Pichler, who wrote a long poem "To Theodor Körner's Mother"; Theodor's fellow Lützower Friedrich Förster; and, more than twenty years later, King Ludwig II of Bavaria. One might expect someone with Ludwig II's psychological make-up to be impressed with the tale of the glamorous and martyred military poet, and he was: "The millenia vanish, fade away, / Kingdoms fall, new kingdoms arise; / Körner! may the name resound gloriously." In Stägemann's sonnet "Dem Angedenken Theodor Körner's," Körner becomes the new Friedrich Barbarossa, sleeping peacefully until "new barbarians" call him forth to defend Germany once again with sword and lyre,[73] while Rückert's Körner arises from the new grave, girds on a sword, takes a lyre from the nearby chestnut tree, and sings his approval of his tomb monument and his place of burial.

Man hat in Fürsten Grüften	They wanted to bury me
Bestatten mich gewollt;	in a princely grave;
Hier in den frischen Düften	here in the fresh-scented air,
Ihr ruhn mich lassen sollt.	you should leave me to rest.
Hier sei noch oft mit Kräuseln	Here may the oak leaves
Der Eiche Laub bewegt,	often flutter about and stir
Wenn in des Windes Säuseln	when in the wind's rustling,
Mein Geist die Saiten schlägt.[74]	my ghost strikes the strings.

(stanzas 14–15 of 15)

On 26 August 1863, fifty years after Theodor's death, there was a national Körner festival in Wöbbelin in which some 3,000 people took part, including Friedrich Förster, who had helped to dig the grave so many years before. Toni, who was still alive; the children of Hugo Helfritz, in whose arms Körner died; Rückert; Marianne Saling, Theodor's oldest surviving childhood friend, and others sent wreaths to be laid on the grave, and Franz Abt, among others, composed music for the memorial observances. This celebration was duplicated on a smaller scale elsewhere in Germany and even in the United States, as newspaper accounts of a Körner-commemoration in Baltimore attest.[75] The festivals inspired another outburst of fiction based on the Körner legend, including Julius Papst's one-act play *An Körner's Grabe* (At Körner's grave), Georg Zimmermann's three-act historical drama *Theodor Körner*, and Heribert Rau's "Fatherlandish novel" *Theodor Körner*,[76] as well as still more music to add to the long list of Körner settings. The repertoire of Körner-lieder and partsongs is music's memorial to the war that finally sent Napoleon "reeling backwards across the Rhine,"[77] a war in which Theodor played a role as standard-bearer, minstrel, and, ultimately, symbol.

"I HEAR DARK CHORDS RESOUNDING": KÖRNER AND MUSIC

The musical adulation of the dead young hero began immediately with the oratorio *Das befreite Deutschland* (Germany liberated), to a text by one of his friends, Caroline Pichler, and music by another, Louis Spohr. *Das befreite Deutschland* includes an accompanied recitative and aria in Part II in which "The Maiden" laments the death of her beloved in battle; that the maiden is Toni Adamberger and the dead hero was Theodor is evident in the acrostic which spells Körner in the second stanza of the aria:

Wie gern wollt' ich zu dieser Höh' mich schwingen,	How gladly I would soar to these heights,
Wie gern mit solchem Heldenblick die Welt,	how gladly I would survey myself, the world,
Mich, und was ich verloren, schauen!	and what I have lost with such a heroic gaze!
Umsonst! Das Herz, in seinen innern Tiefen	In vain! My heart, torn to its very depths,
Zerrissen, blutet, zittert, und vermag	bleeds, trembles, and can feel
Nichts als den schrecklichen Verlust zu fühlen!	nothing other than terrible loss!
Er fiel als Held – ich soll nicht um ihn klagen –	He fell as a hero – I should not mourn for
Ach, und ich kann kaum meinen Schmerz ertragen!	him – Ah, but I can hardly bear my sorrow!

Arie.	Aria.
Er war so gut, er war so bieder,	He was so good, so honorable,
So fleckenlos dieß starke Herz,	this strong heart so spotless,
Und kehrt so früh zum Himmel wieder,	and he has returned to heaven so early
Und läßt mich hier in meinem Schmerz!	and left me here with my grief!
Die Welt neu zu Glück und Lust geboren,	The world is new-born to happiness and joy,
Ich fühle nichts – als daß ich ihn verloren!	I feel nothing, but that I have lost him!

Keine Freude blüht mir mehr,	No joy blooms for me any longer,
Öd ist Alles um mich her,	everything about me is desolate,
Reizlos was ich geliebt habe;	what I have loved is deprived of all allure,
Nirgends strahlet mir sein Blick	nowhere does his gaze shine upon me.
Eines kenn' ich nur als Glück,	In only one thing can I know happiness:
Ruhe, wo Er schläft, im kühlen Grabe.[78]	To rest where he sleeps, in the cool grave.

Johann Tost had proposed this giant cantata to celebrate the emperor's return to Vienna, and Spohr obligingly composed the music between January and mid-March 1814. However, for want of a suitable hall, it was not performed until the Frankenhausen festival of 18 October 1815 in Thuringia, after victory at Waterloo. A premiere in Vienna had to wait until 25 March 1819, when it was received with great enthusiasm, prompting two further performances in the ballroom of the Gesellschaft der Musikfreunde on 28 and 30 November 1819.[79]

Looking at the Maiden's recitative and aria, one can understand both the critical approval in its own time and the subsequent disappearance of this occasional work. The accompanied recitative begins with a beautifully chromatic, appoggiatura-laden introduction for the woodwinds and horns only, followed by the recitative, the cry "Umsonst!" (In vain!) and the broken, rising exclamations "zerrissen, blutet, zitternd" particularly poignant details. The aria, "Er war so gut," begins with a *Larghetto con moto* section ostensibly in G major, but Spohr modulates almost immediately to the flatted mediant key of B-flat major at the words "[und läßt mich] hier / und kehrt so früh zum Himmel wieder, und läßt mich hier in meinem Schmerz" in mm. 8–13 – the music also "kehrt so früh" at the word "hier" (here) to a darker (earthly?) realm. The tonal symbolism is quite moving in the abstract, but the effect is disconcerting because the deflection occurs before G major has even been securely

Example 3.   Louis Spohr, the aria "Er war so gut, er war so bieder" from the oratorio *Das befreite Deutschland* to a text by Caroline Pichler, mm. 1–13.

established (ex. 3). The acrostichon, which constitutes the middle section of this da
capo aria (mm. 31–75), is set as an Allegro moderato in E minor but with occasional
purple patches of intense chromaticism. Spohr, understanding that the maiden's desire
"to rest where he sleeps, in the cool grave" was far from peaceful, set the word
"Ruhe" as a longing *pianissimo* whisper, followed by a "walking bass" pattern in the
low strings, throbbing repeated pitches in the upper strings, chromatic wisps in the
woodwinds, and a twice-stated descent to the grave in the vocal line, the second
time with the Phrygian lowered second degree at the words "im küh*len* Grabe" –

Example 3.   *cont.*

chill indeed. But if details of this aria, in which a particular tragedy is apotheosized as a universal one, are quite beautiful, the larger design, the canvas on which these details are assembled, is not so successful. It would be left to the miniaturists, the song composers, to hymn Körner more effectively; the modestly lovely setting of "Lied aus HEDWIG" from the *Zwölf Lieder und Romanzen*, op. 76, by Conradin Kreutzer (1780–1849), the German-born Kapellmeister of the Vienna Kärntnertor-Theater from 1822 to 1827 and a composer Schubert admired, is a better memorial and more deserving of revival (ex. 4). The poem, which asserts the Romantic doctrine of

Example 3. *cont.*

music's primacy over words, constitutes the entirety of act 3, scene 2 of Körner's tragedy *Hedwig* and was intended for musical setting; Körner directs that Hedwig's gaze should fall upon either a keyboard instrument or a harp, that she should rush wildly over to it, and accompany her own singing.

Worte such' ich mir vergebens	In my heart's fullness of longing,
In des Herzens vollem Drang.	I search in vain for words.
Jede Seligkeit des Lebens	Every rapture in life
Hat nicht Worte, nur Gesang.	has, not words, only song. (stanza 1)

Example 3.   *cont.*

Example 4. Conradin Kreutzer, "Lied aus HEDWIG" from *Zwölf Lieder und Romanzen*, op. 76, Heft 2 (Leipzig, Fr. Kistner), mm. 1–20.

Example 4. *cont.*

Example 4. *cont.*

Wor — te nur Ge — sang.

The repertoire of Körner songs runs the gamut from virtuosic lieder requiring the services of a skilled pianist and singer to the simplest of parlor ditties for the patriotically-minded but musically limited.[80] The lieder and part-song collections begin with Friedrich Heinrich Himmel's (1765–1814) *Kriegslieder der Teutschen* (War-songs of the Germans), settings of patriotic poetry by the likes of Heinrich von Collin, Karl Friedrich Müchler, Elisa von der Recke, her lover Christoph August Tiedge, and Körner himself, the collection published in Breslau by Joseph Max in December 1813. Himmel was the target of a stinging critique by Beethoven, who declared him less skilled at the piano than Prince Louis Ferdinand of Prussia and asked him, at the conclusion of one of Himmel's fantasias, when the piece would begin, since he took what had just transpired to be merely a prelude.[81] Himmel was closely associated with Körner's own circle, including Theodor's godmother Dorothea, Herzogin von Kurland und Sagan, to whom Himmel's settings from Tiedge's *Urania* are dedicated, and the young man's death was more than a statistic to him. The collection of twelve strophic songs, including one choral work ("Siegeslied nach der Schlacht vom 2ten Mai 1813" to a text by Heinrich von Collin) and "Des Vaterlandes Auferstehungsfest. Trinklied" for tenor and chorus, was sold by subscription as a memorial to Körner: "Elevating through melody and feeling, it [the song anthology] has particular worth as a remembrance of Körner, the heroic youth who gave so much for German art, yet bade fair to do so much more, and who breathed forth his blossoming life in a swan-song prayer as he fell in battle for blazing freedom." The collection too is "aufflammend" (blazing), the indication "Feurig" or "Mit Feuer" (fiery) appearing at the start of well over half of these simple songs.

The best songs in the little collection are settings of Körner's *Leier und Schwert* poems "Gebet während der Schlacht," "Lützows wilde Jagd," and the "Reiterlied" (Cavalry song), the three poems most popular with composers. In the latter, Körner delineates in unmistakable terms the homoeroticism of blood-lust and war, in which a true patriot "marries" both the Fatherland and Death – a violent *Liebestod*.

Gar süß muß solch ein Schlummer sein	Such a slumber must be truly sweet
In solcher Liebesnacht;	in such a night of love;
In kühler Erde schlaf' ich ein,	in the cool earth, I will fall asleep,
Von meiner Braut bewacht;	watched over by my bride;

Und wenn der Eiche grünes Holz
Die neuen Blätter schwellt,
So weckt sie mich mit freud'gem Stolz
Zur ew'gen Freiheitswelt.[82]

and when new leaves swell
from the oak tree's green wood,
then she'll awaken me, with joyful pride,
to an eternal world of freedom.

The most famous poem from the collection, however, was "Lützows wilde Jagd," with its potent invocation of the legendary "Wild Hunt of the Dead." Here, the Lützowers become "it," no longer individual soldiers but a mass rendered superhuman and unconquerable, even by death. As a sequence of rhetorical questions unfolds, each query a variation of "What is it?" and each answered by the refrain "It is/was Lützow's wild, daring hunt," a battle runs its course, from the approach of the black-clad corps to the combat itself and to death, with victory and immortality promised at the close. The final stanza, one notices, begins with an extension of the answer at the close of the preceding stanza, thus welding the two verses together for a weightier conclusion to the poem: "It was Lützow's wild, daring hunt ... the Wild Hunt and the German hunt for the executioner's blood and for tyrants." The archetypal galloping rhythms of patriotic poetry, with their rattling, rapid-fire mixture of iambs and anapaests designed to incite frenzy and stir the blood, were perhaps never employed more forcefully than here.

Was glänzt dort vom Walde im Sonnen-
    schein?
Hör's näher und näher brausen.
Es zieht sich herunter in düsteren Reihn,
Und gellende Hörner schallen darein
Und erfüllen die Seele mit Grausen.
Und wenn ihr die schwarzen Gesellen fragt:
Das ist Lützows wilde, verwegene Jagd.

What gleams there in the sunshine, from the
    forest?
Listen to it raging nearer and nearer.
It descends in dark rows
and the piercing horns resound therein
and fill the soul with terror.
And when you ask the black company:
It is Lützow's wild, daring hunt.

Was zieht dort rasch durch den finstern Wald,
Und streift von Bergen zu Bergen?
Es legt sich in nächtlichen Hinterhalt,
Das Hurrah jauchzt, und die Büchse knallt,
Es fallen die fränkischen Schergen.
Und wenn ihr die schwarzen Jäger fragt,
Das ist Lützow's wilde, verwegene Jagd.

What sweeps boldly through the dark forest
and roams from peak to peak?
It lies down in nocturnal concealment,
The "Hurrah!" resounds, and the muskets
explode. The French thugs fall,
and if you ask the black huntsmen,
It is Lützow's wild, daring hunt.

Wo die Reben dort glühn, dort braust der
    Rhein,
Der Wütrich geborgen sich meinte,
Da naht es schnell mit Gewitterschein,
Und wirft sich mit rüstgen Armen hinein
Und springt ans Ufer der Feinde
Und wenn ihr die schwarzen Schwimmer fragt,
Das ist Lützows wilde verwegene Jagd.

Where the grapes glow, there the Rhine
    rushes along,
the ruthless tyrant believed himself hidden.
It nears quickly, like thunder,
and with vigorous arms, throws itself in
and leaps upon the enemy's bank.
And when you ask the black swimmers,
It is Lützow's wild, daring hunt.

Was braust dort im Tale die laute Schlacht,
Was schlagen die Schwerter zusammen?

What wages noisy battle there in the valley,
What do the swords strike together?

Wildherzige Reiter schlagen die Schlacht,	Wild-hearted riders wage the battle.
Der Funke der Freiheit ist glühend erwacht,	The spark of freedom is awakened and
Und lodert in blutigen Flammen.	glowing, and flares up in bloody flames.
Und wenn ihr die schwarzen Reiter fragt,	And when you ask the black riders,
Das ist Lützows wilde verwegene Jagd.	It is Lützow's wild, daring hunt.
Wer scheidet dort röchelnd vom Sonnen-	Who departs from the sunlight there, the
licht,	death-rattle in his throat,
Unter winselnde Feinde gebettet?	lying among the whimpering enemy?
Es zuckt der Tod auf dem Angesicht,	Death convulses their faces,
Doch die wackern Herzen erzittern nicht;	but valiant hearts do not tremble:
Das Vaterland ist ja gerettet!	The Fatherland is truly saved!
Und wenn ihr die schwarzen Gefallenen fragt,	And when you ask the black fallen ones,
Das war Lützows wilde verwegene Jagd.	It was Lützow's wild, daring hunt.
Die wilde Jagd und die deutsche Jagd	The Wild Hunt and the German hunt
Auf Henkers Blut und Tyrannen.	for the executioner's blood and for tyrants.
D'rum, die ihr uns liebt, nicht geweint und	Therefore, you who love us, unwept and
geklagt,	unmourned:
Das Land ist ja frei und der Morgen tagt,	The land is freed, and the new day dawns,
Wenn wir's auch nur sterbend gewannen.	even if we only won it dying.
Und von Enkeln zu Enkeln sei's nach-	And from generation to generation, the
gesagt,	tale will be told:
Das war Lützows wilde verwegene Jagd.[83]	That was Lützow's wild, daring hunt.

Composers could seldom resist the invitation to devise approaching thunder and shrilling horns in the piano accompaniment, and Himmel, in his own modest way, set the tone for what would follow from more extravagant composers. The "brausend" approach of the horde becomes unharmonized rushing-about on sixteenth-note scalar figures, a miniature distillation of battleground noise. At the first mention of "shrilling horns," fanfares blare in the treble, with a special triplet flourish for the verb "schallen," while the trill-accented rising chromatic line in mm. 22–27 ("Und wenn ihr die schwarzen Gesellen fragt"), with its stark unison texture, evokes the vaunted strength of the Volunteers (ex. 5). Similarly, the "Lied der schwarzen Jäger" from the *Sechs deutsche Lieder von Theodor Körner und La Motte Fouqué* by Friedrich Wilhelm Grund (1791–1874), who founded the Hamburger Singakademie in 1819 and composed operas and oratorios,[84] duplicates the formula of warlike noise in the piano, with its buzzing, thrumming "drum-roll" trills and sudden scalar flights, nor is the vocal line a matter for rank amateurs, with its frequent high G's and A's (ex. 6). (His setting of "Lützows wilde Jagd," however, is only marginally "wild," the *Maestoso* lied chock-a-block with root-position chords; one longs for the occasional inversion and something a trifle less foursquare in the accompaniment.) If these songs are hardly vehicles worthy of Thalberg or other virtuosi, if they employ clichés which Carl Maria von Weber and others would shortly thereafter use in more complex and interesting ways, they are nonetheless exemplary of rousing patriotic lieder domesticated for bourgeois parlors at a time of war and demanding at least a modicum of technical expertise.

Theodor Körner

Example 5. Friedrich Heinrich Himmel, "Lützow's wilde Jagd" from the *Kriegslieder der Teutschen* (Breslau: Joseph Max, 1813), mm. 1–22.

Example 6.   Friedrich Wilhelm Grund, "Lied der schwarzen Jäger" from the *Sechs deutsche Lieder von Theodor Körner und La Motte* [sic] *Fouqué* (Leipzig, C. F. Peters), mm. 1–18.

Example 6. *cont.*

Schubert too set "Lützows wilde Jagd" on 26 May 1815 for two unaccompanied voices or two horns, D. 205, the simple piece (even simpler than Himmel's) of interest principally because it is a precursor of "Der Jäger" from *Die schöne Müllerin*. For those in Schubert's and Körner's generation, the word "Jäger" also designated the elite fusiliers' corps that constituted a division within all armies in the German-speaking realms (Schulze joined a *Jägerkorps*), and the word-association that links military history with the folk figure of the hunter is particularly appropriate in this instance. The notably passive, even masochistic miller lad, who would like to kill the hunter but cannot, duplicates the adrenaline-driven, fear-engendered, furious emotions of someone charging into battle; furthermore, the miller depicts the hunter as possessed of the muscular blood-lust of the soldier but directed to sexual conquest rather than annihilation of the enemy. What is overt directive in a war-song becomes murderous subtext in a cycle far from the battlefield, fought instead in the "foul rag-and-boneshop of the heart." One notes that the rhythmic patterns of Körner's poem are similar to the anapaestic tetrameters of Wilhelm Müller's poem, which likewise begins with a rhetorical question, "Was sucht dort der Jäger am Mühlbach hier?" (What does the hunter look for here at the mill-stream?) and impelled from Schubert the same 6/8 rhythms, undifferentiated succession of eighth notes in the melodic lines, symmetrical phrases, and lack of breathing space between phrases that one finds in more primitive form in "Lützows wilde Jagd" (ex. 7).[85] Since Müller would surely have known Körner's poems through the intermediary of Friedrich Förster, it is at least a possibility that "Der Jäger" was modeled directly after "Lützows wilde Jagd." Körner and the War of Liberation thus lurk behind the folk figures of Schubert's song cycle.

Example 7.   Franz Schubert, "Lützows wilde Jagd," D. 205, mm. 1–4. From *Neue Schubert-Ausgabe*, Series III, vol. 4: *Mehrstimmige Gesänge für gleiche Stimmen ohne Begleitung*, ed. Dietrich Berke.

The year after Körner's death, the tempo of new Körner settings picked up apace. Körner had on occasion accompanied himself and his fellow-soldiers on guitar, and it was only to be expected that his *Leier und Schwert* would be set to music for those same forces. Indeed, the Braunschweiger Johann Heinrich Carl Bornhardt (ca. 1770–1843) seems to have been obsessed with Körner and published three volumes of patriotic songs to Körner's poems: (1) *Th. Körner's Gedichte. Leier u[nd]. Schwert: Mit Melodien und leichter Guitarr-Begleitung*, op. 92 (Braunschweig: Spehr [1813]); (2) *Theodor Körners Gedichte. I. Theil*, op. 95 (Braunschweig: Spehr [1814]); and (3) *Th. Körner's Gedichte. II. Theil: Dessen poetischer Nachlass. Op. 96* (Braunschweig: Spehr [1815]). Körner's name even appears in the title of Bornhardt's *Nachklänge der letzten Vergangenheit, als Nachtrag zu Th. Körner's Gedichten*, op. 107 (Bern, 1818), although none of the fourteen songs are settings of Körner. His strophic songs all have simple chordal guitar accompaniments with the vocal part in an unchallenging middle register and narrow compass, devoid of virtuosity, chromaticism, or indeed, any variety of complexity. This is music for the patriotic amateur, but it is not without artistry on occasion, as in "Abschied von Wien," "An die Königin Louise" (Louise of Mecklenburg-Strelitz [1776–1810], Queen of Prussia), and "Abschied vom Leben" (Farewell to life) from op. 95.[86] The latter, which is subtitled "Als ich in der Nacht vom 17. zum 18. Junius 1813 schwer verwundet und hülflos in einem Holze lage, und zu sterben meinte" (As I lay wounded and helpless in the woods on the night of June 17–18 and believed myself to be dying), was one of the lyre-and-sword poems most often set to music – not surprising, as it invites chromatic pathos (or bathos).

Die Wunde brennt, – die bleichen Lippen beben	My wound burns, my pale lips tremble,
Ich fühl's an meines Herzens matterm Schlage,	I feel in my heart's flagging beat
Hier steh' ich an den Marken meiner Tage. –	that here I stand at the end of my days.
Gott, wie du willst, dir hab' ich mich ergeben.	God, as You will, I have surrendered myself
	to You.
Viel goldne Bilder sah ich um mich schweben;	I saw many golden images hover about me,
Das schöne Traumlied wird zur Todtenklage!	the lovely dream-song becomes a death
Muth! Muth! – Was ich so treu im Herzen	lament! Courage! Courage! – what I bear
trage,	so faithfully in my heart, that must
Das muß ja doch dort ewig mit mir leben!	eternally live within me hereafter!

Und was ich hier als Heiligtum erkannte,
Wofür ich rasch und jugendliche entbrannte,
Ob ich's nun Freiheit, ob ich's Liebe nannte,
Als lichten Seraph seh' ich's vor mir stehen, –
Und wie die Sinne langsam mir vergehen,
Trägt mich ein Hauch zu morgenroten Höhen.[87]

And what I here understood as holy,
that for which I, in my bold youth, caught
fire, whether I called it Freedom or Love, as
a glowing seraph, I see it standing before me.
And as my senses slowly fade away, a breath
of air brings me to the dawn-red heights.

From Bornhardt, this sonnet impelled such relatively sophisticated elements as recitative, third-related progressions (the recitative ends on an E major harmony, followed by the C major tonality of "Viel goldne Bilder sah ich um mich schweben"), even a diminished seventh harmony, a rarity in so diatonic an atmosphere (ex. 8).[88]

Example 8. Johann Heinrich Carl Bornhardt, "Abschied vom Leben" from *Th. Körners Gedichte. Erster Theil. Aus Leier und Schwert,* op. 92 (Braunschweig: Spehr [1814]), mm. 1–14.

In another example of a guitar lied in Körner's honor, the guitar virtuoso Mauro Giuliani (1781–1829, a native of Italy but a resident of Vienna from 1806),[89] composed ah setting of Körner's "Der Treue Tod" (The faithful death) wit accompaniment both for pianoforte and guitar and with an additional verse by Karl Schall: "And this poem inspired forebodings of doom – Destiny made it sorrowful truth." In Körner's poem, a departing knight bids his sweetheart farewell before he goes to war, singing, "For my Fatherland and my beloved, I will joyfully go to my death … and fiercely he threw himself into the heat of battle, and thousands fell beneath his blows; they owed the victory to his heroic courage, though he was among the corpses." Such certainties, untainted by fear or ambiguity (they are a defense against such thoughts), impelled from Giuliani the familiar martial dotted rhythms and tuneful diatonicism in the unclouded C major common to the genre.

Perhaps the first to set the "Sterbe-Sonnett" (Death sonnet), as "Abschied vom Leben" was also known, to music was an older Bohemian organist-composer whose nephew Gustav was a comrade of Theodor's: Anton Felix Beczwarzowsky (1753 or 1754–1823), whose small work-list includes the song "Buonaparte's Reise von Elba nach Paris" of 1815 (Bonaparte's journey from Elba to Paris), a set of three victory marches to celebrate the "Battle of the Nations" at Leipzig, and the *Leier und Schwert von Theodor Körner*, privately printed in Berlin in 1814–15.[90] Beczwarzowsky's "Langsam, schwermuthig" (slow, melancholy) setting of the "Sterbe-Sonnett" was conceived in a style midway between aria and lied, a dramatic *scena* from a real-life opera that everyone knew, and its dramatic character is evident from the beginning. The piano introduction begins strikingly with diminished and augmented sixth harmonies *sforzando* and on the weak second beats of mm. 2–3 of the piano introduction, as if in representation of the blow to the poet's head or as an apt musical expression of the anguish that impelled the opening words "Die Wunde brennt." One hears in the tonal indeterminacy of mm. 1–3 – the initial diminished chord (B-flat D-flat E-natural) includes the raised tonic and lowered seventh degrees, hardly a confirmation of E-flat major – the concomitant to the dazed and chaotic mental state of someone weak from pain and loss of blood. But after the introduction, Beczwarzowsky's musical persona "dies" as a precursor of Mimi in *La Bohème*, that is, with sufficient breath and vitality remaining for climactic high G's, A-flats, and even a B-flat, the latter awkwardly set to the unimportant preposition "mit." The hand-crossing for the pianist in mm. 5–11 emphasizes the triplet pulsations in the accompaniment, the "matterm Schlage" rendered as a musical pattern. The declamatory nature of the vocal line in mm. 5–11, with its frequent repeated pitches and dotted rhythms; the change from the "heartbeat" figuration to hymn-like writing for the affirmation "Gott, wie du willst"; the *innig*, chromatically inflected, descending parallel thirds at the words "so treu im Herze trage"; the multiple invocations of the words "das muß ja doch [dort ewig mit mir leben]," including a gasping, fragmentary ascent to the high B-flat; the *morendo* chromatic descent at the words "und wie die Sinne langsam mir vergehen," followed by the climactic, melismatic reference to dawn-lit heights; and the *pianissimo* cadence in the piano alone, with no other postlude – all confirm the dramatic nature of this work. It is surprisingly inspired, passionate, effective music from a composer virtually unknown nowadays (ex. 9). "A lesser composer, if his imagination is stimulated by the poem and a particularly felicitous tune comes into his head," writes J. W. Smeed, "may occasionally transcend himself"[91] – Beczwarzowsky was moved by his friend's death to write music that merits resuscitation, not only the "Abschied vom Leben" but such songs as "Unsere Zuversicht," with its rousing calls for "Tyrannentod." It was clearly an earlier precursor of the Wagnerian *Heldentenor* for whom he composed these clarion calls that vault upwards at the slightest provocation.

Example 9.   Anton Felix Beczwarzowsky, "Abschied vom Leben" from *Leier und Schwert von Theodor Körner* (Berlin: Privately printed, 1814–15), mm. 1–18.

Example 9. *cont.*

Schla - ge, hier steh' ich an den Mar - ken mein - er Ta - ge.

hingebend

Gott, wie du willst: dir hab' ich mich er - ge - ben.

Gott, wie du willst! dir — hab' ich mich er - ge - ben.

Carl Maria von Weber had already lent his compositional gifts to patriotic sentiment when he set Heinrich von Collin's words "Wir stehn vor Gott" (We stand before God) from the *Lieder österreichischer Wehrmänner* (Songs of Austrian soldiers) of 1809 as "Kriegs-Eid" (Oath of war) for a chorus of male baritone, with trumpet, horn, bassoon, and trombone accompaniment (an almost parodistically martial and masculine ensemble), in the summer of 1812. In the *Vossischen Zeitung* for 9 October 1814, the publisher Schlesinger announced "to the friends of the immortal poet Theodor Körner that Herr Kapellmeister Carl Maria von Weber is at this moment working on the composition of this collection of poems and that these works will shortly be published by this firm."[92] The compositions thus heralded were the opp. 41–43 settings of poems from *Leier und Schwert*, beginning with "Lützows wilder verwegener Jagd," op. 42, no. 2 (JV 168) and the "Schwertlied," op. 42, no. 6 (JV 169), composed on 13 September 1814 at Schloß Gräfentonna at Gotha. At Altenburg, on the road between Gotha and Prague, on 23 September, he composed "Männer und Buben" (Men and boys), all three for four-part male chorus; the other *Männerchor* works included in op. 42 are the "Trinklied vor der Schlacht" (Drinking song before the battle) of 19 October 1814 in Prague; "Reiterlied" (Cavalry song), composed 20 October; and "Gebet vor der Schlacht" (Prayer before the battle) of 21 October. The solo lieder published as op. 41 include "Gebet während der Schlacht," composed 19 November 1814 in Prague; "Abschied vom Leben," composed 20 November; "Trost" (Consolation) and "Mein Vaterland" (My fatherland), the latter two from late 1814.[93] Op. 43 is an extended ballad-cantata to Körner's "Bei der Musik des Prinzen Ferdinand von Preussen" (On the music of Prince Ferdinand of Prussia). According to Max Weber, his father's Körner settings cast all previous political songs into the shade; although filial pride is an obvious factor in the pronouncement, he was not far off the mark. Not until the numerous settings of Nicolaus Becker's "Rheinlied" swept the patriotic song-writing market in the 1840s did anything come along to equal the popularity of Weber's nationalistic lieder.[94]

Weber is not a principal focus of this book, nor is there sufficient space to review the entire *Leier und Schwert* corpus, but selected examples, beginning with "Gebet während der Schlacht," op. 41, no. 1, can convey the tone and temper of the rest as well. Xenophobic nationalism and religion were paired in the *Burschenschaften* – "Nur ein Deutscher und ein Christ" was among their mottos – and elsewhere in the German-speaking world, so it was perhaps inevitable that this battle-prayer would be another of the most popular poems in *Leier und Schwert* for musical setting.

Vater, ich rufe dich!	Father, I cry unto You!
Brüllend umwölkt mich der Dampf der Geschütze,	The smoke of roaring guns envelops me,
Sprühend umzucken mich rasselnde Blitze.	Explosive flashes dart all around me.
Lenker der Schlachten, ich rufe dich!	Lord of battles, I cry unto You!
Vater du, führe mich!	Father, lead me!
Vater du, führe mich!	Father, lead me!
Führ' mich zum Siege, führ mich zum Tode,	Lead me to victory, lead me to death,
Herr, ich erkenne deine Gebote;	Lord, I acknowledge Your commands;
Herr, wie du willst, so führe mich,	Lord, lead me where You will.
Gott, ich erkenne dich!	God, I acknowledge You!
Gott, ich erkenne dich!	God, I acknowledge You!
So im herbstlichen Rauschen der Blätter,	In the autumnal rustling of leaves,
Als im Schlachtendonnerwetter,	as in the thunder of battle;
Urquell der Gnade, erkenn' ich dich.	Source of grace, I acknowledge You!
Vater du, segne mich!	Father, grant me Your blessing!
Vater du, segne mich!	Father, grant me Your blessing!
In deine Hand befehl' ich mein Leben,	Into Your hands I commend my life;
Du kannst es nehmen, du hast es gegeben;	You may take it, for You gave it.

Zum Leben, zum Sterben segne mich.
  Vater, ich preise dich!
	Whether for life or death, grant me Your
	  blessing. Father, I praise you!

Vater, ich preise dich!
S'ist ja kein Kampf für die Güter der Erde;
Das heiligste schützen wir mit dem Schwerte:
  Drum fallend und siegend preis' ich dich.
  Gott, dir ergeb' ich mich!
	Father, I praise you!
	This is no battle for the riches of this earth;
	We defend what is holiest with our swords;
	  Therefore, dying and victorious, I praise You.
	  God, I surrender myself to You!

Gott, dir ergeb' ich mich!
Wenn mich die Donner des Todes begrüßen,
Wenn mein Adern geöffnet fließen:
  Dir, mein Gott, dir ergeb' ich mich!
  Vater, ich rufe dich! [95]
	God, I surrender myself to You!
	If the thunder of death greets me,
	If my opened veins flow,
	  To You, my God, I surrender myself!
	  Father, I cry unto You!

Weber seizes upon both the metaphor of battle as a storm and the preposition "während" – a prayer during the battle – in the title as the basis for an incessant storm of thirty-second note figuration in the piano, depicting, according to its composer, not "scene painting" but a storm in the soul (ex. 10).[96] If the song is to be performed at a proper tempo for the singer, the pianist must be Lisztian in virtuosity; the Schubert of "Erlkönig" and "Der Taucher" was not the only composer making extraordinary demands on lieder accompanists at the time, although he far outstripped most of them. The writhing scales and arpeggios ebb and flow in range and dynamics, without a pause until the final chord; when Körner imagines the blood flowing from his veins and life leaving him in the final stanza, Weber, knowing of the hero's actual death, conceives a *morendo* conclusion, with the traditional drum-roll figures from the beginning of the song sounding at its close. Each strophe of this varied strophic lied in C minor begins and ends in the same way, but the interior is differently calculated to the textual content: *fortissimo* horn-calls on E-flat and B-flat harmonies blaring in the left-hand part for the words "Lenker der Schlachten, ich rufe dich" in stanza 1 (this passage returns in stanza 4 at the words "Zum Leben, zum Sterben, segne mich!" and again in the final stanza); the jolt of the V/D minor harmonies at the words "führ mich zum Siege" in stanza 2, the composer leading the poet to a new tonal battle-ground; the plagal harmonies and *cantabile* indication for the words "Urquell der Gnade, erkenn' ich dich" and the affective E-flat minor passing harmony at the words "segne mich" in stanza 3; the blaze of C major for the first time at the words "das Heiligste schützen wir mit dem Schwerte" in stanza 5, with the horn-call motives making yet another appearance in the bass; and the return to C minor in the final stanza. It is no wonder that Weber chose to herald his *Leier und Schwert* settings with this work and almost comically apt that Liszt did not transcribe it for solo piano in his "Leier und Schwert nach Carl Maria von Weber und Körner: Heröide für das Pianoforte." The simpler music of the op. 42 *Männerchor* pieces could be, and was, rendered more virtuosic in Liszt's most brilliant-gaseous manner, but "Gebet während der Schlacht" required no such inflation.

Example 10. Carl Maria von Weber, "Gebet während der Schlacht," from *Leier und Schwert*, op. 41, no. 1 (Berlin: A. M. Schlesinger, 1815), mm. 1–16.

Example 10. *cont.*

brül – lend um – wölkt mich der Dampf der Ge –

– schü – tze,

sprü – hend um – zu – – cken mich ras – – seln – de

Bli – – tze

Example 10. *cont.*

Example 10. *cont.*

Schubert's setting, D. 171 of 1815, is very different in conception from Weber's, even in matters of meter (4/4 rather than Weber's 3/4) and mode (major rather than Weber's minor mode, with an apotheosis in major). Did Schubert, one wonders, know this song, famous from the moment it first appeared, and therefore resolve to treat it differently?[97] It is also less inspired, at least after the "Etwas langsam" setting of stanza 1, which Schubert set as the introduction to the strophic repetitions that follow (ex. 11). As ever, the tumult of battle is assigned to the piano and begins with pianissimo *tremolandi* over a fateful "empty" fifth in the bass – measures 1–8 of the twelve-bar introduction are plotted as a crescendo in which the distant rumble of war at the beginning becomes increasingly louder, swifter, and more chromatically

Example 11. Franz Schubert, "Gebet während der Schlacht," D. 171, mm. 1–12.

fraught. In m. 4, one hears a precursor of a famous Schubertian trill-accented figure, rising chromatically in the bass from D-sharp to tonic G; this same species of trill figure appears later at the invocation of bygone heroes and military glory in the Mayrhofer lied "Auf der Donau" (see chap. 3) – "brüllend" indeed, especially since Schubert uses the figure in "Gebet während der Schlacht" to move to a momentary emphasis on the chord of the flatted seventh degree, or F major. The "rasselnde Blitze," or flashes of rifle-fire and whizzing bullets, become rapid, dotted rhythmic octave figures in the right hand part of mm. 6–7 over augmented triadic harmonies in the bass, indicative of great tension. The "geschwinder werdend" (becoming faster) battle figuration culminates in a brief passage of recitative ("Lenker der Schlachten, ich rufe dich!"), beginning *forzando* on the diminished seventh harmony rife in *recitativo accompagnato* and ending with chromatic descent traced in the bass line and inner voices. This same chromatic descent later appears as the explicit musical symbol of "Untergang," or "doom" near the end of "Auf der Donau." One would have had to be a hermit in 1815 not to know that Körner's plea, "Father, lead me to battle and to death," was answered in the affirmative, and composers signal their knowledge of his fate in various ways when they set his poems to music.

It is only in those three measures at the end of the introduction that the *tremolando* figuration cedes to less vibratory textures, to a clearer atmosphere in which the prayerful words resound starkly. When the body of the song begins with stanza 2, one hears the *tremolandi* resume, this time in the context of the full, rich, repeated chords Schubert would use later, but without the *tremolando* agitation, for his setting of Ladislaus Pyrker's "Die Allmacht," divine power invoked in similar terms of harmonic weight, if not tonal profundity. The initial phrase in the vocal line, "Vater, du führe mich!", repeated to the subsequent related words ("Gott, ich erkenne dich," etc.) at the beginning of each stanza, is a variation in *Terzensteigerung* of the first line of the poem, "Vater, ich rufe dich!", in mm. 2–3; one notices in particular the prolongation of the initial syllable in pleading emphasis, the darkened chord of the flatted sixth degree at the word "Tode" in m. 15, and the chromatic ascent in the vocal line for mm. 16–18, derived from similar voice-leading in the introduction/setting of stanza 1. But what follows is near-exact repetition, written-out for reasons of necessary prosodic adjustments in the singer's part, of the four subsequent stanzas. The lied is thus an odd amalgam: we are led to expect a "Gesang," a longer, through-composed or varied strophic structure of some length, because of the changing textures and recitative in the introduction, but instead we are given a short-breathed "Lied," each strophe a mere nine measures long, with no attempt to differentiate between them. The result is an unrelenting emphasis on tonic G major and on the foursquare rhythms established in the setting of stanza 2. Whether the anti-clerical Schubert was constrained by the religiosity of the text or simply bored by its unchanging form and content cannot be determined, but it is undeniable that he was at a farther remove from this poem than from the dramatic ballad "Amphiaraos" or the non-patriotic works.

Weber's setting of the "Abschied vom Leben" is even more deserving of revival than Beczwarzowsky's. (Grund too included a setting of "Abschied vom Leben" as

Example 12. Carl Maria von Weber, "Abschied vom Leben" from *Leier und Schwert*, op. 41 (Berlin: A. M. Schlesinger, 1815), mm. 22–53.

Example 12.   *cont.*

rasch   und ju-gend-lich ent-brann-te   ob ichs nun Frei-heit,   ob ichs Lie-be

nann — te   als lich-ten Ser-aph seh ich's vor mir

ste-hen   und   wie die Sin-nen   lang-sam mir   ver-ge-hen,

trägt mich ein Hauch   zu   mor-gen-ro — then Hö-hen   trägt mich ein

Example 12.   *cont.*

Hauch zu mor-gen-ro - then Hö - hen.

rallentando

the fourth of his *Sechs deutsche Lieder*, a more complex conception than his other Körner songs.) Unlike his Bohemian contemporary, Weber does not musically depict the blow or the ensuing mental turbulence, but rather begins with the *pianissimo* calm of weakness, with a thinned-out accompaniment in the bass, and only the most minimal of piano introductions. In the fragmented vocal phrases, broken by rests, at the words "die bleichen Lippen beben" and "Herzens matterm Schlage," the latter further pictorialized by means of non-legato "heartbeat" repeated chords and a diminished seventh chord at the word "matterm," one hears the musical signifiers of failing breath and strength. The dramatic economy – intense effects from restricted means – of Weber's interpretive choices is epitomized in the setting of the word "hier!" as an unharmonized leading tone in m. 10, the crucial word of recognition thus isolated before Weber reconnects it to the full poetic line in which it appears ("Hier steh' ich an den Marken meiner Tage"); in the flatted sixth degree that inflects the words "meiner [Tage]"; and in the recitative-like setting (*pianissimo*, not Beczwar-zowsky's *forte*) of the poet's accession to God's will, with its prosodic emphasis on "Gott!" and "dir." Weber repeats both this same affective use of the flatted sixth degree and the ascending D major arpeggio in the piano – the ascent into the "morgenroten Höhen" – that follows it at the end of the song; the imminent death foretold in the first section of this "Abschied" comes to pass at the close.

In Weber's conception, the sparse, deliberately discontinuous first quatrain of the sonnet is succeeded by richer, fuller music in tonalities removed from the earthbound key of D major, the musical concomitant to visions of heavenly glory as earthly senses fade; it may seem fanciful to equate B major, the tonality at the farthest end of the "sharp" keys, with the imagined brightness and richness of the afterlife, but it seems likely that Weber did just that. The visions first materialize from the previous prevailing spare textures in the piano interlude between the first and second quatrains (mm. 20–23) as a harmonic and rhythmic crescendo from unharmonized pitches to full-fledged dominant seventh chords. The visions re-animate the poet, awaken him to new life, and Weber conveys the renewed motion in the repeated chords that sound throughout the remainder of the song, ceding only to the arpeggiated ascent to heaven in the final two measures. But even in the midst of seraphic visions, Weber reminds the listener of the poet's terror in the face of death (the darkening of the harmonic progressions at the words "langsam mir vergehen" is especially notable) and does so in a manner sophisticated beyond Beczwarzowsky's scope (ex. 12).

"Mein Vaterland!", the last of the op. 41 songs, is a dialogue in which an unknown voice (potential recruits?) asks questions about the Fatherland, to which the poet-minstrel replies with patriotic propaganda etched in black-and-white – such shades of gray as German collaborationists with Napoleon are necessarily expunged from mention.

Wo ist des Sängers Vaterland? –	Where is the minstrel's Fatherland? –
Wo edler Geister Funken sprühten,	Where sparks flew from noble spirits,
Wo Kränze für das Schöne blühten,	where garlands bloomed for the beautiful,
Wo starke Herzen freudig glühten,	where strong hearts burned with joy,
Für alles Heilige entbrannt.	afire for everything sacred.
Da war mein Vaterland!	There was my Fatherland!
Wer heißt des Sängers Vaterland? –	What do you call the minstrel's Fatherland? –
Jetzt über seine Söhne Leichen,	Now it weeps under the foreign lash,
Jetzt weint es unter fremden Streichen;	weeps over its sons' bodies.
Sonst hieß es nur das Land der Eichen,	Once it was known only as the land of oak trees,
Das freie Land, das deutsche Land!	a free land, a German land!
So hieß mein Vaterland![98]	That was the name of my Fatherland!

Weber sets the questioner's queries apart as brief passages in 2/4, with no introduction (it is the questions which impel each section of this varied strophic form, not prior instrumental strains) and ending with an upwards, questioning inflection. One notes as well Weber's emphasis on the key words, "Wo," "Wie," "weint," "Wem," "will," and "hofft" and the yearning appoggiatura at every occurrence of the word "Vaterland." The "edler Geister" of stanza 1 impel one of Weber's loveliest lyrical melodies, especially where the heightened supertonic harmonies imbue the "garlands blooming for the beautiful" in mm. 6–8 with elegaic wistfulness. In stanza 2, the "sons' corpses" and "weeping under the foreign lash" turn the harmonic coloration to minor, while the "Wüthrichs Ungewittern" of stanza 3 is accompanied by heavy, martial rumblings in the low bass. Stanza 5 (*Con molto fuoco*) is the peak of intensity, the call for "die Knechte" to strike the Napoleonic bloodhound and drive it from German boundaries; the culminatory cries of freedom ("und frey, die freyen Söhne tragen") resound in a blaze of C major, only to plunge, first, downwards in double-dotted gloom at the words "oder frey sie betten unterm Sand" and then dramatically back up once more for the proclamation "das! das will das Vaterland" – a spiky fever-chart of patriotic fervor and a dramatic conclusion to the op. 41 set (ex. 13).[99] Unlike the settings by Grund, Himmel, and their ilk, this is music that reaches beyond the limited realms of amateur performance for purely patriotic purposes, claiming as well musical status as lied.

Skipping over the op. 42 male-chorus works, we come to Körner's most powerful poem and one of Weber's longest non-operatic vocal works: the op. 43 setting of "Bei der Musik des Prinzen Louis Ferdinand." Here, the poet draws an analogy between the inchoate birth of war-frenzy within the heart and soul and the

Example 13.   Carl Maria von Weber, "Mein Vaterland" from *Leier und Schwert*, op. 41 (Berlin: A. M. Schlesinger, 1815), mm. 34–50.

Example 13. *cont.*

experience of hearing music, the two forces similar in their power to overthrow reason and sway the emotions.[100] The deceased composer whose dark music he hears, the man whose fate he fuses with his own prophesied end, was the so-called "Alcibiades of Prussia," Prince Louis Ferdinand. This handsome, gifted man, a nephew of Frederick the Great, was a virtuoso pianist praised by Beethoven himself, a composer of chamber music and songs, a womanizer whose illegitimate descendants include the playwright Ernst von Wildenbruch, an advocate of reform and critic of the Prussian nobility, and an outstanding soldier decorated for his feats in the campaign of 1792. The last six years of his life were largely devoted to musical interests, pursued with his characteristic intensity but cut short by death: he was one of the first casualties in the battle of Saalfeld on 10 October 1806, a few days before the disastrous battle of Jena.[101] On the evening before his death, he gave his Cremona violin to the French musician Avé Lallemand with the words, "This violin will remain in your possession if I do not return from the battle." To Körner, he was the epitome of the artist-soldier, someone devoted to music who nevertheless charged headlong into battle against terrible odds – Körner's own fate, one he hoped would reverse the humiliation suffered at Jena.

Düstre Harmonien hör' ich klingen,
Mutig schwellen sie ans volle Herz,
In die Seele fühl' ich sie mir dringen,
Wecken mir den vaterländ'schen Schmerz,
Und mit ihren früh geprüften Schwingen
Kämpfen sie im Sturm himmelwärts;
Doch sie tragen nur ein dunkles Sehnen,
Nicht den Geist aus diesem Land der Tränen.

I hear dark chords resounding,
Valiantly they swell within a full heart.
In my soul, I feel them press upon me,
awakening in me sorrow for my Fatherland,
and with their pinions, tested early,
they battle their way heavenwards in the storm,
but they bear only a dark yearning,
not the spirit from this land of tears.

Allgewaltig hält ihn noch das Leben,
Taucht die Flügel in den styg'schen Fluß;
Es ist nicht der Künste freies Schweben,
Nicht verklärter Geister Weihekuß.
Noch dem Erdgeist ist er preisgegeben,
Mit dem Staube kämpft der Genius,
Reißt er auch im Rausche der Gedanken
Oft sich blutend los aus seinen Schranken.

It yet clings with all its power to life,
its wings are dipped in the Stygian river;
it is not the free swaying of the arts,
nor the transfigured spirits' kiss of dedication.
It is still surrendered to the earthly spirit.
The spirit does battle with the dust;
even in the rush of thoughts, it often tears
away, bleeding, from its limits.

Dann ergreift ihn ein bacchantisch Wüten,	Then a Bacchic frenzy seizes it,
Wilde Melodienblitze sprühn;	wild thunderbolts of melody flash;
Aus dem Tode ruft er Strahlenblüten	from the dead, it calls forth flowers of light
Und zertritt sie kalt, sobald sie blühn.	and strikes them cold, as soon as they bloom.
Wenn die letzten Funken bleich verglühten,	When the last spark glows but palely,
Hebt er sich noch einmal, stolz und kühn,	it arises yet again, proud and bold,
Und versinkt dann mit gewalt'gen Schauren	and then, with mighty paroxysms, is engulfed
In den alten Kampf mit dem Zentauren.	in the age-old battle with the centaurs.
Wilder Geist! jetzt hast du überwunden!	Wild spirit! Now you have vanquished!
Deine Nacht verschmilzt in Morgenrot;	Your night melts into dawn; your hours of
Ausgekämpft sind deiner Prüfung Stunden,	tribulation are over and the battle won;
Leer der Kelch, den dir das Schicksal bot.	empty the chalice that Fate delivered to you.
Kunst und Leben hat den Kranz gewunden,	Art and Life have woven the garland,
Auf die Locken drückte ihn der Tod.	Death pressed it on your locks.
Deinen Grabstein kann die Zeit zermalmen,	Time can smash your grave-stone to pieces,
Doch die Lorbeer werden dort zu Palmen.	But there, the myrtles will become palms.
Und dein Sehnen klagte nicht vergebens:	And your yearning did not lament in vain:
Einmal ward's in deiner Seele Tag,	Suddenly day dawned in your soul as your
Als dein Herz am kühnsten Ziel des Strebens	heart, at the boldest goal of its striving, lay
Kalt und blutend auf der Wahlstatt lag.	cold and bleeding at the destined spot.
Sterbend lös'te sich der Sturm des Lebens,	Dying, you were liberated from the storm of
Sterbend lös'te sich der Harfe Schlag;	life; dying, the harp's tones were set free,
Und des Himmels siegverklärte Söhne	and the war-illumined sons of heaven
Trugen dich in's freie Land der Töne.[102]	bore you into the free land of music.

The poem goes beyond the clichés of his own patriotic poetry to explore the process by which an artist, bound to life and creativity, relinquishes art for a soldier's death-seeking blood-lust, for the "age-old battle with the centaurs." In the first two stanzas, Körner traces the initial struggle by which one force begins to overwhelm the other, a combat which inflicts psychic battlefield wounds in the spirit, and then in the third stanza describes what could only be the creation of *Leier und Schwert* itself, songs born of death and created for the purpose of sending others to their deaths. The artist-turned-warrior may, Körner writes, forfeit his prospects for artistic immortality, exchanging the myrtles of an artist's garland for the palms of victory on the battlefield, but he is thereby assured of entry into a Valhalla where music (or poetry) will be restored to him in paradisiacal fullness. If one needed confirmation that Körner *sought* his battlefield death, despite his very human fears, one can find it here.

Weber was the only composer, to my knowledge, who set this work to music and did so as an extended solo cantata-like composition based in part on themes by Louis Ferdinand himself, the dead prince's music designated by the motto "PL" and his own as "CW." After the initial, ominous low bass tremolos and solemn chords, devoid of melody for almost ten measures, Weber sounds "düst're Harmonien" – as one might expect, the Prince's melody – for eight additional measures in the piano as the poet-singer "listens," before joining in. In Weber's conception, the singer first sings a muted commentary on the Prince's music, still sounding in the piano; the "Körner voice" is lower, less obtrusive than the music to which he pays heed, although significantly, the singer chimes in with the Prince's voice at the ends of phrases. Where the singer takes the "Fatherland's sorrow" unto himself ("wecken mir den vaterländ'schen Schmerz"), the Prince's melody becomes entirely his, the accompaniment reduced to subordinate repeated chords and the sorrow rendered dark indeed in a purple patch of chromaticism on and around the flatted seventh degree (ex. 14a). The fusion of Körner and the Prince in Körner's imagination becomes the musical fusion of two composers, one who is now renowned chiefly for the "düst're Harmonien" of the Wolf's Glen – demonic powers of a different sort.

Example 14a.   Carl Maria von Weber, "Bei der Musik des Prinzen Louis Ferdinand," op. 43 (Berlin: A. M. Schlesinger, 1815), mm. 1–32.

Example 14a. *cont.*

The second section, or the setting of stanza 2, is among the most striking sections in this episodic form, the conflict between matter and spirit translated into tonal terms. The "free hovering" of the artistic spirit becomes harmonic hovering in the treble register, the passage laden with diminished seventh harmonies, while the "verklärter Geister Weihekuß" are set to even higher C major strains – clarified and illuminated. Most interesting of all, the spirit's battle to break free becomes a modulatory battleground in which the key of B minor, so near and yet so far from the C major *Ur*-tonality in which the section begins (Wagner was not the only composer to associate C major with "heil'ge Deutsche Kunst," it seems) eventually wins out. B minor is, furthermore, located a tritone away from the principal key of the work, the "Erdgeist" as distant as possible from the F minor "dark harmonies" at the beginning and the F major "palms of victory" at the close (ex. 14b). One glimpses the tonal symbolism of *Der Freischütz* through a glass darkly.

Example 14b.   Carl Maria von Weber, "Bei der Musik des Prinzen Louis Ferdinand," op. 43 (Berlin: A. M. Schlesinger, 1815), the setting of stanza 2.

Example 14b. *cont.*

Example 14b. *cont.*

Example 14b. *cont.*

Ballades and other such mini-operas for solo voice and piano (now thoroughly out of fashion for many decades but once *de rigueur*) were often tonally progressive, ending in a different key after travelling far and wide, but Weber properly understood this poem as a closed circle, the end inherent in the beginning. When the "dark yearning" of stanza 1 recurs in the final stanza, F minor returns, only to cede to F major for the Valhalla-like entry into heaven. The unharmonized figure in the third and second measures before the end of the piano postlude – a last reminiscence of the minor mode – is identified as the Prince's, the final single tonic *major* chord as Weber's. The finicking exactitude may seem a trifle comic at first until one realizes its symbolic meaning: for both the Prince and Körner, life and art alike were cut short, with dark enigmas at the premature close. It was left to Weber to conclude the *Schicksalslied* he had composed in their honor by turning the death-figure, even its rhythmic pattern wrenched awry, into a blaze of fully harmonized resolution in major mode – apotheosis by the most economical of means.

Five years after Weber's *Leier und Schwert* settings, the ballad-master Carl Loewe (1796–1869, born two months before Schubert) set "Treuröschen" (Faithful Rose) from Körner's *Nachlaß* as one of his earliest *Schauerballaden* (horror ballads), a favorite genre of Loewe's. The poem is, typically for Körner, an amalgam of borrowed sources assembled in such a way as to underscore Körner's own obsessions, in this instance, death-weddings – a ballad that would seem on the surface to have nothing to do with impending war is in fact directly premonitory of the lyre-and-sword songs.

Folkish tales of German *Jagdkultur* were, whatever else they might have been, an assertion of *echt Deutsch* identity both then and later, and this ballad has all the requisite ingredients: a hunter, an archetypal folk maiden named Röschen (the beautiful miller maid in Schubert's cycle began life with the same flower-name of Rose), and an enchanted stag who lures the hunter to his death. Musicology in the Third Reich, one is reminded, revived and studied German hunting songs from folk and art repertoires alike,[103] but the subterranean (at times, overt) political implications of imitating folksong were already at work in Körner's day.

Like most writers in their youth, Körner taught himself about various literary genres by imitating, often very closely, the works of those predecessors who excelled in the genre at hand. In "Treuröschen," his debt to August Bürger's "Lenore" of 1773 is obvious; here too, "Die Toten reiten schnell" ("The dead ride swiftly," the otherworldly horseman's sardonic refrain in the latter half of this most famous of all ballads, set to music by Johann Rudolf Zumsteeg). "There once was a hunter bold and brave who wished to make a beautiful Rose bloom," the ballad begins, each stanza ending with the sing-song refrain "Trala, Trala, Trala" – the poem invites musical setting, since the hunter woos his sweetheart with songs and hunting horn-calls, "Sing und Sang, Liederton und Hörnerklang." As in Bürger, Körner's ballad has openly moralistic overtones, a sermonizing message meant to scare the impressionable young reader into sexual or religious conformity. Here, the hunter tells his faithful Rose that their year of betrothal is over, that he will soon lead her to the altar, and the two spend a night of love together, a night for which both pay dearly. (I like to think that Schubert passed over Bürger's famous ballad and Körner's copy because of an aversion to this particular variety of moralising, although I have no verification for such speculation.)

Die Sternlein verblichen, der Morgen graut,	The stars grow pale, the morning dawns gray,
Der Jäger kehrt heim von der süßen Braut,	the hunter returns home from his sweet bride,
Und jagt hinab durch Wald und Flur,	and goes out hunting in the forest and meadow,
Und folgt einem Hirsch auf flüchtiger Spur,	and follows a stag's fleeting trace,
So schön, wie er keinen noch sah!	a stag more beautiful than any he ever saw!
Trala, Trala, Trala.	Trala, trala, trala. (stanza 5)

The stag leaps from a crag into the abyss, the hunter and his horse following it to their deaths. As Röschen weeps in her chamber at midnight, wondering where her lover is, she hears a spectral voice:

Und auf einmal hört sie Hörnerklang	And finally she heard the sound of horns
Und es flüstert ihr leise wie Geisterklang:	and a ghostly sound whispered softly to her:
"Komm Liebchen, bist mir angetraut,	"Come, beloved, you are wedded to me,
Das Bett ist bereitet, komm, rosige Braut,	the marriage bed is ready, come, rosy bride,
Der Buhle ist längst schon da!"	your lover is already long since there!"
Trala, Trala, Trala.	Trala, trala, trala.

Da faßt sie ein Schauer so eisig und kalt,	An icy-cold shudder seized her,
Und sie fühlt sich umarmt von Geistergewalt,	and she felt herself embraced with ghostly force,
Und heimlich durchweht es ihr bebendes Herz	and bridal joy and deathly anguish
Wie Hochzeitlust und Todesschmerz,	mysteriously pervaded her beating heart,
Und zitternd flüstert sie: "ja!"	and trembling, she whispered, "Yes!"
Trala, Trala, Trala.	Trala, trala, trala.
Da stockt das Blut in der klopfenden Brust,	The blood stopped in her palpitating breast,
Da bricht das Herz in Todeslust;	her heart broke in deathly pleasure;
Und der Jäger führt heim die rosige Braut,	and the hunter led the rosy bride home –
Dort oben ist er ihr angetraut,	there above is he wedded to her.
Treuröschen's Hochzeit ist da!	Faithful Rose's wedding is there!
Trala, Trala, Trala! [104]	Trala, trala, trala. (stanzas 9–11 of 11)

However tempting it might be to chuckle at such dated diabolism (as the later nineteenth century did), the ballad becomes less a laughing matter if one speculates that Körner, beset from early on with premonitions of death in battle, may have thus predicted his own death before marriage. Certainly the choice of model is chilling: dead soldiers (Bürger's revenant is a soldier returned from the war) were in all-too-plentiful supply in Napoleon's final years, and Körner would soon be numbered among them.

Loewe's setting,[105] composed in 1819–20 and published in 1824 as op. 2, is rarely performed today, which is a pity; understood in its proper context, this is a riveting work. Loewe indicates that the hollow fifths on the dominant in the piano introduction, the fateful-sounding interval repeated over and over in 6/8 rhythm, should be performed to a crescendo throughout the entire four measures; thus, before the body of the ballad begins in a crystalline-diatonic C major, its storytelling strains initially devoid of menace, we are warned of spectral matters to come. The "Trala" refrains are likewise premonitory of music from the crypt in each instance; Loewe understood them as fragments of song from those eerie forces glad to dance on our graves, and he set them each time to a different "spooky" figure, whether trill-bedecked hollow fifths (the first occurrence in mm. 15–17), grace-noted octaves high in the treble, or more forceful manifestations down below as death draws nearer. This is balladry differently constituted than the Zumsteeg model Schubert preferred, with its mixture of operatic recitative, song sections, and quasi-orchestral passages for the piano; rather, Loewe eschews recitative, deliberately adopts an "erzählend" (story-telling style) manner at the beginning, and continually invents fresh figuration in the piano as his musical tale unfolds in the vocal line. The way in which the motives in the piano plummet from the high treble register into the bass in mm. 34–38, foreshadowing the plunge into the abyss before it occurs; the slightly comic, delighted little thirty-second flourishes that frisk upward in the right-hand part in m. 45 when Röschen says "Yes" to her hunter's promise of marriage; the increasingly rapid motion as the ballad and the hunter head for the precipice; and the *fortissimo* broken octaves in mm. 76–79 that tell us to beware the beautiful stag ("so schön, so schön") are only a few of the inventive details with which this ballad is filled (ex. 15).

Example 15.   Carl Loewe, "Treuröschen," op. 2, mm. 85–101. From *Carl Loewes Werke*, ed. Max Runze, vol. 8: *Geisterballaden und Gesichte / Todes- und Kirchofs-Bilder.*

Example 15. *cont.*

As the tale grows spookier, Loewe comes more and more into his element, putting both the singer and pianist through their dramatic and virtuosic paces – the setting of the initial stanzas may look suitable for amateurs, but the ballad rapidly moves beyond that more limited range – when the hunter plunges from the cliff, the C minor turmoil dying down to hushed measured trills on the tonic and leading pitches; the same "verklingend," dying-away effect returns at the end of the entire ballad. The A minor eeriness with which Loewe heralds the midnight hour ("Und als es kam um Mitternacht, Treuröschen noch traurig im Bette wacht," or "And when midnight came, faithful Rose still sadly kept watch in her bed," mm. 116–30) and the suitably terrifying A-flat minor and D-flat minor chromatic darkness of the ghostly invitation "Komm, Liebchen, bist mir angetraut" (mm. 138–45) are among the most effective passages of a truly gripping work, that is, if one surrenders to the conventions of the genre.

There are many other Körner songs one could mention, including Heinrich Marschner's setting of "Erinnerung" ("Schweigend in des Abends Stille / Blinkt des Mondes Silberlicht") from the *Lieder der Liebe*, op. 44 (Braunschweig: G. M. Meyer, [1828 or 1829?]); the reviewer for the *Allgemeine Musikalische Zeitung* of March 1829 characterized it as having "nothing truly individual, but [the song is] so pleasant that it is bound to find favor," a characterization with which anyone who browses through the charming miniature can agree.[106] Certain poems were repeatedly the target of composers, albeit not so often as the poetry of his more gifted elders and contemporaries – Goethe, Schiller, Eichendorff, and Heine. Nonetheless, another reviewer for the same periodical had reason to observe in a capsule review of "Das war ich!" as set by E. F. Gäbler circa 1840 that this was "a well-known poem." [107] Schubert too was drawn to it, and to other equally well-known Körner poems, and it is to him that we now turn.

ARTISTS IN THEIR YOUTH: THE SCHUBERT–KÖRNER SONGS

Schubert and Körner actually met; Joseph von Spaun befriended the music-loving Körner soon after his arrival in Vienna and introduced him to Schubert after a performance in 1812 of Gluck's *Iphigénie en Tauride* in which Anna Milder and Michael Vogl sang the roles of Orestes and Iphigenia. Spaun recounts the incident in his 1858 "Notes on my acquaintance with Franz Schubert," telling of supper with the gregarious Körner at the Blumenstöckl in the Ballgasse, where a university professor at the next table mocked the two great singers, to Körner's and Schubert's mutual fury. [108] When the poet left the city, Schubert and Mayrhofer took the same room in Madame Sanssouci's rooming house on the Wipplingerstrasse in which Körner had stayed, according to Josef Hüttenbrenner. [109] After Körner's death, his former fiancée also came to know Schubert's music – she says nothing of meeting Schubert himself – and reminisced in later life about an occasion in October 1826 when she sang songs from *Die schöne Müllerin* and the Harper's song "Wer sich der Einsamkeit ergibt" in Franz Grillparzer's hearing. [110] Women evidently performed songs whose poetic personae were male, although one notes that Toni chose the songs of a lovelorn, effeminized (in comparison to the hunter) young man and a tragic outsider, bereft and insane, not a "Prometheus" or "Philoktet" or "Cronnan."

Thirteen of Schubert's fourteen Körner songs belong to the *annus mirabilis* 1815, beginning with "Sängers Morgenlied" (Poet's morning-song), D. 163 of 27 February and D. 165 of 1 March. The two versions constitute a fascinating instance of "Schubert revising Schubert," as they are a study in opposites. For the initial version, Schubert took his point of departure from the first stanza of Körner's six and created a buoyant greeting to the sun in G major, with energetic melismas propelling the vocal line along at strategic points. One notes in particular the unison setting of the words "mit geheimnissvollen Worten" (with secret words) in mm. 9–10 and the chromatic neighbor-notes on either side of the dominant pitch – Schubert would later signify the secretive nature of the wanderer's thoughts in "Letzte Hoffnung" (Last hope) from *Winterreise* in a similar way, a gesture with antecedents in his youth. But the word "Ach" (Ah) at the beginning of stanza 2 of "Sänger's Morgenlied" is the signal for a change of tone, for greater gravity. Schubert did more than merely ignore the *Sehnsucht* (yearning) awakened by the arrival of day in the 27 February version – he set it to the merry strains of the first verse, sound and sense thus at odds throughout the last half of the song.

Süßes Licht! Aus goldnen Pforten	Sweet light! Through golden portals
Brichst du siegend durch die Nacht.	You break victoriously through the night.
Schöner Tag! Du bist erwacht.	Beautiful day! You are awake.
Mit geheimnisvollen Worten,	With mysterious words
In melodischen Akkorden	And melodious sounds,
Grüß' ich deine Rosenpracht!	I greet your roseate splendor!
Ach! der Liebe sanftes Wehen	Ah, the soft breath of love
Schwellt mir das bewegte Herz,	Swells my moved heart
Sanft, wie ein geliebter Schmerz.	As softly as a beloved pain.
Dürft' ich nur auf goldnen Höhen	If only I could wander on golden heights
Mich im Morgenduft ergehen!	In the fragrant morning!
Sehnsucht zieht mich himmelwärts.	Yearning draws me heavenwards.

Presumably disturbed by the discrepancy, Schubert returned to the poem two days later in order to compose a setting whose atmosphere derives from the *second* stanza, not the first, and is therefore reflective of the bulk of the poem. This second version, marked "Langsam" and in a far more reverential mood, entirely devoid of the gaiety of the first version, is a foreshadowing of mm. 16–21 of "Morgengruß" (Morning greeting) from *Die schöne Müllerin*, D. 795 of 1823, at the words "So muß ich wieder gehen" (So I must go away). The morning *mise-en-scène* and the shared yearning, albeit for different objects, might well have impelled the harmonic, motivic, figurational, and rhythmic resemblances eight years later.

It seems only appropriate, given Schiller's influence on Körner, that the Körner songs should be enclosed on either side by Schiller settings, including "Des Mädchens Klage" and "Amalia." The Schiller ballad "Die Erwartung" precedes the Körner songs of spring 1815, and "Des Mädchens Klage" and "Der Jüngling am Bache" follow after, indicative of Körner's utility for Schubert: a newly lyrical impulse and a turn towards smaller-scale songs in this miraculous year, although he never abandoned balladesque dramatic composition and would indeed go on to compose "Kolmas Klage," the first of his Ossian settings, in June. In fact, the most ambitious of the Schubert-Körner works is a ballad which exemplifies as well Schubert's lifelong attraction to classical themes: "Amphiaraos," D. 161, composed on 1 March 1815. It gives one cause to think that while Schubert was writing this ballad as fast as his pen could drive across the page (the autograph manuscript tells us that the ballad was composed in five hours), Körner's arch-enemy Napoleon had just escaped from Elba and was en route to France.

1.   According to Greek myth, Amphiaraos was an Argive warrior, the son of Oïcles and Hypermnestra and a descendant of Melampus, who received his gift of second sight from Zeus and became the great diviner of his day. He drove Adrastus from the throne of Argos, but the quarrel was patched up, and Amphiaraos married Adrastus' sister Eriphyle. Later, knowing that only Adrastus would survive the campaign of the "Seven against Thebes" (the subject and title of a play by Aeschylus which Körner might well have known), he at first refused to join it, but Eriphyle, bribed by Polyneices, forced him to go; one of the marriage stipulations was that Eriphyle's

decision should prevail in any dispute between the brothers-in-law. Amphiaraos made his sons, Alcmeon and Amphilochus, vow to avenge him and then departed, warning repeatedly of impending disaster. The Theban warrior Periclymenus finally overcame Amphiaraos by the banks of the Ismenus, but Zeus saved his protégé by splitting the earth with a thunderbolt, creating an abyss into which Amphiaraos vanished.

Körner, I would guess, saw himself reflected and magnified tenfold in this myth, especially in the Cassandra-motif of the seer who foretells his own death. In the Greek heroic ethos, heroes seek immortality, and Amphiaraos resolves to attain glory by means of a death worthy of Apollo's son – yet another source of Körner's identification with this figure, since Körner too was a poet (a "son of Apollo") who sought a glorious death. (Humility was not demanded of Apollo's scions, hymned here in such phrases as "his great soul … a godlike heart … sacred words … bathed in the holy scent of truth.") With the boldness of youth, Körner half-challenged, half-copied the Dioscurii of his generation, Schiller and Goethe, both of whom peer from behind this ballad: the young hero of Schiller's "Der Taucher" likewise plunges into a maelstrom of death, while Amphiaraos outracing Time, Fate, and all other cosmic forces except death seems akin to Goethe's "son of Apollo" hurtling through life and onwards to death in "An Schwager Kronos."

Vor Thebens siebenfach gähnenden Toren	Outside Thebes' seven gaping gates
Lag im furchtbaren Brüderstreit	Lay, in grim fraternal combat,
Das Heer der Fürsten zum Schlagen bereit,	the princes' armies, ready for battle,
Im heiligen Eide zum Morde verschworen.	and sworn in sacred oath to murder.
Und mit des Panzers blendendem Licht	And clad in dazzling armor,
Gerüstet, als gält' es, die Welt zu bekriegen,	as if intent on conquering the world,
Träumen sie jauchzend von Kämpfen und Siegen,	they dream, rejoicing, of battle and victory,
Nur Amphiaraos, der Herrliche, nicht.	all but the noble Amphiaraos.
Denn er liest in dem ewigen Kreise der Sterne,	For he reads in the eternal course of the stars
Wen die kommenden Stunden feindlich	whom the approaching hours threaten
bedrohn.	with an inimical fate.
Des Sonnenlenkers gewaltiger Sohn	The mighty son of the sun's master sees
Sieht klar in der Zukunft nebelnde Ferne.	clearly into the mists of the distant future.
Er kennt des Schicksals verderblichen Bund,	He understands Fate's pernicious bond,
Er weiss, wie die Würfel, die eisernen, fallen,	he knows how the iron dice fall,
Er sieht die Moira mit blutigen Krallen;	he beholds Fate with her bloody claws;
Doch die Helden verschmähen den heiligen	yet the heroes scorn his sacred words.
Mund.	
Er sah des Mordes gewaltsame Taten,	He saw mighty murderous deeds,
Er wusste, was ihm die Parze spann.	he knew what fate was spinning for him.
So gang er zum Kampf, ein verlor'ner Mann,	Thus he went to battle, a doomed man,
Von dem eig'nen Weibe schmählich verraten.	shamefully betrayed by his own wife.
Er war sich der himmlischen Flamme bewusst,	He was aware of the heavenly flame which
Die heiss die kräftige Seele durchglühte;	burned hotly through his great soul.
Der Stolze nannte sich Apolloide,	The proud man called himself the son of
Es schlug ihm ein göttliches Herz in der Brust.	Apollo; a godlike heart beat in his breast.

"Wie? – ich, zu dem die Götter geredet,
Den der Wahrheit heilige Düfte umwehn,
Ich soll in gemeiner Schlacht vergehn,
Von Periklymenos' Hand getötet?
Verderben will ich durch eig'ne Macht,
Und staunend vernehm' es die kommende Stunde
Aus künftiger Sänger geheiligtem Munde,
Wie ich kühn mich gestürzt in die ewige Nacht."

Und als der blutige Kampf begonnen,
Und die Eb'ne vom Mordgeschrei widerhallt,
So ruft er verzweifelnd: "Es naht mit Gewalt,
Was mir die untrügliche Parze gesponnen.
Doch wogt in der Brust mir ein göttliches Blut,
Drum will ich auch wert der Erzeugers
    verderben."
Und wandte die Rosse auf Leben und Sterben,
Und jagt zu des Stromes hochbrausender Flut.

Wild schnauben die Hengste, laut rasselt der
    Wagen,
Das Stampfen der Hufe zermalmet die Bahn.
Und schneller und schneller noch rast es heran,
Als gält' es, die flüchtige Zeit zu erjagen.
Wie wenn er die Leuchte des Himmels geraubt,
Kommt er in Wirbeln der Windsbraut geflogen;
Erschrocken heben die Götter der Wogen
Aus schäumenden Fluten das schilfichte Haupt.

Doch plötzlich, als wenn der Himmel erglühte,
Stürzt ein Blitz aus der heitern Luft,
Und die Erde zerreisst sich zur furchtbaren
    Kluft;
Da rief laut jauchzend der Apolloide:
"Dank dir, Gewaltiger! fest steht mir der
    Bund.
Dein Blitz ist mir der Unsterblichkeit Siegel;
Ich folge dir, Zeus!" – und er fasste die Zügel
Und jagte die Rosse hinab in den Schlund.[111]

"What? I, whom the gods have addressed,
bathed in the holy scent of truth,
am I to perish in mean battle,
slain by Periclymenos's hand?
I wish to die by the power of my own hand.
Future ages will hear in amazement
from the sacred lips of minstrels,
how I plunged boldly into eternal night."

And when the bloody battle began,
and the plain echoed with murderous cries,
he called out, despairing: "What unerring
Fate has spun for me now approaches with
mighty force. But divine blood flows in
my breast, thus will my death be worthy of
my progenitor." And he turned his horses
    around, for life or for death,
and raced to the river's high-surging flood.

The stallions snort fiercely, the chariot
    loudly rattles,
stamping hooves pound the path.
Faster and faster they approach, as if
attempting to catch fleeting Time itself.
As if he had stolen the torch of heaven,
he rushes onward in a seething whirlwind.
Horrified, the gods of the waves raise their
reed-covered heads from the foaming floods.

But suddenly, as if the heavens were afire,
a thunderbolt falls from the clear air;
the earth is ripped open, a horrifying abyss
    appears.
Then, rejoicing, the son of Apollo loudly
cried: "I thank you, mighty one! My
    covenant stands firm.
Your thunderbolt is my seal of immortality.
I follow you, Zeus!" – and he seized the
reins and spurred his horses down into the
    abyss.

The image of the gaping gates in the first line is striking: in one telling adjective, Körner makes evident the vulnerability of the city. The murderous armies have seven open points of ingress to a city that itself seems a fatally wounded entity, already rent asunder. But despite that evocative opening and Körner's evident familiarity with the conventions of balladry, the work is marred by a revealing flaw. Ballads are customarily narrated by an unidentified poetic speaker who describes an episode from the past, the intermeshed temporal zones thus endemic to the genre. Here, however, Körner veers back and forth in an inconsistent, uncontrolled way between narration in the past and present tenses, whether due to ineptitude or too much identification with the subject – the boundaries between balladesque past and Körner's own foretold fate blurred – or both cannot be determined. The swerve from past to present happens for the first time in stanza 1, in mid-*mise-en-scène* (before one would expect the shift to occur in most ballads) and is emphasized by the concatenation of present-tense verbs in stanza 2 ("reads ... sees ... understands ... knows ... beholds," verbs which underscore Amphiaraos' oracular gifts). In stanza 3, the poet reverts to past-tense narration, then has Amphiaraos himself speak in tones of Promethean scorn and in the present tense in stanza 4 (Prometheus is specifically invoked in stanza 6, line 5: "As if he had stolen the torch of heaven"). The ride into the abyss is depicted in detail and in the present tense in stanza 6 – one notes the striving for epic language in such phrases as "Wild schnauben die Hengste, laut rasselt der Wagen" – before reverting to past tense for the plunge into the chasm. If the vacillation is confusing, it is also touching, if one interprets it as mirroring the poet's identification with the mythic hero. For Körner too, "the convenant stood firm."

Did Schubert read "Amphiaraos" against the backdrop of Körner's own awareness of impending death when the two "murderous armies" of the French allied forces and the Prussians clashed? A fraught, heroic atmosphere prevails in this poem, with no let-up; throughout its entire rattling, clanking amplitude, the ballad affords no opportunities for lyrical interludes, no episodes of "pure song." The banishment of any feminine element (the mention of the wife's perfidy – Körner's poetic persona does not even deign to name her – in stanza 3 only underscores the hyper-masculinity of it all) or even any comrades and the hopelessness of the war preclude any relaxation of tension and temperature. Instead, passages of dramatic recitative alternate with motivic development in a wonderfully flexible way, the one acceding to the other in mid-sentence on occasion. Given Schiller's influence on Körner, it seems only appropriate that Schubert's setting of "Amphiaraos," although self-sufficient in its own right, is also in certain details a preliminary study for his setting of Schiller's "Gruppe aus dem Tartarus," D. 583 of 1817. For example, the setting of stanza 1 of "Amphiaraos" ends in mm. 23–25 with a half-cadence and a fermata-sustained pause, followed by the singer chanting "Denn er liest in dem ewigen Kreise" while the pianist plays a figure premonitory of the similar invocation of Eternity's great wheeling circles at the end of "Gruppe aus dem Tartarus." One notices as well the resemblance between the semitone motive in the piano at mm. 55–58 ("So ging er zum Kampf, ein verlor'ner Mann") with the piano figuration in "Gruppe aus dem Tartarus" at the words "Schmerz verzerret ihr Gesicht" in which the newly dead are impelled to their dread destination (ex. 16). Despite such motivic similarities and the typically Schubertian dramatic nature of the music for both works, they represent different genres: "Amphiaraos" is a dramatic ballad with a single larger-than-life poetic persona at the center of the tale while Schiller's smaller poem is neither narrative in the same sense nor dominated by one giant figure. Indeed, its power derives in some measure from the faceless anonymity of the massed souls Schiller so vividly invokes.

Example 16. Franz Schubert, "Amphiaraos," D. 161 of 1 March 1815, mm. 54–9. Franz Schubert, "Gruppe aus dem Tartarus," D. 583 to a text by Friedrich Schiller, mm. 21–25, from *Neue Schubert-Ausgabe*, Series IV: *Lieder*, vol. 2a, ed. Walther Dürr.

"Amphiaraos" is set in G minor and tonally closed, ending in the same key in which it began, unlike many ballads but chillingly appropriate for this one; Amphiaraos, after all, knows at the start of the ballad that he is to die at this time and in this place, and at the end, he does so. This is not a tonal journey to a destination unknown at the start, like "Der Taucher," but a study in inevitability, the end announced at the beginning. Schubert establishes a portentous, prophetic atmosphere in the piano introduction (mm. 1–5) by means of the mid-measure *forzando* D's and F's high in the treble – the root of the chord, but poised insistently above the level of the martial dotted chords in rising sequence. In retrospect, one hears it simultaneously as the clarion call of Nemesis, appropriately placed above the clamor of human strife, and an insistent tocsin sounding the knell of war, its bitterness and increasing nearness evident in the grinding downbeat dissonances of mm. 4–5. This dramatic passage for the piano, which recurs transposed downward in mm. 12–16, can perhaps be heard as Schubert's vision of an oath-taking ceremony ("im heiligen Eide zum Morde verschworen"), the solemnity and dark violence of the occasion rendered explicit in tones. The "Kraft," or strength, Schubert desired from the performers is implicit in this arresting beginning.

But if the deadly outcome is foretold and the formal structure subsequently plotted as a closed circle, that does not mean an abnegation of chromatic turbulence within those boundaries. This ballad is also exemplary of Schubert's fascination with incessant harmonic and tonal activity in his dramatic lieder after the model of Johann Rudolf Zumsteeg modernised; the radical modulatory motion, the insistence on change, struck some of Schubert's contemporaries as downright eccentric. There is, in this context, something of the inevitability of the forces propelling Amphiaraos to his rendezvous with Death conveyed in the lack of tonal resting places, and yet Schubert does not allow the episodic sectionalization of balladry to become haphazard. The mid-measure prophetic "tolling pitches" reappear in stanza 2, and the military-band dotted rhythmic patterns help to unify the setting of stanzas 1 and 2 and the first four lines of stanza 3 (mm. 1–61), Schubert thus drawing a dividing line between the events leading to Amphiaraos's departure ("So ging er zum Kampf, ein verlor'ner Mann") and the hero's first speech. As so often when Schubert evokes a specific image in his chosen poetry, one catches a glimpse of his own views: his mockery of martial braggadocio and stupidity is perhaps evident in the parade of unvarying B-flat tonic and dominant chords in mm. 20–21 at the words "träumen sie jauchzend von Kämpfen und Siegen." Körner, even in his most rousingly thunderous recruiting poems, never forgot, as these soldiers do, that gore, Bacchic frenzy, and death are the stuff of war. Only Amphiaraos knows the dark truth, and Schubert accordingly heralds him as a hero, trumpeting his name aloud to pitches starkly unharmonized until the diminished sevenths beneath the proclamatory, sustained -a of "Amphiaraos" turn brusquely away from the B-flat clichés. The parallelisms in stanza 2 ("Er kennt … er weiß … er sieht"), recounting those truths only Amphiaraos can discern, are set in mm. 40–45 as a continuation of the dotted rhythmic patterns but with the voice ranging, first down, then up, in arpeggiated configurations, as if to suggest the breadth and depth of the seer's knowledge. Where the other heroes reject Amphiaraos' visions, Schubert turns to recitative, thus bringing narrative to the fore, and turns the flats of the prophet's dark truths into sharps, G-flat major becoming F-sharp major in a visual-verbal-tonal symbol of the soldiers' rejection, of the way in which they transmute Amphiaraos' message to mean something altogether different.

When Amphiaraos himself speaks, the military dotted rhythms are banished; instead, one finds the tremolando chords by which Schubert conveys the turbulent energies of characters such as Atlas or Prometheus and, later, the Fate-induced inner chaos of Mignon as she cries, "Es schwindelt mir, es brennt mein Eingeweide." In Amphiaraos' speech in mm. 75–85, the same enharmonic opposition of truth and delusion previously encountered in mm. 40–48 returns, albeit varied. When Amphiaraos invokes the "holy breezes of Truth" ("den der Wahrheit heilige Düfte umwehn"), the harmonies change momentarily from F-sharp minor chords to darker flatted harmonies, leading to E-flat minor once again, before the mention of Periclymenos, Amphiaraos' appointed killer, returns us to F-sharp major, identifying Fate's assassin among those heroes who scorn the seer's words – typical of the subtle laws of recurrence operating in this ballad. In still another example of similar connecting links, the phrases in mm. 86–92 ("Verderben will ich durch eigene Macht, und staunend vernehm' es die kommende Stunde … "), especially at the beginning, are an altered reprise of the figures from mm. 40–45, the dotted rhythmic pounding chords in the accompaniment (mm. 86–87) more insistent than before and the vocal line again traversing an arpeggiated harmony up-and-down. The section ends with Amphiaraos' words "die ewige Nacht," which Schubert sets as a half-cadence in G minor, ending with an Italian sixth chord and the dominant of G: Night/Death has not yet arrived, but Amphiaraos confronts it directly. Not until the protagonist hurls himself into the abyss does Schubert complete a G minor cadence; none of the seething diminished seventh chords and secondary dominants in the battle scene, which begins in the piano alone with a virtuoso display of Beethovenian arpeggiated rampaging in contrary motion (mm. 93–101), resolves.

The stark, skeletal, triplet figuration that begins in m. 116 as Amphiaraos spurs his horses into action is a preliminary to similar figuration through Schubert's setting, ten years later, of Ernst Schulze's "Über Wildemann," D. 884 (see chapter 4) and in the setting of stanza 5 ("Die kalten Winde bliesen") of "Der Lindenbaum" from *Winterreise*. In all three, the associations are similar: furious, driven motion and Death. But what follows the foaming, rising, dissonance-ridden trills that tell of the water-gods' shock in mm. 135–42 seems, as Graham Johnson has pointed out, perfunctory, "plötzlich" indeed and at a lower level of inspiration than elsewhere in the ballad. The setting of Amphiaraos' cry of triumph as he prepares to follow Zeus into the abyss ("Dank dir, Gewaltiger! fest steht der Bund ... ") is in the B-flat major tonality associated in stanza 1 with heroic dreams of glory and victory – no longer a simple soldier's dream but a hero's reality; one notes in particular the wonderfully dramatic deceptive motion to a G-flat major chord at the word "[Unsterblichkeit] Siegel," as if to set a very heavy seal indeed on the passage. The narrator's final words recounting, as tersely as possible, the ride into the abyss turn the B-flat major of heroic victory into the achieved G minor of Death.

2.   Schubert's second Körner song was entirely unlike "Amphiaraos": a small comic song, "Das war ich" (That was I), D. 174, composed 26 March. In this poem, the poetic persona tells his beloved about his recent dream of her, framed on either side by the dream-embrace at the beginning (stanza 1) and the waking vision of an embrace at the end (stanza 4). The poetic dream – too ordered and purposeful, its goal seduction, to be credible as a "real" dream – is prefaced by the coy evasion, designed to spare maidenly modesty for a moment or two, that the dream-woman merely *resembles* the beloved to an extraordinary degree. Stanza 2 is an archetypal rescue-scenario: the frail maiden of male fantasy is about to be swept away by a floodtide (of passion) and the youth rescues her. It is Love, itself unfettered but binding together youth and maiden, that he faithfully serves, he declares, and yet the chief hallmark of "Das war ich" is delighted narcissism, partly-comic, partly-sweet. "And that was me!", the protagonist announces over and over, impressed at thus finding himself at the center of each romantic image (the sweetheart *does* receive her due – Schubert did not set the pendant poem, "Das warst du," but numerous other composers did). Young love *is*, cynics might say, compounded in greater or lesser measure of narcissism, and Körner indeed seems very young in this poem.

Jüngst träumte mir, ich sah auf lichten Höhen
Ein Mädchen sich im jungen Tag ergehen,
So hold, so süss, dass es dir völlig glich.
Und vor ihr lag ein Jüngling auf den Knieen,
Er schien sie sanft an seine Brust zu ziehen,
Und das war ich.

Recently I dreamt I saw on sunlit heights
a maiden wandering in the early morning, so
gentle, so sweet, that she looked just like you.
Before her knelt a youth,
he seemed to draw her gently to his breast;
And that was I.

Doch bald verändert hatte sich die Szene,
In tiefen Fluten sah ich jetzt die Schöne,
Wie ihr die letzte, schwache Kraft entwich,
Da kam ein Jüngling hülfreich ihr geflogen,
Er sprang ihr nach und trug sie aus den
  Wogen,
Und das war ich!

But soon the scene had changed. I now saw
that beautiful maiden in the deep flood, how
her last remnant of strength was deserting her.
Then a youth rushed to help her;
he plunged in after her and bore her from
  the waves,
And that was I!

So malte sich der Traum in bunten Zügen,
Und überall sah ich die Liebe siegen,
Und alles, alles drehte sich um dich!
Du flogst voran in ungebund'ner Freie,
Der Jüngling zog dir nach mit stiller Treue,
Und das war ich!

Thus the dream was painted in bright colors,
Everywhere I saw Love victorious,
and everything was centered on you!
You sailed on, free and unfettered,
The youth followed you, silently and faithfully,
And that was I.

Und als ich endlich aus dem Traum erwachte,
Der neue Tag die neue Sehnsucht brachte,
Da blieb dein liebes, süsses Bild um mich.
Ich sah dich von der Küsse Glut erwarmen,
Ich sah dich selig in des Jünglings Armen
Und das war ich![112]

And when I finally awoke from my dream,
the new day brought new yearning.
Your dear, sweet image was still with me.
I saw you warmed by the fire of his kisses
I saw you blissful in that youth's arms,
And that was I!

Schubert seems to have understood this poem both as a miniature allegory of Every(young)man's love and the "Ewig-Weibliche" which draws him onward and upward and, perhaps, as a reminiscence of Körner himself. He even employs the "Fate" rhythmic motive of a dotted quarter note and three eighth notes that he would later use in "Der Zwerg" and the Mignon song "So lasst mich scheinen, bis ich werde," in which fate equals death; the pattern unifies both halves of the strophe, the "feminine" half in which the maiden is first described (mm. 1–9, with *pianissimo* dynamics, the texture light and clear, the motion gently flowing) and the "masculine" half (mm. 10–15, filled with *forte-piano*, crescendo, and *sforzando* articulations, more agitated motion, fuller textures) devoted to "das Jüngling auf den Knieen." Whether that particular compositional decision in "Das war ich" was dictated, consciously or unconsciously, by the composer's awareness of Körner's death must remain speculative, but it is a tempting supposition. The indication "erzählend" (in a storytelling manner) is rare in Schubert, both appropriate for the retelling of dreams – always recounted as stories – and, perhaps, for the retelling of a bygone romance which actually happened to someone Schubert knew.

Like most of the Körner songs, "Das war ich" is a strict strophic form and was evidently composed with the words of stanza 1 in mind, the music somewhat less apt for the subsequent three verses. The first half of stanza 1 establishes the *mise-*

en-scène (akin to Mount Parnassus? given Körner's need to insist upon his poetic vocation, the supposition seems likely) and the maiden's presence in a quietly flowing G major passage that never pauses, except for the gentlest of phrase articulations, until the half-cadence at m. 9. This Arcadian dream of blessedness has a placid *gehende Bewegung*, one episode flowing peacefully into the next. The first two symmetrical four-bar phrases, alike but for their endings, are slightly darkened by passing tone E-flats in the inner voice of the piano part (mm. 2 and 5), shading the subdominant chord to minor and foreshadowing the more preponderant minor harmonies of the second half. Minor harmonies are clearly the sounding symbol of youthful, stormy, male passion, already hinted at the beginning of the dream, then bursting forth into full flower in the second half. That passion is forecast not only in the tinges of minor but in the rhythmic diminution of the setting of line 3, "So hold, so süß, daß es dir völlig glich." The melodic line is lifted into a higher tessitura at the words "so gentle, so sweet," as if in rapture, while the rhythmic pattern established in the first two phrases is here compressed and quickened ("daß es dir völlig glich"); those sixteenth notes in m. 8 then become the throbbing chordal figures in the second half.

Both in "Das war ich" and "Liebesrausch," new-found lover's ecstasy is expressed in thrumming chordal figures for the right-hand part, filling the air with sound and throbbing pulsation – in this song, the composer accepts Körner's simplistic categories of mellifluous, gentle feminity and somewhat blustering masculinity. Idealistic, youthful passion takes itself very seriously, so Schubert, whether from fellow feeling or human understanding, invests the harmonic sequences of mm. 10–14 with all the minor-mode coloration due such touching earnestness, with the darkness inherent in passion at any age. The verb "ziehen" ("an seine Brust zu ziehen") is given an appoggiatura raised second degree going to the third scale degree (A-sharp to B, or enharmonically, a hint of the minor mode and B-flat) for additional yearning emphasis – the gesture is inherently "ziehendes" – at the end of a phrase, to match the similar inflection in m. 11 at the word "Knieen." There was a bump, not so much of raw conceit as a strong sense of his own worth, in Körner, evident in the self-satisfied refrain to this poem; Schubert, who did not fail to notice it, emblazons it on the music and even exaggerates it comically. Where Körner merely writes "Und das war ich" at the end of each stanza, Schubert's Körner proclaims "Und das ... " to a *sforzando* subdominant harmony and a dramatic leap of a sixth in the vocal line, followed by the entire refrain. The *piano* dynamics and the high G additionally imply, "Who else could it be but me?" And me and me – the postlude twice more proclaims (softly) "Und das war ich," the sixteenth-note chordal pulsations calmed to broken-chordal figures which are an amalgam of the accompanimental figuration in both halves of the stanza. The instrumental echoes constitute the gentlest of mockery on the composer's part; like Mozart delightedly underscoring Papageno's cowardice and simple self-interest while enlisting our wholehearted allegiance with the bird-catcher's essential goodness, Schubert pokes fun at Körner's narcissism but all in good spirit and with the lightest of touches. Schubert then caps off the song with a charming final gesture: for a dominant seventh chord on the downbeat over a tonic pedal to resolve to tonic on the second or weak beat of the measure (m. 17) is not an uncommon occurrence, but here, the word "ich" resounds in the gesture, emblematic of youthful ardor and egoism. The effect is sweetly comical, the perfect note on which to end this song, and one typical of the lighthearted eroticism in many of Körner's poems. This is the stuff of Singspiele, and Schubert clothes it in appropriately eighteenth-century strains.

3. Körner's poem for "Liebesrausch," D. 179 (this was another of the poems most popular with composers), is disposed in three eight-line stanzas, with the lines in iambic tetrameters, but the poet arrestingly begins with the accented first syllable "Dir," transgressing the meter before it is even established. Love's intoxicating, unsettling power throws him "off his rhythm" immediately. One also notes with amusement how the young poet congratulates himself in this poem, writing of "meine kühne Brust" (my bold heart) and celebrating his own troubadour-like prowess in the songs he composes for the beloved. However, Körner does not rise much above the level of platitude in this love poem, ardent but not inspired. The levelling effect by which love at its most Vesuvian fails to produce the best poetry in ninety-nine out of a hundred cases (the statistical gap is probably even wider than that) is operative here.

Dir, Mädchen, schlägt mit leisem Beben
Mein Herz voll Treu' und Liebe zu.
In dir, in dir versinkt mein Streben,
Mein schönstes Ziel bist du!
Dein Name nur in heil'gen Tönen
Hat meine kühne Brust gefüllt;
Im Glanz des Guten und des Schönen
Strahlt mir dein hohes Bild.

For you, maiden, my heart beats,
gently quivering, filled with love and devotion;
in you, in you, my striving ceases –
you are my life's fairest goal!
Your name alone has filled my bold heart
with sacred tones.
In the radiance of goodness and beauty,
your noble image shines for me.

Die Liebe sproßt aus zarten Keimen,
Und ihre Blüten welken nie!
Du, Mädchen, lebst in meinen Träumen
Mit süßer Harmonie.
Begeist'rung rauscht auf mich hernieder,
Kühn greif' ich in die Saiten ein,
Und alle meine schönsten Lieder,
Sie nennen dich allein.

Love burgeons from tender seeds,
and its blossoms never wither.
You, maiden, live in my dreams
with sweet harmonies.
I am fired with the rapture of inspiration,
Boldly I pluck the strings,
and all my most beautiful songs
utter your name alone.

Mein Himmel glüht in deinen Blicken,
An deiner Brust mein Paradies.
Ach! alle Reize, die dich schmücken,
Sie sind so hold, so süß.
Es wogt die Brust in Freud' und Schmerzen,
Nur eine Sehnsucht lebt in mir,
Nur ein Gedanke hier im Herzen:
Der ew'ge Drang nach dir.

My heaven glows in your eyes,
my paradise is upon your breast.
Ah, all the charms that adorn you
are so fair, so sweet.
My breast surges with joy and pain;
one desire alone dwells within me,
one thought alone lies here in my heart:
eternal yearning for you!

More than Körner, it was Schubert who was "fired with the rapture of inspiration" (stanza 2, line 5, "Begeist'rung rauscht auf mich hernieder"). The verbal phrase that set the song in motion was surely "schlägt mit leisem Beben/ mein Herz" – the triplet chordal eighth notes throughout the song are "heartbeat" pulsations whose thrumming becomes even more urgent in the second half of the stanza, when the left hand as well participates in the threefold animation of every beat. The effect is both reminiscent of another song in which an ardent young poet professes his passion – the Goethe lied "Nähe des Geliebten," D. 162, composed a few weeks earlier on 27 February 1815 – and premonitory of the feverish frustration in "Ungeduld" from *Die schöne Müllerin*. In "Liebesrausch," Schubert for the first time begins a song with the device of a single sustained note or chord in the piano, followed by a fermata-prolonged moment of silence before the texted body of the song ensues and the single initial chord is set into feverish motion. The gesture is dramatic in nature: one imagines the troubadour-poet striking both a loud chord and a loverlike pose before launching into the serenade. Like "Ungeduld," "Liebesrausch" remains in one key throughout the strophe, the lover's single-minded focus on the beloved registered in tonal terms, but moves about restlessly within that key, the changing harmonic inflections of desire acting to destabilize the tonality and disturb it from within. Ardor is immediately evident in the opening leap to high G, the gesture equally apropos to emphasize the words "Dir, *Mäd*-chen" in stanza 1, "Die *Lie*-be" in stanza 2, and "Mein *Him*-mel" in stanza 3; it is also evident in the sequences which fill the entire strophe, rising and falling like the roller-coaster ride that is young love. The music seems tailored most closely to the words of the first strophe, as when Schubert locates the "schönstes Ziel" in mm. 8–9 on B-flat major, the key of the flatted mediant, not the tonic: the "most beautiful goal" – the maiden – has not yet been won and is therefore differentiated from the poet-singer's own G major, the music becoming warmer and softer at the invocation of her beauty.[113] Schubert implies that the poet will make his way to the beloved through painful striving when he darkens G major to G minor en route to the "schönstes Ziel." The brightness of B-natural is reinstated in the second half of the strophe, when light suffuses the images ("Im Glanz des Guten und des Schönen / strahlt mir dein hohes Bild"), and is heightened both in mm. 17–18 at the ecstatic outburst "dein hohes Bild" – "hohe" translated into musical terms – and in the *Schwung*-filled motive echoed between the right and left hands in the postlude.

Schubert borrows the chief compositional gestures of "Liebesrausch" four days later for a passage in his setting of Johann Georg Fellinger's "Die erste Liebe" (First love), D. 182, composed 12 April 1815. At the words "Du siehst nur sie allein im Widerscheine, / Die Holde, der du ganz dich hingegeben" (You see her alone reflected, the fair one to whom you have surrendered yourself) in mm. 31–36, we see a reflection and hear an echo of the Körner lied which likewise tells, if not of "first love," then certainly youthful love (ex. 23). But "Ungeduld" is the culmination of this concatenation of musical symbols for youthful ardor (and it was surely from this model that Schumann found his way to "Frühlingsnacht" at the end of the Eichendorff *Liederkreis*, op. 39); if the Müller-lied is better poetry and music alike than "Liebesrausch," the Körner song is nevertheless an admirable preliminary exercise.

4. Schubert also set Körner's "Sehnsucht der Liebe," D. 180, another song of youthful passion, that same eighth day of April 1815. Here, the poet traces a progression from nightfall to dawn in the course of four stanzas: in stanza 1, night cradles the soul's strivings in sweet slumber and lies gently over the earth; in stanza 3, night goes its quiet path; in stanza 5, humanity and the world scarcely breathe, so deeply immersed are they in slumber; and in the penultimate stanza, "thus the hours go by in their circle until the day dawns in the east." But the poetic persona, although he invokes the sacral quality of nocturnal peace, cannot take part in it because passion does not allow him rest. The change from Nature's nighttime calm to human unrest is heralded by the word "Aber" (But) at the beginnings of stanzas 2 and 4, at which the previous trochaic tetrameters give way to lines lengthened by the addition of dactylic feet. The extra syllables quicken the pace and enliven the rhythm, appropriately so for the restless motions of unstilled desire.

Wie die Nacht mit heil'gem Beben
Auf der stillen Erde liegt!
Wie sie sanft der Seele Streben,
Üpp'ge Kraft und volles Leben
In den süssen Schlummer wiegt!

How with sacred quivering
Night lies over the silent world.
How gently it lulls the soul's strivings,
its abundant strength and rich life
to sweet sleep!

Aber mit ewig neuen Schmerzen
Regt sich die Sehnsucht in meiner Brust.
Schlummern auch alle Gefühle im Herzen,
Schweigt in der Seele Qual und Lust:
Sehnsucht der Liebe schlummert nie,
Sehnsucht der Liebe wacht spät und früh.

But with ever-renewed pain
yearning stirs within my breast.
Though all feeling slumbers in my heart,
though anguish and pleasure are silent in my
soul: Love's yearning never slumbers,
love's yearning lies awake early and late.

Leis', wie Aeolsharfentöne,
Weht ein sanfter Hauch mich an,
Hold und freundlich glänzt Selene,
Und in milder geist'ger Schöne
Geht die Nacht die stille Bahn!

Gently, like the tones from an Aeolian harp,
a soft breeze wafts about me;
friendly Selena shines gently,
and in sweet, spiritual beauty
Night goes its quiet way!

Aber auf kühnen, stürmischen Wegen
Führet die Liebe den trunknen Sinn.
Wie alle Kräfte gewaltig sich regen!
Ach! und die Ruhe der Brust ist dahin!
Sehnsucht der Liebe schlummert nie!
Sehnsucht der Liebe wacht spät und früh!

But on bold, stormy paths
Love leads the enraptured mind.
How all energies are strongly aroused!
Ah! and heart's peace is flown!
Love's yearning never slumbers!
Love's yearning lies awake early and late.

Tief, im süssen, heil'gen Schweigen,
Ruht die Welt und atmet kaum,
Und die schönsten Bilder steigen
Aus des Lebens buntem Reigen,
Und lebendig wird der Traum.

In sweet, sacred silence,
the world rests deeply, scarcely breathing.
The loveliest images arise
from the brightly-colored dance of life,
and dreams come alive.

Aber auch in des Traumes Gestalten	But even amidst the dream-figures,
Winkt mir die Sehnsucht, die schmerzliche, zu,	Yearning beckons sorrowfully to me,
Und ohn' Erbarmen, mit tiefen Gewalten,	and without pity, with profound force,
Stört sie das Herz aus der wonnigen Ruh'.	it wrenches the heart from blissful rest.
Sehnsucht der Liebe schlummert nie,	Love's yearning never slumbers;
Sehnsucht der Liebe wacht spät und früh.	love's yearning lies awake early and late.
So entschwebt der Kreis der Horen,	Thus the hours go by in their circle
Bis der Tag im Osten graut.	until the day dawns in the east;
Da erhebt sich neugeboren	then from the morning's rosy portals
Aus der Morgens Rosenthoren	there arises, new-born, glowing
Glühendhell die Himmelsbraut.	brightly, the heavenly bride.
Aber die Sehnsucht in meinem Herzen	But the yearning in my heart
Ist mit dem Morgen nur stärker erwacht.	awakens more strongly with the morning;
Ewig verjüngen sich meine Schmerzen,	my sorrows are ever rejuvenated,
Quälen den Tag und quälen die Nacht.	troubling the day and troubling the night.
Sehnsucht der Liebe schlummert nie,	Love's yearning never slumbers,
Sehnsucht der Liebe wacht spät und früh.[114]	Love's yearning lies awake early and late.

The contrast between the nocturnal calm and love-born anguish lends itself to a musical strophe likewise split into contrasting sections. The first section, shorter in length but not in duration than the "Schnell" section which follows, begins on a suitably nocturnal E minor, a gentle minor-modal veil lying over the true G major tonality of the song. Schubert must have derived the rising sequence in mm. 6–9 from the words "Seele Streben, / Üpp'ge Kraft und volles Leben," daytime striving and life's energies gently – very gently – invoked in this fashion; by a nice coincidence, it is also suitable for the images of rising motion in lines 3–4 of stanza 5 ("Und die schönsten Bilder steigen / Aus des Lebens buntem Reigen") and stanza 7 ("Da erhebt sich, neugeboren, / Aus des Morgens Rosenthoren"). With the final cadence of the section (mm. 10–12), however, even this quiet motion slows and then stops, the flatted sixth degree E-flat and the lowered third of the tonic chord lulling the music to sleep and darkening it slightly.

After the fermata-sustained pause in m. 13 during which we are invited to imagine everyone else falling asleep (the song falls asleep as well), the contrasting section begins. Schubert makes the contrast as pronounced as possible: cut-time is succeeded by 3/8 meter, the register jolts upward, and full chords give way to a stark unison texture. Even before the word "Aber" is sung, Schubert has the piano plunge downwards, outlining a diminished seventh chord, followed by an F major chord on the word "Aber." This is certainly one sure way of unsettling and displacing G major, especially when the F-natural is sustained for more than a measure and is the highest pitch to that point in the vocal line. The "ewig neuen Schmerzen," ever-new, ever-changing, here become a restless harmonic succession, the dissonance and thrumming beat especially intense at the words "Regt sich die Sehnsucht in meiner Brust." In a variation of the same larger pattern by which slumberous quiet is followed by agitation, the E minor "slumber" harmonies from mm. 1–2 return at the invocation of sleep once again ("Schlummern auch alle Gefühle im Herzen") but with a difference – despite the sustained bass pitches, the throbbing motion on every eighth note beat continues in the right hand, while the vocal line outlines a tritone, subsequently transposed downward for the "easing to sleep" in the words "Schweigt in der Seele Qual und Lust." The setting of the refrain "Sehnsucht der Liebe schlummert nie, / Sehnsucht der Liebe wacht spät und früh" emphasizes the plagal C major harmony avoided until this point in the song.

If there is no piano introduction, there is a lengthy postlude, shading from *piano* to *pianissimo* and concluding with a long-drawn-out plagal cadence. Where Körner insists that desire never sleeps, Schubert thus ends each stanza with a sustained diminuendo, an easing-off to sleep and restfulness. In this lovely passage, typical of Schubert's imaginative additions to his chosen poetry, one hears the composer's voice both depicting the young man falling to sleep at last, his restlessness perhaps eased in the mere telling of its cause, or promising him eventual surcease for his longing. This too is perhaps a poignant reminiscence of Körner himself: Schubert knew that Körner's "yearnings of love" were reciprocated by Antonie Adamberger and that Körner had subsequently died, thus ending all "Sehnsucht" in the ultimate appease-ment of death. Perhaps this revisionary postlude is a wordless elegy for the poet, the musical completion of a poem that ends with its ardor unstilled.

As a teenager, Schubert closely studied the lieder and ballads of Johann Rudolf Zumsteeg, but whether he ever knew any of the lieder by Zumsteeg's daughter Emilie, including her setting of "Sehnsucht der Liebe," op. 6, no. 4 (Stuttgart, G. A. Zumsteeg), is not known. It is, however, a lovely song, within modest boundaries, for mezzo-soprano or contralto (the E a tenth above middle C is its highest pitch), well worthy of revival. Like Schubert's setting, her song is split into an Adagio first half and an Allegro vivace second half which, however, share the same musical material, thus demonstrating the co-existence of nocturnal peace and wakeful human passion. The music she devised for this strophic song was clearly conceived with the first two verses in mind, as the details of word-painting and melodic design correspond exactly to those words and less aptly for the succeeding stanzas. The adjective "heil'gem [Beben]" in m. 1 is inflected by a diminished seventh neighboring harmony and by triplet motion in the vocal line; the same chord enharmonically respelled recurs at the adjective "stillen [Erde]" in m. 3, the composer underscoring the sacral calm by tinting it with chromatic color and at the same time subtly contradicting the assertion of peace. The connotations of disturbance are then made explicit at the beginning of the Allegro vivace when "Aber" resounds *fortissimo* to that same evocative chord. The Adagio section is especially effective, the "soul's strivings" in m. 5 giving rise to an energetic repeated motive spanning a seventh while the section "dies away" in a phrase that begins with a darkened atmosphere created by the flatted sixth degree (Neapolitan to the dominant), sinking back down to the opening C-sharp in the vocal line at the close (mm. 9–13). Emilie reserves "heartbeat" chordal figuration for the refrain, the simplicity particularly effective following the two-against-three rhythmic patterns of the preceding phrase; unlike Schubert, however, there is no consolatory postlude (ex. 17).

Example 17. Emilie Zumsteeg, "Sehnsucht der Liebe," op. 6, no. 4 (Stuttgart, G. A. Zumsteeg), mm. 1–19

Example 17. *cont.*

mei — ner Brust. Schlum-mern auch al — le Ge-füh — le im Her — zen,

5.   On the same day that Schubert set Körner's "Der Morgenstern" and "Lützows wilde Jagd" (26 May 1815), he also set "Liebeständelei" (Flirtation), D. 206, a variation on the familiar "Come and kiss me, sweet and twenty" address to a prospective sweetheart, a bold plea for a kiss which is, in fact, snatched between stanzas 3 and 4 – "*Laß* dich küssen" becomes "*Läßt* dich küssen." In a charming twist on the old theme, the poetic persona tells us in the fourth and final stanza that his song of seduction (Körner, as so often, reminding the reader that he is a poet) was successful, that he has already begun to reap the rewards of his eloquence, cliché-ridden though it is. The poem is thus akin to "Das war ich," with which it shares the same a a b c c b rhyme scheme for its six-line stanzas (lines 1–5 in trochaic tetrameters, the sixth in trochaic dimeters) and the same merry, confident courtship theme. Feminists may also find in this love poem a barely-covert pedagogical intent, a miniature instruction manual on a young woman's "proper" role in life, as well as the assumption that "No" means "Yes" in amatory scenarios, even so lighthearted a one as this; indeed, the assumption is all the more insidious because the context is so sweetly comic. The poet-singer enlists the erotic curiosity of well-bred maidens and tells his beloved that her kisses give him the strength and courage for life (she is to give and exalt, he to take for his own renewal), that the fullness of joy is only to be found in his arms, that her "little heart" must palpitate in time and tune with love, and so on. Not a single cliché is missing.

Süßes Liebchen! Komm' zu mir!	My sweet love! Come to me!
Tausend Küsse geb' ich dir.	I will give you a thousand kisses;
Sieh' mich hier zu deinen Füßen.	see me here at your feet.
Mädchen, deiner Lippen Glut	Maiden, your ardent lips
Gibt mir Kraft und Lebensmut.	give me strength and the courage for life.
Laß dich küssen!	Let me kiss you!
Mädchen, werde doch nicht rot!	Maiden, do not blush!
Wenn's die Mutter auch verbot,	Even though your mother has forbidden it,
Sollst du alle Freuden missen?	are you to forgo all pleasures?
Nur an des Geliebten Brust	Only on your lover's breast
Blüht des Lebens schönste Lust.	does life's most beautiful joy flower.
Laß dich küssen!	Let me kiss you!

Liebchen, warum zierst du dich?
Höre doch und küsse mich.
Willst du nichts von Liebe wissen?
Wogt dir nicht dein kleines Herz
Bald in Freuden, bald in Schmerz?
Laß dich küssen!

My love, why are you so coy?
Listen and kiss me.
Do you wish to know nothing of love?
Does your little heart not surge,
now with pleasure, now with pain?
Let me kiss you!

Sieh', dein Sträuben hilft dir nicht;
Schon hab' ich nach Sängers Pflicht
Dir den ersten Kuß entrissen! –
Und nun sinkst du, liebewarm,
Willig selbst in meinen Arm.
Läßt dich küssen!

See, your reluctance is of no avail;
already, my duty as a singer done,
I have snatched the first kiss from you!
And now, warm with love, you sink
willingly into my arms.
Let me kiss you!

Schubert treats this poem as a tiny (fifteen bars), lighthearted strophic song in the E-flat major horn key he so often associated with his chosen Körner texts. Here, the tonality and everything else in the music recall Papageno, whom one can imagine singing just such a sturdy, folk-like air, but with characteristically Mozartian/young Schubertian text-setting inflections. The first instance of chromaticism (passing motion producing an augmented triad), for example, occurs at the first invocation of the word "Küsse" in m. 3, and when the poetic protagonist kneels, lover-like, at her feet, an appoggiatura-inflected diminished seventh chord emphasizes the word "hier" – he wants satisfaction for his yearning immediately, here and now. There is a delightfully comic dramatic pause in m. 6 during the fermata-prolonged, proclamatory dominant chord at the end of the phrase ("Füssen" heightened still further by a yearningd $\hat{6} - \hat{5}$ appoggiatura in the vocal line); one can virtually see the young man puckering up and waiting for the expected response/resolution. When the desired result is not instantly forthcoming, he resumes the attack, animating the right-hand part with greater motion, sending the vocal line climbing higher than before, and insisting on the dominant pitch in the bass, like a drumbeat of desire, in mm. 6–10. The motion runs right into the multiply repeated pleas, "Lass dich küssen" (this time, the young man is not relying on the maiden to infer what he wants but instead comes right out with an imperative demand), with the emphasis – harmonic and otherwise – on the verb "Lass." She, after all, has to accede. The B-natural of "Küsse" in m. 3 is here respelled as C-flat pitches in accented, mid-measure diminished seventh chords (neighboring harmonies to tonic first-inversion chords). At the third and final plea, "Lass" is comically extended throughout five beats en route to tonic resolution, followed by a minimal instrumental flourish of triumph – this is an impatient young man, his leap of joy typically brief. Even before the dénoument in stanza 4, the poetic protagonist is confident of success. Still another fermata is placed over the quarter-note rest at the very end of the strophe, yet another expectant pause as the suitor waits to hear whether his words have had the desired effect and the maiden will proffer her lips. This song may be undeniably slight, but it is not lacking in dramatic imagination – a charming instance of *Die Zauberflöte's Nachklänge* in Schubert's Vienna.

6. Almost five months later on 15 October 1815, Schubert would return to Körner for a similar comic-erotic piece, "Das gestörte Glück" (Troubled happiness), D. 309, about a young man who wants very badly to kiss his sweetheart but is prevented from doing so time and again. Each effort to kiss his Röschen comes to nought: a pin in her waistband scratches him, and he runs home to bandage it; her old dog bites him in the leg; the ladder he uses in order to climb up to her window, at her invitation, breaks under him; and, to cap it all off, her father appears when he finally manages to embrace her. The maiden comes right out of German folk literature, a stouthearted, sensual creature who is well able to defend herself against hot-blooded importunities and yet eager for them – on her own terms. The young man's self-congratulatory words, "I am very good at kissing," is a delightful comic touch, as is the exaggerated mock-pity and the Cherubino-like invitation to any and all women to kiss him quickly and put him out of his misery. Perhaps the funniest detail of all is the poetic persona's confiding tone: he admits everyone into his confidence, telling them straightaway, with more pride than ruefulness, that he is young and has sex very much on his mind.

Ich hab' ein heisses junges Blut,	I'm young and hot-blooded,
Wie ihr wohl alle wisst,	as you all know,
Ich bin dem Küssen gar zu gut,	and very good at kissing,
Und hab' noch nie geküsst;	yet have never kissed;
Denn ist mir auch mein Liebchen hold,	for although my maiden cares for me,
'Swar doch, als wenn's nicht werden sollt;	it seems as though it will not happen:
Trotz aller Müh' und aller List,	In spite of all my pains and all my cunning,
Hab ich doch niemals noch geküsst.	I've never kissed her.
Des Nachbars Röschen ist mir gut;	Rosie, our neighbor's daughter, is fond of me;
Sie ging zur Wiese früh,	she went to the meadow early one morning,
Ich lief ihr nach und fasste Mut,	I ran after her and took courage
Und schlang den Arm um sie:	and put my arm around her.
Da stach ich an dem Miederband	But then I pricked my hand
Mir eine Nadel in die Hand;	on a pin in her bodice,
Das Blut lief stark, ich sprang nach Haus,	the blood gushed out, I rushed home,
Und mit dem Küssen war es aus.	and that was the end of kissing.
Jüngst ging ich so zum Zeitvertreib,	Recently I went out to pass the time
Und traf sie dort am Fluss,	and met her there at the river.
Ich schlang den Arm um ihren Leib,	I put my arms around her body
Und bat um einen Kuss;	and begged her for a kiss.
Sie spitzte schon den Rosenmund,	She had already pursed up her rosy lips,
Da kam der alte Kettenhund,	when along came her old watch-dog
Und biss mich wüthend in das Bein!	and bit me furiously in the leg!
Da liess ich wohl das Küssen sein.	Then I left off kissing well and truly.
Drauf sass ich einst vor ihrer Tür	Once I sat in front of her door
In stiller Freud' und Lust,	in quiet happiness and joy.
Sie gab ihr liebes Händchen mir,	She gave me her darling little hands,
Ich zog sie an die Brust:	I drew her to my breast:

Da sprang der Vater hinter'm Tor,	Then her father sprang out from behind the door,
Wo er uns längst belauscht', hervor,	where he had been eavesdropping for a long time,
Und wie gewöhnlich war der Schluss:	and the end was just as usual:
Ich kam auch um den dritten Kuss.	The third kiss was lost.
Erst gestern traf ich sie am Haus,	Just yesterday I met her at the house;
Sie rief mich leis' herein:	she called softly to me to come in:
"Mein Fenster geht in 'n Hof hinaus,	"My window goes out into the yard,
Heut' Abend wart' ich dein."	this evening I will wait for you."
Da kam ich denn in Liebeswahn,	When I came, mad with love,
Und legte meine Leiter an;	and put up my ladder,
Doch unter mir brach sie entzwei,	it broke under me,
Und mit dem Küssen war's vorbei.	and kissing was over.
Und allemal geht mir's nun so;	Every time it's the same;
O! dass ich's leiden muss!	How I suffer!
Mein Lebtag werd' ich nimmer froh,	I shall never in my life be happy
Krieg' ich nicht bald 'nen Kuss.	if I don't get a kiss soon.
Das Glück sieht mich so finster an,	Fate is so unkind to me:
Was hab' ich armer Wicht getan?	what have I, poor wretch, done?
Drum, wer es hört, erbarme sich,	So whoever hears this, take pity on me,
Und sei so gut, und küsse mich.[115]	be kind and kiss me.

Schubert matches the merriment of the poem in music of similar lighthearted perfection. In a rustic F major, it begins without a piano introduction, and the folk-like character is further confirmed in the doubling of the vocal part, the syllabic text-setting, the symmetrical phrases, the lightness and clarity of texture, and the *Schwung*-filled 6/8 rhythms. Where it is not folk-like is in the self-evident artistry of the compositional choices, the same true of the poem as well: a Schillerian epigone and modern composer join forces, aping country strains in a sophisticated way in order to tell merry truths about archetypal young men. For example, the lilt and lift imparted by the opening leap of a fifth from the tonic to the dominant pitches is the first of many happy compositional choices in "Das gestörte Glück"; this is then matched by the descending fifth at the start of the consequent phrase, the descending interval placed much higher. For the second group of paired phrases, we hear a slightly ornamented variation of the first pair, ending with a turn to the dominant, the initial kick upwards embroidered with more of the sixteenth notes first heard in the bubbly little piano interlude in m. 4 and the second leap of the fifth transformed by *Terzensteigerung* of the first pitch F into a leap of a seventh from high A — emphasis indeed for the crucial words "*und* hab' noch nie geküsst." Placing the high A on the anacrusis, on the sixth and weakest beat of m. 6, is a delightfully comic touch. The arpeggiated fillip in the piano in m. 8, the smallest of interludes, would later reappear in "Mit dem grünen Lautenbande" from *Die schöne Müllerin* — an exuberant little figure.

To this point, the song is a charming trifle, but from m. 9 to the end, Schubert adds a plethora of particularly delightful details. When the young man plaintively laments his lack of success in obtaining a kiss, even though his sweetheart is fond of him, the composer devises a chromatic sequence of first inversion and incomplete seventh chords, the dominant harmonies each intensified by its Neapolitan neighbor, but the effect is remarkably unmournful. The motion rises and falls like the young man's fortunes, while the secondary dominant chords in mm. 11–13 are all the more irresistible for the bubbling triplet ornaments in the right-hand part. "Trotz aller Müh" (Despite all my trouble) in m. 14 is set as stark unison texture but the grace-noted emphasis on "*al*-ler" sounds more merry than miserable. As a final mock-lamenting fillip, the piano twice repeats a variant of the words "und hab' noch nie geküsst" in the postlude, with the distinctive anacrusis on high A to identify the provenance from earlier in the stanza, but somehow, one doubts the young man's unkissed condition will last for long: such single-mindedness and ingenuity, such infectious high spirits, are assured of eventual success. Certainly Schubert thought so.

7. If Körner's comic Muse tickled Schubert's fancy that October day in 1815, he was also moved to set another poem in praise of love, but this time in a serious vein: the "Wiegenlied" (Cradle Song), D. 304.

Schlummre sanft! – Noch an dem Mutterherzen	Slumber softly! While on your mother's heart,
Fühlst du nicht des Lebens Qual und Lust;	you do not feel life's pain and joy,
Deine Träume kennen keine Schmerzen	your dreams know no sorrows,
Deine Welt ist deiner Mutter Brust.	your world is your mother's breast.
Ach! wie süß träumt man die frühen Stunden,	Ah, how sweetly one dreams in those early
Wo man von der Mutterliebe lebt;	hours when we live by our mother's love;
Die Erinnerung ist mir verschwunden,	my memory of them has vanished,
Ahndung bleibt es nur, die mich durchbebt.	only an impression remains to move me.
Dreimal darf der Mensch so süß erwarmen,	Three times may a man experience such
Dreimal ist's dem Glücklichen erlaubt,	sweet warmth; three times the happy man is
Daß er in der Liebe Götterarmen	allowed to believe in the higher meaning of
An des Lebens höh're Deutung glaubt.	life, cradled in love's divine arms.
Liebe gibt ihm ihren ersten Segen,	Love gives him her first blessing,
Und der Säugling blüht in Freud' und Lust,	and the infant blossoms in joy and happiness.
Alles lacht dem frischen Blick entgegen;	Everything smiles at his fresh gaze;
Liebe hält ihn an der Mutterbrust.	love holds him to his mother's breast.
Wenn sich dann der schöne Himmel trübte,	Then, when the beautiful heavens darken,
Und wenn wölkt sich nun des Jünglings Lauf:	and the youth's path grows clouded,
Da, zum zweiten Mal, nimmt als Geliebte	then, for the second time, love takes him
Ihn die Lieb' in ihre Arme auf.	as her sweetheart in her arms.
Doch im Sturme bricht der Blütenstengel,	But in the storm the flower's stem breaks,
Und im Sturme bricht des Menschen Herz:	and in the storm a man's heart breaks:
Da erscheint die Lieb' als Todesengel,	then love appears as the angel of death
Und sie trägt ihn jubelnd himmelwärts.[116]	and bears him jubilantly to heaven.

No one who knew Körner's fate could have read this without seeing the poet's own life reflected in it. Here, Körner writes a paean to his extraordinary family, in particular, his mother Minna, and converts the familiar theme of "The Three Ages of Man" into "The Three Faces of Love": mother, sweetheart, angel of death. He writes as someone surveying his life from a peak on the border of another world; such surveys are usually the privilege of the old, but Körner, with his uncanny prescience of death, bids the Parcae wield their shears early. In this miniature allegory, he writes as if *his* experiences of love were universal, although he admits the existence of clouded skies after the cloudless Elysium of childhood. If the poem is an idealisation of childhood and love at one level, it is, in fact, true to what we know of his own circumstances.

Schubert, whose mother Elisabeth Vietz died in 1812, might have been drawn to the poem for its evocation of mother-love (if one is lucky enough to have enjoyed a childhood like Körner's), as well as the prophetic summation of Körner's life and early death. The setting in F major, the same key Schubert would later use for the setting of Mayrhofer's "Schlaflied," is without piano introduction, like his setting of Stoll's "An die Geliebte" and "Labetrank der Liebe," Fellinger's "Die Sternenwelten," Johann von Kalchberg's "Die Macht der Liebe," and Deinhardstein's "Skolie" that same October day, replete with song, and many of the other strophic lieder of 1815. Of the 15 October songs, only the delightful "Mein Gruss an den Mai" begins with what would become the more characteristic introductory statement in the piano of the principal musical material of the song. Körner writes the poem in trochaic pentameters, and Schubert then converts them into asymmetrical phrases, remarkable because there is so little regularity to balance the asymmetry and yet one's impression of the song when one hears or plays it is not one of imbalance. The first line of text consumes three full measures; Schubert then elides lines 2 and 3 to produce a five-measure phrase, followed by two statements of line 4, each three measures long, although the second and concluding statement is elongated and elided with the piano postlude. Did Schubert perhaps intend the asymmetrical phrasing to convey something of the sense of disturbance at the heart of this seemingly fatalistic poem, enveloped in a Titian-like golden haze of nostalgic melancholy (from a twenty-year-old!), or was it purely a prosodic exigency? Certainly the asymmetrical phrasing qualifies the hymn-like aura of the lied.

Schubert was perhaps not only drawn to these particular Körner poems in 1815 because he had known the poet and because they accorded well with his interest at the time in more lyrical strophic songs, but because he was responding to an existing set of lieder by an older Viennese contemporary – despite scanty documentation, we can guess that Schubert was keenly aware both of new works by local composers and those more far-flung. Five of the Körner poems Schubert set to music also appear in Stephan Franz's *Sechs Gedichte von Theodor Körner*, op. 10 (Vienna: L. Maisch, [1814]), a memorial to Vienna's adopted son which ends with a setting of the "Abschied von Wien" (Schubert bypassed this poem).

1. Sängers Morgenlied – F major, Mit Ausdruck und Würde
2. Wiegenlied – G major, Mit vieler Zartheit
3. Liebeständeley – C major, Leicht und kindisch
4. Liebesrausch – E major, Sehr leidenschaftlich
5. Das gestörte Glück – G major, Erzählend und naif
6. Abschied von Wien Anno 1813 – A major, Langsam und gefühlvoll

Both composers "speak" to Mozart in these songs, Franz perhaps responding to the Mozartian lied and Schubert responding to both; the beginning of Franz's "Sängers Morgenlied" recalls Mozart's exquisite "Abenddämmerung," although the continuation is different (ex. 18). Franz's light touch is evident in the two delightful

Example 18. Stephan Franz, "Sängers Morgenlied" from *Sechs Gedichte von Theodor Körner*, op. 10 (Vienna: L. Maisch, [1814]), mm. 1–18.

Example 18. *cont.*

comic-erotic songs, in which Franz deftly marries the *Volkston* with the *Kunstlied* in a sophisticated amalgam, not truly "naïf" at all. Every detail of "Das gestörte Glück" impels a chuckle: the vivacious fanfare in the piano at the beginning (an appropriate preliminary for the announcement, "Ich hab ein heißes junges Blut, / wie ihr wohl alle wisst"), the hilarious leap of a sixth for extra emphasis on the words "alle" and "nie" (the leap repeats in higher transposition the initial interval of the *volkstümlich* first phrase), the singer's languishing erotic-chromatic descent over a dominant pedal point at the words "Denn ist mir auch mein Liebchen hold" (repeated, lest we miss the point), and the increasingly elaborate – Franz was more given to frothy, aria-like fioriture and embellishments than Schubert – multiple repetitions of the last line, "Hab ich doch niemals noch geküßt" (ex. 19). These two charming songs are not the equal of Mozart or Schubert, but they do not fall far short.

8.   Körner, a "golden lad" long before A. E. Housman sang of them and their tragic fates, was such an inherently youthful phenomenon that it seems only natural that he should belong almost entirely to Schubert's youth as well; once Schubert's association with the far more serious poet Johann Mayrhofer was underway, he had little further use for this repertoire. He only returned to Körner's poetry once more when he set "Auf der Riesenkoppe" (On the giant peak), D. 611, in March 1818.

Example 19. Stephan Franz, "Das gestörte Glück" from *Sechs Gedichte von Theodor Körner*, op. 10 (Vienna: L. Maisch, [1814]), mm. 1–14.

Hoch auf dem Gipfel	High on the peak
Deiner Gebirge	of your mountains
Steh' ich und staun' ich,	I stand and marvel,
Glühend begeistert,	fervently glowing,
Heilige Koppe,	divine peak,
Himmelsanstürmerin!	heaven-storming one!
Weit in die Ferne	My ecstatic, joyous gaze
Schweifen die trunknen	scans far
Freudigen Blicke;	into the distance;
Überall Leben,	everywhere life,
Üppiges Streben,	luxuriant growth,
Überall Sonnenschein.	everywhere sunshine.
Blühende Fluren,	Blossoming meadows,
Schimmernde Städte,	shimmering towns,
Dreier Könige	the happy realms
Glückliche Länder	of three kings:
Schau' ich begeistert,	I behold these
Schau' ich mit hoher	with rapture,
Inniger Lust.	with sublime inner joy.
Auch meines Vaterlands	I also behold the border
Grenze erblick' ich,	of my fatherland,
Wo mich das Leben	where life
Freundlich begrüßte,	greeted me as a friend,
Wo mich der Liebe	where the holy longing
Heilige Sehnsucht	of love,
Glühend ergriff.	seized me, glowing-hot.
Sei mir gesegnet	Beloved homeland,
Hier in der Ferne	here in the distance,
Liebliche Heimat!	I bless you!
Sei mir gesegnet	I bless you,
Land meiner Träume!	land of my dreams!
Kreis meiner Lieben,	I greet you,
Sei mir gegrüßt![117]	the circle of my loved ones!

Here, Körner's patriotism takes the wholly affirmative form of love for one's home, family and friends, one's first sweetheart, and the summertime luxuriance of his native landscape. To this, Schubert could assent musically in a way he could not to sabre-rattling bloodthirstiness. Körner sets his blessings and greetings in the form of a litany with short-breathed lines in dimeters, specifically, a dactyl and a trochee; the accented beginning of each line bespeaks the poet's fervor, especially when the line starts with the wide-open diphthong -ei, as in "Sei mir gesegnet" or "Kreis meiner Lieben." Later, Schubert would set another litany sung by a poetic persona "In der Ferne" (In a far-off place), the title of his song D. 957, no. 6 to a poem by Ludwig Rellstab, that is, in a manner of speaking, an "anti-'Auf der Riesenkoppe,'" an anti-litany or curse on those who flee their country and hate their mother's house ("Mutterhaus hassenden"). The dactylic rhythms of "In der Ferne" are heavier than Körner's lighter, brighter hymn of praise; here, all is blessedness and blessing, love of one's homeland as a sacred emotion.

In "In der Ferne," Schubert would preserve as best he could in music the symmetries of litany in order to magnify the persona's sense of cursedness, but here, he ignores the poetic form, except in a few telling instances; indeed, the song begins with recitative, as if it were to be a ballad. Schubert, who knew the poet's enthusiasm and verve first-hand, has the pianist charge straight up the mountainside, *forte* and in stark, unharmonized octaves, and then stop at the peak, the motion arrested in hushed awe. The song proper begins in D major in m. 16 at the words "Weit in die Ferne"; the poet, having attained the peak, begins to survey the lands spread out before his gaze, and here, in Schubert's conception, he bursts into genuine song. In accord with his lyrical understanding of Körner, Schubert heightens not the energetic, striving, drunk-with-joy connotations of stanza 2, but instead a quieter, more inward happiness, although he acknowledges "trunk'nen [freudigen Blicke]" in m. 19 and the corresponding repetition of the same gesture at the word "Streben" (beautifully apt for it as well) with an ascending leap upwards of a sixth, this after conjunct descending motion in the vocal line. The directional metaphor by which the topmost voice in the piano and the vocal line in mm. 16–19, 23–25 are inversions of one another, juxtaposed in contrary motion, is beautifully symbolic of the poet's "schweifendes" (sweeping) glance "weit in die Ferne" – an all-encompassing gaze captured in a small musical figure, a wide expanse suggested in the most economical manner. There is something too of Körner's heartfelt directness of feeling conveyed in the downbeat prolongation of the words "Weit" and "schwei - [fen]" in mm. 16 and 18, the expansion into the infinite hinted in the word-music of the diphthong -ei, followed by a scalewise descent whose lyrical simplicity bespeaks the poet's sincere emotion (the beginning of the descent is ornamented at the verb "schweifen," a motivically important ornament that prefigures the expansion of the phrase in mm. 19–21). That descending melody is a further development of the phrase "Himmelsanstürmerin," the last vocal phrase of the recitative section (mm. 11–12), the "heaven-storming" emotion subsumed immediately in a quieter, more lyrical working-out.

In this through-composed song, each section linked by reminiscences and development of prior strains, the first section of the song proper ends with a cadence in the dominant at "Sonnenschein" (sunshine) in mm. 25–27; if the setting of the preceding word "überall" is prosodically awkward, the full-throated emphasis on the concluding noun "Sonnenschein" should resonate with anyone grateful for the sun's brilliance after a period of gloom. Following that cadence, Schubert transports performers and listeners, via one of his characteristic common-tone mediant modulations to F major, the change happening so suddenly that we still half-hear the A major and D major harmonies even as the tessitura shifts to a higher plane and a new pitch is tonicized. There is something wonderfully appropriate about both the pastoral tonality for this hymn to "flowering fields" and the delicate, treble register for someone poised on the heights, surveying that which is beautiful below. The vocal line in mm. 32–39 is an embellished version of the familiar scalewise descent from before, doubled by the "bass" line in parallel sixths (A G F E), while the inner voice is a written-out trill in slurred figures based upon the neighbor-note figures in the inner voice of "Weit in die Ferne." This measured trill – which produces an apt "shimmering" effect, as if the very air were alive with happiness – gently animates the texture, especially when it rises above the vocal line upon repetition of the phrase. With the invocation of "great, inner joy," rapture rises chromatically in the inner voice of mm. 40–42 and then culminates in an emphatic (three *forzandi* in succession) cadence on C and a gentler cadence on G – "inniger Lust." Schubert distinguishes between different shades and types of happiness with great precision.

Schubert divides "Auf der Riesenkoppe" in two recitative-plus-song sets: the *mise-en-scène* and the situation are established in stanza 1 and set as recitative, followed by a tonally progressive song in two sections (stanzas 2 and 3). In stanza 4, the poet again tells us, as he did in stanza 1, that he surveys the countryside – his own country – from his vantage point on the heights, and therefore Schubert returns to recitative, the formal parallelism exact. This in turn is followed by another hymn of praise, a "song" which is also in two sections, but tonally closed; textual repetition stretches the final stanza of text (stanza 5) to almost exactly the same length as the prior "song," which is a setting of two stanzas. In the piano interlude before the second patch of recitative, the grace-noted leaps of a ninth in the right-hand part from G to A and the additional grace-notes in m. 46, such that D is ornamented from both above and below, imbue this passage with an indefinable youthful verve; in retrospect, we are intended to understand that the poetic persona's heart leaps with particular joy on first spotting the boundaries of his own native land. In mid-recitative, Schubert seems as if returning to the tonal sphere of "Weit in die Ferne," back to the D major and dominant A major harmonies of the first "song" at its beginning; the tonal swerve occurs when the poet recalls "love's holy desire" ("Wo mich der Liebe / Heilige Sehnsucht / Glühend ergriff"), the transformative effects of love gently symbolized in harmonic metamorphosis. Only here, at the end of the descent from higher to lower tessituras in the piano interlude (mm. 62–70), does the music come to an expectant halt, a fermata-prolonged pause on A major; everywhere else in "Auf der Riesenkoppe," one section flows into the next as if in mimicry of happy reflections following, stream-like, one upon the other.

What follows the fermata is sheer magic. Where we are led to expect D major and a return to the song of mm. 16f, we hear instead a hymn of blessing ("Sei mir gesegnet") – in B-flat major. There is no transition, no modulation, no preparation, although in retrospect, as our ears adjust to the newly-deepened, newly-serious strains, we realize the relationship with the F major passage in the setting of stanza 3 ("Blühende Fluren, / Schimmernde Städte … ") and understand that the words of blessing have flowered from harmonies and sentiments that appeared earlier in the work, hear as well the motivic and melodic relationships with the setting of stanzas 2 and 3. And there is still more tonal magic to come. At the first invocation of the words "Kreis meiner Lieben" in mm. 91–92, Schubert quietly jolts the harmonic progression up a semitone and sounds two full measures on flat-VI of B-flat major,

Example 20. Franz Schubert, "Auf der Riesenkoppe," D. 611, mm. 88–94.

investing the "circle of my loved ones" with the greatest richness and warmth of all in this song, especially given the sudden *pianissimo* hush and the almost chant-like declamation on a repeated D-flat; both the chanting and the sudden hush have their origin in mm. 57–58 at the words "Wo mich der Liebe [heilige Sehnsucht]," the parallelism between the poetic content obvious (ex. 20). Each time, the four-measure phrase returns to the key of blessing, to B-flat major, for the pendant words "sei mir gegrüsst" (whether coincidence or not, this is also the tonality for the later Rückert song "Sei mir gegrüßt," D. 741), such that the sudden soft, dark warmth is dispelled as quickly as it appeared. The imitation in music of an unheralded rush of heartfelt emotion, manifested by greater quiet rather than heightened volume, which then gives way to a somewhat less intense, more extroverted state is quite precise. In the "verklingend" (dying away) postlude (mm. 98–103), Schubert does what he would later do, albeit in a very different context, in "Mein!" from *Die schöne Müllerin*, a song in which he also modulates to the key of the flat submediant as an expression of warmer, deeper emotion: he sounds a pedal point as the inner voice of the right-hand part, with arpeggiated harmonies branching off above the pedal tones. One of those pedal tones is – must be – D-natural, reestablished after all those D-flats so near the end of the song, although at the very end, we hear the last incarnation of the semitone neighbor-note figure D C-sharp D, the C-sharp an enharmonic final echo of the D-flats. We also hear a premonition of the B-flat "wandering" strains of "Das Wandern" from *Die schöne Müllerin* as well, although less hearty in effect, as if the poetic persona were walking onwards, the sound dying away as he vanishes from sight and sound.

The otherwise hugely disparate poetic worlds of Theodor Körner and Johann Mayrhofer meet in this lied, which begins in one tonal center and ends in another. By the time Schubert composed "Auf der Riesenkoppe," Mayrhofer's darker, grander spheres had replaced the Papageno-like buoyancy of Körner and his ilk, and the result was tonal experimentation of a more radical order than Körner's verse could invite. "Auf der Riesenkoppe" may have beckoned to Schubert in 1818 not only because his mother came from the town of Zuckmantel, near the Riesenkoppe, but because the poet's "sweeping gaze" over different lands and loves lent itself to his musical preoccupations at the time. I wonder whether Mayrhofer, who also knew and admired Körner and who was also an ardent patriot, could have had something to do with Schubert's choice of this text at that time, although this can only be speculation. With that connecting thread between one poet and the next, we now take our leave of Körner.

CONCLUSION

Körner is only marginally among those poets deserving resurrection. For all his facility, he had no opportunity to become anything other than a Schiller epigone (but without the depth and range of his idol)[118] and a fervent patriotic poet, emblematic of all the glory-seeking, idealistic, hot-headed young men who have ever charged into battle. What is so saddening about a perusal of his poems is, paradoxically, the merriment of the early works, the Maytime freshness which then modulates into a Teutonic "Charge of the Light Brigade." "Doch fröhlich geht des Sängers Weg / Durch lauter Frühlingsschein" (The minstrel's path goes merrily through bright spring sunshine), he wrote in "Sängers Wanderlied," which ends with the lines "Und sag' ich einst der Welt Ade / Zieh' ich in Liedern heim" (And if I bid the world farewell one day, I will return home in song). He did just that. Our disillusioned century, knowing what deadly fruit eventually ripened from German nationalism and what became of so many young men with similar ideals, finds the lyre-and-sword poems difficult to stomach, but in his own day and for a long time thereafter, Körner was a beacon of light in the darkness of war and a symbol to inspire love of country in others. Sadly, there are worse fates for such burning patriotism than death.

For Schubert, however, he may also have embodied artistic self-determination. Like Gabriele von Baumberg (but in person), Körner urged Schubert to pursue his artistic calling despite their fathers' mutual worries about profession and a steady income. Given Schubert's support for his fellow-artists' strivings, it is not surprising that he would memorialize in music the friend who had performed so important a service for him, although he did so in accord with his own tastes. He could not engage wholeheartedly in drum-beating patriotic music – it is emblematic that in the autumn of 1813, he set the bloodthirsty poem "Auf den Sieg der Deutschen" (On the German Victory), with its "ravening hyenas" and "bloody altars," as a decidedly unwarlike, almost merry aria for voice, cello, and two violins, D. 81.[119] What Schubert liked best in Körner's œuvre was Körner in love, in lighthearted moods, or musing – but not in the most profound vein – on life, love, and homeland. Of the poems that fit this description, he chose the best and set them in a newly lyrical manner. "Amphiaraos" and "Auf der Riesenkoppe" both transcend the model, but that does not mean the model was unimportant.

I have saved a final tribute to Körner for the last, not only because it comes from Johann Mayrhofer, the subject of the next chapter, but because it is the most beautiful: "Am Grabe Körners" (At Körner's grave).

Nicht ihn, der in dem Kampfgewühl	Do not lament he who fell in the turmoil
Für seine Heimat streitend fiel,	of battle, fighting for his homeland!
Beklaget! selig ist sein Loos,	Blessed is his fate,
Und friedlich in der Erde Schooß.	peaceful in the bosom of the earth.
Es wachsen Veilchen über ihn,	Violets grow over him
Und deuten an ein mildes Blühn:	and hint at a gentle blossoming:
Blühst Liebe ihm und Freyheit nun –	Love and Freedom blossom for him now –
Wer möchte nicht im Grabe ruh'n?	who would not wish to rest in the grave?
Was sehnsuchtsvoll das Herz begehrt,	What the heart longingly covets
Hienieden wird es nicht gewährt;	will not be given to us here below;
Und eine steile Felsenwand	and a steep, rocky wall
Verwehret uns das Blüthenland.	hinders us from the land of flowers.
Und wer sich auch, im kühnen Drang	And whoever, in bold urgency, panting,
Und keuchend, auf die Felsen schwang,	swings up onto the rocks, sees the sea before
Erblickt vor sich die See – und nur	him – and only the meadows of the Hesperides
Umflort die Hesperidenflur.	are veiled in the black crape of mourning.
Nur Fittiche, sie tragen hin,	His wings alone bear him
Wo tausend goldne Früchte glühn.	to where a thousand golden fruits glow.
Uns drängt der schwere Leib zurück	Our heavy bodies drag us back
Vom reinen, fernen Geisterglück.[120]	from the pure, distant happiness of the spirits.

It is an exquisite tribute, as evocative of Mayrhofer's own desire to become spirit, not flesh, as it is homage to his dead contemporary. Körner's ardor, ebullience, and talent touched many; Mayrhofer, alive to beauty of spirit, recognized and lauded it in verse even more compelling than Körner's – but then, Körner died so much younger than Mayrhofer, well before all that gleaming promise could reach either fruition or frustration.

Chapter Three

Chromatic melancholy
Johann Mayrhofer and Schubert

IN THE WORDS OF Johannes Brahms, a lifelong awestruck student of Schubert's lieder, Johann Mayrhofer (1787–1836) was the "ernsthafteste" (the most serious) of all Schubert's friends.[1] Although muted recognition of Mayrhofer's artistry is implicit in the choice of adjective, the standard for comparison is the likes of Franz von Schober, Franz Bruchmann, and Eduard Bauernfeld, not the larger outside world, nor does Brahms fully acknowledge the originality of Mayrhofer's slender poetic oeuvre. Mayrhofer's own sense of unworthiness contributed to the early burial of his works and the subsequent lack of attention even to the many poems Schubert set to music, unfairly so. This complicated man, beset by self-hatred and by emotions whose violence he could not accept, transmuted the conflict-ridden passions of his inner world into poetry whose experimental rhythms and forms, enigmatic language, self-analytical subject matter (inner torment of necessity compels an obsession with that torment), and often powerful darkness deserve renewed attention. If Mayrhofer was not the equal of Hölderlin or the Goethe he so admired,[2] his poems on poetry and on his own tormented condition nonetheless constitute complexly beautiful grapplings with the dark mysteries of time and death. Austrians are quality pessimists, and Mayrhofer was indeed that.

Mayrhofer's influence on Schubert during the period of their close association from autumn 1816 to late 1820 is a well-known fact of Schubert scholarship,[3] but studies of the reclusive poet's verse are few and far between. Although Schubert told Anselm von Hüttenbrenner that he despised "bad poems" and had refused to set mediocre poetry to music,[4] he defined a "good poem" differently from a literary critic; a "good poem" had music in it, his music. By that specialized standard, Mayrhofer's verse was truly "good": forty-seven of his poems, more than any other poet except Goethe, were transmogrified into Schubertian lied. Although the friendship between the two men was assuredly a factor, not even the closest friendship could compel Schubert to set almost fifty poems unless he considered them composable. Many of the poems he chose for musical setting are of greater *literary* merit than one might suppose (and Schubert's concern for literary worth is undeniable, despite the quantity of mediocre verse in his song œuvre). Even where Schubert brutally edited Mayrhofer's bleak imaginings for conversion into lieder, he nonetheless found riches in them that modern readers can rediscover and the impetus for a radically modern approach to the lied.

"THIS EARTH, ALIEN TO IDEALS": MAYRHOFER'S LIFE

Perhaps the best prose-portrait of Mayrhofer comes from one of the poet's contemporaries, a Viennese antiquarian bookseller, editor of the *Wiener Conversationsblatt*, and encyclopedist named Franz Gräffer (1785–1852). The vignettes of "alt Wien" he published in the last years of his life include portrayals of its most distinctive denizens, Mayrhofer among them:

Mayrhofer was always ailing, of sickly complexion, quite bony, but with an abnormal nervous system, totally without elasticity; rigid, icy-cold. Thus also his poetic spirit: elegiac, misanthropic, rancorous, scolding, sarcastic, symbolically inclined; in moments of clarity, even energetic … he could thunder and give off sparks, as in his depiction of Hercules, "In the Smithy." His existence and works were a perpetual, frenzied struggle of matter with soul; he was consumed by this tragic fluctuation. A natural prey to fixed notions, in strife over his situation in life, [he was] strict and parsimonious. Like the miserable Scarron, perhaps he could have been saved if only one had created a new position for him: the Queen's patient. His inner world, which was nearly always clouded and gloomy, nonetheless produced many sweet blossoms, especially in song, which inspired the ardent Schubert, who understood how to complete and illuminate the poems in music. Schubert was full of feeling, like our dear [Ignaz] Castelli – a Lower Austrian, a Viennese: sincerity, warmth, sweetness, profundity, but those from the Enns, more clarity, calm, reflection. Mayrhofer was born in Traunkreise in Steyr, like [Aloys] Blumauer, [Franz Xavier] Süßmayer, and the opera singer [Johann Michael] Vogl.[5]

Gräffer's conclusions were echoed almost a century later by the early twentieth-century psychiatrist Wilhelm Gail, who attempted to formulate a posthumous diagnostic evaluation of Mayrhofer's case in the language of the infant science of psychiatry. Gail wrote:

I would diagnose our poet as a "chronic depressive." Not only his moodiness, but above all his responsiveness to external stimuli attest to this diagnosis. Inhibitions, an inferiority complex, in short, the fact that his vital energies were incompatible with his sensitivities was the hallmark of his life and, so it appears to me, also of his poetic works. The further development of his sickly constitution, partly-reactive and partly the result of innate inclinations, led to paranoid and over-valued hypochondriacal notions. Probably in the beginning, a deep depression, not uncommon among such men, led ultimately to a fixed state, becoming suddenly acute when he heard the news of a cholera epidemic in progress, exciting him to the massive anxiety in which the poet killed himself. (A not-uncommon occurrence.)[6]

The final parenthetical clause is chilling. Noting Mayrhofer's feeling for Nature, Gail further added, "People like Mayrhofer cannot tolerate the influence of other people's emotions, and therefore Nature becomes their dearest friend; they find feelings of release, of redemption, in Nature's life."[7] The descriptions can be confirmed in some measure by the poems themselves, in which Mayrhofer's battles with his own nature, including the heroic and hard-won moments of peace, are recorded. Mayrhofer, one guesses, would not have chosen to make his own torment the principal subject of his poetry; he extolled objectivity over subjectivity and railed against Romanticism, but one has not far to look in his poems to find the poet himself behind the masks of mythological figures, elderly minstrels, birds, and nameless narrating voices. This is not, however, straightforwardly confessional writing; the ambiguities, the gaps implying missing information, the imagery which seems to constitute a coded language, are far from direct. The biographical content which the poet himself allows one to infer from this verse is shrouded in unanswerable questions.

How his "dunkle Lebensangst" ("dark anxiety about life," a beautifully apposite phrase coined by Mayrhofer's first biographer, the philosopher Ernst Freiherr von Feuchtersleben) began is unknown. Mayrhofer was the third of four children (Anaklet, Richard, Johann, and Franziska) born to Magdalena Heizinger and an attorney named Matthias Remigius Mayrhofer, who died in 1798 at age fifty-four when Johann was only eleven years old. The scant biographical facts begin with confusion about the poet's birthdate, Feuchtersleben citing 3 November 1787, while a later scholar, Joseph Bindtner, states that 22 October is the correct date.[8] Apparently, there were two baptismal registers for Mayrhofer's birthplace of Steyr in Upper Austria, the older with the 22 October birthdate, the second, possibly a copy, with 3 November as the date. How the family managed in the years after Matthias Mayrhofer's death, what the "family romance" was, how Mayrhofer felt about his brothers and sister, are matters about which we know tantalizingly little, although Joseph von Spaun relates that he [Mayrhofer] bequeathed his sister 1,200 silver florins at his death and one infers love or, at least, dutiful concern in the bequest. One would like to know more.

For his sparse account of Mayrhofer's early years, Feuchtersleben relied on the reminiscences of Joseph von Spaun (1788–1865), one of Schubert's oldest friends. Spaun later wrote that Mayrhofer, who was a classmate of Spaun's older brother Anton, was always first among his classmates at the gymnasium and the Lyceum, noted for his abilities in Latin and Greek; that he was "ein sittenreiner, liebenswürdiger Jüngling"; and that he was often a guest at the Spaun household, where he felt at ease.[9] In the company of people he did not know well, he was shy and mute, even rude, Spaun reports, and his maladroit social behavior only worsened with time. In accord with his father's wishes, Mayrhofer entered St. Florian's to train for the priesthood and stayed either four years, from 5 October 1806, when he became a novice in the order, to 18 October 1810, or three, as Feuchtersleben states, or two, according to Spaun.[10] Although Mayrhofer reportedly did well as an incipient priest, Feuchtersleben reported that his friend's increasing desire to be a poet, his wish to learn something of worldly life and to be of service to his country, were the reasons for his departure from the monastery. Again, one would like to know more of the matter. Mayrhofer became fiercely anti-clerical, but reading the poems in which he yearns for metamorphosis into the immaterial, one can understand both how he would have been attracted to a spiritual calling and why he would have left. Few people can have considered themselves less holy, less worthy than Mayrhofer.

After leaving the novitiate, Mayrhofer went to Vienna to study law and history. Perennially plagued by poverty, he twice worked as a private tutor in wealthy *bürgerlich* households (whose, when, where, and for how long are not known), but reportedly found the occupation not to his taste – one can hardly imagine so shy and reclusive a person as a teacher – and left voluntarily. During his first years in Vienna, his interest in Herodotus, Horace, and the Stoics intensified (he began, but never finished, a translation of Herodotus). In particular, the pantheism of Heraclitus' fragments in which the universe is conceived as a living organism, everything a member of one rarefied material substance (a kind of mind-fire) in eternal activity, finds its way into Mayrhofer's poetry. In Stoic cosmology, the primordial source of Being produces out of itself the visible world and all within it, thus, Mayrhofer's passionate attachment to Nature constitutes an idiosyncratic appropriation of a pantheism in which Zeus, God, Nature, Providence, Fate, Necessity, Law, and Soul are among many names for the same force. Of all the Stoics, Mayrhofer reportedly had a particular liking for the writings of Marcus Aurelius, in whose disenchantment and depression, grapplings with death, hard-won moments of hope, and wistful longings for love he might have seen his own image mirrored and whose essential goodness is evident throughout the *Meditations*.[11] But the rationally obtained optimism of Stoicism, its insistence that happiness depends solely on the will, was beyond Mayrhofer's powers, however much he may have striven for it.

Mayrhofer gave up his legal studies, worked for a while in a tobacconist's shop, and then in 1816 became a censor for the Metternich regime; he was promoted to second, rather than third, *Bücher-Revisor* in 1832 when the first-in-command at his bureau, Franz Sartori, died.[12] The records of the censorship bureau indicate that Mayrhofer, plagued by chronic faintness, digestive problems, and nervous illnesses, frequently requested sick leave; Mayrhofer himself once wrote, "My persistent abdominal troubles have plagued me for many an evil hour. The worm of spleen gnaws at my life, eating the blossom – can any fruit follow?"[13] Spaun writes sympathetically that only the need to earn his scant living could have driven Mayrhofer, whom he describes as "extraordinarily liberal, indeed democratic in his views … passionate about freedom of the press," to take such a position; when Spaun teased him about the matter, he replied that his opinions were one thing, his job another.[14] Spaun even implies that an unknown quantity of Mayrhofer's poems could not be included in his 1824 *Gedichte* because of their unacceptable political content and that Mayrhofer's verse-tragedies *Timoleon* and *Ulrich von Hutten*, had they ever been performed or published, would have resulted in dire consequences for the poet – no wonder, given the historical Ulrich von Hutten's (1488–1523) fulminations against tyranny, attacks on the Papacy, and ardent nationalism.[15] Nevertheless, Mayrhofer evidently took his position seriously, bringing work home with him when he was too ill to come into the bureau and acting as a strict official in a government that relied on control of all printed matter (Feuchtersleben states that Mayrhofer became markedly more pedantic about his official duties after Schubert's death). There were no prescribed standards for censorship, and the individual censors at every level could decide each case as they wished, often impelled to rejection by fears for their jobs, as appointments to the civil service were extremely difficult to obtain. One wonders what Mayrhofer the classicist privately thought when the Foreign Office censor in 1822 banned a history of Greece, since access to knowledge of ancient democracy was considered dangerous to Hapsburg interests. But despite his stringent performance of his distasteful duties, he was acutely conscious of the contradiction between his literary aspirations and his work as a censor; a poet acting to restrain the free expression of others is a paradoxical and disturbing spectacle. Although psychological speculation is always risky, especially on such scant evidence, it is perhaps possible that Mayrhofer may have perceived himself as "censored" by life and took out his bitterness by censoring, first, others and finally himself. Suicide, after all, is the ultimate censorship.

In Vienna, Mayrhofer belonged to a circle of close friends, most of them from Linz, originating with the Spaun brothers and including Anton Ottenwalt, Josef Kenner, Franz von Schober, Johann Senn, and Franz Bruchmann. Ottenwalt, in a letter of 28 July 1817 to Schober, writes, "It was in the year of the comet of 1811 that we declared that we wanted to be known as brothers because of our common love of the good," a common devotion to the ideal of *Bildung*, or character formation.[16] The "brotherhood" thus began at the Royal Seminary where Schubert received his schooling until October 1813, and Mayrhofer joined a band already dedicated to the concept of "höheres Seyn," or a higher state of being, actively pursued through the medium of the arts; that this was modeled in part on the concept of friendship in classical antiquity and in part on the classicizing tenets of the late eighteenth-century German masters (Herder, Friedrich Jacobi, and above all, Goethe and Schiller) is central to the antiquarian ideals of the group. In 1817, the leaders of the circle – Anton von Spaun, Ottenwalt, Josef Kenner, Josef Kreil, and Mayrhofer – banded together to edit a literary annual conceived as a kind of "missionary outreach" program expressly for youths: the *Beyträge zur Bildung für Jünglinge*, published by Franz Härter, which only lasted two years and two issues before it came under official ban (it is all the more tragically ironic that Mayrhofer himself would soon become a censor) and was cleared from the booksellers' shelves. In the first volume, Mayrhofer contributed the poem "Der Krieger und sein Sohn" (The warrior and his son) and a historical essay entitled "Kunigunde" (pp. 171–93) whose purpose, announced at the outset, was to acquaint readers with an outstanding woman from among the roll-call of great Austrian rulers of the past, although the virtues for which he extols her were purely "feminine," as femininity was then defined. Kunigunde (1465–1520) was not a ruler herself, but the daughter and subsequently the wife of rulers; she was the fourth child of the Hapsburg king Friedrich III (1440–93) and Leonora of Portugal, and she married, after various and sundry trials, Albrecht IV, Duke of Bavaria. Having borne eight children, she retired into a convent upon her husband's death and died as an example of female saintliness. At the end of his essay, Mayrhofer recounts a legend that a hitherto unknown star shone over the cloister when she died. It is an especially interesting choice of subject matter when one weighs in the balance Mayrhofer's fervent patriotism (he clearly considered it important for *Bildung* that one know Austrian history), the pedagogical intent of the journal, and the misogyny one finds elsewhere in Mayrhofer's works (discussed in more detail later in this chapter). One can only speculate about why he chose to write about her: perhaps for "Jünglinge" who might someday become leaders, he points to an instance from Austria's past of a woman who exemplified all the virtues they might hope to find in their wives. That he himself had no such interest is evident in other contexts.

Mayrhofer's contributions to the second volume of the *Beyträge zur Bildung für Jünglinge* include three poems (the beautiful "Mahnung" on pp. 210–11, "Das Leben des Gemüthes" on pp. 297–98, and "Der Schiffer" on p. 325) and a dialogue entitled "Raphael," in which he adumbrates the group's familiar themes of the superiority of Classicism over Romanticism, the necessity to learn from great art and great lives, and the highest ideals of friendship. It is in the section on friendship that the two fictional young men of the dialogue, Willibald and Friedrich, discuss coarse and offensive musicians, Schubert surely the counter-example to such "bad" artists.

Willibald: Dear friend, I've so often been annoyed by musicians who, although they delight others, seem not to feel anything themselves, or who, when they lay their instruments aside, are insignificant or even crude and repulsive people.

Friedrich: If crudeness and one-sidedness are offensive in those who only carry out thoughts, how much more offensive they are in those who think them. The Muses, after all, are sisters who love one another, and whoever offends one is in danger of being abandoned by all at the most decisive moment.[17]

The gem of Mayrhofer's contributions to the *Beyträge*, however, is not his prose but "Mahnung" (Admonition). Here, he holds up his own "long struggle" – the struggle, unhappily, would continue far beyond the disappearance of the journal – and his reverence for Austria's bygone patriarchs as models for youth, who should likewise be "pious and strong." For his quatrains in this poem, Mayrhofer alternates lines in tetrameters with second and fourth lines in dimeters, thereby investing "Zufriedenheit" (contentment), "die schöne Welt" (the beautiful world), and the final admonition with particular intensity because each consumes an entire line. The contrast between "Streit" (struggle) and "Zufriedenheit" in stanza 1 is all the more quietly emphatic because of the rhythmically imposed pause which follows those words.

Ich habe mich zurecht gefunden	I have at last found my way
Nach langem Streit;	after a long struggle;
Mich hat mit ihrem Kranz umwunden	Contentment has encircled me
Zufriedenheit.	with her garland.
Wie himmlisch schläft vor meinen Blicken	How beatifically the beautiful world
Die schöne Welt,	lies asleep before my gaze;
Begränzet durch der Berge Rücken,	bounded by the mountain ridge,
Die Luna hellt.	the moon shines.
Dem schwarzen Dome kühn entsprossen,	Boldly springing from the black dome,
Ragt Stephans Thurm.	the tower of St. Stephan's rises upward.
Der Greise trotzt noch unverdrossen	The old one still patiently braves
Der Zeiten Sturm.	the storms of Time.
Der sah viel sterbliche Geschlechter	That saw many mortal peoples
Um sich vergeh'n,	vanish,
Und denkt noch lang ein ernster Wächter	and imagines that a stern watchman
So da zu steh'n.	stands there.

Er rufe zu dir, o frische Jugend	He calls to you, youth in your freshness,
Der alten Mark:	of olden mettle:
Sey eingedenk der Väter Tugend,	Be mindful of your fathers' virtue,
Sey fromm und stark!	be pious and strong!

It was through Spaun that Mayrhofer met Schubert in late 1814. Although their collaboration began immediately with a setting of "Am See" (By the Lake), D. 124, only one song to a poem by Mayrhofer followed in 1815 ("Liane," D. 298); it was not until 1816, and even more so in 1817, that Schubert began setting numerous works by his friend. In November of 1818, Schubert moved from his father's house to Mayrhofer's lodgings on the third floor of 1 Wipplingerstrasse, above a tobacconist shop owned by the widow of a French emigrant, a woman who described her lodgers as "two somewhat impractical gentlemen" (a delightfully wry under-statement).[18] The two shared the Wipplingerstrasse address for eighteen months, until the end of 1820. Mayrhofer himself characterized the relationship in his elegiac reminiscences of Schubert from 1829, in which he refers obliquely to idiosyncrasies and "sharp edges."

The cross-currents of circumstances and society, of illness and changed views of life kept us apart later; but what had once been was no longer to be denied its rights. I often had to console Schubert's worthy father about his son's future, and I dared to prophesy that Franz would surely win through, nay, that a later world would give him his due, slowly though it came to him at first. While we lived together, our idiosyncrasies could not but show themselves; we were both richly endowed in that respect, and the consequences could not fail to appear. We teased each other in many different ways and turned our sharp edges on each other to our mutual amusement and pleasure. His gladsome and comfortable sensuousness and my introspective nature were thus thrown into higher relief and gave rise to names we called each other accordingly, as though we were playing parts assigned to us. Unfortunately, I played my very own![19]

The "role playing" has been recorded elsewhere: the poet would bandy a stick about like a bayonet, laughing and calling out in Upper Austrian dialect, "Was halt mich denn ab, du kloaner Raker," to which Schubert would reply, "Waldl, Waldl, wilde Verfasser" ("Waldl" a south German name for a dog, "wilde Verfasser" a "savage author"). A mutual friend, the pianist Josef von Gahy, reportedly often witnessed this scene, in which a very odd couple indeed defused at least some of the conflicts between them by attacks in jest, transforming anger into play.[20] Painfully aware of his eccentricities, Mayrhofer attributes paradoxical, untrustworthy behavior to all poets, not merely himself, in "Philisterthum" (Philistine Society):

Dem Poeten sich vertrauen	To put one's trust in a poet
Bleibt doch immer etwas mißlich;	always remains somewhat precarious;
Wo Ihr Bitterkeit erwartet,	where you expect bitterness,
Ist er schonend oft und süßlich;	he is considerate and mawkish;
Wo ihr Honig euch versprachet	where he promises honey,
Läßt er die Orkane brausen;	he lets the tempests roar;
Ach bedenklich, ach bedenklich	Oh, it is risky, risky indeed
Ist's, mit einem Dichter hausen!	to live with a poet!

Metzger, Schmiede, Seifensieder	Butcher, blacksmith, soap-boiler,
Haben ihre Eigenheiten,	have their individual characteristics,
Stattliche Kanzleiverwandte	state chancellery workers
Ihr wunderlichen Seiten;	their odd sides;
Selbst Soldaten – soll man's glauben?	even soldiers – can one believe it? –
Monoton in Marsch und Rocke,	monotone in their marching and their
Kalbfell angethan und Birke,	uniforms, beating on the drums,
Kultiviren das Barocke.	cultivate the baroque.
Wenn prosaische Naturen	If prosaic natures
Sich zuweilen gehen lassen,	now and then let themselves go,
Muß man billig auch Poeten	one must, in fairness, vouchsafe
Nachsichtsvoll gewähren lassen!	indulgence to poets as well!
Ließe man sie nicht gewähren,	If one doesn't grant it to them,
Würde Langweil gar zu mächtig,	boredom would become overwhelming,
Und mitunter die Gesellschaft	and the company occasionally,
So zu sagen niederträchtig.[21]	as it were, abominable.

Beneath the strained poetic rhythms and the awkward attempt at humor (Mayrhofer wrote better poems than this) is a polemic against categorization, one with origins in his own pained sense of difference. Everyone is "odd," he claims, and poets are merely more so than most. Indeed, they are superior to practical beings who "take pains about what happens today," as he writes in the eighth poem of his *Heliopolis* cycle, the manuscript sheaf of six epigrams and twenty poems dated September–October of 1821 and dedicated to Franz von Schober. "The poet's heart is inflamed only by shimmering ideas, which stand on the golden shores of Atlantis like lovely flowers, to be plucked only by a faithful hand," he declares in "Der Reiter liebt sein treues Roß" (The rider loves his trusty steed), and hence, poets stare bemusedly into the distance and pay no attention to their surroundings.[22]

No one knows the precipitating cause of Schubert's and Mayrhofer's estrangement in late 1820 – did the "changed outlook on life" of which Mayrhofer wrote in 1829 have anything to do with the poet's job as a censor? Or did he refer to a changed perspective on *Schubert's* part? It could not have been easy living with a depressed hypochondriac: even before they became roommates, Schubert wrote to Mayrhofer, saying, "Cease ailing, or at least dabbling in medicines, and the rest will come of itself."[23] Will-power alone cannot cure serious mental maladies, but Schubert could not have known this when he advocated what later psychologists would call behavior modification; Mayrhofer's inability to comply with the well-meaning advice may have been a factor in the rupture. Whatever the reasons, the two men parted company; when Mayrhofer's poems were published by subscription in 1824, Schubert's name was not among the subscribers. According to his chroniclers, Mayrhofer was deeply affected by the loss of a friend and collaborator he cherished, and his poetic production suffered as a result; if, as seems likely, he wrote some of his poems specifically for Schubert to set to music, that may very well have been the case.[24] I wonder whether renewed memories of the break with Mayrhofer may have prompted the composer's sorrowful statement on 27 March 1824 in a lost notebook: "There is no one who understands the pain or joy of others! We always imagine we are coming together, and we always merely go side by side. Oh, what torture for those who recognize this!"[25] Four songs to texts by Mayrhofer date from this month, when his erstwhile friend was surely much on his mind ("Der Sieg," D. 805; "Abendstern," D. 806; "Auflösung," D. 807; and "Gondelfahrer," D. 808). No names are cited and the brief passage on the ineradicable solipsism of existence may have some other impelling cause, but the chronology suggests at least the *possibility* of a link with Mayrhofer.

Friends – or former lovers? The controversy about Schubert's supposed homosexuality has aroused heated debate in recent years, although portions of the discussion have been warped by the dissociation of sexuality from those other aspects of personality which inevitably impinge upon it and by the paucity of evidence to support any claim definitively.[26] Nonetheless, it seems likely, if inaccessible to irrefutable proof (seldom forthcoming in these matters), that Mayrhofer was homosexual; this is not, of course, tantamount to an imputation that Schubert was likewise homosexual, since people both then and now have counted those of differing sexual persuasions among their friends, but it does arouse the speculative impulse. Those who deny the possibility that the composer might have been homosexual have sought to extend the umbrella of red-blooded heterosexuality to his circle of friends as well, but Mayrhofer's putative homosexuality is less problematical to infer than Schubert's. There is no mention of any romantic liaisons in the extant accounts of the poet's youth, only Spaun's tale of Mayrhofer writing "a poem on a young woman he barely knew and who only interested him because he saw her weeping in a window across the way."[27] One notes that Spaun discreetly underscores his boyhood friend's lack of "interest" (which can be interpreted as romantic interest, although other shades of meaning are also possible) in the woman, notes as well that Mayrhofer found in her only the occasion for a poetic meditation on grief – he was already a "man of sorrow" and would come to know grief even better in later life. But despite the fact that the disputes over homosexuality in the *Schubert-Kreis* have focused primarily on letters, diaries, and reminiscences such as this anecdote, that is, on non-fiction, I believe that the field of inquiry should also be extended in this instance to Mayrhofer's poetry, in particular, to various poems and epigrams that were only published posthumously in the 1843 *Neue Sammlung* (New collection) edited by his friend Ernst von Feuchtersleben. The considerable dangers of reading biography into poetry are somewhat mitigated here by the fact that Mayrhofer was his own most frequent subject; the "Ich" who speaks in so many of these poems is palpably the poet himself, who fashioned much of his verse from his own beliefs, experiences, and opinions. If such evidence is tantalizingly incomplete and fraught with interpretive difficulties, this does not mean it should be discounted. One cannot, after all, claim to know a poet until one knows his poetry.

Even where Mayrhofer does not speak *in propria persona*, the choice of theme and imagery for poetry, seldom disinterested in any poet's verse, tells of its creator's predilections and obsessions, beyond the framework of the poem itself. One such poem – among Mayrhofer's loveliest – is "Hiacinthe" (Hyacinth) from the *Xenien* (epigrams after the manner of Goethe and Schiller):

Du zarte Blume, füllst mit tiefer Trauer	Tender flower, thou fillest with profound
Das still betrachtende Gemüth:	sorrow the quiet, contemplative soul,
Es fühlt in deinem Ursprung, deiner Dauer,	sensing in thy origins, thy permanence,
Wie jedes Schöne hier verblüht.[28]	that every thing of beauty here decays.

Mayrhofer, steeped in classical myth, knew full well that Hyacinth in Greek mythology was a beautiful youth, loved both by the bard Thamyris and by Apollo himself; according to legend, this was the first time a man loved another man. When the youth was accidentally slain by Apollo with a cast of the discus, a flower that bore on its petals the syllables of lament "ai ai!" sprang from his blood. The hyacinth, like the narcissus, is thus among those flowers long invested with homoerotic significance. Mayrhofer, addressing the flower, does not recapitulate the myth, but rather evokes it, delicately and completely, in the beautiful phrase "thy origins, thy permanence." The aura of heavy, melancholy reverence is almost palpable: the poet worships what he hymns. If he knows that beauty (the charged word "Schöne" in the final line recalls the cult of Beauty in homosexual artistic circles) is transient, subject to death and decay, he can take comfort in its eternal essence. Nor was this the only poem in which the seemingly innocuous subject of flowers is a mask for homosexual content. Mayrhofer had included the equally brief "Die Hyacinthenflor," the fourth poem of the cycle *Auf der Wanderung*, in the 1824 *Gedichte*, the only edition of this poet's verse to appear in his own lifetime.[29] Here, the hyacinths themselves speak, saying:

Wir hauchen reinen Balsam dir entgegen,	We breathe pure balsam toward you,
Und spiegeln hellste Farben vor.	and mirror a dazzlement of brightest colors,
Doch wähne nicht, du stolzer Thor,	but do not presume, you proud fool,
Wir blüheten nur deinetwegen.	that we blossom just for you.
Sind wir begränzt, bist du es minder,	If we are confined and you less so,
Und sind wir nicht desselben Vaters Kinder?	are we not children of the same Father?

This is not as well-written a poem as "Hiacinthe," especially the crucial final couplet, but the appeal to tolerance and the claim to surpassing beauty (one notes the adjective "pure" in particular) are not difficult to decipher.

No one knows when "Hiacinthe" was written; exact dating for many of Mayrhofer's works is beyond ascertaining. But lest one is tempted to take this poem too literally as "proof" of homosexual tendencies Mayrhofer could recognise and acknowledge in himself, still other seemingly autobiographical poems hint at earlier heterosexual involvements. It is possible (especially in the absence of any confirming information whatever) that love for a woman or women, whether genuine or attempted for the sake of convention, was succeeded by recognition of a different orientation, or that the seeming "women" in the poems are actually youths or men, veiled in an identity that would pass muster with the censors, or that the poetic situation was entirely fictional, but whatever the genesis of these works, they impel curiosity. In "Erhebung" (Elevation), like the *Xenien* only published posthumously in the 1843 anthology, the poet first recalls an intense bygone friendship for an unnamed and unknown "friend."

Einst schwärmte ich trunken	Once I revelled, enraptured,
Im Auge des Freundes,	in the eyes of a friend …
Wir träumten uns frei!	we dreamed ourselves free!
Froh schwanden die herrlichen	The glorious hours sped by
Stunden, – noch glüh' ich,	happily … I still glow
Gedenk' ich des Traum's!	when I think of the dream!
Nun ist es wohl anders!	Yet now it is different!
Doch hab' ich gewonnen,	Still, I have won
Und preise mein Glück.	and treasure my happiness. (stanza 1)

What exactly was "different," or "anders" (a charged word in this context)? What was the struggle he had won? What does the title "Elevation" mean? Clarification – of a sort – follows. In the second stanza, he remembers an earlier love for a maiden who seems more poetical than real, a compilation of flowery clichés, and then once again declares himself the victor in this enigmatic struggle.

Einst lieb' ich ein Mädchen,	Once I loved a maiden,
Wie Rosen, so blühend,	as blooming as roses,
Wie Lilien, so rein.	as lilies so pure.
Ich plünderte Wiesen,	I plundered the fields
Ihr Kränze zu flechten,	to weave garlands for her,
Ihr Blumen zu streu'n.	to strew flowers for her.
Wohin sie sich wandte,	Wherever she turned,
Sie sah sich umgeben	she saw herself encircled
Von rührenden Zeichen	by touching indications
Des treuesten Sinn's.	of a most faithful heart.
Nun ist es wohl anders!	Yet now it is different!
Doch hab' ich gewonnen,	Still, I have won
Und preise mein Glück.	and treasure my happiness.

Das Herz, das einst jubelnd,	The heart that once exulted
Für Freundschaft geglüht,	in friendship's flame,
Das Herz, das voll Sehnsucht	the heart that full of desire,
Für Eine gelebt, –	lived for One –
Es hat sich erweitert:	it has expanded.
Nun ruhen in ihm	Now the stars, the worlds,
Die Sterne, die Welten,	the rivers and seas,
Die Ströme und Meere,	and all peoples,
Und alle Geschlechter,	united in love,
In Liebe vereint.	repose within it.
D'rum hab' ich gewonnen,	Therefore I have won
Und preise mein Glück.[30]	and treasure my happiness.

By the end of the poem, we understand that the poet's renunciation of love for individual human beings and its replacement by love on a more cosmic scale, embracing Nature and the amorphous mass of all humanity, was painfully difficult because he had once deeply loved at least two people. The date of the poem is unknown, the time of the renunciation (if real) likewise a mystery, and the identity of those loved and lost an unguessable enigma, especially the cardboard silhouette of the poet's beloved in the second stanza, but the "revelation," however incomplete, is compelling.

Caritas, not *Eros*, was also Mayrhofer's prescription in "Ohne Liebe kein Glück" (Without love, no happiness).

Trübselig Bild von unserm Jagen	Woeful image of our chase after
Nach Lust, die spottend uns entgeht.	pleasure, that, mocking, slips away
Ist's nicht die Fahrt auf einem Wagen,	from us. Is it not a journey in a coach
Der ewig sich im Zirkel dreht?[31]	that eternally goes around in circles?

The investment of all love in a single person would, he believed, exclude him from the larger knowledge he sought, would limit him to an impoverished, domesticated existence, and he furiously rejects the prospect in "Die Liebe währt."

Die Liebe währt; und nur die Gegenstände,	Love endures, and only the objects
Die sie ergreift, verändern sich;	it grasps change;
Wenn ich, wie Abälard, ein himmlisch Weib mir fände	if I, like Abelard, were to find a heavenly wife,
Vom Glück begünstigt wähnt' ich mich.	I would believe myself favored by Fortune.
Doch wär' mein Lieben in ihr abgeschlossen,	But were my love fully contained in her,
So hätte mich das Reich der Geister ausge- stoßen;	the realm of the spirit would have cast me out.
Von Euch geächtet: Kunst und Wissenschaft,	Shut out from you – Art and Knowledge,
Dem All entrückt, – und die Gigantenkraft	distanced from the cosmos – and the colossal
Um Feld und Hütte schmale Pfade bahnend, –	power carving narrow paths from field to
Und über mir die Sterne traurig mahnend, –	hut – the stars a sad reminder overhead –
Armselig Loos! ich will es nicht,	Paltry lot! I won't have it.
Mir leuchte Platon's heilig Licht;	Let Plato's divine light shine for me.
Das Ganze soll sich mir entschleiern,	The Whole shall be revealed to me,
Und durch mein Thun und Lied will ich es feiern.	and I will celebrate it in deed and in song.

The horror of such a diminished fate impels near-incoherent stammering in the middle of the poem. Over and over, he equates love with limitation: those who deed their hearts to a beloved, especially to a woman, are shut out of Mount Parnassus and barred from the all-embracing spiritual knowledge he so prized.

Especially to a woman – for Mayrhofer, love of "das Ganze" went hand-in-hand with misogyny. The poem "Alte Liebe rostet nie" (Old love never tarnishes), set to music by Schubert in September 1816 (D. 477), makes one wonder about Mayrhofer's mother and his subsequent rejection of women. "Since I lost her [my mother]," the poetic persona states, "I have travelled far and wide, but I remain unmoved by the fairest flower of womankind. For in my mind, her image rose chiding, as though opposing them, and such is her magic power that there was only one end to that contest." Although this poetic character is not necessarily to be conflated with the poet himself, Mayrhofer over and over again makes his dislike of women a subject for epigrammatic poems where strong opinions, negative ones in particular, were most conveniently housed. In another of the *Xenien*, he addresses a maiden – and by implication, all like her – and defies her efforts to ensnare him with her beauty and refinement. If she were only truthful and faithful, he declares sarcastically, then she could catch him, implying that such is an impossibility.

Bist du artig, nett und fein,	Should you be well-behaved, pleasant, and refined,
Allerliebstes Mägdelein,	dearest maiden,
Hast Du Ruhm davon und Nutz;	then you will be famed for it and profit thereby,
Doch der Rauhe bietet Trutz.	yet the rough man defies you.
Wirst Du treu und wahrhaft sein –	Will you be faithful and truthful,
Allerliebstes Mägdelein,	oh dearest maiden,
Steckst ihn in die Tasche ein![32]	then you'll have nabbed him!

In two other epigrams from the same set, he asks, "Did I have to burst so many bonds only in order to hem myself in by love?" ("Mußt' ich so viele Fesseln sprengen, / Um mich in Liebe einzuengen?") and then observes that no one who has achieved the ability to think clearly would ever encumber himself with a wife, home, and hearth ("Wer es doch erst zur Klarheit brächte, / Weib, Haus und Herd sei nicht das Rechte!").[33] In the third of his *Sermone* (Sermons), he reiterates the same theme:

Denket Ihr an Frau und Kinder,	Think ye of wife and children,
Haus und Küche mitberechnet!	together with house and kitchen!
Schlägt mein Herz nicht für die Menschheit,	Can my heart not beat for humanity
Weil ein Weib mich nicht gebunden,	because a woman has not bound me,
Weil mir ew'ge Himmelssterne	because eternal stars in heaven
Lieber als zwei Augen sind?[34]	are dearer to me than a pair of eyes?

The "eternal stars," when opposed to the image of "two eyes," additionally suggest Castor and Pollux, the Dioscurii or "Zwillingssterne" of another poem by Mayrhofer ("Hymne an die Dioskuren") who loved each other more than life. "If people want to pair off, they can," he concluded in the ironically entitled "Viaticum"; "I don't want to understand it – best to be alone with *you*, Horace, and good wine!" ("Will Einer auch mit Andern geh'n, / Sie können, – wollen nicht versteh'n; / Am besten bleibt's: allein zu sein / Mit Dir Horaz, und ächtem Wein!").[35]

But if Mayrhofer came to the conclusion (once? twice? many times?) that solitude was best for poets and erotic entanglements a danger to be avoided, there are grounds, however tenuous, for speculation that he did not do so without having experienced what he subsequently renounced. In another of the posthumously published poems (it is, significantly, untitled), he recounts the leavetaking from – a lover? prospective lover? The gender is unspecified, but whoever it was, he or she could not be a fellow-pilgrim in quest of "das Ganze" and was therefore sent away, Mayrhofer congratulating both himself and the would-be lover for the manner in which the parting was accomplished, for the lover's graceful acceptance of the verdict and his own strong-minded resolution. His implicit assessment of the other person as incapable of apprehending the higher ideals which mattered so much to him suggests someone as yet immature, possibly a youth.

Kannst Du mir geben, was ich nicht besitze?	Can you give me what I do not possess?
Vermagst Du es, die Segel anzuschwellen	Is it in your power to unfurl the sails of
Des ernsten Strebens? kräftig aufzuhellen	earnest endeavour? to flood the dark paths
Die dunklen Pfade, gleich dem Blitze?	with radiance, like lightning?
Du schweigest zierlich, und wir sind geschieden.	You fall silent, gracefully, and we are parted.
Wohl mir, daß ich mit Kraft und Mannesklarheit	Good that I, with strength and manly clarity,
Beim ersten Treffen nicht das Wort der Wahrheit	at first encounter did not lose the word of truth
Im blühenden Gesträuch' vermieden![36]	in the blossoming bushes.

The sexual implications of the "blühenden Gesträuch'" are clear, but translating a circumlocution is seldom easy, nor is it so in this instance. "Stillleben" (Still-life) is even more startling from this poet who insisted so often upon the renunciation of physical intimacy. Here, Mayrhofer reverses entirely the relationship of sensuality to the search for truth, declaring the former the victor and abjuring the futile struggle to attain abstractions, which had only proven empty in the end:

Sie beugt den zarten, schlanken Leib	She bends her sweet, slender body
Mir über's Haupt zum Licht,	into the light, over my head,
Und streckt den Arm, und lispelt: "Bleib!	and stretches out her arm and murmurs: "Stop
Dir gilt die Schere nicht!"	… It isn't worth your effort." (stanza 1)

"So I stay still" the poetic persona continues, "and gladly drink in the ardent warmth of life – star on star flickers out yonder, but what does its light matter to me? The tapers that flare more brightly now do not burn as I do; only those who know love's flame understand me and my happiness."

In trauter Stube eingeengt,	Enclosed in a cosy room,
Von Ihrem Hauch belebt,	given life by your breath,
Weiß ich es kaum, daß ich gedrängt,	I hardly recall that I, driven
Von Wünschen einst gestrebt!	by desires, once strove …
Gestrebt – nach Ruhm, nach Wirksamkeit,	Strove – for fame, for effectiveness,
Nach Glück, – und es nie fand,	for happiness – and never found it,
Bis es in diese Einsamkeit	until, in this solitude,
Die zarten Blüten wand![37]	I entwined tender flowers!

"Still-Life" is a beautifully multivalent title, suggesting the quietus attained in love and achieved only by the cessation of active striving for ideals, suggesting as well that love is life itself, opposed to the lifelessness of unhoused virtue. It is, of course, also the designation for a genre of painting in which objects, not people, are customarily depicted, frozen within the frame in a way that paradoxically both contradicts the actual transience of these fruit-and-flower arrangements and reminds one of it – a *memento mori*. "She" in the first line is the only reference to gender; the adjectives "zarten, schlanken" and the blossoms in the final line (a sexually-laden nod to the traditional subjects of still-life canvases) could equally refer to youths, the "woman" a cloak for less admissible desires, but whether this is so, even whether the poem has any autobiographical content at all, remains a mystery.

The precise nature of his relationship with Schubert is likewise a mystery. Mayrhofer freely acknowledged his love for Schubert, whether or not that love was erotic in origin, in his poetry; if he never transgresses the language of passionate friendship common at the time, one would hardly expect open avowals of explicitly homosexual fervor in verse published in the 1820s. "Geheimniß. An F. Schubert" (Secret. To Franz Schubert), which the composer set to music in 1816, is both a hymn of gratitude because Schubert's music could transport Mayrhofer from the "trüber Gegenwart" (dark present times) he detested and a meditation on the mystery – the "secret" of the title – of creativity. If the "secret" has other, more private connotations, they are not evident in the poem.[38] Far more problematical is the first in a mini-cycle of three poems collectively entitled "An Franz," posthumously published in the 1843 *Nachlass*.

Du liebst mich! tief hab ich's empfunden,
Du treuer Junge, zart und gut;
So stähle sich denn, schön verbunden,
Der edle, jugendliche Muth!
Wie immer auch das Leben dränge,
Wir hören die verwandten Klänge.

You love me! deeply have I felt it,
thou faithful youth, sweet and good;
may noble, youthful courage
steel itself then, beautifully united!
However life troubles us,
we hear kindred tones.

Doch, Wahrheit sei's womit ich zahle:
Ich bin nicht, Guter, wie Du wähnst;
Du sprichst zu einem Ideale,
Wornach Du jugendlich Dich sehnst, –
Und eines Ringer's schweres Streben
Hältst Du für rasch entquoll'nes Leben.

But it is truth with which I reckon:
I am not, good one, as you imagined me:
you speak to an ideal
you youthfully long for –
and the difficult grapplings of a striver,
you take for swiftly flowing life.

Was ich gelallt mit schwacher Lippe, –
Hab' ich das Wahre auch erkannt?
Ich schuf – er war ein arm Gerippe;
Hab' ich den Geist je festgebannt?
Konnt' ich den Sinn der Weltgeschichten
Erscheinen lassen in Gedichten?

What I stammered with weak lips –
Did I ever perceive the Truth?
I created – it was a poor skeleton;
Have I ever caught the spirit?
Could I ever convey the meaning
of the world's stories in poetry?

Doch laß uns treu, bis sich dem Willen
Die Bildung und die Kraft gesellt,
Als Brüder redlich bau'n im Stillen
An einer schönern, freien Welt;
Sie ist es nur, der ich gesungen, –
Und ist sie, – sei das Lied verklungen![39]

But let us faithfully, while the will
joins together imagination and craft,
as brothers, quietly and honestly
construct a more beautiful, free world;
it is only this of which I have sung,
and when it is – my song shall die away.

Assigning a date, much less an identity for "Franz," is fraught with unresolvable difficulties, although the mere possibility that Franz *Schubert* might be the person addressed impels examination. The second poem in the set, "Fels auf Felsen hin gewälzet," appeared earlier as the twelfth poem in the 1821 cycle *Heliopolis* and also in the 1824 anthology of Mayrhofer's poems; the poem was subsequently set to music by Schubert as "Aus 'Heliopolis' II," D. 754 of April 1822. Whatever the manuscript source Feuchtersleben used for the trilogy, it contains a significant textual variant: lines 5–6 in the 1821 and 1824 sources read "Einsam auf Gebirges Zinne / Kloster- wie auch Burgruine," while the version published in 1843 substitutes the lines "Einsamkeiten, Abendschimmer, / hoher Burgen graue Trümmer," either an earlier version or a post-1824 revision. The trilogy therefore cannot be definitively assigned the same 1821 date as *Heliopolis*, nor is the addressee of "Du liebst mich! tief hab ich's empfunden," clearly specified. Whoever "Franz" was, he was younger and seems to have shared the same aesthetic-political ideals as the older poet who hymned him – this does not, of course, preclude Schubert, although Mayrhofer's fellow-writer Schober (the dedicatee of *Heliopolis*) is also a viable alternative.[40] As so often in this tale, one would like to know more, but definitive answers are not forthcoming at present. We may never know.

When Schubert died, Mayrhofer wrote, not a conventional elegy, but an ecstatic song in short, breathless lines, enchained as in a litany: "Nachgefühl. An Fr. Schubert (19. Novbr. 1828)," or "Emotion afterward. To Franz Schubert (19 November 1828)." Before winter (old age) can arrive and ravage everything in its path, the privileged songbird escapes and flies away.

Von eines Birnbaum's Zweige	A little bird sang
Da sang ein Vögelein:	from a pear-tree branch:
Der Herbst, er geht zur Neige,	The autumn draws to a close –
Es muß geschieden sein!	I must depart!
Ich flatt're von hinnen	I fly away
Zu wolkigen Zinnen,	to the cloudy pinnacles,
Weit über das Meer;	far over the ocean;
Die Winde von Norden	the north winds
Sie wüthen und morden	rage and kill
Hier Alles umher!	everything here, all about!
D'rum eil' ich zu Auen,	Therefore, I hurry to the meadows
Wo unter dem lauen	where fragrances, consecrating me,
Gekose der Lüfte	and flowers,
Mich segnende Düfte	under the breezes' mild caresses,
Und Blüten erfreu'n;	gladden me;
Wo ewige Lenze	where eternal springtime
Nie welkende Kränze	extravagantly strews
Verschwenderisch streu'n!	garlands which never wither!
Wie will ich dort singen,	How I want to sing there,
Wie soll es nicht klingen	why shouldn't my peaceful song
Mein friedliches Lied, –	resound –
Wenn jubelnd die Seele	when the soul, rejoicing,
Aus schwellender Kehle	issues forth from the swelling throat
Verstandener zieht!	in full understanding!

O selige Wonnen!	O blessed rapture!
Ihr leuchtenden Sonnen,	you shining suns,
Ich fliege zu Euch![41]	I fly to you!

The elegy is all the more poignant when one reflects that the songbird who speaks from line 3 onwards seems a fusion both of Schubert and Mayrhofer himself, longing for the paradisiacal afterlife he envisions as his friend's reward.

The early years in Vienna were the apogee of Mayrhofer's life, but the idyll soon soured irretrievably. In one of his most overtly autobiographical poems, "Tillisberg", he surveys the countryside and the city below from his vantage point on the heights and remembers the happiness he once knew there with a circle of friends. Since that time, life itself had turned on him, love had deserted him, his ideals had betrayed him, and destiny had parted him from those he held most dear. The poem is all the more horrifying because it begins so beautifully, with love of country and gilded memories of youthful friendship, then descends swiftly into an abyss in which he wishes to die but is unable to overcome life's superior force and bring about his own death.

Ich sah zu meinen Füßen ausgebreitet	I saw, stretched out at my feet,
Ein herrlich Land, mein Vaterland;	a glorious land, my fatherland;
Die Donau wälzte fernhin ihre Fluten,	the Danube rolled its tides along into the
Und Berge bildeten den Rand.	distance, and mountains formed its verge.
Gewölke schwammen, wundersam gestaltet,	Beautifully shaped clouds floated above,
Die Schnitter sangen auf der Flur,	the harvesters sang on the banks,
Und Bäume wechselten Gespräch' im Winde,	and trees exchanged conversation in the
Der regsam durch die Äste fuhr.	winds that blew quickly through the branches.
Zur Stadt hin schwärmten meiner Sehnsucht	My longing glances strayed toward the
Blicke;	city;
Dort wandelte so mancher Freund,	many a friend walked there,
Mit dem ich mich, in unvergeß'nen Stunden,	with whom, in never-to-be-forgotten times,
Zum schönen Bunde einst vereint.	I was once joined in a beautiful bond.
Vor meine Seele traten jene Gärten,	Those gardens arranged with many-colored
Die bunter Blumen Flor umspann,	flowers, where life's golden wave flowed along
Wo uns bei jugendlichem Ahnen, Hoffen,	for us, in youthful expectations and hopes,
Des Lebens Welle gold'ner rann.	appeared before my soul.
Ein streng Geschick entrückte mich den	A harsh destiny removed me from the
Kreisen,	circles
Wo Treue schirmend mich umschloß;	where sheltering faithfulness enclosed me.
Von allen alten, traulichen Gesellen	Of all the old, intimate companions,
Blieb nur der Schmerz noch mein Genoss'.	only sorrow still remained with me.
Zerschnitten sind der Liebe zarte Fäden,	Love's sweet cords, on which
An denen froh die Seele hing, –	the soul hung happily, are cut –
Ach, unersetzlich scheint was ich verloren,	Alas, what I have lost seems irretrievable,
Und ohne Werth was ich empfing.	and what I received, without worth.

Dies Herz bedeckt vom heiligen Gewande,	This heart clad in holy raiment
Bebt, ein Lebendiger im Sarg;	trembles, a living creature in the coffin;
Hier, in der freien Schöpfung, thaut die Thräne,	here, in the freedom of creation, tears arise
Die ich den Späheraugen barg.	which I hid from spying eyes.
Mir ist, als müßt' ich von dem Felsen springen	It seems to me as if I must jump from the
In Stromes Flut, – dann wär's vorbei!	rocks into the river – then it will be over!
Die Schlangen ließen ab vom blut'gen Busen,	The snakes will drain out of the bleeding
Vom bangen Geist die Träumerei!	breast, the reveries from out my fearful spirit!

Ich zaud're noch, – welch unbegreiflich Zaudern	I still tarry – from what inexplicable hesitation
Ich sprende die verhaßten Ketten nicht?	can I not burst the hated bonds?
Ich flieh' den Strom, der mir in blauem Schooße	Why do I flee the river, that so faithfully promises me
Beruhigung so wahr verspricht?	peace in its blue depths?
O Leben! Du bist keine weiche Pflanze,	O Life! You are no weak plant,
Du bist ein fester, dunkler Baum,	you are a strong, dark tree –
Es finden zwischen deinen mächt'gen Wurzeln	between your mighty roots, I can
Kaum noch die Kraft zu sterben Raum![42]	hardly find the room or strength to die!

How this man hated himself! – rather than blood draining from the envisioned death-wound, Mayrhofer invokes serpents, lowly, poisonous, and despised creatures, harbored in his breast until death shows them the door. The final image of Life as a giant Yggdrasil-like tree, its massive roots choking the will to die, is truly horrifying. Mayrhofer, it seems clear, contemplated suicide many times before he actually took his own life.

The self-hatred was, as always, conjoined with fear. In stanza 1 of "Zauber" (Magic), he had written, "Do I shy away from the sharp rocks where gray mists swirl? Do I shudder when the smell of putrefaction from the deep abyss surrounds me? *I fear only – myself*" [italics mine]. "Whoever would unveil the deep foundation of this inner fear," he continues, "would heal me," the implicit hope especially pitiable because no such agency was available. In stanza 2 of this particularly beautiful and revealing poem, Mayrhofer writes of seeing an image in the water which looks like him, but light and graceful; divested of his hated corporeal envelope, the *reflet dans l'eau* is fused with a primary element of the Nature he worshipped. Thus to encounter oneself as a disembodied watery *Doppelgänger* seems not only an invocation of death (one recalls that Mayrhofer initially sought death by drowning) but an apt illustration of Freud's theory that such uncanniness ("das Unheimliche") is derived from hidden aspects of the personality come back to haunt the consciousness. For Mayrhofer, it was not merely aspects of the self but the entirety of his being that constituted an eerie mystery; at the same time that he espies the reflection in the water, he invokes a giant creature perched on his shoulder, a creature who cannot be seen and casts no reflection: "Mein Ich," Mayrhofer calls it (and this seventy years before Freud). The sense of a hidden self, of an unknowable being who oppresses him with its weight, is a wonderfully precise image for distress now measured in diagnostic language, for the perception that neither he nor others could see his true self.[43] If he only knew what hidden monster deformed his spirit and his life, perhaps he could banish it.

Mayrhofer's last years are a sad, if remarkably sketchy and incomplete, tale. He had become, just when is not known, a close friend to an elderly professor of law at the University of Vienna named Franz Alois Edler von Zeiller (1751–1828), who, in depression over illness, threw himself into the Danube on 23 August 1828, only three months before Schubert also died. Two years later, so Spaun reported, the July Revolution in France filled the ardently patriotic Mayrhofer with the greatest joy, but two weeks later, infuriated by the outcome, he was reviling Louis Philippe in the strongest terms. Good news about the siege in Poland prompted more outbreaks of "unending hatred against the Russians and all tyrants," according to Spaun. When Mayrhofer heard the news of the fall of Warsaw in 1831, he was maddened by grief and jumped into the Danube, but a fisherman rescued the half-dead poet from the river. In his ironic way, Mayrhofer later commented that he had not thought the river's waters would be so tepid.[44] The Stoics whom he admired held that suicide was justified in some circumstances (both Zeno and his pupil Chrysippus killed themselves), but Mayrhofer's suicidal episodes seem impelled wholly by unbearable psychological distress, not by reason or philosophy. Four years passed: in 1835, the hypochondriac Mayrhofer made a journey to Salzburg for his health and there befriended Johann Ladislaus Pyrker von Felsö-Eör (the poet of Schubert's "Das Heimweh" and "Die Allmacht"), friendship both something of a rarity for the hermit-like Mayrhofer and a treasure he greatly prized.[45] Heartened by the association, he returned to Vienna, where Feuchtersleben found him planning a lengthy narrative poem about medieval monks and knights of which only a fragment remains, entitled "Der Vogelsteller" (The Bird-catcher). In early 1836, he wrote a poem about clouds – his last work, according to Feuchtersleben.

At the same time, another of Vienna's periodic outbreaks of cholera occurred, and Mayrhofer's *idée fixe* on the subject became intolerable. When Mayrhofer was visiting Spaun one day shortly before his death, a young doctor who was present announced the epidemic; when the poet saw Spaun drinking a glass of beer, he commented wistfully that he would like to do so as well but was afraid he would come to harm. A few days later, on 5 February 1836, Mayrhofer went to his office in the Laurenzerberg when a colleague rushed in distraught because his children's nanny had just died of the disease. Mayrhofer quietly said "So" – nothing more, went to the third story of the building, and threw himself out of the window. The reports of his death differ: according to Kreissle von Hellborn, he was taken to the Allgemeine Krankenhaus in the Alservorstadt and lived another forty hours before dying at age forty-eight, while Spaun writes that Mayrhofer lived only long enough to regret his action and died while being transported to the hospital. In his poem "Die erstarrte Amsel" (The frozen blackbird), Mayrhofer told of a bird found dead in winter, a bird who had known many springtime joys, and pleads for the same fate.

Fand am Wege eine Amsel,	I found a blackbird on the path,
Ganz erstarrt, in Schnee gebettet:	completely frozen, bedded in snow:

Vogel! hattest schön gesungen,	Bird, you sang so beautifully
Und nun wirst du nimmer singen!	and now you will never sing again!
Laue Lüfte werden wehen,	Mild breezes will blow,
Bäume werden sich belauben,	trees will leaf out,
Klare Bächlein munter sprudeln,	clear little brooks will murmur merrily,
Und die Rosen sich entfalten;	and the roses unfurl;
Alle Vögel werden zwitschern, –	all the birds will twitter –
Doch die Amsel ist verstummet.	but the blackbird is mute.
War ihr Leben kurz bemessen,	If its life was briefly measured,
Hatt' es dennoch manche Freuden:	it had nonetheless many joys;
Klang sich aus in hellen Tönen	Rang out in bright tones
Eh' der Grimm des Winters nahte.	before the harshness of winter drew near.
Gleiches Schicksal wünscht der Dichter:	The poet wishes for the same fate:
Lenzesfülle, rasches Ende![46]	Springtime fullness, a quick end!

One remembers, sadly, the birdsong elegy to Schubert. If Mayrhofer's end was quick in one sense, it was horrifyingly prolonged in another, since the mental agonies that led to suicide began decades earlier. Indeed, Mayrhofer believed his existence accursed and yet proclaimed his courageous intent to continue his struggle "until my last strength is extinguished, the ground fertilized ['düngen'] with my blood."[47] That last strength was extinguished by fear one day in February 1836.

According to his will, dated 3 October 1829, Mayrhofer wished to be buried in the lowest, meanest grave – this in Vienna, with its "schöne Leiche" cult of magnificent obsequies.[48] It is consistent both with his self-hatred and his detestation of the body that he should wish his remains treated in this way: why expend money and pomp on the interment of a mortal husk he abhorred? (He was perhaps also influenced by Stoic attitudes toward death.) When he was buried on 10 February at 4 o'clock in the afternoon, it was probably in the Währinger Cemetery but all trace of the grave-site has since been lost. Mayrhofer, who wrote in "An die Freunde" ("To my friends," which Schubert set to music in 1819, D. 645) of his wish to be buried without any marker in the forest, would probably have approved. Franz von Schober wrote a sonnet in 1842 about a grave already obscured and in disrepair less than a decade after his friend's death, although one must make due allowance for poetic license.

Ich suchte mir – mein Sinn war trüb umfangen,	I sought out – my spirits were darkly overshadowed – the most deserted
Den öd'sten Platz, wo halbvermorschte Zäune	place, where half-mouldering fences show
Kaum Lebensspuren wiesen. Blass im Scheine	scarcely any signs of life. Pale in the light
Des vollen Monds, der eben aufgegangen,	of the full moon, which had just arisen, the
Lag still die Welt, nur schrille Heimchen sangen.	world lay still; only the shrill crickets sang.
Fahl schimmernd durch die Nesseln, Dornen, Steine	Shimmering palely through the nettles, thorns, stones,
Verriethen klagend menschliche Gebeine,	human bones, lamenting, disclose
Dass jemand hier ein Grab – nicht Ruh empfangen.[49]	that someone found a grave, but not peace, here. (lines 1–8)

That a friend could thus invoke misery's continuation even beyond death is among the most chilling measures of Mayrhofer's unhappiness.

At some unknown time after Mayrhofer's death, Eduard Bauernfeld wrote a detailed portrait of the poet in his *Buch von uns Wienern in lustig-gemütlichen Reimlein* (Book of us Viennese in merry, companionable little rhymes) or the *Rusticocampius*.[50] The poem was later published with extensive additions in Bauernfeld's collected works as "Ein Wiener Censor" (A Viennese censor),[51] Mayrhofer's occupation a crucial element in the unsympathetic portrayal[52] – it is as a "censor," the enemy of poets, not as a "poet," that Bauernfeld designates the dead man. Temperamentally, the two writers were poles apart, and Bauernfeld's dislike of his compatriot is palpable. It seems likely that Mayrhofer may not have bothered to hide his disapproval of Bauernfeld's comedies ("leichten Belletristik"), and the younger writer retaliated with his pen dipped in gall. But Mayrhofer made a deep impression on him nevertheless: the poet's profound response to Schubert's music, his fanatical patriotism, his anti-social behavior, and the paradox of his censorship post are all vividly sketched by someone who knew him – but how well is not known.

Halbvergessen ist Euch jener	The Viennese poet named Mayrhofer
Wiener Dichter, hieß Mayrhofer;	is half-forgotten now;
Viele seiner Poesien	his friend Schubert
Componirte sein Freund Schubert.	composed many of his poems.

this stanza included in the *Rusticocampius*:

So die zürnende Diana	"Die zürnenden Diana,"
Philoktet und manche andre;	"Philoktet," and many others
Waren tief ideenreich	were profoundly thoughtful
Aber schroff, – so wie der Dichter.	but rough – just like the poet.
Kränklich war er und verdrießlich,	He was sickly and peevish,
Floh der heitern Kreise Umgang,	fled the merry circle's dealings,
Nur mit Studien beschäftigt;	occupied himself only with studies;
Abends labte ihn das Whistspiel.	in the evenings, he enjoyed playing whist.
So mit älteren Herren saß er,	So he sat with elderly men,
Mit Beamten, mit Philistern,	with officials, with Philistines,
Selbst Beamter, Bücher-Censor	himself an official, a book-censor,
Und der strengste, wie es hieß.	and among the strictest, so it was said.
Ernst war seine Miene, steinern,	His countenance was serious, stony,
Niemals lächelt' oder scherzt' er.	He never smiled or joked.
Flößt uns losem Volk Respekt ein,	He instilled a sense of respect from us slackers
So sein Wesen und sein Wissen.	with his bearing and his knowledge.

the following three stanzas in the *Rusticocampius* only:

Wenig sprach er, – was er sagte,	He spoke little – what he said
War bedeutend; allem Tändeln	was weighty; he was averse
War er abgeneigt, den Weibern	to all frivolity, to women,
Wie der leichten Belletristik.	to light belles-lettres.

Nur Musik konnt' ihm bisweilen	Only music could at times release
Aus der stumpfen Starrheit lösen,	him from his mute stiffness,
Und bei seines Schuberts Liedern	and his whole being was transfigured
Da verklärte sich sein Wesen.	when he heard the songs of his Schubert.
Seinem Freund zu Liebe ließ er	For love, he allowed his friend
In Gesellschaft auch sich locken,	to entice him into society;
Wenn wir Possen trieben, sah ihn	when we played tricks, I saw him
Stumm dort in der Ecke hocken.	crouching mutely there in the corner.

The remainder is from "Ein Wiener Censor":

Eines Abends, als sich Schubert	One evening, when Schubert
Frei erging im Phantasiren,	indulged in improvisation,
Ueberkam die Dichter-Mumie	deep emotion overcame the poet-mummy
Dort im Winkel tiefes Rühren.	there in the corner.
Des verschrumpften Mannes Körper	The man's shrunken body
Schien sich mächtig auszudehnen,	seemed to expand greatly;
Ueber seine hagern Wangen	hot tears of sorrow
Liefen warme Schmerzensthränen.	ran down his thin cheeks.
Langsam stand er auf vom Sessel,	Slowly, he arose from the armchair
Als die Phantasie zu Ende,	when the improvisation ended,
Und dem Freunde am Klaviere	and he mutely and strongly
Schüttelt stumm und stark die Hände.	shakes the hand of his friend at the piano.
Dann ergreift ein großes Weinglas	Then he takes a large wineglass,
Majestätisch er, bedächtig,	slowly, majestically, he fills it
Füllt es bis zum Rande, stürzt es	to the brim, hurls it down quickly,
Flugs hinunter, rasch und mächtig.	bold and powerful.
Ward gesprächig da und geistreich,	He became garrulous then and witty,
Ueberrascht', erfreute Jeden	astonished and overjoyed everyone
Durch die Frische der Gedanken –	through the freshness of his thought –
Ließen bald allein ihn reden.	we soon let him alone speak.
Oesterreich wurde durchgesprochen	Austria and its future development
Und sein künftiges Entfalten,	was thoroughly discussed,
Wie's vom Weg auch abgekommen,	how it had deviated from its course,
So von Kaiser Joseph's Walten.	since Emperor Joseph's reign.
Kaiser Joseph war der Heros,	Emperor Joseph was the poet's
Den der Dichter sich erkoren,	chosen hero,
Und er klagte patriotisch,	and he patriotically lamented
Daß sein Oesterreich verloren.	that his Austria was lost.
Alle Fehler der Regierung	He set forth in logical array
Setzt' er aus einander logisch,	all the faults of the government,
Immer feuriger die Rede,	the speech became ever fierier,
Ward zuletzt wild-demagogisch –	was in the end wild and demagogic.

Daß er aufsprang so vom Tische,
Und mit Worten, kecken, dreisten,
Nur von Freiheit sprach und Volksthum,
Schäumend, mit geballten Fäusten.

Then he sprang from the table
and with bold, audacious words,
spoke only of freedom and nationhood,
foaming, with clenched fists.

Also sprach er, also tobt' er,
Glas auf Glas hinunterstürzend,
Und mit Witzen, mit Sarkasmen
Seine wilde Rede würzend.

Thus he spoke, raged,
drinking glass after glass,
and spicing his wild speech
with wit and sarcasm.

Und zum Schluß beiläufig sagt' er. –
"Ja, der Geist hat seine Waffen,
Wird sie einst damit zerschmettern
Diese Knechte, diese Pfaffen!

And in conclusion, he said casually,
Yes, the spirit has its weapons,
May they someday be destroyed by them,
these knaves, these clerics!

Nach Jahrhunderten vielleicht erst,
Ueber all' die Leichenhügel
Flattert, jetzt noch Puppe, Menschheit,
Als ein Falter mit dem Flügel.

Perhaps after centuries,
humanity, now only chrysalises,
will flutter like a winged butterfly
above all the grave-mounds.

Doch in jedem der Jahrhundert'
Treibt und wächst der Puppe Leben,
Und zum Licht empor zu dringen
Ist ihr innerstes Bestreben.

But in each century, life grows
stronger within the chrysalis,
and its innermost aspiration is
to emerge into the light.

Ja, ich sag' es Euch prophetisch:
Kommen werden schlimme Zeiten,
Und die Dunkelmänner werden
Gegen Licht und Wahrheit streiten.

Yes, I say to you prophetically:
Bad times will come,
and men of darkness will
battle against light and truth.

Aber kommen wird am Ende
Doch die neue schöne Aere,
Siegen wird der Geist, die Freiheit,
Und die neue Gleichheits-Lehre!"

But in the end
the new beautiful era will come,
the spirit, freedom, and the new
teachings of equality will triumph!

So ein österreich'scher Censor
Sprach vor etwa vierzig Jahren;
Wörtlich weiß ich's nicht – doch schwör' ich,
Daß es die Gedanken waren!

Thus spoke an Austrian censor
some forty years ago;
I don't know it word for word – but I swear
that these were the thoughts!

Und im Leben hat der Mann
So gesprochen wohl nur einmal,
Trocken saß er sonst und stumm,
Wie auf einem Grab das Stein-Mal.

And in life, the man
spoke thus only once.
Usually he sat there mute and dull,
like the stone on a grave.

Und am nächsten Morgen saß er
Als Beamter am Censur-Tisch,
Streng, gewissenhaft und Pflicht-treu
Strich er jede Geistes-Spur frisch.

And the next morning, he sat
as an official at the censor's table,
Strict, conscientious, and duty-bound,
he struck out every trace of spirit.

Einmal kam er frühen Morgens	One time, he came to the office early
In's Bureau, begann zu schreiben,	in the morning and began to write,
Stand dann wieder auf – die Unruh'	then stood up again – unrest
Ließ ihn nicht im Zimmer bleiben.	did not allow him to remain in the room.
Durch die düstern Gänge schritt er	He walked through the dark passageways,
Starr und langsam wie in Träumen,	slow and staring, as if dreaming,
Der Kollegen Gruß nicht achtend,	not heeding his colleagues' greetings,
Stieg er nach den obern Räumen.	he mounted to the upper stories.
Steht und stiert durch's off'ne Fenster,	Stands and stares through the open window,
Draußen wehen Frühlingslüfte,	Outside spring breezes blow,
Doch den Mann, der finster brütet,	but the man, who brooded darkly, breathes
Haucht es an wie Grabesdüfte.	it in as if it were scents from the grave.
An dem off'nen Fenster kreiselt	At the window, flecks of sunlight
Sonnenstaub im Morgenscheine –	circle in the morning light –
Und der Mann lag auf der Straße	and the man lay on the street
Mit zerschmettertem Gebeine.[53]	with shattered bones.

In Bauernfeld's 1835 essay "Die schöne Literatur in Österreich" (Belles-lettres in Austria), Mayrhofer is described as "geistvoll" (gifted), a "strong and manly spirit," who nonetheless lacked true lyrical sweetness and whose poetry was only "complete" when Schubert set it to music.[54] In his diary for 6 February 1836, Bauernfeld wrote, "Yesterday the poet Mayrhofer threw himself out the window. A victim of the Austrian establishment [Ein Opfer des Oesterreichertums],"[55] continuing: "Salon at Eskeles's. Schröder-Devrient sang 'Der Wanderer' [D. 649 to a text by Friedrich von Schlegel, or D. 493, to Georg Philipp Schmidt von Lübeck's words?] and 'Erlkönig' brilliantly." As in the poetic portrait, but more tersely, he evokes the conflict between the dead poet's *Brotwissenschaft* and his beliefs.

Whatever Bauernfeld's disapproval, tainted by personal dislike, the 1824 *Gedichte* met with general approval from the critics when it first appeared.[56] The fact that Ernst von Feuchtersleben, highly regarded as a literary critic in Vienna, compiled the dead poet's *Nachlass* for publication and wrote a lengthy prefatory biography was yet another index of contemporary praise for Mayrhofer, at least in Vienna. (Franz Grillparzer, however, condemned the collection out-of-hand, declaring "These poems should never have been printed! … friends might find much of interest in the manuscripts, but for strangers, whatever counsel they might find is not worth the trouble." When the *Neue Sammlung* appeared in 1843, Grillparzer was less condemnatory, observing somewhat more gently that the verses were, in his estimation, *poesia per musica*.[57] He was not, however, willing to grant them status as self-sufficient works of art.) Tragically, Mayrhofer was just beginning to win outside recognition for his poetic gifts when he killed himself. In 1837, Julius Seidlitz (a pseudonym for Alois Isidor Jeitteles) published *Die Poesie und die Poeten in Österreich im Jahre 1836* (Poetry and poets in Austria in the year 1836), with the following passage about Mayrhofer:

One of the most gifted Austrian poets, but a terra incognita outside that country. A strong but somewhat gloomy character reigns over a self-sufficient reclusivity; he seems like a mimosa in his convulsive twitching-away from every outside contact, and he displays more an inner life of the soul than an outward realm or diverse observations about the external world in his poetry. Many of his best poems were set to music by the unhappily too-soon deceased Schubert. Mayrhofer is one of those young Viennese poets, one out of the crowd who, by concentrating his energies, could ultimately construct an Austrian national poetry not dependent upon the German school.[58]

It is a dreadful irony that the poet was alive when these friendly words were written, dead when they were printed.

Although Spaun records Mayrhofer saying that he only began to like his own poems when Schubert set them to music,[59] Mayrhofer had more in mind than *poesia per musica*, and he made his views about the duties of a poet and the proper nature of poetry the subject of his verse. "Poetry should reconcile, not agitate [Die Poesie soll ja versöhnen, nicht aufregen]," he wrote in a strong statement of his classical ideals and his belief that the soul's harmony should be fostered, even brought into being, through the agency of the poet. In "Objectiv und Subjectiv," the attraction of subjectivity – finding one's own self everywhere and in everything – is measured against what to Mayrhofer was the nobler aim of *submerging* one's identity in order to give poetic bounty to humanity. "Your 'I' is something Other [Entweder ist's dein Ich], which engages you and takes all your imaginative energy to cultivate," he writes, concluding:

Und doch ist es viel edler sich zu opfern,	And yet it is far nobler to sacrifice oneself,
Und lohnender im All zu seyn:	and more rewarding to be in everything,
Der Nährerin und Mutter aller Dinge	to dedicate one's life, like one's song,
Das Leben, wie das Lied zu weih'n.[60]	to the nurturer and mother of all things.

"You," one suspects, is Mayrhofer himself. The poet should, he wrote in "Der Dichter an das Publikum" (The poet to the public), depict passions, hate, love, all lands, all times, in an artist's dispassionate manner, observing, not participating, in the storminess of life and love,[61] although this was not an ideal he could maintain undisturbed from recurrent attack by pathological melancholy. He disliked Romanticism and twitted his confrères for their fascination with "what once pleased the savage Goths," or medieval themes, in "Neue Kunst" (New Art) – did he have the Nazarenes in mind? "The Devil is loose!," he cries, tweaking Romantic love of the supernatural as well.

Dächer, roth und gelb bemalt,	Rooftops, painted red and yellow,
Thürmchen, eckig, spitz und alt,	Little towers, angular, sharp and old,
Bunter Plunder, trüber Dunst:	brightly-colored trash, dark miasmas:
Siehe da die deutsche Kunst!	Behold German art!
Daß es Gothen einst gefiel –	That Gothic was once pleasing,
Sagst Du – kümm're Dich nicht viel?	you say, doesn't that bother you?
Bst! sonst ist der Teufel los,	Pst! the devil is already loose
Und der neuen Schule Troß'![62]	and the new school's camp followers!

This is Mayrhofer at his roughest and most sarcastic, but then he was writing about what mattered most to him. As early as the *Beyträge*, Mayrhofer was already inveighing against the "distortions and mistakes of the German school," that is, the Romantics. This would not last, he predicted; fads for "Gothic poetry or Chinese architecture ... are mere aberrations and nothing more – time will bear me out."[63] Time, often of a disobliging nature, promptly buried Mayrhofer's verse (except in Schubert's lieder) and has preserved the "distortions and aberrations" against which he railed.

The poems of the *Heliopolis* cycle are entirely devoted to the nature of art and the artist's role in society as Mayrhofer conceived them. "We will vary an ancient theme, carried out in the dim past," he announced at the beginning, "We may, though we stumble and lose our way, strive still more often for the sun." The sun was art, Heliopolis the city of art, and artists the children of the light, as we learn in the initial epigrams; if artists do not succeed in the practical world of society, filled with superficial souls who cannot understand them, they can still quietly create "what others cannot hinder" (the third epigram). It is art which constructs, which orders the universe, which produces results, the latter of great importance in an aesthetic which stressed "Taten" (deeds). And yet here, before the poems begin, Mayrhofer's ambivalence about society's capacity to attain betterment through art – Schiller's aesthetic program – and his frequent theme of art as escape from "humans embroiled in controversy" (words from the fifth poem, which Schubert set to music as "Heliopolis I," D. 753) are evident. Heliopolis, as David Gramit has pointed out, is a place from which the world can learn by observation how to worship art – its wider mission – but it is also a walled enclosure in which artists can take refuge from a world of limitation and suppression.

The ambivalence only intensifies when the poems begin (Schubert set no. 4 to music as "Nachtviolen," D. 752; no. 5 as "Heliopolis I" [Im kalten, rauhen Norden]; no. 12 as "Heliopolis II" [Fels auf Felsen], D. 754; and no. 20 as "Lied eines Schiffers an die Dioskuren," D. 360). This is not a narrative cycle by any stretch of the imagination, but neither is it entirely haphazard in design. It begins and ends, one notes, with idealistically optimistic poems in which the symbol for the poet is a sailor ("Schiffer"); Mayrhofer was fond of the antique metaphor of the sailor/soul on the river of time and life, and he uses it in the first poem, "Ein Fischer fuhr den Strom herab" (A fisherman travelled up the stream – the fisherman becomes a sailor in stanzas 4 and 6), when the poetic persona asks the river god to explain the water's power, "its eternal emptying, its eternal presence, for the sailor has to know what it is on which he travels and moves about." When one seeks to understand what one lives on, the poet assures the reader, one will find it, first fragmentarily, then the whole. At the end of the cycle, the sailor returns to sing a hymn of thanks to the twin stars who guide him on his journey (multivalent suggestions of Goethe and Schiller and of Castor and Pollux, the latter resonant of antiquity and, perhaps, homosexuality). There are other bridges spanning successive poems as well: nos. 2 and 3 are linked by references to storms and crashing waters, while nos. 3 and 4 are connected by their central flower imagery of a lily and dame's violets. When the world pales and sinks away at the end of no. 4, "Nachtviolen," we are ready to

enter the city of the sun/the city of art in no. 5, "Im kalten, rauhen Norden."
Nos. 6 and 7 are *Mahnungen*, admonitions for the proper conduct of the poetic life,
injunctions to continue working and to revere Nature, whose creativity surpasses
anything made by mortals. Nos. 8 and 9 are poems about poetry, about the impractical
nature of poets and the "purest ether" in which they move towards the sun. "But
how illumination alters everything!," he exclaims joyously in the ninth poem.

Poetry about poetry in the hemmed-in world of Biedermeier Austria was
Mayrhofer's preoccupation elsewhere as well as in *Heliopolis*. Art was Mayrhofer's
raison d'être, his sole proud defense against the loneliness he laments in "Resultat"
(Result). "Who will dry the tears I have wept for myself? Where was the friend,
with anxious desire to comfort me?," the poetic persona asks, in a melancholy
variant of Goethe's "Trost in Thränen";[64] no one comes, and he continues, "Thus
newborn courage steeled the sad years; I steer and journey on poetic flood-waters."[65]
When all else failed, poetry remained, as Mayrhofer wrote in the couplet: "Die
Freuden gingen in die Weite – / Nur Poesie blieb mir zur Seite" (Joy vanishes in
the distance – only poetry remains by my side).[66] Contrary to the aesthetic ideals
of his youthful circle of friends, he does not often hymn the *vita activa*, or involvement
in the real world, but instead extols poetry's power to veil reality from view
temporarily, if always with the underlying knowledge that horror lurks below the
surface. In "Der Fernen" (The Distant One), he begs the unidentified "Du," surely
his Muse or Poetry itself, to envelop "fearful nights, fearful days" in a gauzy veil of
poetry and asserts that even mountain breezes, art, and music are less effectual
comforts than poetry.[67] In "Geborgenes" (Hidden), his favorite pessimistic leitmotives
nevertheless lead to praise for solitude graced by the Muses and to the desire to
create something praiseworthy.

Der frömmste Wunsch bleibt unerfüllt,	The most pious wish remains unfulfilled,
Die Zukunft uns in Nacht gehüllt,	the future is veiled from us in night,
Und Geist mit Sinnlichkeit im Streite	and spirit in conflict with sensuality
…	…
Was nennst du, Wanderer, noch dein?	What can you still call your own, wanderer?
"Ich bin allein, ja ganz allein –	"I am alone, entirely alone,
Doch quillt mir immer noch im Busen	and yet the courage to do what is
Der Muth, zu thun, was löblich ist;	praiseworthy still wells up in my heart
Und meine Einsamkeit versüßt	and the Muses' sisterly greeting
Der schwesterliche Gruß der Musen."[68]	sweetens my loneliness."

In "Sängers Loos" (Poet's Fate), the poetic narrator describes the sorrowful minstrel,
wandering on bleak paths as if under a curse, and asks whether love has been robbed
from this man, whether it is a sickness of the blood that afflicts him, whether he is
mad that he should seek renewal in a desolate landscape where the storm howls
through withered branches – life as futile effort in a hideous wilderness.[69] Although
the attempt at self-analysis of his ills, falling short of an answer, is tragic, the poem
culminates in a graveyard epiphany of song:

Horch!	Listen!
Was tönt aus jener Hütte für ein Sang?	What song resounds from that cottage?
Wie doch der Töne milde Kraft das Herz	How the gentle power of music stirs the heart
In seinen Tiefen wendet, und ein Land	to its depths and makes a land
Wie das der ersten Liebe uns erschließt![70]	like that of first love appear to us!

One remembers Bauernfeld's description of Mayrhofer listening to Schubert's music and realizes anew that music was one of the poet's few avenues of escape from his misery, notes as well the link between music and idyllic memory.[71] But such consolation was only intermittent; the darkness which was his habitual climate always returned.

Aware that he was suffering some unnameable oppression of the spirit, Mayrhofer writes in "Veränderung" (Transformation) of the depressive's inertia and of the desire for a "tempest of deeds," a frenzy of creativity to revitalize the soul:

Meines Lebens Tage wandern	The days of my life
Zur Unendlichkeit dahin:	stretch out to infinity:
Träge, einer gleich dem andern,	sluggishly, one like the next,
Keiner frisch und keiner grün.	none of them fresh and none of them green.
Nebel hüllen schon die kahlen	Mists already envelop the bare
Bergeshöh'n in Silberfarb,	mountain heights in silvery hues,
Und die holde Macht der Strahlen	and the gentle power of the sun's rays
Hinter den Gewölken starb.	has died behind the clouds.
Walte wieder, Sturm der Thaten!	Rule again, storm of deeds!
Flüst're wieder, Liebeshauch!	Whisper again, breath of love!
Schwanken, meines Herzens Saaten,	Tremble in the breezes, my heart's seeds,
In den Lüften, wie ein Rauch![72]	like smoke!

"Im Sturme" (In the Storm) and "Hinaus" (Out there) tell of the same desire for violent action, both heaven-storming creativity and participation in the world:

Spreite, Sturm, die Geierflügel	Spread your hawk's wings, storm,
Über die Ströme, über die Hügel, –	over the rivers, over the hills –
Rüttle die Thürme mit luftigem Speer	Rattle the towers with airy spears,
Pack' an den flatternden Locken das Meer!	seize the ocean's waving locks!
Sturm ist Leben;	Life is a storm –
Sturm muß heben	Storms must uplift
Geist und Muth;	spirit and courage;
Brause, schöpferische Flut![73]	rage on, creative flood!
Aus schwarzen Wolken zischen scharfe Pfeile	Sharp arrows whiz from black clouds and
Auf's Menschenherz, und bohren Wunden;	strike men's hearts, and pierce them with
Es blutet fort in bangen Stunden,	wounds; they bleed for fear-filled hours –
Die nur dem Glücklichen entfliehen in Eile.	only the lucky ones escape in haste.
Wirst du des Blutes Strömung stets betrachten,	Would you then continually contemplate the
Um deinen Schmerzen nachzuhängen,	flowing stream of blood, surrender to your
Und deine Kräfte einzuengen –	sorrows, confine your forces?

Wo, Armer, bleibt das schöpferische Trachten:	Where, wretched one, is the poetic goal:
Die Welt nach allen Seiten aufzufassen?	to grasp the world from all sides?
Ist es wohl recht, ein junges Leben,	Is it truly right to surrender a young life
Der tiefsten Schwermuth hingegeben,	to the deepest melancholy,
In Selbstsucht und in Thorheit zu verprassen?	to dissipate it in foolishness and egoism?
Hinaus, wo sich Gefahren thürmen,	Go out, where perils loom,
Ins Thatenfeld hinaus geritten!	ride forth into the field of deeds!
Und wird dir auch der Tod erstritten:	And if you are stricken unto death,
Viel schöner bleibt, als siechen, stürmen.[74]	it is much more beautiful to be in the midst of storms than to languish in chronic sickliness.

Unable to surmount his melancholy, he blamed himself for his "failures," and the self-reproaches for "foolishness and egoism," for his sickliness, are painful to read.

Trapped in a psychic malady for which no alleviation was available, Mayrhofer could only conceive of existence itself as inimical to him, and he made his horror of life the subject of many poems, most powerfully in "Der Barde unter Felsen" (The bard amidst the rocks):

Umschränkt von rauhen Klippen,	Surrounded by rough crags
Die nackt und feindlich steh'n,	that stand hostile and naked,
Entfließt das Lied den Lippen,	the song flows from my lips
Um spurlos zu verweh'n;	to vanish without a trace.
Umsonst wend' ich nach Leben	In vain, I turn my sorrowful gaze
Den kummervollen Blick, –	towards life –
Er kehrt mit wildem Beben	with wild trembling, my eyes turn back
Von Nacht und Tod zurück.	to night and death.
Hier blühen keine Blumen,	Here, no flowers bloom,
Hier weilt nicht Hirsch noch Reh,	here, no stag, no doe lingers,
Die Vögel selbst verstummen,	the very birds are mute;
Nur ferne rauscht die See.	the sea but murmurs in the distance.
Die Wolken hängen düster	The clouds hover darkly
In's kahle Thal herein;	in the barren valley.
Der Musen treuen Priester,	Is there no glimmer of hope
Labt ihn noch Hoffnungsschein?	for the Muses' faithful priest?
Ja doch! der Dichtung Schleier	Yes, truly, poetry's veil
Verhüllt die Wüstenei,	cloaks the wilderness;
Er schafft sich mit der Leier	with his lyre, he creates for himself
Ein Leben, schön und frei;	a free and beautiful life,
Bevölkert mit Heroen	peoples the still, rocky land
Das stille Felsenland,	with heroes
Und wandert mit den Hohen,	and wanders hand in hand
Ein Bruder, Hand in Hand.[75]	with the exalted ones as their brother.

Freedom, the brotherhood of heroes, and art could only flourish in imaginary realms; one notes the implicit distinction between the life that blossoms apart from him, upon which he gazes longingly, and the dead, mute, sterile geography of his own soul. Only in privileged poetic moments could he leave earth and roam among the immortals on Mount Olympus, as he writes in "Unter Antiken" (Among the gods of antiquity), freed from the might of "you cold murderers." Who the "kalten Würger" are, he does not say, and the lack of specificity chillingly enlarges the possibilities.[76] And yet, he knew that poetic creativity was a privileged state and wondered in "Frage" (Question) why the Muses had chosen him for such beauty, rare though such moments might be:

Wie kam es denn, daß eine Welt	How did it happen, that a world
Von Schönheit sich vor mir erschließt,	of beauty opened up before me,
Daß milder Glanz die Nacht erhellt,	that the night was illuminated with
Und wie vom Himmel niederfließt?	gentle radiance, as if flowing down
Daß Dichtung mit dem weichsten Moos	from heaven, that poetry covered over
Die Felsen überkleidet, –	the rocks with the softest moss,
Daß ich in eines Traumes Schooß	that I am cradled, unblessed,
Mich wiege unbeneidet?[77]	in the lap of a dream?

One sees the words "Schooß" and "wiegen" and realizes that poetry for Mayrhofer was, in part, a return to childhood, with dream or fantasy as the nurturing force, then sees the adjective "unbeneidet" (unblessed) and realizes once more that he considered himself accursed and could never forget it, even in the midst of creative bliss.

Nature's beauty and capacity for renewal, its phoenix-like awakening from wintry death, gave Mayrhofer his happiest moments and the subjects for his least shadowed poems. "Freudig schaut sich's in die grünen Bäume, / Und erhebend in die Wolkensäume" (Joyfully I look about in the green trees, rising up into the flock of clouds), he wrote in "Am Abend" (In the Evening), and in his final paean to clouds, he again looks heavenward: "Above the earth, / the clouds glide along, changing hues ... the saddened eyes of humanity look up at you with longing."[78] Like the wanderer contemplating the vastness above and below from his Alpine eyrie in Caspar David Friedrich's *The Wanderer Above the Mists*, Mayrhofer too found sublimity in the peaks, removed from the "traurig abgestorb'ne Welt" (the mournful, dying world), as he wrote in "Gebirgslust" (Mountain happiness): "Gray mountains, ancient giants, you who defended the meadow valleys, longingly I go to you – receive me into your kingdom! ... Truth, greatness, beauty are only vouchsafed to men in Nature." In Nature, he could, depending upon the mood and the hour, both relish the present moment, "frei vom War und Werde" ("free of Was and Will Be," of past and future), as he wrote in a beautiful phrase from "Abend. Waldhausen" (Evening. Waldhausen), and reflect peacefully in "Der gezähmte Dach" on the beauty of "what has vanished and of the future" under the trees at twilight. In Nature, he could even, on occasion, take heart and resolve to do as springtime did in "Am Morgen," to "Schaffe, wage und gewinne!" (Create, dare, and win out!).[79] *His* winter, however, was unconquerable.

Ultimately, Mayrhofer's œuvre is dominated by anguished questioning about the meaning, or meaninglessness, of life, no mere revelling in fashionable Melancholia but something blacker and more profound. In the two important linked poems entitled "Akkorde" (implying both chords in music and contracts, the latter of the grimmest cosmic kind?), Mayrhofer uses his characteristic trochaic dimeters and rhyming couplets for their incantatory effect, enhanced by the haunting envelope of empty white space around the brief lines. The concision and the alliterative word-music throughout – for example, the exquisite succession of sibilants in "Sterne säen / Zauberlieder" – testify to Mayrhofer's poetic powers at their best.

1. Tannen düstern,
   Schauer flüstern,
   Und die Zukunft,
   Wie ein Riese,
   Steigt empor
   Auf jener Wiese,
Und auf eines Tempels Trümmer
Fällt des Mondes grauer Schimmer.

   Pine trees darken,
   Terror whispers,
   and the Future,
   like a giant,
   rises up
   in the meadow beyond
and on the ruins of a temple
falls the moon's gray shimmer.

   Tannen düstern
   Schauer flüstern:
   Was die Dunklen
   Dir bereiten,
   Du vermagst es
   Nicht zu deuten;
Was die Thräne längst befeuchtet,
Schau' es traurig klar beleuchtet!

   Pine trees darken,
   Terror whispers:
   What the dark ones
   are preparing for you,
   you are unable
   to understand it;
What tears have long bedewed,
sadly see it clearly-lit!

2. Gedanken gehen
   Auf und nieder –
   Sterne säen
   Zauberlieder;
   Büsche streuen
   Träumerein;
   Geister rathen
   Uns zu Thaten,
   Jene wiegen,
   Diese kriegen,
   Kräfte engen,
   Kräfte drängen
Nichts erzielend, ewig streben –
Ist das Leben?[80]

   Thoughts go
   up and down –
   Stars sow
   magic songs;
   bushes strew
   reveries;
   spirits counsel us
   to act.
   This one cradles,
   that one fights,
   forces confine us,
   forces compel us,
Nothing achieving, always striving:
Is this life?

The evergreens, emblematic of eternity, darken in a numinous cosmos from which the gods of yore have vanished, their disappearance symbolized by the ruined temple. No longer can anyone or anything protect us from what the terrifyingly unspecified "dark ones" do, barred from powerless humanity's understanding ("Du" can be understood as Mayrhofer speaking both to himself and to the reader). Reading these two poems, one recalls Maurice Maeterlinck's Symbolist plays of the 1890s, whose *Märchen*-like characters are similarly ruled by a malevolent, unknowable Destiny, the future always dreadful, action always meaningless. And yet, the immaterial forces who permeate Mayrhofer's poetic cosmos and everything in it are beautiful as well, singers of "magic songs," and it is these forces both light and dark who compel women to one fate, men to another (the conventional division between those who tend cradles and those who fight wars encompassing the entire human race) and ban achieved happiness from either. But the dark powers prevail. In "Der Weltengeist und der Mensch," the World Spirit responds in turn to the Boy, the Youth, and the Man; the latter tells of being imprisoned by sorrows and of his need to wander in the forests and fields with the words of the "Beautiful Ones" stirring within him – even here, in this bleak recounting of the Ages of Man, there is a tinge of beauty, even if it is insufficient to outweigh all that darkness. At the end, the earth quakes and the World Spirit turns on him savagely, saying, "Die, thou worm!"[81] Nihilistic determinism hangs heavy in the air of many such poems, countered only by Mayrhofer's heroic insistence that he not surrender entirely to despair and by hard-won moments of belief in a "milde Land" (gentle land) after death.

Brahms rightly observed that Schubert gravitated to Mayrhofer's poems on mythological themes even more than he did to the nature poems; no friend to the Romantics, Mayrhofer nonetheless is part and parcel of what Friedrich Schlegel foresaw in the first years of the nineteenth century would be a rejuvenation of modern literature by the ancients. Although one of Mayrhofer's biographers rashly compared him to Hölderlin, Mayrhofer's fascination with Greek antiquity – it was his preferred subject matter – was entirely different in character from his great contemporary.[82] Mayrhofer does not mourn the loss of long-vanished Greek glory nor yearn to bring it back; he does not exalt, after Winckelmann's example, the noble simplicity of Greek art, nor, like Goethe, did he seek the model of perfected humanity in ancient Greece. Rather, Mayrhofer found in antiquity an escape from the despised present and the *Urquelle* of his own ideals and obsessions. In the "Gesang der Promethiden" (Song of Prometheus's followers), the adherents of the fettered Titan call out for a savior from among the gods and threaten the immortals with Nemesis, should they fail to respond. "When will we see once again / the beautiful morning glow of freedom?", Mayrhofer the patriot asks, and then proclaims, "Learn, ye godly ones, first to know the free human spirit, and you will call him Friend and Brother!" In his own longing for death and transmogrification, he was particularly fascinated by those moments in which the great Job-figures of Greek literature attained apotheosis or foresaw imminent release in death. The ecstatic Endymion expires in bliss in "Der zürnenden Diana," Orestes begs Diana to relieve him of his accursedness in "Der landende Orest" and "Der entsühnte Orest," and the elderly Oedipus foretells his death in "Antigone und Oedip." For himself, he could foresee no such Elysium.

In his loss of certainty about existence, Mayrhofer seems a proto-Expressionist a century before the fact. The intensity of radical emotions, the perception that truth is spiritual and that the artist must find symbols for its revelation, the combination of abstraction with great subjectivity, the sense of the unbridgeable discrepancy between the dream world and reality, and the concern with the ineffable are all

Expressionistic traits foreshadowed in Mayrhofer, but in his own fashion.[83] If he never goes as far as the "telegraph style" of twentieth-century Germany, he *did* devise a highly concentrated idiom marked by unconventional syntax and by a succession of images with remarkably casual, or even absent, connectives between them, poetry with the terseness of a clenched fist. And like his modern descendants, he too was a *poeta dolorosus*, martyred by his very nature, and like them, he spun poetry from his misery. But in his white-hot yearning for conversion into pure spirit and his idiosyncratic verbal gestures, he is unique. However rough his poetic language on occasion, it can also be both powerful and beautiful – and it inspired many of Schubert's best songs, to which we now turn.

SCHUBERT'S MAYRHOFER LIEDER

1.   I begin, not with the fourteen earliest Mayrhofer songs of 1814–1816, but in January 1817, with "Fahrt zum Hades" (Journey to Hades), D. 526. Although there are wonderful things in the songs which precede this neglected masterpiece, including "Liane," D. 298, "Fragment aus dem Aeschylus," D. 450, and "Wie Ulfru fischt," D. 525,[84] the artistic rapport between poet and composer seems to have begun only slowly; not until this lied did Schubert begin truly plumbing the depths of Mayrhofer's poetic world. He does so with a poem on a classical subject during a year in which such songs proliferate in his œuvre and in which the collaboration between the two friends was at its most intense. I wonder whether Mayrhofer's "Fahrt zum Hades" was perhaps inspired by Schiller's great poem "Gruppe aus dem Tartarus" (Scene from Hades), which Schubert attempted to set to music in March 1816 but soon abandoned (the twenty-three measure fragment is D. 396), returning to it in September 1817 (D. 583), the same year as "Fahrt zum Hades." If so, it seems not at all surprising that Schiller's undifferentiated mass of terrified souls should become a single damned soul – Mayrhofer himself – in the later poem inspired by the earlier masterpiece.

Der Nachen dröhnt, Cypressen flüstern –	The boat moans, the cypresses whisper;
Horch, Geister reden schaurig drein;	Hark, the spirits add their gruesome cries.
Bald werd' ich am Gestad', dem düstern,	Soon I shall reach the shore, so gloomy,
Weit von der schönen Erde sein.	Far from the beautiful earth.
Da leuchten Sonne nicht, noch Sterne,	There neither sun nor stars shine,
Da tönt kein Lied, da ist kein Freund.	No song echoes, no friend is nigh.
Empfang die letzte Träne, [o] Ferne,	Distant earth, accept the last tear
Die dieses müde Auge weint.	that these tired eyes shall weep.
Schon schaue [schau'] ich die blassen Danaiden	Already I see the pale Danaids,
Den fluchbeladnen Tantalus;	and curse-laden Tantalus.
Es murmelt todesschwangern Frieden,	Your ancient river, Oblivion,
Vergessenheit, dein alter Fluss.	breathes a peace heavy with death.
Vergessen nenn' ich zwiefach Sterben.	Oblivion I deem a twofold death; to lose
Was ich mit höchster Kraft gewann,	that which I won with all my strength,

183

Verlieren – wieder es erwerben –	to strive for it once more –
Wann enden diese Qualen? wann?[85]	When will these torments cease? O when?

The poetic speaker is en route from life on the "beautiful earth," which he can see vanishing behind him, to death in a hellish Underworld, from known torments to those guessed but yet to be endured. Here, Mayrhofer imagines the fate of his soul as comparable to that of Danaüs' fifty murderous daughters, who were doomed to draw water in leaking jars that forever had to be refilled. In this personalized damnation where the punishment fits the crime, the poet will forget everything he fought to know, will undergo yet again the pain of acquiring his pessimistic understanding, and then lose it all to the powers of oblivion, over and over again throughout eternity. The reference to "fluchbelad'nen" Tantalus, who stole the gods' nectar and ambrosia and told their secrets to mortals, is similarly laden with symbolic meaning. In Hades, Tantalus stands up to his chin in water, but whenever he bends to slake his thirst, the pool dries up. Boughs laden with fruit hang above his head, but when he tries to pluck the fruit, the wind blows it away, and a stone is forever suspended above him. Mayrhofer's torments will be, he imagines, those of the mind and spirit, not the senses, but as a poet, he too has told the gods' secrets to mortals and tasted nectar – poetic creation – denied to many. In the afterlife, the nectar of poetry and the ambrosia of knowledge will be forever taken away from him. And yet, anticipating torments exquisitely tailored to that which he most treasures, he nonetheless bids farewell to earthly existence with great solemnity and confronts the "todesschwangern Frieden" with dignity (pregnancy bespeaks not life but death in Mayrhofer's chilling oxymoronic neologism "todesschwangern"). When he asks at the end, "When will these torments cease? O when?" one is meant, I believe, to understand "these torments" as both the tortures of hell and present existence, neither life nor the afterlife bearable.

Schubert's setting shares certain elements in common with "Gruppe aus dem Tartarus," in particular, the thrumming triplet eighths – Angst given musical life in fear-filled pulsations – but more Gluckian and restrained. The mass of souls who fill the Stygian air with their pulsating fear in the Schiller lied becomes a single person who struggles to maintain some measure of dignity despite his terror. Schubert, usually prone to higher tessituras in lieder, assigns this and several other Mayrhofer songs to a baritone, the *gravitas* of the poetry impelling heavier, lower vocal registers; perhaps he also had Vogl's roles from Gluck in his mind's ear, even before his first meeting with the singer shortly thereafter. This is Schubert's homage to a Gluckian scena, its tonal language modernised and the whole contained within song dimensions. In the piano introduction (mm. 1–3), Schubert recalls a traditional musical symbol of grief: the *lamentatio* tetrachord descending in inexorable, equal half-notes, the rhythm alone reminiscent of earlier eras, although the antique pattern is here bent to conform to its new poetic and musical context. The fact that the topmost voice in the repeated triplet right-hand chords rises as the bass descends adds yet another element of inexorability and terror, as if fear were rising in direct proportion to the descent into the depths and the whole widening span of the music were poised to engulf the fear-stricken soul (Schubert would use those same thrumming triplets in his setting of Christian Friedrich Schubart's "An den Tod," D. 518, also composed in 1817). When the harmonic rhythm quickens in m. 3, where the scalewise descent in the bass is extended downward an additional whole-step beyond its traditional dimensions of a perfect fourth, the drive-to-cadence (elided, in classic fashion, with the next statement of the pattern) adds to the crescendo of fear even before the singer enters to define the cause and nature of such ominous instrumental strains.

But this is not a ground bass setting throughout – it only begins as one, although transposed and varied statements of the descending bass pattern recur in the second and third sections of the formal structure. Mayrhofer's first line of text ("Der Nachen dröhnt, Cypressen flüstern") is set over a restatement of the left-hand pattern – one notices the evocative leap of a tritone upwards at the word "Cypressen" – and followed by a chromatic variant of mm. 1-2, the tetrachord divided into descending semitone "sighing figures"; the chromatic turning figure in the inner voice on the downbeats of mm. 8–9 is a wonderfully spectral ("Horch, Geister reden schaurig d'rein") intensification of an already fraught gesture (as in Schiller's "Gruppe aus dem Tartarus," we are bidden to listen – "Horch" – to the fearful sounds around us). Most striking of all, the cadential conclusion of the ground bass figure is massively extended and redirected to relative major, or F major, at the words "Bald werd' ich am Gestad', dem düstern / Weit von der schönen Erde sein" (Schubert repeats words to lengthen the phrase even more), the musical patterns "becoming" and "traveling" to a different tonal point of arrival as well. The descent in the bass also lengthens as the song, like the poetic persona, goes down, down into the Underworld, the downward passage extending from D-flat to E (mm. 11–14), while the crucial word "weit," repeated for still more emphasis within this passage, impels neighboring diminished seventh harmonies a semitone apart – quietly "schaurig."

Mayrhofer mingles an encomium to those earthly things he holds most dear (as one might expect from him, they are the light of sun and stars, friends, and music) with a negative description of the horrors of Hades. Hell is the lack of everything one most cherishes on earth, and Schubert therefore signifies a change of place ("Da," or "there") by changes both of meter – from cut-time to 3/4 – and tonality – from D minor to F major, the section heralded by a *mezzo-forte* fanfare. It is, after all, a mighty realm to which he is inexorably bound. It may seem strange at first that Schubert sets the words "Da leuchten Sonne nicht, noch Sterne" at the beginning of stanza 2 to calmly classical F major strains, with none of the claustrophobic darkness one might expect or the throbbing triplet chords of stanza 1. Schubert, knowing the significance of stars for Mayrhofer (they are the symbols of otherworldly beauty and ideal love), emphasizes the word "*Ster*-ne" by means of the raised tonic pitch F-sharp as an appoggiatura to G, followed by a repetition of those words and yet another appoggiatura. Schubert's persona tries to be a true Stoic in the face of death, but almost succumbs, despite himself, to the thickening fear he cannot help but feel. Throughout the setting of stanza 2, the calm restraint of mm. 18–23 gives way by degrees to quickened motion and increasing chromatic darkness. At the words "Da tönt kein Lied, da ist kein Freund," again twice-stated (mm. 24–31), the quarter-note motion quickens to eighth-note motion, and a rising harmonic sequence leads to the phrase on the darker D minor of the opening measures of the song. With the words "Empfang' die letzte Thräne, o Ferne" in mm. 32–36, the harmonies suddenly become darker still, the C-sharp leading tone to D enharmonically transformed to the darker D-flat and the harmonies consisting almost entirely of minor chords and diminished seventh chords, their flatted pitches emblematic of thickening horror, while the repeated chordal pulsations return in the right-hand part, but as duplets, not triplets. Then, in mm. 37–43 ("die dieses müde Auge weint"), the poetic persona regains mastery of his terror and returns to the dignity and restraint of the beginning of stanza 2 and to major mode (B-flat major), but with the D-flat emblems of terror and darkness recurring in mm. 40–41, and 43. The struggle to maintain Stoic dignity, the battle between terror and willed calm, is evident in the mixed modal chord colors of mm. 40–45, but the poet wins the struggle, however briefly. The wavering between D-natural and D-flat culminates with a completed cadence in m. 45, with D-natural in the ascendancy and in the topmost voice.

The fragile, hard-won equipoise is immediately overthrown by fresh horror at the sight of the Danaids. Although the accompanimental figuration changes to a broken-chordal stream surely inspired by the last word of the stanza ("Fluss," or "river"), the harmonies of mm. 46–50 ("Schon schau' ich die blassen Danaiden, den fluchbeladnen Tantalus") are a restatement of those in mm. 32–36 ("Empfang', empfang' die letzte Thräne, o Ferne"). One can only draw the retrospective implication that the dread creatures are already present even as the poetic persona's longing gaze is directed backwards to "the distant one" (a beautifully poignant locution for "the earth"). The telling appoggiatura in the vocal line when the poetic persona designates the "Dana-*i-den*" and the augmented sixth chord with B-*natural* in the voice at the word "*fluch* - [beladnen]" are multiple indices of the horror this sight inspires. With the invocation of "todesschwangern Frieden" and "Vergessen-heit," Schubert descends inexorably into the tonal depths his protagonist has been trying in vain to stave off through the earlier sections of the song; via the chromatic version of the *lamentatio* tetrachord in mm. 51–53, he sinks to D-flat minor. If this key is only a semitone lower than the D minor of the beginning, it is worlds away in tonal terms, truly "fern." In the quarter-note rest at the end of m. 58, the most final of endings resounds … and is rejected immediately.

Mayrhofer did indeed fight against the death-dealing gloom that enveloped him with all his considerable strength of will, and Schubert records the combat, ultimately an unequal one, in tones that are faithful to the bitter heroism of the struggle. Even at the sight of the Danaids, terror is constrained by lyrical melody, symmetrical phrases, and conventional, broken-chordal accompanimental patterns, however dark the harmonies. But with stanza 4, rebellion transgresses the boundaries of lieder altogether, the poet refusing the twofold constraints of song and oblivion alike. Fury and panic surge into dramatic recitative, defiant and then despairing, but always urgent, even in the poignant repetition of the question "Wann enden diese Qualen, wann?". Wrenching away from the D-flat minor of "Vergessenheit," he respells D-flat as C-sharp, F-flat as E-natural, and jolts the A-flat up a semitone to A-natural in m. 59 ("Vergessen nenn' ich zwiefach Sterben"), denying oblivion with every constituent of the chord, but without, one notices, really leaving it altogether. Cloaking it under different names, attempting to turn it in different directions, engaging in furious *forzando* motion, only leads him back to an A-flat *major* chord in m. 62, still in the realm of "Vergessenheit." The violent intervallic gestures at "verlieren — wieder es erwerben" heighten the crucial words after the time-honored manner of operatic *recitativo accompagnato*, before the final question of the poem leads to a half-cadence on the A major chord of m. 59 and the beginning of the recitative, A major as the dominant of D minor.

That is where Mayrhofer's poem ends, with a question he dared not answer, since lurking just behind it was the omnipresent possibility of ending earthly torments at any time he chose. Schubert, however, could not end the lied with so lengthy a stretch of recitative, its imbalancing asymmetries and violent mood-swings demanding a more ordered form to follow, and therefore brings back the opening quatrain, the farewell to "the fair earth." When he does so, he radically alters Mayrhofer's ending, thereby suggesting that the dread vision is a tape loop, that the poet compulsively imagines the approach to Hades over and over again. It is not the first nor the last time that Schubert's personal knowledge of the poet seems subtly to have influenced the compositional decisions he made in setting his friend's verse to music. Perhaps it influenced as well one final, and heart-wrenching, element of the design: when Schubert brings back the first stanza, he thus ends the song in the "Stoic" key of F major. Even though the fear-filled pulsations continue, even though the D-flats of minor mode recur (especially in mm. 83–84, where the singer chants funereally on a repeated F while the bass line descends through a series of flatted pitches in the bass), he thus allows his friend to conclude ascendant over his fears, to leave the scene with the dignity and control he so prized. The poem, one notes sadly, does not end thus.

2. The gloom is no less thick in one of Mayrhofer's most beautiful works: "Auf der Donau" (On the Danube). Here, the landscape comes "alive" – but with ghostly and extinct presences – and threatens, not just the poetic persona, but all who read this *memento mori* with a difference.

Auf der Wellen Spiegel	On the mirror of the waves
Schwimmt der Kahn,	glides the boat;
Alte Burgen ragen	old castles soar
Himmelan,	heavenwards.
Tannenwälder rauschen	Pine forests stir
Geistergleich –	like ghosts –
Und das Herz im Busen	and our hearts within our breasts
Wird uns weich.	grow faint.

Denn der Menschen Werke	For the works of man
Sinken all',	all perish.
Wo ist Turm und Pforte,	Where is the tower
[Turm, wo Pforte],	and gate,
Wo der Wall,	where is the rampart?
Wo sie selbst, die Starken?	Where are the mighty themselves,
Erzgeschirmt,	clad in bronze armor,
Die in Krieg und Jagden	who stormed forth to battle
Hingestürmt.	and the chase?
Trauriges Gestrüppe	Mournful brushwood
Wuchert fort,	grows rampant
Während frommer Sage	while the power of pious myth
Kraft verdorrt:	fades.
Und im kleinen Kahne	And in our little boat
Wird uns bang –	we grow afraid –
Wellen droh'n, wie Zeiten	Waves, like time, threaten
Untergang.[86]	Doom.

In recordings and books of song texts, one usually finds this poem incorrectly printed in quatrains in trochaic pentameters rather than Mayrhofer's eight-line stanzas in alternating trochaic trimeters and dimeters, and yet the poet's formal structure is integral to the meaning of this powerful poem. Rather than cloaking his dark broodings in richly sonorous longer lines, Mayrhofer resorts once again to the tersest of poetic units surrounded by emptiness, the culmination of the poem in doom all the more starkly inescapable when the final line consists of the single word "Untergang." Like the ticking of a giant clock, the trochees are emphasized by their very regularity and by the accented ending to every even-numbered line. After a pause where the absent unaccented syllable at the end of lines 2, 4, 6, and 8 would have been, a pause in which we contemplate our latter end, another two lines in exactly the same rhythmic pattern follow; the unnaturally unvaried rhythmic pulsation underscores the dread awareness of Time's depredations which is at the heart of the poem. The correspondence between form and content is beautifully, horribly precise – and lost from music, which converts all poetic form into prose. Schubert had to find, and did, substitutes from the realm of music for the loss of such expressionistic verbal rhythms.

The tableau of the river, the ancient castles, and the pine forests – the stuff of travel posters – here inspires an Angst-ridden meditation on Time. Mayrhofer resorts to a commonplace metaphor in which a small boat gliding on the water is emblematic of individual human life on the river of Time, a metaphor tinted in blackest nihilism. We are all, he intones, borne helplessly to the obliteration which is the common fate of humankind and everything it has wrought, no matter how massive or magnificent. This is not a poem in the singular: "uns" (us), Mayrhofer twice insists, and inclusion in the mass of humanity is not a comforting thought in this context. The bronze armor and those who wore it are vaguely evocative of ancient Greek soldiers or Renaissance warrior-grandees, but without any chronological specificity that might weaken the suggestive power of the image. If warriors as strong as these perished, along with the ramparts they built, and vanished into nameless oblivion, what chance do weaker mortals such as the poet stand against those same inexorable forces? The rhetorical questions hammered throughout stanza 2 require no answer. Nor is any comfort possible, since "pious myth" – religion – has lost its power. In one of the most vivid phrases of a vivid poem, Mayrhofer writes, "Mournful brushwood grows rampant," no longer magnificent man-made ramparts as in the past but scrubby, wild, natural growth. Existence already reverts to primeval desolation, hostile to human habitation. At the end, it is not "die Zeit" (time) but "Zeiten" (eras) that menace us, the time-scale of the poem thus expanding to awe-inspiring effect. The weight of bygone aeons is more than sufficient to crush the individual human fleck who contemplates their vanishing and shudders in terror, knowing that the same fate awaits him as well.

"Auf der Donau," dated April 1817 in the Witteczek-Spaun catalogue (the autograph manuscript is lost), belongs to a group of more than forty songs by Schubert which end in a different key than the tonality of the beginning, a phenomenon variously labeled "directional tonality," "progressive tonality," "trans-formational tonality," and "double tonality." As Thomas Denny has pointed out, roughly twenty of them are extended ballad settings whose sectional organization renders directional tonality relatively unstartling (indeed, a convention of the genre), while another twenty or so are lieder in true songlike dimensions and forms which clearly prolong at least one key prior to arrival at the ultimate tonic (the setting of Goethe's "Ganymed," D. 544 and the settings of Mayrhofer's "Freiwilliges Versinken," D. 700 and "Orest auf Tauris," D. 548 are examples).[87] All of this latter category are products of Schubert's youth, the majority composed by the end of 1820 and the last specimens in 1823 (Franz Schober's flower-ballad "Vergißmeinnicht" and Schiller's "Der Pilgrim"). 1817 was the peak of his interest in such tonal radicalism, with nine songs in directional tonality, including "Auf der Donau." After all, a closed tonal form, beginning and ending in the same tonality, would have been no more appropriate for this poem than it was for Schiller's "Der Pilgrim" (The pilgrim) and for a similar reason. In Mayrhofer's reckoning, we are all en route from a starting point we deludedly believe to be beautiful and lasting to a culmination in oblivion, a journey he traces in tersest condensation. Schubert accordingly begins by defining a tonic key we deludedly believe to be the tonality of the song and then quickly leaves it, sinking lower and lower until arrival at the true and final tonic, far, far away from the beginning. The initial key is E-flat major, a tonality associated in such songs as Schubert's setting of Ludwig Kosegarten's "An die untergehende Sonne" (To the Setting Sun), D. 457, begun in July 1816 and completed in May 1817, with awe and devotion before Nature (the words "Sonne, du sinkst" with which each stanza of Kosegarten's poem begins may also constitute a link between the two songs). In "Auf der Donau," E-flat is tinged with darkness from the beginning by the flatted sixth degree and is soon supplanted, first, by its subdominant A-flat major, then by the new subdominant C-flat major (the enharmonic subdominant of F-sharp minor, already foreshadowed by the C-flat pitches in m. 2) and finally by F-sharp minor itself. In the final section in F-sharp, virtually all of the material initially given in E-flat, A-flat, and C-flat is recapitulated – "Ma fin est mon commencement," the end already clearly foretold in the beginning, had we but ears to hear it.

If critics in Schubert's lifetime cavilled at such tonal daring, present-day listeners, inured to fin-de-siècle directional tonality and its equally black pessimism, can recognize a masterpiece.[88] Schubert takes his cue from the gliding motion ("schwimmen") of the symbolic boat on the waters, but mutes the onomatopoeic possibilities almost entirely, and rightly so; Mayrhofer's concerns were entirely inward. The piano introduction might seem quiet and simple, with its alternating tonic and dominant bass pitches in the left-hand and its arpeggiated and scalewise figuration in the right hand, but it is, typically, less simple than it appears. The right-hand part in m. 1, with its arpeggiated "tonic" triad and descending scalewise pitches $\hat{4}$ $\hat{3}$ $\hat{2}$ $\hat{1}$, or two appoggiatura figures, with A-flat emphasized at the apex (foreshadowing the importance of A-flat major and minor harmonies in both the A and B sections), then splits at m. 2 into two voices consisting largely of appoggiatura figures derived from the second half of m. 1, rhythmically augmented in the top voice, in sixteenth notes as before in the inner voice. The appoggiaturas spell not only descent but tears, in a doubled reincarnation of the gesture also associated with tears in Schubert's setting of Goethe's "Wonne der Wehmut" ("Trocknet nicht, Tränen der ewigen Liebe!", or "Do not dry up, tears of eternal love") and elsewhere. Gliding on the river does not invite a closed introduction, with a full cadence and a pause before the voice enters, but rather continuous motion which the voice joins in a way that points out yet again Schubert's care for prosodic and poetic details. Mayrhofer's first line is ostensibly in trochaic trimeters ("*Auf* der *Wel*-len *Spie*-gel"), and yet the first trochee in this prepositional phrase is syntactically less important and less deserving of accentuation than the second and third trochees. Schubert, who devised a melodic line for the A sections characterized by prolonged downbeat rhythms and wave-like small sequential figures, mitigates what might otherwise be undue prolongational emphasis on the word "Auf" by bringing in the singer at m. 4, not m. 5, and on the dominant harmony, such that the entirety of m. 4 is heard as an upbeat to m. 5 and the arrival at tonic on the word "Wellen." It is truly a masterful solution.

"Auf der Donau" is tonal "Untergang," and descent permeates structural details both large and small. With the first mention of "der Kahn" (symbolic of the individual human life), the descent already evident in the tear-drop figures and the falling sixths at the end of the first two vocal phrases (at the words "Spiegel" and "Kahn") is manifested as well in the harmonic progression, falling by thirds to C minor submediant (m. 7) and then to A-flat major subdominant in m. 9. As they sink, they darken; it is as if the music, like the poet, were afflicted with progressively worsening melancholia. The "alte Burgen" (old castles) may soar by angular perfect fourths in the vocal line of mm. 9–10, but the harmonies cloud over by slow, inexorable degrees with the addition of D-flats in mm. 9–11, G-flats in m. 12, C-flats in mm. 13–14, and the distinctive, eerie darkness of the F-flats in m. 15, rendered "geistergleich" (ghost-like) by the "rauschendes" *tremolandi*. Nearing the end of the A section, the harmonies continue to darken even more in the cadence on C-flat major in mm. 17–20 ("und das Herz im Busen wird uns weich"). The ascending leap of a sixth in m. 18 (a reversal of the earlier descending sixths in the vocal line) at the word "Busen," as if the poet's heart had suddenly leapt in alarm within his breast before sinking an octave lower in fear by the end of the phrase, is one especially notable detail of a section in which Schubert enacts "sinken all" before the words themselves appear.

Not until we arrive at "doom" is there any possibility of a tonal plateau; the tonal waters flow on without pause or rest toward "Untergang," through the C-flat major cadence at the end of the A section and beyond, to stanza 2. Here, any suggestion of water-music is banished. The poet has gone beyond awareness of the Danube and its castles and has retreated inwards to the grimmest of all speculations: the possibility of extinction, of disappearing without a trace, as if we had never been. Schubert beautifully captures, not only the despair, but the anger in Mayrhofer's words. The short, buzzing trills that explode in the bass, beneath the surface, on the second half of the second beat (the weakest part of the measure); the choppily emphatic chordal punctuation of every sixteenth-note pulsation; the plethora of stark perfect intervals in the vocal line, all evoke a kind of bristling fury, shot through with greater and greater tonal darkness. The F-flat Neapolitan neighbor to the [former] tonic pitch E-flat recurs here, not buried in the depths but out in the open, the twice-stated tritone leap downwards from B-flat in the vocal line a particularly affecting detail of the melodic construction. This passage too sinks inexorably, each question ("Wo ist Turm, wo Pforte, wo der Wall, wo sie selbst ... ") darkening and descending by degrees until the invocation of "die Starken" (the strong ones). For all that Mayrhofer eventually succumbed to acute depression, he fought it all the way; he admired strength, hated passivity and weakness, and desperately wanted to be one of "die Starken." When Schubert respells C-flat and G-flat as B-natural and F-sharp in m. 28, turning sharply (if readers will forgive the pun) to F-sharp minor at just those words, he underscores Mayrhofer's furious attempt to combat the forces of oblivion and win out by violent overthrow of all that flatted-key gloom (ex. 21). But F-sharp minor is, of course, the enharmonic equivalent of the darkest key of all (G-flat major-minor) and – tragic irony – the key of "Untergang." It is also a tonality Schubert had earlier associated with death in the first version of "Auf den Tod einer Nachtigall" (On the death of a nightingale), D. 201, and would later use to the same ends in "Schwestergruß" (A sister's greeting), D. 762, and "Totengräber-weise" (Grave-digger's melody), D. 869. The heroic exertions of "the strong ones" only bring them more swiftly to death and oblivion.

Whoever the bronze-clad warriors were, their battles and hunts resound to appropriately emphatic tonic and dominant harmonies in the new key, their bygone feats of strength additionally impelling the strong, dotted rhythmic scalewise ascent in the melodic line. It was Schubert's brilliant conception to repeat, and very angrily, the question "Wo? Wo?" (Where? Where?) at the end of the B section; he repeats, one notices, no other portion of this text, not another word or phrase. Despite the fact that the words "die in Krieg und Jagden hingestürmt?" end on the dominant, not the tonic, and to an upward turn of phrase, none of the questions sound truly "questioning." The poetic speaker already knows the bleak answer, and Schubert, well aware of his friend's pessimistic convictions, makes it apparent in the melodic and harmonic design for those words. When the last echoes of the word "Wo?" die away in the piano in mm. 34–36, one of the most potent of all of Schubert's enigmatic silences at crucial structural points in a work follows. In that measure of

Example 21. Franz Schubert, "Auf der Donau," D. 553, mm. 22–34, from *Neue Schubert-Ausgabe*, Series IV: *Lieder* vol. 1a, ed. Walther Dürr.

Example 21. *cont.*

extraordinarily resonant silence, one hears the sounds of past heroism die away into nothingness and disappear into the void. One also hears the cosmic refusal of any answer to the question, "What becomes of us and all our striving?" The cadential progression, one notices, stops at the end of m. 36 just short of resolution to a downbeat, root-position tonic chord in F-sharp minor. However insistently, however angrily we ask, silence is the only response.

Something else happens in that multivalent measure of silence as well: aeons of time, compressed into a single bar of 2/4 meter, pass and bring the poet back to the present time and place, the return of the A section recalling the "little boat" and the river's waves once again. Here, tragically, is where resolution occurs, linking the hollow fate of those long gone with the impending fate of the poetic persona; of all the bridges between musical architecture and poetic meaning in "Auf der Donau," this is perhaps the saddest. Literal return of the earlier music is not possible after the soul-shattering questions of stanza 2; even where the recurring strains most faithfully mimic the music of stanza 1, they are dyed in the F-sharp minor hues of "die Starken," the change of mode from major to minor indeed mournful. The river of Time no longer flows to and through other tonal regions but remains fixed in the key of "Untergang," despite the continued wave-like motion and rich chromaticism of the stanza. For example, Schubert sinks downward by thirds through the first nine measures of the stanza, falling slowly from F-sharp through D major to a half-cadence on the subdominant B minor at the point where Mayrhofer denies any palliative for despair from the realms of religion ("während frommer Sage / Kraft verdorrt," mm. 44–47). To do so by means of heightened plagal harmonies and the brightness of a "Picardy third" (a tonic major chord which is actually V/IV) is still more tragic irony in a song replete with bleak transformations of conventional tropes.

The last of those tropes is the most powerful. Mayrhofer confronts his deepest fear – "Untergang" – in the final four lines of the third stanza, and does so with unsparing directness. Schubert matches that unflinching courage when he uses the most unmediated musical symbol for doom: a descending chromatic line. The first faint premonition of "Untergang" sounds in the piano in the last half of m. 47, a chromatic version of the scalewise outlined fourth from m. 1. In the last half of the stanza, Schubert recapitulates the B section as well, in particular, the Angst-filled syncopated chords in the right hand and the ascending perfect fourths in the vocal line, while the river continues to flow deep in the left-hand part, as in the last half of the A section (mm. 13-20). The word "Untergang" is, appropriately, first stated in the starkest possible way: an octave plunge downwards from $\hat{5}$ to $\hat{5}$, then resolution on $\hat{1}$. Immediately upon the final syllable of the word, doom and descent are multiply enacted in the piano accompaniment, first in the bass line and then doubled in the inner voice, while the right hand continues to sound an F-sharp ostinato, like a tocsin for the dead as the bass sinks lower and lower to the very bottom of the fortepiano's range. Horrified, Schubert's poetic persona repeats over and over the word he most fears, "Untergang … Untergang … Untergang," until he too, the vocal line as well as the accompaniment, sinks into the depths. In the postlude, seamlessly elided with the body of the song, Schubert seems to mimic the sempiternal rise-and-fall of human destinies in the rise-and-fall of the broken-chordal harmonies deep beneath the continuing ostinato above it. Dissonant supertonic chords, all the more emphatic for the *forzando* accent on the first sixteenth-note subdivision of the beat, followed instantly by *pianissimo* dynamics, sound at each descent to tonic in the lowest register (mm. 62 and 64), as if the poet-singer were fighting the fall into oblivion's pit with his last failing strength until it is no longer possible to do so. Finally, there is no more dissonance and the left hand simply falls to the lowest possible F-sharp, the struggle and the song both over.

3.   *Sehnsucht* (longing) in German Romanticism tells of the desire for indefinable, unattainable fulfillment. "What is it that tugs at my heart so? What lures me outside, twisting and wrenching me out of my room and my home? … I would like to go there!", Goethe's persona asks in "Sehnsucht" (Schubert's D. 123 of 1814), while Schiller dreams of "a miraculous land of beauty" in his poem of the same name (Schubert's D. 51 of 1813 and D. 636 of 1821?).The longing to be elsewhere (but where?), to be something else (but what?), to travel restlessly in search of unknown experience, is at the heart of *Sehnsucht* as most late eighteenth- and early nineteenth-century writers conceived it. Mayrhofer, however, had something else in mind for

his version of "Sehnsucht":[89] he yearns for a "milde Land" he knew to be unattainable on earth, a realm of pure spirit. "Peering into the blessed land of the free ... o earnest joy of the spirit's life!", as he wrote in "Lösung" (Release), one could even find momentary surcease from life's sorrows.[90] The beautiful image of the cranes – an Oriental symbol for the immortality of the soul – tells us that "the gentle land" in "Sehnsucht" is not the Christian afterlife; reading this poem, one thinks of the many Japanese prints in which cranes seem poised to depart the bounds of the framed image as the soul departs the bounds of earthly existence.

Not even in the "gentle land" could Mayrhofer imagine himself worthy to be there; rather, he wishes to be an "aspiring" companion to the cranes, and the "strebendes" effort impels an extra poetic foot in the penultimate line, pentameters rather than tetrameters (the only other line in pentameters is the second line of stanza 2, "Nur du bist blütenlos, in dich gekehrt"). Schubert, one notices, writes "sterbende," or "dying"; whether Mayrhofer later altered the original word for the 1824 anthology or whether Schubert emended the language on his own cannot be determined. The cranes are a counterpoise to the larks at the beginning, where one finds Mayrhofer's characteristic knotty syntax, difficult to render into English with the same sense of convoluted, effortful thought. It is their *songs*, not the birds themselves, which are "near to the clouds" ("wolkennahe"), the spirit more than the body which soars and sings. Elsewhere, the tortuousness of the language serves to isolate important words and phrases, as at the beginning of the second stanza: "Nie wird, was du verlangst, entkeimen / Dem Boden, Idealen fremd." Like Poe's raven, "Nevermore" tolls at the beginning of the line, while "Idealen fremd" is a characteristically terse expression. The very language is "in dich gekehrt," turned in upon itself as if in mimicry of the state of being it describes. Nor can English adequately convey the different nuances of "erschmettern," not only warbling as in birdsong, but with connotations of violence: "to smash, throw down violently."

Der Lerche wolkennahe Lieder
Erschmettern zu des Winters Flucht.
Die Erde hüllt in Samt die Glieder,
Und Blüten bilden rote Frucht.
Nur du, o sturmbewegte Seele,
Bist blütenlos, in dich gekehrt,
Und wirst in goldner Frühlingshelle
Von tiefer Sehnsucht aufgezehrt.

Nie wird, was du verlangst, entkeimen
Dem Boden, Idealen fremd;
Der trotzig deinen schönsten Träumen
Die rohe Kraft entgegen stemmt.
Du ringst dich matt mit seiner Härte,
Vom Wunsche heftiger entbrannt:
Mit Kranichen ein sterbende [strebende]
    Gefährte
Zu wandern in ein milder Land.[91]

The songs of the cloud-soaring lark
ring out as winter flees;
the earth wraps her limbs in velvet,
and red fruit forms from the blossoms.
Only you, storm-tossed soul,
do not flower; turned in upon yourself,
you are consumed by deep longing
amid spring's golden radiance.

What you crave will never burgeon
from this earth, alien to ideals,
which defiantly opposes its raw strength
to your most beautiful dreams.
You grow weary struggling with its harshness,
ever more inflamed by the
desire to journey to a kinder land as a dying
    [an aspiring]
companion to the cranes.

One could not tell from the lucent piano introduction in the opening key of C major that tonal surprises were in store. In retrospect, one hardly knows whether Schubert was depicting newly-arrived Spring or the "gentle land" of which Mayrhofer dreamed in the piano introduction, with its pure melody in the right-hand part over a chordal accompaniment, and the first nine measures of the song proper. Here is much the same sort of "rein Gesang" (pure song) which Schubert both celebrates and creates in his setting of Friedrich von Schlegel's "Der Fluß" (The River), D. 693, composed in 1820; the later song and the beginning of "Sehnsucht" have an elective affinity in their similar right-hand counter-melodies to the vocal line (the poet and the birds sing simultaneously in the Mayrhofer lied, while the poetic persona and the river are paired in the Schlegel song) and the consummate distillation of diatonic lyricism. One is invited in the introduction to imagine the poet in a state of perfect peace and grace amidst Nature, this in the primordial key of C major, which then darkens slightly to A minor melancholy. In the final measure of the introduction, Schubert turns back to a half-cadence on C major thus rendered unstable, the short-lived nature of its beauty and tranquillity evident. The consequent phrase is, typically for Schubert, asymmetrically extended by the excursion to A minor harmonies and the return to C major, both the G-sharps in m. 4 and the enharmonic A-flat passing tone in m. 5 premonitions of the A-flat harmonies to follow in mm. 10-13, when the earth wraps its limbs in velvet. A-flat is, according to John Reed, a tonality in which Schubert on occasion expresses "faith in the power of Nature to revive and renew," as in "Frühlingsglaube," D. 686; "Im Abendrot," D. 799; or the opening of "Ganymed," D. 544;[92] it has those connotations as well in "Sehnsucht," its flatted submediant relationship to the opening tonality appropriately velvety-rich and warm. The melody of the introduction, repeated and varied by the singer, floats up and down, hovering and then moving on, but it is in the right-hand part of mm. 6–13 where the larks truly sing. Schubert has each of the piano's birdsong phrases, with their trills and sixteenth-note darting-and-swooping passaggi appropriately poised above the vocal line, begin in the *middle* of the singer's phrases, as if to ensure our understanding that there are actually two singers, not one. Throughout the setting of stanza 1, Schubert moves by stages from separate but harmonious melodic voices in the C major "lark song" passage (mm. 6–9) to greater rhythmic alignment of the two melodies in the A-flat springtime passage (mm. 10–13) to the banishment of all but the iconoclastic poet-singer in the tonally restless section which begins with the self-accusatory words, "Nur du, o sturmbewegte Seele" (mm. 14–24). No one and nothing else joins in to sing with the storm-tossed soul, and Schubert accordingly banishes the lovely counter-melodies from before.

In time-honored fashion, the poet observes the burgeoning of new life and energy in spring and compares it with his own misery. His soul bears no blossoms and feels no joy in spring's brightness, and Schubert therefore turns as violently as possible from the A-flat warmth of spring to more storm-tossed tonal climes. A-flat major shades to parallel minor in the brief piano interlude at m. 13; at the words "Nur *du*, [o sturmbewegte Seele]," C-flat and A-flat are respelled as B-natural and G-sharp in a *fortissimo* E major chord, en route through a passage in which C-sharp minor and its dominant are stressed (mm. 15–16) and culminating in cadences on B minor ("in dich gekehrt") and B major ("in goldner Frühlingshelle"). The "Seele" fittingly breathes air in C-sharp minor, so near and yet so far from the crystalline C major of the larks' serenade to spring. Storminess and angry self-hatred are made musically evident in the heavy chords, *fortissimo* dotted rhythms, and declamation on a single pitch – significantly, an abnegation of melody for this proclamation of self-reproach – in mm. 14–15, but we hear the strength drain away swiftly in m. 16. There, the word "du" is prolonged throughout three-quarters of the measure in unmistakeable emphasis while the piano accompaniment is fixed in place on repeated secondary dominant seventh chords; not only does the poetic persona have to steel himself, to pause for an instant before he can bring himself to utter harsh realities, but there is something of the sufferer's self-obsession captured in this gesture. (The motion, however, never ceases throughout virtually the entire song, the only pause being the fermata-prolonged eighth note in m. 5 at the end of the piano introduction, a pause which engenders the flow of thought/song to follow. For Schubert, it was evidently an essential property of Mayrhofer's *Sehnsucht* that it never ceased.) The emphasis on B minor harmonies for the lamenting words "in dich gekehrt" gives way to short-lived warmth in parallel major for the "golden springtime brightness," the D-sharp of major mode prolonged on the downbeat of m. 19, while the melodic line briefly resumes the lilting inflections of the larksong melodies of stanza 1. The ascending leap of a seventh, with the apex on an offbeat, at the word "Früh – [lingshelle]" is especially affecting, while "tiefer Sehnsucht" impels a brief and vivid patch of harmonic motion beneath the prolonged adjective "*tief*-er," a momentary emphasis on D major harmonies before the key signature changes to B minor. D major is, of course, the dominant of G major, the key of the dying soul's journey with the cranes to the "milde Land"; the *Sehnsucht* he invokes at the end of stanza 1 will lead him there, if only in imagination, in the final two lines of the poem.

But first, Mayrhofer laments the impossibility of finding what he so desperately desires on earth. In the first six lines of stanza 2, all traces of spring brightness vanish. Schubert sounds a repeated-pitch ostinato figure in the right-hand, like a tolling bell, on F-sharp in mm. 24–28, then on B in mm. 29–32 (later, Schubert would sound a delicate F-sharp ostinato throughout the B minor lament "Die liebe Farbe" in *Die schöne Müllerin*). One notices in particular how dissonances are clustered at the beginning of this section (mm. 24–25), especially the D against C-sharp clash at "du" on the downbeat of m. 25; Schubert, knowing Mayrhofer's aggrieved sense that Destiny had singled him out for especially harsh treatment, underscores the word "du" wherever it occurs, by prolongation (mm. 14 and 16) and by dissonance on the downbeat. Dissonance-free G major harmonies appear at the words "schönsten Träumen" in mm. 27–28, a premonition of the "gentler land" but one immediately banished by the invocation of "rohe Kraft" in the last half of m. 28 and m. 29, with its Beethovenian *fp* accents on each beat. The merest mention of ideals and of beautiful dreams impels a melodic line briefly lifted to empyrean heights, touching upon the high G that is the tonic pitch of the "gentle land." When, in the final section, with its vision of struggle banished in an idyllic afterlife, we hear the high G once again as the only accented pitch in the vocal line (m. 35, "Ge-*fähr*-te"), we understand why.

Schubert's poetic persona dwells upon the beauty of the final image – the last two lines of the stanza occupy half of the setting of stanza 2. Throughout the utterly diatonic setting of those final lines, Schubert over and over again sounds the familiar horn-call figure: Mayrhofer wants to return to his original home, his ideal land, and Schubert, as in Oedipus' swan-song in "Antigone und Oedip," harps on the motivic figure most emblematic of "home" to nineteenth-century German listeners. Here, movingly, we once again hear a "counter"-melody in the right-hand part, but one that is perfectly consonant with the singer's melody. Like the cranes and the singer, the two lines are truly companions and journey hand-in-hand. The ostinato D (G in the final three measures of the song) chimes through the final section (mm. 34–42), thinner and clearer than the octave-doubled ostinato throughout the previous starker, stronger section, and is, I believe, an earlier version of the "journeying motive" in *Winterreise*: a series of repeated pitches, capable of infinite extension, of immutable transposition and variation. The poet wishes to journey to the "gentle land" ("zu wandern"), and the sheer length of the ostinato in this instance is near-mystical in effect. In the postlude, the distance between the hands widens, as if the soul were ascending and leaving the earth far below, with haunting last echoes of the E-flats that were the pivot tones for the brief turn to A-flat in m. 10. The slight touch of darkness and dissonance, the faint echoes of "rohe Kraft," especially after the utter purity of the final nine measures of the texted song, only make the resolution to those last G major chords all the sweeter, all the more indicative of peace after pain.

4. "Erlafsee" is Mayrhofer at his most experimental. The meters change from iambic trimeters to trochaic dimeters to a single iambic dimeter to trochaic tetrameters in the first eight-line stanza alone, followed by five sestet or quatrain stanzas likewise in fluctuating rhythms – truly a complex formal structure for poetic content of equal, even indecipherable, complexity. Of his friend's six stanzas and thirty-six lines, Schubert set only two stanzas and fourteen lines for his lied, D. 586, composed in September 1817. Of all Schubert's emendations to Mayrhofer's poetry, this is the most drastic – if indeed, it *was* emendation. There are (at least) two speculative explanations, neither one verifiable beyond a shadow of a doubt: Schubert either found nothing "brauchbares für Musik" (usable for music) in the other four stanzas, the reasons for such a massive omission thus cause for further speculation, or else Mayrhofer might have interleaved additional stanzas to an originally much shorter poem before publication of his anthology in 1824. The latter seems possible when one considers that Mayrhofer goes back and forth between natural description in stanzas 1 and 3 and confrontation with a visionary apparition in stanzas 2 and 4; however, one could also argue that it seems unlikely for this particular poet to represent a scene in Nature and then end the poem there, without any symbol-imbued meditation. Did the venue of the song's first appearance in print have something to

do with the matter? The lied (Schubert's first printed song) was published on 6 February 1818 as a *Musikbeilage* in a supplement to Franz Sartori's annual *Mahlerisches Taschenbuch für Freunde interessanter Gegenden Natur- und Kunst Merkwürdigkeiten der Österreichischen Monarchie* (Pictorial Pocket-Book for Friends of interesting regional, natural, and artistic curiosities of the Austrian Monarchy), along with a charming copper engraving of Lake Erlaf.[93] Could Schubert and Mayrhofer have collaborated on a particularly lovely form of tourist enticement (the song was then published by Cappi & Diabelli as op. 8, no. 3 in May of 1822), which Mayrhofer then augmented to other ends for his 1824 anthology? Or did Schubert reject the dark enigmas in the poem? Perhaps having devised an idyll "to be sung on the waters," one in which "wohl" dominates "weh," he did not wish its course altered by the dark visions, questions, and prophecies at the heart of the poem.[94]

Mir ist so wohl, so weh	I am so happy, so melancholy,
Am stillen Erlafsee.	by the calm waters of Lake Erlaf.
Heilig Schweigen	A sacred silence
In Fichtenzweigen	amid the pine branches;
Regungslos	motionless
Der dunkle Schooss;	the dark depths.
Nun der Wolken Schatten flieh'n	Only the shadows of the clouds flit
Ueberm glatten Spiegel hin.	across the glassy surface.
[Feenbild, was willst du mir,	[Visionary image, what do you want from me
So umschwebst du mich auch hier?	that you hover about me even here?
Weiche aus dem Land der Hirten.	Shun the herdsmen's lands.
Hier gedeihen keine Myrthen;	No myrtles grow here,
Schilfgras nur und Tannenwucht	only reeds and scrub-pines
Kränzen diese stille Bucht.]	encircle this quiet bay.]
Frische Winde	Cool breezes
Kräuseln linde	gently ruffle
Das Gewässer;	the water,
Und der Sonne	and the sun's
Güldne Krone	golden corona
Flimmert blässer.	grows paler.
[Ach, weine nicht, du süßes Bild!	[Oh, do not weep, sweet image!
Der Wellendrang ist bald gestillt,	The motion of the waves will soon be stilled,
Und glatter See, und Lüfte lau,	and calm waters and mild breezes
Erheitern dich, du Wunderfrau.	will cheer you, miraculous woman.
Des Sees Rand	The lake's border
Umschlingt ein Band,	is a ribbon
Aus lichtem Grün gewunden:	woven of light green:
Es ist der Fluß,	it is the river
Der treiben muß	that must drive
Die Sägemühlen unten.	the saw-mill further down.

Unwillig krümmt er sich am Steg	Unwillingly it writhes along
Von seiner schönen Mutter weg,	the narrow path, distant from its
Und fließt zu fernen Gründen.	beautiful mother, and flees to far-away lands.
Wirst, Liebe! auch mit holder Hand,	Love, will you too, with gentle hands,
Des Sängers ernstes Felsenland,	entwine the singer's grave, rocky land
Mit Blüthenroth umwinden?] [95]	with blossom-red?]

Mayrhofer's favored themes – Nature and poetry as the only consolations in earthly existence, longing for bygone times, alienation and misanthropy, and the mingling of past, present, and future – appear in this poem but webbed in mystery. "Erlafsee" is akin to Matthäus von Collin's "Wehmut" in the poet's half-melancholy revelling in Nature's beauty, but it is less easily explicable than Collin's poem, intimating a private symbolism for which we lack the Rosetta Stone. Is the *Feenbild* his Muse, who has visited him in a place devoid of myrtles, an antique emblem of poetry? Is she so desirous of peace that even the slightest rippling of the wind and waves causes her (as vulnerable as Mayrhofer himself) to break into tears? Does stanza 5 prophesy the forces of Nature eventually reclaiming the industrial works of humanity, the despoiler of Nature? At saw-mills, the trees which Mayrhofer saw as manifestations of the divine are chopped down and turned to prosaic human use. What is one to make of stanza 6? The river, far away from its origins in the ocean (its "beautiful mother"), is forced to go where it does not wish to go, to flow within confined banks to far-off places – is Mayrhofer hinting that human life flows on the river of time to distant places far removed from childhood, as the river must flow from the sea to places far away? What psychological subtext might underlie the necessary flight from the mother? What do the red blossoms, "Blütenroth" (blossom-red) too close to "Blutenrot" (blood-red) for mere coincidence, signify? Do the mother, the Muse, and Love do him violence at the same time as they seek to make his "rocky, stony land" bloom? Does the river become a river of blood – the poet's – at the end? However moved one might be by the beauty and the strangeness of this poem, certitude is not to be found. Like later modernist poetry, Mayrhofer traffics in withheld information, implying profound meanings about profound matters but without supplying didactic clues or fully-adumbrated connectives between thoughts and images, to disturbing effect.

The composer's choice of the same F major tonality as Mayrhofer's "Schlaflied" and a barcarolle 6/8 meter tells of lulling peacefulness, the poet cradled on the waters. As so often with Schubert, the piano introduction contains in microcosm the elements of the song to come: the descending scalewise motion in the inner voice that is so evocative of slipping gently and by degrees into entranced peacefulness, the A C-sharp D figure in m. 1 that foreshadows the D minor "heilig Schweigen" of m. 11f (the C-sharp also enharmonically foreshadows the D-flat of "*so* weh" in m. 7 – Schubert chromatically darkens the adjective signifying extremity, rather than the melancholy itself), the E-flat passing tones of mm. 1 and 3 that foretell the B-flat major of the cloud-shadows in mm. 17–27, and the striking initial gesture in the melodic line. The chromatic descent from the tonic to the dominant pitch in the inner voice invests the passage with the subtlest hint of erotic pleasure in melancholy, truly "wohl-weh." The initial leap downwards may, speculatively, have its origins in Schubert's knowledge of Mayrhofer's personality. Taking his cue from Mayrhofer's syntax in line 1 ("*Mir* ist so wohl, so weh"), Schubert underscores the poet's solipsistic state by means of large intervallic leaps downward on the anacrusis "Mir," followed in the body of the phrase by less dramatic melodic motion. He even accents the high F at the first statement of this figure on the upbeat to m. 1 and doubles it for further emphasis.

When the texted body of the song begins, the poetic persona sings "Mir ist so wohl, so weh, am stillen Erlafsee" twice in succession, as if so struck by this novel sensation of peacefulness that he must repeat the words again, with no variation other than the bare minimum necessary to make the second phrase-ending in mm. 9–10 more final-sounding. As he notices other elements of the lake at sunset, he leaves F major and heightens harmonies which descend by thirds, from F major to D minor to B-flat. The "holy silence in the pine branches" sounds to D minor harmonies – the slight darkening of relative minor evoking the gravity of things sacred – that only last for four measures (mm. 11–14) and never establish D minor as a tonality. The observation that the blue depths are motionless ("regungslos der blaue Schoß") impels block-chordal writing for a mere two bars (to symbolise the glassy-still waters, there are no inner voices in motion) before the dance-like lilt of the "Wolken Schatten fliehn" in m. 17, the right-hand part and voice flitting after one another in elision like clouds in flight. In the piano interlude in mm. 25–27, we descend from the level of the clouds in the treble to the lower level of the lake (an admittedly fanciful reading), culminating in a fermata-sustained B-flat harmony on the sixth and last beat of the measure, at which the music pauses; "regungslos," we wait for what will happen next. (Similar figuration for a similar "dunklen Spiegel" appears in the setting of Friedrich Schlegel's "Der Schiffer," D. 694.)

The quickened ("Geschwinder") "fresh breezes" of the B section blow to a variation of the same musical elements already "sung on the waters"; indeed, the vocal phrase "Frische Winde," repeated to the succeeding words "kräuseln linde" in a lilting-rhyming fashion, is a variant of the phrase "Mir ist so wohl, so weh," the leap of a sixth that formerly underscored iconoclastic emphasis on the self here becomes a small gust of wind. The whole stanza is set as the kind of dreamy-lazy song one hums over and over again when utterly content and out in Nature, the descending sequential invocations of "das Gewässer" (mm. 32–35) beautifully apt in their incantatory quality; it is here that the bass line begins to move again after the rocking octave ostinato of the first four measures of the section (mm. 28–31). Even the prosodic distortions, the "incorrect" prolongations of "das" in "das Gewässer" and "und" in "und der Sonne güldne Krone," are justified by the primacy of barcarolle-like song over declamation in this context. A transposed version of the same sequence reappears in mm. 50–53 at the words "flimmert blässer," this time to parallel minor harmonies evocative of the slight tinge of melancholy in "wohl-weh" moods; the A-flat of the F minor chord has been foreshadowed by the diminished seventh neighbor-note harmonies of mm. 28 and 30. When Schubert repeats the entire stanza in mm. 56–76, that passage is the only one altered – not parallel minor chords, but German sixth chords en route to the D minor harmonies of "Heilig Schweigen in Fichtenzweigen." Before those harmonies can resolve, however, Schubert shifts in m. 76 to the dominant seventh of F and then pauses, the fermata-sustained harmony and the delayed expectation of resolution all the more evocative for the mediant motion from A to C-natural in the bass.

At the end, Schubert simply returns to the beginning and repeats mm. 3–10, adding on to it a three-measure postlude in which the unresolved C-sharp from earlier is respelled as the flatted sixth degree D-flat and resolved to C, while the neighbor-note motion prevalent in the harmonic progressions and the vocal line of this song receives its last melismatic flourish. Although it is an apt and lovely frame for the song, the flatted sixth degree an assertion that the "wohl-weh" mood is unchanged from beginning to end, it could also, speculatively, betray Schubert's awareness of omitted poetic material. In the fermata-prolonged chords of mm. 27 and 75–76, it is possible, I believe, to hear suppression, or the implication of words withheld.

5.   The text for one of Schubert's most tonally radical lieder, "Freiwilliges Versinken," D. 700, composed in 1817, originates in Stoic physics and eschatology. In Stoic thought, the original source of all things was a "fiery breath," simultaneously spirit and matter. This eternal deity, which consumed all yet was itself consumed by none, from whom everything issued forth, came into being and was then reabsorbed into the divine in each of a never-ending series of cycles, as the Pythagoreans had taught earlier. At the beginning of "Freiwilliges Versinken," an unknown voice urgently asks the Sun God "Wohin?", nothing more – it is a remarkably terse beginning, even for Mayrhofer. Helios replies that he departs to immerse himself in the waters, confident that he will arise again to shed warmth on the earth. The phoenix-like regeneration is common symbolic vestiture for the sun seeming to sink beneath the level of the sea at sunset, but Mayrhofer invests the symbol with sacrificial meaning, that is, a god's volitional descent into death for the sake of others; the epitome of the creative principle, Helios need borrow substance from no one and yet prodigally dispenses bounty. (Mayrhofer's own suicidal impulses – the "freiwilliges Versinken" he himself enacted in 1836 – lurk just beneath the surface.) I wonder as well whether Mayrhofer's Helios was also Goethe, the lordly poet of brilliant light whose departure would allow lesser confederates such as Mayrhofer to emerge by night and cast their own paler glow.

Wohin, o Helios? In [kühlen] Fluten	Whither, o Helios? In cool waters
Will ich den Flammenleib versenken,	I will immerse my burning body,
Gewiss im Innern, neue Gluten	inwardly certain that I can bestow
Der Erde nach Bedarf [Feuerreich] zu schenken.	new warmth upon the earth's fires.
Ich nehme nichts, gewohnt zu geben;	I do not take; I am wont only to give.
[Ich nehme nicht, ich pflege nur zu geben;]	
Und wie verschwenderisch mein Leben,	As prodigal as my life,
Umhüllt mein Scheiden gold'ne Pracht,	my parting is bathed in golden splendor;
Ich scheide herrlich, naht die Nacht.	I depart in glory when night draws near.

Wie bleich [blass] der Mond, wie matt die Sterne! How pale the moon, how faint the stars!
So lang ich kräftig mich bewege; As long as I move on my powerful course;
Erst wenn ich ab die Krone lege, only when I lay down my crown upon
[Erst wenn ich auf die Berge meine Krone lege,] the mountains do they gain strength and
Wird ihnen Muth und Glanz in ihrer Ferne. courage in the far distance.
[Gewinnen sie an Mut und Kraft in weiter Ferne.][96]

Schubert matches the vatic voice of Mayrhofer's Helios with equally prophetic music. Other-worldly and powerful forces are vividly suggested by tonal mystery at the beginning, as Helios begins his lordly departure in the piano part. The recurring trills on the second (weak) beat in the octave-doubled inner voices that traverse an ascending scalewise third impel the motion forward in processional majesty. The questioning voice at the beginning can only interject melodic fragments in recitative style, fragments adapted to the god's harmonies but never conjunct with the beginning of the two-bar units in the piano. Throughout those first six measures, that is, the piano introduction and the unknown speaker's queries "Wohin?", Schubert suggests the god's purposeful progression by slow (*Sehr langsam* is a rare tempo marking in Schubert's songs), inexorable half-note steps towards an unearthly place of rest by means of unconventional harmonies in mm. 1–2, the harmonic succession then repeated in mm. 3–4 for maximum mystification. It is not only the unidentified questioner in line 1, but we the listeners who ask "Wohin?" when we hear the emphasis on C in m. 1, followed by the semitone inflection of root-position B-flat and A major chords in m. 2, the B-flat major harmony all the more solemn and startling in effect for its mediant relationship with the preceding G major chord. The A major harmony is premonitory of the later D minor-D major spheres in m. 16f, but we cannot know that as yet, and the repetition in mm. 3–4 only intensifies the sense of strangeness – that it moves towards a goal is apparent, but what that goal might be is not. In Schubert's conception, the questioner urgently repeats his query, arresting the god's departure on a dominant seventh of F, sustained by a fermata and *forzando*. The god can be in no doubt of the questioner's imperative need to know.

In a brilliantly imaginative detail, Schubert's sun-god then remains in F major, albeit "umhüllt" and unstable, for a moment (mm. 7–14) to answer the earthly inquiry before resuming his journey. Indeed, the entire song is a tonal journey, beginning in mystery, pausing on an other-worldly variant of "F major," resuming its course in D minor, and ending on a remarkably un-final-sounding D major, an apotheosis but not "The End." Everywhere, the tonality is rendered mysterious, shifting, now blazing forth in "gold'ne Pracht" and clarity, now shadowed and enigmatic. In fact, everywhere, the one tonality invades the other, the balance shifting, such that F major is shot through with elements of the emphasis on D and the D major-minor sphere is likewise permeated with elements of F major. It is as if Helios were using mortal speech, mortal music, to address a human questioner, but mortal sounds from an immortal speaker emerge transmogrified. Or perhaps what is at times virtually a double tonic signifies the god's duality of focus, his spirit bent towards one goal while still in transit, or perhaps it is symbolic of the mutability and yet permanence of all things. Such complexity seems multivalent. There is no doubt, however, that Helios' prophesy of rebirth is matched by Schubert's prophesy of "neue Gluthen" in tones. This is music that foretells the later nineteenth century.

By the time he composed "Freiwilliges Versinken," Schubert had already demonstrated many times his willingness to abjure conventional melodic designs, and he does so here. In mm. 7–14, Helios speaks in melodic lines that plunge sharply downwards at the beginning and then rise by scalewise degrees, as if enacting each time the nocturnal plunge into "cool floods" and the subsequent ascent to resurrection. The phrases are made even more austerely majestic by the processional dotted rhythms and the thirty-second figures that invest the approach to a tone with a palpable emphasis and urgency, even at this tempo. Everywhere, there is tonal enigma: although the setting of Helios' words in stanza 1 begins and ends on F major and is articulated by a half-cadence on C major in the middle, even the clearest statements of F major are shot through with chromaticism. The "new warmth" ("neue Gluthen") is indeed rendered "new" by the forceful assertion of an E-flat major harmony as if it were yet another tonic in mm. 11–12 (the A-flats have been enharmonically foreshadowed by the G-sharps in the tenor voice of mm. 7–9), although it is not confirmed as such and the music returns to F major by the cadence at m. 14. The E-flat is intended to sound, and does, as a startling disruption of the F major strains, despite motivic parallels with what precedes it. Common-tone mediant shifts from one major chord to another major chord at the interval of a major third below (the flatted submediant) were relatively common, but this was unconventional both then and later – the musical speech of the gods. It seems only appropriate when the concluding verb, "zu schenken" (to give, in this instance, to humanity) returns to the human realm of F major from this brief excursion into mystery.

Mayrhofer's second and third stanzas constitute two parallel statements, the sun-god each time invoking his power in the second line of the verse ("und wie verschwenderisch mein Leben" in stanza 2, "so lang ich kräftig mich bewege" in stanza 3) and his lordly departure in the third and fourth lines. Schubert accordingly sets those two stanzas to the same music (mm. 16–28, repeated in mm. 29–44), with variations for prosodic adjustments and the longer line lengths of the final stanza. Each passage is a solemn progress from dark majesty in D minor to a cadence on D major. Paradoxically, Helios' greatest glory occurs when he submits to darkness: it is the words "naht die Nacht" (the night nears) and "gewinnen sie" that resound in parallel major, a blaze of light to herald the heroism of willed self-extinguishment. But if D minor and D major stand on either side of the repeated stanzas as a recognizable frame, neither is established at length and neither is stable, in an exact parallel to the clouded treatment of F major in stanza 1. There are no tonal plateaus in this song; however slow and majestic, the motion is inexorable. Each phrase ends at a place other than its beginning; for example, after the turn to D minor in the piano at m. 15, as forcefully (*ffz*) and economically limned as possible, Schubert extends the D minor chord throughout mm. 16–17, but then uses the pitch D-flat as the upper neighbor note to C-natural in a turn to an F major articulation. The F major harmonies of mm. 19–20 are then succeeded by a slow approach to D major, "umhüllt" in its progress. The light at sunset is not constant, but continually alters, and so too does the play of harmonies in Schubert's setting.

Rather than sinking motion in the postlude, Schubert chose the opposite musical metaphor: an ascent that seems doubly symbolic both of the moon and stars rising in the "weiter Ferne" and Helios' apotheosis-through-abnegation, repeated and extended in the piano interlude between stanzas 2 and 3. Here, the dotted processional rhythms become double-dotting, thus emphasizing each stage of the ascent. Of all Schubert's song endings, this is the most open-ended, the composer hinting that the music fades into silence *before* completion. Since Helios eternally comes and goes, vanishes and reappears, there is no ending as such possible, only whatever means will evoke further music beyond the borders of the final barline. The D major chord of resolution in m. 41 is extended throughout four measures in a manner that implies elision of the cadence at "Ferne" with a continuation of which we hear only the beginning. When Schubert darkens the Picardy third with the B-flat belonging to D minor and F major in those final measures (spelled as A-sharp in the rising inner voice) and stops the music on the weakest beat of the measure with the third of the tonic chord in the topmost voice, he denies any sense of closure. Helios, he suggests, may have vanished from our sight and sound, but he still moves purposefully in realms beyond our ken. Extinguishment is not death, the ending not the end, and for such mysteries, Schubert found the concomitant in sound.

6. In "Sternennächte" (Starry nights), the poet, soothed and salved by moonlight, ceases his customary dissension with existence and reflects that even the earth, seen from afar, appears as one of the stars he longs to become. Mayrhofer was captivated by stars as the ultimate symbols of beauty and goodness, and one finds the image in many of his poems. In "Der Schönheit Stern" (The star of beauty), for example, the illumination shed by beauty guides him on life's thorny paths, frees him – when the clouds of illness and age part – from his constraints, and lift his spirits.

In dunkler Nacht, wo Form und Farbe
   schwindet,
Erblinkt ein Stern, – die Guten kennen ihn;
Ob auch durch Dorn und Fels der Weg sich
   windet,
Zu jenem Stern schau' ich vertrauend hin.

Der Krankheit Beute sonst, ein Spiel der Jahre,
Macht mich des Sternes stilles Wirken frei;
Es theilt sich das Gewölk, und ich gewahre
Daß er mein Leiter und Befreier sei.

Ein süßer Wohllaut klingt mich an von oben,
Wie frischer Morgenhauch umweht es mich;
Im Innersten veredelt und gehoben,
Fühl' ich gesund und wieder jugendlich.[97]

In the dark of night, when forms and
   colors vanish,
a star shines – the good know it.
Although the path winds through thorns
   and rocks,
I look trustingly up to this star.

The star's quiet workings make me – a prey
to illness, a plaything of the years – free;
the clouds part, and I see
that it is my guide and liberator.

Sweet music resounds from above;
like fresh morning breezes, it wafts about me.
Inwardly ennobled and elevated,
I feel youthful once again and healthy.

The gentle light of moon and stars, which yet allowed the comfort of enveloping darkness, was a kinder poetic environment for such as Mayrhofer than harsh daylight. In "Lied," he calls the evening star "my sun," while in "Sternenschein" (Starlight), he writes that the Furies rage when "Selene's brother" – the sun – is the only heavenly being present and begs the stars to strew their nocturnal blossoms on those who hope for rescue.[98] In "Sternennächte," Mayrhofer muses that individual human pain is indiscernible across cosmic distances and that earth itself, pervaded by suffering and torment, glows as part of a diadem of stars. We too inhabit a star, and the thought was sufficient to make Mayrhofer cease his bitter wrangles with fate – for the duration of the poem. If such comfort is a short-lived rarity for this poet, it is thereby all the more moving.

In monderhellten Nächten,	On moonlit nights
Mit dem Geschick zu rechten,	my heart has forgotten
Hat diese Brust verlernt.	to quarrel with fate.
Der Himmel, reich besternt,	The heavens, rich with stars,
Umwoget mich mit Frieden;	leave me in peace,
Da denk' ich: Auch hienieden	and I think: even here on earth
Gedeihet manche Blume;	many a flower blooms,
Und frischer schaut der stumme,	and my silent, troubled gaze
Sonst trübe Blick hinauf	brightens as it contemplates
Zu ew'ger Sterne Lauf.	the stars' eternal course.
Auf ihnen quälen Schmerzen,	On them pain torments,
Auf ihnen bluten Herzen,	on them, hearts bleed,
Sie aber strahlen heiter,	but they shine serenely on.
So schließ' ich selig weiter:	And so I happily conclude:
Auch unsre kleine Erde,	even our little earth,
Voll Mißton und Gefährde,	full of discord and danger,
Sich als ein heiter Licht	is a bright light
Ins Diadem verflicht.	woven into this diadem.
So werden Sterne	Stars are made thus
Durch die Ferne![99]	by distance!

The poetic form is ingenious, despite Mayrhofer's carefully simple language, almost conversational in tone; the convoluted syntax of his most depressive, angry, tormented works is in abeyance here. The iambic trimeters dance, but gently, and the poetic sentences cut across and through the rhyming couplets in stanza 1, obviating any danger of jingle-like triviality, while the grammatical structure in stanza 2 follows the couplet form more closely, perhaps an index of even greater peace. The *Kling-Klang* rhyme and rhythms tell of concordance with the dance of the spheres, the poet gratefully tuning his lyre to a higher, harmonious order. For the final couplet of stanza 2, Mayrhofer truncates the lines, abbreviating them from trimeters to dimeters as a signal to the reader that this is the "concluding moral": "So werden Sterne / Durch die Ferne!" Weary of struggles with unremitting inner torment, the poet sought refuge in distances so great that he and all his psychological traumas vanished altogether.

Schubert reversed the first two lines of stanza 2 for his 1819 setting (D. 670), composed in D-flat major but copied in the Witteczek-Spaun collection in B-flat major; this latter version was probably the basis for the first edition, published by Spina in 1862 in B major as op. 165, no. 2, with the title "Die Sternennächte," the inserted definite article added by the publisher. This is one instance in which Schubert's habit of working from a memorized text could be responsible for the switched lines, whose parallelism invites such slips. Here, Schubert combines the chordal texture appropriate to a hymn of gratitude, albeit a non-Christian one; the 6/8 barcarolle rhythms of one cradled, not on the water but in the starry ocean of the firmament; the rare D-flat tonality shared by his setting of Schober's "Am Bach im Frühling," D. 361, another contemplative song inspired by Nature; and passages entirely in the treble register, as in the even more ethereal "Nachtviolen." Where the piano accompaniment doubles the vocal line at the start of a phrase, then branches off to overtop the singer's melody, Schubert thus evokes the discant to a hymn, although other musical elements are less suggestive of the church. The vocal line in the original tonality is poised serenely on high, only occasionally and briefly dipping below D-flat. The fact that the vocal line in the initial phrase (mm. 5–6, repeated in mm. 14–15 and 42–43) emphasizes the third of the tonic chord, only touching upon the root pitch before ascending gently upwards once again, heightens the sense of moonlit release from earthly bonds.

Where other composers might have set this poem as a strophic song in two stanzas to correspond with the poetic form, Schubert created an A B A three–part song form in which lines 1–7 of stanza 1 constitute the A section (ending with the words "gedeihet manche Blume"), lines 8–10 of stanza 1 and lines 1–3 of stanza 2 the B section (beginning with the words "und frischer schaut der stumme, trübe Blick"), and lines 4–10 of stanza 2 the return of the A section, beginning "So schliess' ich selig weiter." In order to make the two halves of the A section symmetrical (eight measures each, with a one-bar interlude in between) and yet still preserve the poetic "sentences" intact (three lines for the first "sentence," four lines for the second), Schubert repeats line 3, "Hat diese Brust verlernt"; when he does so, he quietly emphasizes what an achievement it was for Mayrhofer, of all people, to forget – more precisely, to "unlearn" – his quarrel with fate. It might seem obvious to locate the recapitulation at the point where the poet says, "And so I happily conclude … " but Schubert does so across and through the poetic architecture. Another result of this division of the poem is that the darkness and pain are isolated in the B section, the "darkened gaze," the "bleeding hearts," and anguished sorrows concentrated in the middle of the formal structure. It is those words which are, after all, the measure of how precious such moments of peace were in Mayrhofer's existence. The poet dispels the tell-tale revelation of melancholy with the words "sie aber strahlen heiter" (but they shine on cheerfully); there, Schubert in his turn dispels the chromatic pitches emblematic of darkness and returns to the A-flat major dominant tonality from the beginning of the B section, repeating those words to an embellished cadence in which the singer soars up to the high A-flat of m. 28 – "hinauf" indeed (the embellished cadence, however, was an addition to the Spaun-Witteczek copy and is not in the autograph manuscript). That cadence is somewhat reminiscent of the final setting of the words "Sterne, ach, gar viele" at the end of Franz von Bruchmann's "Am See" (By the lake), D. 746, in which another poet from the Schubert circle contemplates the stars and human destiny.

The peace that envelops the poetic persona lulls him and the music, first, to gentle descent, then to a complete standstill; the A section ends with a quite final-sounding cadence on the tonic, repeated in the piano as the bass line descends almost three octaves from the treble into the low bass and concluding with a fermata-sustained pause. But with the words "und frischer," a brighter, fresher movement commences in the dominant tonality. The piano figuration is set in motion for almost a full measure before the voice joins in with the words "und frischer schaut," the composer thus suggesting that the singer joins in a process already begun before words form and accounting wonderfully for the connective "und." Schubert, who knew just how "trübe" Mayrhofer could be, sets the adjective to a dominant minor harmony (A-flat minor) sustained throughout almost an entire measure and then uses the lowered third C-flat to turn to a cadence on C-flat major for the "ew'ger Sterne Lauf," the C-flat of the "stars' eternal course" indeed distant from the D-flat major of the poet on earth. Both A-flat minor and C-flat major harmonies then recur in that order for the "bleeding hearts" and "sorrows" in mm. 32–35, the "fresh" sixteenth-note motion replaced by the chordal texture once again. Schubert varies the chordal motion by removing the downbeat in the piano, as if to suggest the de-stabilizing effect of pain in that fashion, and by setting the verbs of suffering, "bluten" and "quälen," as appoggiatura motives repeated in *Terzensteigerung* – intensification indeed. And yet, in a tonal subtlety worthy of Mayrhofer's transmogrification of pain into distant light and beauty, the non-chord tone A-double-flat in m. 34 ("quälen") becomes, a mere two measures later, the leading tone to A-flat major (G-natural), the means to turn from gloom to illumination. After the F-flats and C-flats of the darkling episode, the restoration of F and C-natural in m. 36 at the word "aber" (but) seems a repudiation of melancholy effected with the lightest of touches.

In the piano interlude in mm. 40–41, Schubert turns back to D-flat for the return of the A section, simply but with two beautifully subtle details: the vacillation between D-natural and D-flat in m. 40 and the fermata-prolonged dominant seventh in m. 41. The topmost voice remains poised on high G-flat (the seventh of the chord) for a moment, as if to say, "And thus," pausing for maximum anticipatory effect – but delicately so – before the singer steps in to say, "So schliess' ich." It is a charming gesture and one perfectly apt to prepare a closing maxim. Since the final lines of text are a more conclusive summary of the first stanza, Schubert repeats the A section with only skillful adjustments of the form to the shortened text – he masterfully compensates for the abbreviated lines by breaking them apart, his poetic persona musing for a moment in the piano between the two halves of the concluding statement. Measures 14–17 (a repetition to different words of mm. 5–8) are omitted in the final section of the song, Schubert skipping from m. 12 to m. 18 and then extending the final cadence by an extra measure. The mastery with which it is all done is of the sort to mask, not expose, the consummate artistry involved; the song is only "simple" in its inevitability of effect, as if it could only be thus and no other way.

7. In "Nachtstück," Mayrhofer imagines his death as he wished it to be: an "old man" (for all his imprecations against life's miseries, the poet betrays his natural human desire for a long tenure on earth), knowing this night to be his last, departs existence with a song, serenaded and surrounded by Nature until he slips imperceptibly into "the long sleep." There is no suffering, none of the disease Mayrhofer so dreaded, no terror, no loss of his artistic capacity; Death "inclines" to him as a gentle friend making a pre-arranged rendezvous, not as a violent raptor. It is a vision horrifyingly distant from his actual death.

Wenn über Berge sich der Nebel breitet,	When the mists spread over the mountains,
Und Luna mit Gewölken kämpft,	and the moon battles with the clouds,
So nimmt der Alte seine Harfe, und schreitet,	the old man takes his harp and walks
Und singt waldeinwärts und gedämpft:	towards the forest, quietly singing:
"Du heilge Nacht:	"Holy night,
Bald ist's vollbracht,	soon it will be done.
Bald schlaf ich ihn, den langen Schlummer,	Soon I shall sleep the long sleep
Der mich erlöst von allem Kummer."	which will release me from all care."
Die grünen Bäume rauschen dann:	Then the green trees rustle:
"Schlaf süss, du guter, alter Mann";	"Sleep sweetly, good old man";
Die Gräser lispeln wankend fort:	And the swaying grasses whisper:
"Wir decken seinen Ruheort";	"We shall cover his resting place."
Und mancher liebe Vogel ruft:	And many a sweet bird calls:
"O lasst ihn ruhn in Rasengruft!"	"Let him rest in his grassy grave!"
Der Alte horcht, der Alte schweigt,	The old man listens, the old man falls silent,
Der Tod hat sich zu ihm geneigt.	Death has inclined to him.

When Schubert first set this poem in October 1819, he and Mayrhofer were still friends and the composer was not under a death-sentence from venereal disease, although songs about death proliferate in his *œuvre* from the very beginning. When he went back to "Nachtstück" in order to publish it as op. 36 with Cappi in February 1825, the friendship with Mayrhofer was no more and he knew that he himself was dying. One wonders, as he was transposing the original C-sharp minor setting downward to C minor and preparing the second version for publication, what this swan-song for a dying minstrel might have meant to him in the wake of that knowledge.

The body of Schubert's setting, D. 672, published as op. 36, no. 2 in February 1825, is a bipartite formal structure consisting of the old man's death-song and Nature's welcome to him (mm. 18–68), preceded by a similarly bipartite "upbeat" (mm. 1–17), as Graham Johnson aptly calls it. The first section of the "upbeat," consisting of the piano introduction and the brief, evocative description of the nocturnal *mise-en-scène* ("Wenn über Berge sich der Nebel breitet, / und Luna mit

Gewölken kämpft," mm. 1–10), is filled with semitone sighing figures built up at several levels in the right-hand part of the piano introduction (mm. 1–5), as if the very air were saturated with sighs, while the left-hand part descends in a *lamentoso* chromatic line from the tonic pitch to the dominant. One also notices the weak-beat accents, the indices of psychic turmoil and pain in *Winterreise* and elsewhere in Schubert's song *œuvre*, in almost every measure of the introduction. In the last half of m. 4 and the entirety of m. 5, the weak-beat accents disappear, suggesting that Death ultimately eases away all pain. As the topmost and bottommost lines widen in opposite directions throughout mm. 1–3, the tension increases and the dynamics grow louder until the mid-measure arrival at the dominant seventh chord, each harmonization of the dominant pitch in the bass accented like a tolling bell even as the dynamics grow softer once again. In retrospect, it seems a musical symbol *in nuce* of the ever-increasing grief of life, leading inexorably to the death-blow (the accented *forte* dominant seventh chord in the middle of m. 3); what follows the fateful moment is an ebbing-away, a descent and a lessening of tension, filled with softer and softer echoes of the blow. The semitone figures, especially A-flat G, become the whole-step A-*natural* G at the end of the introduction, the A-natural belonging to parallel major mode in a telling hint of the brightness and peace only to be found after departing this "vale of sighs." In Mayrhofer's imagination, death is release from the grief which permeates life, and Schubert encapsulates that realization in this one supremely economical gesture, the effect far in excess of what one might expect from the chromatic alteration of a single note. Fittingly, the resolution of the dominant sevenths in mm. 5 and 10 only comes at the very end of the song, when Death "inclines," as a kind Deity from above, to the old man. Schubert states his musical allegory of grief-filled life, followed by death and the cessation of pain, twice, as the introduction and, transposed an octave lower, as accompaniment beneath the singer's first two phrases for lines 1–2. Before "der Alte" even appears, we are twice told, even if we only recognize it in retrospect, that he will be granted the death he desires.

As the elderly poet takes his harp and walks, singing, to the woods and his appointment with death, the texture and meter both change to the extraordinary starkness one finds elsewhere in the Mayrhofer songs – it is a texture Schubert seems to have associated with this poet alone. The first four bars of the processional to death in "Nachtstück" are a variation, some five or six months later, of the piano part throughout "An die Freunde" (To my Friends), D. 654 of March 1819, in which Mayrhofer instructs his friends to bury him in the forest, without a cross or stone to mark the grave-site (ex. 22). The parallels with the "old man" in "Nachtstück" are poignantly obvious.

Im Wald, im Wald da grabt mich ein,   In the forest, in the forest, there bury me,
Ganz stille, ohne Kreuz und Stein: silently, without cross or stone;
Denn was ihr türmet, überschneit   for whatever you raise up,
Und überwindet Winterszeit.   winter storms will cover with snow.

(stanza 1 of 3)

Example 22. Franz Schubert, "Nachtstück," D. 672, op.36 no. 2, mm. 11–17 and "An die Freunde," D. 654, mm. 1–8.

Throughout "An die Freunde" and in the parallel passage of "Nachtstück," one finds the same funereal quasi-march, with distant origins in Baroque "walking bass" figuration (Schubert would later evoke this particular device even more strongly in his setting of Schober's "Schatzgräbers Begehr," or "The Treasure-Hunter's Desire," of November 1822, perhaps inspired to do so by the phrase "ein alt Gesetz" – "an old law"). In "An die Freunde," each starkly unharmonized pitch is separated by a rest from the next pitch; there is no rhythmic differentiation, only the musical ticking of a giant clock, marking the passage of time which bears the poet, and everyone else, to their deaths. A similarly austere passage also occurs at the beginning of "Aus 'Heliopolis' (I)," D. 753 of April 1822, in which the poet, trapped in "the cold, harsh North," dreams of a city-of-the-sun, part classical allusion ("Heliopolis" was the Greek name for the ancient Egyptian city of Iunu or Onu, where the priapic worship of the sun god Re, or Osiris, was centered), part private vision of an ideal world.[100] The true "kalten, rauhen Norden" was the same miserable existence that the old minstrel of "Nachtstück" is about to depart, and it is just as austerely limned.[101] The minstrel's walk to the woods in mm. 11–17 has another predecessor in the unvarying quarter-note rhythmic tactus throughout the first version of "Harfenspieler II," or "An die Türen will ich schleichen," in which a far more tragic elderly minstrel envisions a *living* death. Perhaps Mayrhofer was not only imagining the death he would most desire but re-writing the Harper's fate.

En route to the old man's swan-song, the texture of "Nachtstück" warms and grows richer in preparation. Already in mm. 12–13, at the words "seine Harfe" (his harp), one hears a four-voice cadential phrase-ending on the relative major (E-flat major) before the austerities resume. One notices in particular the Neapolitan sixth in m. 16, a favorite Schubertian way of darkening the approach to especially significant cadences, and the sighing figures that once again multiply throughout the different voices of mm. 15–17, in particular, the final measure of the section, with its rich harmonization of a final appoggiatura semitone motive. The mournfulness that is about to end is all the more intense for being "gedämpft," or muted.

Swan-songs are traditionally a last glorious outpouring of melody at its sweetest and purest, a "singing to death" in consummate melody. Like an Orpheus-in-reverse who desires death, not life, Mayrhofer's alter ego pleads with Death for an extraordinary boon and does so with all the artifice at his disposal. For the swan-song in mm. 18–39, Schubert gives his minstrel the archetypal broken-chordal mimicry of harp figuration in the right hand, with a simple, deep bass foundation in the left hand, and a beautifully-crafted lyrical melody. Far more often than Mayrhofer's persona, Schubert's old man ecstatically repeats the lines and phrases of his hymn to Night, like a spell repeated over and over again until the magic finally works. After the halting, sigh-laden motion of the introduction and the weary, dragging pace of mm. 10–17, the unbroken rise-and-fall of the arpeggiated figures wonderfully represents not only harp music but a final infusion of strength and motion for this last lyrical outpouring. At the beginning of the old man's song, the initial C minor tonality turns into the E-flat major associated elsewhere in Schubert's songs with awe and devotion (Franz Bruchmann's "Am See," D. 746, Friedrich Rückert's "Du bist die Ruh'," D. 776, and Jacobi's "Litanei auf das Fest aller Seelen," D. 343) as simply and naturally as pain turns to ease, life to death, when surcease from suffering finally appears. Although the sustained dominant seventh chord in m. 17 resolves to the expected C minor harmony at the start of m. 18, thus investing the adjective "heil'ge" with the slight touch of darkness appropriate to sacred mysteries and to night, it becomes apparent that C minor is now the submediant harmony of E-flat major when the initial C minor chord is followed by a plagal progression, its traditional connotations of reverence unmistakable, to the first new tonic harmony on the word "Nacht." The B-flat in the singer's part at the word "Nacht" after the fermata-prolonged leading tone to C just before is almost magical in its sensation of sinking into easeful death.

But life and its griefs are not yet entirely vanquished. The short-lived cadential articulation on G minor at the words "langen Schlummer" (a transposed variant of the phrase "bald ist's vollbracht" in mm. 20–21) in mm. 23–24 garbs the "long sleep" in minor-mode sadness and heaviness. But in the next moment, death begins the process of salvation and release, of "Erlösung," with the rising sequence in mm. 25–27, as if the old man were being drawn upwards by ecstatic stages. Throughout the swan-song, Schubert finds tonal symbols for the way in which life and death are mingled at this moment, the last vestiges of life's darkness in C minor followed in each instance by the E-flat major of release from care. When Schubert's elderly minstrel repeats the entirety of stanza 2 in mm. 30–39, we hear the two worlds, that of life and "easeful Death," struggle with one another for an instant at the beginning of the passage, like dissonant death-throes – mercifully brief. The dominant and tonic pitches of C minor reappear in the bass of mm. 30–31, but the G in the bass is harmonized, not as the dominant of C minor, but as an E-flat augmented triad, containing both E-flat and B-natural, the dissonant harmony accented each time en route to another C minor harmony. Mayrhofer speaks only of release from "all cares," not a final conflict between life and death, but Schubert's death-obsessed imagination could and did supply this vivid addition to the poet's scene.

The swan-song ends each time, one notes, with the pitch G, not tonic E-flat, in the vocal line – the plea for death and surcease is not yet achieved, and therefore tonic closure does not occur. When the old man's song is done, it is left to Nature to sing him to his final sleep. Schubert took his cue for the changed figuration from the rustling branches and waving grasses, each triplet-figure wave of leafy plumage culminating in an offbeat accent on E-flat as chiming echoes of the bass; the quarter-note tactus is in part what distinguishes these inhuman speakers from the old man, with his slower, broader, more lyrical motion. The harmonic emphases change with the change of speaker: the E-flat chords of the swan-song become dominant sevenths of A-flat minor in m. 40, brightening to major at the adjective "guter" and the injunction, "Schlaf süß, du guter, alter Mann" in m. 43. When the grasses whisper, the harmonic inflection again changes, returning once again to the E-flat of the old man's swan-song for the designation of a "Ruheort." Throughout the setting of this entire third stanza, the music, especially the right-hand part, sinks by degrees, as if sinking gently down to the ground in death, although the bass only descends into the "Rasengruft" (grassy grave) at the culminating words "Wir decken seinen Ruheort" in mm. 47–48. But this entire lied is a long, gradual drifting-to-sleep in which the music literally dies away in the protracted final section, and therefore Schubert once again repeats the entire previous passage but with the birds rather than the grasses pleading for the elderly minstrel's ultimate rest in the "Rasengruft" (one remembers that Schubert becomes a bird in Mayrhofer's poetic elegy for his dead friend). When we hear tonic closure in the vocal line at m. 58, we know that death is truly nigh.

Death answers Nature's pleading, not in the E-flat major in which the birds and grasses sing of their concerted longing for the minstrel's death, but by means of an exquisitely gradual progression that sinks by degrees from E-flat major to C major, the Janus-faced twin to life's C minor pain. For the gentle "dying-away" at the end (mm. 59–68), Schubert combines the half-note tactus of the old man's death-song, with its octave bass pitches at the beginning and mid-point of each measure, and the right-hand figuration that accompanies the trees, grass, and birds: the minstrel and his non-human attendants are all attentive presences at the close, and Schubert accordingly combines elements of their entreaties when Death "inclines" to the old man. Surely everyone who hears this passage would long for a death as beautiful as this one in which E-flat major darkens to parallel minor, slips still lower to the warmth and richness of D-flat major and its parallel minor, then at last to C minor and C major. In the descending sequence, we hear Death gently drift down as the old man listens for his coming. Only when Death finally arrives in m. 64 does the song arrive at C major, the ultimate goal of "Nachtstück" as death is the ultimate goal of life. In m. 65, we hear once again the A-natural of m. 5, Schubert and Death providing the complete context for what was hinted so long ago, at the word "[zu] ihm," "to him," as if to underscore how personal the gesture is. When Schubert repeats the last line ("Der Tod hat sich zu ihm geneigt") in mm. 66–68, it is not only over a repeated C ostinato in the bass, but to a vocal line that consists only of neighbor notes around C, Death taking the minstrel into his keeping and holding him close. There is no postlude, only the ebbing-away of the final C major chord as Death stills the minstrel and the song alike.

8.   After the 1822 songs, there was a hiatus of two years during which, for the first time since 1814, there were no Mayrhofer songs. Not until March 1824, between the composition of the string quartets in A minor, D. 804, and D minor, D. 810, did Schubert return to Mayrhofer's poetry for the last time to compose five of his best songs, four for solo voice and one for choral ensemble. Of the solo songs, "Der Sieg" (The victory) for bass is the least well-known, possibly because its subject is suicide.

O unbewölktes Leben!	O unclouded life!
So rein und tief und klar.	So pure and deep and clear.
Uralte Träume schweben	Age-old dreams hover
Auf Blumen wunderbar.	miraculously over the flowers.

Johann Mayrhofer

Der Geist zerbrach die Schranken,	The spirit broke the fetters
Des Körpers träges Bley;	of the body's inert leaden weight;
Er waltet groß und frey.	it roams great and free.
Es laben die Gedanken	The mind is refreshed
An Edens Früchten sich;	by the fruits of Paradise;
Der alte Fluch entwich.	the ancient curse is gone.
Was ich auch je gelitten,	What I have suffered,
Die Palme ist erstritten,	the palm is now won,
Gestillet mein Verlangen.	my longing stilled.
Die Musen selber sangen	The Muses themselves sang
Die Schlang' [Sphinx] in Todesschlaf,	the serpent [sphinx] to the sleep of death,
Und meine Hand – sie traf.	and my hand – it struck the blow.
O unbewölktes Leben!	O unclouded life!
So rein und tief und klar.	So pure and deep and clear.
Uralte Träume schweben	Age-old dreams hover
Auf Blumen wunderbar.[102]	miraculously above the flowers.

Here, Mayrhofer imagines ultimate victory in his war with matter and the flesh and writes this poem as if from the other side of the divide. The Muses, who are his allies and confederates, have sung the tormenting beast within him to sleep in death, and the spirit at last has broken free and emerged into an unclouded existence, joining the other age-old spirits who hover about the paradisiacal flowers. But this is a heaven to which one gains entry by suicide, by killing the "serpent" (according to the 1824 *Gedichte*) or the sphinx (Schubert's text) that is life; whether the composer used an earlier manuscript version of the poem or made the alteration himself (perhaps as a reminiscence of Mayrhofer's "Memnon"?) is not known. In one of the aphoristic *Betrachtungen* (Observations), Mayrhofer explicitly compares life to the sphinx and dreams of its ultimate vanquishment:

Das Leben ist die Sphinx; wen ihre Schöne kirrte,	Life is the Sphinx: whoever would bring its beauty to heel,
Wem Sinnestaumel den Verstand verwirrte,	whoever would confuse the intoxication of the
Er war auch ohne Rettung hin.	senses with reason, he too was without salvation.
Oedip allein erlegt die Fragerin;	Oedipus alone slays the questioner,
Und in denselben Abgrund muß sie sinken,	and it must sink in the same abyss from which
Woraus die Beine ihrer Opfer blinken.[103]	the bones of its sacrificial victims gleam.

If suicide was a sin in Catholic Austria, it was not so among the Stoics, and Mayrhofer proclaims, "My hand struck the blow!" with defiant pride. Like a warrior who slays the enemy in battle, the poet imagines striking the ultimate blow against his worst enemy – his own fleshly envelope – and winning the most difficult victory of all.

Schubert frames his setting on either side with a hymn-cum-solemn march, ten bars of *Reinheit, Klarheit,* and *Tiefe* (purity, clarity, and profundity) that could have issued from Sarastro's halls. After a first phrase in which the pianist doubles the vocal line in the right-hand part, with the bass line doubled in octaves, the singer then doubles the descending left-hand part in mm. 9–10 at the words "Uralte Träume schweben," as if literally descending into caverns of Time; the weighted, yet austere bass line sounds beautifully suggestive of things "uralte." Paradoxically, the poet ecstatically hymns the afterlife, invoking both "the old curse" incurred in the Garden of Eden and the "fruits of Paradise," and yet it is a spirit world to which one gains entry by suicide – and for which Schubert evokes the textures of Christian hymnody. Schubert had also used hymnlike textures the previous year in his setting of Schiller's "Der Pilgrim" (The Pilgrim), D. 794[104] in which a poetic persona initially guided, like Mayrhofer himself, by a "dunkle Glaubenswort" (dark word of faith) struggles mightily to attain his spiritual aspirations but finds – nothing. One wonders whether Schubert saw the parallels between the driven fictional pilgrim and the disappointed idealistic depressive he knew so well.

Mayrhofer may have written in the past tense of bonds already burst and spirit already freed from flesh, but Schubert locates the struggle in the musical present, replacing the former balanced symmetries of cut-time with triple meter, inherently unbalanced, and the diatonicism of the first fourteen measures with chromatic conflict, waged principally between F major and D minor, as if those two tonalities were emblematic of spirit and flesh at war (did Schubert perhaps recall the confounding of F major-D minor/major in "Freiwilliges Versinken" when he composed the later song?). The section begins on the dominant, not tonic, and at the words "Körpers träges Bley" – the tragic weight of flesh – momentarily heightens D minor before shifting yet again to the subdominant for the fortissimo proclamation of greatness and freedom, "groß und frei." Eden's fruitfulness and the vanishing of the "ancient curse" impel six measures of unclouded C major (mm. 22–27, the key of death at the end of "Nachtstück" and the tonality of Eternity at the close of "Gruppe aus dem Tartarus"), almost entirely purified of chromatic "sin," before the invocation of the poet's suffering brings back the dotted rhythmic D minor strains of the "Körpers träges Bley." As before, the singer breaks away from leaden weight and suffering with blatant parallel fifths in the soprano and tenor voices of the hymn texture (the ends of mm. 18 and 29, the beginnings of mm. 19 and 30), as if in miniature demonstration of the radical violence necessary to overcome such restrictive bonds. This time, rather than the prior motion to a cadence on B-flat, the words "gestillet mein Verlangen" (my longing stilled) lead for the first time in this battleground of a middle stanza to a completed cadence on tonic F major, but not until Schubert has prolonged the accented syllable of "ge-*still*-et" while multiple dissonances are stilled beneath it, in a wonderfully graphic illustration both of the intensity of the poet's longing and the quietus wrought by Death.

What follows this passage is even more intense. In the final measures of the middle stanza, Schubert depicts the lulling of the sphinx to death's sleep and the death-blow itself in a passage (mm. 35–43) whose culminating enharmonic transformation foreshadows the more extensive use of similar gestures, as if alternating between death and life (the same tones but transformed, their contexts utterly altered), throughout the setting in 1826 of Franz Xaver von Wssehrd Schlechta's "Totengräber-Weise," D. 869. One does not have far to seek for the traditional symbolism of enharmony in songs such as these. Here, the Muses sing the sphinx to death's-sleep as a hushed vocal descent to low F ("Todesschlaf") through the flatted sixth degree, an appropriately dark and mysterious voyage into the deepest abyss of the song; the pitch D-flat is explicitly identified with the sphinx in both the vocal line and the bass of m. 36. Those D-flats resound even more strongly when the poet-singer vaults suddenly, shockingly, out of the chasm and kills himself ("Und meine Hand, sie traf!"). Without breaking the texture and rhythms already established, Schubert heightens the tension of the moment by placing the connective "und" on the strong downbeat and thereby heightening the element of shock, by quickening the rhythmic pace of the first three words, and by a dramatic vocal break before the climactic words "sie traf." The death-blow in m. 40 sounds as a seventh chord on D-flat, literally striking down the D (natural) minor associated with the hated weight of life. The chord at "traf" is not a root-position triad, but a seventh chord, a wonderfully economical way to suggest that the fatal blow is not the end, to imply that more *must* follow even before the shape-changing harmonic metamorphosis continues in mm. 41–43. The enharmonic transformation from m. 40 to m. 41, a thicket of sharps replacing a thicket of flats, is the visual symbol of the transformation from flesh to spirit, from hated corporeal existence to "unclouded life," from darkness to brightness. The dazzling light we are told that one sees at the moment of death here finds both a visual and an auditory symbol at once. The flash of brightness appears as an F-sharp major six-four chord, so close to F-major tranquillity and yet so distant from it tonally: in mm. 42–43, the lightning bolt of harmonic electricity is dispelled, revealing the dominant of F major (ex. 23) – and then the refrain once again. (This

Example 23.   Franz Schubert, "Der Sieg," D. 805, mm. 35–43. From the *Neue Schubert-Ausgabe*, Series IV: *Lieder*, vol. 13a, ed. Walther Dürr.

time, Schubert had the poet's sanction to repeat the beginning lines at the end, unlike "Erlafsee".) When the hymn of praise, "O unbewölktes Leben!", recurs as the final section, one hears it differently than in the beginning, as hard-won tonal clarity after the fraught chromaticism and tensions of the middle stanza.

The postlude is minimal; there is no need for more. One hears its emphasized subdominant harmony as prayerfully triumphant or triumphantly prayerful, a *forte* reminiscence of "groß und frei" and a final victory over the tonal battles in the middle of the song. Schubert could not, of course, have known that Mayrhofer's hand would strike just such a blow, if less victoriously by far, eight years after his own death, but had he outlived his poet-friend, one can imagine him unsurprised by the eventuality foreshadowed in "Der Sieg."

9. "Abendstern," D. 806, seems at first to be a simpler song than "Der Sieg," but appearances are deceptive.

Was weilst du einsam an dem Himmel,	Why do you linger all alone in the sky,
O schöner Stern? und bist so mild;	fair star? For you are so gentle:
Warum entfernt das funkelnde Gewimmel	why does the host of sparkling brothers
Der Brüder sich vor deinem Bild?	shun your sight?
"Ich bin der Liebe treuer Stern,	"I am the faithful star of love;
Sie halten sich von Liebe fern."	they keep far away from love."
So solltest du zu ihnen gehen,	If you are love,
Bist du der Liebe, zaud're nicht!	you should go to them – do not delay!
Wer möchte denn dir widerstehen?	For who could resist you,
Du süsses eigensinnig Licht.	sweet, wayward light?
"Ich säe, schaue keinen Keim,	"I sow no seed, I see no shoot,
Und bleibe trauernd still daheim."	and remain here, silent and mournful."

In this miniature allegory, an unnamed, unknown voice speaks to the evening star, or Love, asking why it shuns "the host of sparkling brothers" – Mayrhofer underscores the brilliance of the other stars in lines 3 and 4 by suddenly quickening the poetic rhythm at the adjective "funkelnde." The diphthong -ei chimes twice in the first line of stanza 1 ("weilst," "einsam"), the bright, wide-open sound imbuing the question with its own distinctive poetic color; Schubert subsequently heightens the internal rhyme by setting both syllables on the third degree of the tonic chord and lingering on the poignant appoggiatura dissonance at "*ein - sam*." When the questioner then exhorts Love to go to the others, saying that its sweetness is irresistible, Love reveals in more detail the reasons for its solitude. If one understands this poem as self-revelatory, one finds a barely-veiled admission of the poet's likely homosexuality, a love that "sows no seeds, sees no shoots" and therefore remains isolated and apart. Even Love's replies to the poetic speaker are, one notices, set apart formally as a rhyming couplet (lines 5 and 6) that follows a quatrain in an a b a b rhyme scheme, and the couplets are notably terse, with all the brevity of someone too alienated for loquaciousness. The ending is all the more tragic because of Mayrhofer's implicit assertion of uniqueness; he is, after all, the evening star, the emblem of faithful love, and yet he is condemned to existence perpetually apart from the companionship for which he longs. The poet is also the questioner: one can understand the seeming dialogue as two dissenting voices within Mayrhofer himself, the one urging him into the world and the other pessimistically asserting that it is no use – and hinting why.

The pianist Graham Johnson has pointed out the close relationship between "Abendstern" and "Du liebst mich nicht" (You do not love me), D. 756 of 1822, a setting of a pseudo-Persian ghazal by August von Platen-Hallermünde, who was quite certainly homosexual; he could have added as well that the "Fate" rhythmic pattern throughout the song is also reminiscent of Mignon's "So laßt mich scheinen, bis ich werde," D. 877, no. 3 (another song about a poetic creature isolated from "the other stars") and another A minor tale of tragedy, the setting of Matthäus von Collin's "Der Zwerg," D. 771. The relationship to "Du liebst mich nicht" is all the more compelling because similar ostinato bass pitches and chordal texture prevail in both songs, although the writhing, tortured anguish of "Du liebst mich nicht" impels far-reaching tonal excursions of a sort not found in "Abendstern." In the later song, Schubert suggests the faint shimmering aura of starlight by means of the dissonances created between the ostinato pitches in the bass and the moving voices above it, dissonant appoggiaturas which sometimes linger for a beat and a half before resolving; even the "resolution" is often still dissonant because the soprano tone of resolution and the bass ostinato, as in the pitches B and A in mm. 1 and 4, are dissonant with one another. The effect is especially poignant when it underscores such key words as "einsam" and "entfernt." (I wonder whether Hugo Wolf perhaps learned from this song how similarly to suggest ethereal light in sound for his beautiful setting of Goethe's "St. Nepomuk's Vorabend" over sixty years later, another poem in which an extremity of pain – the dismemberment of St. Wenceslas of Bohemia – is converted into points of sparkling light.) The effect of the multiple dissonances unconventionally treated, performed *pianissimo* (except where the dynamics warm to *mezzo-forte* and *forte* when the poetic persona exhorts Love in the first four lines of stanza 2), is beautifully analogous to the shimmer (of other tones) that surrounds a central point of light (the primary chord). In larger symbolic terms, it can also be heard as the conversion of pain into beauty, with the faint echoes of that pain still preserved in the music.

The piano introduction has more subtleties than its brevity and seeming simplicity might initially suggest. After the gently swaying motion on the root and third of the tonic chord and the scalewise descent of a diminished fourth, the yearning leap of a sixth upward at the end is all the more effective – the music itself looking up above in longing. It seems evident that the initial motive of the introduction was conceived to the opening words "Was weilst du einsam," with the verb "weilst" gently stressed in the anacrusis and the crucial word "einsam" doubly stressed on the downbeat of m. 1 – loneliness is the crux of it all. When the singer enters with an extended variant of the introduction, the yearning becomes even more palpable as the vocal line "overshoots" the mark and leaps upwards a diminished seventh to F at the adjective "schöner" (once again, Mayrhofer's significant concern with beauty and the beautiful), prolonged slightly in added emphasis. In stanza 2, when the same music recurs, the urgent leap is equally apropos for the words "bist du [der Liebe]."

In each of the two stanzas, the poetic interlocutor occupies two-thirds of the strophe, while the "treue Stern" speaks in the final third. Schubert mimics the poet's form in his musical structure for the song: in the setting of stanza 1, the questions in the first four lines of each stanza begin in the A minor of Schubertian lamentation (mm. 3–8, ending with a half-cadence on V of C major) and modulate to the relative major (C major) as the questions become more urgent, ending with a half-cadence in A minor in m. 12. The star's reply begins in A major, which slips back to A minor for line 6, the brightness and sweetness of parallel major dimmed by sorrow (mm. 13–18). The ostinato pitches in this form dominated by that particular compositional device are thus A C A, that is, the soprano pitches of the anacrusis preceding m. 1. In his setting of Karl Leitner's "Die Sterne" (The Stars), D. 939, Schubert also suggests via ostinati that the rapt poet-singer stands with his feet firmly rooted in place on terra firma, while the motion happens in higher realms, both in the heavens and in the heart.

The A minor mournfulness brightens to C major in mm. 6–7 for the words "und bist so mild," the star's gentleness prompting the short-lived mitigation of melancholy. It is equally apt for the plea-command, "Zaudre nicht" (Do not delay) in mm. 21–22; in both instances, even though the musical phrase continues seamlessly, without a pause or break, the harmonic change is the corollary of the grammatical inflections in the poetry, the question followed by a statement in stanza 1 ("O schöner Stern? und bist so mild") and the two clauses punctuated by a comma in stanza 2 ("Bist du der Liebe, zaudre nicht"). Surely the sixteenth notes at "funkelnde" were inspired by the twinkling lights of stanza 1, while the climactic high G on the downbeat of mm. 11 and 25 is more apt for emphasis on the initial syllable of "ei - [gensinnig]" in stanza 2. There, as in the emphasis on "einsam," one can detect Schubert's personal knowledge of the "eigensinnig" poet, self-condemned to the solitude he mourns in this poem.

The piano echoes and ornaments the half-cadence on the G major harmony in mm. 7-8, as if not only assenting to the fact that the beautiful star "is so gentle" ("und bist so mild") but insisting upon it – gently. The interlude between the end of the poetic interlocutor's question and the star's reply consists of a far more mystical-sounding gesture: non-legato chiming E's, at first unharmonized but culminating in an A major chord. The effect of unprepared parallel major is nearly as magical as the sudden transformation of D minor into D major for the final stanza of "Gute Nacht" in *Winterreise*. The piano interludes are linked: one notes the non-legato D's in the topmost voice of the piano interlude in m. 7, the non-legato pitches subsequently extracted in m. 12 as the sole element – the "earthly" voices down below no longer sound, and only the celestial chimes remain. In the setting of the second stanza, the first interlude is omitted; the poetic interlocutor's urgency is such that he cannot wait.

The "schöner Stern" sweetly, quietly proclaims his identity in A major with the vocal line moving beneath the E pedal point in the topmost voice of the piano (was it from passages such as this that Brahms learned to do likewise in the Intermezzo in E-flat major, op. 117, no. 1?). Despite the loveliness of the brief patch of A major, tonic minor reappears all too soon, slipping back at the words "halten sich." Schubert delays the reinstatement of C-natural until it appears in the vocal line as well as the inner voice of the piano part, a masterful detail by which to heighten the verb "sich halten" (constrain, keep back, hold out against) in a manner that is almost unbearably poignant, especially given the intervallic tracery of descending thirds in the vocal line – later, Brahms's "death" motif in the *Vier ernste Gesänge* (and Brahms, one remembers, was particularly fond of the Mayrhofer songs) – and the dissonance on the downbeat of m. 16, a virtual tone cluster. When the same passage recurs at the end of stanza 2, however, the last phrase in the vocal line leaps upward unexpectedly to high F at the word "trau - [ernd]" (sorrowfully), a desperate gesture which immediately dies away into resignation and descent. At the end of each stanza, the piano sadly echoes the cadential words "von Liebe fern" in mm. 17–18 and again at the end, but with two additional tonic chords. The final two measures are a richer, rhythmically augmented variant of the anacrusis preceding m. 1 – there is no possibility of a redemptive ending on a Picardy third here. However quietly stated, the poem is a sentence of loneliness pronounced by Mayrhofer's harshest judge – the poet himself; Schubert, recognizing the despair and the (momentary) resignation, refuses any ending that might spell hope.

10.   We end with one of Schubert's most monumental songs, with music to match Mayrhofer's intensity syllable for syllable, note for note. "Auflösung," D. 807, is a setting of one of the poet's best poems, a fiery compound of ecstasy and the desperate desire for death – Schubert, who had prayed for death and rebirth in "Mein Gebet" (My Prayer), written during the height of his medical crisis in May 1823, knew this same desire. If it is difficult to tell the imagined moment of death from the fires of poetic creativity, consuming the artist in an all-too-brief rapture, it is because Mayrhofer conceived them as similar awesome forces. But this is death; how else is one to blot out the sun? Even Nature and music, Mayrhofer's consolations, belonged to an existence he detested; his suicidal wish to obliterate everything and himself is all the more evident when he savagely bids springtime and music to get out of his sight, out of his hearing, so that he might immerse himself entirely in the envisioned act of dying.

Verbirg dich, Sonne,	Hide yourself, sun,
Denn die Gluten der Wonne	for the fires of rapture
Versengen mein Gebein;	burn through my whole being.
VerstummetTöne,	Be silent, sounds;
Frühlings Schöne	spring beauty,
Flüchte dich und lass mich allein!	flee, and leave me alone!
Quillen doch aus allen Falten	From every recess of my soul,
Meiner Seele liebliche Gewalten;	gentle powers well up
Die mich umschlingen,	and envelop me
Himmlisch singen –	with celestial song.

Geh unter, Welt, und störe	Dissolve, world, and never more
Nimmer die süssen, ätherischen Chöre.[105]	disturb the sweet ethereal choirs.

It is not only the world which begins to dissolve, but the poetic form and the metrical rhythms. The lines vary from dimeters ("Verstummet Töne, / Frühlings Schöne") to tetrameters and from trochees to iambs, with dactyls and anapaests intermingled irregularly, the meters altering in unpredictable fashion as the poem lurches desperately along. But if the metrical changes are unpredictable, they are calculated, as when the switch to trochees in stanza 1, line 2 emphasizes the word "Denn" or when the rhythmic accelerando at the phrase "liebliche Gewalten" in the second line of stanza 2 conveys just how eagerly the poet welcomes those "gentle powers." The pace dramatically, wildly quickens in the last half of the last line of stanza 1: one instinctively spits out the words "lass mich allein," the sizzle of the sibilant -ss's in "Lass" heightening the already considerable emphasis of that desperate command. At its culmination, the mouth is wide open on the diphthong -ei as if howling; the word-music is especially compelling because the imperative follows after the verbal darkness of "Verstummet Töne, / Frühlings Schöne." The English phrase "Leave me alone" does not have nearly the same power. Even the rhyme scheme changes from the first stanza to the second, the a a b / c c b pattern of stanza 1 followed by the d d e e f f rhyming couplets of stanza 2. Furthermore, each line has a different number of syllables from the preceding or the following lines, the effect a frighteningly apt poetic approximation of the mind reeling as all former boundaries dissolve and begin to disappear. In the last two lines of the poem ("Geh unter, Welt, und störe / Nimmer die süssen, ätherischen Chöre"), a marvelous enjambement leads from a line filled with percussive -t's to the word "Never," accented on the printed page in an unforgettable way. That word heralds the longest line of the poem, unfurling to eleven syllables as if in delirium. And yet, the stanzaic structure itself remains, however turbulent its internal rhythms; it is as if the world, symbolised by the larger poetic architecture, refuses to melt away altogether. Rather, the poet speaks from within a metamorphosis imagined but not actual and, tragically, uncompleted: he is still aware of the world, and it refuses to allow final passage across the bar.

Schubert, recognising this, composed a setting whose form cleverly mimics dissolution while signalling at the same time that the death so fervently desired, so intensely imagined, does not happen. The song is set in an A A¹ A² form in which the boundaries between sections are blurred, almost but not quite dissolved, in which harmonic events near the end of the A and A¹ sections are fused with the beginning of the next section. The motion is ceaseless throughout, but the formal structure is nevertheless apparent. Schubert translates the all-consuming rapture as a constant flood of sound in motion, with *tremolandi* throughout in the bass and arpeggios that swoop and plunge in the right hand, wave after wave welling up and engulfing the entire hand in an exact analogy to the rapture that engulfs the poet's body and soul at the moment of death. The right-hand G major arpeggiated figure in m. 1, repeated over and over again thereafter, is disposed in such a way as to heighten the sense of ecstasy: the emphasis is on the third and fifth chord degrees, not the tonic root, and each figure plunges downward and then shoots upward, culminating in a rapturous quiver on B and D, as if en route to departure from terra firma. When Schubert reverses the direction of that ecstatic shudder in mm. 3-4 and sends a diminished seventh chord, still over the tonic bass, plunging downwards two octaves into some unimaginable abyss, he renders palpable the sense of an inner world turned topsy-turvy.

And yet the tonic root in the bass remains fixed in place throughout the first ten measures of the song, indeed, throughout much of the song – what more graphic way to show that the swirling, dissolving motion, the spirit in chaos, happens while the singer-poet is rooted in place? The bass does not change until m. 11 at the words "versengen mein Gebein," where Schubert scorches more than bones: he scorches the tonality itself for an instant, just long enough for us to feel the searing heat which harmony can summon into being. In m. 11, the B D pitches are common tones in the mediant chord, whose dominant seventh harmony in m. 12 is succeeded, not by resolution to the mediant-as-briefly tonicized, but by the real tonic, by G major in m. 13 ("Ge - bein"). The tonic harmony subsequently seems not like the tonic at all but rather the result of deceptive motion, as if it too were in the process of transformation, its function and identity undergoing a sea-change. The very same progression, jolted upwards a semitone, recurs in mm. 30–32 at the words "meiner Seele liebliche Gewalten," when the A-flat pedal regnant since m. 20 moves to C minor and its dominant seventh in m. 31, followed by "resolution" not to C minor but back to A-flat. It is the "gentle powers" who scorch the poet's bones, and the harmonic parallel underscores the relationship.

Schubert understood that the experience of "Auflösung" is wholly inward and signals that understanding in many of his compositional choices for this gigantic song, chief among them, the dynamics. As in the later cycle *Winterreise*, the softness spells introversion – death is a wholly private earthquake of the spirit. *Piano* and *pianissimo* dynamics are prevalent in the song, adding enormously to the difficulty for both the singer and the pianist. Only at certain significant moments in the first two sections of the formal structure is the vibration-filled quietude overwhelmed by more overt, and therefore louder, expressions of rapture or desperation, which, however, always and quickly die away, returning to the inward sensations. The *forte* which swells into being at the "Gluten der Wonne" (floods of rapture) and immediately subsides to *piano* dynamics in mm. 9–10 – the use of anticipation tones in the vocal line emphasizes each successive segment of the vault upwards, the *Schwung* simply achieved but unforgettable – is then followed and outdone by the longer crescendo in mm. 17–20 at the words "Frühlings Schöne, flüchte dich / Und laß mich allein, laß mich allein," culminating in one of the most monumental Neapolitan inflections in all of Schubert. That too, however, immediately sinks back down to a *pianissimo* hush. The crescendo which begins at the end of m. 34 builds throughout five measures and explodes in four of the fiercest measures Schubert ever wrote – Mayrhofer's furious Lear-like howl "Begone!" to the world, and yet the words "störe nimmer" restore the *piano* hush, as if the poet-singer recognized that he himself was disturbing the "heavenly singing." But in the final section of the song, the series of crescendi and of *fp* inflections follow one another in such rapid succession that it is virtually impossible for the singer to obey them all precisely – but then, this is a song about impossibility (one cannot die by writing a poem about it or merely wishing for it). Making that impossibility palpable in the vocal line is one of the ways in which Schubert matches musical concept to poetic concept.

The grandiose difficulties at the close are preceded by a *ne plus ultra* of harmonic shock. When Mayrhofer bids all sound to cease and "Spring beauty" to flee, Schubert seems as if to repeat mm. 7–13, the fiery commands to Nature continuing in the same vein as before. But where the mediant harmony appeared before, now we hear a diminished seventh chord G-sharp B D F (the B D common tones again) in m. 19, followed by an enharmonic alteration to A-flat at the words "Und lass mich allein, lass mich allein!", one of the most wrenching progressions in all of Schubert's lieder. The shift upwards a semitone is virtually unprepared and therefore all the more jolting, especially as G major in mm. 1–18 is not defined by conventional means; G major is asserted as tonic by repetition alone, without many other chords of the key to define hierarchical functions. Schubert's Mayrhofer repeats the phrase perhaps most tragically emblematic of him, "laß mich allein" in mm. 20–23, the repetition a wonderful example of Schubert's genius for redirecting the same words and thereby making the listener aware of other inflections. In m. 20, the verb "laß" is sustained on the downbeat, which is the moment of transformation from G-sharp to A-flat; "mich" is set as an accented mid-measure dissonance, a diminished seventh chord on G above the A-flat pedal, and "[al]-lein" returns to the A-flat harmony and sustained downbeat. The second time (mm. 21–23), it is the verb "laß" which sounds to the mid-measure diminished seventh/pedal point dissonance, and the dactylic pattern from before is diminished rhythmically, the final syllable "[al]-lein" sustained for more than a measure. If the passage is dry in description, it is far from dry in actuality.

Such abrupt semitone shifts would not become commonplace until later in the century, and this particular instance is unconventional in the extreme, molded to the extraordinary verse which inspired it. For the next ten measures, Schubert asserts A-flat as tonic in the same fashion he had asserted G major as tonic: by obsessive repetition of the chord, although we hear its dominant seventh as well, unlike the first section of the song. With G major still ringing in our ears, the dominant seventh of A-flat acts to insist all the more emphatically upon the status of A-flat as the new "tonic," as a substitute whose remarkable tension derives from the fact that the flatted second, darker in hue than the tonic, has such a strong gravitational pull back down to $\hat{1}$. The semitone shift also seems, if a bit fancifully so, symbolic: the poetic persona wants nothing more than total transformation and removal to some other sphere of being, and indeed G major and A-flat are distant from one another, different worlds tonally. Yet they are also only the smallest of intervallic steps apart from one another, and the initial key is the stronger of the two, whatever Schubert's insistence on the power of the new tonic.

When the "gentle powers" surround the poet, Schubert evokes metamorphosis, the verb "umschlingen" the catalyst for another enharmonic transformation; G-sharp is respelled as A-flat and surrounded ("umschlingen") with transforming tones, its nature and direction altered as the poet-singer wishes his corporeal substance to be forever altered. In mm. 33–38, A-flat major is transmogrified into C-sharp minor (the appearance on the page of a thicket of accidental flats followed by a thicket of accidental sharps and naturals tells the eye as well as the ear of metamorphosis in mid-stream) as supertonic of B major – "heavenly singing" – but B major never takes root. Although Schubert's poetic persona repeats "Himmlisch singen" more loudly in mm. 37–38, he cannot fully arrive there. In frustration beyond bearing, he returns to the G major in which he first bade the sun begone and bids the entire world "go under," go to hell, leave him alone. The jolt downward in the topmost voice of the piano accompaniment from D-sharp in m. 38 to D-natural in m. 39 is on a par with the other jolts to the central nervous system in this song, all the more so as this passage in mm. 39–42 is – remarkably – not in a key or on a chord. Caught between two worlds, that of the "himmlisch singen" and the key of imperative demands, the singer retains the C-sharp belonging to the previous measures, while the bass "goes under" but not far enough to reach a destination of ultimate descent; indeed, the voice-leading keeps returning to the point of origin, to the furious plea "Geh unter." Pound as hard as he might, the *forzando* accents worthy of Beethoven at his stormiest, the poetic persona cannot make the circular strains go where he wishes and therefore returns to commands-cum-pleas on G major, as in the beginning.

But if the words "Und störe nimmer die süßen, ätherischen Chöre" in mm. 43–48 bring back the G major of the opening section, they do so with a difference. The adjective "sweet" impels a subdominant harmony not heard until this moment, a "sweet" respelling of the dissonance in mm. 40 and 42 in which E in the bass clashes with D (and nothing else) in the topmost voice; no one could mistake the prayerful implications of the tonic-subdominant progression. If the world will not "go under" as bidden, the singer would vault away from it, into the empyrean, by his own mighty resolution and tries it over and over again. The impossibility of the endeavor is signalled in the sheer awkwardness of the weak-beat leaps to high G in each measure of mm. 45–48. It is not in ignorance of "grateful" vocal writing that Schubert composes a passage in this manner – rather, he sought, and found, deliberately difficult and spiky contours in order to convey both the failure to hold on to the "sweet, ethereal choirs" and the repeated attempts to do so. With palpable desperation, the poetic persona, having fallen from the heights, does not wait to take a breath, to gather strength, to approach the peak in a new way, but repeats the same vaults one after another, again and again. He does not even allow himself to fall very far before he breathlessly assaults the peak once more. When it does not work, he furiously (and exactly) repeats both the injunctions "Geh unter, geh unter, Welt" and "störe nimmer." The massive climax at "ätherischen" in mm. 59–60 on a V/V harmony unheard until this moment is, rightly, not "ethereal" at all, but almost too desperate to bear. Unable to hold on to the high G's and stay in the realm of

"Wonne," the poet-singer gathers his strength for one last over-arching leap beyond all the previous high G's to high A-natural, all the more massive in its impact because of the dark residue in the mind's ear from the previous A-*flat* harmonics. This final vault upwards is a rhythmic augmentation of the awkward weak-beat leaps to high G, the climactic high A subsequently tied over the barline; with all his might, Mayrhofer tries to remain in the realm of the "sweet, ethereal choirs."

Defeat is inevitable, and we hear it enacted at the end. By m. 66, the arpeggiation in the right hand is replaced by *pianissimo tremolandi*, the hands far apart; crouched down low within the vibratory quivering and distant from both the right-hand and the left-hand registers, the possibility of dissolution disappearing at either end of the spectrum, the heartbroken singer murmurs "Geh unter, Welt, geh unter, Welt, geh unter" in a way that demonstrates his recognition of defeat. After his supreme effort in mm. 59–63, he has no other resources left with which to vault into the next world by sheer willpower alone. In the flatted $\hat{6}$ - $\hat{5}$ in the vocal line of mm. 67–68, we hear both a last echo of an A-flat major chord tone and the minor mode of tragic disappointment, while the leap from D to B in mm. 68–69 is a lowered, disappointed echo of all those leaps from B to high G. The singer's final G in the lower register in m. 70 sounds a tonic root pitch not to be found at the close of any other phrase in the song – the final admission of defeat. The minimal postlude sets the final seal, the vibration ceasing in the right hand and ceremonial fanfare-like chords descending from the heights, as if reversing the fanfares at the beginning of *Die Zauberflöte*. And yet, when the motion ceases altogether in mm. 73–74, Schubert freezes the G major chord in place with the third and the fifth chord degrees in the topmost voice, as if refusing further descent. Perhaps the chord voicing suggests that the poetic persona will wait, fixed in position, until "Auflösung" is finally attainable.

There is no generalisation by which one can characterize Schubert's forty-seven Mayrhofer songs as a body – they are too diverse, spanning an entire decade of the composer's life and encompassing many genres and types of song. From the distended ballad-cantatas, such as "Uraniens Flucht," D. 554 and "Einsamkeit," D. 620 to such miniature gems as "Schlaflied," D. 527 and "Lied eines Schiffers an die Dioskuren," D. 360, Mayrhofer provided Schubert with the stuff of numerous moods and themes. There is even the unalloyed gaiety of the uncompleted strophic song "Über allen Zauber Liebe" (completed by Reinhard van Hoorickx) to counter the prevailing darkness in which Mayrhofer lived and wrote his verse, however heroically he strove to combat it by imagining mythological apotheoses (Oedipus in the grove at Colonnus in "Antigone und Oedip," D. 542, or "Der entsühnte Orest," D. 699) or exhorting himself to brave action ("Der Schiffer," D. 536). Despite the multiply tragic denouement in, first, rupture and then death, the relationship between these two artists is of incalculable significance, on both sides of the equation: the poet whose verse is filled with signs of struggle, with life and with words alike, would probably not have produced so much poetry had his collaborator not encouraged him, while the composer found in this repertoire the inspiration for radical harmonic and tonal experimentation, for the modern reshaping of Gluckian mythological scenas, for much of his best music.

In the final poem of the 1843 anthology, "Am Eingange des Avernus" (At the entry to Avernus), the poet's soul arrives at the portal of the Underworld, where two sphinxes stand guard and soft voices say, "Hail, thou who art pure of heart!" When the supplicant-poet's heart is tested, it is found to be unworthy; he is rejected from the company of blessed souls and damned to eternal night. The poet's last words are a desperate injunction, ostensibly directed outward to the reader but actually self-admonitory, to leave an immortal work as one's legacy before it is too late.

Wie thöricht dünkt ihn nun sein Streben, –	How foolish his striving now seemed to him,
Wie arm an Liebe seine Brust!	how poverty-stricken his heart in love!
Die Weihe fehlte seinem Leben, –	His life lacked dedication:
Hier wird er furchtbar sich's bewußt.	here, he is fearfully conscious of it.
Weit hinter sich die Luftgefilde,	The wind's realm far behind him,
Vor sich die grauenvolle Nacht,	fearsome night before him,
Verschwunden alle Huldgebilde,	all kind beings vanished,
Todt, was er ewig sich gedacht:	what he had imagined as eternal, dead.
Auf! eh' die dunklen Flügel klaffen,	Arise! before the dark wings gape open,
Eh' Dich die Schattenwelt verschlingt,	before the shadow-world entwines about you,
Ein großes, kühnes Werk geschaffen,	create a great, daring work that
Das Grabesnacht und Zeit bezwingt![106]	will conquer the grave's night and time!

Mayrhofer went to his death believing that the "great, daring work" that would be his bulwark against oblivion had gone uncreated. If it must be conceded that he did in fact fail in his supreme goal and is not to be numbered among the literary immortals, he did not fall as far short as he imagined. He did, after all, write a number of beautiful, if bleak, poems in a unique voice (no one could accuse him, as they rightly accused Körner, of imitation), and he inspired a great composer to create some of his best music. If the immortality he craved has been largely borrowed, it is none the less real for that and none the less deserved. Perhaps now he can emerge from the shadows he himself wove about his own legacy and receive the honor that is his due.

Chapter Four

En route to *Winterreise*: Ernst Schulze and the sisterly muses, or a study in Romantic psychopathy

IN 1825 AND 1826, Franz Schubert set to music ten poems from the *Poetisches Tagebuch* (Verse diary) by Ernst Konrad Friedrich Schulze (1789–1817), published post-humously in 1822.[1] In his enthusiasm for this new-found poetic repertoire, Schubert even hoped for a Schulze opera and attempted, with no success, to persuade his new-found friend Eduard Bauernfeld to adapt Schulze's prize-winning verse-romance *Die bezauberte Rose* (The enchanted rose) as a libretto in March 1825.[2] If the operatic project came to nought, like so many others, the songs more than compensate us for the loss. Several are tours de force whose driving rhythms and pessimism, as John Reed observes, foreshadow *Winterreise*,[3] while "Im Frühling" must be counted among Schubert's most beautiful works. The pessimism is indeed acute. Schulze harps on a single theme throughout the entire 100 poems and five-year span of his verse diary: anguish over unrequited love, or, to be more clinical, erotomania for two sisters. Even where the poet-sufferer could recognize his condition as patho-logical, he could neither heal himself nor relinquish the women who were the center of his delusory world. Although we cannot know with certainty what drew Schubert to this obsessively unhappy poetry, it seems plausible that both artistic reasons, including the challenge of lengthy strophic song-forms, and a more subjectively determined empathy with a tragic, incurable condition (albeit not his own) were at work. Whatever the attraction, he devised music that is both premonitory of his second Müller cycle and beautiful in its own right.

Lied scholars have tended to dismiss Schulze with a few perfunctory biographical observations, where they pay heed to him at all, but the dismissal is undeserved, and not only because Schubert found him "composable." If Schulze cannot join Goethe and Schiller on Mount Olympus, he was nevertheless a true poet, and his poetry was lauded by critics throughout much of the nineteenth century for its elegance and craftsmanship. In assessing his poetry, one must remember that he, like Körner, died young and never attained the years that might have brought about stylistic development, were this even possible for someone trapped in such unyielding psychological distress.[4] However, the impressive quantity of verse he produced before his premature death repays closer study not only for what it tells us about Schulze

Figure 10. Engraving of Ernst Schulze (1789–1817) in 1816 by Ernst Riepenhausen

the poet but for what it simultaneously reveals and conceals of Schulze the man. When one probes beyond the capsule biographies in modern sources, one discovers a bizarre case history in the most powerful of all nineteenth-century myths about creative artists: the notion that they create art from their most personal experiences, thus incorporating their own history into their works. Like many myths, it is both true and false. Autobiography may be avowedly present in a writer's œuvre, but it is always, consciously or unconsciously, edited, refashioned, warped, gilded, exaggerated, diminished, altered in myriad ways en route to petrifaction in the art-work. Furthermore, the relations between life and art are circular: psychological imperatives and events external to art impinge on poet and poetry alike, but an artistic calling also determines crucial aspects of an artist's life. In Schulze, one sees both sides of the equation with a rare clarity and wealth of detail because his confessional instincts led him to write reams of self-revelatory prose. As he told one of his boyhood friends,

"You see that I do not hide my flaws from you, but I count it as one of my strengths that I pay necessary attention to my weaknesses,"[5] and his chronicles constitute a fascinating, if pitiable and often distasteful, record of Romantic psychopathy.

According to one late nineteenth-century writer, however, there are few instances in which life and art had so *little* to do with one another. An apolitical Philistine, Schulze preached patriotism in his verse; mocking the "romantic rigamarole, the mystic and romantic frenzies" of others, he was a Romantic through and through; a sensualist who celebrated frivolity in life, he wrote chaste hymns to love; overbearing, irascible, and often offensive in his dealings with others, he spoke in his poetry as a timid and sweet soul.[6] One looks at the 1816 portrait of the poet engraved by the artist Ernst Riepenhausen (1762–1840) and sees, not the lovelorn minstrel of *Die bezauberte Rose*, but a fiery, handsome rake accustomed to success in his numerous conquests (Fig. 10). And yet, the gulf between Schulze's life and art was more apparent than real, especially when one discovers that Schulze knowingly constructed an outward persona as a role to play in company and with women, claiming social advantage as the rationale but with momentary awareness of profound emptiness and depression lurking just behind his witty, malicious mask. As a university student, he expounded a philosophy of sensualist pleasure in the moment, a dispassionate, mocking stance that should, he felt, insulate him from unhappiness; to skim like a bird above the waves of passion in which others drowned would, he declared, be his modus vivendi. Such rationalizations were a defense against inadmissible pain and, inevitably, inadequate to the task. When all defenses failed and he fell, he fell hard.

The unpleasant truth of Schulze's life gave rise to a biographical cover-up that began shortly after his death. According to the curriculum vitae one finds repeated to the present day, Schulze led a consummately Romantic life: a pure and idealistic youth, he fell in love with a professor's daughter who awakened his nascent poetic gifts, she returned his love, the couple were supremely happy for a time, she died one year after they first met, he was inconsolable, fought in the War of Liberation, wrote sad poetry, and then died a few years later of the same disease that killed his beloved.[7] The reality is far more complex than the myth, purified, as legends so often are, of any ambiguity or ugliness. Not one but two muses haunt Schulze's melancholy poetic world, and they were sisters; the transfer of desire from Cäcilie Tychsen (born 18 March 1794, died 1812) to her older sister Adelheid Sophie Wilhelmine (born 17 February 1793, died 1866) began even as Cäcilie lay dying. The documents that recount his long obsession with the older sister are acutely distressing to read. Schulze, in modern terminology, "stalked" her, visiting her house as often as he could, showering her with poetry and flowers, watching her every move and interpreting it with relation to his own love for her, seeing signs of hope where none existed, and besieging her with letters whose verbosity, anxiety, and delusional content are clear distress signals. Although he did not threaten violence in the extant letters, one cannot be sure that the possibility never existed, since she destroyed all of his letters to her; only those he copied into his diary remain, and he could have expunged any threatening content. Every word Schulze wrote from

1813 to 1817 pertains to her, including the entire *Poetisches Tagebuch*; each of Schubert's Schulze texts thus has an autobiographical backdrop and represents a spike upwards or a downturn in the fever-chart of the poet's obsession with Adelheid. Only his death from tuberculosis ended the siege of a woman who may have been as unworthy as some of the evidence suggests, but did not deserve to be hounded in such a fashion. One feels deeply sorry for her, for her beautiful sister, for Schulze, for everyone involved in this long-drawn-out tragedy.

The tale is exhaustively documented. Well aware of his poetic gifts, narcissistic to the core, certain that his "private" diary would be read by others, possessed by a great need to analyze his own troubled nature, and determined to batter down the doors of Adelheid's resistance by every rhetorical means at his considerable disposal, Schulze wrote gargantuan letters and diaries which constitute a case study in psychopathology. His well-meaning first biographer wished it otherwise and, with the power of the pen, made it so by sins both of omission and commission. But the pathos of Schulze's genuine grief is enhanced, not destroyed, when one knows the truth, rather than the pastel chromo-lithograph of a minstrel *sans peur et sans reproche* that his well-meaning chroniclers put in its place. The revised biography is, furthermore, not even congruent with Schulze's poetry, replete with autobiographical references. It is a testament to the strength of the romantic myth attached to Schulze's name that no one pointed to the incongruity until over fifty years after the bowdlerized account had already become legend.

The initial falsification was the work of Friedrich Bouterwek (1766–1828), a philosopher and literary historian at the University of Göttingen who met Schulze in the autumn of 1806 when the young poet began his studies in philology. Bouterwek provided a biographical preface expunged of all unpleasant truths for his edition of Schulze's complete poetic works, published in 1818–19 when Adelheid Tychsen was still alive, Cäcilie Tychsen dead for only six years, and Schulze himself for one year – all the more reason to suppose that Bouterwek wished to spare those still living and to burnish his protégé's literary reputation after the model Schulze himself had provided in his poetry.[8] The expurgated biography was immediately romanticized still further in the novella "Schulze von Celle und Cäcilie: An Cäcilie in Paris" (Schulze from Celle and Cäcilie: To Cäcilie in Paris) by Heinrich Zschokke (1771–1848), who published the tale in 1819 in his journal *Erheiterungen*. Zschokke, unaware of Bouterwek's falsifications of the record, proclaims, "His [Schulze's] life-history is the best explanation of the poem and the poem the best explanation of his life – both are the same."[9] There could be no balder statement of the conflation of life and art. Nor did Hermann Marggraff's 1855 biography *Ernst Schulze. Nach seinen Tagebüchern und Briefen sowie nach Mittheilungen seiner Freunde geschildert* (Ernst Schulze, depicted on the basis of his diaries and letters, as well as information from his friends) rectify matters.[10] Marggraff, while revealing Schulze's love for Adelheid, omitted anything redolent of mental illness and all mention of how the tale of Schulze and Cäcilie began, thus partially perpetuating Bouterwek's revisionary endeavors. "More confusing than clarifying" was the judgment of Karl Emil Franzos

(1848–1904),[11] the writer who finally filled in the missing pieces of a puzzle no one had realized was a puzzle at all.

Beginning in the late 1880s, Franzos set the record straight in a series of articles published in *Deutsche Dichtung* (German Poetry), a literary journal he founded and edited until 1904.[12] These massive documentary studies in as many as fifteen serial installments – the dimensions of a modest-sized book – are situated at a crucial turning point in Schulze-reception, that is, just as his fame had begun to decline but before he vanished altogether into footnotes and the ranks of the forgotten. By stripping away the biographical falsifications, Franzos hoped to pull the poet back from the brink of oblivion, not by asserting his literary worth but by demonstrating that Schulze exemplified the historical-cultural-social ills of his generation, although he limits the exposition of this thesis to scant interpolated comments sprinkled amidst the documentation in which Schulze appears *in propria persona* for the first time. Criticized by later scholars for his editorial practices in the pioneering edition of Georg Büchner's works, Franzos was largely scrupulous in his transmission of the good, the bad, and the ugly in Schulze. The picture of the poet that emerges is often unsavory, especially in the early stages, but it is always vivid and, ultimately, very moving.

DICHTERLIEBE: SCHULZE'S LIFE AND LOVES

Ernst Schulze was born on 22 March 1789 at the house "Am Großen Plan 1" in Celle, where his father Friedrich Ernst Wilhelm Schulze was a lawyer and where his paternal grandfather, a court book publisher named Johann Diedrich Schulze from Peine, had founded a bookstore in 1746. Ernst's mother, Christine Johanna Hedwig Lampe, was the daughter of a pastor from Bissendorf; Ernst was the second child, his birth coming three years after his brother August in 1786. Christine died of tuberculosis on 7 July 1791 when Schulze was two years old; according to his father and brother, the poet inherited his tendency to illness and his nervous nature from her. Two years after her death, his father married a woman named Karoline Sophie Mittag, who bore two children named Sophie and Peter, before she too died of tuberculosis in 1796. In late 1798, his father married for the third time, an eighteen-year-old woman named Christine Antonia Schwarz. His father's sister Wilhelmine took care of the four children after Karoline's death; of her, Ernst says only that she did not have a talent for raising children. The earliest extant letter by Schulze is one the ten-year-old Ernst wrote "An die Demoiselle Antoinette Schwarz in Harburg" on 24 November 1798, that is, to his father's fiancée shortly before their wedding: "Dearest Mother," he writes, "I have greatly enjoyed the game that you sent me. We both played with it. Father won ... the time seems to go so slowly until you arrive. Good-bye and love me as I love you. Your obedient son." Although he describes her as "a wonderful woman," he also writes that she was too young to be saddled with so many children from the previous marriages. Reading between the lines, one can infer that the mothering this gifted child needed was not available in the midst of multiple losses and alterations in the household.

The young Ernst was described as "an obstinate, uncommunicative boy," and his brother August told Franzos that no one expected Ernst to turn out well because he seemed to have no discipline. Ernst himself writes that he compared badly with August, who was tidy, practical, and had a talent for business. The director of the Ernestinum in Celle, a man named Grünebusch, observed the young Ernst's tendency to lose himself in imagination and dreams, to the detriment of his studies, and tried to comfort Schulze senior by pointing out that the Bürgermeister's namesake was not lacking in talent, only in industriousness.[13] Ernst realized that he was considered a difficult case, especially after a visit to merchant relatives in Hamburg convinced him that he had no interest in business, and came to believe that he was destined to be a ne'er-do-well. In his diary, he wrote that this realization made him feel shy and awkward, as well it might, and led to a double life as a daredevil with his schoolmates and a quiet bookworm at home. His family thought that perhaps he could become a pastor, and he thought so as well, until his first adolescent experience of passion at about age fourteen.[14] The lack of parental understanding, his wish to appear daring and bad to his peers, and his early sexual awakening are crucial elements of his formative years in Celle, in particular, the classic configuration of a child who blames himself for the inability to be and act as expected. One can also see the connection between his bifurcated behavior in childhood and his adult behavior in society (the similar resolution to act daring and "bad" in order to demonstrate his superiority to his peers), between the childhood loss of his mother and his adult behavior towards women, characterized by simultaneous denial of any possibility of lasting emotion and a great need for love. Very little of this, as one might expect, appears in Bouterwek, who relied principally on anecdotes told him by Schulze's father of his son's early interest in *Märchen*, chivalric tales, and books on historical weaponry, youthful passions with an obvious relevance to the later poetic works. Indeed, Bouterwek writes that no one could have foretold from Schulze's youthful cheerfulness the melancholy that would later engulf him. "Cheerfulness [Heiterkeit]" is not really the *mot juste*, unless one adds, as Bouterwek does not, that it was a mask adopted for the purposes of acceptance, a mask that hid his depression from others until the day when no mask was adequate.

One of the principal sources of information about Schulze's experiences is a special diary written for Adelheid Tychsen – whether she ever read it and, if so, how she reacted are not known. In June 1813, Schulze declared: "I belong to you entirely and must not have any more secrets from you, even those whose revelation might make me seem less in your eyes than before."[15] Given his mental distress and his possible awareness of writing for an audience, one takes what he presents as fact with a grain of salt, but warped reporting (if such it was) of events still constitutes a category of psychological truth-telling, or the revelation of more than facts. In this diary, he tells her in great detail about every woman with whom he was ever in love, beginning with Julie von Bülow, his best friend Fritz von Bülow's aunt. He could not confide his feelings to the valleys and rocks, he writes in mockery of Romantic convention, because it was not that kind of landscape, nor could he carve her name onto the trees because the evergreen bark of the nearby pines was not accommodated to such loverlike gestures, but she *did* inspire poetic ideas previously shadowed and unintelligible. From the beginning, he linked love with poetic creation. When the Bülows left Celle in 1805, Schulze wrote a poem on the occasion of his friend's departure, a poem which attracted his family's attention to his poetic gifts for the first time.[16]

Between his fifteenth and seventeenth years, Schulze told Adelheid, an entire world of poetry opened up for him. He often spent weeks alone at an outlying country house at Habighorst several miles from Celle, where he read, walked through the fields, or lay under the fir-trees, cultivating his imagination in solitude. From there, he wrote a letter to Fritz on 10 July 1805, telling of his newly emergent love for the writings of Christoph Martin Wieland (1733-1813), whose rationalistic philosophy, sensual view of eroticism, cosmopolitanism, pre-Romantic fantasy, and stylistic elegance all appealed enormously to Schulze. "Appeal" is perhaps too mild a word: Schulze devoured Wieland's works and rhapsodized about him at every opportunity. At the time, however, he was writing poetry after the manner of Klopstock or Friedrich Matthisson, especially the latter, and did not begin emulating his idol Wieland until the next year; his poem "Der Abend" (Evening), enclosed in a letter to his friend Georg Olbers, is typical of his youthful Matthisson-like productions:

In Ruhe hingegossen,	Lapsed into peacefulness,
Entschlummert die Natur,	Nature goes to sleep.
Vom Purpurlicht umflossen	Flooded in purple light,
Erglänzt die Frühlingsflur,	the spring meadows gleam.
Es tönt der Heerde Läuten	The cowbells chime
Im weidumkränzten Thal,	in the meadowed valley,
Die Fluthen sanft entgleiten	the waves softly slip away
Dem goldnen Wasserfall.[17]	from the golden waterfall.

The poem culminates in the nocturnal appearance of ghosts right out of Matthisson, spectres who exhort the poetic persona to flee lest he join their number prematurely. Schulze was aware of his models; in another letter of 1805 to Fritz von Bülow, he describes an enclosed poem entitled "Klage" (Lament) on the topos of the dead beloved as being "in Matthisson's manner" – long before the encounter with Cäcilie Tychsen, he was drawn to themes of mourning for lost love.

Denn ach, sie ist entschwunden,	Alas, she to whom I dedicated my heart
Der ich mein Herz geweiht,	is vanished.
Kaum hatt' ich sie gefunden	I had scarcely found her
Floh sie zur Ewigkeit.	before she flew away into Eternity.
Ihr Wehmuthsthränen, rinnet,	Run down my cheeks, tears of melancholy,
Erlisch auf stets, mein Blick,	Be forever extinguished, my gaze,
Denn ach, die Parze spinnet	For alas, the Fates do not spin
Den Faden nicht zurück.[18]	the [broken] thread back again.

In another poem, "An den Phöbus" (To Phoebus), written in 1806, Schulze returns to the theme of the too-soon-deceased beloved: "I sit here alone and quiet," he mourns, "hidden in the bushes; in the softly rustling canopy of leaves, a cypress sways, a cypress that arches over the urn which holds the ashes of my dearly beloved."[19] Later that same year, he began imitating Wieland in a series of short pieces mingling prose and poetry, including "Amor und Erato" (Cupid and Erato) and "Amors Wunde" (Cupid's wound), although Wieland also inspired him to write a work more in accord with Schulze's own nature. The older poet's *Oberon*, a work which foreshadows Romanticism, was the model for the schoolboy-poet's *Lancelot vom See* (Lancelot of the lake), now lost.[20]

Returning from poetry to real life, we find a series of early infatuations chronicled in the diary for Adelheid: a crush on a pretty cousin in 1804–5, an episode of calf-love in the summer of 1805 for a young woman named Marianne Meyer in Rehburg, and another for one Johanna Taube in his native Celle.[21] When he went to Göttingen in the autumn of 1806 to begin his university studies, ostensibly in theology but with more emphasis from the beginning on literature, Bouterwek took an interest in the talented but unformed young man and taught him some much-needed social graces by introducing him to a circle of cultured men and women. He also sponsored the publication of Schulze's thoroughly Wielandesque "Amor und Psyche. Ein Fragment aus einem griechischen Märchen" in his literary periodical *Neue Vesta* for 1808. Despite Schulze's depiction of himself to Adelheid as a dissolute wastrel during his University years, his letters to his friends tell of an ascetic's work-schedule and of his rapid progress in Old French, in English literary history, and much else. The inexperience in amatory matters, if such was the case, did not last long, however, and Schulze did indeed have something to confess to Adelheid: his on-again, off-again affair with Sophie von Witzendorff, née Meyer, from 1806 to 1810. Wieland first and then Sophie were, it seems, his chief tutors in the adoption of a lighthearted sensualist's approach to love, or so he insisted.

In a letter of 6 October 1806 to Fritz von Bülow, Schulze recounts the festivities for his aunt's wedding, in particular, his attraction to a merry and lively neighbor named Sophie Meyer, who was shortly to wed a Herr Witzendorff.[22] She was, he tells Adelheid, the prettiest young woman in Celle, and it pleased his vanity to be in her company. He had been at Göttingen for one year when Sophie became a widow; when he rode to Celle to comfort her, he found that doing so was quite easy. After his customary fashion, he analyzes her personality in a search for specifically "feminine" flaws: she loved what glittered more than what was truly beautiful, had more politesse than *Bildung*, and knew how to bind someone to her if she wished – and in his case, she did. He was vain enough to continue the affair, even though he contends that his heart was disengaged, as was hers: they agreed to be good friends, to sleep together so long as they derived pleasure from it, but without protestations of fidelity on either side. In the autumn of 1810, when he was on holiday in Celle, he found that Sophie had returned with one "Caesar G." in tow: purloining a letter in which the affair was revealed, he first played a trick on her, pretending to have sent it by mistake to someone else who would assuredly broadcast the news, then relented and gave her back the letter. At her wedding in mid-November 1810, Schulze, who had sent her a lover-like sonnet that very morning, went up to her after the vows were pronounced and whispered in her ear: "You are now happy – you can help me attain similar good fortune. I love Helene [Helene Jungblut, the fiancée and later the wife of Ernst's friend Bergmann] madly: would you put in a good word to her for me?" "My deceived Laura" (Schulze thought of himself as Petrarch redivivus, casting Sophie as Laura in bitter jest even before he would cast Cäcilie and Adelheid successively in that same role) turned to stone, he vengefully reports. However, the two shortly afterwards put their friendship to rights, Schulze telling her that he had begun as her pupil in such affairs – shouldn't a diligent teacher rejoice when her student outdoes her? His cynical badinage to the contrary, Sophie left her imprint, evident in a series of "Sonnets to S." and other poems, also in comments throughout his diary. In Schulze's scrapbook, one finds Sophie's signature and the message, written 29 September 1810, shortly before her wedding: "I remain eternally your truest, warmest friend; it will heighten my happiness when you are truly fortunate, truly contented." Her knowledge that he was neither fortunate nor contented is implicit in the words. It was Schulze's custom to write an ironic little rhyme or, at least, a biographical notice for each entry in his scrapbook, but Sophie's is the only one lacking any annotation at all.[23]

The eighteen-year-old Schulze described his own character in a letter to Fritz von Bülow of 14–18 October 1807 as "a rare mixture of enthusiasm and coldness which makes me among the most fortunate of men"; to this, he ascribes his ability to enjoy the present moment to the fullest. The pleasures and present moments of which he writes were largely amatory and distinguished by their failure to leave any mark on him. "I believe," he declared "that I could have twelve mistresses without loving one any less than the others," a notably Don Giovanni-esque turn of phrase, but he adds that he is rescued from mere sensuality by the fact that his greatest pleasure is in imagination, hope, and memory rather than the seduction of women – "and these are entirely innocent joys."[24] Not all his joys were so innocent. In 1809, he wrote to a friend to say that he was so exhausted from his debaucheries that he could hardly remain upright in his chair, adding further that he preferred experienced, coquettish, dissatisfied young wives to inexperienced young maidens, so long as they too were eager to play the game.[25] Unlike Don Giovanni, he had no liking for "la giovin principiante." At the time he resolved to seduce Cäcilie Tychsen, he was in the process of disengaging himself from an affair with a certain Celle-born Luise von Pentz, the wife of a major in the Westphalian army and the mother of two small daughters; the Frenchified tale – Franzos dubs it "à l'empire" – began in autumn 1811 when Schulze was not yet twenty-three years old and marks the beginning of Schulze's prose diary and a revelatory predecessor to the story of Schulze and Cäcilie Tychsen.[26] On 13 December 1811, he records the renewed encounter with Cäcilie Tychsen and then writes "I am becoming more and more cool towards the Pentz woman with each day .... I never really loved her, but my vanity made the situation very worthwhile, not so any longer ... now a new sun arises on my heart."[27]

Schulze's cynicism about women extended to all of society. "One can live quite nicely here in Göttingen, if one accommodates oneself to people somewhat and, above all, takes the trouble to employ all of the graces with women. It is, on the whole, the greatest profit one can obtain here – to appear to be what one is not and can never be."[28] In a letter to Fritz von Bülow of 19 March 1810, he wrote that in company, one must adopt a definable character cut to the mold of elegant society, lest one count for nought, and that he had chosen to be a malicious wit who loved nothing better than to satirize others. This, he continued, could not fail to make an impression upon "people of ordinary and unrefined habits of thought."[29] That his grandiosity (the assumption of intellectual superiority is all the more startling when one remembers that university professors were among the company he kept) and contempt for the very people whose approval he was courting were defenses against underlying emptiness did not occur to him, despite his occasional perception that there was something profoundly awry. "Why has Nature given me such a frivolous, inconstant heart and placed such deep inward emotion elsewhere on the scales?", he asked, the hubristic latter half of the question as remarkable as the self-condemnation in the first half.[30] In his diary for Adelheid, he confessed to her both awareness of his cynicism and the desire for betterment during an episode in July 1810, when he journeyed to a place near the small town of Pleßburg in the Harz mountains in order to seek out a beautiful young woman also named Adelheid (the illegitimate daughter of a Count Wernigerode) whom he had encountered on an earlier trip.[31] The mountain idyll was short-lived: Schulze wrote that he felt like the serpent of desire in the garden of Eden and did not want to be responsible for awakening her to the knowledge of good and evil, but the sentimental episode enabled him to include women among those he could respect ... or so he said.

He certainly did not respect Adelheid Tychsen when he first met her. In a letter of 20 January 1812 to a boyhood friend, he described each of the guests at a tea-party held on 12 December 1811 at the home of Johann Tobias Mayer, the natural philosopher whose daughter Karoline was Cäcilie's best friend. He began with the women because "there is customarily more material for caricature in them than in us"; indeed, he waxed so prolific on the subject that he never reached the men, casually dismissed as "a varied lot." It is a nasty letter, one in which he assesses the female company for their sexual availability, worldliness, and physical charms. Here are his character portraits of the Tychsen sisters, beginning with Cäcilie, to whom he was clearly attracted:

Cäcilie Tychsen. A beautiful, sweet, ethereal being, with both spirituality and passion in every feature of her face. She has a brilliant mind and is very refined, but takes great pains to hide these good qualities under a bushel ... she is emotional by nature and coquettish by custom and fashion and perhaps could not love unless she were idolized. I am very much in her favor, because I attribute to her each witty idea which is due to *jeux d'esprit*, but I sank yesterday in her estimation because I explained to her that I consider those people to be fools who would struggle for something which neither one of the two could dare hope to win, since at this time, a couple of her admirers fought over her and won nothing more than, for the one, a gash, and, for the other, *consilium*.

Adelheid Tychsen. The elder sister of the above, who is rather like a bagpipe that does not sound equally pleasant to all listeners. To many, she seems pretty, but to me, she has a monkey's face; to many, she seems clever, but to me, she is insignificant, to say nothing worse about her. It is usually only those poor wretches with no wit to grace their conversation who take her willingness to listen to them and answer them as cleverness; in this too, she is like a bagpipe, since what she has to say comes from other people's breath and wind. These same poor wretches assure me that she is neither coquettish nor affected, and I considered it well worth the trouble to examine such a great wonder in Göttingen female society more carefully. Upon close investigation, I soon discovered, however, that her coquettishness lay precisely in seeming not to be coquettish and that she affected being unaffected. She plays at being natural and unspoiled, but with little success, and it is intolerable when a nineteen-year-old maiden acts like a child of twelve and strikes a pose, as if she could ask, like Agnes in Molière's "L'École des Femmes:" Si les enfants qu'on fait, se faisoient par l'oreille?[32]

Schulze either erred or, more likely, was availing himself of poetic license: it is Arnolphe, who raised the maiden Agnès in utter ignorance, who utters these lines in act 1, scene i, not Agnès herself. In tragic irony, Schulze, who did not at this time cast himself in the role of Horace (Agnès's lover), would have given anything in later years had Adelheid said to him, as Agnès says to Horace in act 5, scene iii, "Non, vous ne m'aimez pas autant que je vous aime." His readiness in 1811 to see insincerity in every woman is apparent when he judges Adelheid's naturalness to be insufferable affectation; the analogy to bagpipe music is, of course, doubly insulting, both to Adelheid and those attracted to such uncouth strains. Drawn to Cäcilie for her beauty and brilliance, he still had to disparage her for coquetry. His character portrait of a certain Auguste G., also present at the tea-party, reveals all too plainly his opinion of women in general: she was, he declared, the only young woman present who had studied the art of coquetry – "her science" – and knew how to exercise it systematically. "Never have I seen such a changeable female Proteus," he wrote, "she can in the space of a single hour be modest and impudent, decent and frivolous, serious and merry, malicious and sentimental, gossiping and good-willed, hot and cold, gentle and furious, in short, she is a *semper variabile monstrum* ... she laughs to enslave men, she weeps to enslave men, she sighs to enslave men, indeed, she yawns to enslave men."[33] He would not be so enslaved, he declared.

When he resolved in December 1811 to seduce Cäcilie, it was out of conceit: it would be no small credit to him, he proclaimed, if he could conquer a beauty who had thus far withheld her favors from all and sundry. The campaign (he uses the age-old amatory language of military maneuvers throughout his chronicle) began two weeks later with a tea on 27 December 1811 at which Cäcilie was present. Opportunistic narcissist that he was, he recalled a riddle on the composite word "holdselig" (most lovely, sweet) that he had composed in other circumstances, presumably romantic, and trotted it out for her delectation as if he were inventing it on the spot for her. On 28 December, he writes of a concert given by Bach's first biographer, Johann Nikolaus Forkel, then the music director in Göttingen, at which he [Schulze] assessed his competition for Cäcilie's favors; it is an ironic consequence of his quasi-military strategy that he had to pay as much (or more) attention to his rivals than to Cäcilie herself, especially to the handsome, spirited Count Solms.

Schulze's diary for the first three months of 1812 is unpleasant reading, and Bouterwek expunged every word of it from his biography. At Forkel's concert, Schulze had promised the musically gifted Cäcilie, who played both the fortepiano and the harp, a hymn to St. Cecilia and promptly wrote one. His poem pleased the company: "They saw me as a genius and marvelled especially at my modesty ... I affected the true [echt] manner of an unselfish artist who does not work for his own glory." "More fools they" is the readily apparent subtext to every word he writes. On 10 January, he went to tea at the Tychsen's and there began to wage war against another suitor named Gustav von Usedom (lesser fry than Solms), who, according to Schulze, relied solely upon his good looks, did not know how to flatter the company, and therefore was no match for him. Schulze took what he considered to be his rightful place next to Cäcilie and was "indescribably malicious," not really the way to her heart, he realized, but then, she appreciated wit as long as it was not being used against her. It is an intolerably knowing passage, all the more so because of the conflict between his cynical façade and what he realised was her fundamental disapproval of such behavior. Indeed, on 31 January, Cäcilie asked him outright why he spoke such ill of others and he told her the truth, that this was a mask in order to make an impression in society. But he would not have told her this, he writes, had he not hoped to win an advantage thereby, since he was already beginning to seem like her "amant déclaré" (declared lover) in the eyes of others. It is a psychological point of interest that the admission left him "completely, unbearably listless."[34]

On 25 February 1812, Schulze crowed with premature triumph in his diary, writing, "The booty is mine, and Solms has had to abdicate the field. I am the declared lover and am privileged as no one else before me has been."[35] The sheer nastiness of referring to her as "the booty" – he had not yet said once that he loved her – is enough to make any reader wince. It happened at a ball, where at first, he remained in the background, from what caprice, he could not say (periodically, he records losing all interest in the hunt and in her), but when Solms appeared to be making headway, Schulze initiated a conversational duel, the exchange of witty pleasantries barely disguising the rivalry beneath the surface of the words. Schulze won the verbal skirmish and wrote in his diary that it would not require much more to make Cäcilie fall in love with him.

But three months later, it was Schulze, not Cäcilie, who was in love – after a fashion. He had hinted previously that he was disturbed by his frivolity and the emptiness it concealed; now, he believed, the gods had given him the perfect antidote. The overweening arrogance that was his defense against insecurities about love and literature alike led him to think that she had indeed fallen in love with him but was merely observing the proprieties and therefore could not express her love fully. Ever the narcissist, he believed that his new-found love had enabled him to discover "a great spiritual sweetness, a truly moral purity and modesty" in himself. In his diary for 28 March 1812, he wrote, "Wonderful heart! you would at this moment sacrifice everything for her; you think of nothing else and dream only of her."[36] But the greatest transformative effects of love were on his poetry, he declared, and it was for that reason above all others that he was grateful for the experience. He had, he writes, just completed a poetic epistle of some 450 lines on the subject of love, with hardly a bad line in the lot, of such "sweetness and profound sensitivity that one might believe it to be spun out of air" (his arrogance was hardly in abeyance). Love of a different sort than he had known before was to be the avenue to a new vein of poetry, to Schulze's literary ambitions as well as his psychological needs.

On 5 April, he wrote of finishing a poem on sorrow that he had begun earlier and sending it to Cäcilie, who was ill and not receiving visitors, on the familiar pretext that he had just written it for her. This is the first mention of illness, and Schulze had yet to discover what real sorrow was lying in wait in real life, beyond the confines of pen and paper. The planned deception about the poem led to the following reflection, both cynical and tragic:

What one cannot be, one must at least appear, and in this art, I have, fortunately, been very successful. In my first years at the University, when I hardly knew anything, people thought I was very learned. When I was introduced into society and, due to my dullness, kept silent, people thought I was very gifted. When, from irritation at the boredom I felt in most company, I waxed malicious, people took me for a thoroughly witty creature. When I did anything praiseworthy, out of a momentary rash impulse, perhaps also out of arrogance, people believed that I must be a paragon of magnanimity and generosity.

> The world wishes to be deceived;
> Therefore I will deceive it.[37]

The emptiness beneath his grandiosity led to spells of overpowering inertia. On 13 June 1812, he wrote that he had to feign a headache because he could not summon the customary ways of disguising his frequent "Geistlosigkeit," or listlessness, which " ... comes upon me so often that I truly doubt whether or not I *have* a spirit."[38]

And what of the woman who prompted his seeming conversion? From the admittedly scant evidence of a posthumous water-color portrait by an unknown artist (Fig. 11), she was indeed beautiful. She was artistic — a charcoal portrait of Peter Paul Rubens and a sketch of a female friend in Göttingen are extant — and loved music, especially Bach's music (no doubt due to Forkel's influence). In his diary for 26 May 1812, Schulze wrote that she had asked him to write a "hymn" on Bach after he had pleased her with his gift of the "Musikalische Phantasie. Für Cäcilie" (Musical fantasia. For Cecilia), a hymn to accompany a painting representing Bach's apotheosis — Schulze's subsequent poem was entitled "Sebastian Bach's Apotheose." She was, he informed her in a letter, almost too well educated for a woman, certainly more than he considered was necessary; she read and spoke English, French, and Italian and was learning Spanish before her illness. Her upbringing in a scholar's household could well account for an unusual access to learning: she was the daughter of Thomas Christian Tychsen (1758–1834), a distinguished orientalist and archeologist, and Wilhelmine Johanne Elberfeld.[39]

Cäcilie and the poet obsessed with her had few tastes in common or even compatible personalities, as Schulze himself came to realize shortly before her death. She was an ardent nationalist who despised the French, whereas he was a thorough-

Figure 11. Portrait of Cäcilie Tychsen (1794–1812) by an unknown artist.
From Hellmut Draws-Tychsen, *Requiem und Hymnen für Cecilie Tychsen* (Diessen
vor München: Danziger Verlags-Gesellschaft, 1930)

going cosmopolitan whose "taste for things foreign" she noted and disliked.[40] On
25 July 1812, she was ill and lying on the sofa (Schulze dismisses the illness as an
insignificant fever) while he read to her; he chose a favorite of his own, the comedies
of the minor eighteenth-century playwright François Poullaine de Saintefoix, and
she rejected his choice, saying that he spoke French like a Frenchman, that she could
hardly believe a German was sitting with her. This, as Schulze knew, was not praise
but an expression of disapproval. Going to the fortepiano, she then played what
Schulze called a "bear dance" and said mockingly, "Voilà de la musique française!"
("That's French music!").[41] They did, at least, have a love of music in common.

Schulze's brother August writes that Ernst "loved music and had attained a certain facility on both the keyboard and the guitar" when he was young, but had not cultivated the art after his boyhood.[42] In his diary, he describes reading Johann Philipp Kirnberger's *Die Kunst des reines Satzes in der Musik* in order to appear more learned about the subject than he was.[43]

Even their literary tastes were dissimilar. On his customary opportunistic note, he records on 16 July that a certain Frau von W. (Sophie von Witzendorff) had given him a beautiful edition of Klopstock's *Messias* and his odes in six volumes; the relationship was no more and therefore he sent the volumes to Cäcilie, who had a particular liking for the works of Klopstock.[44] Most of all, she was offended by his habit of *médisance* and had the spirit to say so. In one such instance on 15 April 1812, he made fun of an elderly gentleman for being in love with Cäcilie; Cäcilie replied that she was not in the slightest ashamed of such love and was delighted to be in the old man's company. When Schulze persisted in his mockery, she refused to speak to him.[45] Her liking for a quiet, domestic existence was not to his taste, either. Shortly before her death, Schulze read a novel entitled *Faublas* by Louvel de Couvray that aroused all his desires for adventures to awaken the imagination and incite fantasy. For the moment, he no longer saw his love for her as the means to more heartfelt poetry but an impediment to the kind of life that fed the writer's spirit.

The frivolity of my nature, that I have veiled for a long time now in piety [!], has stepped forth boldly and baldly once again. I want to go forth into all the brightly colored turmoil of the world, want to play a role in the adventurous and changing dramas of life, want to surrender to every passing whim freely and gaily. No, I was not made for a quiet, domestic life. What use is this ordinary routine? For the heart, perhaps something good can come of it, but there is nothing for the spirit and the imagination.[46]

So dissimilar were they, in fact, that his suit did not go as planned, whatever his initial posturing. "I want her to sidle up to me, to speak only to me, to take my least word as an oracular utterance," he declared on 27 June, making explicit the commonplace of male desire for female hero-worship and his need for the strongest possible assurance that his love was returned. Aggrieved by her lack of response, he protested that the flattery of barons wrongfully outweighed the expenditure of his poetic gifts. "I value my talent too highly to squander it on an ungrateful woman," he proclaimed, adding that "Daily I thank Fate for the great gift of frivolity, of heedlessness." It is the adult version of a hurt child's proclamation, "I don't care," and likewise means just its opposite.[47] He had attempted at a country outing on 14 June to force her to pay attention to him by flirting with the other young women in the group, most notably, with Adelheid, but the ploy had not worked. On 1 August, his patience was at an end, and he lashed out in pain. "I am sick of it; I will not put up with the whims of a coquette any longer. From now on, I'll break off any affair that might cost my heart anything at all."

Not a single kind word, not a glance in return for my sweet, unending love, while at the same time, others, who are not worth as much as my shadow because they speak nonsense, have won her kind attention. Oh God, this time my intuition about people has betrayed me. I have never known a single coquette who made such a show of feeling while being colder than ice. It was a beautiful dream, the most blissful of my life. It has brought me much joy, and I will not be ungrateful. There is no dream without an awakening, and life is only withered prose [the analogy is to love as poetry, life as prose]. I wish I were dead … Oh, if only it were given to me to be as unbearably vacuous and dull as most men![48]

He recovered his optimism briefly and wrote the "Dämmerungsphantasie. An Cäcilie" (Twilight fantasy. To Cäcilie) for her, but on 9 August, he exploded once again, declaring, "She is decidedly a coquette, and the serious portion of this novel is over and done with." Flaunting his French in defiance, he wrote "Adieu pour toujours!" and appended a poem, utterly unlike his youthful imitations of Matthisson and Wieland in its powerful economy of expression:

Löscht aus das Licht, und laßt den Vorhang nieder.	Put out the light, and let the curtain fall –
Es ist vorbei, das weinerliche Spiel,	The sorry play is over.
Verhüllt Euch gut, denn draußen ist es kühl,	Cloak yourselves well, for it's cool outside;
Ins kalte Reich der Prosa kommt Ihr wieder	To the cold kingdom of prose you return.
Drum schnallt es ab, das wächserne Gefieder,	Therefore, unfasten your waxen wings
Und in den Schrank schließt sorgsam das Gefühl.[49]	And put your feelings carefully away in the cupboard.

One reads "Put out the light" and hears Othello on the verge of strangling Desdemona. The beginning of the poem is Schulze at his best, but the continuation has Lucretia in bed with Tarquin for lo these many years and uncaring whether the entire city of Rome sees her; one cannot read it without wincing. But if a poetic Icarus here renounces the vain flight towards the sun that was Cäcilie, "Adieu pour toujours" was only a temporary vow. Over and over that summer, he declares that he cannot stand the situation and will leave, but does not. The tables were indeed turned, and it was he who was caught in her trap.

The dilemma was resolved by Cäcilie's impending death and Schulze's inability to deny it any longer. It is impossible to know from what disease she suffered, although Bouterwek refers to a chill that developed into a mortal affliction.[50] "Nervous disease" (Nervenkrankheit), Schulze's only designation for her illness, could be many things in more precise modern diagnostic parlance; a descendant, Hellmut Draws-Tychsen, ascribes her death to consumption, the same disease that would kill Schulze himself five years later. An episode of illness kept her bedridden in March, and in July, she again fell ill and teasingly had Schulze taste some of her medicine, laughing when he made a face. Since Schulze, for all his efforts, was not her fiancé and there is evidence to suggest that the older members of the family disliked him,[51] he may not have been apprised of the course of her illness, and he was too obsessed with his losing battle for her favors during the summer of 1812 to speak of much else. Having made no mention whatever of mortal illness earlier in the diary, he bursts forth suddenly on 21 August with the recognition that she was soon to die:

Alas, I see only too well how she withers and draws closer to death each minute, and this melancholy thought makes her even more dear to me. Soon this beautiful life will be no more, and with her, many sweet, holy emotions will also slumber beneath the grass. May she die gently – she was not made for this harsh world. Oh, I have a bitter cup to empty soon – I will weep for her eternally.[52]

Two days later, Schulze wrote to Bergmann on2 3 August that "my Cäcilie" will soon die and that he has seen her for a long time wither away towards death.[53] If he did indeed see Freund Hain approaching, there is no evidence of it in the diaries and letters; perhaps the potent combination of denial, narcissism, and obsession conspired to keep his blinkers in place until the impending tragedy could no longer be denied. The suddenness with which the chronicle changes direction and tone is shocking, reminiscent of a medieval morality play in which frivolous humanity comports itself in vain and foolish ways until the skeletal figure of Death bursts unheralded onto the scene and lays waste to all in its path. The whole *histoire* may very well have begun in death: Schulze saw in the dying Cäcilie the image of his half-sister Sophie Elisabeth, who had died at age seventeen on 29 November 1811 of consumption. It seems hardly coincidental that Schulze began his pursuit of Cäcilie, who was so unlike his previous conquests, immediately after Sophie's death.

Schulze persuaded himself that the dying Cäcilie returned his love, but her reciprocity was an illusion on his part. On 13 September, he wrote in his diary: "Cäcilie seems to be deeply moved by my faithful devotion, my unselfish love. When she dies – alas, it is now only too probable, it will be with the thought that I loved her until death and that my love did not depend on her bodily charms."[54] But he also observes that the "other side" of his character is still active, that even while Cäcilie lay dying, he had arranged a rendezvous with Sophie and was conducting another flirtation with one Dorette S. – if Cäcilie would not divulge her "bodily charms," other women would. Two days later, on 15 September, he wrote, "Cäcilie loves me; today, I have looked deeply into her heart." They had never spoken of love before, he revealed, but on this occasion, he cast the two of them in the roles of Petrarch and Laura, or Dante and Beatrice.[55] Whatever his protestations of reciprocated love, Schulze was evidently not even allowed to see her very often that fall as she lay dying. On 20 October, he wrote that he went to the Tychsen's house at Gothmarstraße no. 3 daily in order either to see her or hear news of her, usually the latter and usually from her talkative grandmother, whose lengthy tales he compares to Old French romances or an oriental fantasy à la Scheherazade. When he could not see her, he added wistfully, he was at least consoled by being under the same roof.

Throughout November 1812, Schulze alternated between fear and hope. People had told him that those even nearer to death than Cäcilie had yet lived, he wrote on 19 November, and therefore he took hope, while cautioning himself against reliance on miracles. Near the end of the entry, he notes, "Adelheid is a wonderful girl … such a sweet, caring nature in conjunction with such strength of character is something one seldom finds in women." He had already begun to turn from the near-dead to the living.[56] When on 27 November, Cäcilie relapsed into a moribund state, Adelheid's weeping was what pained him the most.[57] On 1 December, Schulze went to the Tychsens's house and found everyone in tears, with Cäcilie's grandmother saying "O beloved Cäcilie, we will never forget you when you are dead, we will never forget." Schulze believed her already dead and went to sit, despairing, in a dark corner of the room. She had not yet died, however, and even regained consciousness the next day, to the amazement of her doctors. Her imminent death impelled from Schulze a moving lament:

Oh, I would be cold and without feeling. I will bury myself in philology and criticism, I will embrace every conjugation, every contemptible or ingenious disquisition on a word, a syllable, a letter, as if it were the sweetest of brides. I will become learned and will mock those people who hold feeling and imagination to be better than scholarship. I will vegetate, since I can no longer fully live.[58]

The fight for life ended on 3 December at 3 o'clock in the morning. When Schulze first saw her corpse, he wrote that death had restored the beauty that months of dying had robbed from her; the death-mask, taken shortly before her burial three days later, is indeed moving, with its high cheekbones and chiselled, classical features (Fig. 12). Adelheid, he relates, sank on her knees by the deathbed and, weeping, kissed her dead sister's mouth, while Schulze whispered, "Pray for me up above, thou saint! ... Beautiful Laura, I will be your Petrarch ... so long as my poems endure, you will not die."[59] By an ironic twist of fate, a man named Ernst Schulze was buried next to Cäcilie's grave in the Alter Weender Friedhof, not the poet who loved her – although lines by her self-appointed Petrarch adorn her tombstone – but a professor of philology who died in 1833. It is, after all, a common name.[60]

After writing a poem in his diary following her burial on 6 December, he fell silent for more than three months, with the exception of two letters to Bergmann. According to one of those letters, written eight days after the burial, Cäcilie's death was the focal point for a religious crisis. He wanted to believe in an afterlife in which his beloved wandered amidst golden clouds in joy, but the spirit of unbelief all too readily overtook him. And yet she had been, he wrote, the transforming experience of his life: "I was cold as ice and as scornful as a damned soul" before he met her, he continued, but "in Cäcilie, I found myself, but far more pure and chaste, far more beautiful and noble." In the next breath, however, he tells his friend: "Adelheid, Cäcilie's sister, is a wonderful girl. Cursed be the poison that I once poured out in a letter to you, before I knew her. I have never found such a clear, strong, deep spirit in anyone before."[61]

At Cäcilie's deathbed, Schulze had resolved to write a great poetic work after the model of Dante or Petrarch in celebration of his love for her, a romance that would, he declared in a letter of 21 December, have nothing in common with earlier specimens of the genre. Because Cäcilie despised the French and espoused German nationalism, he announced that the subject matter would come from medieval German history and Teutonic myths, with religion as the essence of the romance, in honor of Cäcilie's piety. (Schulze was an ardent participant in the early nineteenth-

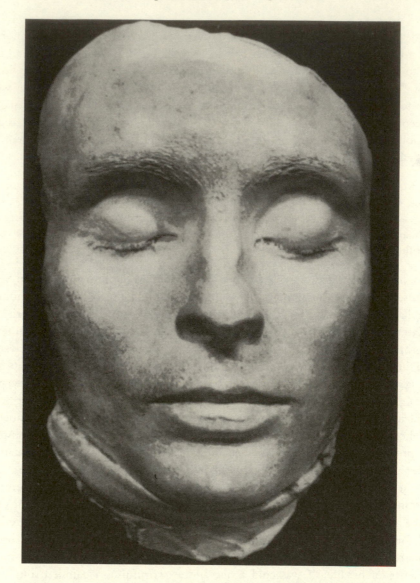

Figure 12. Death-mask of Cäcilie Tychsen. From Hellmut Draws-Tychsen, *Requiem und Hymnen für Cecilie Tychsen* (Diessen vor München: Danziger Verlags-Gesellschaft, 1930)

century revivals of German medieval literature during his first years at Göttingen, so the choice of subject was not entirely dictated by his dead muse's tastes.) The ending, while it could not be happy, should not, he declared, tear at the heart but rather be gently melancholy, like Schiller's "Ritter Toggenburg" or "Thekla's Geister-stimme."[62] All of these ideas and plans were as yet, he told his friend, in an unfinished state, but he planned to spend the Christmas holidays developing an outline for the work. He also revealed that he was physically ill, that he coughed blood at Cäcilie's deathbed and now could taste nothing and was beset with headaches; he could not shake off the premonition he would not long outlive his dead beloved. He was right: he would die a mere four years later, but much happened in the interim between her death and his.

Cäcilie, Ein romantisches Gedicht, completed by December 1815 and published posthumously in 1818–19, fulfills all of the dictates proposed in his letter. It is an epic poem in twenty cantos about the conquest and conversion of heathen Denmark by Otto I, or Otto the Great (936–73) in the tenth century, that is, shortly after the founding of the German monarchy by Otto's father, Henry the Fowler, who was elected king of the Saxons and Franconians in 919 and who established himself as chief of a ducal confederation. His son Otto, determined to be the true ruler of Germany, not merely a ducal chieftain, allied the monarchy with the Church in an attempt to reconstruct and extend the Empire of Charlemagne. Schulze, of course, was not a historian but a poet in search of artistic immortality, and he invented thinly-disguised alter egos for himself and Cäcilie as the principal protagonists of his romance: a minstrel named Reinald whose purity of soul is conveyed in the initial syllable of his name ("rein," or "pure") and his adored Cäcilie, who accompany the army en route to Danish territories. When success finally crowns the expedition, she dies and her soul flies up to Heaven, while Reinald remains below to hymn her beauty and nobility. Schulze announces the memorializing purpose of his enterprise at the beginning, telling his readers that he had made a vow at Cäcilie's deathbed that "You shall not depart unheralded; your dust shall not vanish in the storms of Time."[63] Cäcilie's transfigured spectre in the heavens appears to him, and fantasy opens up "the dark kingdom of saga" to him:

Gigantisch hob sich aus dem nächt'gen Graus	The bold, giant images of the heroic days of
Das kühne Riesenbild der alten Heldentage,	yore arose, gigantic, from the nocturnal terror,
Und sehnsuchtsvolle mit mächt'gem Flügel- schlage	And my intoxicated spirit, full of yearning,
Schwang sich mein trunk'ner Geist ins ferne Land hinaus.	Flew with mighty wings forth to distant lands.
Laut klang der Harfe Gold, um meine Lippen bebte	The golden harp rang out loudly,
Dein Kuß, Cäcilie, und dein Gebild' entschwebte.[64]	Your kiss trembled on my lips, Cäcilie, and your image floated away.

The romance may bear Cäcilie's name, but it has as much and more to do with Adelheid as with her deceased sister. Here, Bouterwek's biographical scissors began working overtime: he omits all but a single cursory mention of Schulze's love for Adelheid from his biographical preface to *Cäcilie* and says nothing about the obsessive nature of Schulze's second courtship in the Tychsen household. That courtship began only a few months after Cäcilie's burial. Schulze resumed writing in his diary in March 1813 in order to dissect his feelings for Adelheid; on 15 March, he wrote, "Cäcilie has been dead for over three months now; it is a question whether I still love her … If I still love her? My grief tells me every day that I do," but at the same time, he asks, "Have I not already so often listened to the gentle desire within me to make Adelheid my wife?"[65]

After Cäcilie's death, it was Schulze's work on the romance in her honor that gave him entrée to the Tychsen household (on 22 March 1813, his twenty-fourth birthday, the Tychsens gave him a card with a lock of Cäcilie's hair and one of her ribbons enclosed in it), and therefore access to Adelheid. Once again, he alternated between false certainty and renewed questioning, telling himself on 25 May that "she loves me, perhaps more than I have ever been loved" and on 26 May that his heart is beset with doubts.[66] Once again, he saw in her the mirror of himself, but purer and better. "It is remarkable," he writes on 28 March, "that I can now see so many similarities in our characters."[67] It was, sadly, not remarkable at all, but a commonplace of narcissistic passion that the beloved should be a mirror for the lover's own reflection, all the more so when the passion is delusory and unreciprocated. As with Cäcilie, he observed her every gesture like a hawk, interpreting them in accord with his own wishes; when he noted that she did not want to be alone with him, he took this as a good sign [!] because it was consonant with her modest character.[68] And always, love was the catalyst for poetry. In an undated letter from late summer or early fall of 1813, Schulze described a nocturnal boat ride with Adelheid, dwelling upon the deep stillness of the night and the loneliness of the watery depths; in short order, he had drafted "a small epic in romantic style."[69]

On 21 April, he wrote that the inner strife between his memories of Cäcilie and his thoughts of Adelheid eased when the two seemed to merge, when he could hardly tell which one he was thinking of at any given moment and which of the two he loved.[70] Certainly Adelheid appears by name in the fifth canto of *Cäcilie* (he wrote six cantos in 1813), an episode which, Schulze confides in his diary, "tells of Adelheid's and my history, as I would have desired its outcome to be. Fate did not allow the sweet dream to come true."[71] What must the Tychsens have thought of a romance in which the "sister's sweet image" sinks rapturously into the hero's arms? The reality was quite different. After a month of Maytime dithering, Schulze proposed marriage on 9 June and was refused with the time-honored bromide that she did not ever intend to marry and could only offer him "the greatest attentiveness and friendship." Like a human Norn, her words "I must take every hope away from you" were to prove prophetic.[72] Schulze could not tolerate the disappointment and wrote her an enormous letter on 11 June, arguing that women can only attain their full being through love and marriage, that it was unthinkable that she should never marry.[73] Four days later, he proposed again and was rebuffed again; when he begged for reasons, Adelheid demurred, promising coyly to bequeath him her diary when she died and then he would know why. Schulze's diary for that day ends with the pathetic resolution, "I will do what I promised her I would do – she shall see me be more cheerful. I will love her, but without passion, and perhaps that way, I can yet be happy."[74]

What Adelheid had refused to tell him was that she was in love with a young lawyer named Johann Nepomuk von Wening (1790–1831), whom Schulze counted as one of his best friends; indeed, Wening set to music Schulze's "Die Maiblümchen an Adelheid" and a "Romanze" for soprano, flute, and guitar, the latter published as a *Musikbeilage* in Schulze's first collection of poems from the firm of Dieterich in Göttingen in 1813. On 10 June, the morning after Adelheid's first refusal, Wening was there, painting Adelheid's portrait, when the obsessed Schulze, like a moth to the flame, went back to the Tychsen's house and wept openly. Schulze's continual attempts throughout the summer of 1813 to speak to Adelheid privately, but with Wening always there, were pure tragi-comedy. Somewhere in his mind, millimeters away from full admission, he knew that there was a strong emotional undercurrent between Wening and Adelheid. On 25 August, he described a musical gathering at which he was miserably conscious of Wening's physical proximity to Adelheid and retaliated by displaying a "Busenkette" (a necklace or garland, given as a token of affection) she had once given him in conjunction with a riddle invented on the spot ("What is as delicate as a spider's web and yet stronger than diamond chains?"). Adelheid was unhappy that he had displayed it so openly, no doubt worried about Wening's reaction, but Schulze misconstrued her concern as a sign of her hidden love for him. Even when she told him in late September that she loved another man, without revealing the name, he would not heed her words and continued, leech-like, to cling to Adelheid and the Tychsen household. But Wening was engaged to a young woman named Amalia in Passau, an engagement that preceded his encounter with Adelheid in Göttingen, and left to return to his home and bride on September 14. The Baroque opera plot duplicated so often in life and literature alike – A loves B who loves C who marries D – played itself out once again in Göttingen that autumn of 1813.

In a letter of 12 July 1813 to his friend Karl Josias Christian Bunsen (1791–1860), later a distinguished statesman and theological scholar in England,[75] Schulze declared that hope, not immersion in memory and grief, is necessary to accomplish the "great work" that all men desire as a bulwark against death. With that significant statement as a prelude, he then analyzed the difference between his love for Cäcilie and his love for Adelheid, although he insisted that it was his love for the dead sister that lived on in his feelings for the living sister.

What draws me to her [Adelheid] above all, what gives her unbounded power over me, is her clear, open-eyed understanding, her refined and yet deep emotions, purified of all mist of passion, her strength of will, which springs from clarity ... Adelheid can never displace Cäcilie, and I could never love her [Adelheid] as much, given my thoroughly romantic disposition, but she can make me happier than her sister, can perhaps succeed in calming and binding this eternally longing heart. Cäcilie was nothing but imagination and emotion; she never belonged to reality and destroyed those who tried to draw closer to her ... love for her was a painful, destructive bliss that would necessarily have ended in entire ruin. Adelheid awakens a pure and restful sensation of well-being. One doesn't want so much to possess her entirely as only to be with her because one feels so much at ease in her presence ...

But what is most alarming about the letter is his declaration: "We love each other – she has told me so herself and treats me as her fiancé, as does the entire city," an outright lie born of pathological delusion. Bunsen might well have wondered what the true state of affairs was when he read: " ... we could both remain unmarried and yet love one another. I do not desire any more than that."[76]

Until now, the great historical events sweeping through Europe seem hardly to have touched Schulze, so preoccupied was he with Adelheid. Göttingen might have been wrapped in cotton wool and put away in a box, isolated from any source of news, for all Schulze mentions of Napoleon, Friedrich Wilhelm III, Franz I, Metternich, Czar Alexander, or any of the other players on the world stage until late summer and autumn of 1813. Even then, this most unpolitical of poets in those most political of times could only think of the war in personal terms, either as a fantasized way of winning Adelheid or the means to an "honorable, glorious death" (one thinks of a child's hurt proclamation, "When I'm dead, you'll be sorry"). Not until 3 August 1813 does he mention the war in his diary, an entry in which he states that only the thought of his parents holds him back from enlisting – a statement one is entitled to question.[77] Once he read aloud to Adelheid from the list of war dead to make her fearful of his possible fate, just as he had earlier read a tale of a suicide for love to her in an attempt to harrow her feelings. On 1 October, beset by longing for her while he was on his usual fall holiday in Celle, he tells her that he has written a thousand novels in his mind, novels in which he rescues her from robbers, from death on desert islands, in which she gives him the victory garland after he saves the fatherland – laughable, he knows, but no less evidence of love than Hero's fall from the rocks by Sestos.[78] Two days later, he wrote an especially emotional letter impelled by the news that a troop of 200 enemy soldiers was nearby. If he should die, he wrote, "I have been fortunate because I have loved you and Cäcilie [one notices the order] and both of you have heeded [geachtet] my love."[79] The choice of verb is significant. The enemy did not advance upon Celle, and Schulze was spared to continue his obsession with Adelheid for four more years.

When he returned to Göttingen, Adelheid evidently expressed unhappiness with the situation; in his diary for 28 November 1813, Schulze records a gloomy dialogue that ended with her silence and his dejected departure. "I would give up my entire future life," he wrote, "if I could buy back last May" when he was with Adelheid, going on walks with her, writing poetry to her.[80] Two months later, on 27 January 1814, he sent her a letter in which he declared his intent to vanish from society and, unknown and unloved in distant lands, remain true to his love.[81]

Once, I thought, the world seemed to be a beautiful, quiet garden ... Now the whole of that blossoming creation is laid waste ... cold and despicable daily life forced itself upon you with its ridiculous distortion and with its boring monotony, and all about your feelings blows the frosty autumn wind, playing mockingly with the withered flowers of your earlier dreams.[82]

Hatred of reality could hardly be expressed more forcefully.

On 8 December 1813, Schulze volunteered for the Göttingen Jäger, a regiment headed by First Lieutenant, later General, von Beaulieu-Marconnay (1780–1858). According to Baroness Bunsen, her future husband Christian, unable to dissuade Schulze from risking his fragile health in the hardships of military service, travelled to Hannover to persuade the Volunteers to give Schulze a staff job.[83] The company did not leave until 15 March 1814, however, so Schulze continued to visit the Tychsens, bring Adelheid his newest poems, and write her copious letters until the day of his departure. There is very little known about his experiences in the final convulsions of the Napoleonic Wars. His commander was a cultivated man who befriended Schulze, making him his secretary and bringing him into the household, which included three gifted daughters by the first marriage of Beaulieu's wife to one Count von Egloffstein: Julie Egloffstein, a painter who corresponded with Goethe and who was Schulze's special confidante; Karoline, a composer; and Auguste, who wrote religious poetry. We know that Beaulieu-Marconnay's battalion joined the "Nordarmee" on 15 March 1814, fought in battles on 4 and 7 April, and went to Hamburg, then besieged by General Davoust's French armies on 30 May; we know as well that Schulze was either wounded or became ill with some unspecified chest ailment. Beyond those bare facts, little else is available.

Certainly the War of Liberation left few traces on his poetic output. One of the only patriotic poems to be found in the *Poetisches Tagebuch* is a paraphrase of Körner's "Lützow's wilde Jagd": "Jägerlied. Moorburg, den 8. April 1814," written the day after the battle on 7 April.

Was blitzt in den Büschen so hell, was schallt	What flashes so brightly in the bushes, what
In dem grünen Gehege so munter?	resounds so merrily in the green enclosure?
Was zieht hervor aus dem dunkelen Wald	What comes forth from the dark forest
Und fern von den Bergen herunter?	and the distant mountains?
Wir sind die Jäger, wir ziehn von Haus	We are the fusiliers: we leave our houses
Und wollen zum Feind in das Feld hinaus,	and meet the enemy on the battlefield.
Zum Krieg,	To war,
Zum Sieg	To victory,
Und zum Siegesschmaus.	And the victory feast.
…	
Denn der größte Jägersmann ist der Tod,	For the greatest hunter of all is Death,
Der will an der Lust nur sich laben;	Who only wants to feast on pleasure;
Wol färbt er mit Blute die Haiden roth	He colors the fields red with blood
Doch die Beute läßt er den Raben.	but leaves his booty to the ravens.
Und er saust und braust mit Sturmes Gewalt	And he rushes and roars, with stormy force,
Hoch über die Berg' und über den Wald;	high over the mountains and forest.
Und es bebt	And whatever lives,
Was lebt,	Trembles
Wenn sein Jagdhorn schallt.[84]	When his hunting horn resounds.

But even though Schulze could imitate the blood-stirring rhythms of Körner's famous collection to a nicety, he wielded lyre and sword alike not out of patriotic sentiment, but for the sole purpose of winning Adelheid's favor and admitted as much in the poem "Am 27. Oktober 1814":

O könnt' ich's ersingen,	Oh, if only I could sing it,
Das goldene Ziel!	the golden goal!
O könnt' ich's erringen	Oh, if only I could win it
Im Schlachtengewühl!	in the tumult of battle!
Vergebens begegnen	In vain,
Sich *Leier und Schwert*, [italics mine]	the lyre and the sword meet –

Sie hält den Verwegnen,	She does not deem the bold one,
Den Milden nicht werth;	the gentle one, worthy.
Und gäb' ich für Liebe	And although I would gladly
Das Leben auch gern,	give my life for love,
Stets bleibt er mir trübe	the gentle star remains
Der freundliche Stern.[85]	forever clouded to me.

Schubert, who must surely have recognized the allusion to Körner, set this poem as the male quartet "Ewige Liebe" (Eternal love), D. 825a.

When the war was over, Schulze hastened back to Göttingen, arriving in early summer of 1814, but Adelheid's feelings about him had not changed or softened – quite the contrary. Schulze ascribed her coldness to inordinate concern for the proprieties (a favorite rationalisation of his), writing that "the secret consciousness of our close relationship" was the cause of her outward coldness to him.[86] The icy reception hurt him even more because he had brought her a sonnet cycle entitled *Reise durch das Weserthal*, each poem containing references to her; for example, the "Zueignung" or "Dedication" of the entire cycle ends with the following tercet: "Mag streng und kalt dein Blick sich von mir wenden / Nie soll mein Hoffen, nie mein Streben enden; / Schön ist die Müh' auch um ein nicht'ges Ziel" (No matter how harshly and coldly you turn your gaze from me, my hopes, my striving, will never end; the labor is beautiful even if it leads nowhere). That this might well have seemed like a threat was something Schulze never considered. In the company of a friend, he made a journey through the Eichsfeld on 22–25 July 1814, and each day, he wrote one or two poems for Adelheid; the texts of Schubert's "Auf der Brücke" and "Im Walde" stem from this journey.

No matter how much he wrote for her, the situation only worsened. His sole consolations that winter of 1814–15 were poetry and the company of a group of distinguished and sympathetic young men: Bunsen; Karl August Brandis, later a philologist at Bonn; Friedrich Lücke, a theologian; and the religious poet and fabulist Wilhelm Hey. Schulze's diary for 1815 continues the wretched tale: he had resolved to go to the Tychsens only on Thursday evenings and fancied that Adelheid was kinder to him as a result. Therefore, between 2 and 22 March 1815, one finds poems in a brighter tone, including "Am 5. März" (Schubert's "Um Mitternacht"). "Am 31. März 1815," which Schubert entitled "Im Frühling," ends with Schulze hoping that he could "remain here on the branches and sing sweet songs to her the entire summer." On 1 April, he wrote "O wie dringt das junge Leben / Kräftig mir durch Sinn und Herz" (Schubert's "Lebensmut"), but this was truly an April Fool's delusion. Indeed, the spell had already been broken on his birthday (22 March), when he expected a present, if only a flower or a garland, to no avail. No one said anything at all, and he was desperately hurt.[87]

The war with France broke out again in 1815, and Schulze briefly considered military service once again, but instead went on a journey to the Harz Mountains. His travels failed to alleviate his worsening depression, especially as the Tychsen family redoubled their efforts to rid themselves of his unwelcome presence. On 22 April 1815, he found some gillyflowers growing beneath his window and sent them to Adelheid with a poetic letter, but the Tychsen's maid returned them. On 10 May, Bouterwek took matters in hand and told Schulze that the Tychsens were furious with him, that he was on no account to go to their house, and that he [Bouterwek] would negotiate on Schulze's behalf with Adelheid and the Tychsens.[88] But on 29 July, Schulze wrote Adelheid yet another gigantic letter in which his promises to leave her alone modulate quickly into abject pleas that she restore to him his former place in the family – a place he never really had. Adelheid and her parents reacted swiftly, banning him from the house altogether, the edict delivered by Adelheid herself. The psychological cloaks which Schulze draped around his own culpability are pitiable: he has, he told her, served the family nobly, with everything that is good and holy in him, and yet now they reject him. He recognised that they had been trying to expel him for quite some time, first, by ignoring or disregarding him, then by outright harshness, finally through the openly expressed desire "to see me *less often*" [italics mine] – one notices with a pang that he still could not admit that they did not want to see him at all.[89] "Inexplicable circumstances," he writes, have parted him from his beloved; he did not become angry in response to her words because she is incapable of thinking and feeling at a sufficiently exalted plane to realise that she owes him thanks for immortalizing her and her family in verse.[90] One can only gasp.

In a letter to Adelheid from Göttingen on 2 September 1815, he briefly rebelled against a mute, numb state he recognized as pathological, even deathly.

No, I cannot any longer stare fixedly into the distance, without tears, without words, without thoughts, almost without feeling. That which moves about confusedly, dark and barren, within me seems more like an unconscious death-struggle than the living sensation of sorrow. I must create a truly great sorrow for myself in order to find consolation.[91]

Yet he still begs for a kind word, telling her that she would not deny alms to a beggar, and he is the poorest and most pitiful of all. She did not, as one might expect, respond as he wished, and this prompted a "farewell" letter – not the first, not the last – on 11 September, in which he tells her that he has turned to God for consolation.[92] Nothing was any use: Schulze could not even bear to leave Göttingen for his usual fall holiday in Celle, and it required repeated and pressing invitations from his father to dislodge him. From Celle, he wrote still more letters, all manifestly frantic, to Adelheid on 21 and 23 September and October 6, 10, 13-16, 18, and 20. The endless sentences and convoluted syntax are painfully accurate mirrors of a warped mind. "I wish that I were a happy person," he writes on 13 October, the sentence trailing off in the mute recognition of impossibility.[93] Five days later, he tells her that he has heard from Wening, who had broken with Amalia and must have apprised Schulze of the facts of his former relationship with Adelheid: "I loved him … perhaps, although I hardly dare to say it, because he loved what I loved … we are yet friends, but must stay apart from one another because neither trusts the other."[94]

Despite his misery, he completed the giant romance *Cäcilie* on 18 December 1815, after less than three years of work. By the time he reached canto 3 (of twenty, plus an additional dedicatory canto "An Cäcilie" at the end), Adelheid had already rejected him, a rejection he recorded in stanza 119 as a death: "Alas, Adelheid, so thou too are departed? What was most beloved and dear to me on earth sways aloft and rests in eternal peace. I remain behind, alone, in sorrow and danger, in night and battle!" Only Adelheid's father thanked him upon receipt of the romance, but Schulze nevertheless remained in Göttingen, still writing poems to Adelheid, still acting in all of the old, hopeless ways. In April 1816, he was persuaded to visit Beaulieu and the Egloffstein daughters, where he remained longer than he had expected: on each scheduled day of departure, he wrote a little verse in the family scrapbook, "Upon my departure ... Upon my real departure ... Upon my unfailing departure ... Upon my unwavering departure," in a comic version of his inability to leave Göttingen and Adelheid. But the end was near. As the *Poetisches Tagebuch* tells us, he went on 27 April to the Giebichenstein and on the next day to the mountain town of Wildemann ("Über Wildemann"), the site of a poem in which he furiously mourns both the stone on Cäcilie's tomb and the stone that was Adelheid's heart. When he returned to Göttingen in May 1816, he wrote two immense farewell letters – this time, truly the last – on 25–6 May: "Farewell, my only beloved. For the last time, I call you 'mine.'"[95] His last diary entry was on 17 July 1816 and recounts the final break with the Tychsen family.

Throughout the summer and fall of 1816, his friends moved heaven and earth to persuade the broken-hearted Schulze to join them in Italy. Christian Bunsen wrote him a letter from Florence on 25 September 1816, urging him to rejoin the real world and make it, not delusion, the basis for poetry. For all Bunsen's diplomacy, it is evident that he feared for his friend's sanity.

Every man, I believe, can only represent in entire truth, whether in life or in any other art, what he has himself really known, beheld, and experienced. Now we find that each individual, more or less, particularly in an age of high culture, has assimilated the forms and ... the phantasms of his epoch. To guard himself against the latter may be difficult for one who, like yourself, is gifted with the seer's wide-reaching and sympathetic vision ... Thus it seems to me that in the past, your poetic soul has seen and represented much, without its being *lived through*, as it were, *in yourself* [the italics are Bunsen's]; you could not therefore inwardly feel this and believe it to be near and real. Now that is exactly what no mortal can do with impunity. Thus you gradually lost the power of believing in what is true in itself, and for all your representations, whether of love, of faith, of all primary ideas in life, you ended by knowing no basis but your own fancy, which was able at any time to destroy the entire fabric of its creation ...

But now ... your life has taken a rare and most salutary turn. With few men has the hand of God shown itself more visibly than in your case. Heavy sorrow has been allotted to you. Truly, if you will but continue to live through in yourself what your verses contain, how glorious is the life that awaits you! The poet's fine perception will find itself combined with a warm love of real life ... Your first step must be to throw off everything which threatens to separate the poet from the man. Tear yourself away – and come to us![96]

It is an eloquent letter and an insightful one. His friends' pleas, their avowal of the beneficial effects that the change of scene would produce, finally persuaded Schulze, who resolved in November to raise the money for the journey. But his friends were too late. After returning to Göttingen from a brief visit in a neighboring town, he suffered a hemorrhage that same month, and thereafter, his health failed precipitously. In mid-January 1817, he had, for the first time, a sense of his impending death, recorded in the poem "Am 17. Januar 1817" (the text of Schubert's "Tiefes Leid"). On the anniversary of Cäcilie's birthday in February, he sent Adelheid, as always, a garland of flowers and a poem, to no avail and for the last time. In March, his condition had deteriorated so much that his stepmother came from Celle to tend him. On 22 April 1817, she wrote a revealing letter to her husband, describing visits to the Bouterwek and Tychsen households, where Schulze's friend Karl von Reck had taken her at her request so that she might thank the women of those households for the services they had rendered her sick stepson. The Tychsen home was the last she visited.

... and from there, we went to the Tychsens. I did not like it there, although they greeted me with every possible courtesy and invited me to tea and supper. When she [Adelheid's mother] spoke of Ernst, tears ran down her cheeks. She called her daughter Adelheid, whom I did not like at all: a little thing, her face not at all to my taste and more hateful than pretty, although her eyes are nice, brown eyes with a striking resemblance to Ernst's. But she did not seem attractive in the slightest; she might very well be clever, but has nothing feminine about her and acted so coldly when the conversation turned to Ernst's illness that it made me furious. I believe I would have encountered greater compassion from a complete stranger than she showed ... Reck then told me that Ernst loved her beyond words, that he grieves constantly for her ... Adelheid was not responsible for the duration of this love, since she had told him that she did not love him and would not marry him or anyone else ... [97]

Evidently, his parents only learned of Schulze's obsession a few weeks before his death.

In May, Schulze went home to Celle to die. In his last days, he received the news that a professorship in Lüneberg awaited him and that he had won a major literary prize from the Brockhaus publishing firm in Leipzig for his romance *Die bezauberte Rose*, although he told his father that it "lacked the right design and had many flaws."[98] Whatever his harsh self-criticism, it was enormously popular and was even translated into English and French; it is no wonder that Brockhaus in 1852 erected a tomb monument at Schulze's grave.[99] Schulze knew nothing of his fame: for him, Destiny "had cast the die maliciously."

Dies sang ich dir, als mit der ersten Rose
Auch mir ein Lenz der neuen Freud' erschien:

Doch tückisch mischt das Schicksal seine Loose,
Ein weißes zeigt's, wenn wir ein schwarzes ziehn.
So ruht auch jetzt schon unter kühlem Moose,
Die freundlich mir die kurze Lust verliehn,
Und mir ist nichts aus jener Zeit geblieben,
Als nur dies Lied, mein Leiden und mein Lieben.

I have sung this to you, as if a springtime
of new rejoicing had also appeared to me
with the first rose.

But Destiny casts the die maliciously,
It draws a white card, we a black one.
She who sweetly granted me brief joy
now already sleeps under the cool moss,
And nothing remains for me of that time
but only this song, my sorrow, and my love.

(the final stanza of *Die bezauberte Rose* – my translation)

In his last days, Schulze could apparently speak of Adelheid calmly and told his brother that if he were to recover, he would never return to Göttingen. Nor did he: he died on 29 June 1817 and was buried in the Bürgerfriedhof by the Hehlentore in Celle. His friend Bergmann wrote that two days after the burial, two women swathed in black veils – surely not Adelheid and her mother, but who were they? – appeared at the cemetery late in the evening and laid two wreaths at the grave before disappearing. Schulze was only twenty-eight; even Schubert was granted a few more years than that.

On 7 December 1864, almost fifty years later, Karl von Reck wrote to the poet's nephew, telling him how the Tychsen family had reacted to the news of Schulze's death. The poet's stepmother had begged Reck to tell them the sad tidings; when he did as she bade, he found only Adelheid and her mother at home. Being a partisan friend of Schulze's, he disliked Adelheid, writing that she did not seem at all moved by her erstwhile suitor's tragic death, that "... her beautiful brown eyes were just as cold, sly, and clever as before," that she was "somebody with whom I could never have fallen in love." Someone else did, however. On 22 July 1819, two years after Schulze's death, she married Ludwig Friedrich Freiherr von Berlepsch (1795–1852), the third son of Friedrich Ludwig von Berlepsch and Dorothee Helene Sievers, née Hämelschenburg (with whom both Bouterwek and Jean Paul Richter had previously fallen in love), for his money, without love, according to the reports of contemporaries. Their first daughter, Thekla Johanne Henriette, was born 15 September 1820 and baptised 4 October in Göttingen, after which the couple moved to Erfurt and finally to Naumburg, where Adelheid died on 26 June 1866. Although three daughters followed Thekla (Agnes Dorothee Friederike, Ottilie Friederike Albertine Auguste, and Karoline Adolfine Asta Justine Charlotte Emma), there was no son born of the marriage and consequently her husband's estate went to a nephew upon his death. When Marggraff's biography appeared in 1855, she reportedly destroyed the poet's letters to her (it is interesting, however, to note that she kept them until then) and ripped every page with any mention of him from Cäcilie's diary. Only in her final year of life did she seem to undergo a transformation: she read his poetic works (for the first time?) and once burst into violent weeping when a niece asked her about Schulze. She seems never to have confided in anyone who thought to record her experiences, and one deeply regrets knowing so little of her or Cäcilie's side of the whole tragic tale, and that only from Schulze and his friends. The poet's floodtide of words only makes the silence on the other side of the story echo more loudly.

If Adelheid truly did read her deceased suitor's poetry in later life, she might well have been especially struck (but in what way, one wonders?) by *Cäcilie*, in which she is a character under her own name, and by the *Poetisches Tagebuch* (Poetic diary), in which his long obsession with her is mapped and charted. Of all Schulze's works, it was the latter collection, first published posthumously in 1818, which most attracted composers, including Schubert; the subjectivity of this verse, in which a soul ceaselessly probes a wound that will never heal, invited, and received, numerous musical realizations. The word "diary" implies intimacy, the admission of the reader into the day-by-day, year-by-year ebb and flow of emotional life ordinarily barred from the public record, although intimacy in this work is paradoxically both a feint and a fact. One learns nothing of Schulze's daily routine, his associates, or his activities, but his fits of despair and hopes for love – not, however, his cynical side or sexual opportunism – are transmuted into lyric verse intended to be read by others. A poet who courted immortality as openly as Schulze did not write these poems for his delectation alone, but if he revised his unhappiness in accord with myths he found more pleasing than reality, he was unable to expunge his pathology completely.

The 100 poems of the poetic diary begin on 29 June 1813, following his springtime "idyll," or so he thought, with Adelheid, and end on 17 February 1817. There is a curious circular relationship between Schulze's erotomania and his poetic output, the one feeding off the other; if depressive emptiness ordinarily deprives its sufferers of the energy, the concentration, the will to do productive work, this was not the case with Schulze. The *Poetisches Tagebuch* is the record of almost unflagging industry, its chronological blank spots mostly accountable to Schulze's military service or to renewed work on the romance. Multiple compulsions fueled such productivity, his quest for poetic immortality, the persistent attempt to compel the world to do his bidding through the power of words alone (a quintessentially Romantic act), and a pathological probing of memory. If he ceased renewing his hopeless love in different meters, forms, images, and words, both he and Cäcilie would die the double death of those whom the world forgets.

But the most bizarre of the *raisons d'être* for the *Poetisches Tagebuch* was Schulze's need to justify his obsession with Adelheid as the continuation of his love for the dead Cäcilie. He proclaims as much in the prefatory poem "Erklärung" (Elucidation).

Mein Singen soll nur eine Herrin preisen,	My song shall praise but one mistress
Die doppelt stets mein zweifelnd Aug' erblickt:	whom my doubting eyes see doubled:
Dort in des Grabes ewig stummen Kreisen,	There in the grave's eternally mute company,
Hier mit des Lebens frischem Reiz geschmückt;	here with life's fresh charms adorned,
Und wenn auch hier zwei Namen sie benennen,	and if I invoke two names here, my heart
Nie kann mein Herz die holden Bilder trennen.	cannot ever separate their gentle images.

(lines 3–8, stanza 1)

If it is indeed "elucidation," it requires decoding. "Erklärung" was written well after the beginning of the poetic diary, since he speaks in stanza 3 of having begun a long journey in order to sing her [Cäcilie's] praises in distant lands and reveals that two years have gone by since he last saw his homeland. The "journey" is the poetic quest to the Teutonic Middle Ages in *Cäcilie*, the journey thus an eloquent metaphor for living in the poem as if it were a foreign country from which he would return when the work was completed. Adelheid had already refused him several times by the time he wrote "Erklärung," and therefore Schulze describes one of the beloved women descending from heaven in order to place the poet's myrtle garland on his brow, while the other's stern glance and proud countenance [Adelheid] strike horror into his soul and extinguish love's bright illumination in night. "Dreams are sweet, but life is hard and cold," writes this poet who hated quotidian reality for its multiple betrayals of his desires, and ends by reassuring himself with the prospect of poetic immortality. Most revealing of all, he admits in "Erklärung" that his love was never reciprocated: "Many will ask about the faithful minstrel who, *though never loved* [my italics], sang only of love,"[100] he writes in the first, but not the only such admission to be found in his diary.

Everywhere, comparisons of this poet with a far greater poet – Francesco Petrarca – beckon: the *Poetisches Tagebuch* was written simultaneously "In vita di madonna Adelheid" and "In morte di madonna Cäcilie." To immortalize Cäcilie Tychsen was the avowed purpose of everything Schulze wrote after her death, just as the poetic apotheosis of "Laura" was Petrarch's intent, and Schulze courts the comparison at every turn; when he includes a "Canzone. Am. 28 Juli 1816" near the end of the collection, he makes the claim of equivalence especially clear. Both of the women thus hymned are similarly shadowy for similar reasons, that is, the focus on the psychology of the lover-poet rather than depiction of the beloved. If we did not possess the documentary evidence of a historical Tychsen family and a real Cäcilie, we too might doubt whether Cäcilie was anything other than a symbol and a pretext for poetry, just as Petrarch's close friend, Giacomo Colonna, expressed doubts about Laura's existence in actuality. Although Petrarch averred that she was real, he did so in a way that left the matter ambiguous, perhaps preferring that her transmutation into poetry take precedence over flesh-and-blood origins. Schulze likewise turns Cäcilie into the febrile impetus for words, into a literary phantom, but with a difference that is fascinating in its psychological complexity. It is one thing to turn a dead woman into Laura, another simultaneously to merge a living and obsessively desired woman into that same poeticized creature.

Other reminiscences of Petrarch's *Rime* abound in the *Poetisches Tagebuch*: in the broodings on memory, the fragmentation of experience, and the placement of longer poems as structural pillars at varying intervals among shorter poems. The avoidance of the factual, the obsession with the mental image of the beloved, the conflicts inherent in sublimation, the quest for poetic glory, and the link between grief and *contemptus mundi* are likewise shared elements, although the contexts in which the turning away from the world occurs are very different indeed; the *concetti*, wit, and mysticism of the *Rime* are absent from the *Poetic Diary*, in which this would-be Petrarch redivivus creates a sadder and more claustrophobic poetic sphere. Because both poets understood that memory transfigures desire, the woman's *imago* had constantly to be renewed by visiting sites associated with the beloved, by seeing her reflection everywhere in nature, by marking anniversaries and the passage of time. Schulze's poetic diary, like all diaries, organized by the measurement of time, includes a poem written on Cäcilie's birthday for three of its four years and ends "Am 17. Februar 1817, dem Geburtstage der Geliebten" (On 17 February 1817, the beloved's birthday). Recreated memory was the sole bulwark – for a time – against disintegration and death.

Both the *Rime* and the *Poetisches Tagebuch* breathe obsession from every page, evident in the sheer number of poems on unresolved grief. "I wept and sang; I cannot change my style, but day and night I vent through my tongue and my eyes the sorrow accumulated in my soul," Petrarch writes in the final tercet of poem 344 in the *Rime*. Schulze did likewise.

"Am 7. Januar 1814":
Wie im Lenz am blüh'nden Zweigen
Immer junge Knospen keimen,
So entsprießt mit ew'gen Drange
Mir im Busen Lied auf Lied.
Singen oder ewig schweigen,
Sterben muß ich oder träumen,
Weil im Traum nur und Gesänge
Mein verwelktes Leben blüht.[101]

"On 7 January 1814"
As in springtime, young buds always sprout
on blossoming branches,
so poem after poem, with eternal urgency,
germinates within my breast.
To sing or be eternally silent,
I must die or dream,
For it is only in dreams and poetry
that my withered life blossoms.

Channeling the vital energy of frustrated love into the sublimated mode of poetry was only achieved at the cost of the poet's natural life. Schulze recognized that only poetry was keeping him "alive," after a fashion, and begged God for death, once *Cäcilie* was completed:

"Am Sonntage den 27. August 1815":
So willst du denn so schnell das Werk
vollenden,
Wozu die Kraft der treuen Brust dich trieb,
Und pflückt so bald mit ungestümen
Händen
Den letzten Schmuck, der deinem Leben
blieb?
Dir blüht das Glück nur noch in süßen
Träumen,
Und feindlich ist dir draußen Lieb' und
Welt ...[102]

"On Sunday, 27 August 1815"
So do you want to finish the work so
quickly,
to which the strength of a faithful heart
compelled you, and, with impetuous hands,
so soon pluck
the last treasure that still remains in your
life?
For you, happiness still blossoms only in sweet
fantasies,
and love and the world outside are hostile to
you ...

Only poetry, he laments in "Am 16. Januar 1816," "has never forsaken me ... let me once more, in wonderful melodies, extol you through you yourself and that which awakens you!" The "wonderful melodies" should, he thought, guarantee him the laurel crown accorded master poets by posterity. That Petrarch won the gamble for immortality and Schulze did not only heightens the pathos.

"Sorrow can only see and give sorrow" ("Schmerz kann Schmerz nur sehn und geben"), Schulze writes in "Am 16. Januar 1816," (a gloss on Goethe's miniature masterpiece of obsessive grief, "Erster Verlust" or "First loss"), and he dissects that sorrow in poem after poem. He is no longer himself, he writes in the ode, "Am 29. Januar. 1816," but a being wracked with pain, trapped eternally by it and in it:

Nichts denken kann ich dann und nichts
beginnen,
Die Lippe schweigt, dich sieht mein Aug'
allein,
Die Welt versinkt vor meinen irren Sinnen,

Then I cannot think, cannot begin anything,

My lips fall silent, my eyes see you alone,

The world vanishes from my dazed mind,

Nichts an mir ist, nichts in mir selbst mehr mein,	Nothing about me, nothing in me is mine any longer,
Und Flammen fühl' ich durch die Brust mir rinnen,	And I feel flames run through my breast
Und kämpfe wild mit Zweifel, Trug und Schein,	And I struggle wildly with doubt, delusion, illusion,
Mit Licht und Nacht in wandelbaren Wogen	With light and night in changeable waves;
Hält Lust und Leid mir Blick und Geist umzogen.	Joy and sorrow envelop my gaze and spirit.
Ich kann nicht nahn, nicht fliehn und nicht verweilen,	I cannot draw near, cannot escape, and cannot tarry,
Es fesselt mich und treibt mich rastlos fort;	It enslaves me and drives me forth restlessly;
Mag Ort und Zeit auch wechseln und enteilen,	however time and place change and rush away, for me
Eins bleibt die Zeit mir ewig, Eins der Ort.	there is eternally but one time, one place.
In tausend Wünsche muß mein Geist sich theilen,	My spirit must split into a thousand desires,
Und alle doch umfängt ein einz'ges Wort;	and yet a single word encompasses them all;
Von tausend Pfeilen ist mein Herz getroffen	My heart is pierced with a thousand arrows
Und bleibt doch stets für neue Wunden offen.[103]	And yet stays open for new wounds.

A psychiatric diagnostician's manual could not describe any more precisely, certainly not more beautifully, the mechanisms of grief, the way in which it alters the sense of space and time and the manner in which it saps strength and substance from the sufferer. In "Am 19. Februar 1816," Schulze writes that grief renders him as light as foam on the ocean, blown hither and yon by forces stronger than the stricken poet. The loss of control inherent in grief, the inability to do anything other than suffer, are vividly described.

Stille Nacht mit kühlem Schatten,	Quiet night, with your cool shadows,
Die du mütterlich den Schleier	You who, like a mother,
Deinen tagesmüden Kindern	draw a veil over the dark eyes
Um die dunkeln Augen ziehst,	of your children, weary from the day,
Kannst du nicht dem Todesmatten	Can you not soothe the poison
Seiner Wunden brennend Feuer,	of these arrows, the poison coursing
Jener Pfeile Gift ihm lindern,	through his veins, the burning fire of
Das die Adern ihm durchfließt?	his wounds, for one weary unto death?
Weh, wie ist das helle Leben	Alas, bright life is transformed for
So zum Traum mir umgestaltet!	me into a dream!
Weh, wie schleudert selbst im Traume	Alas, even in my dreams,
Mich das Leben hin und her!	life tosses me to and fro,
Wie die Lüfte wehn und weben,	blown and tossed about like the wind,
Wie die Welle wogt und waltet,	forced to surge and roll like the waves,
Schwimm' ich gleich zerflossnem Schaume,	I swim, Love, like froth on the waves
Liebe, durch dein wildes Meer.[104]	through your wild sea.

It did not require his friend Bunsen telling him so for Schulze to realize the interpenetration of life and fantasy in his mental illness, such that dreams were permeated with life's suffering while life became as unreal as dreams. He had already diagnosed himself quite accurately, but a cure was beyond his powers.

Because no remedy was forthcoming, nothing ever changes in the *Poetisches Tagebuch*. Time comes and goes, war waxes and wanes, but the forward march of history and the clock only underscores the intolerable stasis at the heart of the anthology. The same conflicts between memory and the present, between life and fantasy, between obsessive grief and the awareness of life outside its narrow boundaries, are played out over and over in the poems cited above and in those Schubert set to music. It is to those poems, and to music, that we now turn.

SCHUBERT AND SCHULZE

Given Schubert's requirements for poetry-for-music, there was only a limited selection possible for him to choose from the poetic diary. Schulze was wont to write lengthy poems in classical meters, far surpassing the bounds suitable for lieder, as in the two-and-a-half pages of classicizing hexameters one finds in "Am 17. Juli 1813."[105] Elsewhere, both sensuous imagery and motion vanish; in "Am 15. November 1813," Nature itself dies and disappears from the poetic persona's cosmos, leaving him with only the endless inward scrutiny of his own bereft condition. Where sensuous imagery and motion disappear, Schubert was left cold. Of two "wandering songs" written on the same day in July 1814, "Im Walde hinter Falkenhagen" and "Auf dem Berge vor Hohlungen," Schubert chose the one in which motion is enacted, not remembered, while another of his choices, "Auf der Bruck," is a study in driven motion. When Schubert had, speculatively, rejected those poems too long for even the most generous song dimensions and poems devoid of Nature and movement, he was left with a limited pool, from which he chose some of Schulze's best endeavours.

The Schulze songs of 1825–6 seem in retrospect like studies for *Winterreise*, D. 911 (this is not to detract from their self-sufficient worth). Schubert could not, of course, have been aware of this when he began gleaning poems from the *Poetisches Tagebuch*, but the resemblances between the two repertoires, both poetic and musical, are very striking. Schulze's exploration of love and loss, of pathological melancholy, of the inability to rejoin and regain life, is differently calibrated than Müller's and more narrowly focussed, but many of their themes are the same. Even the imagery is similar, especially the dichotomy of winter/the present/grief and springtime/the past/love, admittedly, a poetic cliché for centuries. The preference for wintry climes as more consonant with the poet's grief than balmy breezes or blossoming meadows and the sporadic, unsuccessful attempts to jolt himself back to life also reappear, more complexly developed, in Müller's poetic cycle.

The differences are, however, as telling as the similarities, due in some measure to a different relationship between life and the work. It is possible that the unhappy outcome of Müller's love for Luise Hensel might have led, some five years later, to the creation of a winter wanderer impelled by love's loss to self-analysis, but the wanderer is not to be confused with Müller. The poetic voice in Schulze's verse-diary, however, is patently the poet himself *in propria persona*. If he rearranges fact in accord with delusion and art, he is still his own subject and object alike. Mired in his own pathology, he is unable to divine the root causes of his misery, which lie deeper than the loss of his beloved, as the winter wanderer recognizes early in *Die Winterreise* and is finally able to understand, if not accept. The two lovelorn voices even sing for different reasons; where Schulze insistently claims Petrarchan status as a "singer of songs," Müller's winter wanderer sings in spite of himself, without realizing that he is an artist until an epiphany near the end.[106] Whatever the imagery and themes these two poets share, a different aesthetic of poetry divides them.

Schubert responded to Schulze's poetic diary with music whose motion, figuration, tonalities, rhythms, and development often prefigure D. 911, but once again with significant differences. Schulze was a more self-indulgent poet than the healthier Müller, who carefully revised his poems for maximum resonance from minimal words. Within the shorter confines of a typical poem by Müller, more happens, whereas Schulze tends to harp on one string, to play one variation after another on the same theme, in a manner emblematic of obsession. Where Müller's winter wanderer often changes mood between the beginning and end of a poem or arrives at a new insight into his condition by the close, Schulze's poetic alter ego seldom does likewise, or does so only minimally and against the backdrop of unchanging despair. Schubert embodied the poet's pathological fixity in strict strophic form for the majority of the Schulze songs, although it is those poems in which one finds sudden kaleidoscopic shifts of tone and therefore a beckoning to *varied* strophic form ("Der liebliche Stern," "Über Wildemann," and "Im Frühling") that impelled the greatest of the Schulze lieder. The tonal language too tends to be somewhat simpler than in the second Müller cycle, without the proto-Wagnerian modulations and tonal deflections one finds in songs such as "Auf dem Fluße," although there are exceptions in which the Schulze songs seem all the more a forerunner of the winter journey. Schulze's alter ego, fixated on his pain, is tonally bound in place in a way that Müller's wanderer, who continually questions his heart for the Prime Cause of his alienation and therefore casts about both mentally and tonally, is not. But if the futuristic daring of a "Letzte Hoffnung" or "Im Dorfe" or "Einsamkeit" is not to be found in the Schulze songs, the two bodies of lieder are nonetheless akin in many ways, in the prolonged use of unison textures, in the poetic signification of parallel major and minor modes, even in certain evocative details. When Schubert, for the sixth and final stanza of "Der Lindenbaum" (the fifth song in *Winterreise*) lifts an accompanimental pattern above the voice, where formerly the two inhabited the same register, he is putting to new use one of the most poignant aspects of "Im Frühling," while the driven *Bewegung* (motion) of obsession, of frantic grief, is a common element in certain of the Schulze and Müller songs.

What is most compelling about the Schulze songs, however, is the musical mapping of near-insanity, the poet at times straying dangerously close to the borders of irrationality, at times drawing back from the brink by great force of will. Lacking any anecdotal evidence, one cannot help wondering what drew Schubert to this poetry at this time and whether bonds of empathic identification with the tortured poet had anything to do with the choice. By 1825, Schubert was well-acquainted with despair and loss; he too knew what it was to count one's life diminished and abbreviated, unalloyed happiness a mirage and creativity the sole remaining bulwark against encroaching shadows. Although he did not, to our present knowledge, experience erotic obsession as it afflicted Schulze, he would have known the extremity of suffering one finds on every page of the *Poetisches Tagebuch*, would have known too that the dark mysteries of death and sex were implicated in the cause of despair. If he was undoubtedly the best of the composers drawn to Schulze's finely-crafted misery-in-verse, a certain sympathy compounded of suffering and artistry alike could, speculatively, have contributed to these detailed depictions of pathology in sound.

1. Perhaps the first – the chronology is uncertain – of Schubert's Schulze songs was "Im Walde" (In the forest), D. 834, or, to give it the poet's title: "Im Walde hinter Falkenhagen. Den 22. Juli 1814" (In the forest beyond Falkenhagen, 22 July 1814). The autograph manuscripts for the two versions, the first in G minor and the second in B-flat minor, are both lost; there is a copy of the first version, dated March 1825, in vol. 31 (pp. 24–41) of the Witteczek-Spaun collection in the Vienna Gesellschaft der Musikfreunde. When Schubert visited Graz in September 1827, he met the music publisher Josef Andreas Kienreich, who then brought out "Im Walde und auf der Brücke. Zwey Gedichte von Ernst Schulze in Musik gesetzt für eine Singstimme und Pianoforte-begleitung von Franz Schubert während seiner Anwesenheit in Gratz. Op. 90"; the opus number was wrong and was subsequently corrected to op. 93. Kienreich claimed that the songs were composed during Schubert's stay in Graz, but in fact, they were more than two years old when Schubert negotiated the deal for the Graz edition. The first version was published by Anton Diabelli in early 1835, and it is interesting to note that when Schubert recopied the song from memory, he did so in a higher register than the original and an unusual key.

Ich wandre über Berg und Thal	I wander over hill and dale,
Und über grüne Heiden,	and over green meadows,
Und mit mir wandert meine Qual,	and my suffering wanders with me,
Will nimmer von mir scheiden	never leaving me.
Und schifft' ich auch durchs weite Meer,	And were I to sail across the wide sea,
Sie käm' auch dort wohl hinterher.	it would still follow me there.
Wohl blühn viel Blumen auf der Flur,	Though many flowers bloom in the meadow,
Die hab' ich nicht gesehen;	I have not seen them,
Denn eine Blume seh' ich nur	for I see but one flower
Auf allen Wegen stehen.	on every path I tread.
Nach ihr hab' ich mich oft gebückt	I have often stooped down towards it,
Und doch sie nimmer abgepflückt.	but have never plucked it.

Die Bienen summen durch das Gras	The bees hum through the grass
Und hängen an den Blüten;	and linger on the blossoms;
Das macht mein Auge trüb' und naß,	that made my eyes clouded and moist –
Ich kann mir's nicht verbieten.	I cannot help it.
Ihr süßen Lippen, rot und weich,	Sweet lips, so red and soft,
Wohl hing ich nimmer so an euch!	never did I linger so on you!
Gar lieblich singen nah und fern	Far and near the birds sing sweetly
Die Vögel auf den Zweigen;	on the branches;
Wohl säng' ich mit den Vögeln gern,	I should dearly love to sing with the birds,
Doch muß ich traurig schweigen:	but I must keep a mournful silence
Denn Liebeslust und Liebespein,	For the happiness and the pain of love
Die bleiben jedes gern allein.	prefer to remain alone.
Am Himmel seh' ich flügelschnell	I watch the clouds wing their way
Die Wolken weiter ziehen,	swiftly across the sky;
Die Welle rieselt leicht und hell,	the waves ripple softly and brightly –
Muß immer nahn und fliehen;	they must ever come and go.
Doch haschen, wenn's vom Winde ruht,	Yet when the wind dies down, cloud
Sich Wolk' und Wolke, Flut und Flut.	catches cloud in play, and wave catches wave.
Ich wandre hin, ich wandre her	I wander here, I wander there,
Bei Sturm und heitern Tagen,	through storm and fine weather,
Und doch erschau' ich's nimmermehr	yet I shall never again behold it,
Und kann es nicht erjagen.	shall never track it down.
O Liebessehnen, Liebesqual,	O longing and torment of love,
Wann ruht der Wanderer einmal?[107]	when will the wanderer finally rest?

The poet's sorrow is anthropomorphised as if it were a leechlike travelling companion who refuses banishment, a succubus separate from the poet and yet omnipresent. Beyond physical motion from place to place, "wandering" for Schulze meant the soul's search for meaning in a life where his love was not requited, as he admits in this poem and many others. In a barely-veiled euphemism, he laments his failure to possess her sexually: he never "plucked the flower," although he "often stooped down towards it," as poor Adelheid knew to her cost. He never even kissed her, a frustration of desire requiring no evasions by analogy (the imperfect rhyme "weich - euch" in the culminating couplet underscores disjunction). The touch of superiority evident in "stooping" to the flower's level is unpleasant, nor did Schulze question the equally unpleasant assumptions underlying the commonplace analogy of women to flowers: fragile, fixed in place until a superior force breaks them and moves them elsewhere, ornamental, and doomed to wither once plucked. Where so much else was warped, however, one could hardly expect nascent feminism.

The pathology of mental illness is especially evident in stanzas 4-6. In a tangle of associations, the birds Schulze invokes in stanza 4 are multivalent: as erotic symbols, they continue the motif of sexual frustration already limned in stanzas 2 and 3 ("vögeln" a vulgar verb for sexual intercourse). They also represent the love-poet, the singer who serenades his beloved, but Schulze tells us he is barred ("muß") from singing with them as he would like, an analogy easily translatable as the constraint on expression imposed by Adelheid, who did not want to hear him "singing sweetly of love." The final couplet of stanza 4 ("For the happiness and the pain of love prefer to remain alone") is only explicable, despite its plain wording, as an explanation of a *poet's* love, requiring separation from the beloved rather than propinquity and therefore impelling in reaction the wistful voyeurism of stanza 5, in which he watches "couples" in Nature. Tellingly, there is a pursuer and a pursued in these couples: one wave, one cloud, "catches" another. In the final stanza, the twice-repeated "it" is not identified, and one is left to guess its meaning – reciprocated sexual passion? peace? happiness? love? the "flower-maiden" Adelheid? All of that, and more?

Premonitions of *Winterreise*[108] abound in this song. The ceaseless triplet motion and two-against-three patterns remind one of "Erstarrung" and are possibly descended from Beethoven's *An die ferne Geliebte* as well – did Schulze's image of clouds at play, in motion even when the wind dies down, recall Beethoven's cycle to his younger contemporary? Although the triplet motion is omnipresent, Schubert makes a distinction between the figuration in the lengthy piano introduction/inter-ludes/postlude and in the texted sections; in the former, the triplets descend to the bass and become a solid wall of sound at the bottom of the texture, enabling the right hand to state an octave-reinforced melody that both foreshadows or echoes the vocal line (mm. 2–3 are repeated with words added in mm. 9–10) and diverges from it thereafter. When the singer enters, the triplet figures are divided between the two hands. Where Schubert indicates accents in the bass at the beginning and the midpoint of the measure and furthermore alternates octaves and single pitches in the bass, as in mm. 9–10, the effect is eerily reminiscent of the Erl-king's blandishments a decade earlier. The connection is not far to seek and lies in the similar mélange of death and sexual obsession which pervades both poems, despite their obvious differences in other ways.

Like "Erstarrung," "Im Walde" has a lengthy piano introduction preceding a lengthy song, and, as in "Erstarrung," length and text repetition are indices of the protagonist's obsessiveness. The melody first stated in the introduction divides into three two-measure segments: the first diatonic segment outlines both by leap and scalewise motion the interval between tonic and dominant pitches, culminating in a mid-measure accent on $\hat{5}$. The second is chromatic, with the melodic line decorating the dominant pitch by means of its neighbor notes on either side, while the descending chromatic bass line prefigures later instances of linear chromaticism in the song. Furthermore, the G-flat upper neighbor to the dominant pitch in m. 4 will soon after be massively emphasized in the setting of stanza 1 and thereafter. While the chromatic descent continues in the bass, the third and last segment of the right-hand melody traces a descent from $\hat{4}$ to $\hat{1}$. The resemblances to "Erstarrung" are truly uncanny, although in the later song, the driven triplet motion appears in the right-hand part while the left hand searches for melodic souvenirs on the snow-covered ground of the bass line. Could this have been what called "Im Walde" and "Auf der Brücke" to mind when Kienreich importuned Schubert for songs in September 1827, only a few months after the composition of "Erstarrung"?

Schubert brings the incipient insanity of the poem out in the open – if it is clearly evident in Schulze's words, the poet had a stake in hiding its severity from his own awareness, or disguising it as "normal" grief, whereas it was precisely the pathology of it all that Schubert seems to have found "komponabel." At the beginning, Schulze's alter ego states, in an almost matter-of-fact manner, "I wander over mountains and valleys and green fields, and my sorrow goes with me, will never leave me." The sense of a rift in the psyche that opens up between the two halves of that declarative statement is paradoxically underscored by the flatness of tone. Schubert's persona, however, displays near-madness overtly, the composer driving him over the landscape at a more frenetic pace than the poet's initial line might suggest. The naming of his unwanted travelling companion provokes a veritable howl of anguish, a sudden wrenching-away from the diatonic bounds of the first phrase. With the words "Und mit mir wandert meine Qual," the tonic B-flats in the bass continue, but the harmony changes to the submediant, heightened and emphasized by the C-flats and secondary dominants of G-flat in this passage, the B-flat and G-flat harmonies yoked together by their common tones like the persona and his grim travelling companion. With the word "Qual" itself, the singer leaps to the high G-flat and remains there, hammering the words "Will nimmer von mir schei - [den]" in declamatory emphasis, too desperate for melodic inflection, while the pianist pounds the fullest-textured chords of the entire work – the darkness inherent in Neapolitan chords rendered wild. When the singer despairingly repeats the words "Will nimmer von mir scheiden" at a lower, less frenetic level, Schubert writes a measured trill on the third degree of the tonic scale, as if the persona were physically attempting to shake the leech-like presence from him. And Schubert also makes explicit the menace underlying the words "Und schifft' ich auch durch's weite Meer, / sie käm' auch dort wohl hinterher" when he first sets them as a linear chromatic ascent back to B-flat minor in a stark unharmonized texture, followed by a fully-harmonized repetition of the entire couplet in the upper tessitura of greatest desperation. In the final repetition of those words, the vocal line is doubled at the octave in the inner voice of the accompaniment (mm. 24–26), an especially strong texture. The similar chord voicing and much lengthier unison passages of an even wilder Schulze lied – "Über Wildemann," which also shares the same 4/4 meter and triplet figuration – are foreshadowed here in the refrain to stanza 1.

And thereafter, in the refrain to stanzas 3, 4, and 6 – Schubert uses exact or near-exact repetition of entire passages in "Im Walde" as the register of obsession, which cannot change its tune. Where this occurs in stanza 3, the rising chromatic line, fraught with particularly acute tension, sounds to the words "Ihr süßen Lippen, rot und weich, / Wohl hing ich nimmer so an euch"; Schubert could not have epitomized the taint of mental illness and the aura of menace in this seemingly loverlike proclamation more aptly. In the strophic repetitions, we are reminded yet again of "Erstarrung," in which Müller's wanderer atypically repeats the music for stanzas 1 and 2 to the words of stanzas 4 and 5, a rarity in *Winterreise* but not in the Schulze songs; the poetic persona, fixed in place psychologically, repeats himself over and over. Change is kept to a minimum; the bees humming in the grass in stanza 3 and the birds singing on the branches in stanza 4 do so in major mode rather than minor (mm. 66–68, mm. 92–95), but the outbreak of raw despair on all those hammered submediant and Neapolitan chords is unchanged each time – it never softens, it never modulates, it never alters.

Stanzas 2 and 5 are variations which begin on the brighter sounds of dominant and parallel major harmonies, interludes in which the tension slackens notably, although the repetitions cluster just as thick and fast and the figuration and motion remain the same. One notes the anticipation tones in the ascending, arpeggiated vocal line at mm. 39, 43, 122, and 125, and the neighbor-notes and passing tones that ornament mm. 37 and 120, an airy impulsion for the benign analogies in Nature. But with the final couplet ("Nach ihr hab' ich mich oft gebückt / Und doch sie nimmer abgepflückt"), the distinctive tensions of this song return in full force. The tonality darkens to minor once again, and "stooping down" ("bücken") is combined with descending chromatic lamentation in a sequential descent, culminating on F minor. Unable to refrain from repeating, over and over, that which most pains him, he once again proclaims "Und doch sie nimmer abgepflückt" as a dramatic ascent to the higher tessitura and *forte* dynamics of his earlier desperation. The passage might seem at first unsuited to the final couplet of stanza 5, with its "cloud on cloud, wave on wave" at play, even with major mode maintained throughout, but the *lamentoso* chromatic gestures underscore the fact that the poet is not among the happy couples he sees mirrored in Nature.

At the end of "Im Walde," the poetic persona is back where he began, his grief unchanged. Therefore, we hear the piano introduction once more as the postlude, but with an extraordinarily moving difference. At the end of the poem, the poet asks "Love's longing, Love's pain" when "the wanderer" will rest at last. Schubert, who knew that there was no rest accorded the creator of the *Poetisches Tagebuch*, knew furthermore that Schulze was dead, appends a three-bar extension to the postlude in which the panic-stricken triplet motion of the accompaniment is allowed to run down, "spin its wheels" for a moment before it finally stops (he would do likewise at the end of "Erstarrung"). The dying-away progression is premonitory of the similar bone-simple progression, stripped of anything extraneous, with which both the Andantino movement of the piano sonata in A major, D. 959, and the Andante sostenuto of the sonata in B-flat, D. 960, end. After the colossal, roiling crisis in the middle of the Andantino of D. 959, the haunting varied return of the A section dies away in this same fashion, foreshadowed by the valedictory end of "Im Walde." It is perhaps a trifle fanciful, but the close of the lied seems like Schubert's own funerary benediction on Schulze himself, the composer's conferral of peace at last on a poet he knew to be tragically dead at an early age.

2.   The second of the 1825 Schulze group was "Auf der Brücke" (Schubert's title) or "Auf der Bruck. Den 26. Juli 1814" (Schulze's title), published with "Im Walde" in op. 93. Both in Diabelli's edition and the Witteczek-Spaun collection, "Auf der Brücke" is set in G major, but for the Graz edition, Schubert transposed the song to A-flat major.

Frisch trabe sonder Ruh und Rast,
Mein gutes Roß, durch Nacht und Regen!
Was scheust du dich vor Busch und Ast
Und strauchelst auf den wilden Wegen?
Dehnt auch der Wald sich tief und dicht,
Doch muß er endlich sich erschließen,
Und freundlich wird ein fernes Licht
Uns aus dem dunkeln Thale grüßen.

Trot briskly on, my good horse, without
resting or stopping, through night and rain!
Why do you shy at bush and branch,
and stumble on the wild paths?
Though the forest stretches deep and dense,
it must come to an end at last,
and a distant light will greet us warmly
from the dark valley.

Wohl könnt' ich über Berg und Feld
Auf deinem schlanken Rücken fliegen
Und mich am bunten Spiel der Welt,
An holden Bildern mich vergnügen
Manch Auge lacht mir traulich zu
Und beut mir Frieden, Lieb' und Freude,
Und dennoch eil' ich ohne Ruh
Zurück, zurück zu meinem Leide.

I could cheerfully speed over mountain
and meadow on your lithe back
and enjoy the world's varied delights,
its fair sights.
Many an eye smiles at me affectionately,
offering me peace, love, and joy,
and yet I hasten restlessly
back, back to my sorrow.

Denn schon drei Tage war ich fern
Von ihr, die ewig mich gebunden,
Drei Tage waren Sonn' und Stern
Und Erd' und Himmel mir verschwunden.
Von Lust und Leiden, die mein Herz
Bei ihr bald heilten, bald zerrissen,
Fühlt' ich drei Tage nur den Schmerz,
Und ach, die Freude mußt' ich missen!

For three days now I have been far
from her to whom I am forever bound;
for three days, sun and stars,
earth and sky have vanished for me.
Of the joy and sorrow which, when I
was with her, now healed, now broke my heart,
I have for three days felt only the sorrow.
Alas, the joy I have had to forego!

Drum trabe mutig durch die Nacht!
Und schwinden auch die dunkeln Bahnen,
Der Sehnsucht helles Auge wacht
Und sicher führt mich süßes Ahnen.
Weit sehn wir über Land und See
Zur wärmern Flur den Vogel fliegen,
Wie sollte denn die Liebe je
In ihrem Pfade sich betrügen?[109]

So trot bravely on through the night!
Though the dark tracks may vanish,
the bright eye of longing is wakeful, and
sweet presentiment guides me safely onwards.
We watch the birds fly far away
over land and sea to warmer pastures.
How then should love ever
be deceived in its course?

More than a means of conveyance through the nocturnal countryside, "mein gutes Ross" can also be understood as a descendant of Plato's horses in the myth of the soul from the *Phaedo*. In Schulze's variation, the horse symbolizes his heart or soul, his inmost being, which he comforts, encourages — and deceives; this poem could share the title "An mein Herz" with D. 860. As he does elsewhere in the *Poetisches Tagebuch*, Schulze conflates a real and a symbolic journey. In the former, he is acutely aware of his inability to leave the site of his obsession for the world beyond its boundaries, but he "justifies" the irrational fixation by declaring that the beloved is his sole source of joy and sorrow alike, and therefore separation from her deprives him of all joy. In the symbolic journey, his heart falters in the confrontation with night, rain, and wild paths, with the dark forest of his psyche, but he rallies, reassuring himself of a way out and an end to night. Beyond his present travail, he sings, lies morning, and Love will guide him there as unerringly as Nature guides birds to their warm havens during winter. One recalls Müller's winter wanderer, who recognizes this same hope to be illusion; the will-o'-the-wisp who promises "that beyond the ice and night and horror, a bright, warm house, and a beloved soul within" beckon in "Täuschung" (Deception) lies to him, and he knows it. But Schulze, impelled by obsession to lie to himself on a regular basis, does so once again here on a look-out point called "die Bruck" near – where else? – Göttingen. His delusory optimism cannot hide the fact that he is, and would remain, "auf den wilden Wegen" throughout the song and beyond.

The lied, however, places its protagonist on "die Brücke" (the bridge) rather than the "Bruck." Schubert's title is unknown, since the autograph manuscript is missing, and Deutsch subsequently claimed that the "mistake" was the publisher's. John Reed has argued that the original "misunderstanding" could well have been Schubert's,[110] but it seems more likely to me that the composer deliberately altered the title, especially since he eliminated the dates (with one exception) and German place-names from the ten poems he plucked from the *Poetisches Tagebuch* and invented titles *de novo*, I would guess, in order not to circumscribe his songs in time and space. The copy in the Witteczek-Spaun collection is also entitled "Auf der Brücke," still more evidence of the composer's invention of a new title, economically wrought by means of an umlaut and a single additional letter. Symbolically, Schubert's poetic persona rides over a bridge (without ever reaching the other side) between two places and two temporal zones in the geography of the psyche: between the present and the future, between stormy night and sunlit morning to come, between despair and hope. Nor was that Schubert's only editorial revision to the poem. He also placed lines 5–8 of the final eight-line stanza first, ending, not with Schulze's revealing question, "How then should love ever be deceived in its course?", but with the injunction "Trot on" and the declaration that "sweet presentiments" are his [the poetic persona's] guide. Schubert thus alters the poem crucially. In Schulze's formal structure, the poem ends with the awareness of deception present in the very words with which the poet denies it; he falls significantly silent as soon as he asks the question, posed as if it were rhetorical when it is actually nothing of the kind. Schubert, however, does treat it as rhetorical and ends the lied with delusory hope in the ascendent.[111]

It was not that he failed to recognize the self-deception at the heart of the poem – far from it. Indeed, he makes evident a condition far unhealthier and unhappier than the poetic persona would have us believe, his music telling the listener in numerous ways that the optimism is false and that misery lurks just beneath the surface. Schulze begins the poem with an invocation of brisk trotting motion, and Schubert accordingly begins the piano introduction with the cliché of clip-clopping figuration consisting of repeated eighth-note chords in the right-hand (continuous to the end of the entire song) and upbeat figures outlining the motion from the dominant to tonic pitches. Well before the singer enters, the motion manifests itself as "ohne Rast und Ruh'," as sounds perceived by a disturbed mind, when the accents cluster thick and fast in m. 3 and when sequential motion presses upwards in mm. 5–7. When Schubert brings the incipient wildness under control by the end of the piano introduction, he sets the pattern for the entire song to come: brisk hope, manifest disturbance, and the re-establishment of control over encroaching madness. When the song proper begins in m. 11, Schubert differentiates between the metaphorical horse in the bass and its rider in the vocal line, the two parts closely related but with the phrasing staggered to make the distinction clear. In this first phrase, repeated exactly for the second phrase, one notes more than anything else the disturbance created by the accented downbeat A-natural in the bass of m. 13 ("mein *gu* - [tes Ross]") and the voice. Although Schubert might, speculatively, have devised this gesture specifically for the words "[Denn schon drei Tage war ich fern] Von *ihr*, [die ewig mich gebunden]" at the beginning of stanza 3, its initial appearance confers a peculiarly fraught emphasis on the adjective "good." That Schubert could recognize the conflicts attendant upon Schulze's desperate wish to be "good" and could embody that recognition in this significant detail is emblematic of his song-writing art. The raised tonic pitch is the only chromatic element in these first two phrases, signifying disturbance which attacks the very root of the song – and does so from below, beneath the hearty surface.

Schubert divides each of Schulze's stanzas into halves, the first half (with one exception) anchored firmly in tonic A-flat major and the second half diverging from it briefly before returning. What more apt design could he have found for someone who is not truly en route anywhere, who is actually fixed in place? Furthermore, the tonal design is representative as well of delusory brightness barely under control, each strophe defined by divagations into darker, minor-mode realms at midpoint, unseating and unsettling the brisk A-flat major resolutions, and by the manner in which those doubts are dispelled. When the poet in stanza 1 invokes the deep, dark forest in which he is trapped, the bass sinks to the lowest register of the Schubertian fortepiano, where it moves about like some sinister creature in the depths of the mind. The harmonies shift momentarily to relative minor, fixated on the chords of F minor and its dominant as if trapped there. But even before the harmonies are jolted back to A-flat major, the protagonist energetically combats the lapse into darkness; he does not allow himself to linger on the word "[tief und] dicht," but immediately vaults upward, with no break or rest, and proclaims "Doch muß er endlich sich erschließen" to an athletic phrase replete with perfect intervals, stark and strong. The poet does not depict his alter ego tumbling over himself in haste, scrambling to get away from the implications of the words "der Wald … tief und dicht," but Schubert could and did. When the F minor harmonies persist, despite the protagonist's efforts in the vocal line, the piano wrenches away in m. 26, the violence of the procedure only partially mitigated by the continuing *pianissimo* dynamics, and the right hand leaps upward, just as it will subsequently do in m. 57. (There, in the final stanza, the passage is equally appropriate, the F minor depths belonging to the night and the "dark paths," the wrench upwards to tonic emblematic of the "bright, wakeful gaze of longing.") Schubert heightens the jolt all the more when he has the topmost voice leap a diminished octave, from E-natural to the E-flat belonging to the newly-reinstated A-flat major for the words "Und freundlich wird ein fernes Licht / Uns aus dem dunkeln Thale grüßen." The descending chromatic passing tone at the second statement of the word "freundlich" in m. 29 not only prefigures the C-flats clustered thick and fast in the setting of stanza 3, but tells us that the underlying meaning of "freundlich" is erotic, laden with desire and grief alike; the erotic associations are made explicit in the final strophe when the gesture reappears to the words "Der Sehnsucht [helles Auge wacht]." The assurance of a "gentle light" greeting the protagonist from the dark valley (life as a dark vale of tears, love as the beacon) is only achieved by the forcible maintenance of A-flat major optimism, by jumping repeatedly out of the morass of despair back to levels which are not, one notices, that far above the Slough of Despond in the bass.

In the second half of stanza 2 (mm. 53–57), as the poetic persona sings "Manch Auge lacht mir traulich zu / Und beut mir Frieden, Lieb' und Freude" (Many an eye smiles at me affectionately and offers me peace, love, and joy), the listener hears either the composer, from within the wordless fastnesses of the instrumental part, saying, "No, do not believe what he [the poet] says," or the protagonist's foreboding rumbling in the bass, like a sleeping dragon momentarily stirred to wakefulness. Although Schubert lingers here upon the warmer sounds of subdominant D-flat harmonies for the threefold, quasi-religious invocation of "peace, love, and joy," having largely avoided the subdominant until this point, he contravenes its warmth and lessened tension by sinking an ominous trill on low G-flat deep in the bass. What was present but quiescent in m. 53 ("[manch] Auge lacht mir") is roused to momentary, menacing motion in the caverns at the bottom of the Schubertian fortepiano's range. Peace, love, and joy were never in the protagonist's grasp, nor would they ever be, and the truth is told in this abyss of rumbling disquiet far below the level of the words. The protagonist, however, will not have it and banishes the mysterious Fafner from the lied, never to return. Schubert depicts the precise moment of banishment when he suddenly shifts the accompanimental register upwards in m. 57 at mid-measure, with no preparatory rest or break. Not only is the pianist thus forced to enact physically the difficult wrenching-away from doubt, but there is something palpably unbalanced in the maneuver. The mechanisms of mental disturbance here find exact musical expression.

With the third strophe, grief begins to work upon the A-flat briskness earlier than in the two previous strophes. The poet at first sings "For three days now, I have been far from her to whom I am forever bound" to the jog-trotting, wide-ranging briskness of the first vocal phrase of the song but is unable to repeat the phrase literally, to hold on to the earlier optimistic strains. The disappearance of his "sun and star and earth and heaven," the totality of the cosmos emphasized by the reiterated connectives, rapidly darkens the harmonic palette, overshadowing the clip-clop phrase with parallel minor gloom. When the protagonist attempts to combat the encroaching shadows of mm. 78–79 and turn it back into major mode brightness in mid-phrase, he can only manage C-flat major harmonies in mm. 80–83, notably darker than tonic, before losing the battle and lapsing back into parallel minor at the first mention of "Leiden," or "sorrows." For the polarity of "bald heilten, bald zerrissen" (now healed, now tore) that follows in mm. 86–7, the plunge of a diminished seventh in the vocal line at the word "Leiden" reappears at the verb "heilten," aptly undermining the delusory "healing," while the bass figuration beneath the "deep, thick forest" of stanza 1 echoes down below. When the protagonist admits his sorrow openly ("For three days, I have felt only sorrow"), the climactic statement and its pendant ("And, alas, the joy I have had to forego!") are set as deceptive motion to the most intense chromaticism of the entire song. At the line "Fühlt' ich drei Tage nur den Schmerz," one notes that the octaves in the bass double the voice, a manner of emphasis reserved for those words only. The first time Schubert sets the foregone joy to music in mm. 91–92, it is as far removed from the A-flat false briskness as Schubert could go; when he repeats those same words in mm. 94–96, "Freude" (joy) is flung upwards to a high A-flat in the vocal line and the most emphatic downbeat he could devise. Only midway through the piano interlude between stanzas 3 and 4 (m. 102) can Schubert's Schulze win his way back to major mode after a desperate struggle to maintain delusion intact; the first half of the interlude is a capsule recapitulation of the A-flat minor, C-flat major, and D-flat minor harmonies from the chromatic turmoil immediately preceding. At the point where the battle is won, *fortissimo* cedes to *piano* and minor mode to major; the suddenness with which the change occurs is yet another nuance of mental distress, acutely disconcerting to hear.

In the final stanza, the protagonist, presumably having learnt his lesson in the preceding strophe, avoids all mention of anything painful and speaks only of happiness to come. Here, strands from the previous strophes (in particular, the last half of each strophe) are brought back and reconciled in some way with the protagonist's desire for a *lieto fine* in the near future. The F minor strains of the dark forest in stanza 1 recur yet again for the "night and dark paths" in stanza 4, but this time for revisionary purposes. Avoiding the lowest depths of the bass and the ominous sustained tones from before, Schubert instead sounds a brisk trotting rhythm in the bass and proclamatory fanfare-like figures in the voice as the poet bids the "dark paths" vanish. Just as in "Im Walde," nothing changes between the beginning and the end – the delusion stated at the start is reconfirmed at the close – and Schubert consequently repeats the piano introduction as the postlude, with, once again, a telling addition. In the final measures, we hear the receding, dying-away sounds of the horses' hooves as the protagonist rides back to his beloved. It is perhaps worth noting that as the bass line descends, evocative of vanishing hoofbeats, it almost touches the depths of the "dark forest" and low F – but not quite.

3. At the end of 1825, Schubert returned to the *Poetisches Tagebuch* to compose "An mein Herz" (To my heart), D. 860, a setting of Schulze's "Am 23. Januar 1816":

O Herz, sei endlich stille!	O heart, be still at last!
Was schlägst du so unruhvoll?	Why do you beat so restlessly?
Es ist ja des Himmels Wille,	For it is Heaven's will
Das ich sie lassen soll.	That I should leave her.

Ernst Schulze

Und gab auch dein junges Leben
Dir nichts als Wahn und Pein,
Hat's ihr nur Freude gegeben,
So mag's verloren sein.

Und wenn sie auch nie dein Lieben
Und nie dein Leiden verstand,
So bist du doch treu geblieben,
Und Gott hat's droben erkannt.

Wir wollen es mutig ertragen,
So lang nur die Träne noch rinnt,
Und träumen von schöneren Tagen,
Die lange vorüber sind.

Und siehst du die Blüten erscheinen,
Und singen die Vögel umher,
So magst du wohl heimlich weinen,
Doch klagen sollst du nicht mehr.

Geh'n doch die ewigen Sterne
Dort oben mit goldenem Licht
Und lächeln so freundlich von ferne,
Und denken doch unser nicht.[112]

Even though your youthful life
Gave you nothing but delusion and pain,
So long as it gave her joy
Then no matter it was lost to you.

And though she never understood
Your love or your sorrow,
You nonetheless stayed faithful
And God above saw it.

Let us bravely endure
As long as the tears still flow,
And dream of more beautiful days
Long since past.

And when you see the blossoms appear,
When the birds sing all about,
Then you may weep in secret
But you should lament no more.

For the eternal stars above
Move with a golden light,
Smiling so sweetly from afar
And yet with no thought for us.

This poem was written after Schulze had been categorically barred from the Tychsen household and is his summation and justification of an episode even *he* had to recognize at some level was over. As in the letters with which he flayed both himself and Adelheid, his grief is shot through with accusatory anger, boiling through rifts in the leaden depression that was his wont. Near-insanity is writ large in this witches' brew of conflicting statements, devoid of all recognition of their illogic. In the first stanza, he displaces blame for his misery onto Heaven, rather than his beloved, but by the third stanza, unable to maintain the celestial dodge, he accuses her of never having understood him. Even more wildly contradictory is the assertion that if his pain-filled "young life" (he implies that it is already over and, sadly, he was right) gave her joy, his pain does not matter, a statement that imputes sadism to the beloved. Counselling his heart on how to conduct a proper martyrdom, he tells it to weep in secret but not to lament any longer, even as he proclaims his grievance in words intended for publication. His parting from the beloved was, he declares, ordained by heaven itself, the grandiosity of asserting that he is God's victim augmented still more by the declaration that the same God saw his fidelity to this "belle dame sans merci." At the end, he invokes "eternal stars" who smile down kindly but have no thought for "us" (he and his heart); the dead Cäcilie, like the living Adelheid, pays him no heed, and he punishes her for it at the same time he apotheosizes her.

If Schulze could not see that his distress emanated from his own mind rather than the external malevolence of fate or God, Schubert could, and he registers the heart's wild vacillations in every compositional decision he made for this song, set in the A minor tonality of such pathological laments as "Wer nie sein Brot," D. 478, no. 1;

August von Platen-Hallermünde's ghazal "Du liebst mich nicht," D. 756; Matthäus von Collin's "Der Zwerg," D. 771; and "Der Leiermann" from *Winterreise*. Indeed, "Der Zwerg," composed in November 1822 (?), and "An mein Herz" also share the Beethovenian rhythmic motif of Fate from the Fifth Symphony and frequent tritone figures in the bass – Schubert clearly caught the taint of perversion, of revelling in masochism, common to both texts. The "heartbeat" chordal figuration in "An mein Herz" is both constant, an unceasing tactus throughout this lengthy lied, and yet riddled with conflict of all kinds, harmonic, rhythmic, and tonal, especially in the piano introduction. Schubert might well have read the opening injunction of the poem, "O Herz, sei endlich stille" and devised a musical scenario in which the heart/piano beats wildly for eleven measures; the singer then enters and attempts to impose order but with limited success and frequent relapses into distraught violence. Furthermore, one hears in the opening passage a descendant of the panic-stricken "heartbeat" pulsations that accompany the maiden's pleading in "Der Tod und das Mädchen," D. 531, the chords similarly divided between the left and right hands such that the root of the chord only sounds *after* the downbeat in a manner beautifully expressive of turbulence. Beginning with m. 3, Schubert throws the A minor tonality suggested by the initial two measures of nothing but tonic chords into doubt with six measures of harmonic thrashing-about, a passage remarkable for its multiple indices of acute conflict (ex. 24). The accented A minor harmony on the downbeat of m. 3 is succeeded in the next sixteenth-note subdivision of the beat by A reharmonized as the dominant seventh of D minor, all the more emphatic for the persistent offbeat bass pattern. What follows is even more wrenching: a "progression" in which tonic chords alternate with secondary dominants, swinging back and forth between the tritone D-sharp A in the bass for almost two measures. The contrast between *forzando* downbeats in mm. 5-6 and the jolting reinstatement of the initial *piano* dynamics at mid-measure also tells of wild mental vacillation, redolent of near-insanity before a single word is sung. After a pounding apex of fury in mm. 7-8, the paroxysm is followed by comparative calm in m. 9, evident in the *decrescendo*, the regular harmonic rhythm, and diatonic progression. The singer enters only after he has calmed down sufficiently to allow words – the compositional technique that could produce so controlled a musical impression of the impending loss of control is cause for marvel.[113]

When the body of the song begins, Schubert enacts both the poet's attempt to impose control over his emotional state and the heart's refusal to do as it is bid by chaining the bass to an ostinato A throughout mm. 10-17 while the right hand thrums on. The restlessness ("unruhvoll") of this music is further confirmed when the singer declaims his futile initial plea on and encircling the pitch C, unable to alight on the tonic until m. 19, the end of the second vocal phrase. The A minor of desolation becomes A major when the singer proclaims that this is Heaven's will, the surety of its decrees signalled in the more resolute sounds of major mode, but when he states what Heaven has supposedly willed ("that I must leave her"), his agitation is evident in the diminished seventh chord on D-sharp and the tritone leap in the bass, returned from mm. 5-6 of the introduction. Heaven may be strong,

Example 24.   Franz Schubert, "An mein Herz," D. 860, mm. 1–13. From the *Neue Schubert-Ausgabe*, Series IV: *Lieder*, vol. 13a, ed. Walther Dürr.

but he is not, and his irresolution, his unwillingness to comply, are encapsulated in that notoriously unstable harmony. To counteract the collapse into renewed weakness, significantly, at the word "ich," Schubert's persona must then repeat "Es ist ja des Himmels Wille, daß ich sie lassen soll, daß ich sie lassen soll" (mm. 20–25) twofold, both times without the revealing harmonic stammer from before. Schubert's response to every nuance of this pitiable portrayal of obsession is so exact that by the end of the first stanza, one hears the cadential octave leap between "ich" and "sie" in mm. 22 and 24, with "ich" a prolonged downbeat in the topmost end and "sie" at the lower pole and rhythmically weak, as symbolic: the poet-singer pairs "ich" and "sie" on the same pitch, but it is *his* suffering that takes precedence and top billing. No matter that this is a relatively commonplace cadential formula — Schubert expressly tailors it to Schulze's poetic exercise in masochism.

Schubert twice brings back this entire passage (mm. 16–25, "Es ist ja des Himmels Wille, daß ich sie lassen soll"), first, for his setting of the third and fourth lines of the third stanza when Heaven again enters the picture: "So bist du doch treu geblieben, / Und Gott hat's droben erkannt." The poet's fidelity, however diseased, is indeed resolute and brings back the A major certainties, but the diminished seventh chord from m. 18 now sounds at the word "Gott" [!] and, as before, requires a twofold correction. What had formerly signified personal weakness now signals weakness of belief. And the entirety of stanza 1 recurs to the words of stanza 4, the A minor beginning of the musical strophe now expressive of grief-stricken endurance ("Wir wollen es mutig ertragen, / So lang nur die Träne noch rinnt") while the turn to parallel major tells of dreams of better, bygone days (*Winterreise* indeed beckons just around the corner). Here, the tritone leap to the diminished seventh chord and the wonderfully poignant descent from C-sharp to C-natural in the vocal line – traversing the vast distance between happiness and grief, past and present, in the space of a single semitone – underscore the adjective "lange." The poetic persona may speak of courageous forbearance, but the emphasis on "lange," the continued pulsations, and many other details both of the poetry and the music tell us that this is beyond his capacity.

Between each stanza, the unrest of the introduction floods back in the interludes – no matter what the poet says, his heart stubbornly refuses to be calmed. Indeed, his words exacerbate the very condition he seeks to alleviate (a classic vicious cycle), especially in the lengthiest of the interludes (mm. 58–65), eight bars rather than the three-bar interludes between stanzas 1 and 2, 2 and 3, 4 and 5, 5 and 6. It was Schubert's brilliant intuition that the words "I have remained true to you, and God above knows it" should impel a particularly fraught onslaught of instrumental turbulence at the exact midpoint of Schubert's structure, marked by these extended passages of unrest for the piano at the beginning, middle, and end. God is no substitute for the sweetheart who has failed to appreciate "my love and my sorrow," and the heart-piano responds to the false comfort – what does fidelity matter when it is not reciprocated? – with an irrepressible outbreak of violence. Schubert understood that when poetic personae lie to themselves, the music, especially the piano part, can tell the truth (one recalls the dramatically unstable chromatic harmony to which Brahms sets the word "fester" when the deludedly faithful maiden of "Von ewiger Liebe" proclaims "Unsere Liebe ist fester noch mehr").

The words "junges Leben" in stanza 2, especially the adjective "junges," are emphasized by the singer's leap of a seventh to D-natural, momentarily cancelling the D-sharps belonging to the dominant; the poet, in a desperate bid for sympathy, reminds Adelheid – and, although the poem is ostensibly addressed "To my heart," it is actually addressed to her – that he is young, and Schubert heightens both the reminder and the desperation that drives it. Even more telling, he sets the final couplet of the stanza ("Hat's ihr nur Freude gegeben, / So mag's verloren sein") twice, the first time, in accord with the poet's stated proclamation and the second time, in accord with the underlying emotional truth, but returning to grandiosity at the end. Her purported "joy" resounds in the relative major, with, however, the continued agitated "heartbeat" rhythmic patterns and the neighbor-note measured trill from "Im Walde" at the verb "verloren [sein]," contradicting any sense of brightness. The despair of the words "Will nimmer von mir scheiden" from the earlier Schulze song is echoed in this small figure. With the second setting, irresistible truth replaces the false brightness: joy descends precipitously from its peak on high G, and the words "verloren sein" this time impel hollowed-out, fatalistic-sounding fourths and fifths in the lower register. The vocal line of m. 38 is triply doubled in the piano, especially in the bass octaves – like a self-appointed prophet of doom, the poet-singer pronounces a death-sentence on himself in the starkest of tones. (A variant of this same texture will recur in "Über Wildemann.") Determined to be brave about the matter, determined to proclaim his vaunted strength of purpose in martyrdom, the singer then repeats "let it be lost, let it be lost" as he ascends back to the higher register, all the way back up to the high G of m. 36 ("hat's *ihr* nur Freude gegeben"), and reinstates full, diatonic C major harmonies as he climbs upward. The plunge down into the melodic abyss and the immediate scramble back out of it sound patently desperate. Little more than a year later, when Schubert composed "Irrlicht," the ninth song of *Winterreise*, he would again set an ambiguous statement, "[Wie ich einen Ausgang finde] / Liegt nicht schwer mir in dem Sinn" (How I am to find my way out does not trouble my mind), as successive renderings of denial and the truth behind denial, bravado followed by grief. In both songs, consummate compositional finesse is evident in the ways in which music reveals the failure of vaunted insouciance.

The same script is enacted in the setting of the fifth stanza in A major, the change of key signature emblematic of the poetic persona's resolve at the end of stanza 4 to cease living in the doleful present and dream of the beautiful past. Schulze's declaration that he will cease lamenting publicly and only weep in secret produces a *pianissimo* ("heimlich") turn to C-sharp minor, very distant indeed from the C major harmonies of her "joy," while the appoggiatura B-sharps in mm. 87 and 91 create an augmented triad at the word "*wei*-[nen]," the tension of that harmony evocative of acute distress; one thinks of the augmented triad that invests the word "Graus" in "Täuschung" ("die hinter Eis und Nacht und *Graus* ...") with such power. The injunction to cease lamenting in mm. 88–89 impels a return to the A major previously associated with heaven's will, but Schubert's persona cannot leave it at that and repeats both lines. This time, the twofold repetition of the words "klagen, klagen sollst du nicht mehr, klagen sollst du nicht mehr" – the repetitions are themselves a lamentation in defiance of the words – impels, first, a readily-recognizable variation on the doom-laden setting of the word "verloren" in stanza 2 and then an outburst on high A. The stratospheric vocal pitches A D-sharp for the verb "klagen" in m. 94 make explicit what one could already infer was the signification of those same pitches from the introduction onward.

Schubert understood that this poem, like so many others in the *Poetisches Tagebuch*, is a poetic battlefield between self-flagellating grief and the desire for dignified self-control, understood as well that Schulze fought his long-sustained and losing war heroically, with every ounce of strength at his disposal. When the key signature changes to major mode for the final stanza, its brightness seems emblematic both of Nature's blossoms and birdsong, invoked in the initial lines of the stanza, and the poet's resolution to bear his grief nobly, a resolution he could only enact momentarily before slipping back into the grip of obsession. Consequently, Schubert repeats the final line of the poem "Und denken doch unser nicht" (and yet do not think of us) three times, swerving back and forth between major and minor in a palpably unstable manner: in the first instance, we hear a repetition of the diminished seventh chord, disturbing the A-major resolution of mm. 18–19, followed by the restoration of A major, while the second statement brings a swerve back to A minor, followed by a final texted cadence in major. In the painful struggle for self-control enacted in these multiple settings of the most self-flagellating words of the entire poem, Schubert grants the poet victory for the final texted cadence and then reminds us how short-lived such victories were for the tormented creator of the *Poetisches Tagebuch* when he repeats the piano introduction as the postlude. Once again, the poetic persona regains some small measure of self-possession when the postlude, and the entire song, culminate, not in the authentic cadence with which the introduction concludes, but with a prayerful *plagal* cadence. Here, and only here, the throbbing sixteenth-note pulsation slows, then stops altogether. In this most economical of ways, Schubert both suggests that the poet is at last able to calm his restless heart sufficiently to end the song (in prayer to "die ewigen Sterne"? in dreams of the past?) and that the calm is unstable and likely to be short-lived. If this is an ending which seems to differ from Schulze's bitterness at the close of the poem, the difference is more apparent than real. Schubert merely extends the battle for heart's-ease into the instrumental postlude – an unspoken last verse.

4.   "Der liebliche Stern," D. 861, also composed in December 1825, is a setting of Schulze's "Am 28. April 1814."[114]

Ihr Sternlein, still in der Höhe,	Little stars, so silent in the heavens,
Ihr Sternlein, spielend im Meer,	little stars, playing upon the sea,
Wenn ich von ferne daher	when from afar
So freundlich euch leuchten sehe,	I see you glittering so beautifully,
So wird mir von Wohl und Wehe	then for weal or woe,
Mein Busen so bang und so schwer.	my heart grows troubled and heavy.
Es zittert von Frühlingswinden	The sky trembles in the spring breezes
Der Himmel im flüssigen Grün,	above the watery meadows;
Manch Sternlein sah ich entblühn,	I saw many a star blossom,
Manch Sternlein sah ich entschwinden;	I saw many a star vanish,
Doch kann ich das schönste nicht finden,	But I cannot find the most beautiful
Das früher dem Liebenden schien.	that once shone for this lover.
Nicht kann ich zum Himmel mich schwingen,	I cannot soar to the heavens,
Zu suchen den freundlichen Stern,	to seek that kindly star;
Stets hält ihn die Wolke mir fern.	clouds forever conceal it from me.
Tief unten da möcht' es gelingen,	Deep below, there I might succeed

Das friedliche Ziel zu erringen,
Tief unten da ruht' ich so gern!

in reaching the peaceful refuge;
deep below I would gladly find rest!

Was wiegt ihr im laulichen Spiele,
Ihr Lüftchen, den schwankenden Kahn?
O treibt ihn auf rauherer Bahn
Hernieder ins Wogengewühle!
Laßt tief in der wallenden Kühle
Dem lieblichen Sterne mich nahn![115]

Breezes, why do you lull the rocking boat
in gentle play?
Drive it along a rougher course,
down into the whirlpool!
Deep in the cool, turbulent waters
let me draw near to that lovely star.

The poetic form is typically artful, each six-line stanza having the rhyme scheme a b b a a b, or internal rhyming couplets bordered on either side by the contrasting rhyme, the first couplet with accented line endings, the second with unaccented endings. The gently swaying, dancing rhythms of the poem are due in part to the two internal anapaestic feet in each line, the lightness calculatedly at odds with the poetic content by the poem's end. The art of saying bitter, despairing things in a dance-like lilt is a device few poets have used successfully; A. E. Housman was the pre-eminent practitioner of the art in English, but there are not many specimens in German verse. "Der liebliche Stern" (written, one notes, during Schulze's wartime service!) begins with its form and content seemingly in accord, but as the poem unfurls, the misery first evident in the last line of stanza 1 grows blacker and heavier until it is horribly dissonant with the unchanged lilting rhythms. In this context, the discrepancy between the two is expressive, beyond any other means one could imagine, of Nature's and the sweetheart's collective indifference to the poet. His powerlessness to change them, to alter anything in accord with his own desires, is summed up in the way he tunes his misery to their rhythm and is then unable to cease doing so.

"Der liebliche Stern" is among those Schubert songs "to be sung on the water" in which watery reflections of the beloved meld with thoughts of death; "Tränenregen" from *Die schöne Müllerin* and "Widerschein," D. 639 to a poem by Franz Xaver von Schlechta are others, the former particularly striking for its resemblances to Schulze's poem. Schulze's bereft lover sees the star he loved and lost reflected in the waters and longs for death down below, while the miller-lad gazes into the brook in company with the miller maid and hears it beckoning him to follow ("Geselle, mir nach!"). But the miller does not yet realize that the brook beckons him to a watery death and Schulze does; when the miller *does* realize it, he heeds the invitation and drowns himself in the depths of the brook, whereas Schulze, like the wanderer in *Winterreise*, cannot bring himself to commit suicide and longs instead for a tempest to sweep him away to death involuntarily.

Schubert had earlier been drawn to poems of "Wohl und Weh," that untranslatable sense of pleasurable melancholy induced by the contemplation of Nature, for two of his greatest songs, "Wehmut" (Melancholy), D. 772, to a poem by Matthäus von Collin, composed in 1822 (?), and Mayrhofer's "Erlafsee." The phrase recurs in Schulze's "Am 28. April 1814," and it might seem that "Wohl und Weh" were again the inspiration for the unstably shifting alternation between parallel major and minor chords throughout the song.[116] However, the contrast that drives the poem – the nocturnal serenity of the sea counterposed to the poet's mingled fury and pain – is far more extreme than the gentler "Wohl und Weh" of stanza 1. As the poem progresses, the anguish becomes rapidly more intense, culminating in the desire for tempests that would submerge the hated gentle motion in violence. And yet, the crescendo of increasing tension and the progressive darkening of the poem are only allowed flickering, momentary expression in the music. According to John Reed, Schubert "ignores the tragic hints in the last two verses of the poem," while Capell states that "Der liebliche Stern" (which he dubbed a "little pearl") is in "a lighter mood," its "dainty accompaniment figure" reflecting the dancing stars in the lake.[117] But the death-wish in the final stanza is far more than a hint, and it is inconceivable to me that Schubert would thus blot out the most significant level of meaning in the poetic text while still retaining the words in his musical setting. He had no qualms about ignoring certain aspects of a poem (but not the most important ones) or omitting those portions of a text which he found to be incompatible with his purposes, but that is not the case here.

Far from ignoring the poem, I believe that Schubert read it more closely than his commentators. Above all, he paid heed to the frustrated question and fruitless demand, "Breezes, why do you lull the rocking boat in gentle play? Drive it along a rougher course, down into the whirlpool!", in the final stanza. He understood that what has driven the poetic persona to self-destructive fury is precisely the *lack* of response to his wishes on the part of everything around him and his inability to change anything at all, in this lied, the inability to change the music that surrounds him. He is not even permitted to cry "Drive it along a rougher course" in a way that accords musically with the violence of his demand, but is forced to conform to the light, gentle, lulling motion around him, just as the poet's alter ego is forced by his creator to continue the same dance-like rhythms throughout. The peculiar terror of a situation in which one must speak of death while dancing and the horror of Nature's indifference to the human heart are Schulze's macabre achievements in this entry from his diary, magnified all the more by Schubert's music – "light" only in the same sense that "Täuschung" from *Winterreise* is "light ... a naive dance tune." Only madmen dance to such tunes.

In Schubert's conception, despair produces only hints quickly suppressed and replaced by the water music of the introduction. His poetic persona is as if trapped amidst the broken-chordal wavelets, the song accordingly fixed throughout on G major (one notes in particular the G pedal point in the bass through mm. 1–15 and 18–21, the D pedal in mm. 22–31). The fixity of the tonality is among the most significant indices of tragic insight: the poetic persona longs for violent transport to another place, to the realm of Death down below, but Nature refuses his wish, and he remains where he is, accommodating his tune to the watery motion that never stops and never pauses. The only darkening or heaviness is rendered in short-lived hints, such as the G minor harmonies first heard in m. 13 (Schubert shades "Wohl und Weh" in parallel minor, as if to underscore which one predominates) and the emphatic mediant harmonies first heard in m. 16 – "schwer" indeed. But the added weight lasts less than a measure before shading, first, back to tonic minor and then G major in the piano interlude, although the minor subdominant harmony in m. 18 darkens the texture for an instant before being "corrected" to C major in m. 20, dispelling the hint of gloom completely. The purpose of the piano interludes which follow both stanzas 1 and 2 is to reinstate an unsullied G major, purified of even this minute trace of the protagonist's grief. The same progression first heard in mm. 12–16, with its G minor and B-flat major "heaviness," recurs even more emphatically at the words "Doch kann ich das schönste nicht finden" (But I cannot find the most beautiful one) at the end of stanza 2; here, the gently swaying rhythmic pattern is replaced by out-and-outright muffled pounding in the bass and by *Terzensteigerung* in the vocal line. Were the crescendo in mm. 30–32 to continue, the whirlpool might indeed engulf him, but it is checked in m. 33 and brought back to tonic tranquillity in the interlude.

There are even fewer hints of minor when Schulze longs openly for death. Schubert sets the last lines of stanza 3 ("Tief unten, da möcht' es gelingen, / Das friedliche Ziel zu erringen, / Tief unten, da ruht' ich so gern") and the final lines of stanza 4 ("O treibt ihn auf rauherer Bahn, / Hernieder ins Wogengewühle! / Laßt tief in der wallenden Kühle / Dem lieblichen Sterne mich nahn!") to the same music (mm. 47–54 and mm. 62–69), the only hints of disturbance being the diminished seventh chords in mm. 47, 49, 62, 63, and 64 and the erotically-charged rising chromatic configuration in both the vocal line and the accompaniment at the words "ruht' ich so gern" in mm. 51–52 and "tief in der wallenden Kühle" in mm. 66–67. The diminished seventh chords, one notices, are voiced in what seems a symbolically suggestive manner: the chromatic tones surround and enfold the vocal line, which remains diatonic, before reinstating the prior unclouded dominant chords. The singer attempts to enact "Tief unten" and the plea "O treibt ihn [auf rauherer Bahn]" musically by means of octave leaps downward, but the light, lilting patterns continue, nullifying the traces of desperation. The gulf between sound and sense could not be more drastic, especially when the death-haunted words "Tief unten, da ruht' ich so gern!" are set to the most tritely innocuous $\hat{5}\ \hat{4}\ \hat{3}\ \hat{2}\ \hat{1}$ melodic contour imaginable (mm. 53–54). And yet, the hints of tragedy persist, however suppressed. Schubert's heartsick persona at the end pleads "Laßt tief in der wallenden Kühle / Dem lieblichen Sterne mich nahn!" to *pianissimo* plagal harmonies in mm. 70–71, its prayerful connotations unmistakable. Perhaps most affecting of all, major subdominant shades to minor in mm. 75 and 77 of the postlude, reversing the prior relationship, and the oft-repeated accompaniment figure first stated on the second beat of m. 2 is here extended as the final three measures of the postlude, ending with D in the topmost voice. If one hears this figure (albeit with a certain poetic license) as a directional metaphor in music for the poet looking upwards at the inaccessible star, then Schubert tells us in this final gesture that his poetic persona continues to do so after the words cease, indeed, ends by staring fixedly up above. In real life, he did so for three further years of misery after 28 April 1814.

5. "Tiefes Leid," D. 876 is a setting of "Am 17. Januar 1817" from the *Poetisches Tagebuch*. The undated autograph manuscript of Schubert's setting is now in the Bodleian Library at Oxford, where it is entitled simply "Am 17ten Januar 1817." The title "Tiefes Leid" also appears on the manuscript, but not in Schubert's hand – no one knows who selected those key words from the third and final stanza of Schulze's poem for a song first published in 1838 in book 30 of the *Nachlaß*.

Ich bin von aller Ruh geschieden	All peace has forsaken me;
Und treib' umher auf wilder Flut;	I am tossed upon the stormy waters.
An einem Ort nur find' ich Frieden,	In one place alone I shall find peace:
Das ist der Ort, wo Alles ruht.	the place where all things rest.
Und wenn die Wind' auch schaurig sausen	Though the wind may whistle eerily
Und kalt der Regen niederfällt,	and the rain fall coldly,
Doch mag ich dort viel lieber hausen,	I would far rather dwell there
Als in der unbeständ'gen Welt.	than in this fickle world.
Denn wie die Träume spurlos schweben	For as dreams float away without a trace
Und einer schnell den andern treibt,	as one swiftly succeeds another,
Spielt mit sich selbst das irre Leben,	so life is a dizzy whirl:
Und jedes naht und keines bleibt.	everything draws near, nothing remains.
Nie will die falsche Hoffnung weichen,	False hope never fades,
Nie mit der Hoffnung Furcht und Müh;	nor with that hope, fear and toil.
Die Ewigstummen, Ewigbleichen	The ever-silent, the ever-pale
Verheißen und versagen nie.	never promise and never deny.
Nicht weck' ich sie mit meinen Schritten	I shall not awaken them in their dark
In ihrer dunkeln Einsamkeit,	solitude with my footsteps;
Sie wissen nicht, was ich gelitten,	They do not know what I have suffered;
Und Keinen stört mein tiefes Leid.	my deep sorrow disturbs none of them.
Dort kann die Seele freier klagen	There my soul can lament more freely
Bei Jener, die ich treu geliebt;	with her whom I have truly loved.
Nicht wird der kalte Stein mir sagen,	The cold stone will not tell me, alas,
Ach, daß auch sie mein Schmerz betrübt![118]	that my suffering distresses her too.

Bouterwek praised Schulze for his ruthless elimination of rhetorical flourishes from his poetry, and this poem exemplifies that stylistic austerity, in particular, the simple declarative statements of stanza 1. As autobiography, the poem is distressing in its diagnostic accuracy: "False hope never fades," he wrote, "and with that hope, fear and toil." By January of 1817, Schulze, banned from Adelheid's presence and mortally ill, could recognise his pathology, but could not do anything to alter it for the better. The gulf between purely intellectual recognition of mental illness and the capacity to rectify matters could not be more poignantly hymned than here. Beset by the intolerable evanescence of all things, the poet longs for stasis and knows he can only find it in death. Aware that his grief had become oppressive to others, he visits in verse the cemetery where Cäcilie is buried, a ghostly simulacrum of the press of humanity, where he might lament without offending anyone. There is no consolation in the thought of an afterlife; Schulze had long since lost the faith he briefly acquired in the wake of Cäcilie's death, nor does he envision reunion after death with the beloved who was never truly his. The words "auch sie" in the final line of the poem are, one would guess, a reference to Adelheid, "auch" the tiniest of clues that the cold stone (Cäcilie) and "she" are two separate beings. The lamenting exclamation "Ach" divides the two sisters, but belongs more to the living beloved. She, after all, was the more recent loss and elicited sharper pangs of grief.

Schubert, taking his cue from Schulze's contrast between the hurly-burly of grief and life on one hand and the comforting silence of the grave on the other, divides the musical strophe into symmetrical halves of parallel minor-major modes, the first (lines 1–6 of each octave stanza) filled with musical devices to suggest restlessness, the second (lines 7 and 8) marked by the absence of conflict. Schubert forecasts the later appearance of tonic major in mm. 3–4 of the piano introduction, but not the restfulness of the cemetery; the introduction belongs with the first half of the musical strophe, the postlude with the latter half. ("Tiefes Leid" is akin to the Mignon song "Heiss mich nicht reden," likewise composed in January 1826, likewise in E minor with a patch of parallel major, likewise the song of a creature trapped in an "unbeständ'gen Welt.") Schubert lingers over the final two lines of each of Schulze's stanzas – his poetic persona would indeed "viel lieber hausen" in E major peacefulness and dwells upon its strains until his grief drives him back to minor mode and the more frenetic pace of the first half. There, the singer and pianist rush through a line of Schulze's verse in a mere measure-and-a-half, but with the word "*will* [ich dort viel lieber hausen]," the singer lingers on the verb of choice for two full beats – thereafter, a line of text consumes three measures, twice as long, while the lulling syncopated ostinato in the right-hand part could well have been the inspiration for Hugo Wolf's similar rhythmic device throughout "Sterb' ich, so hüllt in Blumen" from the *Italienisches Liederbuch*. The motion almost, but not quite, melts away the barline boundaries, as if the poetic persona were suspended in some hypnotically swaying other-world, no longer earthbound.

Schubert's choice of 3/4 meter for "Tiefes Leid" seems particularly apt because measures in triple meter cannot be divided into equal halves whose symmetry underscores calm or peacefulness; here, the restlessness of grief prevails. For the E minor half of the song, Schubert brings back the neutral chordal pulsations of "Trock'ne Blumen" and then fills the section with a plethora of weak-beat accents. Between the first three vocal phrases, one finds the weak-beat accented semitone figures in the bass that one would later find both in "Um Mitternacht," composed two months later, and in *Winterreise*. The melodic style at the beginning is similar to "Wasserflut" (also in E minor and similarly with cadences on G major) in *Winterreise*, that is, a rising arpeggiated line whose apex on the second beat of the measure is then prolonged; in this way, it is the adjective "aller" rather than the noun "Ruh'" that is stressed in m. 5. Schubert sets the varied echo of those same words in m. 11 ("Das ist der Ort, wo *Alles* ruht") as a more exaggerated prolongational accent: not only do the voice and left hand sustain a fermata-prolonged D (not yet harmonized, for greater austere emphasis on the stressed initial syllable) but the right hand chimes in on the second half of the third beat with its own fermata. There as well, Schubert turns briefly to G major, the key of *Ruhigkeit*, albeit darkened by the flatted sixth degree of G, or E-flat – so near and yet so far from the root of E minor. In the last two phrases of the first half of the musical strophe ("Und wenn die Wind' auch schaurig sausen, / Und kalt der Regen niederfällt"), however, the weak-beat accents disappear, in preparation for the consolatory turn to major mode at the words "Doch will ich dort viel lieber hausen," and the bass descends straight downwards throughout mm. 13–18, from E to G-sharp, downward to the grave.

It is here in mm. 18–36 that one hears a foreshadowing of "Im Wirtshaus," in which the same traits appear more complexly developed. In his setting of stanza 2 of "Das Wirtshaus" ("Ihr grünen Totenkränze / Könnt wohl die Zeichen sein, / Die müde Wandrer laden / Ins kühle Wirtshaus ein"), Schubert has the soprano part in the accompaniment branch off into a higher obbligato voice above the middle register for the singer, an effect similar to *Blaskapelle* music, or solemn wind and brass music to accompany burial. In Johann Gabriel Seidl's "Das Zügenglöcklein," D. 871, possibly also composed in 1826, and in "Des Baches Wiegenlied," the last song of *Die schöne Müllerin*, Schubert similarly associated octave pedal points in the right hand and treble register with peaceful passing, with death as a boon to anguished humanity. And yet the bass line throughout the second half of the stanza never descends to low E, brushing close to the implied bottommost goal, but never achieving the ultimate surcease. When the root of the tonic harmony appears in the final texted cadence, it is in the higher register, the tessitura of the "unbeständ'gen Welt."

6.   Two months later, Schubert returned to the *Poetisches Tagebuch* for the last time to compose three songs and a fragment of a fourth. The March 1826 Schulze songs include "Um Mitternacht," D. 862, a setting of Schulze's "Am 5. März 1815, Nachts um 12 Uhr."

Keine Stimme hör' ich schallen,
Keinen Schritt auf dunkler Bahn,
Selbst der Himmel hat die schönen
Hellen Aeuglein zugethan.

I hear no voice,
no footstep on the dark path;
even heaven has closed
its beautiful, bright eyes.

Ich nur wache, süßes Leben,
Schaue sehnend in die Nacht,
Bis dein Stern in öder Ferne
Lieblich leuchtend mir erwacht.

I alone am awake, sweet life,
gazing longingly into the night
until, in the bleak distance, your star
awakens me with its lovely radiance.

Ach, nur einmal, nur verstohlen
Dein geliebtes Bild zu sehn,
Wollt' ich gern im Sturm und Wetter
Bis zum späten Morgen stehn!

Ah, if I could see your beloved image
but once, secretly,
I should gladly stand until late morning,
even in storm and tempest!

Seh' ich's nicht schon ferne leuchten?
Naht es nicht schon nach und nach?
Ach, und freundlich hör ich's flüstern:
Sieh, der Freund ist auch noch wach.

Do I not see it shining in the distance?
Is it not gradually approaching?
Ah, I hear it whispering gently:
See, your friend is still awake.

Süßes Wort, geliebte Stimme,	Sweet words, beloved voice,
Der mein Herz entgegenschlägt!	at which my heart beats!
Tausend sel'ge Liebesbilder	Your breath has stirred within me
Hat dein Hauch mir aufgeregt.	a thousand blissful images of love.
Alle Sterne seh' ich glänzen	I see all the stars glittering
Auf der dunkelblauen Bahn,	on their dark-blue path;
Und im Herzen hat und droben	the sky has cleared, up above
Sich der Himmel aufgethan.	and within my heart.
Holder Nachhall, wiege freundlich	Sweet echo, now lull my head
Jetzt mein Haupt in milde Ruh,	to gentle rest.
Und noch oft, ihr Träume, lispelt	Dreams, whisper often to me
Ihr geliebtes Wort mir zu![119]	her beloved words.

As in "Der liebliche Stern," the beloved is apotheosized as a star in the heavens, but to consolatory purposes, "Am 5. März 1815" the optimistic obverse of "Am 28. April 1814." This poem epitomizes the machinations of obsession: the fact that Schulze, devoid of any real affirmation of reciprocated love, could continually call up poetic hallucinations and persuade himself of their possible transformation into future reality is precisely why the miserable matter dragged on as long as it did. Like a child who seeks its mother's presence at bedtime as a bulwark against fears of abandonment and death, the poetic persona feels his inner darkness most acutely at midnight, with a long stretch of blackest night left to endure, and calls up a vision of his beloved as comfort. When he does so, her image transforms the darkness into star-spangled clarity, and he can then fall asleep and dream of her, dreams in which she says what *he* would have her say. This is a fantasy with roots in infantile distress, and it seems only fitting that Schulze chose a folk-like form and meter for this lullaby in which he is both mother and child and must sing himself to sleep.

The chordal textures of hymnody – this is also a vigil song in which a latter-day minstrel-knight is rewarded with a vision of his lady – are here disrupted by multiple indices of conflict and disquiet.[120] In the introduction, jostling right- and left-hand weak-beat accents consume the entire second beat in 2/4 meter; the anacrusis perhaps conceived to emphasize the dread adjective "Keine" when the body of the song begins is thus appropriately fraught with rhythmic tensions. When the figure is repeated sequentially, the impression of heavy sighing, of depression and descent (the upbeat pitches are higher than the downbeat resolutions), is all the greater. The motive which follows the accent-laden anacrusis figures foreshadows *Winterreise* perhaps more strongly than anything else in the Schulze songs. In the second line of stanza 1, Schulze invokes a "dark path" with "no footsteps" ("Keinen Schritt auf dunkler Bahn"), an allegorical emblem for life as a gloomy journey in isolation. Schubert, in mm. 2–3 of the introduction, states a motive of four repeated non-legato G minor chords – he would later use that same motive, in many permutations, harmonizations, and guises, throughout "Gute Nacht" and "Der Wegweiser," where it is the musical symbol of the winter journey itself.[121] At the end of the introduction and the end of the song, Schubert lifts the "journeying figure" and its cadential tag into the treble register of sleep and sweet dreams, the second time with two slight but significant alterations: the E-natural in the inner voice of m. 5 and tonic closure in the soprano voice at the very end. Where there were only the non-legato G minor chords before (mm. 2–3), there is now passing motion that leads from minor to major, dark to bright, anguish to peace.

Schubert's musical strophe encompasses two of Schulze's stanzas and is divided into symmetrical halves, each one a variation of the figures from the introduction. Again, Schubert's understanding of his poet seems almost uncanny: the poet's desire for consolation, for the hallucination of love if the real thing could not be had, is epitomized in the hymn-like parallel sixths that fill the song and in such details as the Baroque passing tones and anticipation tones doubled in parallel thirds in m. 10. (According to Spaun's testimony, Schubert assiduously studied the works of Bach and Handel in his youth, and trace-elements of the Baroque are not difficult to locate in his music; however, it is intriguing to speculate that he might also have read the fourth volume of the collected works in his search for composable poetry and therefore discovered the Cäcilie-Bach connection.) But the persona's depression and anxiety are in conflict with the consolatory strains, as in mm. 10–12 at the words "Selbst der Himmel hat die schönen [hellen Äuglein zugethan]." There, one finds, buried low in the bass (much lower than the bass register before and after it), offbeat-accented semitone figures in chromatic descent, the same sort of "sighing figures" that one later finds sprinkled throughout the first half of *Winterreise*, often with similar offbeat accents and dissonant appoggiaturas likewise redolent of psychic distress. Schubert's persona, determined to find consolation, overturns the deep bass sighs by means of the vocal leap upwards to high G-natural, thus replacing the darkened bass G-flat, at the word "hellen" – bright enough to overcome (temporarily) the misery so economically limned in the previous measures.

Such overt hints of distress are largely banned from the second half of the strophe. Instead, on three occasions (the end of the interlude between halves, mm. 22–24, and m. 29), the phrase seems as if about to turn to darker relative minor, whose association with night is spelled out explicitly in mm. 22–24 at the words "Schaue sehnend in die Nacht." Each time, the threat of G minor melancholy is deterred and the music steered back to a brighter, more comforting harmonic realm, a turn whose significance is apparent when "Nacht" on V/G minor in m. 24 is succeeded by dominant seventh chords of E-flat at the words "Bis dein Stern in öder Ferne / Lieblich leuchtend mir erwacht." Refusing to acknowledge the "öder Ferne" in musical terms, Schubert's persona instead sings those words to most un-"öder" plagal harmonies, passing through the "bleak distance" in order to arrive at high G once again for the stressed adjective "lieblich." It is a gesture which epitomizes the whole poem: the lover is determined to bypass the "bleak distances" and fix his attention on the gentle light. That he is only able to do so incompletely is the quiet tragedy of this song, all the more so as the seventh and final stanza of Schulze's poem is set by itself to a repetition of the first half of the musical strophe, but with no second half to follow. Thus, the hopeful words "Und noch oft, ihr Träume, lispelt [ihr geliebtes Wort]" are set to yet another recurrence of the chromatic sighing figures in the low bass. Not even his dreams can banish disquiet entirely. Schubert, after all, did not set this poem as a through-composed progression from blackest night at the beginning to starlit epiphany at the end, but rather as a quietly fraught, strophic hymn-cum-lullaby, the same throughout. Nothing truly changes between the beginning and the end, and Schubert knew it.

7.   That same month, Schubert composed one of the greatest jewels in all of his œuvre: "Im Frühling," D. 882, or "Am 31. März 1815."

Still sitz' ich an des Hügels Hang,	I sit silently on the hillside;
Der Himmel ist so klar,	the sky is so clear.
Das Lüftchen spielt im grünen Thal,	The breeze plays in the valley
Wo ich beim ersten Frühlingsstrahl	where once, in the first rays of spring,
Einst, ach, so glücklich war;	I was, oh, so happy.
Wo ich an ihrer Seite ging	Where I walked by her side,
So traulich und so nah,	so tender and so close,
Und tief im dunkeln Felsenquell	and saw, deep in the dark, rocky stream
Den schönen Himmel blau und hell,	the fair sky, blue and bright,
Und sie im Himmel sah.	and her, reflected in that sky.
Sieh, wie der bunte Frühling schon	See how the colorful spring
Aus Knosp' und Blüte blickt!	already peeps from bud and blossom!
Nicht alle Blüten sind mir gleich,	Not all the blossoms are the same to me:
Am liebsten pflück' ich von dem Zweig,	I like most of all to pluck them from
Von welchem sie gepflückt.	the branch which she has plucked.
Denn Alles ist wie damals noch,	For all is still as it was then,
Die Blumen, das Gefild,	the flowers, the fields.
Die Sonne scheint nicht minder hell,	The sun shines no less brightly,
Nicht minder freundlich schwimmt im Quell	and the sky's bright-blue image
Das blaue Himmelsbild.	bathes in the stream no less cheerfully.
Es wandeln nur sich Will' und Wahn,	Only will and delusion change,
Es wechseln Lust und Streit,	joy alternates with strife.
Vorüber flieht der Liebe Glück,	The happiness of love flies past,
Und nur die Liebe bleibt zurück,	and only love remains behind,
Die Lieb' und ach, das Leid!	love and, alas, sorrow!
O wär' ich doch das Vöglein nur	Oh, if only I were that little bird
Dort an dem Wiesenhang!	there on the sloping meadow!
Dann blieb' ich auf den Zweigen hier	Then I would stay on these branches here
Und säng' ein süßes Lied von ihr	and sing a sweet song about her
Den ganzen Sommer lang.[122]	all summer long.

Only two years had passed between the time that Schulze first began openly courting Adelheid in the early spring of 1813 – "beim ersten Frühlingsstrahl" – and the end of March 1815. In those two scant years, "the happiness of love" had indeed flown, although at the time he wrote this poem, Schulze had deluded himself into thinking that Adelheid was treating him more kindly, that he might perhaps remain nearby on sufferance, if nothing else, and hymn her "den ganzen Sommer lang." Like Dante's Francesco da Rimini in Canto V of the *Inferno*, Schulze sings his own variation on the famous words "Nessun maggior dolore, / che ricordarsi del tempo felice / nella miseria" (There is no greater sorrow than to recall a happy time in wretchedness) and remembers past springtime love through the scrim of present loss, all the sharper because the season and the scene are the same. Sadly, there is a kind of honor in Schulze's poetry; he lied to himself and to his friends about the supposed reciprocal love between him and the Tychsen sisters, but he does not lie in his poems. He recalls the walk by the mountainside lake with Adelheid in 1813 (again, *reflets dans l'eau*), but he does not say that she loved him, and he diagnoses his own condition in the fifth stanza with remarkable clarity. Schulze the inveterate craftsman disposes all this wistfulness and pain into an ingenious stanzaic structure, with each five-line stanza in the rhyme scheme a b c c b, the rhyming second and fifth lines in trimeters and the remaining lines in tetrameters. Every line ends with an accented syllable, thus slowing the tempo of the poem to a reflective pace. Translators, unaware of the background in obsession, render the alliterative "Will und Wahn" in stanza 5 as "will and *whim*,"[123] but "Wahn" is more aptly colored in darker shades as "delusion" or "madness," the same "dunkle Wahn" invoked in "An mein Herz" and "Über Wildemann." Schulze does not once in stanza 5 refer to himself directly, to "me," "mine," or "I," although the implication is clear; in this way, he can both objectify his condition and be spared the additional pain of naming himself as the one buffeted between will and delusion (pain breaks out irresistibly in the exclamation "Ach" in the final line of stanza 5). But, knowing all this, the poet still ends by reverting to "Wahn," by wishing to be a bird that remains nearby and "sings of her" the entire summer long, for all of life's blossoming season.

The magic of Schubert's song begins with the introduction – John Reed calls this the greatest of Schubert's spring songs, and he is right.[124] Was there ever a more affecting use of the initial progression I–III–IV–I or the scale degrees $\hat{8}$-$\hat{7}$-$\hat{6}$ than in m. 1 and thereafter? The music of m. 1 compels a closer look for its assemblage of refined details, the result a grace all its own. The tonic chord stated without anacrusis on the first beat is repeated on the second half of the beat, where it becomes a chordal appoggiatura to the mediant chord with which it is slurred. That mediant chord is then slurred to the subdominant harmony on the third beat, which is also repeated en route to the tonic chord on the fourth beat, after a miniature "drive-to-cadence" in the form of the sixteenth notes in the soprano that retrace the ascent $\hat{6}$-$\hat{7}$-$\hat{8}$. The description is inevitably dry and labored, but not so the musical effect. The slight rhythmic asymmetry (too often glossed over by pianists) produced by the slurred figures in the context of an even eighth-note tactus, by the eighth note – quarter note – eighth note pattern in the inner voices, might here seem evocative of the faint lilt of bygone happiness and the gentle play of the "Lüftchen … im grünen Thal," but it returns in the setting of the fifth stanza (the crux of the poem) in diminution as an index of disquiet and grief and thereafter persists, albeit banished to the bass, in the setting of the sixth and final stanza. Not until the repetition of the words "Ich säng' von ihr den ganzen Sommer lang" in mm. 48–49 can the singer charm away the rhythmic unease born so quietly in m. 1.

Because melodic motion is so restricted in the initial two-measure antecedent phrase, because it is entirely conjunct until m. 4, the effect of the rising gesture, the leap upward to E in the voice above the raised fourth degree in the bass, is disproportionately moving. It becomes even more so at the end of the song in m. 49 when a variation of this same progression is set to the words "den ganzen Sommer lang," with fermatas prolonging the V/V on the second beat of the measure, the apex of the leap upwards on the first syllable of "*gan* - [zen]." But that chord is a *passing* inverted seventh chord on a weak beat, and lingering on it is impossible; if the performers remain there a millisecond too long, listeners fidget, even the musically uneducated subliminally aware that the attempt to hold on to the fermata-sustained chord is futile. Schubert could not have found a more perfect way to represent the impossibility of the poet-singer's desire. Even as he sings "ganzen," it slips away, impelled by the forward impulsion of the harmonic progression, while "lang" endures no more than a beat. If, in describing the introduction, I keep referring to the end, perhaps that will serve to underscore what a perfect unity this song is, how seamless the fabric from beginning to end.

Even though the symmetrical introduction ends with a perfect authentic cadence on tonic G major (the same Nature key as "Der liebliche Stern"), the cadence concludes on the fourth beat, and the voice chimes in with the anacrusis "Still [sitz' ich]" on the second half of that beat. Like the lapping water of the other Schulze masterpiece, one section flows into another without a break. In one of the most exquisite details of an exquisite song, the Andante motion is occasionally suspended, the gentle flow of sound halted – not broken by silence, but lingering on a fermata-prolonged secondary dominant, with the voice leaping upwards to the flatted seventh degree (the first occurrence is in m. 14 at the words "[den schönen Himmel blau] und *hell*"). The heightened tension, however muted by the reflective atmosphere of the song, is undeniable, given the atypical (for this song) large leap upward, the tritone dissonance between the soprano and bass voices, the fermata prolonging the fourth beat of the measure. The drama seems, but only seems, unwarranted by the words. What about the "beautiful, bright blue sky" in stanza 2 could have produced this electric charge of desire? Actually, it seems most likely that Schubert devised the gesture in accord with the fourth line of stanza 6, "Und säng ein süsses Lied von *ihr*" [italics mine], the word "her" invested with all the yearning urgency Schubert could supply, and then applied it earlier in the song. It is almost as apropos in stanza 2 as a desire-laden prelude to the words "Und *sie* im Himmel sah" [italics mine], the mere mention of "her" enough to unleash this quietly fraught passage. Once heard, it is unforgettable. No matter that the phrase is not particularly apt for the lines "Nicht minder freundlich schwimmt im Quell / Das blaue Himmelsbild" in stanza 4: where so much is so right, the occasional discrepancy between music tailored to one verse and the words of another in strophic settings is a small price to pay.

A single poetic "sentence" unfurls throughout stanzas 1 and 2, and Schubert accordingly sets them as a single musical strophe, which is then repeated and varied to the words of stanzas 3 and 4. The way in which Schubert accounts for the fact that stanzas 1 and 2 are part of the same larger statement and yet not really enjambed (there is a semicolon articulation between the two) is masterful: the cadential resolution to G major at the end of stanza 1 is simultaneously the beginning of a restatement of m. 1 of the introduction as the connective between the two halves of the poetic structure. When the singer enters, it is not on tonic harmonies that would make the words sound like the start of another "sentence," but on the supertonic and subdominant harmonies of m. 11. The vocal line of stanza 1 stays within the same octave span from E to E established in the topmost voice of the introduction until the words "… einst, *ach*, so glücklich war, so glücklich war." At the lamenting exclamation "ach," the singer breaks beyond the previous ceiling to the dissonant F-natural appoggiatura to E. Just before, in m. 8, the poetic persona remembers the springtime past, a memory Schubert evokes as a *pianississimo* reference to the supertonic realm, to the A major key so often associated with springtime and love in his songs. It is, poignantly, only a glancing reference, the springtime-bright chords darkening to parallel minor in m. 9. The same progression that leads to A major memories in m. 8 had earlier, in mm. 5–6, led somewhere else, to a brief emphasis on the subdominant harmony at the words "Der Himmel ist so klar," the harmonic skies clearing of all accidentals to produce a brief patch of pellucid C major. Schubert has the singer wistfully repeat the words "so glücklich war" as a sequential descent down a whole-step, from the supertonic to the tonic. The temperature is cooler, more resigned than the first statement, but the brief dissonance in m. 9 created by the flatted sixth degree and the appoggiatura B in the vocal line underscores the adjective "so" all the more. Furthermore, the harmonic rhythm quickens at those words "ach, so glücklich war, so glücklich war," as if the thought of past happiness impelled a touch of agitation. One hears the same quickening of the harmonic rhythm, the same drive-to-cadence, at the words "So traulich und so nah." Remembered intimacy causes the heart to beat faster.

Schulze counterposes remembered sight in stanza 2 to present sight in stanza 3, the one impelling the other: "sah" past tense at the end of stanza 2 is followed by the injunction "Sieh'" in the present. In Schubert's imagination, the bereft lover begins looking about him at the fresh beauties of springtime present in the piano interlude in mm. 17-20, a variation of the introduction from which all the subtle indices of rhythmic assymmetry have been dispelled, "bunte Frühling" clear as a bell. Everything lightens and quickens (eighth notes in the bass, sixteenth notes in the right hand), with the broken-chordal figuration in the right hand lifted an octave higher. When the voice enters, the treble part chimes above the voice, at times dipping below or sounding with it, but mostly set in an ethereal register above it. The slurred motives in the first strophe are now rhythmically altered, the repeated note occurring on the fourth subdivision of the beat. The gentle dancelike lilt is irresistible, but it does not last long. All is not "wie damals noch," and pain comes flooding back in the *minore* variation of stanza 5, which is even in the conventional place for such an episode – near the end.

Here in mm. 33-40, disquiet is manifest in offbeat rhythmic patterns in the right hand, while the sixteenth-note broken-chordal patterns move to the bass, rendering it heavier than in the previous strophes. In the two-bar passage for the piano alone preceding the singer's entrance, the descent G F-sharp E in m. 1 is extended the length of a seventh from G to A, literally a descent into tragedy. What had before been the melismatic play of "Lüftchen spielend im grünen Tal" is now the flight "vorüber" of bygone love's happiness, and the A major springtime harmonies ("beim ersten Frühlingsstrahl" in m. 8) are now Neapolitan A-flat harmonies, one of Schubert's favored ways of darkening and intensifying the descent to tonic minor. The love and the sorrow that remain behind when happiness is gone (mm. 38–39) momentarily come to rest on the A-flat harmonies first stated in the introduction; the hushed warmth of those borrowed chords is all the more moving when one knows that A-flat major is a tonality associated elsewhere in Schubert's songs with secure and reciprocated love, as in Friedrich Rückert's "Lachen und Weinen," D. 777, or Goethe's "Ganymed," D. 544, and "Geheimes," D. 719, although one need not know this in order to feel the effect of the small deflection to A-flat in "Im Frühling" and the relapse into G minor sadness when the singer repeats "und ach, das Leid" in mm. 39–40. (Schubert would later use the Neapolitan chord to unforgettable effect in the final section of another song in G minor, "Der Wegweiser" from *Winterreise*, while the scalewise descent in the piano part of mm. 33–34 through the Neapolitan sixth is premonitory of "Die Krähe.")

Stanza 5 is an abbreviated variation, unlike the paired stanzas of 1 and 2 (springtime past), 3 and 4 (springtime present) – "Will und Wahn" do not bear contemplating. The poet retreats into wishfulness in stanza 6 and longs, not for an end to sorrow (that, he realizes, would be impossible), but, pathetically, for toleration; he would be her poet-minstrel rather than her lover. In the abbreviated piano interlude between stanzas 5 and 6 (m. 40), Schubert tells us exactly when the thoughts of sadness are, first, halted in their course and then shifted into the musical subjunctive, into the realm of wish: he begins a repetition of the same scalewise descent first heard in mm. 33–34 at the start of the *minore* variation, but what had been a G minor chord on the fourth beat of m. 33 is here transformed to G *major* and arrested there, the sad slippage downwards to the Neapolitan and beyond halted in its tracks. Schubert's wishful, wistful poet then brings back the treble springtime beauty of stanzas 3 and 4 for the setting of stanza 6 but is unable to banish entirely the rhythmic traces of his sorrow, even though he buries them in the bass; the effort required to bring the left hand quickly upward from the low bass to levels more than an octave higher for the remainder of the chord on the second subdivision of the beat is a small musical emblem of the laboriousness of sorrow, the way in which it makes everything more difficult, and of the anxiety and tension underlying the words. But at the end, Schubert grants the bereft lover another brief spring idyll in what may well be the most moving detail of the song. At m. 48, the quickened, effortful rhythmic pattern in the bass vanishes, and the unclouded "bunte Frühling" of stanzas 3 and 4 (the second musical strophe) returns, the *pianississimo* dynamics a telling recollection of those "first rays of spring" in m. 8. Schubert foreshadows its return on the first beat of m. 46 at the word "ganzen," the smallest and sweetest of ways to underscore that telling adjective, but the asymmetrical pattern returns immediately thereafter and for a further two measures. Not until he musingly repeats his wish are the rhythms of sorrow banished.

The nature of that summer song is spelled out in one of Schubert's most poignant postludes, its brevity in sad contradiction to the last word of the song. The rising chromatic fragments previously buried in the bass (such as the approach to the dominant pitch through the raised fourth degree in the bass of mm. 2 and 4 in the piano introduction) step to the fore, with all their Mozartian connotations of eroticism delicately apparent. Perhaps most revealing of all, the chromatic anacruses twice lead to cadential resolution *on the weak beat*, the fermata-prolonged final tonic chord placed on the fourth beat of the measure, halted at the same point where the reestablished G major chord had appeared in m. 40. The certainty of sorrow ("und ach, das *Leid*," mm. 39–40) impels a downbeat resolution, but delusional fantasy is rendered as rhythmically off-balance, the "strength" of the authentic cadence and tonic closure in the vocal line countered by deliberate metrical weakness – this too belongs to the lengthy catalogue of musical gestures which indicate Schubert's awareness of Schulze's precarious mental state. It is also the most moving of endings for the most perfect of songs.

8. Schulze, recognizing his condition as pathological, periodically issued an urgent call to himself for revivification, for a phoenix-like renewal of youthful strength, as in "Am 1. April 1815," which Schubert entitled "Lebensmut," D. 883. The poem was, one notices, written the day after "Am 31. März 1815," or "Im Frühling." If the wistful memories of springtime past gave rise to a frenetic surge of energy the next day, it was truly an April Fool's phenomenon.

O wie dringt das junge Leben	How vigorously young life
Kräftig mir durch Sinn und Herz!	pulses through my mind and heart!
Alles fühl' ich glühn und streben,	I feel everything is glowing and aspiring,
Fühle doppelt Lust und Schmerz.	I feel pleasure and pain doubly.
Fruchtlos such' ich euch zu halten,	In vain I seek to restrain you,
Geister meiner regen Brust!	spirits of my quickened breast!
Nach Gefallen mögt ihr walten,	You rule at will,
Sei's zum Leide, sei's zur Lust.	whether it be for sorrow or for pleasure.
Lodre nur, gewalt'ge Liebe,	Blaze on, mighty Love,
Höher lodre nur empor!	blaze higher!
Brecht, ihr vollen Blütentriebe,	Burst open, ripe, blossoming desires,
Mächtig schwellend nur hervor!	swelling abundantly!
Mag das Herz sich blutig färben,	Let my heart be tinged with blood,
Mag's vergehn in rascher Pein;	let it perish swiftly in pain.
Lieber will ich ganz verderben,	I would rather be completely destroyed
Als nur halb lebendig sein.	than be only half-alive.
Dieses Zagen, dieses Sehnen,	This hesitation, this longing,
Das die Brust vergeblich schwellt,	that swells my breast in vain,
Diese Seufzer, diese Thränen,	these sighs, these tears

Die der Stolz gefangen hält,
Dieses schmerzlich eitle Ringen,
Dieses Kämpfen ohne Kraft,
Ohne Hoffnung und Vollbringen,
Hat mein bestes Mark erschlafft.

Lieber wecke rasch und mutig
Schlachtruf den entschlafnen Sinn!
Lange träumt' ich, lange ruht' ich,
Gab der Kette lang' mich hin.
Hier ist Hölle nicht, noch Himmel,
Weder Frost ist hier, noch Glut;
Auf ins feindliche Getümmel,
Rüstig weiter durch die Flut!

Daß noch einmal Wunsch und Wagen,
Zorn und Liebe, Wohl und Weh
Ihre Wellen um mich schlagen
Auf des Lebens wilder See,
Und ich kühn im tapfern Streite
Mit dem Strom, der mich entrafft,
Selber meinen Nachen leite,
Freudig in geprüfter Kraft.[125]

which pride holds captive,
this painful, futile struggle,
this fighting without strength,
without hope and fulfillment,
has sapped my whole being.

Rather let the quick, bold
battle-cry awaken my sleeping mind!
Long have I dreamt, long have I slumbered,
long have I yielded to the chain.
Here there is neither hell nor heaven,
neither frost nor fire.
Up, into the hostile tumult,
briskly beyond it, through the flood!

So that once more desire and daring,
anger and love, weal and woe
pound me with their waves
on life's stormy sea,
and I, bold, struggling bravely
with the current that sweeps me along,
steer my boat myself,
happy in my well-tried strength.

At the beginning, he claims renewed life and redoubled vital forces, but what might have seemed like optimism from someone else is here tainted by the revelation that he is wholly at the mercy of these "spirits of my quickened breast," or the divided and wounded selves at battle within him. When he bids "mighty Love" (one notes the grandiose designation of his obsessive love as "gewalt'ge") blaze higher in stanza 2, it is not, however, for hopeful reasons, but in order that his own heart might be consumed in the flames of a gigantic *Liebestod*. In the last line of stanza 2, we learn that the vitality asserted at the beginning is wish, not reality, that the poetic persona actually leads a sleepwalker's existence, his life sapped by the never-ending struggle with delusion and grief. "Brisk," "lively," "bold," "brave," "quick," "strongly": over and over, he invokes the energy, resolution, and life he no longer has. Of all the poems in the *Poetisches Tagebuch*, this is one of those most redolent of madness, the pitched armies in the battlefield that was Schulze's soul in heated combat. No one could read this poem and think him sane.

"Am 1. April 1815" poses a problem to any composer. How is one to create music that expresses both the impetuous, bold life the poet so desires, attempting to whip it into being merely by saying so, and the apathetic grief in which he is mired? Schubert's solution – a brilliant one – was to compose what one hears in retrospect as a preliminary study for "Mut" in *Winterreise*. There, the winter wanderer likewise longs for devil-may-care courage to overcome all obstacles in life but finds it difficult, and ultimately impossible, to suppress his pathological depression, for all the strenuous effort one hears in the song. The relationship between the two songs extends beyond the obvious kinship of their titles and their tempo designations ("Ziemlich geschwind, doch kräftig" for "Lebensmut," "Ziemlich geschwind, kräftig" for "Mut"): the falsity of the energy both poetic speakers invoke is conveyed by means of blustering over-emphasis, music which "doth protest too much."[126] The bluster is even more bombastic, more frantic, in the Schulze song than in *Winterreise* – but then, Schulze was closer to the brink of insanity than Müller's winter wanderer.

The tonal scheme of the two songs is even akin (the original tonality of "Mut" in the autograph manuscript, however, was A minor, the song subsequently transposed down a whole-step for the first edition). Despair in the principal key of G minor predominates in the later Müller song, but when the wanderer denies his grief most forcefully, he does so to pounding B-flat major chords that seem an echo from "Lebensmut." The signification of the relative major and minor modes is the same as well: the first vocal phrase of "Lebensmut" turns from the tonic B-flat major designating "strong young life" to a cadence on G minor at the words "durch Sinn und Herz," thus hinting at the true state of affairs. The poet's mind and heart are not really pulsating with renewed vitality, and the momentary deflection to relative minor, already foreshadowed in the submediant chords of mm. 1–2, tells us so. Just as in "Mut," the hints of grief demand immediate action, strenuous musical "correction" back to the desired brightness and energy in the piano interlude which follows (mm. 6–7). There, G minor is swiftly wrenched back to tonic major, the directional symbolism of the ascending motion notable as well. "Excelsior!", the music wordlessly cries and charges upward to renewed delusion (by happy coincidence, the cadence on G minor and the subsequent B-flat major cadence in the piano are equally applicable for the words "den entschlaf'nen Sinn!" in stanza 4 and the "Wohl und Weh" of stanza 6). A similar mechanism is operative in the second phrase as well, in which Schubert turns the music towards the subdominant key of E-flat (not, one notices, the strong dominant pole but the weaker subdominant) by the end of the phrase. At the invocation of "sorrow" ("doppelt Lust und *Schmerz*"), we hear a deceptive C minor (VI/IV) resolution on the word "Schmerz," which then must be vigorously corrected to major chord color and a firm cadence on E-flat, again, with a piano interlude which charges upward even higher than before and reasserts artificial energy.

The piano introduction to "Lebensmut" is already rife with signals of disquiet, most prominently in the clustered offbeat accents in the bass (the anacrusis to m. 1, the fourth beat of m. 1, and the second and fourth beats of m. 3). Whether conscious or unconscious echo from the past (probably the latter), the twofold descent in the bass in mm. 1–2 is reminiscent of the piano introduction to the "Lied des Orpheus, als er in die Hölle ging" (Song of Orpheus as he went to Hades), D. 474 of 1816 to a text by Johann Georg Jacobi – Schulze too was a poet-singer whose Eurydice was lost to him and who had descended into a hell of a different sort. The rhythmic figure of an eighth note and two sixteenth notes which fills the piano interludes is furthermore reminiscent of yet another earlier work: the Walter Scott song, "Lied des gefangenen Jägers" (Song of the imprisoned huntsman), D. 843 of April 1825, in which a more literally imprisoned poetic persona longs for the bold, vigorous life he once enjoyed and ends by proclaiming "Dahin ist Lieben und Leben" (Love and life are lost). It is no wonder Schubert recalled this song when he came to compose "Lebensmut" almost one year later.

Schubert sets stanzas 1 and 2 of Schulze's poem to the same music, but clearly shaped the musical strophe to the first stanza. As if the word "Schmerz" in stanza 1, line 4 had made it momentarily impossible to continue his bluster, Schulze laments – but in the same "strong" trochaic tetrameters as the self-exhortations to new vitality – his inability to rule over his tempestuous inner selves ("Fruchtlos such' ich euch zu halten, / Geister meiner regen Brust!"). Schubert registers the Angst and darkness of the words by emphasizing C minor harmonies and by doubling the vocal line, with its rising contour and tension-filled augmented second interval, in octaves in the bass (end of m. 11 through m. 12). Determined to accomplish what he knows to be fruitless, Schubert's Schulze next attempts to constrain the "spirits," to halt the tense, rising motion in its tracks. In a frantic attempt to deny his own words, to drown out the truth that breaks through the thin crust of assumed bravado, the verb "walten" impels an outbreak of the Walter Scott "Jäger" figuration in the piano elided with the verb itself. The reaction is instantaneous. As if unable to keep words he would rather not admit at bay ("Nach gefallen mögt ihr walten, / Sei's zum Leide, sei's zur Lust" in stanza 1, "Lieber will ich ganz verderben, / Als nur halb lebendig sein" in stanza 2), he repeats them over and over in mm. 16–20 but to music of almost featureless heartiness – artificiality becomes *forte* tinniness. Only at the end in m. 19 does "Leide" warp the melodic line into an arpeggiated ascent spanning a diminished octave from G to G-flat, the distinctive tinge of minor coloration immediately "corrected" by the subsequent authentic cadence.

When the words cease, the piano takes over in a lengthy conclusion to the musical strophe (seven measures, one-third of the entire strophe). These instrumental passages are drenched in poetic meaning: they are vivid, wordless enactments of processes within the protagonist's tortured mind. Recognising that the poet cannot stop himself from invoking the very distress he seeks to banish in this poem, Schubert once again, as in the brief instrumental interludes between vocal phrases, depicts an imagined inner struggle to reassert bold vital energies at even greater length and even more bombastically. The result is a musical portrait of insanity. These thundering codas quickly veer out of control, not only in their extended length but harmonically as well. Over and over, Schubert repeats the dominant seventh and tonic chords of B-flat major, with the *forzando* dominant seventh chords accented on the strong beats and the "resolution" to tonic each time occurring on the weak half of the first and third beats of the measure. Accent, meter, and harmonic progression are massively at odds with one another (mm. 22–23 in particular). Furthermore, the left-hand bass part jumps back and forth between high and low registers in a manner both remarkably difficult and palpably lunatic. It is as if the final passage of a Beethovenian coda had gone beserk. Both the insistence on B-flat major – "This must, and shall, be the key of new life," Schubert's Schulze hammers over and over – and the harmonic-rhythmic imbalance shout insanity aloud. *Forzando* hysteria in the middle of the coda is followed by the reinstatement of greater control. At the end of m. 23, Schubert has the pianist break away from the dominant-tonic

Example 25. Franz Schubert, "Lebensmut," D. 883, mm. 20–26.

progression, by now rendered unbearable, to massive repeated subdominant chords, followed by a cadence which concludes with the final measure of the piano introduction. We are thus ready to begin the whole mad roundelay yet again (ex. 25).

It is no longer possible to maintain major mode for the "hesitation, longing, tears, sighs, pained futility" of stanza 3, and Schubert accordingly switches to parallel minor mode and alters the brief interludes for piano such that the ascending figuration now descends sequentially in classic "falling tears" figuration; at the end of the coda, we hear a final echo of this figure high in the treble, the D-flat of minor mode emphasized for the last time before the reinstatement of tonic major. But despite the darkness of minor, the musical material and motion remain much the same as before, the result downright schizophrenic in its internal contradictions. A less perceptive composer might have read this stanza, in part correctly, as a relapse into unalloyed misery and therefore the occasion for contrasting strains, but Schubert continues the prior hearty rhythms (warped on occasion by the telling offbeat accents) and the "Jäger" figuration, disposed in the same formal design as before. The desire for renewed life is still present behind the hopeless words and will shortly give birth to another "call to arms," another self-admonition to charge forth into the "hostile tumult" (Schulze's characterization of life and the world as inimical to him evident once more), and Schubert allows us to hear that determination at work, even in the gloom of this *minore* episode. In a final affective detail, a chromatic passing tone in an inner voice produces a tonic major chord in the first bar of the coda (echoing the bass line from two measures earlier). The impression is that the singer-poet attempts to reinstate major mode vitality in the wake of the tragic final line of the stanza, but is unable to do so for longer than a single quarter-note beat and cannot thereafter dispel the shadows of minor mode until the second call for reawakened vitality in stanza 4 ("Lieber wecke rasch und mutig").

"Lebensmut" has been panned by commentators as "of inferior interest in spite of a brave beginning," lacking the subtlety of the best Schulze songs and filled with wearying repetitions. If the repetitiveness is indeed wearying, it is because what is repeated is unbearable. Schubert was bound to the mask of optimistic bluster Schulze assumes in this poem; although the composer unerringly registers those moments when the mask slips and the underlying truth emerges, it never slips completely and is quickly clamped back down over the abyss beneath. Hence, neither modulation nor far-ranging development is possible, only obsessional repetition and tonal fixity. The fascination of this song lies in the multiple means by which Schubert makes evident the suppression of grief, imminent hysteria, and the threatened loss of control, but it is not a comfortable work to hear, "beautiful" only in its fidelity to a disturbed and disturbing poem.

9.   That same month of March, when Schulze and Schubert were at their most perfectly attuned, Schubert also set "Über Wildemann," D. 884, a setting of Schulze's "Ueber Wildemann, einem Bergstädtchen am Harz. Den 28. April 1816" (Above Wildemann, a mountain village in the Harz Mountains. On 28 April 1816). This was probably the last of the Schulze songs to be composed and one of those most premonitory of *Winterreise* just around the corner.

Die Winde sausen	The winds whistle
Am Tannenhang,	over the pine-slope,
Die Quellen brausen	the streams rush
Das Thal entlang;	along the valley;
Ich wandr' in Eile	I hasten
Durch Wald und Schnee,	for many a mile
Wol manche Meile	through forest and snow,
Von Höh' zu Höh'.	from peak to peak.
Und will das Leben	And though life
Im freien Thal	in the open valley
Sich auch schon heben	already rises
Zum Sonnenstrahl,	to meet the sun's rays,
Ich muß vorüber	I must pass on,
Mit wildem Sinn	disturbed in spirit,
Und blicke lieber	preferring to look
Zum Winter hin.	towards winter.

Auf grünen Haiden,	In green fields,
Auf bunten Aun	in many-colored meadows,
Müßt' ich mein Leiden	I would only contemplate
Nur immer schaun,	my suffering endlessly,
Daß selbst am Steine	knowing that life
Das Leben sprießt,	burgeons from the very stones,
Und ach! nur Eine	and that, alas, only one
Ihr Herz verschließt.	closes her heart.
O Liebe, Liebe,	O love, love,
O Maienhauch!	O breath of May!
Du drängst die Triebe	You force the shoots
Aus Baum und Strauch!	from tree and bush!
Die Vögel singen	The birds sing
Auf grünen Höhn,	on green treetops,
Die Quellen springen	the springs gush forth
Bei deinem Wehn!	when you stir!
Mich läßt du schweifen	You leave me to roam
Im dunkeln Wahn	with my dark imaginings
Durch Windespfeifen	along the rough path,
Auf rauher Bahn.	in whistling winds.
O Frühlingsschimmer,	O gleam of spring,
O Blütenschein,	o sheen of blossoms,
Soll ich denn nimmer	shall I never again
Mich dein erfreun?[127]	delight in you?

"Über Wildemann" is Schulze at his most violent, with its Byronic protagonist striding from peak to peak in a frenzy. Here indeed was motion to inspire a bleak, ferocious song, in which everything rushes and shrieks, Nature and the protagonist alike. One suspects the place name was chosen with more than geographical location in mind: it is indeed a "wild man" who sings in Wildemann. Although Schubert dispenses with much of it, Schulze's longer title and the date of his poetic diary entry confirm the image of a bifurcated world, with spring already arrived in the valleys below but winter regnant on the heights where the poet stands. From his tempest-tossed winter fastness, he can see the verdant beauty below from which he is barred: Love and Nature give to others but not to him. Wherever he is, at whatever season, winter reigns.

"Über Wildemann" is a *Winterreise*, and it impelled an encapsulated foreshadowing of several songs in the later cycle, especially "Erstarrung" and the winter tempest in stanza 5 of "Der Lindenbaum"; the disposition of the triplet figures in the piano accompaniment into an octave-reinforced bass pitch on the first beat and a broken-octave echo in the right hand are the same in "Der Lindenbaum" and "Über Wildemann."[128] The protagonists of "Erstarrung" and this last Schulze song similarly engage in frantic motion because of a "dunkle Wahn" (dark delusion), and their panic-stricken desperation is similarly rendered in rapid triplet figuration, the wheel of obsession running nonstop through both songs; even the semitone figure on which Schubert harps throughout mm. 1–2 of "Über Wildemann" will remind some listeners of the way in which the left-hand melody of "Erstarrung" begins. Schubert would later use the D minor tonality for "Gute Nacht" at the start of the winter journey, perhaps reminded as he did so of this earlier winter journey through a bleak landscape of the soul,[129] while the rhythmic monomania in the vocal part recalls "Rückblick." Angst-ridden motion inspired in each instance the sacrifice of rhythmically inflected melody to the driven quality produced by prosody in equal note values. When the anguished poet invokes hurrying for mile after mile through the mountains, Schubert composes a study for "Der stürmische Morgen," in which the voice and piano in simultaneity also trace diminished seventh harmonies and increasingly larger intervals that rebound wildly from the dominant pitch (mm. 18–19). But despite all the ways in which "Über Wildemann" reminds the listener of Schubert's second Müller-cycle, it also has its own self-sufficient (and virtuosic) identity, compounded in part from the ascending scalewise motion which fills the song. It is as if the musical material itself was a peak the protagonist could, literally, scale in an attempt to outrun his anguish.

The crescendo through the initial two measures of "Über Wildemann," two measures fixated on the tonic and leading-note pitches, seems a mimicry of a mad thought, fixed in place but gaining momentum and then bursting forth into motion away from such a narrow circumference. Indeed, the setting of the first stanza is a study in increasingly larger and more angular motion, by the end expressive of massive desperation. The plunge downwards two-and-a-half octaves in a mere three beats (mm. 20–21) in the piano is shocking in its wildness, especially since the music rushes onwards without any pause. There is no internal acknowledgment that this gesture is extreme; if such extremity is the climate and topography alike of "Über Wildemann," it is nonetheless singular in its fraught tension. The alternation between unison texture and fuller harmonization seems to foreshadow "Die Wetterfahne," marked by the same lengthy stretches of unharmonized writing, while the *forzando* accents on the fourth beat are echoed in many of the songs in *Winterreise*. Those savage accents on the fourth beat thrust the dominant triads and secondary dominants of relative major which alternate with one another in the piano introduction starkly into the forefront, with consequences later in the body of the song, for example, the momentary cadential inflection on C-natural in m. 10 and at the corresponding place in the last stanza. The tonal shock of the first C major chord in m. 3 is all the greater because of the thrumming C-sharps of mm. 1–2. The effect of the alternating D minor and F major chords is that of someone too tormented either to stay in one place or define that place. The dominant chords are all triads, not seventh chords, and are furthermore all in root position: the elemental wildness of this musical landscape is due in some measure to this compositional choice. Nowhere, one notices, is the "wild man" of this song able to remain within an unadulterated D minor but instead reverts to this harmonic gesture whenever the strains from the beginning return, including the postlude. There, the order of events in the introduction is reversed: the restless D minor – F major alternation first, then two measures of thrumming chordal repetition culminating in a *forzando* minor chord.

One hears that final tonic harmony, with its fateful open fifth in the left hand, as a barrier to prevent the manic motion from continuing any longer.

The second and third stanzas of "Über Wildemann" are paired by their similar structures, each one split into contrasting zones of light and dark, the plunge back into darkness in each instance the result of compulsion ("Ich muss ... Müsst' ich"). For the first and brighter half of the second stanza, Schubert banishes the austerity of unison texture and no longer has the octave-reinforced bass line double the singer's part. Against the neutral chordal pulsations in the piano, the singer sings what is a simulacrum − but only a simulacrum − of lyrical song. The repeated D major chord in the accompaniment sounds obsessive, especially since the rhythmic patterns never change; no matter what the invocations of love and spring and brightness, the ostinato drumbeat bass strikes each beat. The dive back into the darkness he never really left is literal, a plunge downwards of a tenth to the lower register of the wintry winds in mm. 7–8. The unison texture and *forte* dynamics return, and the music presses "vorüber" after the static diatonic brightness of the brief patch of parallel major mode in mm. 27–30. One is reminded of the (more leisurely) turn to parallel minor in "Der Lindenbaum" when the wanderer-protagonist of that cycle sings, "Ich mußt' auch heute wandern / Vorbei in tiefer Nacht" − once again, the compulsion ("mußt'") inherent in grief.

The setting of stanza 3 is a variation of stanza 2, one in which the return to darkness occurs earlier than before. Here, sorrow enshadows the "green fields and many-colored meadows" in lines 3 and 4, two lines earlier than in stanza 2, and Schubert accordingly returns to tonic minor while still in the higher register and full-textured harmonization of the D major patch of sunshine. In the *fortissimo* D minor cadence at the end of the stanza, the singer directly names the cause of his grief ("Und ach, nur Eine / Ihr Herz verschließt"), the shattering climax premonitory of the climactic passage in "Die Krähe" from *Winterreise* and most particularly in the gulf that opens up between the left- and right-hand parts. The paucity of rests and pauses in the vocal line should remind the listener of a song from the *first* Müller cycle, *Die schöne Müllerin*: "Der Jäger." It is not possible to sing "Und will das Leben / Im freien Thal / Sich auch schon heben / Zum Sonnenstrahl; / Ich muss vorüber / Mit wildem Sinn" (mm. 27–32) all in one breath, no matter how quick the tempo, and yet that is what Schubert notates, the plunge of a tenth downwards at the words "ich muß vorüber ... " especially desperate for the lack of time in which to prepare for the change of register from high to low. Just as in "Der Jäger," the singer is forced to snatch a revivifying dose of oxygen as fast as possible in the grammatical interstices, reproducing in actuality the gasping breaths of someone driven by mania "for many a mile, from peak to peak." Schubert adds to this induced short-windedness the fact that the vocal phrases tend to be end-directed, to drive relentlessly to a climactic final pitch, to embody a crescendo in their melodic design. This is urgency indeed.

In the second of the three strophic variations (the setting of stanza 4 in mm. 50–61), Schulze addresses Love itself, love as a beneficent force of nature, the power that impels the birds to sing, the streams to flow, the trees and flowers to blossom.

Schubert accordingly bids the piano, in the corridor leading from stanza 3 to 4, descend from the heights of grief and turn to the dominant tonality of A major, the key so often associated with the potent compound of springtime and love in Schubert's songs ("Frühlingstraum," for example). Nowhere does unison texture or minor mode intrude; not until the setting of the final stanza does the wintry musical climate return. The harmonic rhythm is not only swifter, the "dringende" force of love that compels growth and life rendered graphic in sound, but moves by circle of fifths motion, an element found nowhere else in the song and all the more affective for the appoggiaturas in the inner voice of mm. 54–57. The entire passage is sweetly diatonic, so that we may hear not only what the poetic speaker mourns with such desperation but why. Every detail dazzles: the singer never descends to the tonicized A until the last word of the last phrase ("Die Quellen springen / Bei deinem *Wehn*!"), and the voice therefore literally hovers in mid-air, above the lower, darker, despairing register. The melismatic "breath of May" in m. 53 is both a musical "Hauch" and a melodic impulsion to drive the phrase gently onward, "dringen" and "Triebe" in their most lyrical manifestation. The piano accompaniment at the beginning (mm. 51–54) is a variation of the accompaniment at the start of stanzas 2 and 3 ("the open valleys," "green fields," and "many-colored meadows"), but with the right-hand part transposed upwards to the same register as the voice, the effect notably lighter and brighter than before. The words "Lie - [be]," "drängst," and "Baum" in mm. 52, 54 and 55 are the only words on the first beat of the measure to receive the durational emphasis of a dotted quarter note; "Baum" is the sequential consequent of the prolongational accent on the verb "dringen," but it is "Love" and compulsion that Schubert thus subtly underscores. Birdsong in mm. 56–57 becomes incantatory alternation on the interval of a third (C-sharp E), and the springing streams resound to almost folk-like strains in the vocal line of mm. 58–59. And yet, through all of these gestures evocative of love, beauty, and spring, the triplet motion and drumbeat bass continue undeterred by so much as a single beat. Everywhere else in the song, the rhythms are all of a piece with the unison starkness, the frantic swooping gestures from the peaks to the abysses, the *crescendi* and *fortissimo* climaxes, but here, the driven motion is dissonant with what surrounds it, deliberately and powerfully so. It is difficult to imagine a more potent combination of winter and spring than this.

Schubert was fond of unharmonized repeated pitches for transition zones between sections, as in the transition from the A section to the B section in "Im Dorfe" from *Winterreise*, and he resorts to that simultaneously stark and obsessive gesture in m. 62 of "Über Wildemann," the return to unharmonized harshness the signal for winter's return in the fifth and final stanza. Reed writes that Schubert ignores the opportunities for a gentler, more lyrical vein here (those alert to the word music of poetry will note in the last half of the stanza the alliterative brightness of "-schimmer" and "-schein" and the assonance of "ü" in "Frühlingschimmer" and "Blütenschein" at the same place in the poetic line), but Schubert rightly focuses on the "dark imaginings," "rough path," and stormy winds as the occasion to bring back the music of stanza 1 very little changed. The poet can only look longingly at a paradisiacal springtime from within his wintry prison and can only hymn it in winter's strains. The composer's choice not to write another strophic variation but instead to frame the modified strophic form on either side with the same music is the formal embodiment of the poet's unchanged "Wahn," so powerfully evoked in this song. Its bleakness and difficulty for both singer and pianist have meant fewer performances by far than the lyrical melancholy of "Im Frühling," whose melancholy is more lyrically housed, but that should not be the case: the song of winter is as great a masterpiece as its spring companion.

And there, Schubert's involvement with the convoluted tragedy of Ernst Schulze and the *Poetisches Tagebuch* ends. Whether or not the composer ever knew the wretched details of the entanglement with the Tychsens, whether he thought the experience recounted in the verse-diary was factual or fictional or a mixture of both, he seems to have understood the delusory erotomania chronicled in this poetry better than almost anyone else except the poet's own friends, and he had the means to make it audible. I am not therefore implying that Schubert himself was similarly afflicted: great artists can and do re-create human situations not their own, or rather, not precisely their own. The man who told Leopold Kupelwieser in March 1824 that his "most brilliant hopes" had perished, that the "felicity of love and friendship" had nothing to offer but pain,[130] who converted his death-haunted despair into artistry, had, I believe, something crucial in common with the poet he set to music so profoundly.

Musically, the Schulze songs belong to Schubert's long history of tinkering creatively with strophic forms. He had already set obsessive *Dichterliebe* to music in *Die schöne Müllerin*, likewise replete with strophic songs, but the Schulze songs are another matter. At the simplest level, they are far longer than the likes of "Das Wandern" or "Morgengruß," for example; at a more complex level, the balance between reason and unreason in passionate love is differently calibrated, closer to tipping the scales at insanity, and hence, the elements of exact repetition and variation are differently deployed, pushed to the extremes. The sheer boldness of some of these songs ("Auf der Brücke," "An mein Herz," "Über Wildemann") is overwhelming. Even where desperation is not permitted expression ("Der liebliche Stern") or is temporarily held at bay ("Im Frühling"), Schubert reminds us in myriad details that *Wahnsinn* is the ever-present threat in all this poet said and did, a mad insistence that fantasy replace reality and thereafter never change; musical repetition on both a small and large scale, from motivic and phrase repetition to repeated strophes, is deployed in the service of that insistence. Schubert did not subsequently use strophic forms to the same extent or in the same way in *Winterreise*, its monologist a different and more thoughtful creature, but the psychological acuity of his musical portrait of Schulze is indeed both a laboratory for the winter journey to come and a marvel in its own right.

AN ALBUM OF SCHULZE SONGS BY NEGLECTED COMPOSERS

Schubert was not the only composer to discover how beautifully tuned Schulze's poetry was for musical setting; a small throng of obscure and not-so-obscure *Kapellmeister* and *Lieder-Komponisten* did likewise throughout the heyday of Schulze's fame.[131] The reviewer for the *Allgemeine Musikalische Zeitung* for June 1825, in a review of Sigismund Neukomm's setting of "Der Stern der Liebe" (The star of love) from the *Sieben Gesänge*, praised the poet's pictorial imagination – "rich in beautiful and meaningful images" – and the composer's ability to extend the scenic depiction by musical means.[132] Schubert, of course, began composing his Schulze songs that same year, but if he jumped on a bandwagon in company with other song composers, he was among the few to detect true pathology in the poet's grief-stricken screed and to incorporate it in his music. If one studies the Schulze settings of those *Kleinmeister* both during and after Schubert's short stay on earth, one discovers that they are divided unequally between those composers who found only the stuff of sentimental *Liebeslieder*, devoid of any taint of madness, and those who, like Schubert, found the musical realisation of near-insanity an intriguing compositional challenge. Schubert was by far the best of the latter group, but his contemporaries and those who followed after him nonetheless deserve our attention, both for what they can tell us about bygone approaches to song and verse and for the intrinsic worth of some, if not all, of their music. Present-day reviewers might be as favorably inclined as their nineteenth-century forebears, should certain of these songs be revived.

The eldest in the catalogue of Schulze composers was Carl Melchior Jakob Moltke (1783–1831), a descendant of the great Protestant hymn writer Paul Gerhardt (1607–76) and an operatic tenor whose performances as Tamino won praise from Goethe. Moltke chose six poems from the *Poetisches Tagebuch* for musical setting and grouped them into a cycle entitled *Weihe der Liebe: Sechs Lieder von Ernst Schulze*, op. 14 (Leipzig, H. A. Probst).

Weihe der Liebe (Love's Consecration)

1. Der Liebe Freud' und Leid (Love's joy and sorrow) – the text of Schubert's "Im Frühling" – G major
2. Der Liebe Klage (Love's lament, beginning with the line "So scheid' ich denn mit stiller Klage") – Schulze's "Am 6. April 1816" – F major
3. Der Liebe Kunde (Love's message, beginning "Ertönet, ihr Saiten, / In nächtlicher Ruh'" – Schulze's "Am 27. October 1814" – C major
4. Der Liebe Trost (Love's consolation) – the text of Schubert's "An mein Herz" – A minor
5. Der Liebe Blick (Love's glance, beginning "Was siehst du mich so hold und mild") – Schulze's "Am 16. November 1813" – F major
6. Der Liebe Wunsch (Love's wish, beginning "Nicht im Leben, nicht im Lieben, hoff' ich Ruhe mehr und Glück") – Schulze's "Am 22. December 1816" – A major[133]

There is no linear progression of events in the poetic anthology that would invite narrative succession and Moltke therefore goes back and forth between different years and seasons in the diary, the non-chronological unhappiness of it all unified more by recurrent themes and poetic language than by the storyteller's art. And yet, the composer clearly intended *Weihe der Liebe* – a consecration of love in six moods – to be understood as a cycle, evident in the parallelisms of the titles he invented (like Schubert, he eliminates the dates and all references to a diary), in the close tonal relationships between several of the songs, and by a motto beginning in the vocal line for each of the first three songs, varied rhythmically but otherwise similar. It is interesting, and revealing, that Schubert shied away from carving a cycle out of Schulze's multitudinous calendar poems (he preferred his poetic cycles ready-made), but others did not.

Moltke's musical idiom is more conservative by far than Schubert's and betrays a trace of operatic influence on occasion, as when the melody of "Der Liebe Freud' und Leid" blossoms into modestly Mozartian scalewise ascents into the upper register at the close (ex. 26). Although he preferred poems whose melancholy is gentler than the manic misery Schubert found so compelling, Moltke, too, caught the whiff of

Example 26. Carl Moltke, "Der Liebe Freud' und Leid" from *Weihe der Liebe: Sechs Lieder von Ernst Schulze*, op. 14 (Leipzig, H. A. Probst), mm. 15–31.

Example 26. *cont.*

madness in this poetry and included at least one specimen of Schulze at his most unbalanced: the text of Schubert's "An mein Herz," which Moltke entitled "Der Liebe Trost." His musical means of signalling near–insanity were more limited and far less bold than Schubert's, but his recognition of the poet's dire straits is evident in the crescendo from *piano* to *forzando* in the space of slightly more than a measure (mm. 1–2); in the melodic ascent spanning a ninth and culminating in the desperate emphasis on the word "stille" – the very act of bidding his heart to grow calm inducing increased wildness; in the energetic, even frantic melodic profile, dominated by see-sawing intervallic leaps rather than more lyrical scalar motion. Like Schubert, Moltke saw and understood the anguished narcissism of the text, apparent in such details as the downbeat *forzando* emphasis on the word "ich" in the line "dass ich sie lassen soll," while the "heartbeat" repeated chords, the splashes of diminished seventh coloration in mm. 3 and 5, and the A minor tonality are all reminiscent of Schubert's "An mein Herz." There is even a faint family resemblance in their settings of the words "Und gab auch dein junges Leben"; whether these are merely coincidental similarities or not is beyond ascertaining. Schubert's Schulze, however, listens to his chaotic heart pounding throughout a lengthy piano introduction while Moltke's Schulze dispenses with any preliminaries (true of all but one of the six

Example 27. Carl Moltke, "Der Liebe Trost" from *Weihe der Liebe: Sechs Lieder von Ernst Schulze*, op. 14 (Leipzig, H. A. Probst), mm. 1–10.

Example 27. *cont.*

songs) in order to launch directly into a tension-fraught setting (ex. 27). If the extremity of Schubert's conception and the containment of calculatedly wild gestures within the fixity of an unchanging framework penetrate to the core of Schulze's erotomania in a way that this composer could not match, Moltke *did* understand that the matter was one of incipient madness and sought to tell it in his music.

The first of C. Nicola's *Drei Gesänge*, published by Breitkopf & Härtel and favourably reviewed in the *Allgemeine Musikalische Zeitung* for December 1826, is "Das Lied von der Rose" (The song of the rose), a setting of Schulze's "Am 3. Januar 1814."[134] Nicola's strophic setting – he marks the fourth verse as "quicker" until the slowed final line, the fifth verse as "peacefully" – is indeed attractive, its pleasant lyricism more skilfully-crafted than Moltke. This morning serenade to a rose (the customary flower-designation for the beloved, or Adelheid) betrays the poet's pathology in the final verse ("Your pride has truly saddened me, but whoever loves beauty is blessed; therefore I can never leave you and will build myself a quiet arbor and look at you from afar. Tell me, proud little rose, will you suffer it?"), but Nicola chose to interpret "Du zarte Ros' im Morgenthau" as a conventional lover's address, beginning with twelve bars of piano introduction – the lover announcing his presence with instrumental strains – and filled with ingratiating appoggiatura

307

inflexions. The music was clearly conceived to the words of the first verse, with each phrase or thought impelling a fresh change of figuration: the singer's desire for the "sweet rose" is evident in the descending chromatic inner voices of m. 12, the reference to the rose's solitude in mm. 18–19 ("und immer willst du einsam stehn") brings about a turn to the parallel minor, and the rising desire Nicola heard in the line "und nur für dich so frisch und schön" brings about a chromatic ascent to the crucial word "schön" (ex. 28). If pathology is not to be found here, the postlude, with its subdominant minor chords, tinges the closing instrumental passage with the appropriate melancholy.

Example 28.   C. Nicola, "Das Lied von der Rose" from the *Drei Gesänge* (Leipzig: Breitkopf & Härtel, [1826?]), mm. 8–28.

Example 28. *cont.*

im - mer willst __ du ein-sam stehn, und nur für dich so

frisch und schön, den Kranz der Lie-be nim-mer zie - - ren.

Joseph Abenheim (1804–1891), music director at the court chapel in Stuttgart from 1844 to 1848, and Leopold Lenz are two other composers from Schubert's generation, although they long outlived their great contemporary. Abenheim set the first in a cycle of farewell poems "An S.," to Sophie von Witzendorff, as "Abschied" ("Ich liebte dich, und ach, ich muß entsagen! / Nicht zürn' ich dir, ich zürne dem Geschick," etc.), and published it in one of the famous *Orpheon* song anthologies.[135] Although Abenheim perhaps did not do so consciously, the pleasant but superficial lyricism of his F major song matches the elegant, formulaic sentiments, without deep feeling, of the poem to a nicety (ex. 29). Lenz's songs are more attractive: "Nur du!" ("Only you!," Schulze's "Am 4. Mai 1816") and "Zum Geburtsfeier der

Example 29. Joseph Abenheim, "Abschied," op.5, no. 2 (Stuttgart: Karl Göpel), mm. 4–12.

Geliebten" ("On the Beloved's Birthday," or Schulze's "Am 17. Februar 1817," beginning with the line "Blüt' und Ranken weh'n und schwanken"), both from the *Fünf Gesänge*, op. 25, also "In wilder Nacht," op. 21, no. 7 ("On a wild night," a setting of Schulze's "Am 10. Februar 1817," the penultimate poem in the poetic diary).[136] "Nur du!" in particular is a lovely song:

Wenn das Abendroth zerronnen	When dusk has disappeared,
Steigen Mond und Stern' empor	the moon and stars arise,
Und wenn Stern' und Mond erbleichen	and when the stars and moon grow pale,
Tritt die Sonn' aus goldnem Thor.	the sun strides forth from a golden gate.

(stanza 1 only)

The poet surveys every splendor in the heavens by both day and night and sees only "thy face." Lenz correspondingly traverses the harmonic regions round about the E-flat major tonic key, in continual gentle motion, touching on C minor and G minor cadences en route to a tonic cadence delayed until m. 16. The slurred leap upwards of a tenth in m. 4 at the word "empor," acts as the seamless corridor from the first vocal phrase to the second and is particularly striking in a song otherwise devoid of such dramatic intervallic gestures (ex. 30). Beginning in m. 26, Lenz repeats

Example 30.   Leopold Lenz, "Nur du!" from *Fünf Gesänge*, op.25, mm. 1–17.

the first musical strophe but with the right-hand chords animated as sixteenth-note figuration, a gentle register of heightened expressivity at the words "aber wenn Du nah' gekommen" (but when you draw near).

Even royalty turned its hand to the composition of Schulze songs: Georg Friedrich Alexander Carl Ernst August, crown prince of Hanover (27 May 1819–12 June 1878), the son of Ernst August, Duke of Cumberland, and Friederike Charlotte von Mecklenburg-Strelitz. He studied composition and piano as a youth with Karl Wilhelm Greulich (1796–1839) and Friedrich Wilhelm Kücken (1810–1882), the latter a prolific and, for a time, highly-respected song composer. Perhaps due to Kücken's influence, Georg Friedrich, who became blind in 1833 at the age of fourteen, was particularly drawn to vocal composition; he later wrote an essay "Über Musik und Gesang" (On music and song) and elaborated further on what he considered to be proper text-setting principles in his 1858 *Ideen und Betrachtungen über die Eigenschaften der Musik* (Ideas and reflections on the properties of music). Whether the fact that Schulze was a Hanoverian subject had anything to do with it or not, the monarch was truly obsessed (perhaps the appropriate response to an obsessed poet) with Schulze's verses, setting a total of thirty-seven solo lieder, twenty-three unaccompanied male chorus works, a "Hymne an die heilige Cäcilie" for male chorus and solo quartet, and "Sehnsucht" (the text of Schubert's "Der liebliche Stern") for male chorus with piano accompaniment, all to texts by Schulze.[137] The *Sechs Lieder von Ernst Schulze*, published by Bachmann of Hanover in 1838 when the future monarch was barely nineteen years old, are representative of his style:

1. Das Grab der Geliebten ("O Leben, lass von dir hinweg mich scheiden") – Schulze's "Am 19. September 1813" – A-flat major
2. Das Veilchen ("Du Veilchen auf der Frühlingsau") – Schulze's "Am 7. April 1816" – G major
3. Die Rose ("Du zarte Ros' im Morgenthau") – Schulze's "Am 3. Januar 1814" – E major
4. Das Reh ("Durch die Thäler und über die Höhn") – Schulze's "Hildesheim. Den 20. April 1816" – E major
5. Erinnerung ("Still sitz' ich an des Hügels Hang") – Schulze's "Am 31. März 1815" – A major
6. Die Ferne ("Entfaltet lässt die weite Flur sich sehn") – Schulze's sonnet "Fürstenberg" from the *Reise durch das Weserthal* of 1814 – F major[138]

Like Schubert, the prince ranges throughout the poetic diary, selecting individual poems and ordering them in non-chronological succession, even straying outside the diary for the final song. One can spot certain affinities in the set – nos. 2 and 3 are "flower songs," each beginning in 2/4 meter, while nos. 3 and 4 are paired tonally – but closer cyclical procedures are in scant evidence.

The Hanoverian prince weds Schulze's logorrhea and monomania with tonal restlessness verging on the chaotic. The future Georg V insisted upon interpretive inflections of the smallest details of word and image in his chosen poems (the impression that he could not see the forest for the trees is quite strong); distant and radical tonal relationships, drastic sectional contrasts, and constant chromatic roiling-about were his musical corollaries to the diseased mind depicted in the poetry. For

Example 31. Georg Friedrich, crown prince of Hanover, "Das Grab der Geliebten" from *Sechs Lieder von Ernst Schulze* (Hanover: Bachmann, 1838), mm. 5–20.

a song composer in the mid- to late 1830s, he had a predilection for the experimental and modern – he was no *volkstümlich* composer. The first and most impressive song in the set, "Das Grab der Geliebten," for example, has six changes of key signature in the space of 152 bars, from the initial (and closing) A-flat major to F-sharp minor and thence to a thoroughly unstable passage ostensibly in G major, B-flat major, E-flat major, B major, and finally, tonic A-flat, of which one hears very little indeed. Within each tonal episode, ranging from a mere eight measures to some thirty, nothing remains fixed or stable for more than a few measures before the musical quicksand shifts underfoot yet again – shades of Gesualdo. Georg V, like Schubert, read the entire poetic diary and, it would seem, sought to convey the poet's distinctive tensions in the most powerful fashion. If he was no Schubert in compositional inspiration or even cohesion, he had his moments, as the opening of "Das Grab der Geliebten" can attest (ex. 31).

Renaissance composers plucked madrigal texts from Ariosto's giant romance *Orlando furioso* and Tasso's *Gerusalemme liberata*; three hundred years later, August Emil Titl (1809–1882) similarly found lieder texts in Schulze's *Cäcilie*, which is shot through with inset "songs" – stanzas in songlike meters and lines shorter than the prevailing hexameters – for the characters to sing. Titl, who was *Kapellmeister* at the Josefstädter Theater, the Theater an der Wien, and the Burgtheater, set two song texts from an interpolated tale that occupies much of the thirteenth canto: "Wechselgesang" (Dialogue Song) and "Sighilds Klaggesang" (Sighild's song of lamentation), op. 17, published by Schlesinger in Berlin (1840?). The songs found favor with the critic of the *Allgemeine Musikalische Zeitung* for August 1840, the writer characterizing the first as "terrifying and good," the second as "the real thing, great and deeply felt, a draw for a singer of spirit."[139] In Schulze's tale, Sighild, daughter of King Frotho of Sweden, falls in love with the hero Hialmar, son of a smith, and marries him. Hialmar dies in combat with the fierce Angantir, who is also killed; as Hialmar lies dying, his friend Odur finds him, and the two sing a dialogue-song:

[Odur] Wie ist dein Panzer	Why is your armour
Von Blut so roth,	so red with blood?
Wie deine Wange	Why are your cheeks
So bleich vom Tod?	so pale in death?
Kalt liegt Angantir	Cold lies Angantir
Am grünen Hang;	on the green slopes,
Doch schallt von Hialmar	yet from Hialmar rings
Kein Siegsgesang?	forth no song of victory?
[Hialmar] Ist Kleid und Wange	If my garb and my cheeks
Mir roth und bleich,	are red and pale,
So ist's vom Siege	it is from victory
Und Tod zugleich,	and death alike,
Und wenn vom Munde	and when no song
Kein Lied mir schallt,	resounds from my lips,
So folgt dem Todten	thus the victor soon follows
Der Sieger bald.[140]	the dead. (stanzas 1 and 2 of 4)

The Scottish folk-ballad "Edward," another dialogue-poem beginning with the question "'Dein Schwert, wie ist's von Blut so rot? Eduard, Eduard!" (Why is your sword so red with blood? Edward, Edward!) in Johann Gottfried Herder's German translation, is clearly the model for Schulze's first stanza. Were Schulze's wartime fantasies of death in battle and of Adelheid's imagined grief for the slain singer the biographical subtext of this *Wechsellied*? Upon returning, Odur gives Sighild the blood-stained ring that is Hialmar's dying gift to her, and she, after a long silence, sings the "Klaggesang."

So liegst du blutig	So you lie, bloody
Vom harten Streit,	from the harsh battle,
Im Siegeskranze,	in the victor's garland,
Im Grabeskleid?	in your grave-clothes?
So ist dein Busen	Is your breast
Zum Tode wund,	wounded unto death,
Dein Blick so dunkel,	your gaze so dark,
So bleich dein Mund?[141]	your lips so pale? (stanza 1 of 7)

From this grim denouement to Norse gloom, Titl fashioned two beautiful songs deserving of resurrection – one plays them and agrees wholeheartedly with the review from 150 years ago. The "Wechselgesang" alternates between tonic A minor and brief patches of emphasis on F major, with its right-hand triplet figuration throughout reminiscent of "Erstarrung" and likewise evocative of the panic-stricken motion of fresh grief. The sudden eruption of flats that darken the musical landscape at Hialmar's words "[Ist Kleid und Wange mir] roth und bleich" in stanza 2 (equally appropriate for the words "[Dies Ringlein golden, das] blutig raucht" in stanza 4), the vocal line descending the span of a twelfth at the end of stanzas 2 and 4, and the alternation between the doubled submediant and dominant pitches in the postlude – the lamenting semitone thus emphasized – are particularly effective aspects of this beautiful song (ex. 32). In "Sighild's Klaggesang" in G minor, Titl makes use once again of the *lamentoso* semitone in sixteenth-note right-hand figuration throughout stanzas 1 and 2 (also stanzas 5 and 6, repeated to the same music at the end), especially the semitone figures that fill each of the three upper voices in mm. 1–2, the singer entering on the raised fourth degree (C-sharp D) in a way that underscores the initial words "So liegst." Whether or not Titl was consciously recalling the medieval tradition of women's lamentations at the spinning wheel and their later reincarnations (the dialogue-song is also a medieval genre), "Gretchen am Spinnrade" foremost among them, the buzzing, spinning piano figuration of the framing sections, with its touches of asperity, is a haunting backdrop for another of Titl's lyrical melodies, again graced by such details as the Neapolitan darkening at the cadential words "so dunkel, so bleich [dein Mund?]" and the grief-stricken *sforzando* cries "Hialmar, Hialmar." When Sighild sings of her vision of Hialmar's faraway burial-site in the internal stanzas, Titl changes tonality (to the dominant for stanzas 3 and 5, to parallel major for the birds who sing at the hero's grave in stanza 4 – the B section thus an ABA form within a larger ABA structure) and figuration, the repeated chords and drum-roll figures in the bass of stanzas 3 and 5 especially grandiose (ex. 33).

Example 32.   August Emil Titl, "Wechselgesang," op. 17 (Berlin: Schlesinger, [1840?]), mm. 1–12.

Example 33.   August Emil Titl, "Sighilds Klaggesang," op. 17 (Berlin: Schlesinger, [1840?]), mm. 75–100.

Example 33. *cont.*

When ballad composition was at its height of popularity in the 1830s, the Berlin composer Rudolf von Hertzberg (1818–1893) set Schulze's "Elfengesang" as his op. 6 (Berlin: Cranz, 1838).[142] The elf – Schulze cum Alberich – bewails his lovelorn condition from on high, his song resounding in the dark valley below while the winds howl all around him – this is a supernatural variation on "Über Wildemann." "I have red and blue flowers, gleaming with fresh dew; I have gold, so pure and bright, and only love is lacking! … Oh, love's flame! love's joy! never do you warm my wild breast!" and so on and on, until at the end, the bereft creature spreads his wings and fills the night with a storm to match the tempest raging in his own spirit. This is purest balladesque tradition from a poet who wrote very few specimens of the genre; it begins and ends with the archetypal unnamed narrator to establish the appropriately wild, moonlit, tempest-tossed *mise-en-scène* and introduce the elf, who then tells of his longing for a woman to love him. The poorest laborer in the fields has a bride, the creature laments, and the shepherd meets his beloved by the brook, but he, despite all his powers (Schulze's defensive superiority evident yet again), is sorrowful and alone. From this wonderfully dated Romantic kitsch, Hertzberg devised an equally pure specimen of musical balladry in the best Loewe manner and on a par with Loewe's finest ballads; one has cause to regret his small work-list, almost all of it composed before his twenty-fifth year. In fact, the crystalline texture in the G minor sections at the beginning and end (the narrative framework), compounded of "zefiroso" [!] sextuplets on a pedal point tonic G in the right hand and a bass melody that begins with the traditional lamentation interval of the diminished fourth, seems like a simpler precursor of Hugo Wolf's setting of the words "Im nächt'gen Hain, mit Schneelicht überbreitet" from the Mörike lied "Auf eine Christblume I," in which an elf emerges at the end of the song to marvel at the winter flower and then scurry away from its holy vicinity (ex. 34). Schulze's elf first exclaims, "Wie einsam ist es auf den Höh'n! Wie schaurig hier die Winde weh'n!," in dramatic recitative style, with the eerie, unharmonized piano interludes and tremolando chords endemic to the *Schauerballaden* of the ballad master Loewe. This is followed by a stormier version of Loewe's water-music in "Der Nöck," op. 129, no. 2 to a text by August Kopisch, the similarities quite striking; Hertzberg's cascading D minor arpeggiated figuration ends with an unharmonized measured trill in the low bass, a reminiscence of Schubert as well as Loewe. The elf's song proper traverses three sections of the episodic formal structure, first, in B-flat major, then a central episode in E-flat / B-flat minor / E-flat minor-major, and finally returning to B-flat major for the elf's last passionate words. Was Hertzberg quoting the accompanimental figuration for Schubert's "Ellens Gesang I" ("Raste, Krieger, Krieg ist aus"), D. 837, in the right-hand patterns at the elf's words "Ich habe Blumen, roth und blau"? Whether Hertzberg did so tongue-in-cheek or was merely obeying in all sincerity the conventions of the genre, the elfin song in the center of the ballad is lushest sentimentality from start to finish, but colorfully wrought and skillfully done. It is no longer the custom to include an obligatory group of ballads in a recital, as it was in the late nineteenth and early twentieth centuries, but it would be worth reviving the tradition to resuscitate this work, and others like it, in performance.

Example 34. Rudolf von Hertzberg, "Elfengesang," op. 6 (Berlin: Cranz, 1838), mm. 1–41.

Example 34. *cont.*

- klang,   so   schallt   sein   Lied   das

Thal _____ ent - lang.

marcato il basso ma *p*

riten.

morendo

Example 34. *cont.*

Example 34.   *cont.*

Still another *Kleinmeister* and prolific song composer, Otto Tiehsen (1817–1849), set the text of Schubert's "Im Walde" as his own "Lied" from the *Sechs Gedichte von Chamisso, Burns, Eichendorff, Schulze und Rückert*, op. 18, no. 3 (Berlin, Bote & Bock) from the early 1840s(?).[143] He too smelled the taint of near-insanity in this poem (it is hard to miss it) and set it as an Allegro con moto song in E minor; as in Schubert's setting, the triplet figuration in the piano never ceases. Tiehsen had other ways of registering obsession as well: where the first stanza veers from the standard introduction to a *Wanderlied* – "I wander over mountain and meadow" – into mad grief at the words "und mit mir wandert meine Qual, / Will nimmer von mir scheiden," Tiehsen has the singer hammer the text on repeated eighth notes, each syllable accented, while a chromatic right-hand part shifts about underneath, culminating in a repeated howl of distress at the word "nimmer." The darkness of the Neapolitan sixth chord at the first invocation of the word "nimmer" in m. 10 and the quarter-notes in the vocal line, after the previous nine measures of eighth-note tactus, are especially dramatic details. Not until m. 13 are there any rests in the vocal line, the breathlessness this imposes another index of panic-stricken obsession. The last of Tiehsen's musical strophes is a variation in which the final couplet of text ("O Liebessehnen, Liebesqual, / Wann ruht der Wanderer einmal?") is repeated over and over, most dramatically where Tiehsen leaps from the E minor tonic chord to a C minor harmony hitherto unheard in the song (ex. 35).

Example 35.   Otto Tiehsen, "Lied" from the *Sechs Gedichte von Chamisso, Burns, Eichendorff, Schulze, und Rückert*, op. 18, no. 3 (Berlin: Bote & Bock, [early 1840s?]), mm. 37–61.

3. Ich wan - dre hin, ich wan - dre her, bei

Sturm und hei - tern Ta - gen, und doch er - schau' ich's

nim - mer - mehr, und kann es nicht er - ja - - gen, o

Lie - bes - seh - nen, Lie - bes -

Example 35. *cont.*

-qual, wann ruht der Wan - de - rer ein - mal, wann

ruht der Wan - de - rer ein - mal, o Lie - bes - -

- seh - - nen, Lie - bes - - qual, wann

ruht _____ der Wan - de - - rer ein - - mal,

Example 36. Eduard Lassen, "Kleine Lieder, geht nur immer" from *Sechs Lieder*, op. 83, no. 5 (Breslau, Julius Hainauer), mm. 1–13.

A late nineteenth-century Lisztian of the "New German" school, Eduard Lassen (1830–1904), set Schulze's "Am 2. April 1815" as "Kleine Lieder, geht nur immer," op. 83, no. 5. In each of Lassen's two written-out musical stanzas, he traverses a rising chain-of-thirds progression from tonic E major through G-sharp minor to C major and, finally, returning to tonic, in a simpler but still effective version of one of Hugo Wolf's favorite tonal plans; Wolf's favorite syncopated rhythmic pattern is also prominent in an inner voice. Lassen was highly regarded in his own day, and this song is an attractive example of his art, Schulze's wistful text treated in a delicate, restrained manner without the far reaches of late Romantic chromaticism (ex. 36). Another late nineteenth-century composer born the same year as Lassen, Carl Haine (1830–?), turned to the early poems for the text of "Der Stern der Liebe," op. 46

Example 37. Carl Haine, "Der Stern der Liebe," op. 46 (Leipzig, Gustav Lichtenberger), mm. 30–39.

(Leipzig, Gustav Lichtenberger), a far lusher and more over-ripe composition than Lassen's.[144] The piano introduction, with its sighing, gasping, fragmented figures, appoggiaturas, and secondary dominants, establishes the late Romantic atmosphere of the song, which becomes even fervent when the poetic persona sees a vision of the beloved ("Da schwimmt ein leises, liebes Bild"), the swaying, hovering motion rendered as tremolando chords. The passionate *fortissimo* climax at the words "Das ist der Liebe goldner Stern" in mid-lied is indicative of Haine's overblown style (ex. 37).

Of all of Schulze's poems, the one most popular with composers, even passing into folksong, also came from the early repertoire: the "Lied der Vöglein." (Schubert, one notes, was not interested.)

Von Zweig zu Zweig zu hüpfen,	To skip from bough to bough,
Durch Wies' und Busch zu schlüpfen,	to glide through meadow and bush,
Zu ruhn in weichen Grases Schoos,	to rest in the soft lap of the grasses,
Das ist das Loos	that is the lot
Der kleinen bunten Sänger	of the little, brightly-colored singer,
Je länger,	The longer,
Je lieber, süßes Loos!	the lovelier sweet fate!
Schwebt nieder, laue Lüfte,	Sway lower, mild breezes,
O kommt, ihr Wiesendüfte,	Oh come, you meadow scents,
Ihr Schmetterlinge tummelt euch,	butterflies, romp
Von Zweig zu Zweig	from twig to twig,
Mit unsrer Schaar zu spielen	to play with your hosts
Im kühlen,	in the cool,
Im säuselnden Gesträuch![145]	rustling shrubbery!

This is pure *poesia per musica*, and composers promptly identified it as such.[146] Of the numerous settings of this text, with its lark-like alliteration and "musical" variations in line length, one will suffice: the op. 51 duet for soprano and alto composed by the Viennese-born Ferdinand Sieber (1822–95) and published in Magdeburg by Heinrichshof. Sieber's setting in A-flat major has nothing *volkstümlich* whatever about it, replete as it is with birdsong effects of all kinds, both instrumental and vocal. If the duet is far from profound, this text hardly invites profundity, receiving instead fluent, graceful music in a Rossini-esque vein, "un petit rien" – pure *Salonmusik* and an uncharacteristically light note on which to take leave of Schulze and the music he inspired (ex. 38).

"Every man has in his soul a fixed center in which all of his emotions, his hopes and resolutions unite," Schulze wrote on 19 November 1813, "and from which the entire strength and productivity of his life emanate. For some, all of their energies are bent to ambition, for others, to avarice or similar passions. For me, it is love through which every other emotion in my heart draws its sustenance, every power its efficacy; everything I do is for love, and without it, I am nothing."[147] This passage rings true to its creator in its defensive superiority and self-congratulation ("I am

Example 38.   Ferdinand Sieber, "Lied der Vöglein," op. 51 (Magdeburg: Heinrichshof), mm. 1–8.

not as others, and what I desire is not dross"), its beauty of expression, and its pitiable desperation. From the depths of whatever massive psychic wound that never healed, Schulze directed his entire being and his considerable poetic gifts to an unremitting search for love. He never found it, at least, not in any form that would assuage him; not even his poems could provide more than momentary consolation. But that poetry *did* strike responsive hearts among readers Schulze never lived to know, first and foremost among them, Franz Schubert. If Schulze never became the latter-day Dante he dreamed of becoming, it is no mean feat to have inspired so much music, especially such songs as "Im Frühling," "Über Wildemann," "An mein Herz," and "Der liebliche Stern." There are far worse legacies.

Notes

1 "The Sappho of Vienna": Gabriele von Baumberg and the disasters of war

1 Caroline Pichler née Greiner, *Denkwürdigkeiten aus meinem Leben*, ed. Emil Karl Blümml, 2 vols. (Munich: Georg Müller, 1914).

2 Caroline Pichler also wrote a memorial essay on the first anniversary of Gabriele's death: "Gabriele Baumberg. Den. 24 Julius 1840," in *Zerstreute Blätter aus meinem Schreibtische. Neue Folge* (Vienna: A. Pichler's sel. Witwe, 1843), pp. 243–52.

3 Carl Wilhelm Otto August von Schindel, *Die deutschen Schriftstellerinnen des neunzehnten Jahrhunderts*, 3 vols. (Leipzig: F. A. Brockhaus, 1823), vol. I.

4 Ernst August Ballin, in *Das Wort-Ton-Verhältnis in den klavierbegleiteten Liedern W. A. Mozarts* (Kassel and Basel: Bärenreiter, 1984), pp. 80–83, says little about the poets of Mozart's songs.

5 See Anton Schlossar, "Die Wiener Musen-Almanache im achtzehnten Jahrhundert (1777 bis 1796)," in *Österreichische Kultur- und Literaturbilder mit besonderer Berücksichtigung der Steiermark* (Vienna, 1879), pp. 3–64; Anton Ullrich, "Die Musik im Wiener Almanach von 1777–1817" (Ph.D. dissertation, University of Vienna, 1953); and Otto Rommel, "Der Wiener Musenalmanach: Eine literarhistorische Untersuchung," *Euphorion: Zeitschrift für Literaturgeschichte*, ed. August Sauer (Leipzig and Vienna: Carl Fromme, 1906), pp. 1–219. Rommel has harsh words for Gabriele's poetry, condemning her lack of feeling for Nature (but this was never a concern of hers) and characterizing her images as "colorless" (p. 208); he could not understand why she should be included in the literary circle of Alxinger (1755–97), Blumauer, Haschka (1749–1827, the author of "Gott erhalte Franz den Kaiser"), and Leon. The *Wienerischer* (later *Wiener*) *Musenalmanach* was published from 1777 to 1796, with five changes of editorship (Joseph Franz Ratschky 1777–79, Martin Joseph Prandstetter in 1780; Ratschky and Aloys Blumauer 1781–92; Blumauer 1793–94; and Gottlieb Leon); Ewan West, in "Schubert's Lieder in Context: Aspects of Song in Vienna 1778–1828" (D. Phil., Oxford University, 1989), points out that it was "frankly parochial, with contributors almost exclusively of the second rank or lower, the vast majority being Viennese" (p. 153). See also Karl Goedeke, *Grundriss zur Geschichte der deutschen Dichtung aus den Quellen*, 2nd edn. (Dresden: L. Ehlermann, 1884–), vol IV, p. 232; Friedrich Sengle, "Johann Baptist von Alxinger (1755–1797)," in Herbert Zeman ed., *Die Österreichische Literatur: Ihr Profil an der Wende vom 18. zum 19. Jahrhundert (1750–1830)*, (Graz: Akademische Druck- und Verlagsanstalt, 1979), vol. II, pp. 773–804; and Erwin

Ritter, *Johann Baptist von Alxinger and the Austrian Enlightenment* (Bern: Herbert Lang & Co., 1970).

6 Robert Keil, *Wiener Freunde 1784–1808. Beiträge zur Jugendgeschichte der deutsch-österreichischen Literatur* (Vienna: Carl Konegen, 1883), in a letter from Gottlieb Leon to the philosopher Karl Leonhard Reinhold on 2 December 1786, p. 64.

7 Gabriele von Baumberg, *Sämmtliche Gedichte Gabrielens von Baumberg* (Vienna: Johann Thomas Edlen von Trattnern, 1800), pp. 268–69. The poem was not included in the revised and abbreviated edition of her poems, *Gedichte von Gabriele Batsányi geb[oren] Baumberg. Mit einer Abhandlung über die Dichtkunst, von F. W. M.* (Vienna: J. V. Degen, 1805).

8 Gabriele von Baumberg, *Gedichte* (1800), pp. 268–69.

9 Ewan West, "Schubert's Lieder in Context," p. 17.

10 See Constantin von Wurzbach, *Biographisches Lexikon des Kaiserthums Österreich* (Vienna: Druck und Verlag der k. k. Hof- und Staatsdruckerei, 1866), vol. xv, pp. 95–6.

11 Baumberg, *Gedichte* (1800), p. 63. This poem was not included in the revised edition of 1805.

12 See Lawrence Lipking, *Abandoned Women and Poetic Tradition* (Chicago, Illinois: University of Chicago Press, 1988), chapter 3, "Sappho Descending: Abandonment through the Ages," and chapter 4, "Sappho Descending: Abandonment to the Present."

13 See Horváth Balázs, *Bacsányiné* (Kassa: "Szent Erzsébet" nyomda részvénytársaság, 1908). The title means "Mrs. Batsányi" – again, the denial that she had an existence apart from her husband.

14 Her poems include "An meinen lieben Vater zu seinem Namenstage, den 16. May. Eine Erzählung" (To my beloved father on his name-day, 16 May. A tale) and "Oranisa. Eine Erzählung. An meinen Vater zu seiner Genesung" (Oranisa. A tale. To my father upon his recovery). See Baumberg, *Gedichte* (1800), pp. 43–44 and pp. 221–24. There are no poems to her mother.

15 See Ewan West, "The *Musenalmanach* and Viennese Song 1770–1830," *Music & Letters* 67 (1968), pp. 37–49.

16 The poems in the *Musenalmanach* include the following:

(1) *Wiener Musenalmanach auf das Jahr 1787*, ed. Ratschky and Blumauer (Vienna, Christian Friedrich Wappler): "An meine Freundinn Rosalia von Schmerling, geboren von Ehrenbaum," pp. 7–12; "Auf einen schlechten historischen Maler," p. 30; "Widerruf," pp. 54–55; "Auf den Fächer meiner Freundinn," p. 63; "Bittschrift an die Nymphe des Schwefelbrunnens zu Baden," pp. 86–87; and "Abschied an meine Leyer," pp. 124–26.

(2) *Wiener Musenalmanach auf das Jahr 1789*, ed. Ratschky and Blumauer (Vienna, Rudolph Gräffer): "An die Muse," pp. 22–24; "Sophiens Empfindung bey'm Sonnenaufgang," pp. 29–32; "Das liebende Mädchen," pp. 52–54; "Glück und Liebe," pp. 75–76; "Empfindungen in Lascy's Garten. (Dornbach den 10ten August 1787)," pp. 90–95; "Der Schwesterbund," pp. 105-7; and "Selbstgespräch," pp. 144–46.

(3) *Wiener Musenalmanach auf das Jahr 1791*, ed. Ratschky and Blumauer (Vienna, Rudolph Gräffer): "Cora an die Sonne," p. 126; "An einen Freund der Litteratur," p. 34; "Eine Phantasie," pp. 52–54; "Auf das erste Blatt im Stammbuch meiner Freundinn," p. 96; "Schwur und Glaube," pp. 116-18; "Als ein süßes Herrchen seinen Hut auf einem Punschtopf legte," p. 127; "An MV ★ ★. Am Neujahrstag," p. 141. In the last small poem, she writes, "Du wünschest Glück zum neuen Jahre mir, / In dem mich deine Blicke tödten; / Nimm deine Wunsch zurück, und liebe mich dafür, / In deinen Armen hab' ich sonst kein Glück von nöthen."

(4) *Wiener Musenalmanach auf das Jahr 1792*, ed. Ratschky and Blumauer (Vienna, Rudolph Gräffer): "Kennzeichen wahrer Liebe," pp. 23–25; "Lisettens Aeußerung über die Wahl eines Gatten. (Aus einem Gespräche.)," p. 43; "An Fräulein Karoline v. Greiner," pp. 71–73; "Die Schäfchen," pp. 74–77; and "An ★ ★. Bey Erhaltung eines Paars weißer Handschuhe," p. 110. One also finds a poem by Alxinger entitled "In das Stammbuch des Fräuleins G. v. Baumberg geschrieben," p. 94.

(5) *Wiener Musenalmanach auf das Jahr 1793*, ed. Blumauer (Vienna, Rudolph Gräffer): "Glückwunsch zum Namensfest meines lieben Oheims Franz von Rodius, Rittmeisters und Adjutanten der k.k. deutschen adelichen Garde," pp. 50–52 and "Bey Uebersendung meines Porträts. Le Destin nous sépare, le Penchant nous unit," pp. 153–55.

(6) *Wiener Musenalmanach auf das Jahr 1794*, ed. Blumauer (Vienna, Blumauer): "An Fanny," pp. 18–20; "An Franz II, Bey Ueberreichung eines Kriegsbeytrages in zehn Stücken goldener Denkmünzen, acht Dukaten am Werthe," pp. 95–97; and "Zwey Elegien: Auf den Tod eines geliebten Rothkehlchens & Auf den Tod einer geliebten Nachtigall," pp. 124–28.

17 Pichler, *Denkwürdigkeiten aus meinem Leben*, vol. 1, p. 153.

18 "Das gefährliche Spiel" was first published in 1813 in the *Taschenbuch für Damen auf das Jahr 1814* (Tübingen, 1813), pp. 18ff, and later included in her *Sämmtliche Werke*, vol. 31: *Kleine Erzählungen, Dritter Teil* (Vienna: Anton Pichler and Leipzig: August Liebeskind, 1829), pp. 7–67.

19 Maria Christina Baumberg supported the suit of a court clerk who was the nephew of Johann von Sedlnitzky, the secretary of state for internal affairs. When Gabriele announced that she would only marry a Freemason, her persistent suitor joined the "Wahre Einheit" lodge and arranged for Gabriele to receive the white gloves awarded to women the order considered meritorious. Although she wrote a poem about the gloves, she continued to reject his suit.

20 Baumberg, *Gedichte* (1800), p. 135.

21 See Ernst Wangermann, *From Joseph II to the Jacobin Trials: Government Policy and Public Opinion in the Habsburg Dominions in the Period of the French Revolution*, 2nd edn. (Oxford: Oxford University Press, 1969).

22 There is some confusion about Batsányi's birthdate. Constantin von Wurzbach cites 11 May 1763 as his date of birth. That Batsányi was not of aristocratic birth was evident from the fact that his name ended with "i" and not "y."

23 Cited in Lóránt Czigány, *The Oxford History of Hungarian Literature from the Earliest Times to the Present* (Oxford: Clarendon Press, 1984), p. 93. Anthologies of Batsányi's poetry include *Poetische Arbeiten* (Buda: Universitätsbuchdruckerei, 1835) and *Versek*, ed. D. Keresztury and A. Tarnai, 4 vols. (Budapest: Akadémiai Kiadó, 1953–67). See also Moritz Csáky, "Die Präsenz der ungarischen Literatur in Wien um 1800," in *Die österreichische Literatur: Ihr Profil an der Wende vom 18. zum 19. Jahrhundert (1750–1830)*, vol. 1, pp. 483–84.

24 From an undated letter to Johannes von Müller in Eva Zadányi, *Batsányi János és Johannes von Müller* (Budapest: Minerva, 1941), pp. 28–29.

25 Ignác Martinovics, the leader of the conspiracy, was an unfrocked monk and Freemason, perhaps a former agent provocateur of the Austrian secret police. After he organized the discontented radical intelligentsia into a secret society modeled after Jacobin societies in France, the Austrian police uncovered the plot in 1794; Martinovics and many of his conspirators were executed in 1795.

26 Zadányi, *Batsányi János és Johannes von Müller*, p. 13.

27 János Batsányi, "Der Kampf (A Viaskodás)," in *Összes Müvei*, ed. Dezsö Keresztury and Andor Tarnai (Budapest: Akadémiai Kiadó, 1967), p. 11.

28 Ibid., p. 13.

29 Ilona Vajda, *Batsányi János és Baumberg Gabriella. I. 1799–1809* (Budapest: Magyar Egyetemi Nyomda Könyvesboltja, 1938), pp. 18–19.

30 Ibid., pp. 19–21.

31 Ibid., p. 21.

32 Ibid., pp. 27–28.

33 Ibid., letter of 26 December 1799, p. 30.

34 Ibid., p. 35.

35 Three of Gabriele's poems in the *Gedichte* of 1800 bear the subheading "after the French of Madame Deshoulières": "Die Schäfchen" (The little sheep), modeled on "Les Moutons. Idylle" (The sheep. Idyll) of 1674; "Sonnett nach dem französischen der Madame Deshoullieres" (Sonnet, after the French of Madame Deshoulières), modeled after a "Chanson" beginning "Ah! que je sens d'inquiétude"; "Robert an die Liebe nach dem französischen der Madame Deshoullieres" (Robert to Love, after the French of Madame Deshoulières), renamed "An Amor" in the 1805 edition and modeled after a "Madrigal." See Baumberg, *Gedichte* (1800), pp. 102–4, 133, and 198, respectively. See also *Œuvres de Madame et de Mademoiselle Deshoulières*, 2 vols. (Paris: Stéréotype d'Herhan, 1803), pp. 24–26, and 142–43. Three other poems by Gabriele are labelled "After the French," without further designation: "Ihr Bild" (Your picture), pp. 24–27; "Schwur und Glaube" (Vow and belief), pp. 89–90; "Selbstgespräch" (Conversation with myself), p. 74 in the 1805 edition; and "An Lina. Abendständchen" (To Lina. Evening serenade).

36 Cited in A. Fabre, *De la Correspondance de Fléchier avec Mme. Des Houlières et sa fille* (Paris: Didier et Cie., 1871), p. 1. There is an eerie, if only partial, parallel between Antoinette's fate and Gabriele's: Antoinette was married to Guillaume de La Fon de Boisguérin, seigneur des Houlières, who fought in the Fronde. After the rebellion collapsed, she endured imprisonment and exile in the Spanish Netherlands along with her husband. In one of her late, powerful poems on death and love (*Réflexions Diverses*), she wrote, "Man perishes imperceptibly, bit by bit. The name of 'Death' given to our last hour is only the completion."

37 Lipking, *Abandoned Women and Poetic Tradition*, p. 62.

38 Baumberg, *Gedichte* (1800), p. 205. The poem was omitted from the 1805 second edition, along with many of its ilk. Did Batsányi find them insufficiently elevated in tone?

39 Baumberg, *Gedichte* (1805), pp. 21–22. The poem is not in the earlier edition.

40 Ibid., p. 23. In the *Gedichte* (1800), the title is "Auf eine weggeworfene Rose" with the first stanza as follows: "So lang' die Ros' am dunkeln Strauche glühte, / War sie der Wunsch des Jünglings, bald sein Raub. / Und da sie nun an seiner Brust verblühte, / So wirft er sie, o Undank! in den Staub" (p. 199).

41 Baumberg, *Gedichte* (1805), p. 35, 3rd and final stanza.

42 Baumberg, *Gedichte* (1800), pp. 89–90, and pp. 69–70 in the 1805 edition.

43 Baumberg, *Gedichte* (1805), pp. 143–45, stanzas 2, 3, and 8 of 8.

44 Ibid., pp. 21–23.

45 Ibid., p. 130.

46 Vajda, *Batsányi János és Baumberg Gabriella*, p. 38.

47 Ibid., p. 47.

48 Ibid., pp. 56–57.

49 Ibid., p. 57.

50 Ibid., p. 67.

51 Ibid., p. 58.

52 Ibid., p. 63.

53 Ibid., p. 74.

54 Balázs, *Bacsányiné*, p. 27.

55 Baumberg, *Gedichte* (1805), p. lix.

56 Ibid., pp. lxi–lxii.

57 Schindel expresses similar views in the prefatory essay, "On women's writing and their literary calling," to vol. 3 of *Die deutschen Schriftstellerinnen*. At the heart of the matter, according to Schindel, was the question of compatibility with "female destiny," that is, whether a woman's "great and beautiful" calling to be wife and mother could co-exist with a literary occupation. What, he asks, of unmarried women without the duties of a wife and mother, what of widows, what of those whom circumstance has left bereft, like "the unfortunate Gabriele v. Betsany [sic]"?

58 Baumberg, *Gedichte* (1805), pp. 146–52.

59 Vienna: Johann Vincenz Degen, 1807.

60 In the third canto, one learns that the two kingdoms of Love and Hymen were divided by the storm-tossed river of passion, on which ships of all sizes filled with people of all ages are tossed about at the whim of the whirlwinds; on board these ships are an allegorical company of vices, including Pride of Birth (one wonders if Gabriele was urged by her husband to reproach herself for that particular flaw). In the fourth canto, a couple asks Wisdom for her guidance as they navigate the waters of passion en route to Hymen's kingdom. Gabriele repeats the myth of male strength and female dependence when the woman wavers and asks her lover if he wishes to return to Love's kingdom, should marriage not crown their hopes with good fortune. He vehemently swears that they shall be like the oak's trunk – the man – sweetly entwined by clinging ivy – the woman.

61 Eduward Wertheimer, "Auf dem Leben einer Wiener Dichterin," in the Vienna *Neue Freie Presse* (5 September 1884).

62 See *Correspondance de Napoléon Ier* (Paris: Imprimerie Impériale, 1865), vol. 19, pp. 13–14.

63 See Gilbert Schuy, *Bacsányi János és I. Napoleon 1809-ki Proclamatiója a Magyarokhoz* (Budapest: Stephaneum Nyomda, 1914).

64 In a desperate letter of 7 March 1810 to Hammer's wife, she writes, "Oh, I would give anything if he had not followed the advice of his apprehensive friends!" See Pál Margit, *Batsányi Párizsban 1810* (Budapest: Danubia Könyvkiadó, 1943), pp. 11–12.

65 Ibid., p. 14.

66 Ibid., p. 15.

67 Ibid., p. 21.

68 Ibid., p. 23. In her letter to her husband, Gabriele altered the wording of the notice as it appeared in the *Vaterländische Blätter für österreichischem Kaiserstaat*, vol. 2, nos. 65–67 for Friday 16 March and Tuesday 20 March 1810 (Vienna: Degen, 1810), p. 385. There, the writer (probably Joseph von Hormayr, the editor of the journal) observes that "Batsany, a man of true talent, is nonetheless known in the publishing world only as the husband of the poetess Gabriele Baumberg." Also in the same letter to Batsányi, Gabriele writes that as she was going home from Mass, she encountered the king and made her obeisance.

The king thanked her and then turned back as he was departing to look at her fixedly once again. He was, she says, in doubt as to her identity, so much had she aged.

69 Another poem "Auf die Vermählung der Erzherzogin Louise" (On the marriage of the Archduchess Louise) was printed anonymously and rumored as being by Gabriele, who sent it to Batsányi. He too mistook it as hers (how interesting that she did not correct the mistaken impression) and wrote slightingly that the misprints must be corrected – nothing more.

70 Pál Margit, *Batsányi Párizsban 1810*, pp. 29–33.

71 Ibid., p. 31.

72 Ibid., p. 34.

73 Ibid., p. 35.

74 Ibid., p. 35.

75 Ibid., p. 38.

76 Sz. Nemes Éva Margit, *Batsányi Párizsban Találkozás Gabriellával 1810–1811* (Budapest: Danubia Könyvkiadó, 1942), p. 8.

77 From a letter of 10 July 1810 in ibid., p. 6.

78 From Gabriele's letter of 12 September 1810 in ibid., p. 9 and Batsányi's reply of 14 October in ibid., p. 16.

79 From a letter of 4 October 1810 in ibid., p. 14.

80 From a letter of 14 October 1810 in ibid., p. 16.

81 Ibid., p. 12.

82 Ibid., pp. 9–10.

83 Ibid., p. 16.

84 Ibid., pp. 19–23.

85 Ibid., pp. 24–26.

86 Ibid., pp. 26–28.

87 Ibid., p. 29.

88 Ibid., pp. 33–34.

89 Ibid., pp. 49–50.

90 Ibid., p. 40.

91 From a letter of 6 January 1811 in ibid., p. 43.

92 Ibid., p. 56.

93 *Die deutsche Muse, am 10. November 1816* (Vienna: J. C. Akkermann, 1816). Twenty years earlier, she had written a similar poem for Maria Christina, the bride of Archduke Karl of Teschen, younger brother of the Emperor: *Danklied zur Ehre Karls, gesungen an Seinem Namenstag den 4. Nov. 1796* (Vienna: A. Blumauer, 1796).

94 "Schillers Bild" appears on pp. 84–87, "An Füger" on pp. 88–91 of *Aglaja. Ein Taschenbuch für das Jahr 1816* (Vienna: Johann Baptist Wallishauser, 1816).

95 The fragments have been published in Franz Schubert, *Neue Ausgabe sämtlicher Werke*, series IV, ed. Walther Dürr (Kassel, Basel, London: Bärenreiter, 1969), vol. 6, pp. 157–70 and pp. 171–79. D. deest is entitled simply "Gesang in c," while D. 39 is entitled "Ich saß an einer Tempelhalle," with the annotation "Poet unknown" [?]. However, the first four lines of Gabriele's "Lebenstraum" appear intact, with only one small alteration: Gabriele's line 1, "Ich sass *vor* eines Tempels Halle," becomes Schubert's "Ich saß *an* einer Tempelhalle." See Maurice J. E. Brown, "Some unpublished Schubert songs and song fragments," *The Music Review* 15 (1954), pp. 93–102; by the same author, "Schubert: Discoveries of the Last Decade," *The Musical Quarterly* 47 (1961), pp. 296–97; Reinhard

van Hoorickx, "Schubert: Songs and song-fragments not included in the collected edition," *The Music Review* 38 (1977), pp. 267–92; by the same author, "Schubert's Earliest Preserved Song-Fragments," *Revue belge de musicologie* 36–38 (1982–84), pp. 145–61; and Christa Landon, "Neue Schubert-Funde: Unbekannte Manuscripte im Archiv des Wiener Männergesang-Vereines," *Österreichische Musikzeitschrift* 24 (1969), pp. 299–323, translated as "New Schubert Finds," in *The Music Review* 31 (1970), pp. 215–31.

96 Baumberg, *Gedichte* (1805), p. 8.

97 Ibid., p. 12.

98 The sketch on the Wiener Männergesang-Verein ms. A is printed in the *Quellen und Lesarten* appendix to the *Neue Schubert-Ausgabe*, Series IV, vol. 6, p. 31. On p. 172 of vol. 6 itself, readers will notice that Prof. Dürr has guessed that the text for mm. 23–5 might be a repetition of the words "im sanften Abendschein"; however, the *pianississimo* hush suggests the initial statement in the next poetic line, "Kein Lüftchen wehte," while prosodic considerations in the phrase which follows confirm that this is probably the case.

99 *Schubert: The Complete Song Texts*, trans. by Richard Wigmore (New York: Schirmer Books, 1988), p. 114.

100 Graham Johnson, "Lieder der Nacht," notes to *The Hyperion Schubert Edition*, vol. 15 with Margaret Price, soprano, and Graham Johnson, pianist (Hyperion Records Ltd., 1992, CDJ33015), p. 15.

101 John Reed, *The Schubert Song Companion*, p. 7.

102 Ewan West, in "Schubert's Lieder in Context," p. 144, has pointed out that the text of "Lob des Tokayers" first appeared in the *Wiener Musenalmanach auf das Jahr 1796* under the pseudonym "von Traubenberg," but was then reprinted in the *Sämmtliche Gedichte* of 1800. Schubert's source was the anthology, not the periodical, as he reproduced all the minor differences in punctuation and spelling of the second source. I am indebted to Graham Johnson's essay-booklet entitled "An 1815 Schubertiad - II," vol. 22 of *The Hyperion Schubert Edition* (CDJ33022, 1994), pp. 30–31, for the miniature disquisition on Tokay wine; repayment in the tipple itself seems only appropriate.

103 János Batsányi, *Összes Müvei*, vol. 1, *Versek*, p. 175. The first poem was entitled "In das Stammbuch meiner Gabriele (am 29 December 1799)," or "In my Gabriele's album, on 29 December 1799": "Nimm diesen Schatten denn zum Angedenken hin, / O süsse Freundin meines Herzens Du! / Du weisst am besten, Teure! wer und was ich bin; / Schreib' ich den Namen gleich dir nicht dazu. / 'Du bist das Liebste mir auf Gottes weiter Erde!' / Auch das ist Dir bekannt, Du holde Schwärmerin! / O denke stets, dass ich auch dann dein Freund sein werde, / Wenn ich für Andre längst schon nichts als—Schatten bin! / / Dann mag die Welt in deinem Buche lesen, / Wer dieser Freund, und was er Dir gewesen." See ibid., p. 161. Another poem "A ma Gabrielle" was written in French in 1814: "Sur mon destin sois plus tranquille; / Mon nom passera jusqu'à toi: / Quelque soit mon nouvel asyle, / Le tien parviendra jusqu'à moi. / Trop heureux, si tu vis heureuse, / A cette absence douleureuse / Mon coeur pourra s'accoutumer: / Mais ton image va me suivre; / Et si je cesse de t'aimer, / Crois que j'aurai cessé de vivre." See ibid., p. 174.

104 Johann Gabriel Seidl, *Dichtungen*, vol. 1: *Balladen, Romanzen, Sagen und Lieder* (Vienna: J. P. Sollinger, 1826), p. 185.

105 Gabriele revised "Als Luise die Briefe" for the *Gedichte* of 1800 (p. 78) and yet again in the 1805 revised edition (p. 48). In both editions, the final line of stanza 1 is "Der schöne

Taumel ist vorbey" (The beautiful rapture is over), rather than the line "Ihr Kinder der Melancholie" (You children of melancholy). Stanza 2, line 3 of Mozart's text is "Und all die *schwärmerischen* Lieder" (And all the songs of tender passion), altered to "Und all die *schmeichlerischen* Lieder" (And all the flattering songs) in 1800 and again to "Euch, und die *heuchlerischen* Lieder" (You, and the deceitful songs) in 1805. Furthermore, Gabriele eliminated the entire original stanza 3 in both editions: "Ihr brennet nun, und bald, ihr Lieben, / Ist keine Spur von euch mehr hier: / Doch ach! der Mann, der euch geschrieben, / Brennt lange noch vielleicht in mir" (Now you are burning, and soon, dear letters, there will be no trace of you: but alas! he who wrote them to me may perhaps burn forever within me).

2 The lyre and the sword: Theodor Körner and the lied

1 Ulrich Völkel, *Mit Leier und Schwert: Roman um Theodor Körner* (Berlin: Verlag der Nation, 1986). Earlier novels include Christian Ludwig Zander's *Die Lützower*, 3 vols. (Berlin: L. Schlesinger, 1847) and Heribert Rau, *Theodor Körner* (Leipzig: Thomas, 1863). The plays include "Theodor Körners Anwerbung durch Frau von Lützow" of 1863 by Gustav Putlitz; Georg Zimmermann's "Theodor Körner" ed. Johann Conrad Herber (Darmstadt: Diehl, 1863); Gustav Burchard, "Lützows wilde Jagd" (Berlin: F. Fontane, 1891); Wilhelm Schröder's "Studenten und Lützower" (Hanover: Pockwitz, 1863); Friedrich Oels's "Lützows Lager" (Berlin-Friedenau: K. Fischer, [1913?]), and Hedda Zinna's "Die Lützower" (Berlin: Henschelverlag, 1961). The works for youthful readers include Heinrich Smidt, *Theodor Körner. Ein Dichter- und Heldenleben* (Neuruppin: Alfred Oehimgke, 1866) and Gustav Höcker's *Theodor Körner, der Sänger und Held von Lützows wilder Jagd* (Glogau: Carl Flemming, 1889), also "Aus Theodor Körners Leben" for *Buntes Jahr. Kinder-Kalender 1890* (Berlin: A. Hofmann, 1890). Wendelin Weißheimer's five-act opera *Theodor Körner* (Leipzig: H. Matthes, 1867), libretto by Luise Otto-Peters with quotations from Körner's writings, was performed in 1872.

2 John Reed, *The Schubert Song Companion* (Manchester: Manchester University Press, 1985), p. 468.

3 Körner brought eleven poems of what became *Leier und Schwert* with him to Leipzig in 1813 and gave them to his friend Wilhelm Kunze, to whom he dictated a twelfth poem: "Lützows wilde Jagd (Auf dem Schneckenberge bei Leipzig, am 24 April 1813)." The *Zwölf freie deutsche Gedichte* (Twelve free German poems) appeared in November 1813 and included an appendix containing additional poems ("Trost, als Rundgesang zu singen," "Mannestrost nach der Schlacht bei Lützen," "Reiterlied," "Abschied vom Leben," and "Schwertlied"). The edition of *Leier und Schwert* edited by Theodor's father was first published by Nicolai (Dresden, 1814); another collection of *Leier und Schwert* poems was edited by the Countess Elise von der Recke and one Herr von Freymann [a pseudonym?] with the title *Theodor Körners Nachlaß oder dessen Gefühle im poetischen Ausdruck, bei Gelegenheit des ausgebrochenen deutschen Freiheitskrieges. Aus dem Portefeuille des Gebliebenen* (Leipzig: Baumgärtner, 1814). See Emil Peschel, *Theodor Körner's Tagebuch und Kriegslieder aus dem Jahre 1813* (Freiburg: Friedrich Ernst Fehsenfeld, 1893).

Regarding the orthography of *Leier und Schwert*, the older form *Leyer und Schwerdt* is widely used in the earliest editions. Later editions use the modern spelling. I have used the latter in all cases for consistency.

4 The *contrafactum* melody brings with it many of the same associations as the newly-written poem. The "Lied der schwarzen Jäger" is set to the tune "Am Rhein, am Rhein," the "Reiterlied" to "Es gibt nichts Lust'gers auf der Welt," the "Gebet" to "O sanctissima," "Unsere Zuversicht" to "Wer nur den lieben Gott läßt walten," "Männer und Buben" to the eighteenth-century folk-tune "Brüder, mir ist alles gleich," "Letzter Trost" to "Es heult der Sturm, es braust das Meer," "Zueignung" to "Ich will von meiner Missetat," "Jägerlied" to "Auf, auf, ihr Brüder und seid stark," and the "Trinklied vor der Schlacht" to "Feinde ringsum."

5 Fritz Jöde, *1813 im Liede: Eine Sammlung von Volks- und volkstümlichen Liedern aus der Zeit der Befreiungskriege* (Essen: G. D. Baedeker, 1913), including Körner's "Männer und Buben" (pp. 24–26, to an "old folk-tune"), "Jägerlied" (pp. 34–35, to a Sicilian folk-tune), "Gebet" (p. 49), "Bundeslied vor der Schlacht" (pp. 50–52, by Johann Heinrich Christian Bornhardt), "Trinklied vor der Schlacht" (p. 52), "Lützows wilde Jagd" (p. 54–55, Carl Maria von Weber), "Gebet während der Schlacht" (pp. 55–56, Friedrich Heinrich Himmel), "Lied zur feierlichen Einsegnung des preußischen Freikorps" (pp. 59–60, to the chorale "Aus tiefer Not"), and "Schwertlied" (pp. 61–63, Carl Maria von Weber).

6 W. Emil Peschel and Eugen Wildenow, *Theodor Körner und die Seinen*, 2 vols. (Leipzig: E. A. Seemann, 1898), vol. 1, pp. 13–14.

7 See Christian Gottfried Körner, "Ueber Charakterdarstellung in der Musik" (On character-painting in music) in *Gesammelte Schriften*, ed. Adolf Stern (Leipzig: Fr. Wilhelm Grunow, 1881), pp. 87–106.

8 Christian Gottfried, the Stocks, and Huber resolved to demonstrate their admiration for the young playwright by sending him an anonymous letter, although the veil of anonymity fell quickly. Upon Schiller's reply, Körner wrote back on 3 January 1785, saying, "We must be friends. We know enough of you to offer you our entire friendship, but you do not know us well enough as yet. So, come here as soon as possible!" See Peschel and Wildenow, *Theodor Körner*, vol. 1, p. 24.

9 Ibid., p. 108.

10 Ibid., p. 105.

11 Ibid., p. 117, stanza 3.

12 Theodor Ziolkowski, in chapter 2, "The Mine: The Image of the Soul" of *German Romanticism and Its Institutions* (Princeton: Princeton University Press, 1990), cites Körner's 1810 poems "Bergmannsleben" and "Der Kampf der Geister mit den Bergknappen," also his 1811 opera libretto *Die Bergknappen*, as examples of mines in which the struggle between good and evil takes place (see pp. 40–42).

13 Peschel and Wildenow, *Theodor Körner*, vol. 1, p. 155.

14 Ibid., p. 191.

15 Ibid., p. 200.

16 His father's letters from 1809 in ibid., pp. 172–73, are extraordinary for their understanding. "I too was once in a similar situation," he tells his son, "and had to choose between the lesser of several evils in order to make a living and be self-sufficient … strive only for the highest goals—no mediocrity, no flagging efforts! Seriousness and love, which so suit the German temperament [Christian Gottfried thus appealing to his son's patriotism], will lead you to a worthy goal" (p. 173).

17 Ibid., pp. 221-22.

18 *Theodor Körner's Sämmtliche Werke*, ed. Karl Streckfuß, 2nd edition (Berlin: Nicolai, 1835 and Vienna: Carl Gerold, 1835), p. 15, final stanza.

19 Peschel and Wildenow, *Theodor Körner*, vol. 1, pp. 248–49.

20 *Der Meistersänger* was set to music by Karl Borromäus von Miltitz. Augustin Gürrlich (1761–1817) began but never completed the music for *Alfred der Große*, while Theodor began, but never finished, an opera-text entitled *Chlotilde* for Friedrich Heinrich Himmel.

21 Peschel and Wildenow, *Theodor Körner*, vol. 1, pp. 261–62.

22 Ibid., pp. 267–68. The unchastened Theodor wrote the poem "Toll aber klug" in a Berlin album for 16 April 1811: "Ausgeschmiert und relegiert, / Hat mich alles nicht gerührt! / Bin drauf nach Berlin spaziert; / Doch, trotz der Philosophie, / Blieb ich ein fideles Vieh. / Pereat Sulphuria! / Dein Freund, Bruder und Landsmann Theodor Körner aus Dresden, rel. cons. carcerisque Candidatus." Ibid., p. 265.

23 Theodor's love of music is evident in "Das Reich des Gesanges" (The kingdom of song), "Die menschliche Stimme" (The human voice), "Beim Alexanderfeste" (At the performance of [Handel's] *Alexander's Feast*), "Die heilige Cäcilie" (Saint Cecilia), and "An Corona [Schröter] als sie gesungen hatte" (To Corona Schröter, after she sang). He also wrote German *contrafacta* for Italian operatic airs, including Giovanni Paisiello's "Nel cor più non mi sento" from *L'amor contrastato, ossia La bella molinara* (Love contested, or The beautiful miller maid) of 1788.

24 Peschel and Wildenow, *Theodor Körner*, vol. 1, p. 269. See Gustav Parthey, *Das Haus in der Brüderstraße. Aus dem Leben einer berühmten Berliner Familie*, ed. Gabriele Koebel (Berlin: Das neue Berlin, 1955, 2nd edn. 1957) in which Friedrich Parthey's son Gustav (1798–1872) recounts Theodor's first visit to the house when Gustav was twelve-and-a-half years old. Evidently, Theodor was a romantic apparition, dressed all in black, with a bandage across his forehead, but he won the children over with his guitar-playing and singing (pp. 97–101).

25 Peschel and Wildenow, *Theodor Körner*, vol. 1, pp. 276–77, a letter of 6 March 1811.

26 Ibid., p. 296.

27 *Das Fischermädchen* was set to music, among others, by Goethe's son Walther Wolfgang von Goethe in 1839 and *Der Kampf mit dem Drachen* by Adalbert Gyrowetz.

28 *Der Nachtwächter* was later set to music as an operetta by Friedrich Krug in 1846, by E. T. Recknitz in 1865, and by Viktor Neßler in 1871.

29 Peschel and Wildenow, *Theodor Körner*, vol. 1, p. 306.

30 See Hans Ludwig Krticzka, Freiherr von Jaden, *Theodor Körner. Neue Körner-Erinnerungen in Wort und Bild: Ein unbekanntes Porträt und ein unveröffentlichtes Gedicht Theodor Körners* (Vienna: Ferdinand Wurst, 1913) and the same author's *Theodor Körner und seine Braut: Körner in Wien, Antonie Adamberger und ihre Familie* (Dresden: Wurst, 1896), also Friedrich Latendorf, *Aus Theodor Körners Nachlaß: Liedes- und Liebesgrüße an Antonie Adamberger* (Leipzig: Bernhard Schlicke, 1885).

31 See Hans Zimmer, *Theodor Körners Braut: Ein Lebens- und Charakterbild Antonie Adambergers* (Stuttgart: Greiner & Pfeiffer, n.d.).

32 See Alfred Ritter von Arneth, *Aus meinem Leben*, vol. 1: *Die ersten dreißig Jahre (1819–1849)* (Vienna: Privately published, 1891), pp. 61–62.

33 Ibid., p. 68. See also Peschel and Wildenow, *Theodor Körner*, vol. 1, p. 315.

34 Arneth, *Aus meinem Leben*, vol. 1, p. 70.

35 Peschel and Wildenow, *Theodor Körner*, vol. 1, p. 316. In *Die Braut*, a father and son (who do not know of their relationship) both woo a coquette at the same time. See also Eduard Wlassak, "Theodor Körner und das Burgtheater," in *Chronik des k. k. Hof- Burgtheaters* (Vienna: Rosner, 1876).

36 Caroline Pichler was a friend of the prolific historian Joseph Freiherr von Hormayr, who took part in the 1809 Tyrolean uprising against Napoleon. See André Robert, *L'Idée nationale autrichienne et les guerres de Napoléon: L'Apostolat du Baron de Hormayr et le Salon de Caroline Pichler* (Paris: Librairie Félix Alcan, 1933), chapter 5: "Caroline Pichler et le salon du renouveau national," pp. 302–47. See also Caroline Pichler, *Denkwürdigkeiten aus meinem Leben,* ed. Emil Karl Blümml (Munich: Georg Müller, 1914), vol. 1, pp. 386–92, and Peschel and Wildenow, *Theodor Körner,* vol. 1, pp. 322–23.

   Henriette Freiin von Pereira-Arnstein was the granddaughter of the distinguished Jewish Berlin banker, Daniel Itzig; her mother, the Freiin Fanny von Pereira-Arnstein, also presided over a salon and was a gifted pianist who founded the "Gesellschaft adliger Frauen zur Beförderung des Guten und Nützlichen" in Vienna. The society's success in staging benefit concerts led to the formation of the "Gesellschaft der Musikfreunde." Mozart was a guest in 1781–82 at Fanny Arnstein's house and salon. Henriette married the banker Heinrich von Pereira and continued her mother's tradition with her own salon after Fanny's death in 1818. For more on the Arnstein salons, see Peter Gradenwitz, *Literatur und Musik in geselligem Kreise: Geschmacksbildung, Gesprächsstoff und musikalische Unterhaltung in der bürgerlichen Salongesellschaft* (Stuttgart: Franz Steiner Verlag, 1991), pp. 187–91.

37 Peschel and Wildenow, *Theodor Körner,* vol. 1, p. 342–44.

38 *Theodor Körner's sämmtliche Werke,* ed. Karl Streckfuß (Berlin: Nicolai and Vienna: Carl Gerold, 1835), p. 147, Act 4, scene 4.

39 Ibid., p. 151, Act 4, scene 9.

40 Arneth, *Aus meinem Leben,* vol. 1, p. 70.

41 *Theodor Körner's sämmtliche Werke,* ed. Streckfuß, p. 222.

42 Peschel and Wildenow, *Theodor Körner,* vol. II, pp. 4–5.

43 See Johann Friedrich Gottfried Eiselen, *Geschichte des Lützowschen Freicorps* (Halle: Eduard Anton, 1841); Fritz von Jagwitz, *Geschichte des Lützowschen Freikorps; nach archivalischen Quellen bearbeitet* (Berlin: E. S. Mittler, 1892); Wenzel Krimer, *Erinnerungen eines alten Lützower Jägers, 1795–1819* (Stuttgart: R. Lutz, 1833, 4th edn. ed. Adolf Saager [1913?]); Fritz Lange, *Die Lützower: Erinnerungen, Berichte, Dokumente* (Berlin: Rütten & Loening, 1953); Adolph Schlüsser, *Geschichte des Lützowschen Freikorps. Ein Beitrag zur Kriegsgeschichte der Jahre 1813 und 1814* (Berlin: Ernst Siegfried Mittler, 1826); J. A. Voigt, *Skizzen aus dem Leben Fr. David Ferdinand Hoffbauers, weiland Pastors zu Ammendorf. Ein Beitrag zur Geschichte des Lützow'schen Corps* (Halle: Buchhandlung des Waisenhauses, 1869); and Christian Ludwig Enoch Zander, *Geschichte des Krieges an der Nieder-Elbe im Jahre 1813* (Lüneberg: Herold & Wahlstab, 1839, reprinted Buchholz: LTR, 1991).

44 Peschel and Wildenow, *Theodor Körner,* vol. II, pp. 7–8.

45 Louis Spohr, *Selbstbiographie,* ed. Eugen Schmitz (Kassel and Basel: Bärenreiter, 1954, reprint of 1st edn., Kassel: Georg H. Wigand, 1860), vol. 1, p. 191.

46 Ignaz Franz Castelli, *Memoiren meines Lebens: Gefundenes und Empfundenes, Erlebtes und Erstrebtes,* ed. Dr. Josef Bindtner (Munich: Georg Müller, 1913), vol. 1, pp. 295–96. Castelli published Körner's Singspiel *Haß und Liebe* (Hatred and love) in the *Wiener Hoftheater-Taschenbuch auf das Jahr 1815,* vol. 12 (Vienna: Wallishauser, 1815), pp. 63–109.

47 Peschel and Wildenow, *Theodor Körner,* vol. II, p. 30.

48 Ibid., p. 32.

49 Friedrich Förster, *Geschichte der Befreiungs-Kriege 1813. 1814. 1815* (Berlin: Ferdinand Dümmlers Verlagsbuchhandlung, 1889), vol. 1, pp. 36–37. Förster had met the Körners

when he and Theodor were both mining students in Freiberg; see Förster's memoirs *Kunst und Leben. Aus Friedrich Försters Nachlaß*, ed. Hermann Kletke (Berlin: Verlag von Gebrüder Paetel, 1873), in particular, pp. 64–77. Förster's accuracy as a historian was later questioned by Friedrich Latendorf in *Friedrich Försters Urkunden-Fälschungen zur Geschichte des Jahres 1813 mit besonderer Rücksicht auf Theodor Körners Leben und Dichten* (Poeßneck: C. Latendorf, 1891).

50 Peschel and Wildenow, *Theodor Körner*, vol. II, pp. 39–40.

51 *Theodor Körner's sämmtliche Werke*, ed. Karl Streckfuß, p. 91.

52 Peschel and Wildenow, *Theodor Körner*, vol. II, pp. 44–45.

53 Ibid., p. 48.

54 Cited in John V. A. Fine, *The Ancient Greeks: A Critical History* (Cambridge, Massachusetts: Harvard University Press, 1983), p. 141.

55 Friedrich Schulze, ed., *Die deutschen Befreiungskriege 1813-1815 geschildert von Zeitgenossen* (Leipzig: R. Voigtländers Verlag, 3rd edn.), pp. 88–89.

56 Theodor Rehtwisch, *Das Volk steht auf, Der Sturm bricht los! Geschichte der Freiheitskriege in den Jahren 1812–1815* (Leipzig: Georg Wigand, 1909), pp. 465–69. Friedrich Förster, in *Geschichte der Befreiungs-Kriege 1813. 1814. 1815*, vol. I, also tells the tale at great length (pp. 402–4). See also Peschel and Wildenow, *Theodor Körner*, vol. II, p. 71, and Adolf Brecher, *Napoleon I. und der Überfall der Lützowschen Freikorps bei Kitzen: Ein Beitrag zur Geschichte der Befreiungskriege* (Berlin: R. Gaertner, 1897).

57 See Ludwig Schlosser, "Rettung Theodor Körners," in Karl-Heinz Börner, ed., *Vor Leipzig 1813: Die Völkerschlacht in Augenzeugenberichten* (Berlin: Verlag der Nation, 1988), pp. 67–70, reprinted from Schlosser, *Erlebnisse eines sächsischen Landpredigers in den Kriegsjahren von 1806 bis 1815* (Leipzig, n.d.).

58 See Emil Staiger, "Georg Friedrich Kersting: 'Lesender beim Lampenlicht.' Eine kultur-geschichtliche Betrachtung," in *Vor Drei Bildern* (Zürich: Artemis Verlag, 1983), pp. 11–33; Kurt Karl Eberlein, *Deutsche Maler der Romantik* (Jena: Diederichs, 1920), pp. 63–75 and the same author's "Kersting's patriotische Kunst," *Der Cicerone* 16 (1924), pp. 846–54.

59 See Theodor Rehtwisch, *Das Volk steht auf, Der Sturm bricht los! Geschichte der Freiheitskriege in den Jahren 1812–1815*, vol. III, p. 43. The three reports (by his fellow soldiers Hugo Helfritz, Ferdinand Zenker, and Anton Probsthan) can be found in Peschel and Wildenow, *Theodor Körner*, vol. II, pp. 111–12. Theodor may have countermanded an order to retreat and led the charge in defiance of instructions.

60 "Wie und durch wem starb Theodor Körner den Heldentod?" in *Allgemeine Theater-Zeitung*, ed. Adolph Bäuerle, no. 298, 35. Jahrgang (Vienna, 14 December 1842), p. 1310.

61 Theodor Rehtwisch, *Geschichte der Freiheitskriege in den Jahren 1812–1815*, vol. III, pp. 43–46.

62 Friedrich Förster, *Geschichte der Befreiungs-Kriege 1813. 1814. 1815*, vol. I, pp. 850–53. Förster also includes a poem (pp. 852–53) entitled "Unter Theodor Körners Eiche. (D. 28. August 1813)."

63 The remaining Lützowers, by then incorporated into the army, took part in the Battle of the Nations, however. See Paul Burg, *Die Lützower in der Leipziger Völkerschlacht; Ein Streifritt durch drei grosse deutsche Tage* (Leipzig: Xenien-Verlag, [1913]).

64 Peschel and Wildenow, *Theodor Körner*, vol. II, p. 121.

65 Ibid., pp. 121–22. "Am 26. August dieses Jahres fiel unter den Kämpfern für Deutschlands Rettung mein Sohn Karl Theodor Körner, Lieutenant bei dem von Lützowschen Freicorps, in einem Gefechte zwischen Schwerin und Gadebusch, nachdem er in seiner kurzen Lauf bahn – er hatte das 22. Jahr noch nicht vollendet – die Freude und der Stolz der

Seinigen gewesen war. Ungeachtet einer Todesanzeige in den Berliner Zeitungen blieb mir nach späteren Nachrichten immer noch einige Hoffnung übrig, bis ich gestern die traurige Gewißheit gehielt.

Diese Bekanntmachung darf daher nicht länger anstehen, und ich rechne dabei auf das Mitgefühl aller, die den Verstorbenen gekannt haben.

Einen solchen Verlust zu überleben, findet der Vater Kraft in der Religion und in dem herzerhebenden Gedanken um den nunmehrigen Sieg der guten Sache, für die so mancher Tapfere Blut und Leben geopfert hat. Gott wird auch die Mutter und Schwester stärken. Großenhain, am 9. November 1813."

66 On the back, one reads "Karl Theodor Körner, / geboren zu Dresden am 23. September 1791, / widmete sich zuerst dem Bergbau, / dann der Dichtkunst, / zuletzt dem Kampfe für Deutschlands Rettung. / Diesem Beruf / weihte er Schwert und Leier / und opferte ihm / die schönsten Freuden und Hoffnungen / einer glücklichen Jugend. / Als Lieutenant und Adjutant / in der Lützowschen Freischar / wurde er bei einem Gefecht / zwischen Schwerin und Gadebusch / am 26. August 1813 / schnell durch eine feindliche Kugel / getötet." The quotations from Körner's poems are as follows: "Dem Sänger Heil, erkämpft er mit dem Schwerte, / Sich nur ein Grab in einer freien Erde!" and "Vaterland! Dir woll'n wir sterben, / Wie Dein großes Wort gebeut, / Unsre Lieben mögen's erben, / Was wir mit dem Blut befreit. / Wachse, du Freiheit der deutschen Eichen, / Wachse empor über unsre Leichen!"

67 Peschel and Wildenow, *Theodor Körner*, vol. II, p. 128.

68 Ibid., p. 129.

69 Ibid., pp. 132–33. Before leaving for Wöbbelin, she wrote "It seems impossible that I have entirely lost him. There, where his earthly shell rests, every dream is destroyed, and that which cannot be changed in our destiny stands cold and harsh before my mind." The first house one comes to in Wöbbelin, she wrote, is the house where Theodor's body lay until its burial; the nearby farmers told the family that they had seen the body, its features unaltered and bright, as if in the sweetest sleep.

70 See Alfred Arneth, *Aus meinem Leben*, part 1, p. 71, also Peschel and Wildenow, *Theodor Körner*, vol. II, pp. 138–45.

71 Arneth, *Aus meinem Leben*, pp. 70–71.

72 The hostility to Antonie Adamberger later found expression in Alfred Kaiser's "Theodor Körner, ein musikalisches Schauspiel" (London: privately published, 1912). Antonie is characterized as a two-timing flibbertygibbet who becomes engaged to Arneth while Theodor is still alive.

73 See Theodor Körner, *Leier und Schwert* (Berlin: Nicolai Buchhandlung, 1858), p. 81, for Ludwig II's encomium, and ibid., p. 89 for Stägemann's sonnet.

74 *Rückerts Werke*, vol. 1: *Vaterland*, ed. Elsa Hertzer (Berlin and Leipzig: Deutsches Verlagshaus Bong & Co., n.d.), p. 56, stanzas 14–15 of 15.

75 See "Theodor Körner und die National-Körnerfeier," in the Leipzig *Illustrirte Zeitung* no. 1036 (Leipzig: J. J. Weber, 1863); "Körnerfeier," in the *Schlesische Zeitung* no. 397 (1863); "Theodor Körner's Tod," in *Coburger Zeitung*, nos. 198, 199, and 200 (1863); "Körner's Tod" and "Noch eine Erinnerung an Wöbbelin," in *Die Gartenlaube*, no. 50 (Leipzig, 1863), pp. 189 and 489; Karl Deutsch, "Der Tod des Dichterhelden," in *Der Hausfreund. Illustrirtes Familienbuch*, ed. Hanns Wachenbusen (Vienna: Förster, 1863), p. 601; "Eine deutsche Todtenfeier in Amerika," in *Die Gartenlaube*, no. 50 (Leipzig, 1863), p. 180; and Friedrich Förster, *Geschichte der Befreiungs-Kriege*, vol. 1, p. 857.

76 For the works by Rau and Zimmermann, see note number 1. See also Julius Papst, "An Körner's Grabe, Vorspiel in einem Act" (Dresden: Meinhold und Söhne, 1863).

77 James J. Sheehan, *German History 1770–1866* (Oxford: Clarendon Press, 1989), p. 323.

78 Caroline Pichler, *Sämmtliche Werke* (Vienna: Anton Pichler, 1829), vol. XXVI, pp. 267–68. The text was first published in the Taschenbuch *Minerva* for 1815.

79 There is a review of the Frankenhausen performance in the *Allgemeine musikalische Zeitung*, vol. 21 (Leipzig, 1819), pp. 272f and a review of the Viennese performance in *Der Sammler*, vol. 11 (Vienna, 1819), p. 580, also the *Allgemeine Musikalische Zeitung*, vol. 22 (Leipzig, 1820), p. 56. See also Clive Brown, *Louis Spohr: A critical biography* (Cambridge, England: Cambridge University Press, 1984), pp. 92–93; Paul Katow, *Louis Spohr: Persönlichkeit und Werk* (Luxembourg: RTL Edition, 1982), p. 128, in which Katow points out the similarity of performing forces to Carl Maria von Weber's "Kampf und Sieg"; and Dorothy Moulton Mayer, *The Forgotten Master: The Life & Times of Louis Spohr* (London: Weidenfeld and Nicolson, 1959), p. 84.

80 Ben Arnold, in *Music and War: A Research and Information Guide* (New York and London: Garland Publishing, Inc., 1993), pp. 51-88, discusses symphonies, piano battle-pieces, cantatas, and choral works, but not song, in "War Music of the Classic and Early Romantic Period: 1750–1827."

81 Himmel's teacher Neumann once said that had Himmel applied himself more, he could have been one of the greatest composers of the age – the archetypal excuse for also-rans. See Carl Freiherrn von Ledebur, *Tonkünstler-Lexikon Berlin's von den ältesten Zeiten bis auf die Gegenwart* (Berlin: Ludwig Rauh, 1861), pp. 243-47.

82 *Theodor Körners sämtliche Werke*, ed. Christoph August Tiedge (Stuttgart: Macklot, 1822), vol 1, p. 25, stanza 4 of 6.

83 Ibid., pp. 174–75.

84 *Allgemeine Deutsche Biographie*, vol. 10 (Berlin: Duncker & Humblot, 1968), p. 35. For this same opus, Grund also composed an Adagio male chorus setting of Körner's "Morgenlied der Schwarzen" (Morning song of the black-clad ones) as the fifth work in the set and a setting of Körner's "Trost, als Rundgesang zu singen" (Faith, to be sung as a group), with its choral refrain at the end of each stanza, as the final expression of German patriotism in his first published opus.

85 Franz Schubert, *Neue Ausgabe sämtlicher Werke*, series 3, vol. 4: *Mehrstimmige Gesänge für gleiche Stimmen ohne Begleitung*, ed. Dietrich Berke (Kassel and Basel: Bärenreiter Verlag, 1974), pp. 46–47. Müller was a wartime friend of Graf Friedrich von Kalckreuth, a general's son who knew Körner personally. Müller, Wilhelm Hensel, Friedrich von Kalckreuth, Georg von Blankensee, and Wilhelm von Studnitz together published a volume of patriotic poems entitled *Die Bundesblüthen* ("Flowers of the League," Berlin, 1816).

86 For more on Bornhardt, see the *Allgemeine Deutsche Biographie*, vol. 3 (Berlin: Duncker & Humblot, 1967), p. 175. The other songs in op. 95 are "Die Eichen," "Mein Vaterland," "Trost: Ein Rundgesang," "Jägerlied," "Lied der schwarzen Jäger," "Bundeslied vor der Schlacht: Am Morgen des Gefechts bei Dannenberg," "Gebet während der Schlacht" (to Himmel's melody), "Missmuth, als der Dichter bei Sandau lange Zeit die Ufer der Elbe bewachen musste," "Reiterlied," "Trost," "Trinklied vor der Schlacht," "Lützows wilde Jagd," "Männer und Buben," and the "Schwerdtlied."

87 *Theodor Körner's sämtliche Werke*, ed. Tiedge, vol. 1, p. 173.

88 Another such collection of guitar-accompanied Körner settings is Albert Gottlieb Methfessel's *Lieder von Körner für vier Stimmen mit Begleitung der Guitarre*, published in

Leipzig by Hofmeister in 1814. Methfessel (1785–1869), a court Kapellmeister in Braunschweig, was well-known in his day as a singer, pianist, guitarist, and compiler of one of the most famous *Commersbücher* of the era, the product, as he relates in the foreword to the fifth edition, of his *Burschenschaft* experiences in 1813. See *Allgemeine Deutsche Biographie*, vol. 21 (Berlin: Duncker & Humblot, 1970), pp. 511–14.

89 In about 1814, he became a "virtuoso onorario di camera" to Empress Marie-Luise, in whose honor Gabriele von Baumberg had written "Das Waisenlied." See Thomas F. Heck, "The Birth of the Classic Guitar and its Cultivation in Vienna, Reflected in the Career and Compositions of Mauro Giuliani (d. 1829)," dissertation, Yale University, 1970, and the following articles by the same author: "Mauro Giuliani: Birth and Death Dates Established," *Guitar News* 114 (1971), p. 4; "Mauro Giuliani (27 July 1781–8 May 1829): Birth and Death Dates Confirmed," *Guitar Review* 37 (1972), p. 14; and "Giuliani in Italia," *Fronimo* 8 (1974), p. 16. In 1989, Ian Partridge, tenor, and Jakob Lindberg, guitarist, recorded Giuliani's *Sechs Lieder*, op. 89 on a compact disc entitled *Romantic Songs for Tenor and Guitar* from Pearl Records (SHE CD 9608).

90 See Carl Ledebur, *Tonkünstler-Lexicon Berlin's*, pp. 33–34. Heft 1 of the *Leier und Schwert* includes "Mein Vaterland," "Missmuth," "Reiterlied," "Trost," "Schwerdtlied," and "Bundeslied," while Heft 2 includes "Trost," "Unsere Zuversicht," "Abschied vom Leben," and "Lützow's wilde Jagd" as the rousing conclusion to the collection.

91 J. W. Smeed, ed., *Famous Poets, Neglected Composers: Songs to Lyrics by Goethe, Heine, Mörike, and Others* (Madison, Wisconsin: A-R Editions, 1992), p. ix.

92 See Max Maria von Weber, *Carl Maria von Weber. Ein Lebensbild* (Leipzig: Ernst Keil, 1864), vol. 1, p. 343, and Carl Maria von Weber, *Mein vielgeliebter Muks: Hundert Briefe Carl Maria von Webers an Caroline Brandt aus den Jahren 1814–1817*, ed. Eveline Bartlitz (Munich: C. H. Beck, 1987), pp. 31–32.

93 John Warrack, *Carl Maria von Weber* (Cambridge: Cambridge University Press, 1976, 2nd edn.), pp. 162–65. Warrack points out that Weber paid a price for his patriotism: Friedrich Wilhelm took offence when the songs were adopted by the Landwehr, rivals with the King's regulars, and in Dresden, Friedrich August, an ex-ally of Napoleon, also took a dim view of Prussian victory songs (p. 162). See Ernest Legouvé, "Weber et Körner," in *Gazette musicale* 5 (1838), pp. 415–17; Georges Servières, "Les Lieder de Weber," in *Episodes d'histoire musicale* (Paris: Fischbacher, 1914), pp. 187–223; Max Degen, *Die Lieder von Carl Maria von Weber* (Freiburg: Herder, 1924); Julius Kapp, *Carl Maria von Weber: Eine Biographie* (Berlin: Max Hesse, 1931); Felix von Lepel, "Carl Maria von Weber als Liederkomponist," in *Zeitschrift für Musik* 87 (1920): 432–43; Jürgen Mainka, "Carl Maria von Weber und die antinapoleonische Unabhängigkeitsbewegung," in *Beiträge der Musikwissenschaft* 29/1 (1987) 73–75; Hans Joachim Moser, "Weber und das Klavierlied der Biedermeierzeit," in *Das deutsche Lied seit Mozart* (Berlin and Zürich: Atlantis Verlag, 1937), vol. 1, pp. 141–63; Max Maria von Weber, "Wie und wo Körner's Leyer und Schwert von Carl Maria von Weber komponiert wurde," in *Berliner Musikzeitung Echo* 39 (27 September 1863) 305-8; 40 (4 October 1863) 313-17.

94 Max von Weber, *Carl Maria von Weber*, p. 454. His account of the composition of the *Leier und Schwert* songs and choruses follows on pp. 465–68, and an account of a concert on 6 January 1815 in Prague at which "Lützow's wilde Jagd" and the "Schwertlied" were performed by a chorus of sixteen men is on p. 471.

The threat of war in 1840 inspired Nicolaus Becker's (1809–1845) poem "Der deutsche Rhein," first printed in Becker's *Gedichte* (Cologne: M. DuMont-Schauberg, 1841), pp.

216–18, and beginning with the lines "Sie sollen ihn nicht haben, / Den freien deutschen Rhein." Ernst Challier's *Grosser Lieder-Katalog* of 1885 (pp. 163–64) lists sixty-five settings of the famous poem, including those by Sigismund Neukomm, Albert Methfessel, Robert Schumann, Conradin Kreutzer, and Adalbert Gyrowetz.

95 *Theodor Körners sämtliche Werke*, ed. Tiedge, vol. 1, pp. 167–68.

96 Weber made the statement in a letter to Johann Friedrich Rochlitz on 14 March 1815; see Warrack, *Carl Maria von Weber*, pp. 162–63.

97 The first sketch – fMS Mus 99 in the Houghton Library at Harvard University – is dated 15 March 1815; the completed song was first published as one of the *Acht Geistliche Lieder* by Anton Diabelli in 1831 (*Nachlaß-Lieferung* 10). There is also a copy of "Gebet während der Schlacht" in the Witteczek-Spaun collection, vol. 80, pp. 45-48, "verändert von M[ichael] Vogl."

98 *Theodor Körners sämtliche Werke*, ed. Tiedge, vol. 1, pp. 147–49, stanzas 1–2 of 6.

99 Franz Liszt transcribed op. 42, ending with "Lützows wilde Jagd" (arrangements of the "Schwertlied" and "Gebet vor der Schlacht" constitute the first and second sections of this work, which approaches one-movement sonata structure).

100 Op. 43 was published with a prefatory poem "Im Namen des Carl Maria von Weber" by Clemens Brentano.

101 The first song in Fritz Jöde's *1813 im Liede* (pp. 1-2) is "Prinz Louis Ferdinands Tod. 10. Oktober 1806." See Hans von Arnim, *Louis Ferdinand, Prinz von Preußen* (Berlin: Haude & Spener, 1966); Burkhard Nadolny, *Louis Ferdinand: Das Leben eines preußischen Prinzen* (Düsseldorf & Cologne: Eugen Diederichs Verlag, 1967); and Peter Gradenwitz, *Literatur und Musik in geselligem Kreise*, pp. 197–200. See also Fritz von Unruh's play "Louis Ferdinand Prinz von Preußen" (Berlin: Verlag Erich Reiß, 1922); Hans Wahl, *Prinz Louis Ferdinand von Preußen, ein Bild seines Lebens in Briefen, Tagebuchblättern und zeitgenössischen Zeugnissen* (Weimar: Kiepenheuer Verlag, 1917); Carl Ledebur, *Tonkünstler-Lexicon Berlin's*, pp. 334–36; and Louis Spohr, *Selbstbiographie*, vol. 1, pp. 85 and 93. For his musical works, see Louis Ferdinand, *Musikalische Werke*, 2 vols., ed. Hermann Kretzschmar (Leipzig: Breitkopf & Härtel, 1915-17) and *Lieder für Solostimme und Klavier*, 5 vols. (Wilhelmshaven: Heinrichshofen's Verlag, 1981). Franz Liszt wrote an "Elégie sur des motifs du Prince Louis Ferdinand de Prusse," recorded on Hyperion CDA 66357 (1989), *The complete piano music of Franz Liszt*, vol. 4, with Leslie Howard, pianist.

102 *Theodor Körner's sämtliche Werke*, ed. Tiedge, vol. 1, pp. 146–47.

103 See the collection *Musik und Jägerei: Lieder, Reime und Geschichten vom Edlen Waidwerk*, 3 vols., collected and edited by Carl Clewing (Neudamm: J. Neumann and Kassel-Wilhelmshöhe: Bärenreiter, 1937). On the dedicatory page after the title page, one sees an engraving of a swastika mounted between a stag's horns.

104 *Theodor Körner's Vermischte Gedichte und Erzählungen*, ed. C. A. Tiedge (Leipzig: Johann Friedrich Hartknoch, 1815), pp. 65–67, stanzas 9–11 of 11. What, one wonders, would Körner have made of the French fascination with this ballad, exemplified in Gérard de Nerval's translation and Ary Scheffer's and Horace Vernet's paintings of 1830 and 1839 respectively, in the years after Napoleon's downfall? For younger Frenchmen, this ballad must have expressed something of their own situation, in which dead men were indeed riding fast, and history had let them down. See Michel Le Bris, *Romantics and Romanticism* (New York: Rizzoli International Publications Inc., 1981), pp. 150–53.

105 Carl Loewe, *Werke*, ed. Max Runze, vol. 8: *Geisterballaden und Gesichte / Todes- und Kirchhofs-Bilder* (Leipzig: Breitkopf & Härtel, 1900), pp. 2–10.

106 *Allgemeine Musikalische Zeitung* for 1829, no. 11 (Leipzig: Breitkopf & Härtel), p. 188.

107 Ibid., August 1840, no. 32, p. 657. Other Körner settings reviewed in the AMZ include "Worte der Liebe" by Eduard Tauwitz (August 1838, no. 32, p. 524); "Gebet," "Zur Nacht," "Die drei Sterne," and "An meine Zither" by Jacob Rosenhain (November 1835, no. 46, p. 765); "Das warst du" by Otto Tiehsen (January 1839, no. 5, pp. 83–84); "Gute Nacht" by Wilhelm Nedelmann (December 1835, no. 48, p. 797); "Wiegenlied" by Gustav Reichardt (October 1827, no. 40, p. 687); and the *Drey Lieder von Theodor Körner* by Friedrich Knuth (September 1831, no. 38, p. 636).

108 Otto Erich Deutsch, *Schubert: Memoirs by His Friends*, trans. Rosamond Ley and John Nowell (London: Adam & Charles Black, 1958), p. 129. In one version, Mayrhofer is named instead of Körner.

109 Ibid., p. 75.

110 Ibid., pp. 224–25.

111 Körner, *Sämmtliche Werke*, p. 41.

112 Ibid., pp. 41–42. The pendant poem "Das warst du" is found on p. 42 and begins as follows: "Der Morgen kam auf rosichtem Gefieder, / Und weckte mich aus stiller Ruh', / Da wehte sanft Begeist'rung zu mir nieder, / Ein Ideal verklärten meine Lieder, / Und das warst Du!"

113 Hearing the beginning of "Liebesrausch," one is reminded of the sustained chord and the fermata-held pause which begin "Mit dem grünen Lautenbande" from *Die schöne Müllerin*, although the dramatic context and signification are very different; the sustained chord extends both the tonality and the dramatic situation of the preceding song "Pause" and is then broken by musical recollection of the miller maid's entrance. In still another example for yet another purpose, "Abendlied," D. 382 (haunted by Mozart's "Abend-empfindung") also begins with a single arpeggiated tonic chord which gives the singer the simplest orientation for the opening pitch and quietly underscores the hymn-like mood of reverence.

114 Körner, *Sämmtliche Werke*, p. 42.

115 Ibid., pp. 51–52.

116 Ibid., pp. 47–48.

117 Ibid., p. 44. The poem is the seventh and last in the cycle *Erinnerungen an Schlesien* (Memories of Schleswig). John Reed, in *The Schubert Song Companion*, p. 59, writes that the poem was originally entitled "Sonnenaufgang auf der Riesenkoppe" (Sunrise on the giant peak), but that work is the sixth in the set and begins "Die Erde ruht in tiefer, ernster Stille / Und alles schweigt, es dringt kein Laut zum Ohre."

118 See Gustav Reinhard, *Schillers Einfluß auf Theodor Körner* (Straßburg: Karl J. Trübner, 1899).

119 See Franz Schubert, *Neue Ausgabe sämtlicher Werke*, Series 4: *Lieder*, vol. 14b, ed. Walther Dürr (Kassel & Basel: Bärenreiter Verlag, 1988), pp. 188–93. The following stanza of the text by an unidentified poet is typical: "See how the French creatures have turned German fields into bloody altars. The ravening hyenas have devoured Hermann's noble sons for more than twenty years." "Hermann" refers to Arminius, who in 9 A. D. annihilated a Roman army in the Teutoburg Forest; he was subsequently defeated by Germanicus in 16 A. D. and assassinated by rivals five years later, while his wife Thusnelda was captured by Germanicus (see Friedrich Klopstock's "Hermann und Thusnelda," set to music by Schubert, D. 322, in 1815).

120 Johann Mayrhofer, *Gedichte* (Vienna: Friedrich Volke, 1824), pp. 98–99. Mayrhofer also wrote another tribute entitled "Den Manen Theodor Körners" (To the Shade of Theodor

Körner). "On my life's first paths, there came to me, in a beautiful hour, a heroic youth who gave me his hand in friendship's bond," he begins; "the strong one bore me on his young eagle's wings to the purest starry realm of poetry, where neither sorrow nor lamentation penetrate ... he taught me how from decay and blood comes salvation ... He fell! in unweakened fullness, the youth was received into Odin's sacred grove where spirits in the quiet oaks rejoice in the salvation of their people – Here Achilles died! Let every descendant from German soil become as Thetis!" (the sea-goddess Thetis brought a golden urn for Achilles' ashes after his death.) Johann Mayrhofer, *Gedichte von Johann Mayrhofer. Neue Sammlung*, ed. Ernst von Feuchtersleben (Vienna: Ignaz Klang, 1843), pp. 51–52.

3 Chromatic melancholy: Johann Mayrhofer and Schubert

1 Max Kalbeck, *Johannes Brahms* (Vienna and Leipzig, 1904), vol. 1, p. 230. The quotation comes from a letter to Geheimrat Wendt in Thun in 1887. "The true successor to Beethoven is not Mendelssohn, whose artistic cultivation was quite incomparable, also not Schumann, but Schubert. It is unbelievable, the music he put in his songs. No composer understands proper declamation as he did ... Of his friends, Mayrhofer was the most serious, and Schubert is surely not to be reproached for setting all sorts of mythological poems [by Mayrhofer] to music."

2 In Ernst Freiherr von Feuchtersleben's biographical foreword to the *Gedichte von Johann Mayrhofer. Neue Sammlung. Aus dessen Nachlasse mit Biographie und Vorwort* (Vienna: Ignaz Klang, 1843), p. 7, Feuchtersleben writes that the younger generation, which studies Goethe only as if he were a "dead language," cannot realize how important Goethe was for their forebears, such as Mayrhofer. In 1810 and 1816, the firm of Anton Strauß in Vienna published an edition of Goethe's and Schiller's works respectively, and from then on, the lyric poetry and ballads of the two Weimar masters exercised an enormous influence on Austrian writers and composers. Mayrhofer, Feuchtersleben notes, was less interested in the "allbewunderte Goethe" – the Goethe everyone acclaimed – than in such works as the scientific studies of nature, *Die Wahlverwandtschaften*, and *Der West-östliche Divan*.

3 In "Notes on my association with Franz Schubert" from 1858, Spaun wrote, "During this period I introduced him to my closest friends, first and foremost to the poet Johann Mayrhofer, my countryman and oldest friend. He had an exceptionally good ear and a great love for music. When Mayrhofer had heard some of Schubert's songs, he reproached me for having been much too modest in my praise of Schubert's talent. Mayrhofer sang and whistled Schubert's melodies the whole day long, and poet and composer were soon the best of friends." See Otto Erich Deutsch, *Schubert: Memoirs by his Friends*, trans. Rosamond Ley and John Nowell (London: Adam and Charles Black, Ltd., 1958), pp. 129–30.

4 In Deutsch, *Memoirs*, pp. 182–83, Anselm Hüttenbrenner reported that Schubert once said to him, "With a bad poem one can't make any headway; one torments oneself over it and nothing comes of it but boring rubbish. I have already refused many poems which have been pressed on me."

5 Franz Gräffer's *Kleine Wiener Memoiren*, 3 vols. (Vienna, 1845) and *Wiener Dosenstücke*, 2

vols. (Vienna 1846) were republished as *Kleine Wiener Memoiren und Wiener Dosenstücke*, (Munich: Georg Müller, 1928); see vol. 1, pp. 199–200 for the vignette of Mayrhofer.

6 Moritz Bauer, "Johann Mayrhofer," in *Zeitschrift für Musikwissenschaft*, ed. Alfred Einstein, Fünfter Jahrgang, October 1922 – September 1923 (Leipzig: Breitkopf & Härtel, 1923), pp. 83–84.

7 Ibid., p. 86.

8 The confusion about Mayrhofer's birthdate is elucidated in Michael Maria Rabenlechner's biographical study of the poet in the Wiener Bibliophilen-Gesellschaft reprint of the *Gedichte von Johann Mayrhofer*, "Nachwort des Herausgebers. (Johann Mayrhofers Leben)" (Vienna, 1938, reprint of the edition from 1824), pp. 21–23. Joseph Bindtner's research into the conflicting *Taufbücher* was first published in "Schuberts Freund Johann Mayrhofer," in the *Wiener Zeitung* for 8 September 1920, p. 186. See also Ernst Feuchtersleben's biographical preface to his edition of Mayrhofer's *Neue Sammlung*, pp. 1–25; Heinrich Kreissle von Hellborn, *Franz Schubert* (Vienna, 1865), pp. 43–55; Ernest Mayerhofer, "Johann Mayrhofer, der Dichterfreund Schuberts," in *Österreichische Rundschau-Land-Volk-Kultur*, vol. 2 (Vienna, 1938), p. 63; and Karl Kaspers, "Schuberts Jugendfreunde," in the *Wiener Zeitung* for 18 November (1928), no. 266, p. 3. Spaun criticizes Kreissle for describing Mayrhofer as a person of vulgar appearance; in Deutsch, *Memoirs*, p. 367, he writes that Mayrhofer "had a very intelligent appearance, with beautiful blue eyes, full of life, a delicate well-formed nose and a charming mouth with satirical cast. His appearance, it is true, could not exactly be called very handsome, but it was intelligent and attractive."

9 Carl Glossy, "Aus den Lebenserinnerungen des Joseph Freiherrn von Spaun," in the *Jahrbuch der Grillparzer-Gesellschaft*, vol. 8 (Vienna: Carl Konegen, 1898), pp. 293–98. See also Deutsch, *Memoirs*, p. 354 from Spaun's "Memoirs" of 1864 and Spaun's 1858 "Notes on my association with Franz Schubert," in Deutsch, *Memoirs*. Spaun noted that "poor as Mayrhofer was, every time an opera by Mozart or Gluck was given, he was to be seen in the fifth tier of the Kärntnertor Theatre. At home and in the street, he always used to whistle and sing bits from 'Die Zauberflöte,' which was his favorite opera. He learned to play the guitar so that he could accompany his own singing which, by the way, was not exactly beautiful."

10 In Rabenlechner, "Nachwort," pp. 215–16, the author quotes the Stiftsarchivist of St. Florian, Franz Linninger, regarding Mayrhofer's studies for the priesthood: "Der in Steyr am 3. November 1787 geborene Joh. B. Mayrhofer wurde am 8. Oktober 1806 eingekleidet und verliess St. Florian wieder am 18. Oktober 1810." Fritz List, in his doctoral dissertation for the University of Munich, "Johann Mayrhofer: ein Freund und Textdichter Franz Schuberts" (1922), repeats those same dates. Feuchtersleben, in his foreword to Mayrhofer, *Neue Sammlung*, p. 4, states that Mayrhofer studied theology "als Kleriker des Stiftes St. Florian durch drei Jahre, ebenfalls mit Auszeichnung." Feuchtersleben is frustratingly imprecise about dates, places, any particularities, saying "Denn die folgende Blätter enthalten weniger eine Geschichte als eine Darstellung; schildern weniger ein Leben als eine Denkweise" (p. 2).

11 The singer Johann Michael Vogl was also fond of this writer, as was Schubert, who mimics the Roman emperor's meditations somewhat in his diary for 8 September 1816. See Deutsch, *Schubert: A Documentary Biography*, pp. 70–71.

12 Cited in Rabenlechner, "Nachwort," p. 220. In the Schematismus for 1835, the last year in which Mayrhofer appears, he is still listed among the *Revisoren*, but with the additional note, "K. K. nö. Regierungskonzipist."

13 Fritz List, in "Johann Mayrhofer," cites on pp. 17–18 a list of Mayrhofer's requests for leave and the reasons given, including the sad "zerrüttete Gesundheit" in 1827.

14 Glossy, "Aus den Lebenserinnerungen des Joseph Freiherrn von Spaun," p. 295. Nothing external by itself can affect us, according to the Stoics; it is not until we inwardly assent to it or refuse it that harm or benefit can result.

15 It is easy to imagine that Mayrhofer might be drawn to this figure, among the most passionate and dynamic of the German humanists, a man constantly embroiled in confrontations with powerful forces. There are many parallels between Ulrich and Mayrhofer, for all the obvious differences of time, place, historical context, and personal history: Ulrich was originally intended for monastic life, then planned to devote himself to learning (he was diverted from this path when his cousin was murdered by Duke Ulrich of Württemberg in 1516, and Hutten embarked on a feud against the powerful prince), and he was a poet (he was crowned as such by Emperor Maximilian I) who wrote Lucian-like dialogues about his misfortunes, his sickness, his nationalism and attacks on tyranny.

16 Ottenwalt's letter is in the collection of the Vienna City Library WStB 36529 and is cited in David Gramit, "The intellectual and aesthetic tenets of Franz Schubert's circle" (Ph.D. dissertation, Duke University, 1987), p. 32. The Linz circle is discussed in two dissertations: Helga Prosl, "Der Freundeskreis um Anton von Spaun: Ein Beitrag zur Geistesgeschichte von Linz in der Biedermeierzeit (1811–1827)" (Ph.D. dissertation, Leopold-Franzens Universität, Innsbruck, 1951), and Dieter Lyon, "Anton von Spaun: Ein Beitrag zur Geistesgeschichte des Vormärz" (Ph.D. dissertation, Karl-Franzens Universität, Graz), 1964. As Gramit observes (p. 31), Prosl was more concerned with the intellectual background of the Linz circle, Lyon with the political background. Gramit also refers the reader (p. 36) to Walter Horace Bruford, *The German Tradition of Self- Cultivation: "Bildung" from Humboldt to Thomas Mann* (Cambridge: Cambridge University Press, 1975), with pp. 1–57 particularly relevant to Schubert's era. Schubert was most closely associated with members of the Linz circle from 1814 on; Gramit (p. 1) reminds readers that Schubert was described shortly after his death by Matthias Franz Perth, who had not known the deceased composer personally, as "an educated man" ("gebildeter Mann"). See also Herbert Zeman, "Franz Schuberts Teilhabe an der österreichischen literarischen Kultur seiner Zeit," in *Schubert-Kongreß Wien 1978: Bericht*, ed. Otto Brusatti (Graz: Akademische Druck- und Verlagsanstalt, 1979), pp. 285–304, despite the mistaken statement that only one volume of the short-lived literary annual *Beyträge zur Bildung für Jünglinge*, which Mayrhofer helped to found, was published (there were actually two issues).

17 *Beyträge* 2, pp. 302–3, also cited in Gramit, "The intellectual and aesthetic tenets of Schubert's circle," pp. 72–73. There is another historical article in vol. 2 of the *Beyträge*, this one on the tenth century Emperor Otto, which could possibly be by Mayrhofer, but which is unsigned; the next volume, which never appeared, was supposed to include the continuation.

18 Deutsch, *Memoirs*, p. 130. See also Kreissle von Hellborn, *Franz Schubert*, pp. 47–48n.

19 Deutsch, *Memoirs*, from Mayrhofer's "Recollections of Franz Schubert" (*Neues Archiv für Geschichte, Staatenkunde, Literatur und Kunst*, Vienna, 23 February 1829), pp. 13–14.

20 Kreissle von Hellborn, *Franz Schubert*, p. 51n.

21 Mayrhofer, *Neue Sammlung*, pp. 78–79.

22 The *Heliopolis* cycle (now in the collection of the Vienna City Library) is the subject of

an article by David Gramit, "Schubert and the Biedermeier: The Aesthetics of Johann Mayrhofer's 'Heliopolis'," in *Music & Letters*, vol. 74, no. 3 (August 1993), pp. 355–82. "Der Reiter liebt sein treues Roß" appears on p. 376 (German text) and p. 380 (English translation).

23 Deutsch, *A Documentary Biography*, no. 134, p. 100. The letter was written on 8 September 1818, before Schubert and Mayrhofer began to room together. The injunction to "Cease ailing" is preceded by reassuring words about their future plans: "Dear Mayrhofer, my longing for November will hardly be less than yours."

24 In Deutsch, *Memoirs*, p. 56, the Linz physician Adam Haller wrote in 1858 that "Feuchtersleben used often to say to me: 'Mayrhofer's genius is drying up, for the harmony of his life faded out with Schubert's death.' A deep melancholy, a bitterness against the wickedness of life, now filled Mayrhofer's being, and I found that the perceptive poet had become a misanthrope, for he inveighed against everything to an abnormal degree and mankind he found base and wicked." See also Rabenlechner, "Nachwort," p. 233.

25 Deutsch, *A Documentary Biography*, no. 451, p. 336.

26 See Maynard Solomon, "Franz Schubert and the Peacocks of Benvenuto Cellini," *19th-Century Music* 12 (Spring 1898) 193–206, the fount and origin of the controversy, and *Schubert: Music, Sexuality, Culture*, ed. Lawrence Kramer, a special issue of *19th-Century Music* 17/1 (Summer 1993).

27 Carl Glossy, "Aus den Lebenserinnerungen des Joseph Freiherrn von Spaun," in the *Grillparzer-Jahrbuch*, vol. 8, pp. 293–98. The anecdote is quoted in Rabenlechner, "Nachwort," p. 215.

28 Mayrhofer, *Neue Sammlung* (1843), p. 227.

29 Mayrhofer, *Gedichte*, p. 128. The anthology of 118 poems was subsequently reproduced in 1938 as a "rarissimum" of the Viennese Biedermeier by the Wiener Bibliophilen-Gesellschaft (Society of Bibliophiles), with a lengthy biographical "Afterword" by Rabenlechner and a facsimile of Mayrhofer's handwriting from a dedicatory poem in Helen von Feuchtersleben's album. The original publication costs were subsidized by subscribers, including many from the Schubert circle; the list of "Subscribenten" is found on pp. iii–vi of the 1824 edition and includes Johann, Frau and Fraulein Justina, Isabella, and Franz von Bruchmann; Karl Enderes; Anna Honig and her husband; Anselm, Heinrich, and Joseph Huttenbrenner; Anton Ottenwalt; Mayrhofer's former landlady Anna Sanssouci; Anton, Franz, Joseph, and Max von Spaun; Carl Schoberlechner, Caroline Pichler, Moritz von Schwind, Leopold Sonnleithner, Anna Watteroth, Caroline von Pasqualati, Franz von Schlechta, Franz von Schober, and Johann Michael Vogl, who often sang Schubert's Mayrhofer settings. In Spaun's reminiscences, found in Deutsch's *Memoirs*, p. 132, the works the composer brought for Vogl when the composer and singer first met in February or March 1817 included the Mayrhofer settings "Augenlied" (which Spaun calls "a pretty, very melodious, but not important song") and "Memnon." Spaun also relates that "When the song 'Die Dioskuren' ['Lied eines Schiffers an die Dioskuren,' D. 360] came to his notice he declared it to be a magnificent song and said it was frankly incomprehensible how such depth and maturity could emanate from the little young man." Spaun, in Deutsch, *Memoirs*, p. 139, tells of Vogl's unforgettable singing of Schubert's songs, including the "Fragment aus dem Aeschylus," "Der entsühnte Orest," and "Die zürnende Diana" (*sic*). Bauernfeld (ibid., p. 240) in 1872 also mentions Vogl's singing in his later years of "Memnon," "Antigone und Oedip," "Philoktet," and "Orest [auf Tauris]."

30 Mayrhofer, *Neue Sammlung* (1843), pp. 107–8.

31 Mayrhofer, *Gedichte* (1824), "Ohne Liebe kein Glück", p. 51.

32 Mayrhofer, *Neue Sammlung* (1843), pp. 238–39.

33 Ibid., p. 323.

34 Ibid., p. 247.

35 Ibid., p. 227.

36 Ibid, p. 238.

37 Ibid., p. 101, stanzas 4 and 5 of 5. Another love-poem in the *Neue Sammlung* which arouses curiosity is "An die Geliebte" (To the beloved), with its lines "Distanced from you, I strive to return to you – does life have any worth without you? ... I want only you" (p. 99).

38 Mayrhofer, *Gedichte* (1824), p. 9.

39 Ibid., pp. 43–44.

40 Could "Braun" (brown) be a reminiscence of Schubert? "In place of brighter colors, I choose brown, only brown, o gentle brown! It flowed from the beloved's eyes and had its source in the beloved's hair," Mayrhofer writes in the first stanza. Given the plethora of brown-eyed, brown-haired people in the world, one hesitates to speculate further. See Mayrhofer, *Neue Sammlung* (1843), p. 63. And could the poem "An Eccho" (*Neue Sammlung*, p. 49) also be an encoded lament for Schubert? The third and last stanza is: "Mancher Ton dringt schmeichelnd an die Ohren; / Einer nur vereinte das Zerstückte, / Einer wär' es, der mich noch beglückte, – / Aber ach, ich habe ihn verloren!"

41 Mayrhofer, *Neue Sammlung*, pp. 151–52.

42 Ibid., pp. 53–54.

43 Ibid., pp. 178–79.

44 Kreissle von Hellborn, *Franz Schubert*, p. 53.

45 Pyrker, later an archbishop, was the dedicatee for Schubert's op. 4 songs, published in May of 1821, and the two Pyrker settings of Op. 79 ("Das Heimweh" and "Die Allmacht"), published in May 1827.

46 Mayrhofer, *Neue Sammlung* (1843), p. 150. Horribly, this poem is followed by "Nachgefühl. An Fr. Schubert (19. Novbr. 1828)," a death-song to his erstwhile friend, who *did* know "Lenzesfülle, rasches Ende!" as Mayrhofer did not. One notes that it is a blackbird, the traditional messenger of ill-tidings in folklore.

47 Ibid., p. 177. The poem begins: "Often a bolt of lightning with glowing red flames flashes through my fearful mind, and night and the dense clouds both disappear, and the landscape becomes green. Oh, if only I could hold on to the ray of light: my life would then be calmed, the battle that destroys it set aright, and gentle beings would hover about me! Yet – night again! And the battle is renewed."

48 "In Bezug auf mein Leichenbegängnis will ich in der letzten, d. h. schlechtesten Klasse beerdigt werden." See Rabenlechner, "Nachwort," pp. 238–41, for an account of Mayrhofer's end (the will is quoted on p. 240). The *Sterbebucheintragung* for 1836, folio 62, of the parish for the Heilige Dreifaltigkeit in the Alservorstadt includes Mayrhofer's death notice: "Am 5. Februar der in der Stadt Steyr geborne ... in der Leopoldstadt Nr. 498 wohnhaft gewesene Mayrhofer, Johann, ledig, Revisor des k. k. Büchereirevisionsamtes, 48 Jahre alt, infolge der durch einen Sturz erlittenen Verletzungen, hat sich selbst entleibt ... stürzte sich vom 3. Stock des Lorrenzer Gebäudes in den Hof" (Rabenlechner, "Nachwort," p. 239). It was, Spaun writes, a testament to his modest way of life that Mayrhofer could leave his sister 1,200 silver florins. See Carl Glossy, "Aus den Lebens-erinnerungen des Joseph von Spaun," p. 298.

49 Rabenlechner, "Nachwort," pp. 241–42, ll. 1–8. The final sestet of Schober's poem is remarkably enigmatic.

Für einen zweiten Gast war's wohl erneuet;	It was renewed for a second guest,
Und was dem Ersten Liebe mitgegeben,	And what love gave to the first,
Sein Totenschmuck, die Spende treuer Seelen,	its death-adornment a gift from loving souls,
Lag mit den Knochen nun umhergestreut;	now lay strewn about with the bones;
Mich trieb's, den unscheinbaren aufzuheben –	I felt compelled to raise up what seemed
Und sieh! es waren köstliche Juwelen.	dull – and look! it was precious jewels.

What is symbolized by the seemingly dull grave-adornments that were actually precious jewels? Was the "first guest" possibly Schubert, who was originally buried in the Währinger Cemetery?

50 Kreissle von Hellborn, *Franz Schubert*, p. 50.

51 Eduard von Bauernfeld, *Gesammelte Schriften*, vol. XI, *Reime und Rhythmen* (Vienna: Wilhelm Braumüller, 1873). "Ein Wiener Censor" also appeared in the collection *Neue Zeit*, pp. 84–87. See also Eduard Bauernfeld, *Erinnerungen aus Alt-Wien*, ed. by Josef Bindtner (Vienna, 1923), pp. 75, 87, 95, 468, 512 for brief invocations of Mayrhofer's name and association with Schubert.

52 Bauernfeld had several brushes with the censors, including rejection of his libretto for the unfinished opera in collaboration with Schubert, *Der Graf von Gleichen*. In *A Documentary Biography*, no. 716, p. 561, Deutsch includes a note from Bauernfeld's diary for October 1826: "The libretto prohibited by the censorship. Schubert wants to compose it all the same." Bauernfeld, like Goethe and Mayrhofer, wrote "Xenien," including one on Schubert (Bauernfeld, *Gesammelte Schriften*, vol. II, p. 129): "Hat er studirt, speculirt? Der Lieder entzückende Springflut, / Sonder Pumpe, sie quillt frisch aus der fühlenden Brust" (Has he studied [and] pondered? The enchanting spring-tide of songs flows freshly from the feeling heart without a pump). In the poem "Jugendfreunde" ("Youthful Friends," Bauernfeld, *Gesammelte Schriften*, vol. II, p. 50), Bauernfeld mourns Schubert's death and Moritz von Schwind's departure for Munich.

53 Eduard Bauernfeld, *Gesammelte Schriften*, vol. IX, pp. 84–7.

54 Eduard Bauernfeld, *Gesammelte Aufsätze*, ed. Stefan Hock (Vienna: Verlag des Literarischen Vereins in Wien, 1905), pp. 163–64.

55 Carl Glossy, "Aus Bauernfelds Tagebüchern," in *Jahrbuch der Grillparzer-Gesellschaft*, vol. 5 (Vienna: Carl Konegen, 1895), p. 75.

56 Fritz List, "Johann Mayrhofer: Ein Freund und Textdichter Franz Schuberts," pp. 96–101, lists citations from contemporary reviews. An anonymous critic writing in the *Allgemeine Literatur-Zeitung*, vol. 41, no. 130 (Halle, 1825) about the 1824 *Gedichte* said that much in these verses recalled Goethe's objectivity, chided Mayrhofer for the occasional poor rhyme, and said that the poet could have eliminated some of the more unclear poems and thereby strengthened the anthology. The reviewer for the *Leipzig Literarische Conversationsblatt* for 1824, vol. 2, no. 155 (p. 619) likewise pointed out the debt to Goethe and stated that the anthology could have been made better by the omission of some half of the poems, but praised the profundity: "He does not always succeed in his wish, but many [of these poems] would not be out of place in the *West-östlicher Divan*" – high praise indeed. A review in the *Blätter für Literatur, Kunst und Kritik, Beilage zur Österreichische Zeitschrift für Geschichts- und Staatenkunde* for 6 August 1826, vol. 2, no. 63, was brief but warm, with no reservations. The reviewer for *Der Gesellschafter, oder Blätter für Geist und*

Herz, ed. F. Gubitz, vol. 9 (Berlin, 1925) was complimentary at even greater length. However, List also combed through a lengthy list of journals and newspapers, many of them from outside Vienna but some local as well, hunting for mention of Mayrhofer and met with disappointment (List, p. 107).

57 Franz Grillparzer, *Samtliche Werke*, 5th edn., (Stuttgart, n.d.), vol. XVIII, pp. 133 and 233 respectively.

58 Julius Seidlitz, *Die Poesie und die Poeten in Österreich im Jahre 1836* (Grimma: J. M. Gebhardt, 1837), vol. 1, p. 140. There is evidence of at least one posthumously-printed *Nachklang* of (limited) local acclaim: Mayrhofer's "Befriedigung," "Nahes und fernes Leid," "Im Sturme," "Die Kerze," and "Schlachtgefühl" are included in S. Mosenthal's *Museum aus den deutschen Dichtungen österreichischer Lyriker und Epiker der frühesten bis zur neuesten Zeit* (Vienna: Carl Gerold & Sohn, 1854).

59 Deutsch, *Memoirs*, pp. 130 and 354 (the anecdote twice told). Mayrhofer was not a facile poet. Feuchtersleben recounts an occasion when Mayrhofer came to him in jubilation and said, "I finally have the last two verses for the 'Glücklichen,' after working [Mayrhofer used the evocative verb 'kauen,' meaning 'to gnaw'] on them for a week." See Feuchtersleben's foreword to Mayrhofer, *Neue Sammlung*, p. 20.

60 Mayrhofer, *Gedichte* (1824), p. 142.

61 Mayrhofer, *Neue Sammlung*, p. 37.

62 Ibid., pp. 74–75.

63 *Beyträge* 2, pp. 305–6, cited in Gramit, "The intellectual and aesthetic tenets of Schubert's circle," p. 72.

64 According to Feuchtersleben, Mayrhofer once wrote to Goethe, but no trace of the letter remains, nor any record of an answer. See Feuchtersleben's foreword to Mayrhofer, *Neue Sammlung*, p. 7. Several of Mayrhofer's titles or first lines are clearly borrowed from the older master, but with the younger poet's own melancholy twist, as in "Trost der Trennung." Mayrhofer's "Tasso und Manso," "Faust," "Mephistopheles," and the Iphigenia poems are later variations on Goethe's plays. The *Xenien* too are modelled on Goethe's *Xenien*, although the sentiments are not Goethe's.

65 Mayrhofer, *Gedichte* (1824), p. 5.

66 Mayrhofer, *Neue Sammlung*, p. 48.

67 Ibid., p. 104. In the second stanza, he asks whether spring and summer and the horde of stars can ever alter his darkened mind.

68 Mayrhofer, *Gedichte* (1824), p. 90.

69 Mayrhofer, *Neue Sammlung*, pp. 39–41.

70 Ibid., p. 5, the end of the tenth and final stanza.

71 In "Den Manen Beethoven's. März 1827" (An Elegy for Beethoven. March 1827), Mayrhofer again reveals his love of music: "Bedarf der Genius das arme Wort, – / Das Wort, so, kaum gesprochen, schon verhallt? / Sein unermeßlich Wirken dauert fort, / Und Zeit und Raum verlieren die Gewalt." Mayrhofer, *Neue Sammlung*, p. 61.

72 Mayrhofer, *Neue Sammlung*, p. 66.

73 Ibid., pp. 70–71. "Im Sturme," stanzas 1 and 2. It was not often or for long that Mayrhofer saw the world as "joyfully extending a thousand arms to embrace him" – a reminiscence of Goethe? The older poet's use of the adjective "tausend" to indicate infinite multiplicity reappears here.

74 Mayrhofer, *Gedichte* (1824), p. 125, "Hinaus."

75 Mayrhofer, *Neue Sammlung*, pp. 33–34.

76 Mayrhofer, *Gedichte* (1824), p. 143.

77 Mayrhofer, *Neue Sammlung*, p. 31.

78 Ibid., pp. 167–68. It is especially in his nature poems that one finds the short-breathed lines and changeable meters typical of Mayrhofer at his most experimental, as in "Tannenhymnus" (Hymn of the pine forest). See Mayrhofer, *Gedichte* (1824), pp. 179–80.

79 Mayrhofer, *Neue Sammlung*, pp. 110, 111, 122, and 117, respectively.

80 Ibid., pp. 259–60.

81 Mayrhofer, *Gedichte* (1824), pp. 91–93.

82 Rabenlechner, "Nachwort," p. 231.

83 See Walter H. Sokel, *The Writer in Extremis: Expressionism in Twentieth-Century German Literature* (Stanford University Press, 1959).

84 A complete list is as follows: "Am See," D. 124 of 1814; "Liane," D. 298 of 1815; "Fragment aus dem Aeschylus," D. 450; "Liedesend," D. 473; "Abschied. Nach einer Wallfahrtsarie," D. 475; "Rückweg," D. 476; "Alte Liebe rostet nie," D. 477; "Der Hirt," D. 490; "Geheimnis," D. 491; "Zum Punsche," D. 492; "Abendlied der Fürstin," D. 495 of 1816; "Augenlied," D. 297; "Der Alpenjäger," D. 524; and "Wie Ulfru fischt," D. 525 of 1817.

85 Mayrhofer, *Gedichte* (1824), p. 155.

86 Ibid., pp. 18–19.

87 See Thomas A. Denny, "Directional Tonality in Schubert's Lieder," in *Franz Schubert – Der Fortschrittliche? Analysen-Perspektiven-Fakten*, ed. Erich Wolfgang Partsch (Tutzing: Hans Schneider, 1989), pp. 37–54.

88 Several critics who reviewed op. 21 (which also includes "Der Schiffer," D. 536, and "Wie Ulfru fischt," D. 525), published by Sauer & Leidesdorf in June of 1823, were taken aback. Although Gottfried Fink, writing for the Leipzig *Allgemeine Musikalische Zeitung* on 24 June 1824, praised the "fresh courage of youth, [which] disdains the old, well-trodden ways and clears a new path," he was dismayed by the "want of inner unity, order, and regularity." He especially inveighed against "the unwarrantably strong inclination to modulate again and again, with neither rest nor respite, which is a veritable disease of our time and threatens to grow into a modulation-mania to which unfortunately even famous composers succumb, either willingly or for the sake of following fashion." Deutsch, *A Documentary Biography*, pp. 352–55.

89 There is some question about when Schubert composed this song (D. 516, published by Cappi and Diabelli on 9 May 1822 as op. 8, no. 2, along with "Der Jüngling auf dem Hügel" to a poem by Heinrich Hüttenbrenner and Mayrhofer's "Erlafsee," D. 586 and "Am Strome," D. 539), possibly in 1816. A sketch with the inscription "Sehnsucht" appears, along with sketches for the Adagio in C, D. 349, on the back side of what had begun as the manuscript of the Minuets and Trios for piano, D. 41 (Vienna City Library, MH 154/c). Other scholars have proposed a somewhat later date of 1817, perhaps because "Sehnsucht" is another tonally progressive song of the sort mostly clustered in the years 1817 to 1820.

90 Mayrhofer, *Gedichte* (1824), p. 170.

91 Ibid., p. 100.

92 Reed, *The Schubert Song Companion*, p. 492.

93 Facsimiles of both the song and the engraving appear in *Franz Schubert. Dokumente 1817–1830*, vol. 1: *Texte. Programme, Rezensionen, Anzeigen, Nekrologe, Musikbeilagen und andere gedruckte Quellen*, ed. Till Gerrit Waidelich (Tutzing: Hans Schneider, 1993), pp. 3–6.

94 Walter Gerstenberg, in "Schubertiade. Anmerkungen zu einigen Liedern," in *Festschrift*

Otto Erich Deutsch (Kassel: Bärenreiter, 1963), p. 233, proposed that the frequency with which Schubert's song texts diverge from the poetic text might be explained by Schubert's habit of working from a memorized text, although he recognized that there were instances in which the divergences were too drastic for this explanation to suffice. Maximilian and Lilly Schochow, in *Franz Schubert. Die Texte seiner einstimmig komponierten Lieder und ihre Dichter*, 2 vols. (Hildesheim: Georg Olms, 1974), cite the variants between Schubert's and Mayrhofer's texts in vol. 2, pp. 316–58, and ascribe the striking differences between Schubert's texts and Mayrhofer's published poems to Schubert's superior poetic judgement: he *improved* the poems. Dietrich Berke, in "Schuberts Liedentwurf 'Abend' D 654 und dessen textliche Voraussetzungen," in *Schubert-Kongreß Wien 1978*, ed. Otto Brusatti (Graz: Akademische Druck- und Verlagsanstalt, 1979), in response to the errors in the Schochow compendium, proposed that a *Textvorlage* which corresponds to the text in a Schubert song must exist, whatever reasonable discrepancies are explicable as slips of the pen or the memory. But this does not account for all such instances, as Kristina Muxfeldt has pointed out in "Schubert Song Studies" (Ph.D. dissertation, State University of New York at Stony Brook, 1991); see chap. 3, pp. 75–126.

95 Mayrhofer, *Gedichte* (1824), pp. 94–95. The omitted verses are given in brackets. Even in the portions of the text Schubert retained, there are discrepancies with Mayrhofer's published version. Mayrhofer's line "Der dunkle Schoos" becomes "der blaue Schoos" in Schubert and "Überm *glatten* Spiegel" become "Überm dunklen Spiegel." The somewhat gloomier shading of the poet's published wording in the first instance is literally lightened.

96 Mayrhofer, *Gedichte* (1824), p. 175.

97 Mayrhofer, *Neue Sammlung*, p. 154.

98 Ibid., pp. 41–42 and 135–36 respectively. The second stanza of "Sternenschein" resembles "Tillisberg" in its image of serpents harbored within the breast and its evocation of horrific suffering and guilt: "Von Täuschungen, melodischen Sirenen, / Wird er in Todesschlaf gelullt; / In's Unbegränzte greift sein töricht Sehnen, / Für Glück erbeutet er die Schuld, – / Dann lagern hurtig sich der Reue Schlangen / An's Menschenherz; sein Blut entquillt, / Und wird von ihnen lechzend aufgefangen, / Bis sie den Busen ausgewühlt." Herbert Zeman discusses Mayrhofer's "Sternenschein" as an example of how Goethe's influence affected Austrian literature in the early nineteenth century and compares the initial two lines – "Des Tages schwere Mühen sind vollendet, / Und schweigend naht die heil'ge Nacht" – to Matthäus von Collin's "Nacht und Träume" ("Heil'ge Nacht, du sinkest nieder"). See Zeman, "Die österreichische Lyrik des ausgehenden 18. und des frühen 19. Jahrhunderts – eine stil- und gattungsgeschichtliche Charakteristik," in *Die Österreichische Literatur: Ihr Profil im 19. Jahrhunderts (1830–1880)* (Graz: Akademische Druck- und Verlagsanstalt, 1982), pp. 541–45.

99 Mayrhofer, *Gedichte* (1824), p. 141.

100 See Graham Johnson, "Death and the Composer," in *The Hyperion Schubert Edition: Complete Songs*, vol. 11, with Brigitte Fassbaender, mezzo-soprano, and Graham Johnson, pianist (Hyperion CDJ 33011, 1990), pp. 29–30.

101 The mordents and grace-noted turning figures in mm. 2–3 of "Heliopolis I" recur in "Der greise Kopf" from *Winterreise* when the wanderer believes himself transformed into an old man who can therefore expect imminent death.

102 Mayrhofer, *Gedichte* (1824), pp. 64–65. Wigmore, *Schubert: The Complete Song Texts*, pp. 121–22, breaks Mayrhofer's middle stanza into four separate tercets.

103 Mayrhofer, *Gedichte* (1824), p. 72.

104 Did Brahms (whose homages to Schubert in his own lieder merit fuller exploration) have the end of "Der Pilgrim" in mind when he composed the ending of "Denn es gehet dem Menschen wie dem Vieh," the first of the *Vier ernste Gesänge*, op. 121? The gloomy passage in Ecclesiasticus 3: 18–22 ends with the question "For who shall bring him [mankind] to see what shall be after him?", the existential doubt and pessimism akin to Schiller's pilgrim.

105 Mayrhofer, *Gedichte* (1824), p. 122.

106 Mayrhofer, *Neue Sammlung*, p. 296.

4 "En route to *Winterreise*": Ernst Schulze and the sisterly muses, or a study in Romantic psychopathy

1 No one knows when, how, or where Schubert discovered these poems. The *Poetisches Tagebuch* was first published in Ernst Schulze, *Sämmtliche poetische Werke*, vol. 3 (Leipzig: Brockhaus, 1819, 2nd edn., 1822). A different edition followed in 1824 from the publisher W. A. J. Roßnagel in the town of Dillingen an der Donau, but not until 1827 did the firm of Mausberger publish an edition in Vienna. Otto Erich Deutsch felt that the 1822 second Brockhaus edition, which was disseminated far and wide, was the likeliest candidate for the text source, but the Dillingen edition could also have reached Schubert through various intermediaries in Vienna. The bass Karl Friedrich Weinmüller, court chapel singer since 1800 and a man who knew Johann Michael Vogl well, was born in Dillingen and could have been the middleman, as could the court opera singers Antonie and Cäcilie Laucher, whose brother was a schoolteacher in Dillingen. See Adolf Layer, "Karl Friedrich Weinmüller (1763–1828), ein Wiener Sänger der Beethovenzeit," in *Jahrbuch der Historische Vereins Dillingen*, Jahrgang 1962–3, pp. 95–114, and Hans Böhm, "W. A. J. Roßnagels deutsche Klassikerausgaben," in ibid., pp. 129–32.

2 *Die bezauberte Rose* has three principal strands: (1) a sleeping beauty scenario in which an enchanted maiden awaits a man's "magic" act to turn her into a woman; (2) the Orpheus myth of a poet-singer named Alpino whose art is all-powerful; and (3) the fairy-tale theme of multiple suitors contesting with one another for the prize of the princess's hand. One wonders whether Schubert was drawn to this tale not only as an opportunity for the then-fashionable *Zauberoper* but for its allegory of art's transformative power. On 31 May 1824, Moritz von Schwind wrote to Leopold Kupelwieser to say: "Schubert has left for Count Esterhazy's in Hungary. He has an opera libretto with him, on the subject of the enchanted rose, worked up by Dr. Bernhardt, and he has also resolved to write a symphony." See Otto Erich Deutsch, *Schubert: A Documentary Biography*, trans. Eric Blom (New York: Da Capo Press, 1977), pp. 347–48. Schubert asked Eduard Bauernfeld in March 1825 for an "Enchanted rose" libretto, but Bauernfeld, already devising the "Count of Gleichen," was uninterested (ibid., p. 410). Schubert's hopes came to an end by June 1826 when he wrote to Bauernfeld to say, "'The enchanted rose' has already been taken from you: the burgomaster of Teplitz has treated it operatically" (ibid., p. 532). The "burgomaster of Teplitz" was one Josef Maria Wolfram (1789-1839), the librettist was Eduard Heinrich Gehe (1793-1850, a youthful friend of Theodor Körner), and the opera was entitled *Maja und Alpino, oder die bezauberte Rose*, first performed in Prague on 24 May 1826; a review appears in the *Allgemeine Musikalische Zeitung*, vol. 29,

no. 15 (April 1827), pp. 259–60. See Harald Müller, "Ernst Schulzes Werk in Vertonungen: Zur Wirkungsgeschichte des Celler Dichters in der Musik," from the *Celler Chronik*, vol. 1 (1978), pp. 112–59.

3 John Reed, *The Schubert Song Companion* (Manchester: Manchester University Press, 1985), p. 478.

4 Jules Le Fevre-Deumier, in *Célébrités Allemandes: Essais Bibliographiques et Littéraires* (Paris: Firmin-Didot et Cie., 1894), pp. 238–39, writes that Schulze flowered early, died young, and accomplished all he was capable of creating.

5 Karl Emil Franzos, "Ernst Schulze und Cäcilie Tychsen. Nach den ungedruckten Tagebüchern, Gedichten und Briefen Schulzes," *Deutsche Dichtung*, vol. 12 (April–September 1892), p. 223. Franzos published the diary and letters pertaining to Cäcilie Tychsen in a ten-part series appearing in vols. 11 and 12 as follows: (1) vol. 11 (October 1891–March 1892): pp. 119–28, 171–76, 196–201, 244–51, and 294–300; (2) vol. 12: pp. 198–200, 221–25, 245–52, 267–76, and 294–99.

6 Ludwig Geiger, "Ernst Schulze," *Deutsche Dichtung*, vol. 5 (March 1889), pp. 272–75.

7 John Reed's capsule biography in *The Schubert Song Companion*, p. 478, is the latest to repeat the idealized version of Schulze's life. One also finds it in Jörg-Dieter Schwethelm, *Sie machten die Geschichte: Menschen aus Göttingen* (Göttingen: Th. Weinobst Buchvertrieb, n.d.), in the entry for "Cäcilie Tychsen," p. 118, and, in its most sugary form, in Emma Merkel, "Riekchen Färber und 'Die bezauberte Rose'" from *Alt-Göttinger Geschichten* (Osterode: Verlag Giebel & Oehlschlägel, 1956), pp. 113–15. A descendant of the Tychsen family, an ethnologist and poet named Hellmut Draws-Tychsen (born 1904), both cites Franzos' investigations and perpetuates the "saintly Cäcilie and her minstrel" myth in his 1954 *Requiem und Hymnen für Cecilie Tychsen* (Diessen vor München: Jos. C. Huber, 1954, 2nd edn.; 1st edn. Danziger Verlags-Gesellschaft, 1930). Draws-Tychsen criticizes Germans for honoring the "creatively feeble" Theodor Körner while ignoring Schulze (p. 16); although he describes the fusion of Cäcilie and Adelheid in the *Poetisches Tagebuch* as "seltsam-schizoïd und traumhaft-wahnvoll," he says little about Adelheid or Schulze's behavior.

8 Friedrich Bouterwek, "Biographische Vorrede" to Ernst Schulze, *Cäcilie. Ein romantisches Gedicht in zwanzig Gesängen*, 2 vols. (Vienna: B. Ph. Bauer and Reutlingen: J. J. Mäcken, 1820), pp. v–xxxix.

9 Heinrich Zschokke, *Novellen und Dichtungen*, vol. 11 (Aarau: H. R. Sauerländer, n.d.), p. 338.

10 Hermann Marggraff, *Ernst Schulze. Nach seinen Tagebüchern und Briefen sowie nach Mitteilungen seiner Freunde geschildert* (Leipzig: F. A. Brockhaus, 1855).

11 Franzos is known to musicians primarily as the first editor of Georg Büchner's works (he is the source of Alban Berg's misspelling "Wozzeck"). He was himself a writer, whose works include *Der Wahrheitssucher* (1893). He was indeed a "Wahrheitssucher" (seeker after truth) in Schulze's case.

12 Franzos's other publications pertaining to Schulze are as follows:

(1) "Zur Charakteristik Ernst Schulze's. Nach ungedruckten Quellen," *Deutsche Dichtung*, vol. 6 (April–September 1889), pp. 23–31, 49–56, 146–52, 223–38, and 245–52.

(2) "Ernst Schulze in Göttingen. Nach ungedruckten Quellen," *Deutsche Dichtung*, vol. 7 (October 1889–March 1890), pp. 50–54, 97–103, 170–73, and 193–95.

(3) "Ernst Schulze und Adelheid Tychsen. Nach den ungedruckten Tagebüchern, Gedichten und Briefen Schulze's," *Deutsche Dichtung*, vol. 17 (April–September 1894),

pp. 28–32, 47–52, 68–78, 92–99, 115–23, 142–49, 165–73, 194–99, 217–26, 240-48, 265–72, and 287–95.

(4) "Thekla. Aus Ernst Schulze's Tagebüchern," *Deutsche Dichtung*, vol. 8 (April–September 1890), pp. 198–203.

(5) "Elegie von Ernst Schulze (Ungedruckter Nachlaß)," *Deutsche Dichtung*, vol. 7 (October 1889–March 1890), pp. 279–82. On 4 February 1817, the seriously ill Schulze began work on a large (132 lines) elegy in hexameters, beginning "Was mir die Liebe beschied, den unendlichen Schmerz der Entsagung."

(6) "Ein Liebeshandel à l'empire. Aus den ungedruckten Tagebüchern, Gedichten und Briefen Ernst Schulze's," *Deutsche Dichtung*, vol. 24 (April–September 1898), pp. 22–27, 48–55, 73–79, 91–100, 118–24, 140–46, 169–75, 196–202, 217–22, 247–51, 264–66, and 285–86.

(7) "Karl Lachmann und Ernst Schulze. Mit ungedruckten Briefen Lachmanns," *Deutsche Dichtung*, vol. 33 (October 1902–March 1903), pp. 30–32.

(8) "Christian August Brandis und Ernst Schulze. Mit ungedruckten Briefen Christian August Brandis," *Deutsche Dichtung*, vol. 34 (April–September 1903), pp. 267–72 and 293–96.

13 Franzos, "Ernst Schulze und Cäcilie Tychsen," vol. 11, p. 120.

14 Ibid., pp. 120–21.

15 Franzos, "Zur Charakteristik Ernst Schulze's," p. 24.

16 Ibid., p. 26.

17 Ibid., pp. 51–52, stanza 1 of 11.

18 Ibid., p. 52, stanza 4 of 9.

19 Ibid., p. 54.

20 Ibid., p. 56.

21 Schulze describes the first episode as a "tragi-comic tale." Because the cousin had been ill in 1804, she came to stay in town with the Schulzes, where Ernst would read to her as she lay in bed and bring her tea. After she returned to her family, Ernst was invited to spend a holiday with them in the winter of 1804–5; when he arrived, it was in time to celebrate her betrothal to a young man from the vicinity. One notes the pattern of the attraction: the young woman was ill, he was her "preux chevalier" to sit by her bedside, and she did not return his love. See Franzos, "Zur Charakteristik Ernst Schulze's," p. 28.

22 Ibid., p. 29 and again on p. 245.

23 The tale of Schulze and Sophie Meyer appears in the diary for Adelheid on 20 and 23 June 1813. See Franzos, "Zur Charakteristik Ernst Schulze's," p. 245–47. The sonnets can be found in the *Werke*, 3rd edn., vol. 4, pp. 176–86. See Franzos, "Zur Charakteristik Ernst Schulze's," pp. 248–49, for the poems "Der Schmetterling und die Rose" (The butterfly and the rose) and "Die Liebe" (Love).

24 Franzos, "Zur Charakteristik Ernst Schulze's," p. 228, also in "Ernst Schulze und Cäcilie Tychsen," vol. 11, p. 121.

25 Franzos, "Ernst Schulze und Cäcilie Tychsen," vol. 11, p. 122.

26 See Franzos, "Ein Liebeshandel à l'empire," for the tale of Schulze and Luise von Pentz. Schulze was already in the habit of recording every action and reaction in excruciating detail: he copies into his diary a poem she wrote to him but corrects the imagery and versification lest his vanity be offended by mediocre rhymes in his honor, tells of trying to fondle her breasts under her cloak while company was present, recounts his attempts to combat the "cold frost" suddenly besetting his spirit by means of champagne

debaucheries (he would then dramatize the romantically dishevelled, lovelorn aspect conferred by a hangover the next morning), and so on.

27 Franzos, "Ernst Schulze und Cäcilie Tychsen," vol. 11, p. 125, and Franzos, "Ein Liebeshandel à l'empire," p. 142.

28 Franzos, "Ernst Schulze und Cäcilie Tychsen," vol. 11, p. 122.

29 Ibid., p. 122.

30 Marggraff, "Ernst Schulze. Nach seinen Tagebüchern," p. 99.

31 The most complete testimony about the adventure with Adelheid of the Brocken comes from a letter of 7–10 July 1810 to Bergmann, reproduced in part in Marggraff's biography, *Ernst Schulze. Nach seinen Tagebüchern*, and in full in Franzos, "Ernst Schulze in Göttingen," pp. 171–72. See the latter, p. 193, for Schulze's diary-confessional to Adelheid Tychsen, 7–8 May 1813, with an account of the incident.

32 Franzos, "Ernst Schulze und Cäcilie Tychsen," vol. 11, p. 123.

33 Ibid., p. 124.

34 The anecdotes in these two paragraphs come from ibid., pp. 125–26.

35 Ibid., p. 171.

36 Ibid., p. 173. Bouterwek cites passages from this diary entry in the "Biographische Vorrede," p. 101. So preoccupied was Schulze with amatory matters that he barely mentions in passing the completion of his dissertation, "Incerti auctoris Pervigilium veneris Commentario perpetuo illustratum, prooemio et lectionis varietate instructum," accepted on 12 March 1812. From that time on, he worked as a private tutor at the University.

37 Franzos, "Ernst Schulze und Cäcilie Tychsen," vol. 11, p. 174 and (in shortened form) Bouterwek, "Biographische Vorrede," p. 105.

38 Franzos, "Ernst Schulze und Cäcilie Tychsen," vol. 11, pp. 198–99.

39 See Schulze, *Sämtliche Poetische Werke*, vol. 4 (3rd. edn., 1855), p. 202, for the "Musikalische Phantasie." Thomas Christian Tychsen's works include a "Hymne an Teutschland nach der Rettungsschlacht bey Leipzig 16–18 Oktober 1813" (Göttingen: Vandenhoeck, 1814), or "Hymn to Germany after the battle of deliverance at Leipzig, October 1813"; Cäcilie's nationalistic sentiments, it would seem, were also a family matter.

40 Franzos, "Ernst Schulze und Cäcilie Tychsen," vol. 11, p. 197.

41 Ibid., p. 246.

42 Franzos, "Zur Charakteristik Ernst Schulze's," p. 26.

43 Franzos, "Ernst Schulze und Cäcilie Tychsen," vol. 11, p. 175.

44 Ibid., vol. 11, p. 244. See also Bouterwek, "Biographische Vorrede," p. 113.

45 Franzos, "Ernst Schulze und Cäcilie Tychsen," vol. 11, pp. 174–75.

46 Ibid., vol. 12, pp. 222–23.

47 Ibid., vol. 11, p. 199.

48 Ibid., p. 247. Marggraff, *Ernst Schulze. Nach seinen Tagebüchern*, pp. 118–19, omits the references to Cäcilie as a coquette and the arrogant, misery-laden statement about other men's vacuousness.

49 Franzos, "Ernst Schulze und Cäcilie Tychsen," vol. 11, p. 249.

50 Bouterwek, "Biographische Vorrede," p. xxi.

51 On Sunday 14 August, Schulze twitted Cäcilie about her black dress and gold cross, observing that she was dressed like a nun – did she perhaps seek repentance for her sins? Cäcilie's grandmother took offence and retorted that the world would be a better place if everyone had as few sins to confess as her granddaughter. See Franzos, "Ernst Schulze und Cäcilie Tychsen," vol. 11, pp. 249–50.

52 Ibid., vol. 11, p.250 and (abbreviated) in Bouterwek, "Biographische Vorrede," p. 136.

53 Franzos, "Ernst Schulze und Cäcilie Tychsen," vol. 11, p. 294, and (abbreviated) in Marggraff, *Ernst Schulze. Nach seinen Tagebüchern*, p. 126.

54 Franzos, "Ernst Schulze und Cäcilie Tychsen," vol. 11, pp. 297–98, and Marggraff, *Ernst Schulze. Nach seinen Tagebüchern*, p. 140.

55 Franzos, "Ernst Schulze und Cäcilie Tychsen," vol. 11, p. 299, and Marggraff, *Ernst Schulze. Nach seinen Tagebüchern*, p. 140.

56 Franzos, "Ernst Schulze und Cäcilie Tychsen," vol. 12, p. 223, and Marggraff, *Ernst Schulze. Nach seinen Tagebüchern*, p. 148. Marggraff does not include the passage in which Schulze tells of Adelheid playing a Bach chorale. At the thought of Cäcilie's love of Bach, she broke off playing and went to a corner, where Schulze saw her weeping. Schulze then left, not wishing Adelheid to see his own tears, and went to Auguste G., where he writes that he restrained himself from the malice he desired as an antidote to his grief. It is a revealing episode.

57 Franzos, "Ernst Schulze und Cäcilie Tychsen," vol. 12, p. 225, and Marggraff, *Ernst Schulze. Nach seinen Tagebüchern*, p. 150.

58 Franzos, "Ernst Schulze und Cäcilie Tychsen," vol. 12, p. 225, and Marggraff, *Ernst Schulze. Nach seinen Tagebüchern*, p. 154.

59 Franzos, "Ernst Schulze und Cäcilie Tychsen," vol. 12, p. 245, and Marggraff, *Ernst Schulze. Nach seinen Tagebüchern*, p. 156.

60 Her tombstone bears her name and birth- and death-dates (18 March 1794 – 3 December 1812) on one side and lines by the poet who loved her on the other: "Welkst Du, liebliche Blume, zu zart für die Stürme der Erde, / Ach, so früh! Dich nahm, der Dich uns schenkte, zurück, / Doch uns lebt Dein heiliges Bild im sehnenden Herzen, / Bis wir in Edens Flur himmlisch erblühend Dich schaun."

61 Franzos, "Ernst Schulze und Cäcilie Tychsen," vol. 12, p. 246–47.

62 Ibid., p. 247, and Marggraff, *Ernst Schulze. Nach seinen Tagebüchern*, pp. 164–65.

63 Schulze, *Cäcilie*, Canto 1, stanza 5, p. 5.

64 Ibid., Canto 1, stanza 10, p. 8.

65 Franzos, "Ernst Schulze und Cäcilie Tychsen," vol. 12, p. 250.

66 Ibid., p. 275.

67 Ibid., p. 267.

68 Ibid., p. 274.

69 Marggraff, *Ernst Schulze. Nach seinen Tagebüchern*, p. 195.

70 Ibid., p. 179.

71 Ibid., p. 173.

72 Franzos, "Ernst Schulze und Cäcilie Tychsen," vol. 12, p. 296, and Franzos, "Ernst Schulze und Adelheid Tychsen," pp. 28–29.

73 Franzos, "Ernst Schulze und Adelheid Tychsen," pp. 29–31.

74 Ibid., p. 32.

75 See Frances Baroness Bunsen, *A Memoir of Baron Bunsen, Late Minister Plenipotentiary and Envoy Extraordinary of the Majesty Frederic William IV at the Court of St. James*, 2 vols. (London: Longmans, Green, and Co., 1868), in particular, chaps. 1 and 2 of vol. 1. The memoirs were published in German as *Christian Karl Josias von Bunsen: Aus Briefen und nach eigenen Erinnerungen geschildert von seiner Witwe*, 3 vols. (Leipzig, 1868–71). On p. 45 of the original (English) edition, Bunsen's wife cites a passage in a letter her husband wrote in 1841: "He [Schulze] was one of my dearest friends, after whom I named my

son Ernest. Of a circle of nine who lived together at Göttingen in the momentous years from 1809–1814, he was the first who left this earth; his affection towards those left behind, you will see expressed in his poem 'Cecilia.' There never was a nobler mind; he was a poet by nature, of chivalrous patriotism, despite bodily debility; of immense learning, and as a friend, faithful and affectionate." But according to the Baroness Bunsen, Schulze had "even in such early youth, lost the freshness and elasticity of the moral fibre, so that a morbid longing after excitement, in order to escape self-consciousness, destroyed all capability of joy, or satisfaction in existence: and he died heart-broken, from having wilfully built on the sand. Poems of his were published and are still much read, all showing poetic powers of a high order employed on insignificant subjects." See Bunsen, *A Memoir of Baron Bunsen*, p. 47.

76 Franzos, "Ernst Schulze und Adelheid Tychsen," p. 50.

77 Ibid., p. 51.

78 Marggraff, *"Ernst Schulze. Nach seinen Tagebüchern,"* p. 235.

79 Franzos, "Ernst Schulze und Adelheid Tychsen," p. 116, and Marggraff, *Ernst Schulze. Nach seinen Tagebüchern*, p. 227.

80 Franzos, "Ernst Schulze und Adelheid Tychsen," p. 148, and Marggraff, *Ernst Schulze. Nach seinen Tagebüchern*, pp. 246–47.

81 Marggraff, *Ernst Schulze. Nach seinen Tagebüchern*, p. 250.

82 Franzos, "Ernst Schulze und Adelheid Tychsen," pp. 97–98, and Marggraff, *Ernst Schulze. Nach seinen Tagebüchern*, p. 220.

83 Frances Baroness Bunsen, *A Memoir of Baron Bunsen*, pp. 47–48.

84 Ernst Schulze, *Poetisches Tagebuch*, in *Sämmtliche poetische Werke*, vol. III (Leipzig: F. A. Brockhaus, 1855, 3rd edn.), p. 64, stanzas 1 and 8 of 9.

85 Ibid., p. 85, stanza 3 of 5.

86 Franzos, "Ernst Schulze und Adelheid Tychsen," p. 194.

87 Ibid., p. 218.

88 Ibid., p. 221.

89 We hear of the ban in a letter to Bunsen and Brandis of 13 August 1815.

90 Franzos, "Ernst Schulze und Adelheid Tychsen," p. 240.

91 Ibid., p. 268.

92 Ibid., p. 270.

93 Ibid., p. 276.

94 Ibid., p. 266.

95 Ibid., pp. 270-71 and 287–88.

96 Francis Bunsen, *A Memoir of Baron Bunsen*, pp. 100–101.

97 Franzos, "Ernst Schulze und Adelheid Tychsen," pp. 292–93.

98 Ibid., p. 294. The dying Schulze also told Bouterwek that only the versification was good – nothing else. See Bouterwek, "Biographische Vorrede," p. xxxviii.

99 Brockhaus announced a poetry competition in the *Taschenbuch Urania* for 1816 (the venue, twelve years later, for the first twelve poems of Wilhelm Müller's *Die Winterreise*). See the publisher's notice in Ernst Schulze, *Die bezauberte Rose. Romantisches Gedicht in drei Gesängen* (Leipzig: F. A. Brockhaus, 1818), pp. 149–50.

100 Schulze, *Poetisches Tagebuch*, pp. 3–6.

101 Ibid., p. 43.

102 Ibid., p. 110.

103 Ibid., pp. 131–32, stanzas 7 and 8.

104 Ibid., pp. 153–54, stanzas 2 and 3.

105 Ibid., p. 18.

106 See the author's *Retracing a Winter's Journey: Schubert's Winterreise* (Ithaca, NY and London: Cornell University Press, 1991).

107 Schulze, *Poetisches Tagebuch*, pp. 72–73.

108 Franz Schubert, *Neue Ausgabe sämtlicher Werke*, series IV: *Lieder*, vol. 5a, ed. Walther Dürr (Kassel and Basel: Bärenreiter Verlag, 1985), pp. 16–27. The first version in G minor is in ibid., vol. 5b (Kassel and Basel: Bärenreiter-Verlag, 1985), pp. 202–13.

109 Schulze, *Poetisches Tagebuch*, pp. 77–78.

110 Reed, *The Schubert Song Companion*, p. 57.

111 The second version is printed in Franz Schubert, *Neue Ausgabe sämtlicher Werke*, series IV, vol. 5a, pp. 28–36, the first version in G major in vol. 5b, pp. 214–22.

112 Schulze, *Poetisches Tagebuch*, pp. 125–26.

113 Franz Schubert, *Neue Ausgabe sämtlicher Werke*, series IV: *Lieder*, vol. 13, ed. Walther Dürr (Kassel and Basel: Bärenreiter Verlag, 1992), pp. 186–91.

114 The manuscript containing the autograph of this song, together with the first draft of "Über Wildemann," was split into two parts shortly after the publication of the song in 1832 as part of book 13 of the *Nachlaß*. The first contained measures 1–34, the second section was further subdivided sometime in the 1950s, and all three portions have subsequently vanished.

115 Schulze, *Poetisches Tagebuch*, pp. 65–66.

116 Franz Schubert, *Neue Ausgabe sämtlicher Werke*, series IV, vol. 13, pp. 192–96.

117 Reed, *The Schubert Song Companion*, p. 116, and Capell, *Schubert's Songs*, p. 216.

118 Schulze, *Poetisches Tagebuch*, pp. 205–6.

119 Ibid., pp. 93–94.

120 There are two versions of this song, different in small details. The autograph manuscript of the first version, dated December 1825, has been divided into two portions: the first twenty-three measures of the strophic setting are now in the Library of Congress in Washington, D. C., while the remaining twelve measures are in private hands in the United States. The fair copy has been lost, but it presumably was where Schubert cancelled the earlier version, replacing it with the version first published by Thaddäus Weigl in December 1827 as op. 88, no. 3. The catalogue of the Witteczek-Spaun collection dates the song March 1826, possibly the date of the lost fair copy. See Franz Schubert, *Neue Ausgabe sämtlicher Werke*, series IV: *Lieder*, vol. 4b, ed. Walther Dürr (Kassel and Basel: Bärenreiter-Verlag, 1979), pp. 236–39.

121 The figure also occurs much earlier, in the setting of the final stanza of Ludwig Hölty's "Klage (An den Mond)," D. 435 of 1816, when the protagonist envisions the moon shining down upon his grave at the end of life's journey.

122 Schulze, *Poetisches Tagebuch*, pp. 102–3.

123 Richard Wigmore, *Schubert: The Complete Song Texts* (New York: Schirmer Books, 1988), p. 245. "Whim" is not incorrect, merely less dark than I would prefer.

124 John Reed, *The Schubert Song Companion*, p. 279. Of the sources for Schubert's setting, the first draft, formerly in the collection of the Paris Conservatoire, now in the Bibliothèque Nationale, is dated March 1826 and is marked *Langsam*. The fair copy made for the printer is now missing. The song was first published on 16 September 1828 as a supplement to the *Wiener Zeitschrift für Kunst, Literatur, Theater und Mode*; at the end of the year, it appeared as the first of the four songs of op. 101 from Probst of Leipzig, and

in 1835, it was included in book 25 of the *Nachlaß*.

125 Schulze, *Poetisches Tagebuch*, pp. 104–5.

126 The last of the Schulze songs is a fragment, a dialogue-poem between a flower and a stream that must have called up vivid memories of *Die schöne Müllerin*: "O Quell, was strömst du rasch und wild," D. 874, or "Am 8. Januar 1814." Schubert's sketch, unfinished and untitled, is written on the last sheet of a manuscript which contains "Tiefes Leid." Witteczek dates both songs January 1826, but this may be a misunderstanding of the title Schubert gives to the latter song, "Im Jänner 1817." The sketch includes a four-bar introduction, complete with articulation markings, and fourteen measures of melody, with a single scanty two-voice sketch of a piano interlude and bass D's in the last five measures; although a fascinating glimpse into Schubert's workshop, it was never completed. Could it have been the resemblance to the piano introduction of "Eifersucht und Stolz" from *Die schöne Müllerin* that impelled Schubert to abandon the work? It has been completed for performance purposes and privately printed in 1959 by Reinhard van Hoorickx with the title "Die Blume und der Quell." Schubert subsequently used the mordent-accented right-hand figures in m. 4 of the introduction in much of the accompaniment to "Hippolit's Lied," D. 890, composed in July 1826 to another text about hopeless passion by Friedrich von Gerstenberg.

127 Schulze, *Poetisches Tagebuch*, pp. 181–82.

128 Schubert's fragmentary first draft of this song, formerly in private hands, is now missing. An autograph copy, apparently the one used for the first edition, is now in private possession and has the tempo indication "Nicht zu schnell" rather than the indication "Schnell" one finds in the first edition. The catalogue of the Witteczek-Spaun collection dates the song as March 1826, and it was first published by Maximilian J. Leidesdorf as op. 108, no. 1 in January 1829, shortly after the composer's death. See Reinhard van Hoorickx, "Un manuscrit inconnu de Schubert," *Revue belge de musicologie*, vols. 28–30 (1974–6), pp. 260–63.

129 "Über Wildemann" has a gentler twin in a song also composed in March 1826: Johann Gabriel Seidl's "Sehnsucht" (Longing), D. 879. The same D minor tonality and triplet figuration assume a softer guise in this song, whose bereft protagonist is able to find consolation for the pain of distance from his beloved in the songs he creates to tell of it. Schulze, for all his attempts, could find no such consolation.

130 Deutsch, *Schubert: A Documentary Biography*, p. 339.

131 A partial list of other Schulze settings includes Carl Eberwein, *Lieder von Ernst Schulze* (Hamburg, Böhme); Theodor Gäde, *Gesänge aus Cäcilia von Ernst Schulze*, op. 10 (Berlin, Ende); Sigismund Neukomm, *Sechs Gesänge von Ernst Schulze* (Berlin, Schlesinger); Emil Kauffmann, "Reinald, aus Cäcilie, von Ernst Schulze," in *Lieder und Gesänge für Mezzo-Sopran oder Bariton*, erstes Heft; Schubert's friend and fellow student of Antonio Salieri, Benedikt Randhartinger, "Elfengesang" for alto or baritone (Vienna, Diabelli); Luise, Gräfin von Stolberg-Stolberg, *Poetisches Tagebuch von Ernst Schulze* (Leipzig, Klemm); Salomon Burkhardt, "Unter bläulichen Gewässern" from *Cäcilie*; Karl Geissler, "Minne-dienst," "Die Schäferin," "Die Macht des Blicks," and "Lied der Vöglein" from the *Lieder der Unschuld, Liebe und Freude*, op. 16, nos. 1, 2, 4, and 5, also "Die Liebe" ("Weißt du, was die Liebe ist") and "Amor ist ein zarter Vogel," op. 17, nos. 2 and 3; Joseph Joachim Raff, "Was blitzt in den Büschen" for male chorus, op. 122, no. 8; Therese Schäffer, "Ferne wohnt die Sonn' im Blauen," op. 28, no. 4; Moritz Hauptmann, "Wehe nur du Geist des Lebens" and "Kleine Blumen, kleine Lieder" from the *Acht Gedichte*, op. 14,

nos. 1 and 3; Leopold Lenz, "Alles wo ich weil und gehe" from the *Drey Gesänge*, op. 22, no. 3 and "In wilder Nacht" from the *Deutsche Lieder und Gesänge*, op. 21, no. 7; and Karl Banck, "In wilder Nacht bei Sturm und Wetter," op. 12, no. 5.

132 *Allgemeine Musikalische Zeitung*, vol. 42, no. 32 (Leipzig: Breitkopf & Härtel, 1840), p. 716.

133 "Am 6. April 1816" is found on pp. 164–65 of the *Poetisches Tagebuch*, op. cit., "Am 27. October 1814" on pp. 84–86, "Am 16. November 1813" on p. 33, and "Am 22. December 1816" on p. 198. C. F. Whistling's *Handbuch der musikalischen Literatur* (Leipzig: Friedrich Hofmeister, 1845), p. 151, cites an edition by Kistner in Leipzig; one can speculate that the original edition appeared during the 1828–44 gap in the Whistling-Hofmeister catalogues.

134 Schulze, *Poetisches Tagebuch*, pp. 36–37.

135 Schulze, *Sämmtliche poetische Werke*, vol. 4, pp. 178–80.

136 *Poetisches Tagebuch*, pp. 186 and 214–15 respectively. Leopold Lenz was a royal Bavarian court opera singer, who was pensioned off in 1855 and then went from Munich to Münster. He wrote almost nothing but songs, many of them attractive.

137 See Karl Bloetz, "König Georg V. von Hannover als Musiker," in *Allgemeine Musikalische Zeitung*, vol. 41 (1914) and Georg Friedrich Dammers, *Erinnerungen und Erlebnisse des königlich hannoverschen General-Major Georg Friedrich Dammers, letztem General-Adjutanten des Königs Georg V. von Hannover 1819–1878* (Hanover: Helwing, 1890). The king's complete Schulze settings are listed in Harald Müller, "Ernst Schulze's Werk in Vertonungen," pp. 127–28; the solo songs include 29 poems from the *Poetisches Tagebuch*. Of the texts Schubert set, the crown prince also set, with different titles, "Über Wildemann," "Im Frühling," "Im Walde," and "Um Mitternacht."

138 Schulze, *Sämmtliche Werke*, vol. III: "Am 19. September 1813" on pp. 19–20, "Am 7. April 1816" on pp. 166–67, "Am 3. Januar 1814" on pp. 36–37, "Hildesheim. Den 20 April 1816" on pp. 169–70, and the sonnet "Fürstenberg" on p. 230.

139 Titl's op. 17 is cited in Hofmeister's catalogue for 1844–45; see C. F. Whistling's *Handbuch der musikalischen Literatur* (1844–45), p. 182. In the review in the *Allgemeine Musikalische Zeitung*, vol. 42, no. 35 (August 1840), p. 715, listeners are invited to think of bygone eras with tears in their eyes.

140 Schulze, *Cäcilie*, vol. II (Reutlingen: J. J. Mäcken and Vienna: B. Ph. Bauer, 1820), stanzas 84–87, pp. 225–26.

141 Ibid., stanzas 94–100, pp. 230–33.

142 Rudolf von Hertzberg (born 1818) studied piano and composition with Ludwig Berger, won acclaim as a pianist, and became music director of the Dom-Chor in Berlin. His small list of compositions, all from his early years, includes settings of poetry from Heinrich Stieglitz's *Bilder des Orients* for alto or baritone, op. 1 (Berlin: Fröhlich, 1836). The "Elfengesang" was briefly reviewed in the *Allgemeine Musikalische Zeitung*, vol. 41, no. 46 (November 1839), p. 891, along with Herzberg's *Sechs Gesänge für Alt oder Bass*, op. 4; the ballad was judged to be more successful than the lieder.

143 C. F. Whistling's *Handbuch der musikalischen Literatur* (1844–45), p. 182. Hofmeister also cites "Unruhe. Gedicht von E. Schulze," op. 19 on the same page.

144 Schulze, *Sämmtliche Werke*, vol. III, p. 245.

145 Ibid., pp. 154–55, stanzas 1 and 2 of 4.

146 Other settings include: Martin Blumner, *Sechs Lieder*, op. 13, no. 5; Paul Julius Alexander Dorn (1833–?), *Fünf Lieder*, op. 1, no. 3; Richard Kleinmichel (1846–1901), op. 32, no. 7; Gustav Emil Fischer (1791–1841), *Zwölf Gesänge*, op. 1, no. 3; Paul Hoppe (born *c.* 1845),

op. 31, no. 1; Woldemar Voullaire (1822–1902), *Fünf Lieder*, op. 14, no. 2; Eduard Thiele's op. 10, no. 3; Franz von Holstein, *Zweistimmige Lieder*, op. 8, no. 2; Robert Radecke, *Vier Terzette*, op. 27, no. 4.

147 Franzos, "Ernst Schulze und Adelheid Tychsen," p. 145.

Select bibliography

Adel, Kurt. *Geist und Wirklichkeit: Vom Werden der österreichischen Dichtung.* Vienna: Österreichische Verlagsanstalt, [1967].

Alberti-Radanowicz, Editha. "Das Wiener Lied: 1789–1815" in *Studien zur Musikwissenschaft,* vol. 10 (1923), pp. 37–78.

Alxinger, Johann Baptist von. *Briefe des Dichters Johann Baptist von Alxinger,* ed. Gustav Wilhelm. Vienna: Carl Gerold's Sohn, 1898.

Anderson, Eugene Newton. *Nationalism and the Cultural Crisis in Prussia, 1806–1815.* New York: Octagon Books, Inc., 1966.

Andrus, John Clarke. "Schubert and his Public: The Songs from 1817 to 1828," Ph.D. dissertation, University of California, Santa Barbara, 1974.

Ardito, Pietro. *Carlo Teodoro Körner e la poesia nazionale.* Venice: Grimaldo, 1870.

Arndt, Ernst Moritz. *Arndts Werke,* vol. 1: *Gedichte,* ed. August Leffson. Berlin and Leipzig: Deutsches Verlaghaus Bong & Co., n.d.

Arneth, Alfred Ritter von. *Aus meinem Leben,* 2 vols. Vienna: Privately published, 1891.

Assing, Ludmilla. *Gräfin Elisa von Ahlefeldt, die Gattin Adolphs von Lützow, die Freundin Karl Immermanns.* Berlin: Franz Duncker, 1857.

Balázs, Horváth. *Bacsányiné.* Kassa: "Szent Erzsébet" nyomda részvénytársaság, 1908.

Ballin, Ernst August. *Das Wort-Ton-Verhältnis in den klavierbegleiteten Liedern W. A. Mozarts.* Kassel and Basel: Bärenreiter, 1984.

Batsányi, János. *Összes Müvei,* vol. 1: *Versek,* and vol. 4: *Der Kampf (A Viaskodás),* ed. Dezsö Keresztury and Andor Tarnai. Budapest: Akadémiai Kiadó, 1953 and 1967.

Batsányi (née Baumberg), Gabriele. *Amor und Hymen. Ein Gedicht zur Vermählung einer Freundinn.* Vienna: Johann Vincenz Degen, 1807.

Bauer, Moritz. "Johann Mayrhofer" in *Zeitschrift für Musikwissenschaft,* Fünfter Jahrgang (October 1922–September 1923), pp. 70–99. Leipzig: Breitkopf & Härtel, 1923.

Bauernfeld, Eduard. *Gesammelte Schriften,* vol. XI: *Reime und Rhythmen,* and vol. XII: *Aus Alt- und Neu-Wien.* Vienna: Wilhelm Braumüller, 1873.

 Aus Alt- und Neu-Wien, with an afterword by Rudolph Latzke. Vienna: Österreichische Schulbücherverlag, 1923.

 Erinnerungen aus Alt-Wien, ed. Josef Bindtner. Vienna: Wiener Drucke, 1923.

Baumberg, Gabriele von. *Danklied zur Ehre Karls, gesungen an Seinem Namenstag den 4. Nov. 1796.* Vienna: A. Blumauer, 1796.

Die deutsche Muse, am 10. November 1816. Vienna: J. C. Akkermann, 1816.

Sämmtliche Gedichte Gabrielens von Baumberg: Vienna: Johann Thomas Edlen von Trattnern, 1800.

Gedichte von Gabriele Batsányi geb. Baumberg. Mit einer Abhandlung über die Dichtkunst, von F. W. M. Vienna: J. V. Degen, 1805.

Berde, Juliánna Maria. *Bacsányiné Baumberg Gabriella élete és költészete.* Kolozsvár: Step Jenö és társa könyvsajtója, 1912.

Biedermann, Woldemar Freiherr von. "Goethes Beziehungen zur Familie Körner" in *Goethe und Dresden.* Berlin: Hempel, 1875.

Blümml, Emil Karl and Gugitz, Gustav. *Von Leuten und Zeiten im alten Wien.* Vienna & Leipzig: Gerlach & Wiedling, 1922.

Blumauer, Aloys. *Beobachtungen über Österreichs Aufklärung und Litteratur.* Vienna: Joseph Edlen von Kurzbeck, 1782.

Böckh, Franz Heinrich. *Wiens lebende Schriftsteller, Künstler und Dilettanten im Kunstfache. Dann Bücher-, Kunst- und Naturschätze und andere Sehenwürdigkeiten dieser Haupt- und Residenz-Stadt.* Vienna: B. Ph. Bauer, 1821.

Bothe, Heinrich. *Geschichte des Thüringischen Ulanen-Regiments Nr. 6.* Berlin: Decker, 1865.

Bouterwek, Friedrich. "Biographische Vorrede," pp. v–xxxix, to Ernst Schulze, *Cäcilie. Ein romantisches Gedicht in zwanzig Gesängen*, 2 vols. Vienna: B. Ph. Bauer and Reutlingen: J. J. Mäcken, 1820.

Branscombe, Peter, ed. *Austrian Life and Literature 1780–1938: Eight Essays.* Edinburgh: Scottish Academic Press, 1978.

Brasch, Friedrich. *Das Grab bei Wöbbelin, oder Theodor Körner und die Lützower.* Schwerin: Stiller'sche Hofbuchhandlung, 1861.

Brecher, Adolf. *Napoleon I. und der Überfall des Lützowschen Freikorps bei Kitzen. Ein Beitrag zur Geschichte der Befreiungskriege.* Berlin: R. Gaertner, 1897.

Brown, Clive. *Louis Spohr: A Critical Biography.* Cambridge, England: Cambridge University Press, 1984.

Brusatti, Otto, ed. *Schubert-Kongress Wien 1978.* Graz, 1979.

Bunsen, Baroness Frances, *A Memoir of Baron Bunsen, Late Minister Plenipotentiary and Envoy Extraordinary of the Majesty Frederic William IV. at the Court of St. James*, 2 vols. London: Longmans, Green, and Co., 1868.

Burchard, Gustav. "Lützow's wilde Jagd: Ein dramatisches Festspiel in einem Aufzuge." Berlin: F. Fontane, 1891.

Burg, Paul. *Die Lützower in der Leipziger Völkerschlacht: Ein Streifritt durch drei grosse deutsche Tage.* Leipzig: Xenien-Verlag, 1913.

Cämmerer, Rudolf von. *Die Befreiungskriege 1813–1815. Ein strategischer Überblick.* Berlin: E. S. Mittler und Sohn, 1907.

Capell, Richard. *Schubert's Songs.* London: Pan Books Ltd., 1973, reprint of 1st edn., London: Gerald Duckworth & Co. Ltd., 1928.

Chandler, David. *The Campaigns of Napoleon.* New York: Macmillan, 1966.

Corell, Linda. "The Songs of Louis Spohr" in *The Music Review*, vol. 34 (1978), pp. 31–8.

Dahlhaus, Carl. "War Wien im frühen 19. Jahrhundert das musikalische Zentrum Europas?" in *Wien und Europa zwischen den Revolutionen (1789–1848)*, ed. Reinhard Urbach, pp. 349–61. Vienna & Munich: Jugend & Volk, 1978.

Debryn, Carmen. *Vom Lied zum Kunstlied: Eine Studie zu Variation und Komposition im Lied des frühen 19. Jahrhunderts.* Göppingen: Kümmerle Verlag, 1983.

Degen, Max. *Die Lieder von Carl Maria von Weber*. Freiburg: Herder, 1924.

Deutsch, Otto Erich. *Franz Schubert: Thematisches Verzeichnis seiner Werke in chronologischer Folge*. Kassel & Basel: Bärenreiter, 1978. Abbreviated as *Franz Schubert: Werkverzeichnis*. *Der kleine Deutsch*, ed. Werner Aderhold, Wather Dürr, and Arnold Feil. Kassel: Bärenreiter, 1983.

Franz Schuberts fünf erste Lieder. Musikalische Seltenheiten: Wiener Liebhaberdruck, iv. Vienna & New York, 1922.

"Leopold von Sonnleithners Erinnerungen an die Musiksalons des vormärzlichen Wiens" in *Österreichische Musikzeitschrift*, vol. 16 (1961), pp. 42–62, 97–110, and 147–57.

Schubert: A Documentary Biography, trans. Eric Blom. London: J. M. Dent, 1946, and New York: Da Capo Press, 1977.

Schubert: Memoirs by His Friends, trans. Rosamond Ley and John Nowell. London: Adam and Charles Black Ltd., 1958. First published as *Die Erinnerungen seiner Freunde*. Leipzig: Breitkopf & Härtel, 1957.

Draws-Tychsen, Hellmut. *Requiem und Hymnen für Cecilie Tychsen*. Diessen vor München: Danziger Verlags-Gesellschaft, 1930.

Dürr, Walther. "'Manier' und 'Veränderung' in Kompositionen Franz Schuberts" in *Zur Aufführungspraxis der Werke Franz Schuberts*, ed. Roswitha Karpf, pp. 124–39. Munich & Salzburg: Musikverlag Emil Katzbichler, 1981.

"Schubert and Johann Michael Vogl: A reappraisal" in *19th-Century Music*, vol. 3 (November 1979), pp. 126–40.

Dürre, Ernst Friedrich. "Erlebnisse im Lützowschen Freikorps" in *Dr. Chr. Eduard L. Dürre. Aufzeichnungen, Tagebücher und Briefe aus einem deutschen Turner- und Lehrerleben*. Leipzig: Ed. Strauch, 1881.

Eiselen, Johann Friedrich Gottfried. *Geschichte des Lützowschen Freicorps*. Halle: Eduard Anton, 1841.

Erhard, H. W. *Theodor Körner. Sein Leben, nebst einer ausführlichen Beurtheilung seiner Schriften*. Arnstadt: Hildebrand, 1821.

Erk, Ludwig, and Böhme, F. N., eds. *Deutscher Liederhort: Auswahl der vorzüglicheren deutschen Volkslieder, nach Wort und Weise aus der Vorzeit und Gegenwart gesammelt und erläutert*, 3 vols. Leipzig: Breitkopf & Härtel, 1893–94.

Ernouf, Baron Alfred Auguste. *Maret, duc de Bassano*. Paris: G. Charpentier, 1878.

Fichte, Johann Gottlieb. *Addresses to the German Nation*, trans. G. A. Kelly. New York and Evanston, Illinois: Northwestern University Press, 1968.

Förster, Friedrich. *Die Sängerfahrt. Eine Neujahrsgabe für Freunde der Dichtkunst und Mahlerey*. Berlin: Maurer, 1818, facsimile edn. published Heidelberg: Lambert Schneider.

"Erinnerungen aus den Befreiungskriegen" in *Deutsche Pandora. Gedenkbuch zeitgenössischer Zustände und Schriftsteller*. Stuttgart: Litteratur-Comptoire, 1840.

Geschichte der Befreiungs-Kriege 1813. 1814. 1815, 3 vols. Berlin: Ferdinand Dümmlers Verlagsbuchhandlung, 1889.

Kunst und Leben. Aus Friedrich Försters Nachlaß, ed. Hermann Kletke. Berlin: Verlag von Gebrüder Paetel, 1873.

Frankl, L.A. *Erinnerungen*, ed. Stefan Hock. Prague: Calve, 1910.

Franzos, Karl Emil. "Christian August Brandis und Ernst Schulze. Mit ungedruckten Briefen Christian August Brandis," *Deutsche Dichtung*, vol. 34 (April – September 1903), pp. 267–72 and 293–6. Berlin: Concordia Deutsche Verlags-Anstalt, 1903.

"Ein Liebeshandel à l'empire. Aus ungedruckten Tagebüchern, Gedichten und Briefen Ernst Schulze's," *Deutsche Dichtung*, vol. 24 (April – September 1898), pp. 22–27, 48–55, 73–79,

91–100, 118–124, 140–46, 169–75, 196–202, 217–22, 247–51, 264–66, 285–86. Berlin: Concordia Deutsche Verlags-Anstalt, 1898.

"Elegie von Ernst Schulze. (Ungedruckter Nachlaß)," *Deutsche Dichtung*, vol. 7 (October 1889 – March 1890), pp. 279–82. Dresden: L. Ehlermann, 1890.

"Ernst Schulze in Göttingen. Nach ungedruckten Quellen," *Deutsche Dichtung*, vol. 7 (October 1889 – March 1890), pp. 50–54; 97–103; 170–73; and 193–95. Dresden: L. Ehlermann, 1890.

"Ernst Schulze und Adelheid Tychsen. Nach den ungedruckten Tagebüchern, Gedichten und Briefen Schulze's," *Deutsche Dichtung*, vol. 17 (April–September 1894), pp. 28–32; 47–52; 68–78; 92–99; 115–23; 142–49; 165–73; 194–99; 217–26; 240–48; 265–72; and 287–95. Berlin: Verlag von F. Fontane & Co., 1894.

"Ernst Schulze und Cäcilie Tychsen. Nach den ungedruckten Tagebüchern, Gedichten und Briefen Schulzes," *Deutsche Dichtung*, vols. 11 and 12 (October 1891 – March 1892 and April–September 1892): vol. 11, pp. 119–28; 171–76; 196–201; 244–51; 294–300, and vol. 12, pp. 198–200; 221–25; 245–52; 267–76; and 294–99. Dresden: L. Ehlermann, 1891–2.

"Karl Josias Christian Bunsen und Ernst Schulze," *Deutsche Dichtung*, vol. 33, pp. 225–28, 247–51, 270–76.

"Karl Lachmann und Ernst Schulze. Mit ungedruckten Briefen Karl Lachmanns," *Deutsche Dichtung*, vol. 33 (October 1902 – March 1903), pp. 30–32. Berlin: Concordia Deutsche Verlags-Anstalt, 1903.

"Thekla. Aus Ernst Schulze's Tagebüchern," *Deutsche Dichtung*, vol. 8 (April–September 1890), pp. 198–203. Dresden: L. Ehlermann, 1890.

"Zur Charakteristik Ernst Schulze's. Nach ungedruckten Quellen," *Deutsche Dichtung*, vol. 6 (April–September 1889), pp. 23–31; 49–56; 146–52; 223–28; and 245–52. Dresden: L. Ehlermann, 1889.

Frenzel, Fritz. *Theodor Körner, Dichter und Held in den Kämpfen des Lützow'schen Freicorps. Ein Gedenkblatt dem deutschen Volke zum 100jährigen Geburtstag des Heldendichters gewidmet.* Leipzig: Max Sängewald, 1891.

Geiger, Ludwig. "Ernst Schulze" in *Deutsche Dichtung*, vol. 5 (October 1888 – March 1889), pp. 272–75. Dresden: L. Ehlermann, 1889.

Gelber, Lucy. "Die Liederkomponisten August Harder, Friedrich Heinrich Himmel, Friedrich Franz Hurka, Carl Gottlieb Hering. Ein Beitrag zur Geschichte des musikalischen Liedes im Anfang des 19. Jahrhunderts," Ph.D. dissertation, Berlin, 1936.

Georgiades, Thrasybulos G. *Schubert: Musik und Lyrik.* Göttingen: Vandenhoeck & Ruprecht, 1967.

Glossy, Carl. "Aus den Lebenserinnerungen des Joseph Freiherrn von Spaun" in *Jahrbuch der Grillparzer-Gesellschaft*, vol. 8, pp. 275–303. Vienna: Carl Konegen, 1898.

"Aus Bauernfeld's Tagebüchern" in *Jahrbuch der Grillparzer-Gesellschaft*, vol. 5: ix–xviii, pp. 1–217. Vienna: Carl Konegen, 1895.

Goedeke, Karl. *Grundriss zur Geschichte der deutschen Dichtung aus den Quellen*, 2nd edn. revised, 4 vols. Dresden: L. Ehlermann, 1884–.

Gräffer, Franz. *Kleine Wiener Memoiren und Wiener Dosenstücke*, ed. Anton Schlossar and Gustav Gugitz, 2 vols. Munich: Georg Müller, 1918.

Gramit, David. "The Intellectual and Aesthetic Tenets of Franz Schubert's Circle," Ph.D. dissertation, Duke University, 1987.

"Schubert and the Biedermeier: The Aesthetics of Johann Mayrhofer's 'Heliopolis'" in *Music & Letters*, vol. 74, no. 3 (August 1993), pp. 355–82.

"Schuberts 'bildender Umgang': Denken und Esthetik bei Schuberts Jugendfreunden" in *Schubert durch die Brille: Mitteilungen des internationale Franz Schubert Instituts*, vol. 8 (1992), pp. 5–21.

Grasberger, Franz and Wessely, Othmar, eds. *Schubert-Studien: Festgabe der Österreichischen Akademie der Wissenschaften zum Schubert-Jahr 1978*. Vienna: Verlag der Österreichischen Akademie der Wissenschaften, 1978.

Heck, Thomas F. "The Birth of the Classic Guitar and its Cultivation in Vienna, Reflected in the Career and Compositions of Mauro Giuliani (d. 1829)," dissertation, Yale University, 1970.

Heuss, Alfred. "Franz Schuberts und Friedrich Zöllners 'Das Wandern ist des Müllers Lust'" in *Zeitschrift für Musik*, vol. 96 (1929), pp. 5–10 and 65–70.

Heussner, Horst. "Das Biedermeier in der Musik" in *Die Musikforschung*, vol. 12 (1959), pp. 422–31.

Hilmar, Ernst. *Franz Schubert in His Time*, trans. Reinhard G. Pauly. Portland, Oregon: Amadeus Press, 1988. First published as *Franz Schubert in seiner Zeit*. Vienna, Cologne, Graz: Hermann Böhlaus, 1985.

Höcker, Gustav. *Theodor Körner, der Sänger und Held von Lützows wilder Jagd. Der deutschen Jugend erzählt*. Glogau: Carl Flemming, 1889.

Hoorickx, Reinhard van. "Schubert songs and song fragments not included in the collected edition," *The Music Review* (1977), pp. 267–92.

Horánszky, Lajos. *Bacsányi János és kora*. Budapest, 1907.

Jagwitz, Fritz von. *Geschichte des Lützowschen Freikorps; nach archivalischen Quellen bearbeitet*. Berlin: E. S. Mittler, 1892.

Jansen, Lena. *Karoline Pichlers Schaffen und Weltanschauung im Rahmen ihrer Zeit*. Graz: Wächter-Verlag, 1936.

Jonas, Fritz, ed. *Ansichten über Aesthetik und Litteratur von Wilhelm von Humboldt in seinen Briefen an Christian Gottfried Körner 1795–1830*. Berlin: Schleiermacher, 1880.

Kaiser, Alfred. "Theodor Körner, ein musikalisches Schauspiel." London: Privately Published, 1912.

Kammerhoff, Ernst. *Theodor Körner*. Bielefeld and Leipzig: Velhagen & Klasing, n.d.

Katow, Paul. *Louis Spohr: Persönlichkeit und Werk*. Luxembourg: RTL Edition, 1982.

Keil, Robert, ed. *Wiener Freunde 1784–1808. Beiträge zur Jugendgeschichte der deutsche-österreichischen Literatur*. Vienna: Carl Konegen, 1883.

Kern, Reinhold. *Beiträge zu einer Charakteristik des Dichters Tiedge*. Berlin: Speyer & Peters, 1896.

Kind, Friedrich. "Die Körners-Eiche und die deutschen Frauen. Eine Phantasie." Leipzig: G. J. Göschen, 1814.

Körner, Alfred. *Die Wiener Jakobiner*, trans. Franz-Jospeh Schuh. Stuttgart: J. B. Metzler, 1972.

Körner, Christian Gottfried. *Gesammelte Schriften*, ed. Adolf Stern. Leipzig: Fr. Wilhem Grunow, 1881.

Körner, Theodor. *Leier und Schwert*. Dresden, 1st and 2nd edns. 1814, 3rd edn. augmented by Christian Gottfried Körner, Berlin: Nicolai, 1815 and Vienna: Haas, 1815. Subsequent edns. in 1817, 1819, 1824, 1834, 1848, 1858, 1863, 1867, 1868, etc.

Leier und Schwert. Neue illustrierte Prachtausgabe zur 50jährigen Gedächtnißfeier des Dichters. Berlin: Nicolai, 1st edn. 1863, 2nd edn. 1883.

Leier und Schwert. Gedichte, nebst einer Biographie des Dichters von Friedrich Förster. Berlin: Gustav Hempel, 1879.

Lieder- und Liebesgrüße an Antonie Adamberger. Aus Theodor Körner's Nachlaß, ed. Friedrich Latendorf. Leipzig: Elischer Nachf., 1885.

Poetischer Nachlaß, 2 vols. Leipzig: Hartknoch, 1815, subsequent edns. 1816, 1817, 1818, 1822, 1823.

Theodor Körner's Nachlaß oder dessen Gefühle im poetischen Ausdruck, bei Gelegenheit des ausgebrochenen deutschen Freiheitskrieges. Aus dem Portefeuille des Gebliebenen. ed. Freymann. Leipzig: Baumgärtner, 1814.

Theodor Körner's sämmtliche Werke, 2 vols., ed. Christoph August Tiedge. Stuttgart: Macklot, 1822.

Theodor Körner's sämmtliche Werke, ed. Karl Streckfuß. Berlin: Nicolai and Vienna: Carl Gerold, 1st. edn., 1834, subsequent edns. in 1835, 1837–38, 1847, 1858, 1861, 1866, 1871, 1881.

Sämmtliche Werke, 4 vols., ed. Karl Streckfuß. Berlin: Nicolai, 1st edn., 1838, subsequent edns. in 1842, 1847, 1855, 1863, 1867, 1871, 1879.

Theodor Körner's Tagebuch und Kriegslieder aus dem Jahre 1813, ed. Emil Peschel. Freiburg: Friedrich Ernst Fehsenfeld, 1893.

Zwölf freie deutsche Gedichte. Leipzig, 1813, 2nd edn. Leipzig: Weygand, 1814.

Kohut, Adolph. *Theodor Körner. Sein Leben und seine Dichten*. Berlin: Slottko, 1891.

Kosáry, Domokos. *Napoléon et la Hongrie*. Budapest: Akadémiai Kiadó, 1979.

Kramer, Lawrence. "The Schubert Lied: Romantic Form and Romantic Consciousness" in *Schubert: Critical and Analytical Studies*, ed. Walter Frisch, pp. 200–36. Lincoln, Nebraska: University of Nebraska Press, 1986.

Kramer, Richard. "Distant Cycles: Schubert, Goethe and the *Entfernte*" in *The Journal of Musicology*, vol. 6, no. 1 (1988), pp. 3–26.

Krasa, Selma. *Josef Kriehuber 1800–1876. Der Porträtist einer Epoche*. Vienna: Christian Brandstätter Verlag, 1987.

Kreissle von Hellborn, Heinrich. *Franz Schubert*. Vienna: Carl Gerold's Sohn, 1865.

Kreutzer, Hans Joachim. "Schubert und die literarische Situation seiner Zeit" in *Franz Schubert: Jahre der Krise 1818–1823: Arnold Feil zum 60. Geburtstag am 2. Oktober 1985*, ed. Werner Aderhold, Walther Dürr, and Walburga Litschauer, pp. 29–38. Kassel & Basel: Bärenreiter, 1985.

Kreyenberg, Gotthold. *Karl Theodor Körner. Ein Lebens- und Charakterbild*. Dresden: L. Ehlermann, 1892.

Krimer, Wenzel. *Erinnerungen eines alten Lützower Jägers, 1795–1819*. Stuttgart: R. Lutz, 1833 [4th edn., ed. Adolf Saager, Stuttgart: R. Lutz, 1913?].

Krticzka, Hans Ludwig, Freiherr von Jaden. *Theodor Körner. Neue Körner-Erinnerungen in Wort und Bild: Ein unbekanntes Porträt und ein unveröffentlichtes Gedicht Theodor Körners. Zum 100 Todestage des Heldensängers (26. August 1813)*. Vienna: Ferdinand Wurst, 1913.

Lachèvre, Frédéric. *Les Derniers Libertins*. Paris: Librairie Ancienne Honoré Champion, 1924.

Landau, Anneliese. *Das einstimmige Kunstlied Conradin Kreutzers und seine Stellung zum zeitgenössischen Lied in Schwaben*. Leipzig, 1930 (reprinted Leipzig, 1972).

Lange, Fritz. *Die Lützower: Erinnerungen, Berichte, Dokumente*. Berlin: Rütten & Loening, 1953.

Latendorf, Friedrich. *Aus Theodor Körners Nachlaß: Liedes- und Liebesgrüße an Antonie Adamberger*. Leipzig: Bernhard Schlicke, 1885.

"Der deutsche Tyrtäus und seine Braut" in *Aus allen Zeiten und Landen*, vol. 3. Leipzig: B. Schlicke, n.d.

Friedrich Försters Urkunden-Fälschungen zur Geschichte des Jahres 1813 mit besonderer Rücksicht auf Theodor Körners Leben und Dichten. Poeßneck: C. Latendorf, 1891.

Ledebur, Carl Freiherrn von. *Tonkünstler-Lexikon Berlin's von den ältesten Zeiten bis auf die Gegenwart.* Berlin: Ludwig Rauh, 1861.

Le Fevre-Deumier, Jules. *Célébrités Allemandes. Essais Bibliographiques et Littéraires.* Paris: Librairie de Firmin-Didot et Cie., 1894.

Legouvé, Ernest. "Weber et Körner" in *Gazette musicale*, vol. 5 (1838): pp. 415–17.

Lehmann, Friedrich Wilhelm. *Lebensbeschreibung und Tödtenfeier Carl Theodor Körners.* Leipzig: Industrie-Comptoire, 1819.

Lepel, Felix von. "Carl Maria von Weber als Liederkomponist" in *Zeitschrift für Musik*, vol. 87 (1920), pp. 432–43.

Liess, Andreas. *Johann Michael Vogl, Hofoperist und Schubertsänger.* Graz and Cologne: Hermann Böhlhaus, 1954.

Lipking, Lawrence. *Abandoned Women and Poetic Tradition.* Chicago, Illinois: University of Chicago Press, 1988.

List, Fritz. "Johann Mayrhofer: ein Freund und Textdichter Franz Schuberts," Ph.D. dissertation, University of Munich, 1922.

Loewe, Carl. *Gesamtausgabe der Balladen, Legenden, Lieder und Gesänge für eine Singstimme*, ed. Max Runze. Leipzig: Breitkopf & Härtel, 1899–1904.

Lyon, Dieter. "Anton von Spaun: Ein Beitrag zur Geistesgeschichte des Vormärz." Ph.D. dissertation, Karl-Franzens Universität, Graz, 1964.

Mainka, Jürgen. "Carl Maria von Weber und die antinapoleonische Unabhängigkeitsbewegung" in *Beiträge der Musikwissenschaft*, vol. 29, no. 1 (1987), pp. 73–75.

"Das Liedschaffen Franz Schuberts in den Jahren 1815 und 1816: Auseinandersetzung mit der Liedtradition des 18. Jahrhunderts," Ph.D. dissertation, Technische Universität Berlin, 1958.

Mareck, Johann Baptist. *Verzeichniß österreichischer deutscher Dichter.* Published as *Österreichs erste Literaturgeschichte aus der 2. Hälfte des 18. Jahrhunderts*, ed. Kurt Adel. Vienna: Schendl, 1972.

Marggraff, Hermann. *Ernst Schulze. Nach seinen Tagebüchern und Briefen sowie nach Mittheilungen seiner Freunde geschildert.* Vol. 5 of Schulze, *Sämmtliche poetische Werke*, 3rd edn., Leipzig: F. A. Brockhaus, 1855.

"Schillers und Körners Freundschaftsbund," introduction to *Schillers Briefwechsel mit Körner*, 2nd edn. Leipzig: Veit & Comp., 1859.

Margit, Pál. *Batsányi Párizsban 1810.* Budapest: Danubia Könyvkiadó, 1943.

Márki, Sándor. *Les Jacobins hongrois.* Maon, 1901.

Martersteig, F. *Theodor Körner. Cyclus in 8 Blättern nach Original-Cartons.* Munich: Bruckmanns Verlag, 1871 [with a prefatory biography of Körner by the Brahms poet Hermann Lingg].

Marx, Julius. *Die Österreichische Zensur im Vormärz.* Munich: Verlag R. Oldenbourg, 1959.

Mayrhofer, Johann. *Gedichte.* Vienna: Friedrich Volke, 1824.

Gedichte von Johann Mayrhofer. Neue Sammlung. Aus dessen Nachlasse mit Biographie und Vorwort. ed. Ernst Freiherr von Feuchtersleben. Vienna: Ignaz Klang, 1843.

McConkey, Elizabeth. "Körner's Personality as Revealed in his Works." Master of Arts thesis, University of Chicago, 1915.

Meinecke, Friedrich. *The Age of German Liberation, 1789–1815.* Berkeley, California: University of California Press, 1977.

Meissner, Georg. *Karl Friedrich Curschmann. Ein Beitrag zur Geschichte des Deutschen Liedes zu Anfang des XIX. Jahrhunderts.* Bautzen: E. M. Monse, 1899.

Moore, Gerald. *The Schubert Song Cycles.* London: Hamilton, 1975.

Moser, Hans Joachim. "Weber und das Klavierlied der Biedermeierzeit" in *Das deutsche Lied seit Mozart*, vol. 1, pp. 141–63. Berlin and Zürich: Atlantis Verlag, 1937.

Musiol, Robert. "Theodor Körner in der Musik" in *Neue Zeitschrift für Musik*, nos. 30, 32, 34 (18 July 1879; 1 August 1879; 15 August 1879), pp. 301–3; 317–320; 337–38, 352–53, and 359–362. Scarsdale, N. Y.: Annemarie Schnase – Reprint Dept., 1964 reprint.

Mustard, Helen Meredith. *The Lyric Cycle in German Literature*. Columbia University Germanic Studies 17. New York: King's Crown Press, 1946.

Muther, Richard. *Anton Graff*. Leipzig: E. A. Seemann, 1881.

Muxfeldt, Kristina. "Schubert Song Studies." Ph.D. dissertation, State University of New York at Stony Brook, 1991.

Nemes, Eva Margit. *Batsányi Párizsban. Találkozás Gabriellával 1810–1811*. Budapest: Danubia Könyvkiadó, 1942.

Nemoianu, Virgil. *The Taming of Romanticism: European Literature and the Age of Biedermeier*. Cambridge, Mass.: Harvard University Press, 1984.

Neubauer, Friedrich. *Preußens Fall und Erhebung 1806-1815*. Berlin: Ernst Siegfried Mittler und Sohn, 1908.

Oels, Friedrich. "Lützows Lager: Ein Vaterländisches Volksschauspiel." Berlin-Friedenau: K. Fischer, [1913?].

Oertel, Hugo. *Karl Theodor Körner. Ein Lebensbild aus der Zeit des deutschen Freiheitskampfes*. Wiesbaden: Niedner, n.d.

Orel, Alfred. *Der junge Schubert: Aus der Lernzeit des Künstlers*. Vienna: A. Robitschek, 1940.

Papst, Julius. "An Körner's Grabe. Vorspiel in einem Act." Dresden: Meinhold und Söhne, 1863.

Paret, Peter. *Yorck and the Era of Prussian Reform, 1807-1815*. Princeton, New Jersey: Princeton University Press, 1966.

Partsch, Erich Wolfgang, ed. *Franz Schubert – Der Fortschrittliche? Analysen-Perspektiven-Fakten*. Tutzing: Hans Schneider, 1989.

Peschel, Emil. *Körner-Bibliographie. Zum 23. September 1891 dem hundertjährigen Geburtstage Theodor Körners*. Leipzig: Ramm & Seemann, 1891.

Peschel, W. Emil and Wildenow, Eugen. *Theodor Körner und die Seinen*, 2 vols. Leipzig: E. A. Seemann, 1898.

Pichler, Caroline. *Denkwürdigkeiten aus meinem Leben*, 2 vols., ed. Emil Karl Blümml. Munich: Georg Müller, 1914.

"Gabriele Baumberg. Den 24. Julius 1840" in *Zerstreute Blätter aus meinem Schreibtische. Neue Folge*. Vienna: A. Pichler's sel. Witwe, 1843.

Primmer, Brian. "Unity and Ensemble: Contrasting Ideals in Romantic Music" in *19th-Century Music*, vol. 6, no. 2 (1982), pp. 97–140.

Prohaska, Gertrude. "Der literarische Salon der Karoline Pichler," Ph.D. dissertation, University of Vienna, 1946.

Prosl, Helga. "Der Freundeskreis um Anton von Spaun: Ein Beitrag zur Geistesgeschichte von Linz in der Biedermeierzeit (1811–1827)." Ph.D. dissertation, Leopold-Franzens Universität, Innsbruck, 1951.

Rabenlechner, Michael Maria. "Nachwort des Herausgebers. (Johann Mayrhofers Leben)," in *Gedichte von Johann Mayrhofer*. Vienna: Wiener Bibliophilen-Gesellschaft, 1938, reprint of the edition from 1824.

Rassmann, Christian Friedrich. *Pantheon deutscher jetzt lebender Dichter*. Helmstädt, 1823.

Rau, Heribert. *Theodor Körner*, 2 vols. Leipzig: Thomas, 1863.

Reed, John. *The Schubert Song Companion*. Manchester, England: Manchester University Press, 1985.

Rehtwisch, Theodor. *Das Volk steht auf, Der Sturm bricht los! Geschichte der Freiheitskriege in den Jahren 1812–1815*, 3 vols. Leipzig: Georg Wigand, 1909.

Reinhard, Gustav. *Schillers Einfluß auf Theodor Körner. Ein Beitrag zur Litteraturgeschichte*. Straßburg: Karl J. Trübner Verlagsbuchhandlung, 1899.

Reininghaus, Frieder. *Schubert und das Wirtshaus: Musik unter Metternich*, 2nd edn. Berlin: Oberbaumverlag, 1980.

Reissmann, August. *Das deutsches Lied in seiner historischen Entwicklung*. Kassel: Bertram, 1861.

Ritter, Erwin Frank. *Johann Baptist von Alxinger and the Austrian Enlightenment*. Bern: Herbert Lang & Co., 1970.

Robert, André. *L'Ideé nationale autrichienne et les guerres de Napoléon: L'Apostolat du Baron de Hormayr et le Salon de Caroline Pichler*. Paris: Librairie Félix Alcan, 1933.

Rogge, Bernhard. *Theodor Körner, ein Sänger und ein Held. Zum hundertjähriges Gedächtnis seines Geburtstages dem deutschen Volke gewidmet*. Wittenberg: R. Herrosé's Verlag, 1891.

Rommel, Otto. "Der Wiener Musenalmanach: Eine literarhistorische Untersuchung," in *Euphorion: Zeitschrift für Literaturgeschichte*, ed. August Sauer. Leipzig and Vienna: Carl Fromme, 1906, pp. 1–219.

Rosenwald, Hermann. *Das deutsche Lied zwischen Schubert und Schumann*. Berlin: B. Balan, 1930.

Rühle, A. H. *Theodor Körner's Lehrer, David Samuel Roller. Lebensbild eines sächsischen Pfarrers aus der ersten Hälfte dieses Jahrhunderts*. Leipzig: Justus Naumann, 1878.

Sayous, Edouard. *Histoire des Hongrois et de leur Littérature Politique de 1790 à 1815*. Paris: Librairie Germer-Baillière, 1872.

Schindel, Carl Wilhelm Otto August von. *Die deutschen Schriftstellerinnen des neunzehnten Jahrhunderts*, 3 vols. Leipzig: F. A. Brockhaus, 1823.

Schleiber, Ludwig. "Franz Schuberts einstimmige Lieder nach österreichischen Dichtern" in Hugo Botstiber, ed., *Musikbuch aus Österreich*, vol. 5 (Vienna & Leipzig, 1908), pp. 3–15.

Schlossar, Anton. "Die Wiener Musen-Almanache im achtzehnten Jahrhundert (1777 bis 1796): Ein Beitrag zur Geschichte des geistigen Lebens in Österreich" in *Österreichische Kultur- und Literaturbilder mit besonderer Berücksichtigung der Steiermark*. Vienna, 1879, pp. 3–64.

Schlosser, Ludwig. *Erlebnisse eines sächsischen Landpredigers in den Kriegsjahren von 1806 bis 1815*. Leipzig. n.d.

"Rettung Theodor Körners" in *Vor Leipzig 1813: Die Völkerschlacht in Augenzeugenberichten*, ed. Karl-Heinz Börner. Berlin: Verlag der Nation, 1988.

Schlüsser, Adolph. *Geschichte des Lützowschen Freikorps. Ein Beitrag zur Kriegsgeschichte der Jahre 1813 und 1814*. Berlin: Ernst Siegfried Mittler, 1826.

Schmidt, Lothar. *Organische Form in der Musik: Stationen eines Begriffs 1795–1850*. Kassel and Basel: Bärenreiter, 1990.

Schnapper, Edith. *Die Gesänge des jungen Schubert vor dem Durchbruch des romantischen Liedprinzips*. Bern, 1937.

Schubert, Franz. *Franz Schuberts Werke: Kritisch durchgesehene Gesamtausgabe*. Series 16, 18, and 20. Leipzig: Breitkopf & Härtel, 1884–97.

Neue Ausgabe sämtlicher Werke. Internationale Schubert-Gesellschaft, Series IV, ed. Walter Dürr. Kassel: Bärenreiter, 1969.

Schulze, Ernst. *Cäcilie. Ein romantisches Gedicht in zwanzig Gesängen*. Vienna: B. Ph. Bauer and Reutlingen: J. J. Mäcken, 1820.

Die bezauberte Rose. Romantisches Gedicht in drei Gesängen, 3rd edn. Leipzig: F. A. Brockhaus, 1820.

Sämmtliche poetische Werke, 3rd edn., vol. 3: *Poetisches Tagebuch; Reise durch das Weserthal; Psyche. Ein griechisches Märchen in sieben Büchern*. Leipzig: F. A. Brockhaus, 1855.

Sämmtliche poetische Werke, vol. 4: *Elegieen; Episteln; Vermischte Gedichte*. Leipzig: F. A. Brockhaus, 1822.

Sämmtliche poetische Werke, 3rd. edn., vol. 5: Hermann Marggraff, *Ernst Schulze. Nach seinen Tagebüchern und Briefen sowie nach Mittheilungen seiner Freunde geschildert*. Leipzig: F. A. Brockhaus, 1855.

Schulze, Friedrich, ed. *Die deutschen Befreiungskriege 1813–1815 geschildert von Zeitgenossen*, 3rd. edn. Leipzig: R. Voigtländers Verlag, 1912.

Schumacher, Andreas, ed. *Lebensbilder aus Oesterreich. Ein Denkbuch vaterländischer Erinnerungen*. Vienna: Tauer & Sohn, 1843.

Schuy, Gilbert. *Bacsányi János és I. Napoleon 1809-ki proclamatiója a Magyarokhoz*. Budapest: Stephaneum Nyomda, 1914.

Seidler, Herbet. *Österreichischer Vormärz und Goethezeit: Geschichte einer literarischen Auseinandersetzung*. Vienna: Verlag der Österreichischen Akademie der Wissenschaften, 1982.

Sengle, Friedrich. *Biedermeierzeit. Deutsche Literatur im Spannungsfeld zwischen Restauration und Revolution 1815–1848*. Stuttgart, 1971–80.

Sheehan, James J. *German History 1770–1866*. Oxford: Clarendon Press, 1989.

Silbermann, Adalbert. *Ernst Schulzes Bezauberte Rose*. Berlin: E. Ebering, 1902.

Smeed, John William. *German Song and Its Poetry: 1740–1900*. London: Croom Helm, 1987.

Smidt, Heinrich. *Theodor Körner. Ein Dichter- und Heldenleben. Der deutschen Jugend erzählt*. Neuruppin: Alfred Oehimgke, 1866.

Smith, Barbara Herrnstein. *Poetic Closure: A Study of How Poems End*. Chicago: University of Chicago Press, 1968.

Spilling, Willy. "Die Problematik des Schubertschen Liedes um das Jahr 1815." Ph.D. dissertation, University of Prague, 1931.

Spohr, Louis. *Selbstbiographie*, 2 vols., ed. Eugen Schmitz. Kassel and Basel: Bärenreiter, 1954, reprint of 1st edn., Kassel and Göttingen: Georg H. Wigand, 1860.

Szinnyei, Ferencz. *Bacsányi János, 1763–1845*. Budapest: Hungarian Society for History, 1904.

Tiedge, Christoph August. *Sämtliche Werke*, 10 vols. in 3. Leipzig: Renger'sche Buchhandlung, 1841, 4th edn.

Tornius, Valerian Hugo. *The Salon: Its Rise and Fall. Pictures of Society through Five Centuries*, trans. Agnes Platt. London: T. Butterworth, 1929.

Toscano del Banner, Jos. G. *Die deutsches Nationalliteratur des gesammten Länder der österreichischen Monarchie von den ältesten Zeiten bis zur Gegenwart*. Vienna: Jasper, Hugel & Manz, 1849.

Treuenfeld, Bruno von. *Das Jahr 1813 bis zur Schlacht von Groß-Görschen*. Leipzig, 1901.

Vajda, Ilona. *Batsányi János és Baumberg Gabriella. I. 1799-1809*. Budapest: Magyar Egyetemi Nyomda Könyvesboltja, 1938.

Valentin, E. "Mozart und die Dichtung seiner Zeit" in *Neues Mozart-Jahrbuch*, vol. 1 (1941), pp. 79–113.

Waidelich, Till Gerrit, ed. *Franz Schubert. Dokumente 1817–1830*, vol. 1: *Texte, Programme, Rezensionen, Anzeigen, Nekrologe, Musikbeilagen und andere gedruckte Quellen*. Tutzing: Hans Schneider, 1993.

Weber, Max Maria von. "Wie und wo Körners LEYER UND SCHWERT von Carl Maria von Weber komponiert wurde" in *Berliner Musikzeitung Echo*, vols. 39 and 40 (27 September 1863 and 4 October 1863), pp. 305–8 and 313–317.

Welsmann, H. *Theodor Körners Leier und Schwert, vom biographischen, ästhetischen und kulturgeschicht-lichen Standpunkte ausbetrachtet.* Leipzig: Gustav Fock, 1891.

Wertheimer, Edouard. "Aus dem Leben einer Wiener Dichterin" in *Neue Freie Presse,* Vienna: 5 September 1884.

West, Ewan. "Lieder Composition in Vienna in the 1820s," Ph.D. dissertation, Oxford University, 1992.

"Schubert's Lieder in Context: Aspects of Song in Vienna 1778–1828," D. Phil., Oxford University, 1989.

Wigmore, Richard. *Schubert. The Complete Song Texts.* New York: Schirmer Books, 1988.

Winter, Robert. "Paper Studies and the Future of Schubert Research" in *Schubert Studies: Problems of Style and Chronology,* ed. Peter Branscombe and Eva Badura-Skoda, pp. 209–75. Cambridge: Cambridge University Press, 1982.

Wiora, Walter. *Das deutsche Lied: Zur Geschichte und Aesthetik einer musikalischen Gattung.* Wolfenbüttel: Mösler Verlag, 1971.

Wlassak, Eduard. "Theodor Körner und das Burgtheater" in *Chronik des k. k. Hof-Burgtheaters.* Vienna: Rosner, 1876.

Wolff, Ad. *Theodor Körners Leben und Briefwechsel.* Berlin: Mertens, 1858.

Theodor Körner. Sein Leben, sein Tod im Gefechte bei Rosenberg und sein Grab bei Wöbbelin in Mecklenburg-Schwerin. Eine Erinnerung an den 26. August 1813, dem deutschen Volke gewidmet. Schwerin: Oertzen & Comp., 1863.

Theodor Körner. Der Sänger, Wecker und Liebling der deutschen Burschenschaften und des deutsches Volkes. Dresden: Rob. Nitzsche, 1865.

"Théodore Körner" in *Ecrivains et poètes de l'Allemagne,* ed. Henry Blaze. Paris: Michel Lévy frères, 1851.

Wurzbach, Constantin von. *Biographisches Lexikon des Kaiserthums Österreich: enthaltend die Lebensskizzen der denkwürdigen Personen welche 1750 bis 1850 im Kaiserstaate und in seinen Kronländern gelebt haben,* 60 vols. Vienna: k.k. Hof- und Staatsdruckerei, 1856–91.

Zadányi Eva. *Batsányi János és Johannes von Müller.* Budapest: Minerva, 1941.

Zander, Christian Ludwig Enoch. *Geschichte des Krieges an der Nieder-Elbe im Jahre 1813.* Lüneberg: Herold & Wahlstab, 1839, reprinted Buchholz: LTR, 1991.

Erinnerungen aus den deutschen Befreiungskriegen von 1813 und 1814. Frankfurt am Main: Hermannsche Buchhandlung, 1847.

Die Lützower. Historische Roman, 3 vols. Berlin: L. Schlesinger, 1847.

Ein Streifzug der Lützow'schen Reiterschaar und der Überfall bei Kitzen. Geschildert von einem alten Lützower. Berlin: Schlesier, 1863.

Zeman, Herbert. "Dichtung und Musik: Zur Entwicklung des österreichischen Kunstliedes vom 18. bis zum 19. Jahrhundert" in Herbert Zeman, ed., *Musik und Dichtung: Festschrift Anton Dermota zum 70. Geburtstag,* pp. 20–34. Vienna, 1980.

ed. *Die österreichische Literatur: Ihr Profil an der Wende vom 18. zum 19. Jahrhundert (1750–1830).* Graz: Akademische Druck- und Verlagsanstalt, 1979.

"Die österreichische Lyrik des ausgehenden 18. und frühen 19. Jahrhunderts: Eine stil- und gattungsgeschichtliche Charakteristik" in Herbert Zeman, ed., *Die österreichische Literatur: Ihr Profil im 19. Jahrhundert (1830–1880),* pp. 513–47. Graz: Akademische Druck- und Verlagsanstalt, 1982.

"Die österreichische Lyrik der Haydn-Zeit" in Gerda Mraz, ed., *Joseph Haydn und seine Zeit (Jahrbuch für österreichische Kulturgeschichte,* vol. 2), pp. 121–46. Eisenstadt, 1972.

Zimmer, Hans. *Theodor Körners Braut: Ein Lebens- und Charakterbild Antonie Adambergers.* Stuttgart: Greiner & Pfeiffer, n.d.

Zimmermann, Ewald. "Gestaltungsfragen in klassischen und romantischen Liederzyklen," Ph.D. dissertation, Bonn, 1952.

Zimmermann, Georg. "Theodor Körner. Historisches Drama in drei Acten," ed. Johann Conrad Herber. Darmstadt: Diehl, 1863.

Zinner, Hedda. "Die Lützower: Schauspiel in 5 Akten." Berlin: Henschelverlag, 1961.

Zschokke, Heinrich. "Schulze von Celle und Cäcilie. An Cäcilie in Paris" in *Novellen und Dichtungen*, vol. 11. Aarau: H. R. Sauerländer, 1845.

Index